The Routledge Handbook of German Politics & Culture

The Routledge Handbook of German Politics & Culture offers a wide-ranging and authoritative account of Germany in the 21st century. It gathers the expertise of internationally leading scholars of German culture, politics, and society to explore and explain:

- historical pathways to contemporary Germany
- the current 'Berlin Republic'
- society and diversity
- Germany and Europe
- Germany and the world.

This is an essential resource for students, researchers, and all those looking to understand contemporary German politics and culture.

Sarah Colvin is the Schröder Professor of German at the University of Cambridge, UK.

Mark Taplin is a freelance scholar, editor, and translator.

The Routledge Handbook of German Politics & Culture

Edited by
Sarah Colvin

Assistant Editor
Mark Taplin

LONDON AND NEW YORK

First published in paperback 2018
First published 2015
by Routledge
2 Park Square, Milton Park, Abingdon, Oxon OX14 4RN

and by Routledge
711 Third Avenue, New York, NY 10017

Routledge is an imprint of the Taylor & Francis Group, an informa business

British Library Cataloguing in Publication Data
A catalogue record for this book is available from the British Library

Library of Congress Cataloging in Publication Data
Routledge handbook of German politics & culture/
edited by Sarah Colvin.
  pages cm
  Summary: "The Routledge Handbook of German Politics and
  Culture offers a wide-ranging and authoritative account of Germany
  in the 21st century. It gathers the expertise of internationally leading
  scholars of German culture, politics, and society to explore and
  explain – historical pathways to contemporary Germany – the
  current 'Berlin Republic' – society and diversity – Germany and
  Europe – Germany and the world. This is an essential resource
  for students, researchers, and all those looking to understand
  contemporary German politics and culture"– Provided by publisher.
  Germany–Politics and government–21st century. 2. Germany–Social
  life and customs–21st century. I. Colvin, Sarah.
  DD290.29.R68 2014
  943.088–dc23   2014017199

ISBN: 978–0–415–68686–0 (hbk)
ISBN: 978–0–8153–7757–3 (pbk)
ISBN: 978–1–315–74704–0 (ebk)

Typeset in Bembo and Stone Sans
by Florence Production Ltd, Stoodleigh, Devon, UK

Contents

Contents

Illustrations

Figures

Tables

Contributors

Jeffrey J. Anderson is Graf Goltz Professor and director of the BMW Center for German and European Studies in the Edmund A. Walsh School of Foreign Service, Georgetown University, Washington, DC. He researches and teaches at the intersection of comparative political economy and European integration. His publications include *German Unification and the Union of Europe* (Cambridge University Press, 1999) and two co-edited volumes: (with G. John Ikenberry and Thomas Risse) *The End of the West?* (2008) and (with Eric Langenbacher) *From Bonn to the Berlin Republic* (2010).

Clare Bielby is lecturer in German at the University of Hull, UK. She is the author of *Violent Women in Print: Representations in the West German Print Media of the 1960s and 1970s* (2012) and co-editor of *Women and Death 3: Women's Representations of Death in German Culture since 1500* (2010).

Rob Burns is professor emeritus of German at the University of Warwick, UK. He has published widely on postwar German politics and culture and is the author (with Wilfried van der Will) of *Protest and Democracy in West Germany: Extra-Parliamentary Politics and the Democratic Agenda* (1988) as well as the editor of *German Cultural Studies: An Introduction* (1995).

Paul Cooke is Centenary Chair in World Cinemas at the University of Leeds. He is the author of *Speaking the Taboo: A Study of the Work of Wolfgang Hilbig* (2000), *The Pocket Essential to German Expressionist Film* (2002), *Representing East Germany: From Colonization to Nostalgia* (2005), and *Contemporary German Cinema* (2012).

Beverly Crawford is adjunct professor of Political Science and co-director of the European Union Center of Excellence at the University of California Berkeley. She is the author of *Power and German Foreign Policy* (2007) and has written numerous articles on German politics. She is co-editor of several volumes on Germany, Europe, and the European Union.

Fatima El-Tayeb is associate professor of Literature and Ethnic Studies and associate director of Critical Gender Studies at the University of California, San Diego. She is the author of two books, *European Others: Queering Ethnicity in Postnational Europe* (2011) and *Schwarze Deutsche: Rasse und nationale Identität, 1890–1933* (2001), as well as of numerous articles on the interactions of race, gender, sexuality, and nation. Before moving to the US, she lived in Germany and the Netherlands, where she was active in black feminist, migrant, and queer of color organisations. She is also co-author of the movie *Alles wird gut/Everything will be fine* (Germany 1997).

Contributors

Ute Frevert is director at the Max Planck Institute for Human Development, Berlin, and professor of Modern History at the Free University Berlin, Germany. Her publications include 'Vertrauensfragen: Eine Obsession der Moderne' (2013), *Gefühlspolitik: Friedrich II. als Herr über die Herzen?* (2012), *Emotions in History – Lost and Found* (2011), *A Nation in Barracks: Modern Germany, Military Conscription and Civil Society* (2004), *Eurovisionen: Ansichten guter Europäer im 19. und 20. Jahrhundert* (2003), *Men of Honour: A Social and Cultural History of the Duel* (1995) and *Women in German History* (1989).

Anne Fuchs is professor of German at the University of Warwick, UK. Book publications include: *After the Dresden Bombing. Pathways of Memory 1945 to the Present* (2012), *Phantoms of War in Contemporary German Literature, Films and Discourse. The Politics of Memory* (2008), *Debating German Cultural Identity since 1989* (ed. with Kathleen James-Chakraborty and Linda Shortt, 2011), *German Memory Contests* (ed. with Mary Cosgrove and Georg Grote, 2006).

Mary Fulbrook, FBA, is professor of German History, dean of the Faculty of Social and Historical Sciences, and director of the European Institute at UCL, UK. She is the author of numerous books, including particularly works on the GDR, on 20th-century Germany, on historiography, and on the history and legacies of the Holocaust.

Lothar Funk is professor of Economics and International Economic Relations, Department of Business Studies, Düsseldorf University of Applied Sciences. He has co-authored and co-edited several books and articles on issues of macroeconomics, labour markets, and industrial relations as well as comparative economic policy studies on Germany. He has been co-editing the peer-reviewed German journal *Sozialer Fortschritt* for more than a decade.

Jonathan Grix is reader (associate professor) in Sport Policy and Politics at the University of Birmingham, UK. His work focuses on the political use of sport by governments. Major recent books include *Sport Politics: An Introduction* (2015) and *Leveraging Legacies from Sports Mega-Events* (ed.) (2014), *Understanding UK Sport Policy in Context* (ed.) (2014) and *Sport Under Communism: The East German 'Miracle'* (2012) (with Mike Dennis).

Randall Hansen is director of the Centre for European, Russian & Eurasian Studies, Munk School of Global Affairs, University of Toronto, Canada. He is the author of *Citizenship and Immigration in Post-War Britain* (2011), (with Matthew Gibney) *Immigration and Asylum from 1900* (2005), *Fire and Fury: The Allied Bombing of Germany* (Penguin, 2009), (with Desmond King) *Sterilized by the State: Eugenics, Race and the Population Scare in Twentieth Century North America* (2013), and *Disobeying Hitler: German Resistance after Valkyrie* (2014).

Alexandra Hausstein is a sociologist and German Studies scholar. Her research focuses on the interrelatedness of culture, communication, and knowledge, with special attention to identity politics, knowledge governance, and scientific epistemology.

Rainer Hillebrand is professor of International Economics at Fulda University of Applied Sciences. His research interests include German and European political economy, international economics, and environmental and energy policy. His publications include 'Climate protection, energy security, and Germany's policy of ecological modernisation' in *Environmental Politics* (2013), and *Rationale Umweltpolitik und Globalisierung* (2004).

Patricia Hogwood is a reader in the Department of Politics and International Relations at the University of Westminster, UK. She writes on the politics of German identity; consumerism and wellbeing in Germany; and the securitisation of immigration control.

Kurt Hübner is professor of European Studies and Jean Monnet Chair at the Institute of European Studies at the University of British Columbia, Canada. He has authored, co-authored, and edited numerous scholarly volumes on Europe, political economy, and globalisation.

Volkhard Krech is professor of the Study of Religion at Bochum University, Germany. He is the author of *Wo bleibt die Religion? Zur Ambivalenz des Religiösen in der modernen Gesellschaft* (2011), *Götterdämmerung: Auf der Suche nach Religion* (2003), *Wissenschaft und Religion: Studien zur Geschichte der Religionsforschung in Deutschland 1871 bis 1933* (2002), and *Religionssoziologie* (1999). He has published numerous articles on religion and art, religion and society, religion and violence, and the theory and practice of religions.

Eric Langenbacher is a faculty member and director of the honours programme in the Department of Government, Georgetown University, where he also received his PhD in 2002. He is the co-author of *The German Polity* (2013) and the co-editor of *From the Bonn to the Berlin Republic: Germany at the Twentieth Anniversary of Unification* (2010) and *Dynamics of Memory and Identity in Contemporary Europe* (2013).

Frauke Matthes is lecturer in German, University of Edinburgh, UK. She is the author of *Writing and Muslim Identity: Representations of Islam in German and English Transcultural Literature, 1990–2006* (2011) and is currently working on a monograph on discourses of masculinity in contemporary German literature and culture.

Hanns W. Maull retired in March 2013 from the chair of Foreign Policy and International Relations at the University of Trier, Germany. His book publications include (as editor) *Germany's Uncertain Power – Foreign Policy of the Berlin Republic* (2006), and (with Sebastian Harnisch) *Germany as a Civilian Power? The Foreign Policy of the Berlin Republic* (2001); he is also the author of 'Germany and Japan – The New Civilian Powers', *Foreign Affairs* (1990–1) and numerous articles and essays on German foreign policy.

Laurence McFalls is professor in Political Science and director of the Canadian Institute for German and European Studies, University of Montreal, Canada. In addition to his research on eastern Germany, McFalls's recent publications draw on a cross reading of Max Weber and Michel Foucault to propose a critique of humanitarian interventions and other forms of therapeutic domination in the contemporary neoliberal order.

Gregory Paschalidis is associate professor of Cultural Studies at the Department of Journalism and Mass Communications at Aristotle University of Thessaloniki, Greece. His publications and research interests are in the fields of cultural and media theory, visual culture, cultural policy, and cultural diplomacy.

William E. Paterson is honorary professor of German and European Politics at Aston University. He previously held chairs at Warwick, Edinburgh, and Birmingham. Cofounder of *German Politics*, he also co-edited the *Journal of Common Market Studies*. He has authored, co-authored, or co-edited 27 books and published over 160 articles. Professor Paterson succeeded Douglas Hurd as chairman of the German British Forum (2005–2011) and has been a director of the

Königswinter Conference since 1996. He was awarded an OBE in 1999 and a Bundes-verdienstkreuz 1. Klasse in 1998. He has been honoured for lifetime achievements in Political Science, the study of German Politics, and EU Studies by the relevant professional associations.

Ritchie Robertson is Taylor Professor of German at the University of Oxford, UK. His book publications include *Kafka: Judaism, Politics, and Literature* (1985); *The 'Jewish Question' in German Literature, 1749–1939* (1999); most recently, as editor, *Lessing and the German Enlighten-ment* (2013).

Thomas Saalfeld is professor of Comparative Politics at the University of Bamberg, Germany, and director of the Bamberg Graduate School of Social Sciences (BAGSS). He is the author of *Parteien und Wahlen* (2007) and a co-editor of *The Oxford Handbook of Legislative Studies* (2014). He was elected to the UK Academy of Social Sciences (AcSS) in 2008 and is the managing academic editor of *German Politics*. His research interests include legislative studies and political representation.

Harald Schoen is professor of Political Psychology at the University of Mannheim, Germany. His research interests and publications are in the fields of political behaviour, public opinion, political communication and political methodology.

James Sperling is professor of Political Science at the University of Akron, OH. His most recent publications include the co-authored *EU Security Governance* (2007) and *NATO's Post-Cold War Trajectory* (2012), the edited *Handbook of Governance and Security* (2014), the co-edited *National Security Cultures: Patterns of Global Governance* (2010), *European Security Governance: The European Union in a Westphalian World* (2009), and *Global Security Governance* (2009). He is Fernand Braudel Fellow at the European University Institute and will be Senior Visiting Fellow at the Institute of Advanced Studies, University of Bologna, in 2015.

Alex Street is assistant professor of Political Science at Carroll College. He has published a number of journal articles including 'My Child will be a Citizen: Intergenerational Motives for Naturalization', *World Politics* (2014); 'Representation Despite Discrimination: Minority Candidates in Germany', *Political Research Quarterly* (2013); 'Naturalization Dynamics in Immigrant Families', *Comparative Migration Studies* (2013).

Stuart Taberner is professor of Contemporary German Literature, Culture and Society, University of Leeds, UK, and a research associate in the Department of Afrikaans & Dutch, German and French at the University of the Free State, South Africa. His research deals with contemporary German literature, particularly in relation to transnationalism, cosmopolitanism, the after-effects of the Holocaust, Jewish-German writing, aging, and national identity. His most recent monograph is *Aging and Old-Age Style in Günter Grass, Ruth Klüger, Christa Wolf, and Martin Walser: The Mannerism of a Late Period* (2013).

Wilfried van der Will is honorary professor of Modern German Studies at the University of Birmingham, UK, and a co-founder of the Institute for German Studies there. His books include *Der deutsche Roman und die Wohlstandsgesellschaft* (1968, with R. Hinton Thomas); *Arbeiterkulturbewegung in der Weimarer Republik* (2 vols, 1982); *Protest and Democracy in West Germany* (1988), both with R.A. Burns; *The Nazification of Art* (1990, ed. with Brandon Taylor) and *The Cambridge Companion to Modern German Culture* (1998, ed. with Eva Kolinsky).

Andrew Webber is professor of Modern German and Comparative Culture, University of Cambridge, UK. His publications include *The European Avant-garde: 1900–1940* (2004) and *Berlin in the Twentieth Century: A Cultural Topography* (2008).

Christel Weiler is senior assistant professor at the Institute of Theatre Studies at the Free University, Berlin, and programme director of the Centre for Interweaving Cultures in Performance, Berlin, Germany.

Helen Williams is lecturer in Politics at the University of Nottingham, UK. Her research interests are theories of institutional change, migration studies, and higher education pedagogy. Her recent publications include 'Das britische Integrationsmodell', *Zeitschrift für Ausländerrecht* (2013); 'Changing the national narrative: Evolution in citizenship and integration in Germany, 2000–2010', *Journal of Contemporary History* (2013); and 'Crossing the divide: building and breaking down borders through discourse on citizenship and naturalisation policy in Germany and the UK, 2000–2010', *Eurostudia* 7 (2011).

Preface

Sarah Colvin

In 2014, the centenary year of World War I, Germany looks back at a troubled hundred years: bellicosity, defeat, and enforced territorial changes. At the same time, since 1945, Germany has been at the centre of notably and remarkably peaceful processes of change, as its postwar transformation into a Federal Republic (now often called the Bonn Republic) and an East German state was followed by a further transformation in 1990 into a larger Federal Republic (now often called the Berlin Republic) at the end of a Cold War that never fulfilled its threat.

The focus of this *Handbook* is contemporary Germany – the Berlin Republic – in the cultural and political context of the 'two Germanies' that were unified to constitute it, and of Germany's difficult history as a nation. This is, after all, a country which was unified as a nation only in 1871, under Bismarck; whose borders changed with relentless regularity throughout the 20th century; and which still today is grappling with the question not only who is and who is not German, but what makes up the mysterious quality of German-ness. It is deliberate that this is a handbook not of politics and society but of politics and culture. Historically, Germany's self-definition as a nation is peculiarly linked to the idea of culture, and – as the chapters in this *Handbook* collectively and very stimulatingly demonstrate – understanding its politics or society is enabled by understanding that. Germany's complexity as a nation resides not only, but not least, in its relationship with the idea of culture, which has been read both as a distraction from atrocity or even a licence for it (as Ritchie Robertson outlines) and as a cohesive force in a multicultural society that is historically linked with an ideal of holistic education (*Bildung*) that develops the humane in human beings. There seems to be, for example, a beginning process of empowerment through theatre in the Berlin Republic, which is described in Chapter 14 by Christel Weiler; and certainly the idea of culture and of the *Kulturnation* still informs national and regional policymaking in Germany: Wilfried van der Will and Rob Burns cite a Federal parliament report of 2007 that asserts 'culture is not an ornament. It is the foundation on which our society rests and on which it builds'. It is also, as both Paul Cooke and Gregory Paschalidis note, a vital element in Germany's exercise of soft power. The Federal Republic's foreign cultural policy, writes Paschalidis, is 'not about "the good, the beautiful, and the true", but about scientific exchange and the promotion of civil society'; and that is a very significant part of what has led to contemporary Germany's external 'recognition as an agent of peace and cooperation'.

Another element in that process has of course been the Federal Republic's proactive participation in the European project. Ute Frevert cites a poll published in late 2013, in which 84 per cent of Germans viewed their country as a European country (compared with 59 per cent of those questioned in France and just 40 per cent in the UK). Europe, then, has not only been the Federal Republic's political and economic project, but is part of a national identity. Again, that can and probably should be read both positively and negatively: Germany's 'reflexive multilateralism' in the European context is a useful counterforce to limiting nationalistic approaches, and European identity has enabled Germans to move past the vexed issue of being German after World War II; at the same time, as Fatima El-Tayeb asks, what is the strategic, legitimising, political force of the notion of 'being European' or having a 'shared European identity'? Who is 'in' and who is 'out' when the production of continental identity turns into continental gatekeeping?

Since the US financial crisis of 2008, which in the eurozone became a 'euro crisis', the German/European relationship has been challenged and questioned, both inside and outside the country. Among other things, as Jeffrey Anderson outlines, 'being German' means being part of a country internationally regarded as an economic powerhouse, with a highly distinctive economic model. Both Lothar Funk (in Chapter 22) and Kurt Hübner (in Chapter 24) offer accounts of how distinctively German 'ordoliberal' approaches provided a basis for the social market economy (*soziale Marktwirtschaft*) that characterised the postwar Federal Republic. The social market economy, by which the free market is supported in conjunction with social welfare, indicates what might be a characteristically German tendency to make policy on the assumption that 'doing the right thing' can be synergetic with economic success – this is reflected again in Germany's programme of ecological modernisation, as described in Chapter 23 by Rainer Hillebrand. That does not stop Germany from being perceived, still, as an actual or potential hegemon, 'reluctant' (in William Paterson's phrase) or not. But what is a hegemon – primarily an ideological bully, or primarily a practical provider of the resources necessary to enable cross-national cooperation? That question is asked by Beverly Crawford, who suggests that, if the latter answer is true, the eurozone might currently stand in great need of Germany's 'hegemonic leadership', and that the more worrisome question is whether Germany is willing and able to provide it.

Has a 21st-century Federal Republic moved away from its 'European vocation'? For some, Germany's focus on the national self-interest in the context of the eurozone crisis is a sign of 'normalisation' (where national self-interest is held to be a marker of normality). For others Germany's participation in international warfare (described by Hanns Maull and James Sperling) marks a return to 'normality' (where the West German Basic Law of 1949 had forbidden it). But is 'normalisation' in the sense of a political and cultural shift away from the dominant presence of the (Nazi) past something to be welcomed – should the Germans be allowed to forget? That might depend on who one thinks 'the Germans' are. Contemporary united Germany, as Anne Fuchs explains, has acknowledged that it has 'turned into a multicultural society with citizens of diverse ethnic backgrounds and belief systems, divergent generational perspectives, and fractured formative experiences'. There is a risk that a 'continuing emphasis on the moral responsibilities of Germans in the post-Holocaust era' will perpetuate, in Mary Fulbrook's words, 'an essentially ethnically defined notion of citizenship', where the idea of citizenship seems to have a dynamic potential beyond that of ethnic or cultural-historical identity. There seems to be a need both to remember (or memorialise) and to avoid fetishising the responsibility to remember as a key marker of national identity.

The 'positives' of normalisation might well be seen to include the normalisation of Germany's citizenship laws seen in the international context (as Helen Williams points out in Chapter 8), or indeed the effects of high-profile events like the 2006 World Cup, which not only rather 'normalised' the perception of Germany abroad but for many Germans enabled a kind of 'normal patriotism' (as Jonathan Grix describes it) that had not otherwise seemed possible after 1945.

But 'normality' is also a problematic concept because it depends, necessarily, not only (in the specifically German context) on relinquishing the strong emphasis on a post-Holocaust responsibility to remember, but also more generally on a counterpart notion of what is abnormal or deviant. It is unavoidably a notion in flux: even those who choose to queer normality – for example, in a contemporary 'queer Berlin' that has re-established its identity as a 'centre for queer sexualities and genders' (Clare Bielby and Frauke Matthes) – will eventually find themselves inhabiting a queer normality that has its own Others and outsiders. In Andrew Webber's words, 'any notion of normality needs to be qualified carefully [. . .], understood as a field of contesting normative and counternormative positions'. One might think that becoming old was the most normal thing in the world (in the standard phrase, rather better than the alternative); in late capitalist Germany, however – in Stuart Taberner's account of Germany as an advanced exemplar of an ageing society – there seems to be a growing need to account for the position of the elderly in that society. Those who do not provide the reference culture must needs address their place in it, and in contemporary Germany that is true also for those whose identity is East German – being East German in the Berlin Republic is both a geopolitical impossibility and, in Laurence McFall's words, 'an emotional and political reality' that impacts, as Patricia Hogwood demonstrates, on the individual's sense of wellbeing in society.

A central question any handbook on contemporary Germany and the Germans needs to address, then, is: who or what *is* 'German' in a multi-ethnic, multifaith (Krech), post-communist unified Republic in which a once nationally defining memory of the Nazi past is fast becoming postmemory. Is diversity an aspect of normalisation or antithetical to it? It seems important to recognise, as Alex Street and Randall Hansen among others in this volume argue, that German-ness is a highly differentiated thing – that renders the idea of integration (into what? out of what?) problematic. This *Handbook*, therefore, takes a deliberately differentiated approach, offering a collective perspective on contemporary Germany that is both international and cross-disciplinary. Eminent specialists from politics and international relations, political sociology, economics, literary and cultural studies, German history, European studies, religion, and theatre studies come together in the *Handbook*. That is not to claim that all possible perspectives are covered, but it does mean that the volume as a whole provides a complex and various view of a complex and various nation. When conceiving of it, and 'arranging' its chapters, I could not but be aware that one is always telling a story; but it seemed important that the narrative should be multifaceted. I have, therefore, not interfered as editor when contributors' *interpretations* of contemporary Germany – their reading of its policies, and of its cultural and societal practices – differed. Readers are invited to read across chapters and sections (which will almost inevitably also mean reading across disciplines, and across national perspectives); in that way justice is hopefully done both to the contributors' unique expertise and to the complexity of contemporary German politics and culture.

The chapters fall into thematic groups not only within the five sections of the volume but across those five sections. Issues of importance in contemporary German Studies recur throughout, and include the idea of culture and the *Kulturnation* (particularly in Chapters 2, 13, and 28), cultural diversity (in Chapter 18 as well as the chapters in Part III), and cultural activity, including sporting activity, as a form of soft power (particularly in Chapters 13, 19, and 27); issues around memory, the German past, and memorialisation (in Chapters 1, 4, 10, and 11) as well as cultural and political approaches to the problem of the past (*Aufarbeitung der Vergangenheit*) (particularly in Chapters 3, 11, 25, 26, and 28); Germany's European 'vocation' (in Chapters 1 and 24 as well as the Chapters in part IV), and its economy and industry (in Chapters 5, 22, 23, 24, and 25); as well as the 21st-century process of 'normalisation' (particularly in Chapters 6, 9, 10, 20, and 25). The contributors have risen magnificently to the challenge of providing chapters that are both accessible to the lay reader and interesting to experts, and for that, as well as for the extraordinary breadth, precision, and efficiency of my assistant editor Mark Taplin, I am extremely grateful.

Sarah Colvin
Cambridge, March 2014

Part I

Pathways to contemporary Germany

1

The history of a European nation

Ute Frevert

Translation: Mark Taplin

What is a European nation?

This chapter's title might come as a surprise, and it does raise some questions. What is a European nation? What makes contemporary Germany into one? And how far back does the concept of a 'European nation' go, in the German case?

We could look for easy answers. A European nation is a nation in Europe, and geography tells us that Germany is placed firmly in the centre of the European continent. We could go on to write contemporary German history as one that starts at the end of World War II, with the division of the continent and the nation into two antagonistic parts. And we could finish with reunification and its aftermath, using Willy Brandt's famous quote of 10 November 1989 as a leitmotiv: 'Jetzt wächst zusammen, was zusammengehört' (what belongs together will now grow together). We could even present reunified Germany as a model or case study for what has happened in Europe at large: East and West moving towards each other and striving to overcome the rift created by the Iron Curtain during the Cold War period.

But that is not how the history of Germany as a European nation will be told here. For Germany to be called a European nation demands more than geographical evidence: it calls for a deeper and more complex understanding of what Europe actually means. Is there anything like a common understanding of a nation's Europeanness? Has Europe been a national point of reference, and if so, in what way? Has it been used as a historical or political argument, in a strategic or legitimising sense? And have there been attempts to turn Europe into more than an argument by, for example, fostering institutional ties on a decidedly European level? Has Europe been a realm of experience (Koselleck 1989), and has it set the horizon of expectations for German citizens?

Focusing on contemporary Germany, all these questions might easily be answered in the affirmative: yes, today the Federal Republic does consider itself part of a European project defined in political, economic, and cultural terms; yes, politicians and public opinion constantly refer to Europe as a frame of reference and as an argument; yes, there are strong institutional ties on all levels and in many spheres, ranging from student exchanges and city twinning arrangements to financial policies, a common currency, and infrastructural support. Much of this is channelled through the organising power of the European Union, which has developed into a supranational structure integrating close to 30 European nation states. While the FRG (Federal Republic of Germany) was one of six founding members of the EU's forerunner, the European Economic Community (EEC), it is now widely seen as the Union's most important and powerful member state, at least when it comes to economic and financial issues.

That said, contemporary Germany appears as a clear case – even a showcase – of a European nation. As early as 1949, the preamble to the Basic Law (Germany's constitution) stated that the German people not only wished to preserve (or rather, regain) national and state unity, but also strove to support world peace as a 'gleichberechtigtes Glied in einem vereinten Europa' (an equal member of a unified Europe). Germany's new postwar identity and politics were thus clearly situated in a European context. In 1992 parliament added a clause that confirmed the Federal Republic's status as a member state (*Bundesstaat*) of the European Union. Taking a similar, though semantically restricted stance, a Supreme Court judgment from 2009 saw the Basic Law as authorising policies to contribute to and develop a European association of states (*Staatenverbund*).[1] And when asked about their country's Europeanness, German citizens overwhelmingly testify to their affinity for Europe. In an opinion poll published in December 2013, 84 per cent of Germans answered the question 'Is your country today European or not European?' in the affirmative, compared with 59 per cent in France and just 40 per cent in the UK.[2]

History and memory

How do we explain the striking attachment to Europe – the European identity, even – of the Germans and of Germany today? What experiences lie behind it, what aspirations are linked to it, and what interpretations of history have fed into it? I argue that history is of key importance in helping us to understand Germany's relationship with Europe. By history, I mean not so much the past per se as the ways in which it is interpreted. Two examples will serve to illustrate the point.

Example 1: Commemorating the Battle of the Nations in Leipzig

On 18 October 2013, a ceremony was held in Leipzig to commemorate the bloody battle fought out near the city, over three days, between the army of Napoleon and his allies and their opponents exactly 200 years earlier. In Napoleon's ranks were not just Frenchmen but soldiers from Italy and the Confederation of the Rhine, made up of various German states, while the opposing forces included Russians, Prussians, Austrians, and Swedes. In total, almost 600,000 men took part in the engagement, in which around one soldier in six was either killed or wounded. The battle continued to be remembered not just because of its gigantic scale, but because of its outcome – a decisive defeat for the French Emperor, halting his triumphal progress – which assured it a prominent place in the European history books. In Germany, it represented the culmination of the so-called wars of liberation, which in the 19th century came to be seen as an important factor in the process of German nation-building. Veterans' associations celebrated its anniversary and boasted of their contribution to national unification. At the start of the battle, Prussia had confronted Bavaria and Saxony as enemies, yet by the end the Saxons and Bavarians, too, had gone over to the coalition against Napoleon.

The events of 1813 seemed to prefigure the national unification eventually achieved following the victories at Wissembourg and Sedan in 1870. The date was commemorated as a 'feast day' on which – as the propagandist Ernst Moritz Arndt proposed as early as 1814 – all citizens would assemble for a 'großes teutsches Volksfest' (great festival of the German people) in honour of the 'erste große Gemeinsame, das uns allen angehört' (first great collective event to which all of us can lay claim). Alongside this national festival, which was to become 'ein starkes und mächtiges Bindungsmittel aller Teutschen' (a strong and powerful unifier of all Germans), Arndt planned a national 'Ehrendenkmal' (memorial) near Leipzig, which he envisaged as 'groß und herrlich' (large and magnificent), 'wie ein Koloß, eine Pyramide, ein Dom in Köln' (like a colossus, a pyramid, or Cologne cathedral) (Arndt 1814: 8–9, 18, 20–1).

But it took time for the colossus to become a reality; its official opening was delayed until the 100th anniversary of the battle, in 1913. At 91 metres high, the monument towered over the flat surrounding countryside and was visible from miles around. It may have been built using modern materials (concrete), but its iconographic scheme was highly traditional. Guarding the entrance was a supersized image of the archangel Michael, patron saint of all soldiers. The circular interior housed a crypt, which served as a symbolic tomb for the fallen and contained four statues, each almost 10 metres high: the *Totenwächter* (Guards of the Dead) representing the four virtues of the German people during the wars of liberation, namely courage, faith, national vigour, and self-sacrifice. The monument was financed through private donations; neither the state of Saxony nor the German Empire (nor the Kaiser himself) was a major contributor. Instead, a patriotic association drummed up support by mobilising the network of sports clubs, singing clubs, shooting clubs, and veterans' associations scattered across Germany. It was, therefore – just as Arndt had intended – an initiative from below, a 'volkstümliche That' (act of the people) through which donors affirmed the 'Geburtstag des deutschen Volkes' (birthday of the German people) in the 'Volkskrieg' (people's war) against Napoleon (Spitzner 1897: 12–13, 33). The project can be seen as a manifestation not just of bourgeois self-confidence, but of the rampant nationalism to be found throughout Europe during this period. The flip side of pride in one's own 'national vigour' was contempt for other nations, especially the French. Even former allies, whose crowned heads attended the opening ceremony in 1913, found themselves sidelined in the iconography for this 'purely German' monument (Poser 2003).

By 2013 all trace of this nationalist reading of history had vanished. This time the celebration was for a double anniversary, commemorating both the battle of 1813 and the unveiling of the memorial 100 years later. And it was organised with a critical eye to history. For many decades, this monumental colossus had been commandeered for national or nationalist purposes. During the Nazi period, huge parades had been staged there, while later, under the German Democratic Republic (GDR), it was the place where new recruits to the East German army (NVA) were sworn in and initiated into the tradition of brotherhood in arms with the Soviet Union (Bauer 1988: 57–9; Johnson 2008: 37–8). Now, however, the dominant theme was European unity. Even back in the 1990s, the director of the Leipzig historical museum (Stadtgeschichtliches Museum) had proposed that it take its place in a 'Verbund von Friedensdenkmalen' (chain of peace memorials) extending from Spain (Guernica) to Russia (Stalingrad). The symbols that commemorated and bore witness to wars waged within Europe were to be reconstituted as monuments to peace, as befitted the self-image of the new Europe, united within the European Union, as a zone of peace. In this context, the city fathers and mothers of Leipzig were able to throw a party for the whole of Europe, with the 'Ball of the Nations' as its climax. There were performances by European choirs and a re-enactment of the battle of 1813 by 6,000 people from both Germany and other countries; services of reconciliation were held in the churches, while young people from 11 European nations read out a message of peace. In his speech for the occasion, the President of the European Parliament, Martin Schulz, described the monument as a European place of memory, and expressed delight at the fact that 'fortunately, we in Europe have managed to overcome the ultranationalist mentality' expressed in its original design (*Frankfurter Allgemeine Sonntagszeitung* 2013; Keller 2012).[3]

Example 2: World War I

Although the phrase 'ultranationalist mentality' is perhaps too strong and does not fully reflect the political complexity of the original Leipzig ceremony in October 1913, it is understandable that today people should want to link the event to the world war that broke out only a few months later. However, those present for the unveiling of the colossus could not have known that this was taking place 'am Vorabend des Ersten Weltkrieges' (on the eve of the First World War), as the President of the European Parliament put it. It was possible to make such connections only in hindsight – and even then there has been an excessive tendency to see outcomes as preordained. In 1913–14 the people of Europe were not, in fact, clamouring for a new war or doing all they could to bring one about. Every country had its nationalist fanatics, there was the odd journalist ranting on about war as a cure for decadence and feminisation, and some young students were anxious to prove their manhood in the heat of battle, but these groups did not set the tone for society at large. As late as July 1914, anti-war demonstrations in Germany and France were attended by many hundreds of thousands of people. In the following month, we find evidence of a surge of enthusiasm for the war, but the phenomenon seems to have been confined largely to the cities – and even there it did not last long (Verhey 2000; Ziemann 2006). It was this that led the warring governments to set up propaganda departments, which inundated citizens with an unprecedented stream of images and texts. The propaganda they produced, in which the enemy was painted in the blackest colours, seems to have been most effective on the homefront. Many serving soldiers, by contrast, tended to dismiss such caricatures, despite – or, indeed, because of – the direct contact they had had with the enemy (Schmidt 2006; Lipp 2003; Reimann 2000: 178ff.).

Experiences of and discourses about the war also played a crucial political role, especially once the great slaughter had come to an end. The Weimar Republic experienced political fragmentation and social militarisation in which the memory of the war – and the losses suffered by Germany as a consequence – acted as a driving force. Before the war, Germans had felt surrounded by enemies jealous of their country's success; after 1918, this feeling turned into a cast-iron certainty. The Treaty of Versailles, which labelled Germany as solely to blame for the war and used this to justify the imposition of massive reparations, was regarded as shameful victors' justice by politicians of all stripes. The country's political ostracisation, in the form of exclusion from international organisations (the League of Nations, academic associations, etc.) and events such as the Olympic Games, was also universally resented. The humiliating occupation of the Ruhr by French and Belgian troops in 1923 served only to reinforce the sense that Germany was being isolated and treated like a pariah. In the first half of the 1920s, the country was further from being a 'European nation' than at any other time.

Fast-forward to 2014, when a huge round of commemorations was scheduled to mark the 100th anniversary of the start of the war. Events were planned in almost all European countries, not just in capital cities and at major battlefields but at a local level, in both towns and rural districts. Even before the ceremonies had got underway, the memory of the war was being invoked for the sake of domestic political interests. In November 2013, France's embattled and much-criticised President, François Hollande, used a formal address in honour of the victims of the world war to call on his compatriots to come together. Echoing the appeal in 1914 to the *union sacrée* of the French people, transcending political, social, and religious differences, Hollande emphasised the need for national solidarity, even though in 2014 the battles to be fought and won were economic rather than military. By remembering their victory in the world war, the French people could gain the self-confidence they desperately needed to overcome their current economic plight (Hollande 2013).

However, Hollande's choice of battle imagery was far from apposite. International economic competition, unlike war, is not about shedding blood or about weakening or even destroying one's opponent. Hollande also risked creating the impression that once again France saw its enemy as lying east of the Rhine, in the economic superpower that is Germany – a country with which, moreover, it is allied within Europe. The French President sought at once to dispel this impression, repeatedly stressing his country's commitment to the project of European unification and to its close relationship 'with our German friends'. What is more, he invited the German Federal President to Paris for 3 August 2014, the 100th anniversary of the start of the war.

In doing so, Hollande was continuing a political tradition that had begun in the 1980s. In September 1984, Federal Chancellor Helmut Kohl and President François Mittérand made a joint visit to the battlefields of World War I. For the first time, a French president set foot in a German military cemetery and, together with the German Chancellor, laid a wreath in memory of the dead. Afterwards they travelled together to the ossuary at Douamont, home to the mortal remains of 130,000 fallen soldiers of different nationalities. When the Marseillaise was played, Mittérrand suddenly took Kohl's hand. There could be no more powerful way of sending out the message, 'We are reconciled. We have come to an understanding. We are friends'.[4]

While politicians committed themselves to reconciliation, mutual understanding, and friend-ship over the graves of the fallen, academics worked on a reappraisal of World War I designed specifically to exclude narrow nationalist readings. In the mid-1980s, planning began for a new museum at Péronne on the Somme, where more than a million French, German, and British soldiers were killed or wounded, went missing in action, or were taken prisoner within five months during the summer of 1916. The museum, opened in 1992 as the Historial de la Grande Guerre, looked at the war from the perspective of social history and the history of mentalities, highlighting the close parallels in mindset and attitudes between the warring nations. Rather than focusing on the course of the war and the experience of battles and military combat, it placed the everyday lives of soldiers (and civilians) centre stage: issues such as diet, hygiene, and health care, but also the soldiers' grief at the loss of comrades and the atmosphere before an attack. The philosophy behind both the research centre linked to the museum and the exhibition itself was internationalist. Thus the exhibition was organised by topic rather than by country, while all the items on display had accompanying captions in English and German as well as French. The large number of visitors attracted to the museum, including many families, school-children, and young people, were presented with an image of the war that, without erasing the different histories of the nations involved, sought to bring out the elements of shared experience. These included an intensive and far-reaching campaign of 'intellectual mobilisation' that saw the population supplied with mental 'arms' in the form of nationalist posters, postcards, and cartoons, and enlisted in the struggle against a barbarised foe.[5]

On seeing this prewar and wartime propaganda, no visitor to the Historial could fail to be struck – if they were not aware of it before – by the distance separating them from World War I, even though its traces were all about in the surrounding battlefield landscape. This new era, in which old enmities are gradually fading away, has also had an impact on the way in which battlefield tours are organised and conducted. When I accompanied German history students on a trip to Verdun and Péronne in July 2000, everywhere we went we came across evidence of the war being commemorated across national boundaries. At British war cemeteries we found tokens of remembrance left by German visitors, and vice versa. In the crater-strewn countryside around La Boisselle on the Somme, where on 1 July 1916 nearly 60,000 British soldiers were mown down by German artillery, among the many poppy wreaths laid by British tourists I found one dedicated to Ernst Jünger, a German writer who took part in World War I as a young lieutenant and later wrote militaristic books about his experiences. French and English translations of these books, which appeared as early as 1929 and 1930, found an enthusiastic readership even among non-German participants in the war (and among later generations, including some of those laying wreaths in 2000). Clearly Jünger had used a language and form of narrative that reflected soldiers' experiences and how they understood them, regardless of nationality.

A hundred years after the start of the Great War, as it is still known in France and Britain, the old stereotypes prevalent before, during, and long after the war have lost much of their potency. Since the 1980s, the war has been commemorated at a European level, and this is reflected in the events to mark its 100th anniversary. For the historian Joseph Zimet, director of the Mission du Centenaire established by the French government, it is essential that Germany and France remember the war in partnership. Even though World War I plays nothing like the same role in Germany's collective memory that it does in France or Britain, having been quickly overshadowed by the losses and experiences of World War II, Zimet sees a *centenaire* without German involvement as impossible: 'Europe cannot commemorate the First World War without Germany'. Rather, in both France and Germany remembrance is 'very closely linked to the idea of Europe' (*Weltweit vor Ort* 2013).

This idea of Europe was also in the background, no doubt, when Mittérand and Kohl symbolically held hands in 1984, just as it was the inspiration for the researchers, museum experts, and politicians involved in setting up the Historial at Péronne. Yet in 1984 it was clearly still too weak to allow the other 'great war' to be commemorated as a European event. The German Chancellor was not invited to the ceremony marking the 40th anniversary of D-day, the Allied landings in Normandy. Even 10 years later, on the 50th anniversary, the French President did not feel able to ask his friend Helmut to attend. There was also no German representative at the ceremony staged by the British in Portsmouth – the point of departure in 1944 for many of the ships involved in the D-day operations – to witness heads of state and government from countries as far apart as Norway and Greece, Belgium and Canada, and Poland and France celebrate their nations' history of brotherhood in arms. Only with the dawn of the new millennium did it become possible to commemorate World War II, too, in inclusively European terms. On the 60th anniversary of D-day, in 2004, the German Chancellor Gerhard Schröder was finally allowed to take his place alongside other leaders. Unlike his predecessor Kohl, who had waited in vain for this symbolic gesture, he received an official invitation to Normandy from Mittérand's successor, Jacques Chirac. Chirac added to the symbolism by welcoming Schröder with an embrace and explicitly mentioning Schröder's father, who had been killed in the war and whose son had never had the chance to get to know him.

The history of commemoration of the two world wars, which brought both massive destruction and fundamental change to Europe during the 20th century, bears witness to a slow but sustained process of rapprochement and reconciliation between former wartime opponents. This did not unfold automatically or 'naturally', but rather as the product of political will and within an institutional framework. The presence of delegations from France, as well as former allies in the resistance to Napoleon, at the ceremonies marking the 200th anniversary of the Battle of the Nations, and the fact that in 2014 the 100th anniversary of the outbreak of World War I is being commemorated in the spirit of 'European integration' (Zimet), while German statesmen are able to celebrate the liberation of Europe from Nazi rule alongside representatives of the country's former enemies, are inconceivable without people's experiences of 'Europe' since the 1950s. For Germany, the effect of those experiences has been particularly dramatic and profound. That is the main reason why today such a high proportion of German citizens – twice as many as in Great Britain – describe their country and themselves as 'European'.

Europe as will and representation

If a similar poll on the issue of European consciousness or identity had been conducted in the 1920s, it is very likely that it would have yielded different results. We cannot even be sure that people would have understood the question. After World War I, people throughout Europe were busy mourning their own dead and caring for veterans who had returned from the war with severe psychological and physical injuries. Each nation was preoccupied with its own suffering, and each manufactured its own interpretations of the past to honour the victims and justify their sacrifice. This process was particularly difficult for states on the losing side, which also had to cope with serious losses in territory and economic and political power.

Not until the mid-1920s were there signs – slow and cautious at first – of a change in mood; the era of national navel gazing seemed to be coming to an end. At the Locarno Conference in 1925, Germany, France, and Belgium concluded an arbitration agreement and guaranteed the inviolability of their respective borders. This was accompanied by treaties between Germany, Poland, and Czechoslovakia that created a mechanism for the peaceful resolution of all disputes, although these did not extend to a permanent settlement on borders. In 1926 Germany joined the League of Nations and the ban on German academics attending international conferences was lifted.

At the same time, clearly pro-European movements and ideas were starting to gain ground. Those who used Europe as an argument and point of reference in political discourse did so essentially for two reasons. For some, the war and experience of the war were the key factor. They dreamed of establishing a strong and solid 'European community' to prevent any further 'fratricidal wars'. For the liberal academic Arnold Bergsträsser (1896–1964), and others of his generation, 'the war had made Europe a reality for the first time'; according to Bergsträsser, the 'Kameradschaft à l'ombre des épées' (comradeship in the shadow of swords) he had experienced placed him under an obligation to campaign for the 'Einheit unseres abendländischen Kontinents' (unity of our Western continent) (Müller 2001: 262; see also Conze 2005). For others, geopolitical considerations were paramount. The weakening of Europe brought about by the war led them to reflect on the means by which it might recover its strength. In 1924 Heinrich Mann predicted, 'Bevor Europa Wirtschaftskolonie Amerikas oder Militärkolonie Asiens wird, einigt es sich' (Before Europe becomes an economic colony of America or a military colony of Asia, it will unite) (Mann 1987: 100). If Europe's decline was to be halted and then reversed, the antagonism and rivalry between European states would have to end. Only a political federation could reinvigorate Europe and equip it for its role as global leader. A supranational construct of this kind would bring with it considerable economic benefits, as it would mean the creation of a large single market and the consolidation of industrial production capacity (Stirk 1996: 26ff.; Ambrosius 1996: 67ff.).

Many different bodies launched initiatives in support of European integration *avant la lettre*. The League of Nations set up a commission of inquiry 'for the European Union', which met several times (though to no avail) (Wilson and van der Dussen 1993: 101ff.; Orluc 2000). In its 1926 party programme, the German Social Democratic Party (SPD) backed the 'aus wirtschaftlichen Ursachen zwingend gewordene Schaffung der europäischen Wirtschaftseinheit' (creation of a European economic union, for compelling economic reasons) and pushed for the 'Bildung der Vereinigten Staaten von Europa' (establishment of the United States of Europe). The most enthusiastic advocate of a political federation of European states (though without Britain and Russia) was the Pan-European Union, under the energetic leadership of the Austrian Count Richard Coudenhove-Kalergi. The union had the support of leading figures in politics, science, and the arts (including Konrad Adenauer, Albert Einstein, and Thomas Mann)

9

and campaigned for the 'spiritual unification of Europe' on the basis of 'Western' traditions and the achievements of European high culture (Ziegerhofer-Prettenthaler 2004; Schöberl 2008). And indeed, it was the European arts and music scene that took the lead in reforging the connections severed by the war. The 'golden '20s' saw a lively exchange of ideas, styles, and people between Berlin, Paris, Milan, Barcelona, and Moscow. Men and women from many nations worked together at the Bauhaus school in Weimar and Dessau, and the architects of the modern age were all in close contact.

There were signs of tentative progress even with regard to treatment of the war dead. The Treaty of Versailles had placed a duty on all governments to treat war graves with respect and ensure that they were kept in good repair. Requests for the repatriation of remains were to be honoured, where possible. However, there were significant obstacles to implementing these provisions in practice. The first discussions between the French war graves service and the German War Graves Commission (Volksbund Deutsche Kriegsgräberfürsorge) did not take place until 1926. Henceforth the commission had a say in the layout and maintenance of German military cemeteries in France, where it was able to develop its own distinctive designs and symbols, although it took until 1937 for a meeting of all the countries concerned to be organised. Only then did the international cooperation first enjoined back in 1919 finally begin to take shape.

By that point, the national socialist regime in Germany had already rechristened the national day of mourning introduced in the 1920s as 'Heldengedenktag' (heroes' memorial day), infusing it with a triumphalist spirit: it now became a 'Tag der Erhebung' (day of uprising) and 'Hoffens auf das Aufgehen der blutigen Saat' (hope that the seed sown in blood will rise forth anew) (Behrenbeck 1996: 293; Kaiser 2010). This seed did indeed rise forth, with even bloodier consequences than in World War I. From 1939 onwards, Germany plunged nearly the whole of Europe into war. At first the Nazi regime tried to give the impression that it sought only a revision of the terms of Versailles, but the seizure of Prague and Warsaw in 1939 made clear that it had much more expansionist ambitions. Such a policy could not be accommodated even within classic models of a German-dominated *Mitteleuropa*, which had been the subject of ongoing debate since the end of World War I. It was clear that this was no attempt to modify the outcomes of that war; this was a new Napoleonic-style landgrab, designed to transform the whole of Europe and to turn Germany into a 'European nation' of a very particular kind.

Europe was surprisingly important as a theme in Nazi arguments. Clearly the impact of the debate on Europe during the 1920s had been sufficiently profound and far-reaching that even the hypernationalist Nazi regime felt the need to continue it. Of course, the annexation of land in the east, in particular, in order to create 'Lebensraum' (living space) for the German people was in no one's interests but Germany's, but there were attempts to give the policy a European gloss. 'Soviet Russia' was portrayed as the biggest danger to the Western world, and Germany as charged with protecting that world, and with it 'Europe', from 'bolschewistischen Angriffen' (Bolshevik attacks). Talk of a European 'mission' was not confined to Adolf Hitler; Franz Justus Rarkowski, the 'field bishop' or senior Catholic chaplain to the German military, used similar language, placing the invasion of the Soviet Union in 1941 in the medieval tradition of eastward colonisation by military orders of knights and hailing Germany as the 'Herzvolk' (nation at the heart of Europe) that was again, 'wie schon oft in der Geschichte' (as has been the case many times in the past), acting as the continent's saviour and vanguard (Michalka 1985, vol. 1: 188–9; vol. 2: 145). At the same time, the regime's minister of propaganda, Joseph Goebbels, noted the popularity in Spain's Francoist press of the image of a 'crusade' by the Christian West against godless Bolshevism: 'In Europe something like a unified front is taking shape. Ideas of a crusade are starting to appear. We can make use of them' (Fröhlich 1987: 713).

Also useful as propaganda were the ideas concerning the 'Europa-Frage' (European question) developed by the German Foreign Ministry as a means of attracting support. Although the ministry left no doubt that the survival of 'das künftige Europa' (the future Europe) would depend on 'einer voll durchgesetzten Vormachtstellung des Großdeutschen Reiches' (the total supremacy of the Greater German Reich), the key principles for the establishment of a European union of states submitted by its European committee in 1943 were enticing inasmuch as they placed great emphasis on federal structures and a 'Gemeinschaft souveräner Staaten' (community of sovereign states). But Germany had long since begun creating facts on the ground through its economic policy. Since 1940, it had been working to construct a 'europäische Kontinental-wirtschaft unter deutscher Führung' (continent-wide European economy under German leadership), in which the national economies of the countries under occupation were made totally subservient to the needs of the Greater German Reich. This exposed the contradiction between Germany's determination to rule over and dominate other European countries and its promise to uphold their sovereignty, severely limiting the appeal of what Goebbels termed Germany's 'Europaparole' (message on Europe) elsewhere (Michalka 1985, vol. 2: 151–2, 155–7, 141; Fröhlich 1987: 738).[6]

Nonetheless, German and Allied propagandists clashed repeatedly on the issue of the re-ordering of Europe after the war. There were also many plans and projects in circulation among groups active in the resistance and in exile. The 'White Rose' student resistance group wanted to create a 'neues geistiges Europa' (new spiritual Europe). The participants in the plot to assassinate Hitler on 20 July 1944 called for the establishment of a European union of states dominated by neither Germany nor any other power, and in which borders between European countries might become less and less significant. In documents produced by the dissident group known as the Kreisau circle, there was talk of setting up a political order that respected the individual states and operated with the free consent of all the peoples concerned. The Buchenwald manifesto proposed a European community of states to renew Europe's cultural mission in the world ('Europas kulturelle Mission in der Welt'). Collaboration between Germany and both Poland and France, as well as Germany's entry into the Anglo-Saxon cultural sphere, were seen as the preconditions for a new pan-European consciousness ('europäisches Gesamtbewußtsein') that was the only means of safeguarding peace between nations (Michalka 1985, vol. 2: 355, 359–60; Lipgens 1968: 153–5; Mommsen 1994: Schilmar 2004; Bailey 2013).

But the definitive plans for the future of Germany and Europe were drafted not in Berlin, Munich, Kreisau, or Buchenwald but in Tehran, Yalta, and Potsdam, where the postwar European order was hammered out between the 'Big Three': the USA, Great Britain, and the Soviet Union. After its surrender, Germany was the object, not the subject, of political decisions. The country lost its sovereignty and was divided into four Allied occupation zones and spheres of influence. It was only the start of the Cold War between the Soviet Union and the English-speaking powers that led to the establishment, four years after the end of the war, of two new states. The three former western zones combined to form the Federal Republic of Germany (FRG), while the eastern zone became the German Democratic Republic (GDR). One of the conditions of statehood was that both entities be bound into their respective power blocs. In 1950 the GDR joined the Council for Mutual Economic Assistance (Comecon), set up the previous year, and in 1955 it signed the Warsaw Pact on 'Friendship, Cooperation and Mutual Assistance', which set out the Eastern bloc's common defence policy. This step was mirrored by the Federal Republic's accession to NATO in 1955. Previously the three western zones had been involved in the establishment of the OEEC (Organisation for European Economic Cooperation) and had benefited from reconstruction assistance under the Marshall plan (Kleßmann 1982).

Two nations, two Europes

So what became of Germany as a 'European nation'? The question can be answered only in the context of Europe as a whole. No European nation experienced the division of Europe after 1945 more intensely than Germany. The Iron Curtain ran right through the middle of the country, from the Baltic to the Bavarian forest, as well as through the middle of its former capital, Berlin. In 1961 the GDR sealed off its border with the Federal Republic and West Berlin with a wall, barbed wire, and a heavily guarded 'death strip' to halt the flood of refugees from East to West. Despite their public commitment to reunification, both German states settled down more or less comfortably in their respective halves of Europe. From Bonn, the new federal capital on the Rhine, people looked to the West; from East Berlin, the capital of the GDR, eyes were trained on the East. Both the Federal Republic and the GDR became more and more entrenched – politically, economically, and militarily – in the 'alliances' of which they were members. As a result, they belonged to different 'Europes', into which they became increasingly integrated over time.

Of key importance for Western Europe was the fact that its protector – or 'big brother' – was located outside Europe. Whereas in World War I the USA intervened at a late stage, only to withdraw swiftly from the settlement process after 1918, after World War II it established a permanent presence on the European continent. The USA had emerged from what Ernst Nolte describes as the 30-year European civil war as indisputably the world's strongest country. After 1945 Europe's loss of power, which in the 1920s had still seemed reversible, was a fact all European nations had to come to terms with in one way or another.

This was less of a problem for Germany than for France and Britain, which also had to deal with the loss of their colonial empires after the war. Until recently, Germany had been an extremely strong and successful country – in military, technological, and economic terms – so shifts in the centre of gravity within and outside Europe paled into insignificance compared with its own total, devastating loss of power. The fact that it had now surrendered its leadership role to a non-European country – whose support, along with every ounce of its own energy, was needed if it hoped to match the Soviet Union – was less of a blow to national self-regard than the moral 'chasm' ('Abgrund') that, as Hannah Arendt wrote to Dolf Sternberger in Heidelberg in 1948, 'seit Beendigung des Krieges zwischen Deutschen [. . .] und anderen Völkern geöffnet hat' (has opened up between the Germans and other peoples since the end of the war) (Arendt 2013: 79).

The Cold War provided a welcome bridge over this chasm. Although it served to consolidate and entrench the division of Germany, which had initially been seen as temporary, it also made it easier for the two German states to reinvent themselves as loyal allies of their respective 'protectors'. By taking on the role of buffer states and adopting a mutually antagonistic stance, they quickly managed to earn political credit and to emerge from the shadow of the 'Third Reich'. While the Bonn Government cultivated a close relationship with the USA, its counterpart in East Berlin strove to win recognition from the Soviet Union by behaving as a model pupil. While the GDR outdid other Eastern bloc countries in its zeal and eagerness to conform to the Soviet model, the Federal Republic was among America's most loyal allies.

America's influence was felt not just politically and militarily but in economic and cultural terms. It was an influence that proved impossible to resist, and some longstanding reservations and prejudices against America that had only recently been reinforced under the 'Third Reich' were thereby neutralised and overcome.[7] In the 1920s, there was still massive resistance to what went under the heading of 'Americanisation', but after 1945 there was no alternative in the West to the American model of modernity. Economically, the Marshall plan set its beneficiaries on a clear capitalist course, and from the 1950s onwards large sections of the West German population came to see the USA's consumer society, which was more advanced than that of Europe, as a hugely attractive prospect. When the Federal Republic was admitted to NATO in 1955 and then permitted to set up its own army, the new uniforms were modelled on those of the American military; the only protest came from a small number of right-wing politicians who thought this shameful and undignified. Most citizens had been won over by an American charm offensive that began with GIs handing out chocolate, continued with the 'raisin bombers' (*Rosinenbomber*) that carried out the dramatic airlift to West Berlin in 1948, and culminated in the formal declaration with which General Eisenhower exonerated the soldiers of the Wehrmacht in 1951: 'The German soldier fought bravely and honorably for his homeland' (Frevert 2004: 260–1). Henceforth serious criticism of the USA was almost non-existent in the Federal Republic; even during the Vietnam War, the political establishment refused to disown its great friend and 'big brother'. That task was left to young left-leaning students, who, rather than resort to crude anti-Americanism of the traditional variety, did so by expressing solidarity with the anti-war movement both internationally and in the USA itself.

The student movement of the 1960s and 1970s provides a vivid illustration of how westernised the Federal Republic had become. For the 'Kinder von Marx und Coca Cola' (children of Marx and Coca Cola) – as the subtitle to the German version of Jean-Luc Godard's film *Masculin, Féminin* (1966) put it – it was natural to look westwards, not just to Paris and Milan but to Berkeley and New York (della Porta 1998; Schmidtke 1998; Davis *et al.* 2010; Horn 2008; Gildea *et al.* 2013; Doering-Manteuffel 1999). Even the New Left did not model itself on the Soviet or East German version of Marxism, drawing inspiration instead from Rosa Luxemburg, Antonio Gramsci, or Herbert Marcuse. Politically and ideologically it was much closer to 'eurocommunism', which had its origins mainly in Italy and Spain, than to the 'actually existing socialism' on the other side of the Iron Curtain.

This affinity with the West (both Europe and America) was not confined to politics. It was also about more than just the economic integration of the Federal Republic of Germany, France, Italy, and the Benelux countries, a process that that had been gaining momentum since the establishment of the European Coal and Steel Community in 1951. Eventually this would develop into a comprehensive blueprint for Europe, with far-reaching consequences, but in the short to medium term cultural influences and contacts had a much more profound impact. In Bonn, Munich, and Frankfurt, people wore fashions designed in Paris, Milan, or London; they listened to music imported to Hamburg from Liverpool, and ate the gyros, pizza, spaghetti, and paella introduced to Germany by Greek, Italian, and Spanish *Gastarbeiter* (guest workers; see Chapter 12). The works of French existentialists were read in West German schools, while plays by Ionescu and Beckett were staged in West German theatres. Visits and exchange programmes took young people to the UK, where, like Karl Heinz Bohrer in 1953, they came to know and value British institutions, the British way of life, and especially kindness, that 'untranslatable English quality' ('unübersetzbare englische Eigenschaft') (Bohrer 2012: 284). From the 1960s onwards, the Franco-German Youth Office (Deutsch-Französisches Jugendwerk) arranged exchanges for millions of German and French young people – often hosted by local families – that allowed them to practise their language skills and learn about the culture of their neighbours over the border. Twinning arrangements between municipalities brought both local politicians and ordinary citizens into contact across national boundaries. Students jumped at the chance to spend a year or a semester at a university in another European country, a trend boosted by the introduction of the Erasmus programme in 1987.

All these experiences helped strengthen West Germans' sense of themselves as Europeans. In polls carried out in the late 1970s and the 1980s, around two thirds of those surveyed agreed with the idea of Europe as a 'Vaterland' (homeland); 67 per cent were 'entirely' or 'mostly' proud to be Europeans. Among younger people, in particular, national pride was outweighed by pride in European identity: in 1984 only 56 per cent of 16 to 29-year-olds reported that they were 'entirely' or 'mostly' proud to be German (Weidenfeld and Piepenschneider 1987: 26–31). This reflected a widespread suspicion of national, patriotic, and, especially, nationalistic affirmations and symbols. After the excessive nationalism of the 'Third Reich', people were extremely cautious about the use of flags, public declarations, and anthems. For many, the *Verfassungspatriotismus* (constitutional patriotism) advocated by Dolf Sternberger and Jürgen Habermas seemed more appropriate to a democracy than identification with an ethnically or historically defined nationality. As German history afforded few positive points of reference, it made more sense to commit oneself emotionally to the values and institutions enshrined in the *Grundgesetz* (Basic Law) than to membership of some mythical German 'Volk' (Sternberger 1990; Habermas 1992: 632–60; Müller 2010).

This created space for a 'European' sense of identity that found expression not just in polls on people's attitudes towards Europe but in high levels of support for European unification. In this context, 'Europe' usually stopped at the Elbe: when asked whether the eastern European states and the Soviet Union should be included in a united Europe, in 1984 the vast majority of people answered no. Older people, who had lived through the 'hottest' phase of the Cold War, were particularly resistant to this idea, but even those aged between 30 and 50 were for the most part unwilling or unable to contemplate a partnership extending beyond the countries of Western Europe. Also, the more the existence of two German states seemed set in stone, the less people saw (western) European unification as an obstacle to German unification, which now seemed a very distant possibility (Weidenfeld and Piepenschneider 1987: 28, 38). In the 1950s, the German Social Democrats had bitterly resisted the integration of the Federal Republic into the West on the grounds that it would entrench the division of Germany, but 30 years later such hopes or fears were a thing of the past.

West Germans had made a success of life in their part of Europe and felt increasingly at ease there. Looking back, Hans Magnus Enzensberger observed that the idea of Europe had provided them with 'eine zweite, entlastende Identität' (a second, liberating identity) (Enzensberger 1994: 501), offering them the prospect of a bright future in which the things that bound Europeans together would count for much more than their differences. Against this background, it became possible to take a more critical look at the nation's past. In the 19th century, if not earlier, it was argued, Germany had deviated from the standard Western European course of development, with disastrous consequences; what Friedrich Meinecke dubbed the 'deutsche Katastrophe' (German catastrophe) was the result of having taken this 'special path' ('deutscher Sonderweg'). The task now for Germany was to complete its long, all too frequently interrupted and abandoned 'Weg nach Westen' (journey to the West; Heinrich August Winkler) and to touch down safely in the Western democratic camp – and, if possible, to blaze new trails for democracy beyond the narrow bounds of the nation-state.[8]

But what was happening in the GDR, the second of the two German states founded after the war? What ideas and behaviours linked the citizens of the GDR to 'Europe'? How closely was the state integrated into the eastern European economic and military alliances laid down by the Soviet Union? What cultural influences and connections were at work in this part of Europe? And how did the GDR understand its own history and relationship with 'Europe'?

In eastern Europe, the situation was different in one striking respect: unlike the West's 'protector', the USA, the Soviet Union was geographically part of Europe, although it also included areas east of the Urals that extended far into Asia. It was literally close by, sharing borders with Poland, Romania, Hungary, Czechoslovakia, and the Baltic States, then under direct Soviet rule. This allowed it to impose a political and military hegemony that prevented the countries of eastern Europe from enjoying any sort of autonomy or pursuing an independent course. The nature of these relationships was reflected in political language. When in the GDR people talked about their socialist 'Bruderstaaten' (brother states), they meant to include the Soviet Union only in a limited sense. Rather, the Soviet Union was, in Stalinist parlance, the 'fatherland of all workers', or the 'motherland and advance guard of socialism' (*Neues Deutschland* 1963).[9] Regardless of whether it was termed a father or a mother, the Soviet Union was seen as an authority figure that was owed obedience and gratitude by its 'sons'. At official level, the notion of friendship served to gloss over the dependence and subordination this entailed. With 6 million members in 1985, the Society for German-Soviet Friendship (founded in 1949, the successor organisation of the *Gesellschaft zum Studium der Kultur der Sowjetunion* of 1947), was one of the largest mass-membership bodies in the GDR, organising study visits, holiday camps for children, and cultural encounters. Yet such programmes had only limited appeal. The propaganda effort that went into promoting them was out of all proportion to the success they enjoyed at grass roots, among the general population.

Even less successful were the many other friendship societies and committees that made up the *Liga für Völkerfreundschaft* (International Friendship League). The GDR had loose ties, at best, with its 'brother states' in eastern Europe. GDR citizens did visit the 'befreundetes sozialistisches Ausland' (allied socialist countries), spending their holidays on Lake Balaton in Hungary or at the Bulgarian Black Sea coast. Even work-related migration was not unheard of in the Eastern bloc states, which were at different stages of development, but it occurred at levels well below those achieved in Western Europe. The 'brother states' of Comecon were much more cut off from one another economically, socially, and culturally than the countries of the EEC; right to end, they remained more 'national' – and nationalist – societies (Wilson and van der Dussen 1993: 156ff.; Stirk and Weigall 1999: 182ff.; Judt 1996: 64).

This was especially true of the GDR, which – precisely because its political system was in competition with that of the Federal Republic – went to great lengths to reinvent itself as a socialist German state. The East Berlin Government set much greater store than its counterpart in Bonn on rituals and symbols that both reaffirmed the GDR's sovereignty and connected it to positive aspects of the German past. Patriotic tub thumping of a sort that hardly ever featured in the Federal Republic was de rigueur in the GDR. It could be seen at the military parades staged to mark national holidays, at flag-raising ceremonies and in banner displays, and in the goose-stepping of the guards at the Neue Wache, the main memorial in East Berlin to the victims of war and fascism. The GDR quickly developed a view of history that placed it on the side of the victors; unlike the Federal Republic, it did not see itself as the legal successor of the 'Third Reich' and refused to accept any responsibility for the consequences of Nazi policies. Instead, its leaders endlessly repeated the mantra that, thanks to Soviet help, imperialism, capitalism, and militarism had been eradicated root and branch, leaving the GDR free to confront the challenges of the future unburdened by Germany's 'dark' past.

At the same time, the GDR sought to cobble together a 'bright' past it could be proud of – and that could be usefully deployed against the rival German state. While the Federal Republic was seen as the embodiment of everything nasty and contemptible in German history, the GDR assumed the mantle of Germany's 'progressive' traditions, from the Peasants War of the early 16th century, now characterised as an 'early bourgeois revolution', through German classicism, down to Karl Marx and the 19th-century socialist workers' movement. Proclaiming itself the rightful guardian of this 'legacy', the GDR used it to strengthen its sense of national identity (Assmann and Frevert 1999). Political legitimation of the GDR, in competition with the Federal Republic, was central to its positive reappropriation of German history: the new socialist state wanted to present itself to its citizens not as a Soviet import, but as the triumph and fulfilment of the best German traditions.

This self-understanding was one of the main drivers for the GDR's peaceful revolution of 1989. When Easterners changed their slogan from 'Wir sind *das* Volk' (We are *the* people) to 'Wir sind *ein* Volk' (We are *one* people), they were evoking a sense of historical shared identity that had almost disappeared in the Federal Republic. At the same time, their call for reunification reflected the continuing appeal of West Germany, which – as East Germans could see every day on television – was able to offer a far higher standard of living, greater freedoms, and a more cosmopolitan outlook. The inhabitants of Leipzig, Magdeburg, or Rostock had always paid much more attention to developments in the West than to those in the East. After 1990, they looked not just to Hamburg, Frankfurt, or Munich, but to Amsterdam, Brussels, and Paris as well. Russian, which had been a compulsory subject in the GDR, was cast aside as they began to learn and speak English, the lingua franca of the late 20th and 21st centuries.

Conversely, in the old West people began to take a much closer look at what was happening in Warsaw, Prague, and Budapest. After the fall of the Wall and the Iron Curtain, the newly unified Germany lobbied enthusiastically for the eastwards expansion of the European Community. By embracing closer European unity as laid down by the Treaty of Maastricht (1992), the Federal Republic also sought to dispel any remaining doubts about its commitment to Europe and European identity. Having just become the largest, most populous, and most economically powerful nation state in Europe, dominating the heart of the continent, it was anxious to demonstrate that it had no intention of once again going it alone or taking a 'special path'. Quite the reverse: the Federal Republic chose to act as an engine of European integration. It was even prepared to give up its only true national symbol, the German Mark, as a confidence-building measure (Küsters and Hofmann 1998: 638).

There is no doubt that Germany has benefited – and continues to benefit – hugely from this positive approach to Europe. German exports have soared thanks to both the opening up of eastern European markets and the adoption of the euro as a common currency. However, in recent years attitudes towards 'Europe' have become more ambivalent, and eurosceptic movements are now on the rise. The louder the clamour from foreign observers for Germany to take on a leadership role in the financial and euro crisis that began in 2008, the more reluctant the federal government has been to do so. The austerity that it has promoted in Italy, Cyprus, and Greece may reflect German experiences and sensibilities, but it has stirred up anti-German feeling – with the German Chancellor being branded 'Hitler Merkel' – and exposed political and intellectual fault lines in the European project that were thought to have long since healed (Garton Ash 2013; Minton Beddoes 2013). In the current crisis, the tendency throughout Europe is for people to want to revert to national models and traditions and to lick their own wounds. For a 'European nation' such as Germany, which has carefully cultivated an international sense of mission over a long period, a return to nationalism of this kind is harder to contemplate than elsewhere. Yet Germany cannot resolve the European crisis on its own. To quote Timothy Garton Ash, one of the leading foreign experts on Germany, 'Only together can we generate the policies and institutions, but also that fresh breeze of poetry, to get the European ship sailing again'.

Yet 'visionary leadership', accompanied by 'pulse-quickening oratory', is not necessarily the only way to generate the 'breeze of poetry' Garton Ash seeks. An alternative approach – possibly with more lasting results – is through historical memory that avoids the pitfalls of national chauvinism and provincialism and uses the dramatic conflicts, enmities, and catastrophes Europe has suffered as a reason and incentive to seek peaceful, continent-wide solutions to problems. This can take a variety of forms, from official commemorative ceremonies of the sort planned for 2014, large-scale popular celebrations like those to mark the bicentenary of the Battle of Leipzig, and the naming of cities as European capitals of culture, through to Europe-wide history competitions such as those run by *eustory*, the history network for young Europeans, since 2001. Unsurprisingly, this project is the brainchild of a German institution, the Körber Foundation.[10]

Notes

1   See www.bverfg.de/entscheidungen/es20090630_2bve000208.html (accessed 6 December 2013).
2   See http://opinium.co.uk/sites/default/files/opin-inouteurope.pdf (accessed 13 December 2013).
3   For the German text of Schulz's speech, see http://www.europarl.europa.eu/the-president/en/press/press_release_speeches/speeches/sp-2013/sp-2013-october/html/leipzig-1813–1913–2013-jubilaum-v-lkerschlacht-und-v-lkerschlachtdenkmal-rede-von-martin-schulz-prasident-des-europaischen-parlaments (accessed 11 February 2014).
4   See www.volksbund.de/kriegsgraeberstaette/consenvoye.html (accessed 17 December 2013).
5   See the Historial's website, www.historial.org (accessed 17 December 2013), and the many works published by its research centre (e.g. Harel 1998; Huss 2000).
6   On its positive reception by the Vichy regime in France, however, see Bruneteau (2003); Mazower (2009): 553–75.
7   Although traces of these attitudes remained, as events from 2003 onwards were to demonstrate. When Germany opposed American foreign policy for the first time over the Iraq war, the pleasure that it took in dissociating itself from the US was unmistakable; anti-American stereotypes and clichés were also quick to resurface.
8   On the long debate concerning the German 'Sonderweg', see Kocka 1999 and Schulze 2002.
9   *Neues Deutschland* was the official mouthpiece of the ruling Socialist Unity Party and the GDR's most important and influential daily.
10 See www.koerber-stiftung.de/en/education/eustory.html (accessed 31 December 2013). The 'Report on Historical Memory in Culture and Education in the European Union', drafted by a committee of the European Parliament in August 2013, argues that historical 'memory, nurtured among other things by educational activities and cultural events, will reinforce genuine reconciliation between nations and authentic European integration'. See www.europarl.europa.eu/sides/getDoc.do?type=COMPARL&reference=PE-516.702&format=PDF&language=EN&secondRef=01 (accessed 31 December 2013).

Bibliography

Ambrosius, G. (1996) *Wirtschaftsraum Europa*, Frankfurt a.m.: Fischer.
Arendt, H. (2013) *Wahrheit gibt es nur zu zweien: Briefe an die Freunde*, ed. I. Nordmann, Munich: Piper.
Arndt, E.M. (1814) *Ein Wort über die Feier der Leipziger Schlacht*, Frankfurt a.m.: P.W. Eichenberg.
Assmann, A. and Frevert, U. (1999) *Geschichtsvergessenheit, Geschichtsversessenheit: Vom Umgang mit deutschen Vergangenheiten nach 1945*, Stuttgart: DVA.
Bailey, C. (2013) *Between Yesterday and Tomorrow: German Visions of Europe, 1926–1950*, New York: Berghahn.
Bauer, F. (1988) *Die Völkerschlacht bei Leipzig Oktober 1813*, Berlin: Militärverlag der DDR.
Behrenbeck, S. (1996) *Der Kult um die toten Helden: Nationalsozialistische Mythen, Riten und Symbole 1923 bis 1945*, Vierow: SH-Verlag.
Bohrer, K.H. (2012) *Granatsplitter: Erzählung einer Jugend*, Munich: Hanser.
Bruneteau, B. (2003) *'L'Europe Nouvelle' de Hitler: Une illusion des intellectuels de la France de Vichy*, Monaco: Editions du Rocher.
Conze, V. (2005) *Das Europa der Deutschen: Ideen von Europa in Deutschland zwischen Reichstradition und Westorientierung 1920–1970*, Munich: Oldenbourg.
Davis, B., Mausbach, W., Klimke, M., and MacDougall, C. (eds) (2010) *Changing the World, Changing Oneself: Political Protest and Collective Identities in West Germany and the US in the 1960s and 1970s*, Oxford: Berghahn.
della Porta, D. (1998) '"1968"–Zwischennationale diffusion und transnationale strukturen: eine forschungsagenda', in I. Gilcher-Holtey (ed.) *1968: Vom Ereignis zum Gegenstand der Geschichtswissenschaft*, Göttingen: Vandenhoeck & Ruprecht, 131–150.
Doering-Manteuffel, A. (1999) *Wie westlich sind die Deutschen? Amerikanisierung und Westernisierung im 20. Jahrhundert*, Göttingen: Vandenhoeck & Ruprecht.
Enzensberger, H.M. (1994) 'Brüssel oder Europa – eins von beiden (1989)', in P.M. Lützeler (ed.) *Hoffnung Europa: Deutsche Essays von Novalis bis Enzensberger*, Frankfurt a.m.: Fischer, 500–6.

Frankfurter Allgemeine Sonntagszeitung (2013), 20 October, 41.

Frevert, U. (2004) *A Nation in Barracks: Modern Germany, Military Conscription and Civil Society*, Oxford: Berg.

Fröhlich, E. (ed.) (1987) *Die Tagebücher von Joseph Goebbels*, vol. 4, Munich: K.G. Saur.

Garton Ash, T. (2013) 'The New German Question', *New York Review of Books*, 15 August. Available at: www.nybooks.com/articles/archives/2013/aug/15/new-german-question (accessed 15 February 2014).

Gildea, R., Mark, J., and Warring, A. (eds) (2013) *Europe's 1968 Voices of Revolt*, Oxford: Oxford University Press.

Habermas, J. (1992) 'Staatsbürgerschaft und nationale Identität' (1990), in *Faktizität und Geltung*, Frankfurt a.m.: Suhrkamp, 632–60.

Harel, V. (ed.) (1998) *Les affiches de la Grande Guerre*, Péronne: Martelle.

Hollande, F. (2013), 'Rede von Staatspräsident François Hollande zum Beginn der Gedenkfeierlichkeiten 100 Jahre Erster Weltkrieg', 7 November. Online. Available at: www.ambafrance-de.org/IMG/pdf/hollande_14–18–2.pdf (accessed 17 December 2013).

Horn, G.-R. (2008) *The Spirit of '68: Rebellion in Western Europe and North America, 1956–1976*, Oxford: Oxford University Press.

Huss, M.-M. (2000) *Histoires de famille: Cartes postales et culture de guerre*, Paris: Editions Noêsis.

Kaiser, A. (2010) *Von Helden und Opfern: Eine Geschichte des Volkstrauertags*, Frankfurt a.m.: Campus.

Keller, K. (2012) 'Die Völkerschlacht bei Leipzig', in P. den Boer *et al.* (eds) *Europäische Erinnerungsorte*, vol. 2, Munich: Oldenbourg, 421–30.

Kleßmann, C. (1982) *Die doppelte Staatsgründung: Deutsche Geschichte 1945–1955*, Göttingen: Vandenhoeck & Ruprecht.

Kocka, J. (1999) 'Asymmetrical historical comparisons: the case of the German "Sonderweg"', *History and Theory*, 38: 40–51.

Koselleck, R. (1989) '"Erfahrungsraum" und "Erwartungshorizont" – zwei historische Kategorien', in *Vergangene Zukunft: Zur Semantik geschichtlicher Zeiten*, Frankfurt a.m.: Suhrkamp, 349–75.

Küsters, H.J. and Hofmann, D. (eds) (1998) *Deutsche Einheit: Sonderedition aus den Akten des Bundeskanzleramtes 1989/90*, Munich: Oldenbourg.

Johnson, M.W. (2008) *Training Socialist Citizens: Sports and the State in East Germany*, Leiden: Brill.

Judt, T. (1996) *A Grand Illusion? An Essay on Europe*, New York and London: New York University Press.

Lipgens, W. (ed.) (1968) *Europa-Föderationspläne der Widerstandsbewegungen 1940–1945*, Munich: Oldenbourg.

Lipp, A. (2003) *Meinungslenkung im Krieg: Kriegserfahrungen deutscher Soldaten und ihre Deutung 1914–1918*, Göttingen: Vandenhoeck & Ruprecht.

Mann, H. (1987) 'VSE (Vereinigte Staaten von Europa)', in P.M. Lützeler (ed.) *Plädoyers für Europa: Stellungnahmen deutschsprachiger Schriftsteller 1915–1949*, Frankfurt a.m.: Fischer, 98–108.

Mazower, M. (2009) *Hitler's Empire: Nazi Rule in Occupied Europe*, London: Penguin.

Michalka, W. (ed.) (1985) *Das Dritte Reich*, Munich: dtv.

Minton Beddoes, Z. (2013) 'Europe's Reluctant Hegemon', *The Economist*, 15 June. Available at: www.economist.com/news/special-report/21579140-germany-now-dominant-country-europe-needs-rethink-way-it-sees-itself-and (accessed 15 February 2014).

Mommsen, H. (1994) 'Die künftige Neuordnung Deutschlands und Europas aus der Sicht des Kreisauer Kreises', in P. Steinbach and J. Tuchel (eds) *Widerstand gegen den Nationalsozialismus*, Berlin: Akademie, 246–61.

Müller, G. (2001) 'Jenseits des Nationalismus? "Europa" als Konzept grenzübergreifender adlig-bürgerlicher Elitendiskurse zwischen den beiden Weltkriegen', in H. Reif (ed.) *Adel und Bürgertum in Deutschland*, vol. II, Berlin: Akademie, 235–68.

Müller, J.W. (2010) *Verfassungspatriotismus*, Berlin: Suhrkamp.

Neues Deutschland (1963) 'Mutterland und Vorposten des Sozialismus', 2 June, 7.

Orluc, K. (2000) 'Decline or Renaissance: The Transformation of European Consciousness after the First World War', in B. Stråth (ed.) *Europe and the Other and Europe as the Other*, Brussels: Lang, 123–55.

Poser, S. (2003) 'Die Jahrhundertfeier der Völkerschlacht und die Einweihung des Völkerschlachtdenkmals', in V. Rodekamp (ed.) *Völkerschlachtdenkmal*, Leipzig: Verlag DZA, 102–15.

Reimann, A. (2000) *Der große Krieg der Sprachen: Untersuchungen zur historischen Semantik in Deutschland und England zur Zeit des Ersten Weltkriegs*, Essen: Klartext.

Schilmar, B. (2004) *Der Europadiskurs im deutschen Exil 1933–1945*, Munich: Oldenbourg.

Schmidt, A. (2006) *Belehrung – Propaganda – Vertrauensarbeit: Zum Wandel amtlicher Kommunikationspolitik in Deutschland 1914–1918*, Essen: Klartext.

Schmidtke, M.A. (1998) 'Reform, revolte oder revolution? Der sozialistische deutsche studentenbund (SDS) und die students for a democratic society (SDS) 1960–1970', in I. Gilcher-Holtey (ed.) *1968: Vom Ereignis zum Gegenstand der Geschichtswissenschaft*, Göttingen: Vandenhoeck & Ruprecht, 188–206.

Schöberl, V. (2008) *'Es gibt ein großes und herrliches Land, das sich selbst nicht kennt . . . Es heißt Europa': Die Diskussion um die Paneuropaidee in Deutschland, Frankreich und Großbritannien 1922–1933*, Münster: Lit Verlag.

Schulze, W. (2002) 'Vom "Sonderweg" bis zur "Ankunft im Westen": Deutschlands Stellung in Europa', *Geschichte in Wissenschaft und Unterricht*, 53: 226–40.

Spitzner, A. (1897) *Das Völkerschlacht-National-Denkmal: Eine Denkschrift des Deutschen Patrioten-Bundes*, Leipzig: Dt-Patriotenbund.

Sternberger, D. (1990) *Verfassungspatriotismus*, Frankfurt a.m.: Insel.

Stirk, P.M.R. (1996) *A History of European Integration since 1914*, London: Pinter.

Stirk, P.M.R. and Weigall, D. (eds) (1999) *The Origins and Development of European Integration*, New York and London: Pinter.

Verhey, J. (2000) *The Spirit of 1914: Militarism, Myth, and Mobilization in Germany*, Cambridge: Cambridge University Press.

Weidenfeld, W. and Piepenschneider, M. (1987) *Jugend und Europa: Die Einstellung der jungen Generation in der Bundesrepublik Deutschland zur Europäischen Einigung*, Bonn: Europa Union Verlag.

Weltweit vor Ort. Magazin der Max Weber Stiftung (2013) 'Globalisierung der Erinnerung: Ein Interview mit Joseph Zimet', 2: 16–17.

Wilson, K. and van der Dussen, J. (1993) *The History of the Idea of Europe*, London: Open University.

Ziegerhofer-Prettenthaler, A. (2004) *Botschafter Europas: Richard Nikolaus Coudenhove-Kalergi und die Paneuropa-Bewegung in den zwanziger und dreißiger Jahren*, Vienna: Böhlau.

Ziemann, B. (2006) *War Experiences in Rural Germany: 1914–1923*, Oxford: Berg.

2

Humanität, Bildung, Kultur

Germany's civilising values

Ritchie Robertson

Present-day Germany is a society in which culture enjoys high status: theatres and libraries are generously (even if with difficulty) subsidised by governments; the utterances of Günter Grass receive far more attention than those of any British or American writer could expect in their countries. It can also claim to be one of the world's most successful democracies and economies, with a prudent foreign policy that has largely avoided the military involvements of some other Western nations. *Kultur* and associated concepts provide a set of threads linking the Germany of today to its conflicted past.

Although the terms *Humanität, Bildung*, and *Kultur* are notoriously hard to translate, together they denote, very broadly, a conception of humanity that can be developed by education (*Bildung*) and finds expression in culture. This cluster of ideas emerges from the Enlightenment, and may be called the legacy of the specifically German Enlightenment (Reed 2009). Their spokesmen, often grouped together under the label 'Weimar Classicism', include Johann Wolfgang Goethe (1749–1832), Friedrich Schiller (1759–1805), Johann Gottfried Herder (1744–1803), Immanuel Kant (1724–1804), and Wilhelm von Humboldt (1767–1835).

The value of this legacy, however, has been challenged, especially in the light of German history between 1914 and 1945. In the 1930s the concentration camp Buchenwald was set up just outside Weimar. When some woods were being cleared to put up camp buildings, care was taken to preserve an oak tree under which Goethe used to sit with his friend Charlotte von Stein (Roth 1939). Was this not proof that the values of Weimar Classicism were ineffectual against 20th-century inhumanity? Worse still, that they could even on occasion license inhumanity? Hence the critique to which the legacy of Weimar Classicism has been subjected (Wilson and Holub 1993; Dörr and Hofmann 2008).

It has, further, been claimed that the concept of 'Enlightenment' – and hence the others that emerge from it – is corrupted by an inbuilt dialectic, so that innovations designed to benefit humanity end in devastation (Horkheimer and Adorno 2002). The conquest of nature, it is said, leads inexorably to the massacre of conquered populations, whether in European colonies or in the mid-20th-century Europe that witnessed the Holocaust and the gulags. However, this thesis not only rests on very slight historical knowledge about the Enlightenment, but identifies it narrowly with scientific progress. The thesis denies human agency and sees life as subject to an inexorable logic. Against this, I assume historical contingency, not philosophical necessity.

History results from the intersection and clashing of people's actions, and there is always room for the unexpected. Horkheimer and Adorno illustrate a version of the cultural pessimism which flourished in Germany – understandably – in the early and mid-20th century, and of which we shall presently meet a representative in Oswald Spengler (1880–1936).

Weimar values do indeed have weaknesses, which will be acknowledged in the following account. But they also form a valuable and still living tradition. Their proponents' rich and diverse body of thought and literature cannot be reduced to a formula. Nevertheless, the following principles can be distinguished:

1   Humanity is deeply embedded in nature, though it may still have a divine or supersensible component.
2   Immanent in nature is a plan whereby all beings are to realise their potential.
3   Humanity's purpose is to move ever closer to perfection – the realisation of its full potential (*Humanität*) – albeit over an unimaginably long period and with innumerable setbacks.
4   It does so through education, which is an active, creative process of *Bildung*: self-formation or self-cultivation (Bruford 1975).
5   Crucial to *Bildung* are the aesthetic categories of unity and harmony.

Further: the development of *Humanität* entails an ongoing critique of one's own current culture, in the light of ideals pointing towards a better future. In this sense, the cultural critiques delivered by Jean-Jacques Rousseau in his two *Discourses* of the 1750s can be seen as landmarks in the exploration of *Humanität*. 'Rousseau deserves the place at the gateway to the new intellectual world', wrote one of *Humanität*'s classic expositors, 'because he first reflects on what we may call the *self-criticism of modern culture*' (Spranger 1928: 11).

Herder and *Humanität*

Among his many achievements as scholar, theologian, literary and cultural critic, and philosopher, Herder formulated conceptions of *Humanität*, *Bildung*, and *Kultur* that had a lasting impact on the Weimar Classicism that centred on Goethe and Schiller. He presented them most comprehensively in his *Ideas for a Philosophy of the History of Mankind* (*Ideen zur Philosophie der Geschichte der Menschheit*, 1784–91). He presupposes that the organic world forms a great unity, powered by a single vital energy, with no sharp distinction between spirit and matter, mind and body, humans and animals. All are linked in the chain of being, a recurrent image that Herder borrows especially from Leibniz. The analogy between the growth of a human being from an embryo, and of a plant from a seed, illustrates this unity.

Human life has a purpose: the realisation of our *Humanität*, our full humanity. This may sound tautologous, but is not, for *Humanität* comprehends seven main human attributes (Herder 1989: 154–64). The first is peacefulness, for our physical form is not designed for aggression. Second comes the sexual urge, which finds its best expression in marriage based on mutual consent. Third, our ability to hear what other people say grounds our sympathy with others. Fourth, maternal love, combined with a child's long period of dependence on parents, is the foundation of social life. Fifth, our relations with others are kept on an equal footing by our sense of fairness (Herder prefers the tolerant-sounding *Billigkeit* to the severe *Gerechtigkeit* [justice]). Sixth comes *Wohlanständigkeit* (decency and comeliness of appearance), which brings out the beauty and shapeliness of the human body, instead of disfiguring it with the elaborate hairdos of some members of the upper classes or the piercings and mutilations reported by travellers beyond Europe. Finally, true humanity includes religion, which is essentially the hope for immortality.

Humanität can only be realised in the individual; otherwise it would be a meaningless abstraction. Each individual is situated in a particular place, connected via the family with a wider people (*Volk*), whose national character is expressed in its language. The individual is further connected with the rest of humanity through the chain of cultural transmission. This cultural chain enables us to be rational. For Herder, reason is not, as for early Enlightenment rationalism, a timeless, quasi-logical faculty; it means refining and applying the sedimented wisdom of previous generations ('das fortgehende Werk der Bildung des menschlichen Lebens') (Herder 1989: 144). Chains of tradition and sympathy always converge here and now in the unique individual: 'What each person is and can be, must be the purpose of the human race; and what is this? *Humanität* and happiness in this place, to this degree, as this particular link in the chain of *Bildung* that stretches through the entire race' ('Was also jeder Mensch ist und sein kann, das muß Zweck des Menschengeschlechts sein; und was ist dies? Humanität und Glückseligkeit auf dieser Stelle, in diesem Grad, als dies und kein anderes Glied der Kette von Bildung, die durchs ganze Geschlecht reichet') (Herder 1989: 342).

In history, each people makes its own contribution to *Humanität* through its distinctive culture. No people is wholly without culture. Herder writes about 'primitive' people with sympathy and defends them against their detractors. Cultural diversity expresses the richness of *Humanität*. History recounts the progress, even the perfectibility, of our species. Herder is no cloudy-headed optimist: he acknowledges atrocities, massacres, long periods of despotism in history, calling them 'errors and failures' (Herder 1989: 633). But, like storms in the atmosphere, violent passions and conflicts are necessary in history and spur us on. Even war generates new inventions. The increased deadliness of weapons means that only potentates, not marauding chieftains, can now wage war, and increases the chances of peace. Thus progress is indirect, irregular, like a mountain torrent, or even like humanity's basic action of walking:

> The whole course of culture on our earth, with its broken corners and rough edges, hardly ever resembles a gentle stream, but rather a torrent plunging down the mountains. [...] As our gait is a constant falling to right and left, and yet we advance with each step, so also is the progress of culture in human generations and entire peoples.

> (Überhaupt zeigt der ganze Gang der Kultur auf unsrer Erde mit seinen abgerissenen Ecken, mit seinen aus- und einspringenden Winkeln fast nie einen sanften Strom, sondern vielmehr den Sturz eines Wildwassers von den Gebürgen. [...] Wie unser Gang ein beständiges Fallen ist zur Rechten und zur Linken und dennoch kommen wir mit jedem Schritt weiter: so ist der Fortschritt der Kultur in Menschengeschlechtern und in ganzen Völkern.)

> (Herder 1989: 655)

These ideas, expressed with Herder's infectious enthusiasm, are inspiring, but also liberal and generous. Since he finds some value in every culture, Herder is no nationalist, although his ideas may subsequently have been misused by 19th- and 20th-century upholders of German supremacy. Nor is he a complete relativist for whom different cultures are incommensurable (Berlin 1976: 153; see also Sikka 2011; Maurer 2012). His conception of *Humanität* offers normative standards by which cultures may be judged. All cultures contribute something, but not all are equally valuable: Herder praises the peaceful Egyptians, the inventive Greeks, and the industrious Phoenicians, but deplores the Romans' urge for conquest. Yet Herder's standards are also very broad: monogamy, for example, may take a variety of institutional forms. *Humanität* is a work in progress that cannot be defined in a narrow, restrictive way.

Some incoherence arises from Herder's concern for the individual. He opposes the idea, put forward by Kant in 'Idea for a Universal History with a Cosmopolitan Purpose' (1784), that while individuals must fail, in a greater or lesser degree, to fulfil their potential, the potential unrealised in the individual would ultimately be realised in the species; thus hope was transferred to future earthly history (Kant 1991: 41–53). Herder objects to having *Humanität* deferred to a remote future, and claims that each individual realises *Humanität* in a unique way. Yet since clearly many lives are blighted and wasted, the theologian Herder falls back on the unprovable claim that our potential will be fully realised in a future existence – a claim surprisingly often made in late 18th-century Germany, when orthodox Christianity had become largely incredible to critical thinkers (Kurth-Voigt 1999). While Herder attacked Kant, Kant criticised the *Ideen* in two reviews for relying on dubious analogies and mixing natural science with metaphysics. Their public controversy embittered both thinkers.

Goethe and *Bildung*

Goethe worked closely with Herder, first as a student at Strasbourg in 1770, later from 1783 to 1786 in Weimar, where Herder was superintendent of the Lutheran clergy. Both were fascinated by natural science, conceived of nature as an organic unity, and believed in continuous development, not revolutionary disruption, in both geology and politics. Thus Goethe preferred the 'Neptunian' theory that minerals originated from a slow process of sedimentation and from the gradual withdrawal of the oceans, to the 'Plutonian' theory of volcanic catastrophes; and he was among the few German intellectuals who (like Edmund Burke in Britain) rejected the French Revolution from its very outset. Goethe himself perceived the analogy between geological and political cataclysms (David 1974).

Goethe's conception of development, or *Bildung*, found expression in his novel *Wilhelm Meister's Apprenticeship* (*Wilhelm Meisters Lehrjahre*, 1795–6). This is commonly considered the exemplary *Bildungsroman*, or novel of development, though the term *Bildungsroman* was not used till the 1870s, when the cultural needs of the new German Empire required a specifically 'German' type of novel, focused on the hero's inner life (Steinecke 1991). Although the concept of the *Bildungsroman* screens out the large body of realistic fiction produced in 19th-century Germany, it reminds us how widely *Meister* was read as a pedagogical work showing how a young man matures into a useful member of society. In retrospect, however, such a reading seems inadequate to the complexities of Goethe's novel.

Discussion of *Meister* as *Bildungsroman* often starts from the letter Wilhelm writes to his friend Werner, declaring that his middle-class status denies him the 'harmonious development of my personality' (Goethe 1989: 175) ('harmonischen Ausbildung meiner Natur') (Goethe 1986–2000: 9, 659) for which he longs, and that since in his Germany only aristocrats can develop a rounded personality, he as a born *Bürger* can develop himself only by acting as a noblemen on the stage. By this time, Wilhelm and his travelling theatrical troupe have spent time at a noble mansion, where the nobility have cut distinctly unimpressive figures, and his own acting talents have been shown to be limited. So his letter can hardly express his real goal. Soon afterwards, Wilhelm visits another mansion that turns out to be the seat of the Society of the Tower (*Turmgesellschaft*), which has been monitoring his progress through life. His apprenticeship over, he is admitted to a society where each individual's talents contribute to a greater whole. 'All men make up mankind and all forces together make up the world. These are often in conflict with each other, and while trying to destroy each other they are held together and reproduced by Nature' (Goethe 1989: 338) ('Nur alle Menschen machen die Menschheit aus, nur alle Kräfte zusammengenommen die Welt. Diese sind unter sich oft im Widerstreit, und indem sie sich zu zerstören suchen, hält sie die Natur zusammen und bringt sie wieder hervor') (Goethe 1986–2000: 9, 932–3). Here again we see the influence of Kant's 'Idea for a Universal History', particularly of Kant's idea that society progresses through conflict. Man is a social animal, but also seeks to develop his individuality. Hence our social life is always conflicted, but our conflicts press us to develop our natural capacities. We therefore need 'a society which has not only the greatest freedom, and therefore a continual antagonism among its members, but also the most precise specification and preservation of the limits of this freedom in order that it can coexist with the freedom of others' (Kant 1991: 45).

The Society of the Tower may be seen as foreshadowing such a society. To get there, Wilhelm has himself developed. But his *Bildung* has not been smooth. His psychological course veers between depression and ecstasy. He has fathered an illegitimate child, whose mother Mariane has, unknown to him, died in misery. He has misused his father's money to finance an acting troupe in hopes of a theatrical career for which he is ill suited. Was this a waste of time? Or worse? Yet without his theatrical adventure he would not have met Natalie, his perfect partner, to whom he finally becomes engaged. Nor would he have met the strange child Mignon, who first arouses his paternal emotions. And in assuming responsibility for his own child, he acquires all the virtues of a good citizen, not through instruction, but through the promptings of nature. Hence the Society declares his misguided actions to be not crimes or sins, but necessary aberrations, and tells him not to torment himself with futile guilt: 'You will not regret any of your follies, and will not wish to repeat any of them. No man could have a happier fate' (Goethe 1989: 303) ('Du wirst keine deiner Torheiten bereuen und keine zurück wünschen, kein glücklicheres Schicksal kann einem Menschen werden') (Goethe 1986–2000: 9, 873–4).

This is an optimistic message. It recalls Herder's view that the horrors of history are mere 'errors and failures'. Goethe and Herder, accordingly, both rejected Kant's belief, expressed in his *Religion within the Bounds of Mere Reason* (1793), in 'a *radical* innate *evil* in human nature' (Kant 1996: 80; emphasis in original). Yet the novel, with the honesty of fiction, shows that Wilhelm's path, despite his good intentions, is strewn with corpses (Mariane's and Mignon's). Narrative irony exposes Wilhelm, not as a criminal, but as emotionally unstable, a blunderer, and even a bore. Although Wilhelm is nominally integrated into society, Goethe, even in the sequel, *Wilhelm Meister's Journeyman Years* (*Wilhelm Meisters Wanderjahre*, 1829), never got round to showing Wilhelm and Natalie as a married couple. Goethe's confidence in nature is undercut by darker suggestions that only a determinedly upbeat reading could ignore.

Schiller: freedom through art

The progressive optimism favoured by many intellectuals was challenged by the French Revolution. The fall of the Bastille, the formation of the National Assembly, and the Declaration of the Rights of Man and the Citizen aroused enthusiasm abroad. But the subsequent execution of the king and queen, and the reign of terror in which, executions aside, some 10 per cent of the French adult population spent time in prison, aroused horror like that produced by the Chinese Cultural Revolution in the 1960s. What had gone wrong?

This question prompted Schiller's *Letters on the Aesthetic Education of Mankind* (*Über die ästhetische Erziehung des Menschen in einer Reihe von Briefen*, 1795–6). There had, in Schiller's view, been a brief opportunity to replace traditional authority with law, reason, and freedom. But it was not taken, because the people to whom it was offered were morally unprepared for it.

The lack of moral freedom reflects a wider problem of modern society, of deep concern to Weimar Classicism: that of the division of labour (Pascal 1962). Schiller notes that there are thinkers who know nothing of practical life, and practical men, men of affairs, who despise ideas. Up to a point this antagonism of opposing forces is a necessary conflict, an instrument of *Kultur*. Like Kant and Herder, Schiller thinks that progress happens through productive conflict. But such conflict is not itself *Kultur*. The development of culture requires that these antagonisms be softened and eventually overcome.

To explain how, Schiller resorts to anthropology in its late 18th-century sense – the study of human nature. Having in his youth studied medicine, he posits three psycho-physical drives in humanity. The 'sensuous drive' ('Stofftrieb' or 'sinnlicher Trieb'; Schiller 1967: 79) springs from our physical, sensual nature and enables us to deal with particular objects. A person dominated by the *Stofftrieb* lives from moment to moment. The 'formal drive' (*Formtrieb*) springs from our rational nature and is concerned with abstractions, with principles, with what is timelessly true. These two principles are not in direct conflict. We need both. But they have to be held in balance, and to do so is the task of culture (*Kultur*). Life should not be dominated either by sensuality or by rationality.

The balance between the formal drive and the sensual drive is maintained by the *Spieltrieb* or urge to play. This drive is basic to humanity. It shows itself as soon as primitive people begin to decorate their bodies, to practise rituals, to organise their spontaneous movements into rhythmic dances. When people imagine their gods not as terrible tyrants who need to be propitiated, but as beautiful beings, the aesthetic sense opens the way for further intellectual and moral development, as with the Greeks, who, as the most civilised society, idealised their gods by imagining them as constantly at play, enjoying leisure on Mount Olympus. The experience of beauty, which may take various forms, brings the sensual person closer to abstraction, and brings the abstract thinker closer to the sensory world. Schiller then argues that there is an intermediate state between matter and form, between passivity and activity. In this state, the mind is active, yet not under constraint; it is a state of free activity. Schiller calls it the aesthetic condition. In this condition, all our faculties are called into play, but by an object that is not real.

Schiller is not here talking about the external effect that art may have on us. He is describing how the play-drive and the experience of beauty can modify human nature by bringing about the aesthetic condition within us. Through the aesthetic condition, humanity moves from a subjection to physical needs and to brute force towards a condition of freedom in which people can voluntarily obey the demands of morality and reason. The aesthetic condition is a psychological one that also corresponds to a stage in the development of society. At this stage, our dealings with one another acquire an aesthetic element; roughness yields to politeness; kindness and consideration become the social norm. Schiller attacks those critics of culture (meaning mainly Rousseau) who deplore modern politeness as mere insincerity. Beauty is essential to sociability: it shapes the way we live together in society.

And here the *Aesthetic Letters* are revealed as a profoundly political text. The French Revolution failed because people tried to leap straight from a condition of coercion to a society based on reason. Yet neither coercion nor reason can make people good. The state should not try to educate people morally, because it merely limits their freedom. Only aesthetic experience, by transforming human nature and making people capable of freedom, can open the way to true sociability and to the civic virtue that Schiller, following the republican tradition, thought the best foundation for the state (Beiser 2005: 125).

Schiller's *Letters* exercised an immense influence not only on the social critique offered by his contemporaries and by the Romantic generation that immediately followed, but also on the Marxist tradition. Karl Marx, like Schiller, saw the division of labour as a social evil that forced each person into a single sphere of activity. Only in communist society, Marx thought, could this confinement be overcome, because there 'society regulates the general production and thus makes it possible for me to do one thing today and another tomorrow, to hunt in the morning, fish in the afternoon, rear cattle in the evening, criticise after dinner, just as I have a mind, without ever becoming hunter, fisherman, cowherd or critic' (Marx 1977: 169). The Western Marxists of the Frankfurt School drew from Schiller a different utopian conception in which art provided a realm of freedom and a vantage-point from which to reveal the alienation of capitalist society (Jameson 1971: 83–116).

The Greeks

The ideal of harmony that runs from Schiller to Marx and beyond was often thought to have been best embodied in the ancient Greeks. While the Renaissance concentrated on rediscovering Latin literature, 18th-century Germany exalted Greece above Rome, Homer above Virgil, Sophocles above Seneca. The art historian Johann Joachim Winckelmann (1717–68) held up Greek art as an unsurpassable ideal that the moderns should imitate. Goethe took the Greeks, especially in his classical drama *Iphigenie auf Tauris*, as the model for his human-centred worldview: 'The Greeks sought not to render the gods human, but to render humankind divine' (Goethe 1986–2000: 20, 293). Schiller's poem 'The Gods of Greece' ('Die Götter Griechenlands') contrasted the Greek view of nature as populated by divine beings with the disenchanted, mechanical universe of modern science. Friedrich Schlegel extolled the Greek achievement in poetry, politics, social life, and science:

> Only the development of pure humanity is true *Bildung*. Where has free humanity attained such pervasive dominance in the mass of the population as among the Greeks? Where else was *Bildung* so genuine, and genuine *Bildung* so public?
>
> (Nur Entwicklung der reinen Menschheit ist wahre Bildung. Wo hat freie Menschheit in der Masse des Volks ein so durchgängiges Übergewicht erhalten als bei den Griechen? Wo war die Bildung so echt, und echte Bildung so öffentlich?)
>
> (Schlegel 1970: 174)

Friedrich Hölderlin's mature poetry celebrates Greek civilisation as inspired by the gods. In his novel *Hyperion* (1797) the hero denounces, by contrast, the fragmentation of the modern Germans, who may be artisans, thinkers, priests, but never 'Menschen', whole human beings (Hölderlin 1969: 1, 433). Marx struggled to explain how Greek art could still provide unattainable models when Greek society had been at such an early stage of development, and concluded, implausibly, that though the Greeks inhabited the childhood of society, they were normal and hence delightful children (Prawer 1976: 278–88).

This Graecomania was occasionally qualified. Herder, in the chapter of *Ideen* celebrating the Greeks, also criticises them for their constant internecine wars and their harsh treatment of defeated enemies (Herder 1989: 535). Although Goethe read Homer constantly and made a close study of the *Iliad*, he also said, presumably with its atmosphere of perpetual warfare in mind, that it helped one to imagine hell (letter to Schiller, 13 December 1803). Late in the 19th century, the Swiss historian Jacob Burckhardt presented a critical picture of Greek civilisation, bringing out the Greeks' cultivation but also their pessimism, malevolence, and misogyny, and finding in the shortcomings of Athenian democracy a warning for his own day (Burckhardt 1998). However, a conception of ancient Greece as both exemplary and culturally homogeneous, underplaying the Greeks' debts to Egypt and Asia (Bernal 1987), was to be institutionalised in the educational system.

The institutions of *Bildung*

Herder is suspicious of the state, considering it at best a necessary evil. The institution required by nature is the family. The state closest to nature is therefore an extended family whose members all belong to the same *Volk*. Large states, in which different peoples are mingled, are therefore contrary to nature, and so are all established social ranks, since they hamper people's freedom to develop. Rulers, who all owe their power originally to war and conquest, offend nature as soon as they try to regulate their subjects' lives. 'As soon as a ruler seeks to occupy the place of the Creator and, whether from caprice or passion, make the creature into something God did not intend, this heaven-defying despotism becomes the father of disorder and inevitable misfortune' (Herder 1989: 370).

In a similar spirit, the young Wilhelm von Humboldt argued in *A Proposal to Determine the Limits of State Action* (*Idee zu einem Versuch, die Gränzen der Wirksamkeit des Staates zu bestimmen*, 1792) for a conception of the state that now seems astonishingly minimalist. The state should require no positive duties from its citizens. It should limit their liberty only by forbidding such actions as might reduce the freedom of others. It should permit no hindrance to the free development of the individual. 'The true end of Man, or that which is prescribed by the eternal and immutable dictates of reason, and not suggested by vague and transient desires, is the highest and most harmonious development of his powers to a complete and consistent whole' (Humboldt 1969: 16) – a passage later quoted admiringly by John Stuart Mill in *On Liberty* (1859). The individual needs not only freedom, however, but also variety, for monotony impedes one's development. Yet if one follows a variety of pursuits, one may dissipate one's energies and achieve little. The answer to this problem is first, that each person should combine his diverse faculties in order to reach his goal; and second, that he should join together with other people, each of whom is developing his particular abilities, in a common endeavour. The basic form of such a union is the alliance between a man and a woman; beyond that, the associations and societies, founded on personal friendship, which we find especially among the ancient Greeks. The state cannot legislate for such endeavours, but should leave them to voluntary associations. It should not even institute a national system of education, but should leave education to parents and to private schools. For any national system of education will impose some uniformity on the pupils and thus hinder their free development. This ideal conception of the minimalist state ignores the fact that the German principalities all had large bureaucracies ensuring public order and amenities in the name of the *Polizeistaat* or 'police state', a term that had not yet acquired its 20th-century authoritarian meaning (Raeff 1983); the state apparatus would grow throughout the 19th century in all European countries. It may be considered a weakness of Weimar Classicist thought that it failed to address the relation between the individual and the actually existing state.

Ironically, Humboldt in 1809 found himself in charge of Prussia's schools and universities when, in the wake of Prussia's defeat by Napoleon, the ministers leading the Reform movement got him appointed director of the Section for Religion and Public Instruction within the newly reorganised Ministry of the Interior. He sought to institutionalise the principle of free *Bildung*. Vocational education, while necessary, should be strictly separated from the teaching that sought to enlarge people's humanity by arousing their intellect and imagination, and that should be available to all classes. For young children Humboldt prescribed the teaching methods of the Swiss Johann Heinrich Pestalozzi (1746–1827), who encouraged children to learn actively, to deal with realities rather than abstractions, and to develop their individuality. At secondary level, the 'Latin schools' with their dreary and ineffectual teaching should be replaced by *Bürgerschulen* whose pupils should study Latin, history, mathematics, and technical subjects, specialising

27

according to their talents, and by Humboldt's great innovation, the humanistic *Gymnasium*, which prepared pupils for university. The *Gymnasium* centred on classical languages, together with history and mathematics, and aimed – though practice often fell short of precept – to teach those languages not in a dry-as-dust way, but as a means of understanding both the form of a language (Humboldt was among the founders of linguistics) and the spirit of the ancient world.

Humboldt's best-known achievement was founding the university at Berlin that now bears his name. In planning a university, Humboldt shared the conviction, first formulated in the inaugural lecture delivered by Schiller at Jena 20 years earlier, that university study was not for the 'Brotgelehrte' (scholar earning his bread) who simply sought a professional qualification, but for the 'philosophical mind' selflessly devoted to knowledge and to seeking its underlying principles (Schiller 1958: 4, 750–3; Ziolkowski 1990: 237–52). In contrast to the specialised *grandes écoles* established by Napoleon, the university should form the pinnacle of the nation's 'moral culture' ('moralische Cultur') and provide its denizens with *Bildung* in both intellectual matters and social ethics (Humboldt 1964: 4, 255). While the school presents its students with already established knowledge, university students and faculty together should pursue knowledge as something not fixed but always in the process of being discovered and elaborated. The school should develop all its students' abilities harmoniously, so that those impelled towards higher study can discover their vocation and pursue it at university, both through solitary study and through cooperation. For this, the institution of the seminar, pioneered by the classical philologist Christian Gottlob Heyne at Göttingen from 1764, permitted an ideal union of teaching and research (Clark 2006: 158–79). Humboldt admitted that only a few students would devote themselves to the highest intellectual ideals, but expected them to exert a wide influence. Although reality was inevitably more mundane, he established a model for the university that had wide influence, especially in the United States, and contrasts both with the long-established view of the university as a means of professional training and its more recent assimilation to a business model.

Bildung and *Kultur* from the Napoleonic Wars to World War I

In the repressive political climate that followed the defeat of Napoleon, when the Karlsbad Decrees of 1819 required even university lectures to be submitted to censorship, the *Bildung* envisaged by Humboldt had little chance to transform public life. *Bildung* was a possession of many individuals, and sometimes primarily a sign of social status, embodied in editions of Goethe and Schiller that gathered dust in glass-fronted bookcases but attested to their owners' membership of the *Bildungsbürgertum* or educated middle class. Humboldt's conception of the state as confined to safeguarding individual freedom was contradicted by the steady growth of administration and government in Germany's numerous states and, from 1871, in the German Empire.

The new Empire's appropriation of *Kultur* and *Bildung* was most vehemently opposed by Friedrich Nietzsche (1844–1900), who also demanded a reinterpretation and revaluation of these concepts. He attacked the chauvinist illusion that Prussia's victory over France had resulted from the supposed superiority of German *Kultur*. In fact, Nietzsche charged, the triumphalist new Empire threatened to destroy the German spirit (*Geist*). The new Germany had produced the cultivated philistine (*Bildungsphilister*), who trumpeted the excellence of 'German culture' but had no idea what culture really meant. Culture, according to Nietzsche, is not book-learning, but a way of life, characterised by 'unity of artistic style in all the expressions of the life of a people' (Nietzsche 1982: 5). It could be found in Renaissance Italy or among the ancient Greeks, but not in present-day Germany, which offered only a hotchpotch of different styles from diverse periods and countries. The Greeks could no longer provide a model, because the German universities did not supply *Bildung*, but only knowledge about *Bildung*. To a modern student, the Greeks would probably seem uneducated, while to them, with his head stuffed full of knowledge, his awkward body and ugly clothes, he would appear like a walking encyclopaedia, bearing the title 'Handbook of inward culture for outward barbarians' ('Handbuch innerlicher Bildung für äußerliche Barbaren') (Nietzsche 1982: 79). To the degraded versions of *Bildung* and *Kultur* that he found all around him, Nietzsche opposed a heroic ideal of self-development towards what he defined as the basic idea of *Kultur*: 'to promote the production of the philosopher, the artist and the saint within us and without us and thereby to work at the perfecting of nature' (Nietzsche 1982: 160).

The broad tendency of Nietzsche's later writing is to separate aesthetics firmly from morality and politics. 'Nietzsche', wrote Thomas Mann in 1947, 'is the most uncompromisingly perfect aesthete in the history of thought' (Mann 1958: 172). In *Also sprach Zarathustra* (*Thus spoke Zarathustra*, 1883–5) *Bildung* is again mocked as a sterile conglomeration of incompatible fragments, while the state is denounced as 'the coldest of all cold monsters' (Nietzsche 1969: 75). By inquiring, especially in *The Genealogy of Morals* (*Zur Genealogie der Moral*, 1887), how morality itself came into being, Nietzsche seeks to inaugurate a world without morality, beyond good and evil, governed by 'the innocence of becoming' (Nietzsche 1968: 65). In his heady visions of humanity's future, two figures can roughly be discerned. One is Zarathustra, the solitary prophet, mocked by the shallow populace, who denies the supernatural, affirms life on this earth, loves humanity for its potential, and practises a noble self-discipline unknown to the hypocritical moralists of the present. Zarathustra foretells the advent of the *Übermensch* (Superman or Overhuman), a terrifyingly strong-willed, dominating figure, generous, warlike, and cruel, who rejects compassion and is prepared to shape humanity through violence, like a sculptor working on recalcitrant material. Here again the world is seen as an aesthetic phenomenon. Humanity will be reshaped with the ruthless detachment of the artist. *Kultur* has been made absolute.

In the less exalted discourse of late 19th-century Germany, *Kultur* became a heavily charged word. In contrast to the universal implications of French 'civilisation' and to Matthew Arnold's insistence that 'the expansion of our humanity, to suit the idea of perfection which culture forms, must be a general expansion' (Arnold 1969: 48), *Kultur* retained the implication of personal development. To liberals, it offered an alternative to a nationalist politics that claimed support from biology for doctrines of racial superiority. In this liberal, anti-biological sense, the German-Jewish anthropologist Franz Boas, who emigrated to the USA in 1886, took the concept of *Kultur* with him (Kuper 1999: 60–2). Resisting the biological and racial paradigms that still dominated their discipline, Boas and his followers, especially Margaret Mead and Ruth Benedict, analysed distinct 'cultures' (in the plural), and 'culture' in this sense – a body of social practices based on implicit shared assumptions – survives in diluted form whenever we talk about 'dependency culture' or 'research cultures'.

Back in Germany, *Kultur* was increasingly played off against *Zivilisation* (Elias 1964: 3–9, 1976: 1–7). *Zivilisation* was material, technical, external, and associated with Britain and especially with France. While the material progress of *Zivilisation* threatened to make the world boringly uniform, *Kultur* expressed the specific character of a nation, and Germany's *Kultur* was inward, profound, artistic, and philosophical.

Kultur was mobilised as a slogan in World War I. While British and French publicists proclaimed a war for civilisation, their German counterparts called it a war for *Kultur* (Kramer 2007: 159). In September 1914, 93 eminent German intellectuals, describing themselves as representatives of German scholarship and *Kultur*, published an 'Appeal to the Cultured World' ('Aufruf an die Kulturwelt'), denying German responsibility for the war and protesting against allegations of German atrocities in Belgium. Yet, as historians have confirmed, the German invaders not only treated civilians with deliberate brutality, but also destroyed monuments of culture, notably Louvain University Library and Rheims Cathedral (Horne and Kramer 2001). In a much-read patriotic pamphlet, the distinguished economist Werner Sombart took the glorification of *Kultur* to extremes by identifying militarism with the pinnacles of German culture: 'Militarism is *Faust* and *Zarathustra* and a Beethoven score in the trenches' (Sombart 1915, 84–5).

This discrepancy resulted not from some fault implicit in the concept of *Kultur*, but from historical contingencies. The cultural achievements of the age of Goethe were appropriated to help legitimise the German Empire. At the same time, Germany had a military system that was more self-contained, immune to intervention by civilian politicians, than in Britain or France (Hull 2005). Military methods became ends in themselves, and were pursued to extremes without political, practical, or humanitarian considerations. The insistence on total victory, which was achieved in the Franco-Prussian War, let soldiers discard all restraints when fighting rebellions in Germany's African colonies. In World War I, rigid military thinking encouraged troops to continue fighting futilely long after the war was lost, and also to terrorise the populations of occupied territories by shooting suspected resisters indiscriminately, mercilessly requisitioning food and possessions, deporting many for forced labour, and treating prisoners of war with extreme harshness. To point this out is not to demonise Germany, nor to revive the obsolete thesis of a German 'special path' ('Sonderweg') (Blackbourn and Eley 1984), but to draw attention to unpalatable but well-attested historical facts that cast a long and dark shadow over succeeding decades.

Thomas Mann

Welcoming war in 1914, Thomas Mann played off a full-bodied though often bloody *Kultur* against a bloodless *Zivilisation*:

> Culture is unity, style, form, attitude, taste, is some spiritual organization of the world, however eccentric, grotesque, savage, bloody and frightful it may be. Culture can include oracles, magic, pederasty, Vitzliputzli [an Aztec god], human sacrifice, orgiastic cults, Inquisitions, *autos da fé*, St Vitus' dance, witch-trials, poisoning, and the most colourful atrocities. Civilization, however, is reason, enlightenment, mildness, morality, scepticism, dissolution – spirit.

> (Kultur ist Geschlossenheit, Stil, Form, Haltung, Geschmack, ist irgendeine gewisse geistige Organization der Welt, und sei das alles auch noch so abenteuerlich, skurril, wild, blutig und furchtbar. Kultur kann Orakel, Magie, Päderastie, Vitzliputzli, Menschenopfer, orgiastische Kultformen, Inquisition, Autodafés, Veitstanz, Hexenprozesse, Blüte des Giftmordes und die buntesten Greuel umfassen. Zivilisation aber ist Vernunft, Aufklärung, Sänftigung, Sittigung, Skeptisierung, Auflösung, – Geist.)

> (Mann 2002b: 27)

Thus the ancient Greeks, the Aztecs, the Middle Ages, the Italian Renaissance, whatever their excesses, possessed culture, whereas modern civilisation by comparison was safe, bland, and dull.

In his self-justifying book *Reflections of an Unpolitical Man* (*Betrachtungen eines Unpolitischen*, 1918) Mann still upheld a German *Kultur*, represented especially by the trinity of Schopenhauer, Wagner, and Nietzsche, against French and Italian *Zivilisation* associated with the un-German values of democracy and socialism, and embodied in his left-wing brother Heinrich. Reading

Oswald Spengler's huge treatise on world history, *The Decline of the West* (*Der Untergang des Abendlandes*, 1918–22), Mann was pleased to learn that history was a succession of mutually independent cultures ('Kulturen'), each including *Zivilisation* as a phase of decline. The decline of the West, in Spengler's view, had set in with the technical, philistine, commercial *Zivilisation* of the 19th century (Spengler 1972: 44). Spengler's cultural pessimism matched the mood of a defeated Germany.

In the aftermath of the war, Mann painfully rethought his position. The outcome was his great novel *The Magic Mountain* (*Der Zauberberg*, 1924), arguably a *Bildungsroman* whose covert subject is the author's own education (Reed 1974: 226–74). It dramatises a debate between *Kultur* and *Zivilisation* in which *Kultur* narrowly gains the victory. But this cannot be simply the benevolent but shallow, enlightened, progressivist worldview professed by Mann's fictional Italian humanist Settembrini. A modern conception of *Humanität* must acknowledge the undeniable facts of illness, bodily decay, and mortality. Hence Mann sets his novel in a Swiss sanatorium, where death is constantly present. And though *Bildung* may have degenerated into superficial book-learning, as Nietzsche charged, Mann puts his hero through a course of scientific reading, especially in biology and physiology, and thus provides a modern counterpart to Herder's concept of humanity as embedded in organic nature.

Although *The Magic Mountain* is a novel of ideas, the ideas are embodied in colourful characters and in fictional experiences. Settembrini's vision of 'homo humanus', inspired by the Renaissance, the Enlightenment, and the French Revolution, is contrasted with the image of 'homo Dei' put forward by his antagonist Naphta, a Jesuit who foretells that the unity of the Christian Middle Ages will soon be restored by a communist autocracy. While the trained dialectician Naphta scores many points and exposes the hypocrisy mixed in Settembrini's liberalism, the values that he lives, as opposed to those he professes, are clearly animated by hatred, and inferior to the kindness apparent in Settembrini. Thus Mann, without moralising, responds to Nietzsche's aestheticism by discreetly reintroducing the question how we are to live with one another.

The most problematic part of the novel is the symbolic hallucination that the protagonist, Hans Castorp, experiences when lost in the Alpine snow. First he envisions a Mediterranean coast where good-looking young people are playing sports and showing civilised respect for a nursing mother. From this paradise of healthy bodily culture and friendly intercourse – Mann's homage to German Graecophilia – his gaze turns to a grim temple, in whose recesses he finds two hags conducting a human sacrifice. This vision seems to reconcile the antithesis Mann had presented ten years earlier between *Kultur* and *Zivilisation*: the dark side of humanity, denied by *Zivilisation* but acknowledged by *Kultur*, must somehow be incorporated into a fully human way of life, without impairing the kindly sociability shown by the young people in the vision. Castorp draws the (typographically emphasised) conclusion: '*For the sake of goodness and love, man shall grant death no dominion over his thoughts*' (Mann 1995: 588) ('*Der Mensch soll um der Liebe und Güte willen dem Tode keine Herrschaft einräumen über seine Gedanken*'; Mann 2002a: 748). Death must be faced – the whole novel is an exploration of death – but it must not be allowed to dominate our lives as it would in the Christian theocracy extolled by Naphta.

Thomas Mann remains a probing commentator on German culture and politics. His famous statement on emigrating to the USA – 'German culture is where I am' ('Wo ich bin ist die deutsche Kultur') (quoted Reed 1974: 1) – was not a boast, but a denial that the Third Reich could lay any claim to the German cultural tradition. His novel *Doktor Faustus* (1947) addresses this issue in a more nuanced way, suggesting an analogy between the barbarism of the Nazis (and of proto-Nazi intellectuals) and the single-minded devotion to *Kultur* at the expense of *Zivilisation* shown by the transgressive modernist composer Leverkühn, who is observed with partial comprehension by the 'good German' Zeitblom.

Present-day Germany may be called Zeitblom's Germany. Zeitblom's narrative can be seen as the first step in the complex and painful process of *Vergangenheitsbewältigung* (coming to terms with the past) that, after some delay, began properly in the 1960s; Günter Grass's *Die Blechtrommel* (*The Tin Drum*, 1959) was an important landmark. In examining its past, modern liberal Germany has much to confront, but it can also draw on the values expressed by the concept of *Humanität*.

Note

With quotations from German sources, the original is given for literary passages or those including important uses of the words *Humanität*, *Bildung*, or *Kultur*. Translations are my own unless otherwise stated.

Bibliography

Arnold, M. (1969) *Culture and Anarchy*, ed. J.D. Wilson, Cambridge: Cambridge University Press.

Beiser, F.J. (2005) *Schiller as Philosopher: A Re-Examination*, Oxford: Clarendon Press.

Berlin, I. (1976) *Vico and Herder*, London: The Hogarth Press.

Bernal, M. (1987) *Black Athena: The Afroasiatic Roots of Classical Civilization, Vol. 1: The Fabrication of Ancient Greece 1785–1985*, London: Free Association Books.

Blackbourn, D. and Eley, G. (1984) *The Peculiarities of German History: Bourgeois Society and Politics in Nineteenth-Century Germany*, Oxford: Oxford University Press.

Bruford, W.H. (1975) *The German Tradition of Self-Cultivation: 'Bildung' from Humboldt to Thomas Mann*, Cambridge: Cambridge University Press.

Burckhardt, J. (1998) *The Greeks and Greek Civilization*, trans. S. Stern, London: HarperCollins.

Clark, W. (2006) *Academic Charisma and the Origins of the Research University*, Chicago: University of Chicago Press.

David, C. (1974) 'Goethe und die Französische Revolution', in *Deutsche Literatur und Französische Revolution*, Göttingen: Vandenhoeck & Ruprecht, pp. 63–86.

Dörr, V.C. and Hofmann, M. (eds) (2008) *'Verteufelt human'? Zum Humanitätsideal der Weimarer Klassik*, Berlin: Schmidt.

Elias, N. (1964) *The Civilizing Process*, trans. E. Jephcott, Oxford: Blackwell.

Elias, N. (1976) *Über den Prozeß der Zivilisation*, Frankfurt a.m.: Suhrkamp.

Goethe, J.W. (1986–2000) *Sämtliche Werke: Briefe, Tagebücher und Gespräche*, ed. F. Apel *et al.*, 40 vols, Frankfurt a.m.: Deutscher Klassiker Verlag.

Goethe, J.W. (1989) *Wilhelm Meister's Apprenticeship*, trans. E.A. Blackall, New York: Suhrkamp.

Herder, J.G. (1989) *Ideen zur Philosophie der Geschichte der Menschheit*, ed. M. Bollacher, Frankfurt a.m.: Deutsche Klassiker Verlag.

Hölderlin, F. (1969) *Werke und Briefe*, ed. F. Beissner and J. Schmidt, 2 vols, Frankfurt a.m.: Insel.

Horkheimer, M. and Adorno, T.W. (2002) *Dialectic of Enlightenment: Philosophical Fragments*, trans. E. Jephcott, Stanford, CA: Stanford University Press.

Horne, J. and Kramer, A. (2001) *German Atrocities 1914: A History of Denial*, New Haven and London: Yale University Press.

Hull, I.V. (2005) *Absolute Destruction: Military Culture and the Practices of War in Imperial Germany*, Ithaca: Cornell University Press.

Humboldt, W. von (1964) *Werke*, ed. A. Flitner and K. Giel, 5 vols, Stuttgart: Cotta.

Humboldt, W. von (1969) *The Limits of State Action*, ed. J.W. Burrow, Cambridge: Cambridge University Press.

Jameson, F. (1971) *Marxism and Form*, Princeton: Princeton University Press.

Kant, I. (1991) *Political Writings*, ed. H. Reiss, trans. H.B. Nisbet, 2nd edn, Cambridge: Cambridge University Press.

Kant, I. (1996) *Religion and Rational Theology*, trans. A.W. Wood and G. di Giovanni, Cambridge: Cambridge University Press.

Kramer, A. (2007) *Dialectic of Destruction: Culture and Mass Killing in the First World War*, Oxford: Oxford University Press.

Kuper, A. (1999) *Culture: The Anthropologists' Account*, Cambridge, MA: Harvard University Press.

Kurth-Voigt, L.E. (1999) *Continued Existence, Reincarnation, and the Power of Sympathy in Classical Weimar*, Rochester, NY: Camden House.

Mann, T. (1958) *Last Essays*, trans. R. Winston and C. Winston, New York: Knopf.

Mann, T. (1995) *The Magic Mountain*, trans. J.E. Woods, New York: Knopf.

Mann, T. (2002a) *Der Zauberberg*, ed. M. Neumann, Frankfurt a.m.: Fischer.

Mann, T. (2002b) *Essays 1914–1926*, ed. H. Kurzke, Frankfurt a.m.: Fischer.

Marx, K. (1977) *Selected Writings*, ed. D. McLellan, Oxford: Oxford University Press.

Mason, E.C. (1964) 'Goethe's sense of evil', *Publications of the English Goethe Society*, 34: 1–53.

Maurer, M. (2012) 'Herder als Theoretiker der interkulturellen Beziehungen', in C. Couturier-Heinrich (ed.) *Übersetzen bei Johann Gottfried Herder*, Heidelberg: Synchron, pp. 29–44.

Nietzsche, F. (1968) *Twilight of the Idols* and *The Anti-Christ*, trans. R.J. Hollingdale, Harmondsworth: Penguin.

Nietzsche, F. (1969) *Thus Spoke Zarathustra*, trans. R.J. Hollingdale, Harmondsworth: Penguin.

Nietzsche, F. (1982) *Untimely Meditations*, trans. R.J. Hollingdale, Cambridge: Cambridge University Press.

Pascal, R. (1962) '"Bildung" and the division of labour', in *German Studies Presented to Walter Horace Bruford*, London: Harrap, pp. 14–28.

Prawer, S.S. (1976) *Karl Marx and World Literature*, Oxford: Clarendon Press.

Raeff, M. (1983) *The Well-Ordered Police State: Social and Institutional Change through Law in the Germanies and Russia, 1600–1800*, New Haven and London: Yale University Press.

Reed, T.J. (1974) *Thomas Mann: The Uses of Tradition*, Oxford: Clarendon Press.

Reed, T.J. (2009) *Mehr Licht in Deutschland: Eine kleine Geschichte der Aufklärung*, Munich: Beck, 2009.

Roth, J. (1939) 'Die Eiche Goethes in Buchenwald', in his *Werke*, ed. K. Westermann and F. Hackert, 6 vols, Cologne: Kiepenheuer & Witsch, 1989–91, 3: pp. 945–6.

Schiller, F. (1958) *Sämtliche Werke*, ed. G. Fricke and H.G. Göpfert, 5 vols, Munich: Hanser.

Schiller, F. (1967) *On the Aesthetic Education of Man in a Series of Letters*, ed. and trans. E.M. Wilkinson and L.A. Willoughby, Oxford: Clarendon Press.

Schlegel, F. (1970) *Kritische Schriften*, ed. W. Rasch, Munich: Hanser.

Sikka, S. (2011) *Herder on Humanity and Cultural Difference: Enlightened Relativism*, Cambridge: Cambridge University Press.

Sombart, W. (1915) *Händler und Helden: Patriotische Besinnungen*, Munich and Leipzig: Duncker & Humblot.

Spengler, O. (1972) *Der Untergang des Abendlandes: Versuch einer Morphologie der Weltgeschichte*, Munich: dtv.

Spranger, E. (1928) *Wilhelm von Humboldt und die Humanitätsidee*, Berlin: Reuther & Reichard.

Steinecke, H. (1991) 'The novel and the individual: The significance of Goethe's *Wilhelm Meister* in the debate about the Bildungsroman', in J.N. Hardin (ed.), *Reflection and Action: Essays in the Bildungsroman*, Columbia, SC: University of South Carolina Press, pp. 69–96.

Wilson, W.D. and Holub, R.C. (eds) (1993) *Impure Reason: Dialectic of Enlightenment in Germany*, Detroit: Wayne State University Press.

Ziolkowski, T. (1990) *German Romanticism and its Institutions*, Princeton: Princeton University Press.

3

Legacies of a significant past
Regimes, experiences, and identities

Mary Fulbrook

A distinguishing feature of contemporary Germany is a widespread public concern – one might even say, an obsessive concern – with the past. And not just with any past, nor indeed with any single past, but with multiple difficult pasts. No day goes by without a story – whether headline news, or inner pages paragraph, or cultural supplement review – dealing with some aspect of Germany's past: and, more specifically, with the two contrasting dictatorships, the Third Reich and the German Democratic Republic (GDR). The debates about these regimes are at times heated, stirred up by a particular incident, exhibition, anniversary, and at times muted, a background chorus of local scandals or specific discoveries. But these two dictatorships represent, to adapt the controversial phrase applied by the conservative German philosopher Ernst Nolte, 'pasts that will not pass away': pasts that refuse to become 'history' (Nolte 1986).

One reason why these dictatorships continue to fascinate and irritate, to have emotional reverberations even decades after their demise, is because the people who live in Germany today are still intrinsically affected by them. They have not yet become 'history' in the sense of a primarily cognitive, non-emotional body of knowledge about a particular past: a past that is interesting, even possibly emotive and engaging on a personal level, but not of direct personal significance. Nor, however, are these pasts for the most part a matter of 'memory', certainly no longer for the more distant decades. Those who have personal memories of the Weimar Republic and even of the Third Reich are ageing and becoming a tiny minority of the population; the 'death of the eyewitness' has been bemoaned many times, well before the actual physical demise of those who can remember these times, as though a crucial lifeline to the pre-1945 past is being gradually severed. And while the GDR is still very much a matter of living memory, there are already generations coming to adulthood who have no direct memories of this far more recent past. However far back, these pasts remain in some sense 'live', with a continuing salience way beyond the chronological end-dates of their defunct regimes or the inexorable decline and disappearance of the eyewitness generations. The German regimes through which people lived over the last century were more than just political forms; and they continue to shape identities and perceptions in the present.

The massive regime transitions of 20th-century German history need little rehearsal. Defeat in World War I was accompanied by the collapse of the Imperial system in November 1918 and its replacement by the short-lived experiment in democracy, the Weimar Republic. Barely had this established a precarious stability, having weathered the acute political and economic crises of the early 1920s, than it was overwhelmed and eventually swept away by political radicalisation in the economic depression following the Wall Street Crash of 1929. From his appointment as chancellor in January 1933 until his suicide at the end of April 1945, Adolf Hitler presided over a genocidal dictatorship responsible for unleashing World War II, costing more than 50 million lives worldwide, and organising the mass murder of some 6 million people on 'racial' and political grounds. Following four years under Allied administration, two new German states were formed in 1949: in the Western zones of occupation, the democratic, capitalist Federal Republic of Germany (FRG), often now called the 'Bonn Republic' in light of the location of West Germany's 'provisional' capital in the Rhineland; and, in the Soviet zone of occupation, the communist German Democratic Republic (GDR), which, even though Berlin remained nominally under four-power control, had its seat of government in East Berlin or, as the East German Government liked to call it, 'Berlin, capital of the GDR'. While West Germany was the beneficiary of American Marshall Aid and basked in the 'economic miracle' that provided the basis for the stabilisation of the democratic system, East Germany's fate within Soviet-dominated eastern Europe was less fortunate. Berlin, a divided city, was notoriously at the frontline of the Cold War; its Wall, erected in 1961 to stem the flow of refugees to the West, became a symbol of the division of Europe. Despite achieving international recognition and some measure of domestic stability in the early 1970s, East Germany faced economic decline and domestic political challenges within a changed international situation in the 1980s, heralding the end of the Cold War. Following the collapse of the communist regime and the breaching of the Berlin Wall in November 1989, a process was inaugurated that culminated in the absorption of the newly recreated regional states or *Länder* of the former GDR into an enlarged Federal Republic of Germany on 3 October 1990. Within a few years of unification, the capital relocated to the now unified Berlin, giving rise to the appellation 'Berlin Republic' for this latest manifestation of the Federal Republic of Germany.

The political history of these states is related easily enough. Far harder to grasp are the ways in which the different regimes affected generations of people whose lives could not so neatly be pigeonholed into one or another regime, but rather spanned the decades across regime transitions. Social identities were constrained, shaped, and reshaped, as people faced the challenges posed by radical historical transformations and rapid transitions from one system to another. Even so, the acute instability, unrest, and violence that characterised the first half of the century eventually gave way to a degree of stabilisation over much of the latter half. The early periods of radical upheaval and violence have captured public attention to such a degree – and for quite understandable reasons – that it often seems as if the 13 years of Weimar democracy, or the 12 years of Hitler's rule, lasted far longer than the 40 years of the two German states in the period of division. Moreover, the fact that one of these two states ultimately collapsed and was absorbed into the other has led to a degree of teleology in recounting its history, as though the end were built in from the very start. Yet viewed from the perspective of individual lives, the stretches of time take on a quite different appearance. The passage of generations is key to understanding how different the latter half of the 20th century was from the previous 30 or more years of almost incessant involvement in violence both abroad and at home.

People do not just inhabit the present, they also incorporate the past: they are shaped by the past and live with the lingering consequences and continuing significance of that past. Yet we are still searching for adequate approaches to interpreting the complexities of our being within time. In what follows I will distinguish between 'communities of experience', defined as those who actually lived through key events or periods, and 'communities of connection and identification', referring to those who are affected by the impact of a significant past on people with whom they are closely connected (such as family or friends), or on a wider collective to which they feel they belong (such as a nation or a religious, political, or ethnic group) or with which, whatever their own background, they come to develop a strong sense of identification. The structures of postwar states and their changing locations within a wider international political context and transnational cultural system filter and transform the interrelationships among these different communities.

Whichever way these questions are addressed, Germany today is pervaded by a sense of having a particularly significant past, and one that raises political and moral questions of continuing and far broader relevance.

The transformation of identities under Nazism

Identities are not simply given; they are formed and reformed, constantly reshaping under changing historical conditions. This is far harder to capture than are the outlines of the historical events themselves. Who, then, are 'the Germans' whose history we seek to recount?

A major way in which social identities were transformed during the Third Reich was in the everyday application and enactment of 'racial' theories, alongside Nazi practices of terror targeting communists, socialists, and other political opponents. It was made clear from the very start, with the boycott of Jewish shops at the beginning of April 1933, and the law that followed a few days later excluding Jews from professional occupations, that there was to be, as so many phrased it, no future for people of Jewish descent in Nazi Germany. With extraordinary rapidity, everyday racism was enacted; people of Jewish descent were identified and degraded, and friendships broken up well before the Nuremberg Laws officially turned Jews into second-class citizens. Even in the 'peacetime' years, brutality and murder were tools frequently deployed by the Nazis, most visibly in the November pogrom of 1938 (*Kristallnacht*) and in the horrendous experiences of the adult male Jews arrested en masse after this and forced into the increasingly overcrowded concentration camps of Dachau, Sachsenhausen, Buchenwald, and elsewhere. Other groups, too, were rapidly victimised in the 'racial state'. Some 400,000 people held to be carrying supposedly hereditary diseases, including even alcoholism, were subjected to compulsory sterilisation; homosexuals were at risk of severe penalties, including incarceration in conditions such that around 10,000 did not survive; those carrying out abortions were severely punished; Jehovah's Witnesses, Sinti and Roma, and many others eventually suffered imprisonment and murder.

With the outbreak of war in 1939 the violence against civilians intensified. Mass murder of civilians was not a later development coming only after the invasion of Russia in 1941. Special killing squads, or *Einsatzgruppen*, whose activities in the wake of the army's invasion of the Soviet Union have become so notorious, were coordinated already in mid-August 1939, and were active following the invasion of Poland at the beginning of September. In occupied Polish territories in the early weeks of autumn 1939, synagogues were set on fire, and Jewish civilians – in total probably several thousands, although the figures are not exact – were burned alive in places of worship and in their own homes and other buildings. Members of the Polish elites – civilian professionals as well as army officers – were captured, imprisoned, and in some infamous cases massacred. Among 'Aryan' Germans, those deemed to be 'lives unworthy of living' by virtue of physical or mental disabilities were put to death in the misnamed 'euthanasia' programme that started on an order of Hitler dated September 1939 and, despite its official termination following widespread protests two years later, continued unofficially until the end of the war, claiming some 200,000 lives.

While people were stigmatised both officially and informally, those doing the discriminating themselves changed; racism affected the identities of members of the 'master race' as well as its victims. 'Ordinary men' became perpetrators in police battalions and army units on the eastern front; people on the home front mourned their losses of sons, brothers, husbands, fathers in stereotypical terms, seeking solace in reassurances that they had 'fallen for the *Führer*, *Volk*, and Fatherland'.[1] Others, by virtue of political commitments or religious or moral qualms, remained impervious to Nazi ideology or even became resisters, ultimately often also becoming victims of the regime of terror. The Nazi era was a maelstrom that makes nonsense of any generalisations about 'the Germans'. There were many different communities of experience during this period, which left its mark on all who lived through it in ways that could not be ignored in the aftermath.

In the early years after World War II, there was not only widespread relief that a period of suffering had finally come to an end, but also a degree of anguish in facing the uncertainties of the postwar world. Many victims of Nazi persecution were only now, on liberation, able to register the extent of their diminution and, in a still weakened state, to agonise over the loss of loved ones, the difficulties of the present and the challenges of trying to make a new life. The anguish of those who survived Nazi persecution has been largely written out of the script of 'German' history: they become 'survivors', 'Jews' who left for other shores, 'communists' who sought to institute a new dictatorship on the ruins of the old, or homosexuals, whose activities were still criminalised until the late 1960s. The notion of 'Germans' was paradoxically (in light of the history) even after the war still implicitly restricted to those who had been included in Hitler's 'ethnic community'. And their primary concerns and sympathies were not with the victims of Nazi persecution, of the slave labour camps and the death marches, but rather with their own missing and dead, their own hunger, their sense of powerlessness and dislocation; the fates of refugees and expellees from lost territories in eastern Europe, of prisoners of war and missing soldiers, took precedence over the fates of survivors.

There had emerged, in short, quite different, distinct, communities of experience. However shocked and appalled many Germans professed to be on watching films of concentration camp footage, such as the American-produced 'Death Mills' (*Todesmühlen*, 1945), the majority treated denazification procedures – in all the zones of occupation – with a degree of pragmatic cynicism, reorganising their life stories and acquiring credentials (often dubbed 'Persil certificates' as part of the general whitewash) to ensure the most beneficial classification on the five-point scale from 'major offenders' to 'exonerated'. The trials of prominent Nazis carried out under the auspices of the Nuremberg International Military Tribunal in 1945–6 and the successor trials carried out by the Allies, again shocking in what they revealed of Nazi crimes, were widely disregarded as 'victors' justice'; and putting the major Nazis on trial only served to confirm the convenient postwar myth that just a handful of individuals at the top had been responsible for the evils of Nazism. Through the later 1940s and 1950s, German 'war stories' were ones that focused on individual heroism and survival, excluding almost entirely any uncomfortable questions concerning widespread involvement in Nazi crimes.

The notion of German victimhood, sometimes seen as developing more than half a century later, was certainly alive and widespread in the early postwar years, which many Germans both at the time and later considered to be the worst years of their lives. The 'myth of silence' on the part of the victims, too, was born at this time (see e.g. Cesarani and Sundquist 2012). While many survivors in Displaced Persons (DP) camps talked incessantly about their experiences among themselves, and had their stories actively elicited by the (eastern European-born, Jewish) American Professor David Boder, who conducted the earliest tape-recorded interviews with victims of racial persecution, they lacked an audience across the borders of other communities of experience (see Rosen 2010). Bound up in their own concerns, Germans on the other side of the now persisting 'racial' divides simply did not want to listen at this time. Nor was there much of a sympathetic audience for those who left the DP camps and sought to return to former homes or to relocate to other countries: neither in newly communist-dominated Poland, where anti-Semitism flared up again very soon after the war, nor in France, where the Gaullist myth of national resistance conveniently papered over the gulf between different groups, nor in many parts of the USA, where even Jewish relatives often proved uncomprehending, nor even in Palestine/Israel, where Zionist heroism seemed incompatible with sympathy for downtrodden victims. And very soon, the Cold War posed new challenges in an era of a divided world and a divided nation.

'Reckoning' with the Nazi past in divided Germany

For those who remained on German soil, the postwar moment meant not only rebuilding from the rubble, mourning, awaiting news of loved ones who were still missing, or dealing with the return of often physically and psychologically wounded former prisoners of war, but also – in different ways in East and West – building up new states and societies under the pretence of a 'return to normality'. Part of this pretence was the construction of a sense of domestic stability, understood in terms of a 'private life' with a home, a family and secure employment, leisure, friends, hobbies, and holidays, unhampered by the unwelcome intrusions of 'History' in the form of major social and political events, whether revolution, violence on the streets, economic depression, war, expulsions, air raids and mass bereavement. Part of it also was a reckoning with the past, in order to demonstrate that those who had been responsible for recent aberrations and atrocities had been brought to justice; at the same time, the desire to 'draw a line under the past' was a recurrent refrain.

The first postwar chancellor of the Federal Republic of Germany, Konrad Adenauer (1876–1967), initially set the parameters in the West for a public culture of responsibility – and hence shame – without much admission of guilt. He had a distinct preference for adopting the passive mood, as in his 1951 speech declaring that 'unspeakable crimes have been committed in the name of the German people', as though very few Germans had been actually involved in perpetrating these crimes. He was concerned for West Germany's international reputation: political ends were well served by his 1952 agreement to offer 'reparations' to Israel as well as the FRG's belated expressions of sympathy with the victims of anti-Semitism. Moreover, this stance was accompanied by a practical policy of reintegrating former Nazis and providing a broad amnesty for large numbers of people who had been complicit in the murderous regime. In the FRG of the 1950s, tens of thousands of civil servants who had faithfully served Hitler's state returned to their jobs or were awarded full pensions; local and regional government, the judiciary and the police services, hospitals, universities, and schools were staffed by innumerable people who had implemented Nazi policies only a few years earlier. Even Adenauer's chief aide in the Chancellery, Hans Globke, had been involved in writing the official commentary for Hitler on the Nuremberg Laws. It was not difficult for East German communist leaders to find ammunition in their campaign to portray the Bonn Republic as a home for former Nazis. Prominent targets of GDR propaganda campaigns included Adenauer's Minister for Refugees, Theodor Oberländer, who was a former convinced Nazi, an expert adviser on Hitler's 'Germanisation' measures and ethnic cleansing policies in Poland, and controversially associated with a military unit involved in massacres in Ukraine. A determination on both sides to appear the 'better Germany' in terms of 'overcoming the past' meant that pursuit of former Nazis could never come off the agenda. The international position of both German states remained key to domestic developments in this area.

The particular community of experience that was dominant in West Germany had a sympathetic understanding of those who had gone along with the Nazi regime, and gave priority, in matters of welfare and compensation, to the millions of Germans who had suffered in the postwar upheavals and expulsions. The 1952 Equalisation of Burdens Law (*Lastenausgleichsgesetz*) was a public expression of the privileged voice given to this significant constituency of voters, providing compensation for those who had lost their homes and livelihoods as a result of the war. Although this included survivors of the camps, the vast majority of beneficiaries were 'ethnic Germans' who had resettled in the Federal Republic after having fled or been expelled from lost eastern territories. In contrast, for decades there was no recognition of any need to compensate those who had suffered in slave labour camps or as forced labourers in Germany, or victims of Nazi sterilisation policies, or homosexuals who had been imprisoned. The policies enacted by the politically dominant elites were thus broadly in line with, indeed responded to, views prevalent among broader circles of society, even where there remained distinctions between tales told in the privacy of the family and public expressions of shame. People's own experiences, whether at the front or at home, or on the move, were for most individuals more significant than the 'Nazi crimes' allegedly committed by others; and anti-communism took precedence over dealing with the legacies of Nazism.

It took the interventions of key individuals from a quite different community of experience, that of resistance and victimhood, to change the course of developments in West Germany. But these individuals, representative only of a minority, were able to act as catalysts of change because of the relatively open political system in the West. By the later 1950s attempts to prosecute former Nazis were flagging. From 1958, however, the newly founded Central Office of the State Judicial Authorities for the Investigation of National Socialist Crimes (*Zentrale Stelle der Landesjustizverwaltungen zur Aufklärung nationalsozialistischer Verbrechen*), based in the small south-west German town of Ludwigsburg, began to coordinate the efforts of different Länder. Following the capture of Adolf Eichmann, whose trial in Jerusalem in 1961 aroused international interest and controversy, Nazi crimes were back in the spotlight. Much of the impetus for the Frankfurt Auschwitz trial of 1963–5 came from two men who, as far as communities of experience are concerned, were drawn from the side of the victims. Fritz Bauer, the Attorney General of the West German Federal state of Hesse, was a committed socialist of Jewish descent. He had lost his professional position under Hitler's Law for the Restoration of a Professional Civil Service (*Gesetz zur Wiederherstellung des Berufsbeamtentums*) in April 1933, and was forced to flee Germany during the war, first for Denmark and then for Sweden. He had played a role in tracking down Eichmann in South America before making it his mission to bring to trial in Germany a handful of those responsible for crimes committed at Auschwitz. Against considerable opposition, in the midst of a legal profession pervaded by former Nazis, Bauer and his associate, the Auschwitz survivor Hermann Langbein, ensured that a credible trial could be mounted. For the first time in West Germany the voices of victims were heard in public; more than 200 survivors came to bear witness, often speaking out for the first time to a wider audience, in the face of hostile questioning from lawyers for the defence of the perpetrators.

Despite ambivalent responses at the time, a new era had opened: the desired line under the past could not easily be drawn. Even as legislation to lift the statute of limitations for prosecution of murder was being hotly debated, wider groups became involved: younger historians, students, and others began to explore more proactively the crimes of the Nazi era. Those who by family ties or sense of national identity felt a connection with the perpetrators began increasingly to identify with the victims, as West German political culture was transformed from the later 1960s onwards.

Over the following decades, despite growing knowledge and attention, older West Germans clung to the defence of having 'only followed orders' or having 'known nothing about it'. Even in autobiographical writings and oral history interviews towards the end of the century, this community of experience tended to respond in pre-emptively defensive terms that bore traces of the challenges of public debates and wider discourses of self-justification. Meanwhile, younger West Germans came to adulthood who had been brought up with a complex sense of personal connection with members of their parents' generation and wider identification with what was presented as a 'German nation' persisting across time, an imagined community with a particular burden of responsibilities for the past. They learned that they should 'be ashamed' of their nation's past. For many, this brought with it a heightened sensitivity, an identification and empathy with experiences of the victims, and a commitment to engage with an uncomfortable past.

The same situation did not obtain in the GDR, where open discussions of the Nazi past were constrained by official parameters and formulae, and where the new state refused to take responsibility for the consequences of crimes committed by the Nazi regime. The founding fathers of the GDR, drawn from Germany's pre-1945 left, were – with good reason – profoundly distrustful of the majority of their compatriots. Many Germans had gone along with Hitler's murderous regime, and former Nazis and fellow travellers still harboured anti-communist sentiments whipped up by Hitler and exacerbated by brutal treatment at the hands of the Red Army. The politically dominant community of experience in the GDR – those who had been opposed to Nazism – tended to marginalise the suffering of those who had been persecuted on 'racial' or religious grounds, portraying them as passive victims rather than 'antifascist resistance fighters'. It is striking that, even during the very early postwar period, people who had suffered under Nazism sought to constrain their self-representations into the newly dominant mould; people who had been persecuted on grounds of 'race', for example, were already somewhat defensively adding that for this reason they had not been able to be as politically active as they might have liked; others, who had been politically active, were downplaying their own suffering as victims or indeed the plight of close relatives on 'racial' grounds.[2] But they too were a tiny minority. The broader community viewed the new regime with scepticism and widespread dislike.

Former perpetrators were pursued proactively through the East German judicial system, at times clearly for political effect – as in the trials and sentencing *in absentia* of prominent Nazis who had fled to quieter havens in the West – but also simply in order to ensure their prosecution and punishment, a fact often underplayed in the secondary literature. Few East German trials captured international attention in the way that those in the West did, but former Nazis were still being hunted down, put on trial and harshly punished, even where there was little publicity, right through the 1980s. Often individuals who had played comparatively minor roles in the Nazi system received severe sentences, in contrast to the staggering leniency of sentencing in comparable cases in the West. But the GDR leadership also provided ways of exonerating former Nazis and 'fellow travellers' if they were prepared to commit themselves to the new state, and sought to foster a wider sense of pride by propagating the myths of antifascist resistance and 'liberation' rather than defeat.

The political instrumentalisation of the past, along with the GDR's refusal to represent itself as the successor state to Nazism, meant that younger East Germans did not develop a strong sense of connection with this past as part of a persisting 'national community'. There was often some awareness of dissonance between stories told at home and the official version of history propagated in schools, in youth groups, and on visits to former concentration camps such as Buchenwald, which became something of a GDR political shrine. But the Nazi past was far less of an issue than were the challenges of the communist present. A culture of shame about being German was not developed and transmitted across generations in the same way as in the West. Nor, incidentally, did comparable developments take place in Austria, where the convenient 'myth of innocence' was only really challenged with the Waldheim affair of the 1980s. Thus the acute emotion of shame experienced among younger West German communities of connection and identification was not paralleled in the GDR and Austria. Nor, arguably, was it paralleled among Germans who had moved abroad.

There was also, in the later 20th century, a broadening of transnational cultural currents. This was arguably more significant for developments in West Germany, where such phenomena were widely discussed, than in the GDR. If earlier generations could claim that they had 'not seen' and 'knew nothing about it', this was not the case for those living in an age of mass media with global reach. Again, it was individuals drawn from communities of experience and connection with the victims, and often located outside Germany, who were significant catalysts of change in the cultural sphere: Gerald Green's *Holocaust* (1978), Claude Lanzmann's *Shoah* (1985), and Steven Spielberg's *Schindler's List* (1993), for example, portray very different perspectives on the past than does Edgar Reitz's *Heimat* (1984), and all three externally produced depictions arguably had a major impact on growing public identification with victims.

There was, in fact, increasing willingness to give victims a hearing, in ways not possible when post-Nazi communities of experience still dominated the West German landscape of public discourse. In a post-Vietnam era of sympathy for individuals suffering from the newly defined post-traumatic stress disorder (PTSD), victimhood became an acceptable rather than a derided status, and 'victims' transmogrified into 'survivors' who had ever-widening audiences for their stories.

In the GDR, the Nazi persecution of the Jews had been more widely discussed and presented in memorial sites and educational materials than is generally realised; but these developments, while registered and 'known' at a cognitive level, appear not to have been of much immediate personal significance to younger East Germans.[3] The official myth of the 'antifascist state', entailing a lack of collective responsibility for the Nazi past, meant that younger East Germans did not feel a strong sense of identification with a national (imagined) community persisting across time and over the divide of 1945 in quite the same way as younger West Germans were made to do. At the same time, their own experiences of accommodation with the demands and constraints of the Socialist Unity Party (SED) dictatorship rendered them far more likely to be sympathetic to the ways in which their parents and grandparents had participated in the structures of the Third Reich. The level of identification within the family, while acknowledging the crimes of the rejected Nazi regime, thus played out rather differently in East Germany than in the West.[4]

The explanation of these shifts is complex and cannot be adequately addressed here. But a key element has to do with shifts in the imagined communities of those with whom one feels a sense of empathy. For most East Germans, the predominant concerns of the day were with a difficult present that was overwhelming in its demands. Failure to identify fully with the 'antifascist state' was accompanied by a degree of understanding for relatives who were former Nazi fellow travellers, and widespread lack of emotional involvement in the fate of the victims. In West Germany, among those who had been adults during the Third Reich, there was also relatively little interest in the experiences of victims of Nazi policies; even former perpetrators or fellow travellers were already casting themselves in the role of victims of war and expulsion, and were primarily concerned with (and often overwhelmed by) their own problems. Yet here the state was more aligned with popular concerns, and thus the expressions of continuing responsibility for the past fell on more receptive ears. There was then a growing willingness among later West German communities of connection and identification to give a sympathetic hearing to the problems of victims. By the 1980s, victims were not so much 'given a voice' – this they had always had – as given a wider audience. At the same time, those survivors who had been young at the time of the Holocaust were now entering retirement and old age; their personal concerns had shifted from building a bearable present for themselves and their families to a concern with revisiting the past for purposes of educating for the future.

'Building a better Germany': East and West German identities

On each side of the Iron Curtain the new states were created with an eye to creating a better future.

In West Germany, the Nazi dictatorship was replaced by a parliamentary democracy, its constitution informed by the perceived shortcomings of the Weimar Republic. The multiparty system slowly shook down, following further reforms to the voting system, into one where two major parties, the conservative CDU/CSU and the social democratic SPD, vied for the support of the small (and in many respects right-wing) liberal party, the FDP. Over the 40 years of division, the political colour of the West German Government changed only as a result of the shifting support of the FDP, which notably switched to support the SPD in 1969, and swung back to the CDU in 1982 (see Chapter 6).

The capitalist economy continued to develop in the West, now reframed in terms of a 'social market economy', and characterised by a corporatist system brokering deals between managers and workers. The FRG was at the forefront of moves towards closer European integration as well as playing a role in Western international alliances at the frontline of the divided Cold War world – both also conveniently part of Adenauer's strategy for re-entering the community of acceptable nations. Despite major continuities, with an ever more affluent middle class benefitting from the Marshall Plan and the 'economic miracle', there were key social changes. Women, who had been drawn into Hitler's war effort, were persuaded back into the home, and only began to raise their voices in favour of 'emancipation' in the era of social movements from the late 1960s onwards. Expellees and refugees from lost territories in eastern Europe made up around a fifth of the FRG's population by the early 1960s. When this flood dried up, the continuing demand for cheap, mobile labour was met by the 'guest worker' (*Gastarbeiter*) programme, drawing in an infinitely less privileged group of foreign nationals who, having no citizenship entitlement or vote in West Germany, were more readily exploited, their concerns more easily ignored (see Chapter 12). Workers from Mediterranean countries – predominantly from Italy at first, but increasingly from Turkey – took up the lowest paid and most menial jobs. By the 1970s and 1980s, when other European economies were challenged by the oil crises and recession, West Germany's affluent democracy appeared to stand as a model for all. Despite continued controversies over attempts to 'normalise' the past in the 1980s, a now thoroughly discredited nationalism appeared (at least among articulate left-liberal elites) to be displaced by 'constitutional patriotism', a term proposed by the philosopher Jürgen Habermas. Whatever people made of this concept, and it was far from generally accepted, life in the increasingly urbanised, politically stable, and affluent West was relatively easy for many.

The transition for those who found themselves on the East German side of the 'Iron Curtain' dividing Europe was far more challenging. Under the communist-dominated Socialist Unity Party, backed by Moscow, there was a major social revolution. Landed estates of more than 100 hectares were expropriated in September 1945 and redistributed among small peasants and landless labourers; waves of agricultural collectivisation followed, such that by the early 1960s the vast majority of East German agriculture was run under the auspices of collective farms (*Landwirtschaftliche Produktionsgenossenschaften* or LPGs). Industry and finance were nationalised, with a gradual squeezing-out of capitalists and independent tradespeople, leaving only a tiny minority of enterprises in private hands by the start of the 1970s. The working classes now found themselves nominally the new ruling class in the 'Workers' and Peasants' State' (*Staat der Arbeiter und Bauern*), although conditions of work in the new 'People's Own Enterprises' (*Volkseigene Betriebe*, VEB) often seemed little different from in earlier decades; with lack of adequate investment, equipment and machinery became ever more rusty and outdated. Formerly bourgeois occupations were transformed: independent managers of industry gave way to loyal communist functionaries running the new economic combines; doctors gave up independent practices and collaborated in work-based polyclinics; teachers, journalists, and lawyers became servants of the new communist state. Women were proactively recruited into the workforce, for pragmatic reasons to do with labour shortages as well as an ideological commitment to emancipation. Many found combining production and reproduction to be a 'double burden', but there was nevertheless a transformation in gender roles. While East Germany did not urbanise as rapidly as the West, housing shortages were tackled by a combination of prestigious new towns and building projects as well as the construction of cheap high-rise estates. The socialist new town of Stalinstadt, later renamed Eisenhüttenstadt, on the border with Poland near Frankfurt an der Oder, and East Berlin's Stalinallee, renamed Karl-Marx-Allee in 1961, stand as prominent examples of the former; the housing 'silos' so evident on the outskirts of many of eastern Germany's cities bear lasting testament to the latter.

Within these reshaped physical landscapes emerged a quite different form of social and institutional landscape. The State Security Police (*Staatssicherheitspolizei*, or Stasi), formally established in February 1950, was expanded after the unsuccessful uprising of June 1953 and continued to develop thereafter, playing a significant role in suppressing potential unrest in 1968. Many people learned to live in the shadow not only of the Stasi but also of the more visible fortified inner-German border and the Berlin Wall, erected in August 1961 to stem the population haemorrhage to the West. Following the accession to power of Erich Honecker in 1971, replacing Walter Ulbricht as SED leader, and with key developments in the early 1970s (international recognition, new social and economic policies, a policy of 'no taboos' in socialist culture, the Helsinki Declaration on Human Rights), many East Germans harboured hopes for continued improvements in the future, even despite continuing frictions and constraints in the present. But the Stasi grew exponentially in the 1970s and 1980s, following the recognition of the GDR by the FRG in 1972 and the growth of Western influences with greater mobility of both people and media.

The '1929ers', born in the declining years of the Weimar Republic, were arguably the cohort most widely experiencing a personal sense of shame with respect to the Nazi era; and they became the most committed to the East German system. They took advantage of the new educational and professional opportunities for those of modest social backgrounds and appropriate political standpoints, and benefitted from the upward social mobility of the 1950s and 1960s. They became the key functionaries of the new regime; and, once within the system, they were somewhat trapped within its parameters. Those a few years younger, born during the Third Reich, were the most sceptical, the most distanced from any form of politics. The postwar cohorts 'born into' the GDR, educated by the state and socialised in the Free German Youth (FDJ), were – unlike their contemporaries in the West – relatively unconcerned with the legacies of Nazism, increasingly seen as a matter of official rhetoric and political ritual. Organised in collectives in workplaces, participating in state-controlled political, social, and leisure organisations, learning the new rules of the game, younger East Germans developed very different attitudes and outlooks from those who had lived under previous regimes. They faced far more immediate challenges dealing with the communist present; they became the GDR's most explicit critics as early idealism gave way to disillusion.

A period of cultural clampdown in the GDR in the later 1970s was accompanied by growing economic and political crises. The roots of popular discontent had been laid down earlier, but new dissident and reform movements were able to grow under the partially protective umbrella of the Protestant churches, which achieved a degree of recognition in the Church-State agreement of March 1978. The economic troubles following the second oil crisis of 1979, and the renewed Cold War with the Soviet invasion of Afghanistan and debates over stationing of nuclear missiles on German soil, contributed to heightened tensions in the early 1980s. The accession to power in the Soviet Union of Mikhail Gorbachev in 1985 gave hope to reformers and precipitated the series of events in eastern Europe that ultimately led to the collapse of communist regimes in 1989–90.

Topographies of past and present in united Germany

A striking feature for anyone arriving in Berlin, capital of the contemporary Federal Republic of Germany, is the sheer extent of memorialisation (see Chapter 11). Associated with the extraordinary scope is the distinctive character of the representation of the past in united Germany. Berlin is possibly the only capital city in the world to display and indeed 'celebrate' (if this is not an inappropriate word) not pride in the nation but rather shame. The Memorial to the Murdered Jews of Europe stands at the heart of the capital, next to the Brandenburg Gate. Even beyond the capital, in every corner of the Federal Republic, there is memorialisation of Nazi crimes: there are the ubiquitous small 'stumbling stones' (*Stolpersteine*) dedicated to victims of deportation and murder, huge signs listing former concentration camps headed 'sites of terror that we may never forget', small monuments or plaques commemorating the sites of former synagogues or of places of round-ups and deportations. Absence is made present.

These are phenomena produced by distinctively West German communities of identification. The experiences and legacies of the GDR, the 'second German dictatorship', also fed into the ways in which the past continued to play a significant role after unification in 1990, under the auspices of an expanded West German political system. But physical sites of memory still differ across the former inner-German border, where the old politically dominant community of 'antifascist resistance' visually predominates. In Buchenwald, for example, the massive statue designed by Fritz Cremer celebrating communist resistance and self-liberation towers over the hillside, providing a somewhat distorted framing narrative for the camp. In Sachsenhausen, a block has been reserved for displaying GDR exhibits, traces of the recent past within the broader exhibit of the Nazi dictatorship. There have been fierce debates over how to deal with the 'double legacies' of some sites, including the postwar Soviet Special Camps based in the former Nazi concentration camps of Buchenwald, Sachsenhausen, and Ravensbrück. Attempts to commemorate victims of Stalinist terror are complicated by the fact that many (though far from all) of these victims had themselves formerly been Nazi perpetrators; survivors were horrified that their former persecutors could now be remembered in the guise of victims. The highlighting of communist distortions of the Nazi past has partially deflected attention from earlier aspects of the politicisation of the past in pre-unification West Germany, where – despite the later proliferation of memorial sites – memorials had been far slower to emerge and had frequently been the subject of furious contests, against strong local opposition to any physical, visible reminders of the Nazi past.

However contested the memorialisation of the Nazi past might have been, approaches to the legacies of the GDR are more ambivalent. Nor do they attract the same level of international interest as do the legacies of Nazism: the comment that the GDR was merely 'a footnote in

German history', however offensive to those who lived through it, has been partially enacted in memorialisation. The remnants of the Berlin Wall, the former Stasi prison at Hohenschön-hausen, and other museums and exhibitions of the peculiar combination of repression and accommodation that marked the East German dictatorship attract many visitors in Berlin; elsewhere, however, attempts to portray GDR life, as in the Museum for Everyday Life in Eisenhüttenstadt, have attracted insufficient interest and public funding. The afterlife of the GDR is secured, more visibly but also problematically, in media debates over the Stasi, and in films and works of literature that have sometimes castigated the repressive dictatorship, as in Florian Henckel von Donnersmarck's *The Lives of Others* (2006), but more frequently demonstrated an ironic, humorous approach, as in *Good Bye Lenin!* (2003). All these developments have played a role in the continuing, if changing, tensions between people from eastern and western areas of Germany.

Little noticed, but closely connected, are changing conceptions of German citizenship – of what it means to be a citizen of Germany today (see Chapter 8). Citizenship is a contested concept. It establishes a relation between states and individuals, regulates principles of inclusion and exclusion, bestows rights and obligations, according to criteria that vary across different times and places. It may carry with it associations that are not inherent in citizenship itself, but become emotionally attached to it; it may embody less well-articulated assumptions, which become explicit only when they are suddenly challenged or perceived to be under threat.

It is possible to distinguish between quite different concepts of citizenship in modern nation states. Although there are always qualifications, two general principles are readily identifiable: that of *ius sanguinis*, the right to citizenship by virtue of descent or 'blood'; and *ius soli*, the right to citizenship by virtue of the 'soil', the ground on which a person was born. The latter principle has been predominant in Germany's western neighbour France: those born on French soil can become French citizens. Since the Reich Citizenship Law of 1913, the former principle, that of descent, has been of major significance in Germany. This law was intended as a means of ensuring that all those who held citizenship in one of Imperial Germany's constituent states would also automatically be citizens of the Reich; it was not originally ethnically exclusive, since it included, for example, people of Slavic descent in Prussia's eastern territories. Under Hitler, in the Nuremberg Laws of 1935, notions of German citizenship assumed an explicitly ethnic tone and excluded those designated by the Nazis to be 'racially' inferior by virtue of Jewish descent. Hitler's racist restrictions were lifted after the war, but there were problematic legacies. In West Germany, three generations of 'guest workers' or *Gastarbeiter* were denied easy access to citizenship; this situation changed only in the decade after unification.

At the same time, with the public culture of shame about the past, conceptions of citizenship had strongly moral overtones and associations. Even though many East Germans did not and do not share this sense of 'national shame', having quite different emotional relationships with the Nazi past, it has continued to dominate the memorial and imaginative landscape of what it means to be 'German' in unified Germany. But what does this mean for those who have acquired, or feel they should be entitled to acquire, German citizenship in more recent years, and whose parents or grandparents did not live through the Nazi Third Reich? They have no personal connections with the imagined community of post-Nazi Germans persisting across time. Young Germans of Turkish descent may well feel, as members of the human race, that a common humanity demands empathy with the sufferings of Jews at the hands of Hitler – but also that this should be no different for them, as holders of German passports, than for holders of any other passport in the world, and that they need not participate in the public culture of shame that is so prevalent among West German communities of connection and identification.

The continuing emphasis on the moral responsibilities of Germans in the post-Holocaust era is, ironically, perpetuating an essentially ethnically defined notion of citizenship in a way that runs counter to the practical opening-up of the category since the mid-1990s.

There are several possible ways in which this may develop – and there is much evidence of conflicting processes. The resurgence of active racist attacks in the early 1990s gave way to a more emphatic insistence on developing new ways of thinking about multiculturalism and tolerance of diversity, precipitating the reform of citizenship laws. Yet repeated controversies demonstrate just how readily the Nazi era continues to resonate. One possibility is that communities of identification and empathy will shift and broaden: not only self-identifying 'Germans' should feel they have heightened moral responsibilities arising from humanity's violent past. Another, alongside this, is an arguably growing dissociation of formal citizenship entitlement from a personal sense of identity: passports may increasingly be seen as a pragmatic means to rights of residence and employment, irrespective of questions of descent or constructions of 'national identity'. An instrumental, rather than affective, relationship may be developing between citizens of an increasingly mobile, global, cosmopolitan world and the identity papers they require to travel, to settle, and to make a living. Citizenship, even in Germany, may ultimately come to be disassociated from Germany's troubled history, as the new identities and experiences of the 21st century finally displace the reverberations of the old. In the meantime, the legacies of the past continue to resonate, feeding into and echoing the tensions of a later date.

Conclusion

All this has made 'history' a particularly painful process for many in Germany over the last century – painful not only in the obvious sense of experiencing war, destruction, bereavement, and even a continuing fear and uncertainty in the era of national division, but also in the sense of dealing with questions of personal identity as well as a now doubly challenging past. These uncertainties and challenges have been far higher at some periods than others, and for some people than others; but they have stamped their mark on the ways in which people interacted with one another, and the ways in which ruptures in the past repeatedly reverberated in a later present. Reckoning with the past could never be purely a matter of cultural representations and political debates over particular issues; it was about far more than that.

Notes

1　The term 'ordinary men' derives from Christopher Browning (2001); see also Fulbrook (2011).
2　I have explored this in further detail in 'East Germans in a post-Nazi state: Communities of experience, connection and identification', in Fulbrook and Port 2013.
3　My remarks are partly based on findings of a study carried out by the Leipzig Institute for Youth Research in the late 1980s: Bundesarchiv (BArch) DC 4/305, Zentralinstitut für Jugendforschung, Dr Wilfried Schubarth, 'Zum Geschichtsbewusstsein von Jugendlichen der DDR'.
4　This area is still relatively under-researched. For recent relevant contributions see, for example, Jensen 2004; Moller 2003.

Bibliography

Biess, F. (2006) *Homecomings: Returning POWs and the Legacies of Defeat in Postwar Germany*, Princeton and Oxford: Princeton University Press.
Browning, C. (2001) *Ordinary Men: Reserve Police Battalion 11 and the Final Solution in Poland*, London: Penguin.

Caplan, J. (ed.) (2008) *Nazi Germany*, Oxford: Oxford University Press.

Cesarani, D., and Sundquist, E. (eds) (2012) *After the Holocaust: Challenging the Myth of Silence*, London: Routledge.

Fox, T. (1999) *Stated Memory: East Germany and the Holocaust*, Rochester, NY: Camden House.

Frei, N. (2002) *Adenauer's Germany and the Nazi Past: The Politics of Amnesty and Integration*, New York: Columbia University Press.

Friedländer, S. (1998) *Nazi Germany and the Jews: Vol. 1, The Years of Persecution, 1933–1939*, London: HarperCollins.

Friedländer, S. (2007) *Nazi Germany and the Jews: Vol. 2, The Years of Extermination, 1933–45*, New York: HarperCollins.

Fulbrook, M. (2005) *The People's State: East German Society from Hitler to Honecker*, London: Yale University Press.

Fulbrook, M. (2011) *Dissonant Lives: Generations and Violence through the German Dictatorships*, Oxford: Oxford University Press.

Fulbrook, M. and Port, A. (eds) (2013) *Becoming East German: Socialist Structures and Sensibilities after Hitler*, New York: Berghahn.

Good Bye Lenin! (2003) [Film] Wolfgang Becker. Germany: Warner.

Heimat (1984) [TV series] Edgar Reitz. Germany: Studiocanal.

Holocaust (1978) [Film] Written by Gerald Green, directed by Marvin J. Chomsky. USA: NBC.

Jarausch, K. (ed.) (1999) *Dictatorship as Experience: Towards a Socio-Cultural History of the GDR*, New York: Berghahn.

Jensen, O. (2004) *Geschichte machen. Strukturmerkmale des intergenerationellen Sprechens über die NS-Vergangenheit in deutschen Familien*, Tübingen: edition discord.

Ladd, B. (1997) *The Ghosts of Berlin*, Chicago: University of Chicago Press.

Mandel, R. (2008) *Cosmopolitan Anxieties: Turkish Challenges to Citizenship and Belonging in Germany*, Durham, NC: Duke University Press.

Moeller, R. (2001) *War Stories. The Search for a Usable Past in the Federal Republic of Germany*, Berkeley and Los Angeles: University of California Press.

Moller, S. (2003) *Vielfache Vergangenheit: Öffentliche Erinnerungskulturen und Familienerinnerungen an die NS-Zeit in Ostdeutschland*, Tübingen: edition discord.

Niethammer, L., von Plato, A., and Wierling, D. (1991) *Die volkseigene Erfahrung*, Berlin: Rowohlt.

Niven, B. (2002) *Facing the Nazi Past: United Germany and the Legacy of the Third Reich*, New York: Routledge.

Nolte, E. (1986) 'Die Vergangenheit, die nicht vergehen will. Eine Rede, die geschrieben, aber nicht gehalten werden konnte', *Frankfurter Allgemeine Zeitung*, 6 June, reprinted in *'Historikerstreit': Die Dokumentation der Kontroverse um die Einzigartigkeit der nationalsozialistschen Judenvernichtung*, Munich: Piper, 1987.

Nothnagle, A. (1999) *Building the East German Myth*, Ann Arbor: University of Michigan Press.

Pence, K. and Betts, P. (eds) (2008) *Socialist Modern. East German Everyday Culture and Politics*, Ann Arbor: University of Michigan Press.

Rosen, A. (2010) *The Wonder of their Voices: The 1946 Holocaust Interviews of David Boder*, Oxford: Oxford University Press.

Schindler's List (1993) [Film] Steven Spielberg. USA: Amblin Entertainment, Universal Pictures.

Shoah (1985) [Film] Claude Lanzmann. France: BIM.

Staiger, U., Steiner, H., and Webber, A. (eds) (2009) *Memory Culture and the Contemporary City: Building Sites*, Basingstoke: Palgrave Macmillan.

The Lives of Others (2006) [Film] Florian Henckel von Donnersmarck. Germany: Touchstone.

Todesmühlen (1945) [Film] Billy Wilder and Hanuš Burger. USA and Germany: United States Department of War.

Weinke, A. (2002) *Die Verfolgung von NS-Tätern im geteilten Deutschland*, Paderborn: Ferdinand Schöningh.

Wierling, D. (2002) *Geboren im Jahr Eins*, Berlin: Ch. Links Verlag.

4

World War II in German cultural memory

Dresden as *lieu de mémoire*

Anne Fuchs

Introduction

German and British memory of World War II could not be more polarised. In the UK, national memory culture clings to the fantasy of a 'good war' that showcased the moral strength of the nation. The tabloidisation of 'Britain's finest hour', the endless recycling of the war on British TV in the BBC 'reality show' *Wartime Farm* (2012), for example, or the perennially popular comedy *Dad's Army* (1968–77), whose characters 'are bumbling and incompetent certainly, but determined to die if necessary for their country' (Ramsden 2010: 34) are only some of the symptoms of a pervasive myth that makes the past the source of a comforting national self-image based on collective endurance, self-sacrifice, and stoicism.[1]

German memory of warfare is the negative imprint of British remembrance culture: World War II is generally associated with trauma, carnage, historical guilt, the destruction of infrastructure, and the division of Germany. To an extent, of course, this negative memory is an objective reflection of Germany's moral, cultural, psychological, and physical ruination at the end of the war; and there was also embittered remembrance of population flights and loss of territory. Germany's national self-image as a *Kulturnation* steeped in the tradition of *Bildung* (see Chapter 2) lay in tatters in 1945. German cultural memory[2] of World War II today, however, is arguably the outcome less of historical defeat than of intense, often explosive, emotionally fraught, highly polemical, and thoughtful memory debates. After unification, engagement with the long-term legacy of National Socialism was rekindled because Germans now had to come to terms with multiple pasts. This chapter sketches the broad history of German memory of World War II and illustrates contemporary German attitudes to warfare with reference to one of the most iconic sites of war memory: the city of Dresden, targeted by Allied bombers between 13 and 15 February 1945 in several attacks (see Bergander 1994; Taylor 2004).

Memory politics in the 'two Germanies' after World War II

In the Weimar Republic, the loss of World War I was often associated with national shame, widespread resentment that the conditions of the Treaty of Versailles were unjust, and the perception that Germany had been emasculated – a chain of ideas that later fuelled National Socialist propaganda (see Ulrich and Ziemann 1997). After 1945, the memory of World War I was obscured by the more recent experience of defeat, dislocation, death, and the near-complete destruction of Germany's infrastructure. The flattened cities, the arrival of millions of German refugees from the eastern territories, the high death toll amongst civilians and soldiers in the final phase of the war, and the visibility of disabled people in postwar society were constant reminders of total collapse in the aftermath of the Nazi era:[3] 'the war was so strongly present that it was not necessary to recall it' (Schildt 2010: 206). While the disastrous effects of the war were ubiquitous, the division of Germany and the emergence of the Cold War created new geopolitical conditions that hindered the emergence of a united national memory culture (Herf 1997; Assmann and Frevert 1999; Niven 2002). The German Democratic Republic (GDR) cast itself in the role of the anti-fascist state with no responsibility for the Nazi era. Communist resistance to National Socialism became the cornerstone of a memory politics that not only overstated the role of communist resistance but also ascribed a leading role to the working class in the struggle against fascist Germany (Niven 2002: 64). Because Nazism was viewed first and foremost as an emanation of imperial capitalism, the Holocaust was considered merely a secondary effect of imperialist practice. Even though the GDR recognised Jews as victims of fascism, the state refused to pay restitution to individuals or to Israel. It was only after the collapse of the regime that East Germany's first democratically elected government approved a resolution on 12 April 1990 that accepted 'joint responsibility on behalf of the people for the humiliation, expulsion, and murder of Jewish women, men, and children. We feel sad and ashamed and acknowledge this burden of history' (cited in Herf 1997: 365).

The Federal Republic under Chancellor Adenauer, who had opposed National Socialism, pursued a reparations treaty with Israel 'to bring about a solution of the material indemnity problems, thus easing the way to the spiritual settlement of infinite suffering' (cited in Moeller 2001: 26). Such measures were a positive step because they formally acknowledged responsibility for the crimes committed during the National Socialist period. But by dealing with the burden of the past through a financial compensation mechanism, these policies did not 'illuminate the origins of National Socialism' and its place in the history of modern Germany (Moeller 2001: 31). Domestically, Adenauer championed the reintegration of the masses of so-called *Mitläufer* (ordinary Nazi supporters) into postwar society, a policy that was designed to lead to the gradual but steady democratisation of West German society through the creation of economic wealth.[4] High-ranking Nazi officials and even Nazi criminals managed to resume leading positions (Frei 2003; Friedrich 2007). The protest generation of 1968 challenged such continuities in the judiciary, education, politics, and industry (see Seidl 2006; Koenen 2002; Aly 2008; Kraushaar 2008). Besides their overt political aim to oust what they perceived as a rotten establishment, the generation of 1968 was motivated by the desire to reject the stigmatised German identity that they had inherited from their parents (see Moses 2007).[5] Collective German pride at the massive reconstructive effort in the 1950s – captured in the adage 'Wir sind wieder wer!' (we are somebody again!) – clashed with the 68ers' sweeping accusation that the Federal Republic was a totalitarian variant of the fascist state. While the revolutionary language of the student protests was far-fetched, 1968 was a turning point in the history of West Germany.[6] On the one hand, it marked the beginning of a period of violent confrontation between the state and the terrorist Red Army Faction that, throughout the 1970s, turned revolutionary rhetoric into brutal practice (Koenen 2002; Colvin 2009). On the other, the battles between the members of the protest generation who did not support terrorism and the political establishment prepared the ground for institutional reform and a more pluralistic society. When the generation of 1968 began to assume positions in academia, in the teaching profession, in the judiciary and within the political domain, they enacted a reformist version of the revolutionary slogan of the 'long march through the institutions'. At the height of the student protests, a prominent leader of the 68er generation, Rudi Dutschke, had coined this phrase in analogy to Mao Zedong's 'long march' to instigate revolutionary action amongst the students (Kraushaar 2008: 81–8). However, instead of destroying the state from within the institutions, the former protesters settled for a process of democratic reform.

From the end of the 1960s, West Germany founded its sense of identity on the idea that the past had to be publicly debated before it could be put to rest (Niven 2002; Reichel 2001; Assmann 2006a). This shift towards a memory culture of atonement found emblematic expression in Willy Brandt's visit to the Warsaw ghetto in 1970. In a gesture that had not been agreed by diplomatic protocol, the chancellor knelt down at the memorial for the victims of the ghetto uprising. The Warsaw genuflection signalled responsibility for the past for all postwar Germans, not least because Brandt himself, who had spent the Nazi years in Norwegian exile, was an untainted figure. The photograph of this event quickly reached a global audience. As a 'secular icon' (Brink 2000) it provided an instantaneous and em7otional connection with a deeply personal and yet highly symbolic gesture. President Richard von Weizsäcker's speech on 8 May 1985, the 40th anniversary of Germany's capitulation, was another historic moment: describing the wide spectrum of experiences amongst Germans for whom the end of the war could unleash not only feelings of relief and liberation or the hope for a new beginning but also sentiments of despondency over the loss of 'Heimat' in the eastern territories and an embittered sense of defeat, Weizsäcker then redefined 8 May 1945 as a day of liberation. He argued that, as a symbolic date, 8 May required a form of remembrance that connected Germany's total defeat in May 1945 back to its origins on 30 January 1933 when Hitler rose to power.[7] Weizsäcker's speech enacted an inclusive mode of remembrance by interweaving the narrative of German suffering with the emphatic acknowledgement of the victims of National Socialist persecution and warfare. He referred especially to the European Jews, the Sinti and Roma, homosexuals, and all the European peoples – above all Soviet and Polish citizens – who had been the object of systematic oppression and genocidal intentions. While such top-down memory politics undoubtedly shaped West German cultural memory, it is important to note that increased media coverage of the Holocaust and of Nazi crimes created a broader audience. The US melodrama *Holocaust* (1978) was screened across four evenings in January 1979 and watched by 40 per cent of the West German viewership (Reichel 2004: 249).[8]

Germany's memory culture since unification: from *Vergangenheits-bewältigung* to memory contests and political normalisation

From the 1970s, the term *Vergangenheitsbewältigung* (coming to terms with the past) came to denote an official programme of commemoration and education (see Niven 2002; Fritzsche 2006; Reichel 2001; Eitz and Stötzel 2007). Since unification, however, *Vergangenheitsbewältigung* has become a dated notion that captures neither the pluralisation of German memory nor the new reality of a multicultural Germany. The 1990s were characterised by a wave of heated 'memory contests' that concerned both postwar Germanies alongside a new interest in the transgenerational emotional legacies of World War II.[9] Furthermore, the diversity of generational perspectives, the growing distance from the Third Reich, and the disparity of formative life experiences in East and West ruptured the consensus that the legacy of the Third Reich remains the defining historical epoch for present and future generations (Fuchs and Cosgrove 2006b:

1–23). After the millennium, 'the long shadow of the past'[10] appeared to have shrunk: the arrival of the information age and globalisation was posing radically new geopolitical challenges for unified Germany.

The political normalisation of Germany took on an altogether new dimension when, at the end of the 1990s, the coalition government of the Social Democrats and the Green party authorised the participation of the German Luftwaffe in NATO air strikes during the Kosovo war (see Chapter 25). Constitutionally this was made possible by designating the mission a humanitarian intervention, and as such a non-aggressive operation. But the fact that the Luftwaffe was bombing targets in Europe left many Germans uneasy because of the deep-seated cultural memory of the carpet-bombing of Germany during World War II. In 2001 Germany sent troops to Afghanistan as part of the International Security Assistance Force (ISAF) mission, again reflecting a shift in German foreign policy since unification (see Chapters 25 and 26). While the German public is generally in support of Germany's enhanced international role, this does not translate into support for war.[11] Attitudes to military intervention are still shaped by the cultural memory of World War II as a national trauma with long transgenerational effects.

The period since the 1990s has seen a remarkable upsurge of interest in the long aftermath of the trauma of warfare. Elderly Germans who had lived through the war as children now began to talk with a new urgency about their experiences of the air war, flight, expulsion, food shortages, life in the postwar ruins, and the death of family members. Robert G. Moeller suggests that the lifting of the Iron Curtain made it 'possible for Germans to reflect on what all Germans had suffered, re-examining parts of their past that had been subordinated to Cold War priorities' (Moeller 2006: 110). As a historical turning point of global significance that had been anticipated neither by politicians nor by historians or other social and political commentators, it invited broad reflection on the social, cultural, as well as psychological effects of Germany's division. In a context of intense preoccupation with German national and cultural identity at the end of the 20th century, German wartime suffering was rediscovered as a topic that could now be explored without the ideological biases of the Cold War. The popularisation of the notion of trauma in Holocaust discourse and a general recognition of the long-term effects of extreme violence further fuelled the public rediscovery of German suffering and loss (Caruth 1996; Felman and Laub 1992). It is important to note that the defeat at Stalingrad, the Allied air war, the expulsions from the East and, more generally, the hardship of the postwar era had already featured prominently in West German memory discourse of the 1950s (Moeller 2001; Süß 2010). These memories were now legitimised through a national trauma narrative that was made possible by unification. But this new discourse of victimhood did not establish a moral equivalence between the German perpetrators and their non-German victims. Rather, it signalled a shift towards a multivocal memory culture that placed German stories about suffering in a broader narrative frame about National Socialism and World War II (see Niven 2006; Schmitz 2007; Schmitz and Seidel-Arpaci 2011). The intensity of some of this debate, exemplified in the controversy around Jörg Friedrich's contentious history of the air war, Der Brand (2002; The Fire, 2008), points to the deep emotional resonance of the war to this day. For some, Friedrich's emplotment of the Allied air war from the perspective of German civilians offered a fresh perspective that communicated a collective trauma. For others, it was a reckless exercise in historical revisionism because of a descriptive vocabulary that created subliminal associations between the Allied strategy of carpet-bombing and the Holocaust.[12] Such memory contests not only expose the gap between an increasingly ossified official remembrance culture and people's private war memories, but also advance competing claims about vastly different historical experiences (Fuchs, James-Chakraborty, and Shortt 2011: 1–14).

The bombing of Dresden in GDR memory discourse

In the aftermath of the bombing of Dresden in February 1945, a wide range of genres and media communicated the belief that the destruction of the city had been a gratuitous act of disproportionate violence. Most German cities had been flattened by 1945, and other attacks were to follow that left a proportionally higher death rate elsewhere.[13] But it was the destruction of Dresden that impinged on the popular imagination as an icon of wanton and excessive violence. The high death toll amongst women, children, and refugees, the lateness of the attack in the war, and the city's 'cultural innocence' are persisting motifs that quickly solidified into a narrative template. Templates are particularly tenacious forms of cultural self-representation that solidify deeply held beliefs by providing the 'stock of stories' that shape a society' (Wertsch 2009: 128). In analogy to Vladimir Propp's idea of generalisable narrative functions, James V. Wertsch has argued that templates 'exert a conservative, yet often unrecognised force on collective memory' (Wertsch 2009: 130). This is so because those who subconsciously use them 'look right through them without recognising their power to shape how we represent the past' (Wertsch 2009: 130).

The traumatic nature of the Allied destruction of Dresden has been a prominent theme in German cultural memory. In the immediate postwar period, photography and film documented the destruction with the dual aim of articulating the collective experience of loss and of converting the German defeat into a reconstructive effort that encompassed the physical, economic, political, cultural, and moral fabric of society. West German photo narratives about destroyed German cities often adopted a Christian register of sin and redemption. A prominent example is Hermann Claasen's photo book about the destruction of Cologne, *Gesang im Feuerofen. Köln: Überreste einer alten deutschen Stadt* (Song from the Furnace. Cologne: the Remnants of an Old German City, 1947), which embeds the bombing of the German cities in a biblical narrative. In contrast, the East German variant attempted to channel the feelings of despair and loss into the construction of a socialist society. Richard Peter's photo narrative *Dresden: eine Kamera klagt an* (Dresden: A Camera Accuses, 1949) about the destruction of Dresden gained iconic status in the postwar German imaginary and has remained in circulation with reprints in the 1980s and 1990s, and after the millennium. Published in Dresden in 1949, its appearance was accompanied by a nationwide poster campaign that advertised it with the slogan 'A book for all Germans – available in all bookshops'. While the book's accusatory title illustrates the desire for German exculpation as well as GDR Cold War rhetoric, the affective power of this photographic story arguably lay in the provision of a narrative template for the experience of traumatic loss.[14] In spite of the book's title, the photo narrative includes no images of the Allied air raids, and there is only a handful of images towards the end that show corpses and piles of bodies that were burnt on the market square. Of the 104 photographs, which are spread across 86 pages, more than half depict the ruined city. The book opens with three images of Dresden's prewar glory and ends with a section on the collective effort to build a new city. This structure accentuates the narrative intention to convert despondent feelings of irredeemable loss into historical optimism and belief in a bright future in a socialist society.

And yet, the real force of the book lies in the serialisation of image after image of architectural wreckage. By remediating the idea of an excessive and disproportionate loss in a sequence of images, the photo story assumes an allegorical commemorative perspective that elides the analysis of historical cause and effect. One picture in particular (Figure 4.1) – the photograph of the ruined cityscape with a female sculpture in the foreground – has become the single most iconic photograph of Germany's ruination: it features regularly on the cover page of journals and magazines, and in many historical accounts of the bombing.[15] Because this image is not framed

Figure 4.1 Richard Petersen, 'Bonitas' (1949)
Courtesy of SLUB Dresden/Deutsche Fotothek, Richard Petersen

by a margin that contains this endless site of ruination, it creates the impression of a never-ending destruction that extends beyond the horizon. The figure in the foreground adopts a decidedly melancholic gesture that displays the ruination not just of Dresden but of all human history. Seen from this perspective, the destruction of Dresden represented not just a locally disastrous event but, on the level of allegorisation, the dreadful wreckage of human history that solicits deep emotional engagement.

The idea of the excesses of history became a powerful template that made the link between war and trauma in German collective consciousness inseparable. In the postwar German imagination, the destruction of Dresden was continually reworked across a wide range of genres and media, including fine art, film, and literature. For example, in the immediate aftermath of the bombing, the Dresden artist Wilhelm Rudolph produced *Das zerstörte Dresden* (Destroyed Dresden), a cycle of 150 drawings of the destroyed city centre that has been regularly exhibited. Filmic representations range from documentary accounts to fictional renditions, exemplified in the award-winning documentary *Das Drama von Dresden* (The Drama of Dresden), screened by the public broadcaster ZDF a few days before the 60th anniversary of the bombing in 2005, and the two-part TV drama *Dresden*, also shown by ZDF in March 2006. Both films attracted broad audiences: the TV drama *Dresden* was watched by more than 12 million viewers on its first night, and even the documentary reached 4.6 million viewers. The persistent remediation of this trauma narrative across several decades has created a framework for the German perception of warfare as such. This also means that trauma is not necessarily locked into cultural silence, as poststructuralist theories argue.[16] Although historical traumas may defy immediate articulation and reception – as exemplified in the delayed global reaction to the Holocaust as a genocide of unprecedented proportions – they are often subjected to multiple acts of remediation.

In the immediate postwar period the GDR leadership attempted to steer the population away from the idea of a traumatic destruction towards the creation of a socialist society. In order to overturn the attachment to the old Dresden, documentaries and newsreel coverage generally focused on progress and the reconstruction of the destroyed cities in the GDR. For example, in 1946 the East German weekly newsreel *Der Augenzeuge* (The Eyewitness) covered a wide range of Dresden-related topics, such as the exhibition *Das neue Dresden* (The New Dresden), which showcased models of a new socialist city, the reconstruction of a children's hospital, Dresden's first postwar art exhibition, the opening of the Technical University, or voluntary Sunday work.[17] The newsreel made no mention of the air war beyond general references to 'Hitler's war'. After the beginning of the Cold War, a change in vocabulary occurred in the GDR coverage: in 1948 the destruction of Dresden features for the first time as the direct effect of the Allied air campaign. From 1952 the references to 'Anglo-American terror from the air' and 'terror attacks' are a regular feature in official GDR memory discourse, which from now on attempted to use the template of the gratuitous destruction of the city for a Marxist view of history. In 1950 Dresden organised its first annual commemoration of the bombing, which soon established a fixed repertoire. This involved local rallies in schools and workplaces, the laying of wreaths at various symbolic sites in the city centre and at the Heidefriedhof (the cemetery where the majority of the victims were buried), the halting of all traffic for one minute at midday, a central commemorative event with political and cultural representatives, and above all, a mass demonstration in the city centre (Neutzner 2005: 148).

And yet, although the destruction of the city by Allied bombers served the GDR's anti-imperialist rhetoric, the persistence and depth of the collective memory of the bombing as an apocalyptic event disrupted a Marxist perspective. In their attempt to invest in a better future, socialist politicians and policymakers often underestimated the emotional attachment to a lost past that was retrospectively imbued with nostalgia. For centuries Dresden had been perceived as a seat of the most refined European art and culture. In the collective imagination Dresden's Baroque architecture, the vast art collections, the city's vibrant cultural and musical life, and its association with fragile porcelain symbolised a feminine playfulness and theatricality that appeared untouched by Nazi ideology.[18] Dresden's implication in the history of the Third Reich did not feature in a postwar cultural narrative that cast Dresden in the role of innocent victim of history's cruel hand. This is unsurprising given the impatience of collective memory with historical ambiguity. According to Wertsch, collective memory – unlike historical consciousness – filters a commemorative voice through a 'single committed perspective' that is normally divorced from historical interpretation (Wertsch 2009: 127) The inflated death toll is a case in point: although the body count of the immediate postwar period resulted in a fairly accurate number of a maximum of 35,000 deaths, for decades the myth persisted that in Dresden far more than 100,000 people had perished. While these inflated figures seemed to corroborate the popular belief that the destruction of Dresden was by far the worst bombing in the history of World War II, in reality it was the underlying narrative template of a wanton act of destruction that motivated such inflated figures. Faced with the persistence of the myth, the city of Dresden set up a historical commission in 2004 to investigate this issue. In its report of 2010, the commission gave an upper limit of 25,000 deaths (see Müller, Schönherr, and Widera 2010).

Dresden as *lieu de mémoire* in unified Germany

The capital of Saxony, Dresden, illuminates the complex circuit of exchange between Germany's changing cultural topography since 1989 and deep-seated emotional legacies. Dresden's symbolic currency derives from its status as a European cultural treasure trove that, from the perspective of the post-1989 collective imagination, rose from the ashes of World War II, withstood the GDR's plans for a socialist city, and, since unification, has found its identity as a site of national and international reconciliation in the present.[19] Apart from the traumatic legacy of World War II, the city now represents resilience during GDR times when socialist planners attempted to build a new socialist city that bore little resemblance to the old Dresden (Lerm 2000; Fuchs 2012: 70–115). In retrospect, the sharp disagreements between socialist planners and preservationists were seen as evidence that in the postwar period Dresden was the scene of a heroic struggle over cultural heritage. But Dresden's contemporary transformation into a symbolic site of trauma, resilience, and recovery stands for a more substantial recalibration of collective memory. Even though the memory of the Dresden bombing continues to mobilise established narrative schemas, remembrance has now taken on a much more critical edge through exposure to the broader memory discourse of the post-1990s era. As previously argued, templates are mostly unconscious, unanalytical, and as such blind to their modes of emplotment. Since unification the memory of the bombing has undergone shifts that show that templates can be modified and changed through critical examination and historical reflection.

The remainder of the chapter explores those shifts in the Dresden memory since unification that are indicative of its historicisation and contextualisation. The exploration of three contemporary *lieux de mémoire* – a Baselitz exhibition in the Zwinger, the Military-Historical Museum, and the Frauenkirche – and comparison with one historical site (the Heidefriedhof) suggests that, although the memory of the destruction of Dresden is still permeated by trauma, it has become more ambiguous, comparative, and open to contestation than it was in the postwar period. Besides a new preoccupation with the transgenerational effects of trauma, the bombing has been historically contextualised and placed within a transnational culture of reconciliation. Arguably, the latter idea could emerge only since unification and in the context of the global debate on Holocaust remembrance and post-conflict resolution (Levy and Sznaider 2001; Assmann and Conrad 2010). The chapter concludes with Dresden's response to neo-Nazi attempts to hijack the memory for right-wing historical revisionist aims.

Georg Baselitz – Dresdner Frauen

The significance to this day of the trauma narrative in Dresden's cultural memory is underlined by an exhibition of the artistic work of Georg Baselitz in the Gallery of the Old Masters in Dresden's Zwinger in 2009, on the occasion of the 20th anniversary of the fall of the Berlin Wall. Entitled *Georg Baselitz – Dresdner Frauen* (Georg Baselitz – Women of Dresden) the exhibition focused on Baselitz's artistic engagement with the long-term memory of the destruction of Dresden.[20] Baselitz, one of Germany's finest contemporary artists, was born in 1938 as Hans-Georg Bruno Kern in Deutschbaselitz near Dresden. In 1961 he adopted Baselitz as his *nom de plume* to accentuate the importance of a particular memoryscape for his artistic production. His figurative work resonates with references to Germany's changing historical and cultural conditions throughout the 20th century. In 1989, shortly before the fall of the Berlin Wall, he began to work on a monumental painting that thematises the end of the war. Entitled *'45*, it consists of 20 panels, the majority of which show the image of a mostly pink-faced woman amidst a dense network of lines that are scratched into the paintings. One panel depicts three upside-down hares; another, elongated shapes that are reminiscent of urns. The scarred surface of these panels and the thick paint leave a charred effect that is evocative of the violence of the air raids. The women, who (like all figures in Baselitz's work) are depicted upside-down, appear suspended in mid-air and exposed to a destructive force that envelops everything. Although the panels emphasise the similarity of their experience through serialisation, the artist is careful to allude to their individuality through changes in their facial expressions. In this way the painting evokes both the universality and particularity in the experience of trauma. Baselitz's *'45* does not explicitly refer to the destruction of Dresden, but its few compositional elements mobilise the pre-existing interpretive template of the magnitude of the event. While the scratched surfaces evoke the relentlessness and terror of the bombing, the figurative representation of women taps into another key element of the Dresden trauma narrative: the idea that the city was full of women and children when it was attacked. German cultural memory about the war and its aftermath is peopled by the iconic figure of the 'rubble woman' who was involved in clearing the rubble by hand or with hand-pulled wagons. The rubble women's hard labour, resilience, and heroism had already featured in Walter Reinhold's monument *Trümmerfrau* (Rubble Woman), which was erected in front of Dresden's Rathaus in 1952. Gender became an essential element in a trauma narrative that foregrounds the overwhelming nature of the event by emphasising the vulnerability of the city and of its inhabitants. And yet, as a self-conscious art work Baselitz's *'45* invites the viewer to problematise the relationship between artistic representation and historical reality. The women in these images are engulfed in a historical reality that remains obscure and inaccessible in spite of the painter's empathy for his subjects.

The Baselitz exhibition of 2009 juxtaposed this altar-like piece with sculptures that Baselitz had also produced in 1989 and 1990. These large-sized wooden sculptures show the heads of 13 women, who carry personal names such as Karla, Hanka, and Uta, or generic names such as 'the visitor from Prague', 'the sick woman from Radebeul', or 'the Russian woman'. Again the artist emphasises the similarity of the traumatic experience by painting all heads in a bright yellow colour and marking the sculptures with deep incisions. The colour yellow is evocative of the sandstone of Baroque Dresden and as such of the city's former glory; the incisions on the women's faces, necks, and heads are the painful scars of the war. Although these women are injured, they have not lost their sense of individuality, uniqueness, and personality. For Baselitz his *Women of Dresden* stand in the tradition of Goya's graphic series *Los Desastres de la Guerra* as well as Jean Fautrier's *Têtes d'Otages*, which represent mutilated heads of French victims of German atrocities committed during the German occupation of France (Baselitz 2009). The history of art thus provides its own powerful templates for the representation of trauma. By telescoping unconscious narrative schemas into self-reflective artistic frames, art stimulates a reflective stance in the viewer that can take care of the affective imprints of memory while recognising the need for critical distance. Baselitz's sculptures contribute to the reworking of the established trauma narrative by raising questions about whether we see representatives or individuals in these sculptures and faces. The curatorial decision to place both Baselitz's *Women of Dresden* and his huge 20-panel painting *'45* in the first room of the Gallery of Old Masters through which all visitors have to pass accentuated the importance of Baselitz's contribution to Dresden as a *lieu de mémoire* in transformation.

The Heidefriedhof and the Militärhistorisches Museum der Bundeswehr

The historical contextualisation of the bombing is inescapable in the design and exhibition of the Military-Historical Museum, which reopened in Dresden in 2011 with a new permanent exhibition and the addition of a wedge-like building by Daniel Libeskind. Before examining the interrelationship of architecture and the exhibition, which together accentuate the analysis of the causes and consequences of warfare, it is necessary briefly to discuss the way in which the GDR had already contextualised the destruction of Dresden through the memorial at the Heidefriedhof, the cemetery on the outskirts of Dresden where the majority of the victims of the air raids were buried. Both the Heidefriedhof and the Military-Historical Museum are in themselves richly textured sites of memory that reflect the changing ideological settings of German history throughout the 20th century.

From the 1950s official memory discourse in the GDR had represented the destruction of Dresden as proof of National Socialist and Anglo-American imperialism. In the early years after the war, many Dresdners had begun to place flowers and crosses on individual graves when they knew that a relative was buried in a particular spot. This practice ran counter to the symbolic role of the cemetery in the official commemorations that, from the 1950s, involved city officials, high-ranking GDR politicians, and Soviet and GDR military personnel. In 1950 the East German press invited the East German people for the first time to mark the destruction of Dresden by Anglo-American bombers with peace rallies. In Dresden the commemorations quickly developed a fixed repertoire that included the laying of wreaths at the Heidefriedhof

Figure 4.2 Heidefriedhof, central monument

Photograph by the author

Figure 4.3 Heidefriedhof, commemorative columns
Photograph by the author

and at various symbolic sites in the city centre, the halting of all traffic for one minute at midday, a central commemorative event with party representatives, and a mass rally in the city centre. Once the annual commemorative ritual was established, the cemetery became an increasingly important site of remembrance that required a new commemorative frame. A central monument was then erected that remembered the 'nameless and uncounted victims' (Figure 4.2), thus replacing individual graves in favour of a particular collective narrative. Although the tenor of the commemorations was ideologically charged, the design of the area put emphasis on remembrance of the dead in a natural environment without the shrill political overtones that accompanied the official commemorative language of the Anglo-American terror bombings. By the 1960s the city had sufficient funds to build a memorial for the victims of fascism on the Heidefriedhof, with the aim of placing the GDR in a heroic anti-fascist tradition. Four-teen columns with inscriptions commemorating the victims of National Socialist violence are arranged in a circle: while seven columns list the names of cities that had been destroyed by Germany during the war, including Coventry, Rotterdam, and Leningrad (Figure 4.3), seven further columns list the names of concentration camps. In this way a pathway of commemoration was created that led the visitor from the memorial for the victims of fascism on to the victims of the Dresden bombing. While this embedding of Dresden into a broader commemorative context serviced the communist narrative of the GDR as the first and only anti-fascist German state, the juxtaposition of the two memorials on the Heidefriedhof was nevertheless a significant step towards historical contextualisation.

After unification a new language of contextual commemoration had to be found. The old Military-Historical Museum in Dresden has a layered history. Originally the building was part of a barracks complex; towards the end of the 19th century it became the Royal Saxon Military Museum. After World War II it was used as a municipal hall for some time, before the militarisation of the GDR in the context of the Cold War led to huge ideological investment in military history. In the 1970s the GDR's German Armed Forces Museum – created in 1961, the year of the Berlin Wall – was relocated from Potsdam to the arsenal building in Dresden.

As Rogg comments, the narrative focused on the 'revolutionary military traditions' of the working class in Germany, and the armed organs led by the Socialist Unity Party (SED) were presented as marking the preliminary climax of their development' (Rogg 2012a: 12). After unification the museum was assigned to the Bundeswehr and renamed the *Militärhistorisches Museum der Bundeswehr* (The Military-Historical Museum of the Bundeswehr). Its challenge was to create a modern military museum that would 'contribute to a cultural history of violence' and provide 'a forum for critical, differentiated and honest debate about the military, war and violence in the past and present' (Rogg 2012a: 13). Furthermore, the museum needed to be mindful of its special location in Dresden, where the power of collective and cultural memory is omnipresent. The architectural design of the new extension became one vehicle for articulating the dialectic between historical continuity and rupture, while also creating a symbolic link between the city centre and the museum, which is located in the northern part of the city. Libeskind simultaneously disrupted and respected the old building by slicing a wedge-like extension into the left wing (Figure 4.4). However, the entrance and the right wing maintain the old arsenal's imposing façade and classical style, thus drawing attention to the museum's own historicity. The new wing interrupts the idea of continuity not only by cutting through the old building but also through the stark contrast between the shiny aluminium exterior and the sandstone of the old building. The tip of the wedge points into the air and can be interpreted as a symbol of both violence and hope. The visitor has access to a platform on the top floor of the new wing, which offers a panorama of Dresden through aluminium slats. Dresden's city centre is visible in the distance with the cupola of the rebuilt Frauenkirche, the single most prominent memory site in Dresden's cultural topography. But this sight-line makes another historical reference. As Matthias Rogg explains, it is

> exactly directed to the point in Dresden's Friedrichstadt district where the first British aircraft dropped their light markings which guided the following bomber formations during that night-time bombing raid in 1945. With an angle of 40.1 degrees, the wedge exactly describes the crater of destruction which transformed the historical centre of Dresden into a desert of rubble.
>
> (Rogg 2012b: 19)

Inside the museum, the permanent exhibition alternates between historical and thematic explorations of the causes and effects of warfare (Pieken 2012: 21–38). It emphasises contrasting perspectives throughout, creating visual references between objects and themes to accentuate how violence permeates society. For example, a huge German V2 rocket from World War II stands on a launching pad on the ground floor but reaches up into the second floor where toys are featured, including a doll's house that was owned by a girl in London during the blitz. She had made her doll's house fit for war by, for example, blackening out the windows and making Anderson shelters in the garden. On the ground floor, the V2 rocket is next to objects that survived the inmates of the concentration camp Mittelbau-Dora, who were enslaved to build the rocket underground.

The bombing of Dresden features specifically on the top floor of the Libeskind wing. Again the architecture and content of the exhibits exemplify a radically contextualised approach. Visitors who take the lift to the fourth floor enter an asymmetrical room that leads to the Dresden panorama. Before reaching the platform, they pass three displays that showcase the effects of aerial bombing raids in exemplary fashion. Pavement slabs from Wieluń in Poland with traces of the German attack foreground unlawful German aggression (Figure 4.5).

Figure 4.4 Daniel Libeskind's extension of the Military-Historical Museum

Photograph by Helen Doherty

Figure 4.5 Museum display of the German attack on Wieluń, 1939

Photograph by Helen Doherty

Figure 4.6 Museum display of the German attack on Rotterdam, 1940
Photograph by Helen Doherty

Figure 4.7 Museum display of the Allied attack on Dresden, 1945
Photograph by Helen Doherty

This small Polish town was raided by the Luftwaffe prior to a declaration of war in the early hours of 1 September 1939, killing 1,200 people. German aggression and violence is further underlined by the display of remnants of a sculpture from an orphanage in Rotterdam, which was bombed in May 1940 to force the neutral Dutch government to surrender (Figure 4.6). In similar fashion, the bombing of Dresden is represented by slabs bearing marks of the aerial bombing; incendiary bombs, which were found in the ground beneath in 2007, caused the visible holes (Figure 4.7).

Explanatory panels provide historical context as well as the life stories of two inhabitants of each place. The panels about Dresden juxtapose the biography of Manfred Pucks, who lost both his parents and his four siblings during the night of 13 February 1945, with that of Henny Brenner, born as the daughter of a Jewish mother and a Protestant father. The experiential gap between different sides and moral ambiguity are brought to the fore: the Brenner family received its deportation papers on 13 February 1945 and was therefore saved by the Allied air raids. The arrangement of these three fairly understated displays thus creates a contextual space that interweaves the historical narrative of cause and effect with a comparative narrative of human suffering. The visitor who steps out onto the platform then views Dresden through a slanted grid that draws attention to the multiplicity of historical perspectives, held together by historical knowledge.

The Frauenkirche

The third element in the Dresden narrative since unification is the promotion of an inclusive and reconciliatory culture of remembrance that overcomes national resentment and former divisions by way of carefully choreographed gestures of reconciliation. One powerful example of this was the consecration of the rebuilt Frauenkirche in 2005 (Figure 4.8): the event was staged as a symbolic act of reconciliation that recognised the memory of the past, while gesturing towards a new beginning.

Designed by George Bähr, the church was originally built in the mid-18th century to appease Protestant citizens who were less than enamoured when Augustus the Strong converted to Catholicism. A symbol of religious and civic tolerance and architectural perfection, the church collapsed on 15 February 1945 after the firestorm of the previous day. The ruin was not rebuilt for decades after the war: the GDR had no interest in church property, and the Lutheran church in the GDR had other priorities, above all to sustain its precarious position in the socialist state. In the 1980s the church ruins became the site of the emerging protest culture in the GDR, when members of the peace movement called for a sit-in at the ruins of the Frauenkirche. This marked the beginning of a new commemorative practice that targeted militarism in East and West. Instead of orchestrated demonstrations and political speeches by SED officials, the participants in this alternative event stood in silence at the ruined church with lit candles. From now on the citizens of Dresden increasingly asserted an alternative memory culture by holding counter-cultural commemorations in silence. In 1985 the Lutheran church commemorated the bombing of Dresden separately from the state in a ceremony with guests from Coventry, Leningrad, and the neighbouring countries of Poland and Czechoslovakia (Lindemann 2009, 79–90). In the late 1980s the Lutheran and Anglican churches managed to organise simultaneous memorial services in Coventry and Dresden (Neutzner 2005, 160).

This new transnational phase of reconciliation came to full fruition after the fall of the Berlin Wall, when in 1995 the 50th anniversary of the end of the war became the stage for the performance of an inclusive ceremony. Besides a wide range of German politicians, the German President Roman Herzog, church representatives, and ordinary Dresdners, participants also

Figure 4.8 The rebuilt Frauenkirche in Dresden

Photograph by the author

included the Duke of Kent. There were delegates from Coventry, Rotterdam, St Petersburg, and other partner cities, as well as military leaders from Germany, the United States, and Great Britain, amongst others.[21]

In the meantime the campaign to rebuild the church, launched in 1990 by the Förderkreis zum Wiederaufbau der Frauenkirche Dresden e.V. (Association for the Reconstruction of the Frauenkirche), had gained momentum. In contrast to other building projects in unified Germany, the reconstruction of the Frauenkirche was not steered by the city, the Lutheran church, the state of Saxony, or the Federal Parliament in Berlin; while all these institutions eventually supported the plan, it remained first and foremost a citizens' initiative. The Förderkreis ran a very effective national and international campaign by emphasising the redemptive function of the project.[22] The response was overwhelming, and donations began to flow in from all over the world, including from the British Dresden Trust, which made a major contribution to the rebuilding project. A symbol of this reconciliatory ethos is the new golden cross that adorns the church tower today: it was made by the son of a British pilot involved in the attacks on Dresden. In line with this inclusive approach to commemoration, the consecration of the rebuilt Frauenkirche on 30 October 2005 assigned a central role to the former Allied forces. The opening was staged as a global TV event, synchronising a global audience 'in a collective heart beat' (Dyan and Kath 1992: 9). In Germany it was watched by millions of (mostly older) Germans who perceived the ceremony in terms of the symbolic recuperation of their fractured cultural identity.

Conclusion

Trauma, historical contextualisation, and reconciliation are the three dominant interpretive schemas that have shaped a self-conscious memory of the Dresden bombing since German unification. Trauma is the oldest and deepest-rooted trope in postwar German memory, which, in its initial stages, masked German collective responsibility behind the idea of victimhood. The German postwar memory of the bombing of Dresden gave prominence to women, children, and refugees because they accentuated the central idea that, prior to its destruction, Dresden had been a playful, feminine, and ultimately historically innocent city. This was a myth that conveniently ignored Dresden's history during National Socialism: the deportation of its Jewish citizens and its strategic importance as a transport hub during the war. However, the trauma narrative should not be misread as only reflecting the exculpatory tendencies of the postwar period: its persistence to this day also attests to the long-term effects of the experience of violence. The passage of time and the popularisation of the idea of trauma in the public domain in recent times enabled many survivors of the air raids to talk about their horrific experiences from an experiential perspective.

Since the 1990s, the long aftermath of the war has been a particular concern of German cultural memory: the transgenerational effects of the war have been addressed in many public debates, in popular family novels, autobiographies, films, history books, and countless TV documentaries (Assmann 2007; Fuchs 2008). From 1945 the destruction of Dresden symbolised not just the death of a particularly beautiful city with a long cultural history, but the excessive and traumatic wreckage of human history as a whole. Along with the Holocaust and the bombs dropped on Hiroshima and Nagasaki, Dresden became a universally recognisable icon of a destructiveness that could not be understood in terms of cause and effect alone. Dresden transmuted into a carrier of an affective memory of the war that, for all the ideological appropriations across the postwar period, remained tied to an overwhelming experience of violence. This required an emotional response alongside rational analysis.

As this chapter demonstrates, however, the trauma narrative is contained by the two other elements in German cultural memory: contextualisation and transnationalisation (Assmann and Conrad 2010). A degree of historical contextualisation already featured in the GDR, which promoted an anti-fascist narrative that explicitly referred to the non-German victims of German fascism. However, the commemorative narrative of the GDR was limited because it presented an idealised view of communist resistance. After unification a much more critical and self-reflective form of contextualisation was required. On the one hand, Germany now had to deal with multiple pasts (the Nazi period and the legacies of the two postwar Germanies, which included the SED dictatorship, the role of the Stasi in the GDR, the events of 1968, and the state's response to left-wing terrorism in West Germany). On the other, united Germany finally acknowledged that it had turned into a multicultural society with citizens of diverse ethnic backgrounds and belief systems, divergent generational perspectives, and fractured formative experiences. As the group of those with firsthand experiences of World War II was diminishing, the question of how to foster German cultural memory of the war, while also making room for alternative narratives, became ever more pressing. The Military-Historical Museum in Dresden resolves this tension between an enshrined memory and a pluralisation of perspectives by squarely placing World War II in a comparative context that contributes to a cultural history of violence. The thematic explorations of the connections between the military and politics, music, fashion, art, language, games, and technology invite viewers to consider how deeply violence penetrates society, how it is legitimised by the state, and its disastrous effects and long aftermath, which is addressed through themes such as animals in war, the human body, death, trauma, and the transgenerational memory of war. This creates a comparative and multiperspectival context for the bombing of Dresden that carefully balances the recognition of trauma with historical understanding.

The shift towards an inclusive memory culture was paradigmatically enacted through the rebuilding of the Frauenkirche, which has become a symbol of transnational reconciliation. By appealing to a worldwide community, the association that drove the project mapped local identity onto global citizenship, thereby responding to the challenge 'that the integrating force of homogeneous national memories is dwindling' (Assmann and Conrad 2010: 2). The creation of a global public in an age where history is often witnessed in real time brings with it the challenge of a competition for attention. In the case of Dresden, the sustained global reverberation of the cultural memory of the Dresden bombing was helped by the power of templates, which provide interpretive schemas for otherwise overwhelming events. Although these schemas are often unconscious and unreflective, they can be changed in line with new historical perspectives, shifting attitudes, and new political contexts. The cultural memory of Dresden has been transformed in the years since unification: Dresden no longer symbolises gratuitous destruction and trauma but rather the disastrous consequences of warfare and the possibility of recuperation through the creation of a global civic public.

In the case of Dresden this newly contextualised and inclusive approach to cultural memory has to assert itself afresh every year when, on the anniversary of the bombing, extreme neo-Nazi groups from across Europe gather in Dresden to exploit the city's destruction for their perverse historical views. The fundamental democratic right to demonstrate – a right that was swiftly eradicated by the Nazis after 1933 – poses a challenge to Dresden, which must respect this right while making every possible effort to counter such attempts to instrumentalise cultural memory. For example, on the occasion of the 65th anniversary of the bombing in 2010, neo-Nazi groups from across Europe assembled in Dresden's Neustadt on the other side of the river Elbe with the aim of marching towards the city centre. But the city council prevented a symbolic takeover by staging a counterdemonstration that was attended by thousands of Dresdners, trade union members, the entire spectrum of Germany's democratic parties, and various youth and church groups from all over Germany. A human chain was formed that ran from the river Elbe across the Altmarkt to the rebuilt Frauenkirche to prevent the infiltration of this symbolic space. Meanwhile, on the Neustadt side of the river Elbe the police contained frustrated right-wing demonstrators who were not allowed to cross the river and demonstrate in the old city centre. In this way, the city managed to uphold the democratic rights of a repugnant minority while simultaneously aborting the takeover of its sites of memory. The co-occurrence of civic demonstrations in the city centre and neo-Nazi gatherings in the Neustadt and the resulting tensions are now a regular feature of Dresden's annual commemorations. A critical memory culture depends on active engagement by a civic public that resists the ossification of history through rigid interpretive schemas.

Notes

1 In 2012 the unveiling of the Bomber Command memorial in London for the 55,000 pilots who died on their Allied mission provided a further example of a rather triumphalist memorial register that threatens to eclipse the moral complexity of the air war. With its classical style and inscriptions by Churchill and Pericles, such a monument thwarts critical engagement with the public function of memorials in the 21st century and with the difficult question of how a multicultural and ethnically diverse society can maintain the notion of a shared cultural memory.

2 Collective memory refers to the experiential memory of history that normally forms the life horizon of up to three generations. Collective memory is informal and unstable, and relies on oral modes of transmission. Cultural memory denotes the totality of mediatised and archived memories that can be used to authorise cultural identity. Literature, art, films, museums, national archives, and memorials all feed into cultural memory. On collective memory see Halbwachs 1992; on cultural memory see Assmann 2011; Erll and Nünning 2010; Erll 2011.

3 According to estimates, two million refugees died on their treks, 500,000 civilians died during the Allied air raids, and four million soldiers died during the war; see Overmans 1999. On the expellees see Benz 1985; Hoffmann *et al.* 2000. On the air war and its effects, see Groehler 1990.

4 The philosopher Hermann Lübbe argues that the 1950s were characterised by an 'asymmetrical discretion' between the minority of Nazi opponents and the majority of ex-Nazi supporters. For Lübbe this discretion was essential as it enabled former Nazis to buy into the emerging democratic order (see Lübbe 1983: 329–49).

5 According to Dirk Moses, it was the generation born around 1930 that 'commenced the task of subjecting the national intellectual traditions to a searching critique in light of their experiences of 1945' (Moses 2007: 9). Famous German intellectuals who represent this generation are Jürgen Habermas, Niklas Luhmann, Hans and Wolfgang Mommsen, and Ralf Dahrendorf. According to Moses they shared 'a deep distrust of their German element in their own selves' that they channelled into a rejection of irrational nationalism (Moses 2007: 70).

6 In 2008 – the 40th anniversary of 1968 – the impact of 1968 on West German political culture was the topic of an intense debate. Many former protagonists themselves were now critical of the high price of a political discourse that had aggressively silenced alternative voices. See Kraushaar 2008; Aly 2008; Schneider 2008.

7 See www.hdg.de/lemo/html/dokumente/NeueHerausforderungen_redeVollstaendigRichardVon Weizsaecker8Mai1985/ (accessed 10 October 2012).

8 After the screenings, the Bundeszentrale and Landeszentralen für politische Bildung (the federal and state agencies for political education) received half a million requests for educational material. According to an opinion poll that was conducted immediately after the screening, 80 per cent of the viewership felt the need to talk about the Holocaust with family members and friends (Reichel 2004: 252).

9 The notion of memory contests emphasises the dynamic nature of debates enabling a pluralistic memory culture. Memory contests help to challenge and overturn enshrined understandings of the past in favour of a multivocal history (see Fuchs and Cosgrove 2006a: 3–10, 2006b: 1–21). Prominent examples are the Walser-Bubis controversy, the Goldhagen debate and the discussion about the Holocaust memorial in Berlin. More recent controversies include the discussion about the fate of the communist-era Palast

der Republik or the debate surrounding plans for a national unification monument (see Fuchs, James-Chakraborty, and Shortt 2011: 3–4).

10 This is the title of a monograph by Aleida Assmann (2006a); see also Frei (2005).

11 In 2010 an opinion poll by the Allensbach Institut showed that 59 per cent of the population believed that German participation in the war in Afghanistan had been a mistake. See 'Wird Deutschland am Hindukusch verteidigt?', *Frankfurter Allgemeine Zeitung*, 26 May 2010. Although the image of the Bundeswehr is generally positive, Germans continue to reject warfare as a means of policy change. According to an opinion poll by Forsa in 2011, 88 per cent rejected German participation in the air strikes against the Gaddafi regime; a large majority of 70 per cent favoured trade embargoes instead. See http://www.handelsblatt.com/politik/deutschland/libyscher-buergerkrieg-deutsche-lehnen-bundeswehr-einsatz-ab/3956510.html (accessed 12 September 2012).

12 For a critical analysis of Friedrich's book see Assmann 2006a: 187–200; Kettenacker (ed.) 2003; Greiner 2003: 42–4; Naumann 2003: 40–60.

13 The small town of Pforzheim in the southwest of Germany was attacked in March 1945. It had a population of 60,000 of whom approximately 17,000 were killed, proportionally the highest death rate in all German cities.

14 For a more detailed interpretation see Glasenapp 2008: 100–32; Mielke 2007: 125–80 and Fuchs 2012: 32–42. Both Glasenapp and Mielke read Peter's photo book from the perspective of a polemical socialist poem that precedes the photos, a reading that short-circuits the semantic of Peter's photography considerably.

15 The political magazine *Der Spiegel* used the photo twice for its cover image; see *Der Spiegel*, 2 (2003) and 'Spiegel spezial': *Als Feuer vom Himmel fiel: Der Bombenkrieg gegen die Deutschen*, 1 (2003). It also featured in *Bild am Sonntag* when the tabloid polemicised against Frederick Taylor's book; see *Bild am Sonntag*, 16 January 2005.

16 The history as trauma view was promoted by Cathy Caruth in her influential book *Unclaimed Experience* (1996). The idea of history as trauma gained even greater currency through the debate on postmemory. In her book *Family Frames*, Marianne Hirsch coined the term postmemory to capture the mediated and transgenerational memory of the Holocaust by those who did not experience it directly (Hirsch 1997). For a discussion of postmemory see Long 2006; on trauma and postmemory see Fuchs 2008: 47–52.

17 See *Der Augenzeuge* nos 6 (1946), 8 (1946), 14 (1946), 15 (1946), 16 (1946), 22 (1946), 26 (1946), 34 (1946), 36 (1946). See Bundesarchiv (Filmarchiv), FIN 122.

18 The importance of porcelain as a trope of memory is underlined by Durs Grünbein's cycle of poems *Porzellan. Poem vom Untergang meiner Stadt* (Porcelain. Poem about the Demise of My City, 2005), which thematises the destruction of Dresden. For an interpretation see Fuchs 2011: 184–204.

19 On the history of Baroque Dresden see Watanabe-O'Kelly 2002. On Dresden's symbolic currency as an iconic site of war remembrance see Fuchs 2012; *Deutsches Hygiene-Museum Dresden* (2006); Schmitz 2005; Neutzner 2005: 128–63.

20 The art works under discussion are reproduced in the exhibition catalogue: Bischoff and Henning 2009.

21 See the following newspaper articles: A. Funk, '"Ein Mahnmal, das den Namen Dresden trägt": offizielles Gedenken und stille Trauer', *Frankfurter Allgemeine Zeitung*, 14 February 1995; C. Habbe and D. Koblitz, 'Dresden's Undying Embers', *New York Times*, 12 February 1995. For an analysis of the changing role of the Ehrenhain at Dresden's Heidefriedhof see Hertel 2000: 83–6.

22 For a detailed chronology see Fischer, Jäger, and Kobuch 2006: 321–50.

Bibliography

Aly, G. (2008) *Unser Kampf 1968: Ein irritierter Blick zurück*, Bonn: Bundeszentrale für politische Bildung.

Assmann, A. (2006a) *Der lange Schatten der Vergangenheit: Erinnerungskultur und Geschichtspolitik*, Munich: Beck.

Assmann, A. (2006b) 'On the (In)compatibility of Guilt and Suffering in German Memory', *German Life and Letters*, 59: 187–200.

Assmann, A. (2007) *Geschichte im Gedächtnis: Von der individuellen Erfahrung zur öffentlichen Inszenierung*, Munich: C.H. Beck.

Assmann, A. (2011) *Cultural Memory and Western Civilization: Functions, Media, Archives*, Cambridge: Cambridge University Press.

Anne Fuchs

Assmann, A. and Conrad, S. (2010) *Memory in a Global Age: Discourses, Practices and Trajectories*, Basingstoke: Palgrave/Macmillan.

Assmann, A. and Frevert, U. (1999) *Geschichtsvergessenheit – Geschichtsversessenheit. Vom Umgang mit deutschen Vergangenheiten nach 1945*, Stuttgart: Deutsche Verlagsanstalt.

Baselitz, G. (2009) *Dresdner Frauen*, ed. U. Bischoff and A. Henning, Cologne: Dumont.

Benz, W. (ed.) (1985) *Die Vertreibung der Deutschen aus dem Osten: Ursachen, Ereignisse, Folgen*, Frankfurt a.m.: Fischer.

Bergander, G. (1994) *Dresden im Luftkrieg: Vorgeschichte, Zerstörung, Folgen*, Cologne, Weimar, and Vienna: Böhlau.

Bischoff, U. and Henning, A. (eds) (2009) *Georg Baselitz – Dresdner Frauen*, Cologne: Dumont.

Brink, C. (2000) 'Secular Icons', *History and Memory: Studies in Representations of the Past*, 12: 135–50.

Caruth, C. (1996) *Unclaimed Experience: Trauma, Narrative, and History*, Baltimore and London: The Johns Hopkins University Press.

Claasen, H. (1947) *Gesang im Feuerofen. Koln: Überreste einer alten deutschen Stadt*, Düsseldorf: L. Schwann.

Colvin, S. (2009) *Ulrike Meinhof and West German Terrorism: Language, Violence, and Identity*, Rochester, NY: Camden House.

Dad's Army (1968–77) [TV series] Directed by D. Croft, H. Snoad and B. Spiers, UK: 2entertain.

Deutsches Hygiene-Museum Dresden (ed.) (2006) *Mythos Dresden: Eine kulturhistorische Revue*, Cologne: Böhlau.

Dyan, D. and Kath, E. (1992) *Media Events: The Life Broadcasting of History*, Cambridge, MA: Harvard University Press.

Echternkamp, J. and Martens, S. (eds) (2010) *Experience and Memory: The Second World War in Europe*, New York and Oxford: Berghahn.

Eitz, T. and Stötzel, G. (eds) (2007) *Wörterbuch der 'Vergangenheitsbewältigung': Die NS-Vergangenheit im öffentlichen Sprachgebrauch*, Hildesheim: Olms.

Erll, A. (2011) *Memory in Culture*, Basingstoke: Palgrave/Macmillan.

Erll, A. and Nüning, A. (eds) (2010) *A Companion to Cultural Memory Studies*, Berlin and New York: De Gruyter.

Felman, S. and Laub, D. (1992) *Testimony: Crises of Witnessing in Literature, Psychoanalysis and Art*, New York and London: Routledge.

Fischer, C., Jäger, H.-J., and Kobuch, M. (2006) 'Chronologischer Abriß zur Geschichte des Wiederaufbaus der Frauenkirche 1945–2005', in L. Güttler (ed.) *Der Wiederaufbau der Dresdner Frauenkirche: Botschaft und Ausstrahlung einer weltweiten Bürgerinitiative*, Regensburg: Schnell & Steiner: 321–50.

Frei, N. (2003) *Hitlers Eliten nach 1945*, Munich: dtv.

Frei, N. (2005) *1945 und wir: Das Dritte Reich im Bewußtsein der Deutschen*, Munich: Beck.

Frei, N. (2012) *Vergangenheitspolitik: Die Anfänge der Bundesrepublik und die NS-Vergangenheit*, Munich: Beck.

Friedrich, J. (2002) *Der Brand, Deutschland im Bombenkrieg 1940–1945*, Munich: Propyläen.

Friedrich, J. (2007) *Die kalte Amnestie: NS-Täter in der Bundesrepublik*, Munich: List.

Fritzsche, P. (2006) 'What exactly is *Vergangenheitsbewältigung*?', in A. Fuchs, M. Cosgrove, and G. Grote (eds) *German Memory Contests. The Quest for Identity in Literature, Film, and Discourse since 1990*, Rochester: Camden House: 25–41.

Fuchs, A. (2008) *Phantoms of War in Contemporary German Literature, Films and Discourse: The Politics of Memory*, Basingstoke: Palgrave/Macmillan.

Fuchs, A. (2011) 'Cultural Topography and Emotional Legacies in Durs Grünbein's Dresden Poetry', in Fuchs, James-Chakraborty, and Shortt (eds): 184–204.

Fuchs, A. (2012) *After the Dresden Bombing: Pathways of Memory, 1945 to the Present*, Houndmills, Basingstoke: Palgrave/Macmillan.

Fuchs, A. and Cosgrove, M. (2006a) 'Memory Contests' (special issue), *German Life and Letters*, 59(2): 3–10.

Fuchs, A. and Cosgrove, M. (2006b) 'Introduction', in A. Fuchs, M. Cosgrove, and G. Grote (eds) *German Memory Contests: The Quest for Identity in Literature, Film, and Discourse since 1990*, Rochester: Camden House: 1–23.

Fuchs, A., James-Chakraborty, K., and Shortt, L. (eds) (2011) *Debating German Cultural Identity since 1989*, Rochester: Camden House.

Glasenapp, J. (2008) *Die deutsche Nachkriegsfotografie. Eine Mentalitätsgeschichte in Bildern*, Munich: Fink.

Greiner, B. (2003) '"Overbombed": Warum die Diskussion über die alliierten Luftangriffe nicht mit dem Hinweis auf die deutsche Schuld beendet werden darf', *Literaturen*, 3: 42–4.

Groehler, O. (1990) *Bombenkrieg gegen Deutschland*, Berlin: Akademie-Verlag.

Halbwachs, M. (1992) *On Collective Memory*, trans. from the French by L.C. Coser, Chicago and London: Chicago University Press.

Herf, J. (1997) *Divided Memory: The Nazi Past in the Two Germanys*, Cambridge, MA: Harvard University Press.

Hertel, C. (2000) 'Dis/Continuities in Dresden's Dances of Death', *The Art Bulletin* 82: 83–116.

Hirsch, M. (1997) *Family Frames: Photography, Narrative and Postmemory*. Cambridge, MA: Harvard University Press.

Hoffmann, D., Krauss, M., and Schwartz, M. (eds) (2000) *Vertriebene in Deutschland: Interdisziplinäre Ergebnisse und Forschungsperspektiven*, Munich: Oldenbourg.

Holocaust (1978) [TV miniseries] Directed by M.J. Chomsky, USA: NBC.

Kettenacker, L. (ed.) (2003) *Ein Volk von Opfern? Die neue Debatte um den Bombenkrieg 1940–1945*, Berlin: Rowohlt.

Koenen, G. (2002) *Das rote Jahrzehnt*, Frankfurt a.m.: Fischer.

Koenen, G. (2005) *Vesper, Ensslin, Baader: Urszenen des deutschen Terrorismus*, Frankfurt a.M: Fischer.

Kraushaar, W. (2008) *Achtundsechzig: eine Bilanz*, Berlin: Propyläen.

Lerm, M. (2000) *Abschied vom alten Dresden: Verluste der historischen Bausubstanz nach 1945*, Rostock: Hinstorff.

Levy, D. and Sznaider, N. (2001) *Erinnerung im globalen Zeitalter*, Frankfurt a.M: Suhrkamp.

Lindemann, G. (2009) 'Innergesellschaftliche Konflikte seit 1978 und die Christen', in H. Starke (ed.) *Keine Gewalt. Revolution in Dresden 1989*, Dresden: Sandstein: 79–90.

Long, J. J. (2006) 'Monika Maron's Pawels Briefe: Photography, Narrative and the Claims of Postmemory', in A. Fuchs, M. Cosgrove and G. Grote (eds), *German Memory Contests*, Rochester NY: Camden House, 147–65.

Lübbe, H. (1983) 'Der Nationalsozialismus im politischen Bewusstsein der Gegenwart', in M. Broszat (ed.) *Deutschlands Weg in die Diktatur*, Berlin: Siedler: 329–49.

Mielke, C. (2007) 'Geisterstädte. Literarische Texte und Bilddokumentationen zur Städtebombardierung des Zweiten Weltkrieges und die Personifizierung des Urbanen', in A. Böhn and C. Mielke (eds) *Die zerstörte Stadt: Mediale Repräsentationen urbaner Räume von Troja bis SimCity*, Berlin: Transcript: 125–80.

Moeller, R.G. (2001) *War Stories. The Search for a Usable Past in the Federal Republic of Germany*, Berkeley, Los Angeles, and London: University of California Press.

Moeller, R.G. (2006) 'On the History of Man-Made Destruction: Loss, Death, Memory, and Germany in the Bombing War', *History Workshop Journal*, 61: 103–34.

Moses, D. (2007) *German Intellectuals and the Nazi Past*, Cambridge: Cambridge University Press.

Müller, R.-D., Schönherr, N., and Widera, T. (eds) (2010) *Die Zerstörung Dresdens 13. Bis 15. Februar 1945 – Gutachten und Ergebnisse der Dresdner Historikerkommission zur Ermittlung der Opferzahlen*, Göttingen: V&R unipress.

Naumann, K. (2003) 'Bombenkrieg – Totaler Krieg – Massaker. Jörg Friedrichs Buch *Der Brand* in der Diskussion', *Mittelweg*, 36: 40–60.

Neutzner, M. (2005) 'Vom Anklagen zum Erinnern. Die Erzählung vom 13. Februar', in O. Reinhard, M. Neutzner, and W. Hesse (eds) *Das rote Leuchten: Dresden und der Bombenkrieg*, Dresden: Edition Sächsische Zeitung: 128–63.

Niven, B. (2002) *Facing the Nazi Past: United Germany and the Legacy of the Third Reich*, London and New York: Routledge.

Niven, B. (ed.) (2006) *Germans as Victims: Remembering the Past in Contemporary Germany*, Basingstoke: Palgrave/Macmillan.

Novick, P. (1999) *The Holocaust and Collective Memory*, London: Bloomsbury.

Overmans, R. (1999) *Deutsche militärische Verluste im 2. Weltkrieg*, Munich: Oldenbourg.

Peter, R. (1949) *Dresden: Eine Kamera klag an*, Dresden: Dresdner Verlagsgesellschaft.

Pieken, G. (2012) 'Concept and Structure of the Permanent Exhibition', in G. Pieken and M. Rogg (eds) *Militärhistorisches Museum der Bundeswehr: Exhibition Guide*, Dresden: Sandstein: 21–38.

Ramsden, J. (2010) 'Myths and Realities of the "People's War" in Britain', in Echternkamp and Martens (eds): 40–52.

Reichel, P. (2001) *Vergangenheitsbewältigung in Deutschland: Die Auseinandersetzung mit der NS-Diktatur von 1945 bis heute*, Munich: Beck.

Reichel, P. (2004) *Erfundene Erinnerung: Weltkrieg und Judenmord in Film und Theater*, Munich and Vienna: Carl Hanser Verlag.

Rogg, M. (2012a) 'The Historic Place', in Pieken and Rogg (eds): 7–13.

Rogg, M. (2012b) 'The Architecture', in Pieken and Rogg (eds): 15–21.

Schildt, A. (2010) 'The Long Shadows of the Second World War: The Impact of Experiences and Memories of War on West Germany', in Echternkamp and Martens (eds): 197–213.

Schmitz, H. (ed.) (2007) *A Nation of Victims? Representations of German Wartime Suffering from 1945 to the Present*, Amsterdam: Rodopi.

Schmitz, H. and Seidel-Arpaci, A. (eds) (2011) *Narratives of Trauma: Discourses of German Wartime Suffering in National and International Perspective*, Amsterdam: Rodopi.

Schmitz, W. (ed.) (2005) *Die Zerstörung Dresdens: Antworten der Künste*, Dresden: Thelem.

Schneider, P. (2008) *Rebellion und Wahn: Mein 68 – eine autobiographische Erzählung*, Munich: Kiepenheuer & Witsch.

Seidl, F. (2006) *Die APO und der Konflikt mit der Vätergeneration: NS Vergangenheit im Diskurs der '68er*, Nuremberg: Verlag Seidl.

Süß, D. (2010) 'The Air War, The Public and Cycles of Memory', in Echternkamp and Martens (eds): 180–97.

Taylor, F. (2004) *The Bombing of Dresden: Tuesday 13 February 1945*, London: Bloomsbury.

Ulrich, B. and Ziemann, B. (eds) (1997) *Krieg im Frieden: Die umkämpfte Erinnerung an den Ersten Weltkrieg*, Frankfurt a.m.: Fischer.

Wartime Farm (2012) [TV series] Directed by S. Elliott and N. Benson, UK: Acorn Media.

Watanabe-O'Kelly, H. (2002) *Court Culture in Dresden: From Renaissance to Baroque*, Basingstoke: Palgrave/Macmillan.

Wertsch, J.V. (2009) 'Collective Memory', in P. Boyer and J.V. Wertsch (eds) *Memory in Mind and Culture*, Cambridge: Cambridge University Press: 117–37.

5

Modell Deutschland

From the Bonn to the Berlin Republic

Jeffrey J. Anderson

In November 2013, two news articles appeared in the span of three days that captured perfectly the conflicted international status of the German model. The first piece to appear was in *Spiegel Online*, which ran a major story detailing the coalition agreement that had just been hammered out between the centre right (CDU/CSU) and centre left (SPD) negotiating teams. The article highlighted the apparent internal contradictions of the future government's pledges simultaneously to raise the minimum wage, lower the official retirement age, and hold the line on tax increases – all while preaching austerity to the rest of Europe. The message was as clear as the article's title – Germany is no longer a role model for Europe. Two days later, in the 'Business Day' section of the *New York Times*, an article appeared that showcased several successful industrial apprenticeship programmes in South Carolina that have taken their inspiration from the experience of the German vocational training system. Here, too, the underlying message was clear – Germany is worth emulating.[1]

Perhaps these articles tell a subtle story of situational relevance: at the same time as Germany's role as a template for Europe is becoming more problematic, even contested, its experiences have a growing application in other parts of the world. Even if there is nothing more than coincidence in the nearly simultaneous appearance of these contrasting takes on the German way of doing things, we have come a long way since the early 1980s, when Modell Deutschland was held up worldwide as one of several coherent and successful models of political economy – other examples included the Swedish model and Japan Inc. – that had made their mark on the global economy (see also Chapter 24). That each of these distinctive models has fallen on hard times is indicative of broader economic and social transformations that have undercut the varied settlements that emerged out of the early postwar period.

The focus in this chapter is on the evolution of the German model of political economy from its inception in the years immediately following the end of World War II, through unification, to the present day. After locating the study of the German model in the broader social science literature, the chapter will survey the origins and components of Modell Deutschland after 1945 until the so-called *Wende* (turnabout) that followed the collapse of the German Democratic Republic in 1989, and the model's evolution after the unification of the 'two Germanies' in 1990. I argue that the German model achieved a notable level of coherence and success up through the 1970s, but began to experience considerable pressures and undergo significant changes well before the shock provided by unification. Since 1989, the combined impact of two integration projects – Europe and Germany – has led to a deep and permanent alteration in the component parts and internal workings of the German political economy, resulting in a system that is now less clearly defined, less coherent, and less inclusive in terms of its capacity to generate prosperity for all at home and for its neighbours in Europe. Modell Deutschland, to the extent that it now exists, still works, but it is much less apt to be described as appropriate for emulation or export in its entirety. Individual components of the model (e.g. vocational training) remain attractive to the outside world, however.

Some preliminaries: Germany as a model, Germany as a case

The term 'model' has two distinct yet interrelated meanings. The first was outlined above – namely, that empirically there are organised ways of doing things that are recognised and occasionally even exalted by policy experts for the manner in which they function and the outputs they generate. Once established, models become part of the currency of discourse, as advocates and detractors hold them up as reference points in the discussion of options for action. Models can be treated holistically, as integrated systems, or they can be conceived of as packages of component parts, capable of being unpacked. Models can and often do travel, as actors look abroad for examples of 'best practice' that can be imported into the home context. Models can also play a powerful role in internal debates, as a template or reference point that sets limits on what is possible and what is not. All of this, as we will see, is relevant to the discussion of Modell Deutschland.

The term 'model' also carries a separate yet related meaning, one originating in more abstract, academic endeavours. One way to think about models in this vein is to contemplate the question 'What is this a case of?' (Ragin 1992). Models, or cases, play an important role in the accumulation of knowledge within academic disciplines; they are the mainstay of inquiry in political science, history, anthropology, and sociology. Modell Deutschland is one of several examples of pivotal cases in scholarly inquiry drawn from the German experience. For both historians and political scientists, Weimar Germany is an illuminating case of democratic breakdown, just as Nazi Germany is a case of fascism or totalitarianism. Students of political culture look to the postwar Federal Republic for insights into political socialisation or development and the politics of memory, and political economists have derived fascinating insights into the consequences of late industrialisation from the Imperial German case (Gerschenkron 1965).

The elements of the postwar German model

Just as it is tempting but wrong to think that the version of parliamentary democracy established after 1945 in Germany was derived from the democratic experiences of one or more of the occupying powers, it is misguided to look to the United States, the United Kingdom, or France for the inspiration behind the postwar model of the German political economy. Of course, the postwar German economy was capitalist to the core, populated by actors – organised labour, business, consumers, agricultural producers, and state institutions – comparable to those in neighbouring countries of Western Europe, and ultimately it pursued the same output objectives. Its composition, as well as the underlying principles on which it operated, however, was distinctive, and as such deserving of the label 'essentially German'. In this section, the main components of Modell Deutschland are outlined, with special emphasis on how each related to and interacted with other elements in the model to produce a coherent and reasonably harmonious whole.

The survey will begin with the ideas or doctrines informing the model, and then move to the institutions and actors that gave it substance in the Bonn Republic.

Ideas: the social market economy

The postwar German model of political economy rested on a consensus across the left–right and labour–capital divides about the relationship between state and market (see Chapter 22). The 'social market economy' (SME), as the name suggests, is based on a fusion of principles. At the core is a bedrock commitment to the market. The primary responsibility of the state is to support and facilitate the self-regulating economic order, first and foremost through the creation of transparent and comprehensive frameworks of rules and regulations (Müller-Armack 1948). The SME doctrine also carries strong implications for the state's macroeconomic and foreign economic policy. German governments on both the left and the right eschewed an open commitment to demand management (Keynesian) policies, opting instead to prioritise price stability, a policy objective that was formally the preserve of an independent central bank, the Bundesbank. Foreign economic policy objectives revolved around a stable and preferably undervalued currency and free trade.

Alongside the obligations to the market, however, SME doctrine prescribes a social role for the state in ameliorating the disruption and occasional destruction that markets generate. This translates into support for comprehensive social welfare programmes as well as the notion that, frequently, the state will have to intervene with industrial, regional, and labour market policies to address the negative externalities of market forces. When the German state intervened to address sectorial crises in coal and steel production, or sought to address rural underdevelopment, it did so with an eye to facilitating adjustment to market forces, not fighting or reversing them.

The SME also shaped the German state's objectives regarding European integration. Germany threw its weight behind the European project for reasons other than economic interest, to be sure, but once it became a founding member of the European Economic Community it sought to create a supportive policy and regulatory environment. The Federal Republic is often described as having pursued altruistic goals at the European level – sublimating concrete interests to the broader objective of peace and security in Europe. There is nothing inherently flawed in this portrayal; it is only part of the story, however. German governments of both left and right sought to erect institutional and normative frameworks at the European level that would nurture Germany's successful domestic economic formula. Europe's common market and free trade orientation vis-à-vis the rest of the world were essential to German domestic economic objectives. German policymakers consistently backed proposals for EC-wide harmonisation in the areas of economic and monetary cooperation, industrial policy, and regional assistance programmes, all to preserve a level field of competition for German firms (*Ordnungspolitik*) and to reduce the negative consequences of other countries' policy decisions, such as imported inflation. The 'social' dimension of the social market economy found expression and support in European environmental policy, the Common Agricultural Policy (CAP), competition and regional policies, and social policy.

The broadly shared doctrine of the social market economy places the German state in a distinctive category. Because the market is respected, but neither worshipped nor slavishly obeyed, the German state is a far cry from the night watchman state championed by neoclassical economists and many politicians on the right; at the same time, it falls well short of the interventionism and omnipresence of its counterparts in Japan and France. The doctrine of the social market economy in no way dictated political processes or outcomes in postwar Germany, and these principles relating state and market did not rule out hard-fought, even divisive conflicts between left and right over economic and social policies. Rather, debates unfolded within parameters set broadly by the doctrine. Left and right might have disagreed vehemently over the limits of state intervention or the construction of the welfare state, but at no time during the postwar period were core institutional and ideational features of the West German political economy at stake.

Institutions: the coordinated market economy

The German model that quickly emerged and consolidated in the postwar period has been described as a 'coordinated market economy', a term that points to a set of distinctive and interlocking institutional characteristics. The West German private sector featured an 'articulated industrial system' (Shonfield 1965: 247) based on close relationships among firms and between firms and universal banks; these institutional links led managers to adopt long-term planning and investment horizons, and they conferred on the private sector the capacity to undertake sectorial adjustment in the context of industrial crisis. Industrial relations in the Bonn Republic were also characterised by concertation and coordination, in which powerful, well-organised representatives of labour and capital engaged each other in an institutionalised process of negotiated adjustment that unfolded primarily at the sectorial and plant level, lending the German system a decentralised cast.

The industry-finance nexus

In spite of the actions undertaken by the Allied powers to break up cartels and unbundle large firms, particularly those involved in the war effort, the postwar German economy retained many of the distinctive institutional features bequeathed to it by late industrialisation. Large-scale, export-oriented manufacturing concerns dominated the traditional industrial sectors; these firms maintained close ties to small and medium-sized suppliers, often regionally concentrated, that competed with one another but also engaged in important cooperative initiatives involving research and development as well as vocational training.

Germany's finance/banking sector was also large in scale, dominated by investment banks with close ties to industry. Three 'universal banks' – the Deutsche Bank, the Dresdner Bank, and the Commerzbank – enjoyed a commanding position within the financial sector, setting the tone for the thousands of smaller banking institutions in Germany. These major banks owned equity shares in industrial enterprises that entitled them to representation on company boards. The resulting web of interlocking directorships introduced mechanisms for coordination and concertation that were simply not possible in other advanced industrial democracies. By the early 1980s, 'banks voted 70 percent of the shares of the largest 425 firms in Germany. 318 of the top 400 companies had two bank representatives on their supervisory boards' (Hall 1986: 235).

This tight industry-finance nexus carried significant implications for the broader workings of the political economy. In contrast to nations in which firms relied on the stock market or retained earnings to finance new investments, German enterprises could count on long-term financing proffered by banks, which in turn were permitted to shepherd these investments through representation on company boards. The result: 'patient capital', which allowed firms to focus on the medium- to long-term horizon, with salutary implications for management-labour relations, capital investment strategies, and sectorial adjustment without direct government intervention. Expanding profit margins and rising shareholder dividends, while not inconsequential for many German firms, simply did not loom as large in the calculations of company managers as in countries like the United States and the United Kingdom.

The labour-capital nexus

Modell Deutschland was based on organised capitalism. Three separate peak associations represented business interests in the Federal Republic of Germany: the Bundesverband der Deutschen Industrie (BDI), representing industry interests not directly tied to collective bargaining; the Bundesvereinigung der Deutschen Arbeitgeberverbände (BDA), representing employers' interests in collective bargaining; and the Deutscher Industrie- und Handelstag (DIHT)[2], representing the chambers of industry and commerce. At first glance, this method of organising capital might seem to guarantee duplication of effort and increase the likelihood of cross-pressuring and even outright mutual cancelling of interest, but in fact it enabled a broad range of business interests to exercise leverage across a wide range of issues and areas. The BDI concentrated on the general or common interests of business (irrespective of size, market orientation, etc.) as well as sectorial issues pertaining to trade, regulation, and the like; its membership was dominated by large and medium-sized firms, which, it must not be forgotten, were also ably represented by powerful and well-organised sectorial or industry-specific business associations. The BDA was free to focus exclusively on employer interests in the collective bargaining process. The regionally and locally specific interests of small and medium-sized firms found expression in the myriad local chambers of industry and commerce, which were represented at the national level by the umbrella association of the DIHT.

Labour contributed its part to Germany's organised capitalism. After 1945, the principle of autonomous organisations representing the interests of working men and women was resurrected in the new German democracy. In industry, workers were reorganised into 16 separate unions based on distinct industries or sectors of the economy (coal, chemicals, metalworkers, etc.). These sectorial unions in turn belonged to a national (or 'peak') labour federation, the Deutscher Gewerkschaftsbund (DGB). The principles of industrial unionisation, operating under a central federation, created a powerful social partner capable of entering into longstanding and stable agreements with employers. Although formally apolitical, the DGB frequently sided with the political left on a range of economic and social issues, providing critical support at election times at the local, state, and Federal levels. Separate unions were established to represent white-collar workers and civil servants. Although important in their own right, these organisations played less of a determining role in the functioning of the classic German model of political economy.

The organised power of labour is at the heart of three distinctive, even unique features of the German model. The first is a well-established principle of worker participation in the management of the firm. In any firm with more than five full-time employees, workers are entitled to elect a works council, which is entitled by law to negotiate a range of issues with owners, including hiring, overtime and part-time work, the introduction of new technology and production regimes, and – in the case that mass lay-offs are needed – agreement on social plans covering retraining, redeployment, and severance and early retirement packages. In companies employing 2,000+ employees, workers are entitled to 'co-determination' (*Mitbestimmung*), which entails formal representation on the management supervisory board (*Aufsichtsrat*), and the right to participate in all matters that come before this important body, including investment projects and strategies, mergers and acquisitions, and the appointment of the firm's management leadership. The employees who serve on works councils and supervisory boards are almost always members of their sectorial union. Union officials who are not employees of the firm are also permitted by law to serve on supervisory boards; for companies with between 2,000 and 20,000 employees, two of the 12 or 16 (depending on firm size) worker representatives may be union officials not affiliated with the firm, and for companies employing more than 20,000 workers, up to three may be union officials.

The second notable attribute of the German model that can be traced back to the organisational power of labour is the national system of collective bargaining. Although decentralised in appearance, with 16 separate industrial unions – to say nothing of their counterparts in the white-collar and civil service sectors – responsible for hammering out agreements with employers, in practice the system worked in a highly coordinated manner that resulted in a notable level of centralisation. Typically, IG Metall, the largest and most powerful of the industrial unions, took the lead in setting wage norms that were then observed by other unions under the DGB umbrella. The resulting two- to three-year contracts provided for both predictable and stable industrial relations, and typically sprang from the principle of wage restraint, which was critical to management's interest in export competitiveness and labour's interest in sustained full employment.

The third notable institutional feature of the labour-capital nexus in Germany is the vocational training system (Culpepper 2000). This thoroughly institutionalised and highly effective nationwide system integrates hands-on apprenticeships in enterprises with formal education/training at vocational schools in over 300 distinct fields. The system is based on longstanding partnerships between individual firms, sectorial business associations, the chambers of commerce, trade unions, and subnational (*Länder*) governments.

Modell Deutschland and semi-sovereignty

Many if not all of the components of the German model of political economy described so far have analogues or close parallels elsewhere in the advanced industrial world. Indeed, ambitious and illuminating attempts to classify political economies have typically grouped Germany with other countries, like Austria and Switzerland, that share many of its economic attributes. Hall and Soskice place the German model in a broad category of 'coordinated market economies' (Hall and Soskice 2001). What makes Modell Deutschland archetypical, even unique, is both the combined presence and interaction of these attributes within the industry-finance and labour-capital nexuses and their embedding in a broader, distinctive political system. Peter Katzenstein coined the term 'semisovereign' to describe a set of complex but constructive political arrangements that worked in harmony with the organised capitalism of the private sector (Katzenstein 1987). In employing this term, Katzenstein adapted a self-evident characteristic of the German state – its lack of complete sovereignty in the international system – and applied it to the internal attributes of the state.

The postwar German polity was semi-sovereign in a variety of ways. In terms of the vertical distribution of authority, the framers of the constitution, or 'Basic Law', opted for a strong form of administrative federalism, in which the 11 Federal states (*Länder*) not only were allocated significant areas of policy autonomy (e.g. education and regional economic development) but were also tasked with implementing laws decided at the national level. The horizontal distribution of authority at the national level was similarly unconcentrated, both by design and in practice. An independent constitutional court (Bundesverfassungsgericht), a strong upper chamber of the legislature (Bundesrat), the recurrence of coalition government: all these elements combined to ensure that majoritarian impulses, common in other parliamentary democracies like the United Kingdom, were sublimated in favour of concertation and cooperation among actors and institutions. In the realm of economic governance, the hallmark characteristic of the German semi-sovereign state was the central bank, the Bundesbank, which was constitutionally shielded from political control and tasked with the responsibility of protecting the value of the currency (Goodman 1992: 58–102). Central bank independence thus translated into a freedom to focus narrowly and exclusively on price stability and holding inflationary impulses in check.

The resulting separation of monetary policy instruments (Bundesbank) from fiscal policy instruments (Ministry of Finance/Chancellery) cemented the separation of powers. Overall, the end result of semi-sovereignty was a decentralised yet capable state presiding over a centralised society (Katzenstein 1987: 15).

Modell Deutschland and performance

During the four decades of the Bonn Republic, Modell Deutschland was synonymous with success. Its credentials were established early on, as Germany's 'economic miracle' (*Wirtschaftswunder*) unfolded over the course of the 1950s. The combination of a decentralised state and highly organised capitalism produced enviable results across a range of indicators:

- *Exports*: Up until 1989, Germany led its European partners year in and year out in the US dollar value of exports in goods. The country ran a close second to the United States, world leader during this period, and consistently outperformed Japan, another advanced industrial democracy known for its export prowess.[3]
- *Growth, inflation, and employment*: During this period, Germany emerged as Europe's dominant economy. After a decade of explosive expansion in the 1950s, as industry rebuilt and retooled, the German economy settled into a period of stable, respectable growth. Even more impressive, solid growth was accompanied by the lowest inflation rates in Europe (indeed, in the advanced industrialised world) and by one of the lowest unemployment rates. These impressive achievements can be traced back directly to the combination of Bundesbank autonomy and the framework of business-labour cooperation, especially where wage bargaining is concerned.
- *Strikes*: Unlike France, the United Kingdom, Italy, and Greece – to name just a few neighbouring countries – Germany enjoyed a reputation for relative labour peace during the years of the Bonn Republic. Strikes, official or wildcat, were not an ever-present feature of the landscape. Clearly, this had much to do with the growth and employment performance of the national economy: the pie was growing, so there was less to fight about. The role of institutionalised labour inclusion, via the works councils and co-determination, cannot be overlooked, however (Gourevitch *et al.* 1984). And labour conflict was not entirely absent from the scene. During the 1980s, for example, the unions called for nationwide work stoppages in disputes with employers over the introduction of the 35-hour working week.
- *Sectorial adjustment*: Finally, the German model of political economy equipped actors to cope with downturns and crises, which surfaced regularly in Germany as in other advanced industrial democracies during the postwar period. The coalmining industry began to feel the effects of international competition as early as the 1960s, with massive lay-offs and resulting negative ripple effects for the surrounding regional economies very much on the cards. Similar stories can be told for the steel and shipbuilding industries in the 1970s and 1980s. In each instance, although the labour-managements conflicts were bitter, and often spilled over into inter-party conflict between the Social Democratic Party, which invariably had strong political ties to the affected unions and regions, and the Christian Democratic and Free Democratic parties, which tended to side with employer interests, the outcomes were textbook examples of the social market economy in action – industry contraction and restructuring in a manner consistent with the inexorable pressures of (global) market competition, but with compensation and adjustment assistance for workers pushed out through early retirement and lay-offs.

The Berlin Republic: beginning of the end of Modell Deutschland?

In the Berlin Republic, Modell Deutschland no longer exists, at least not in its Bonn incarnation. The changes to its internal constitution are both complex and varied. Some have resulted from conscious decisions taken by elected politicians, business interests, or unions. Others have come about through subtle, incremental adjustments to changing contexts, both domestic and external. Taken together, these changes have altered the model's constituent parts and interconnectedness in each of the three areas surveyed above: the state, the industry-finance nexus, and the labour-capital nexus.

The sources of these changes date back to before the collapse of the GDR and unification in 1989–90. There are in fact two distinct yet overlapping and reinforcing sources of change in the German model: those external to the national model, originating in globalisation and European integration; and those internal to the model, emanating from the process of German unification. Together, they have produced far-reaching changes in the German model of political economy.

Globalisation and European integration

Globalisation and European integration are two sides of the same coin. The growth of global economic and financial interdependence, and the attendant sharpening of competition and the pressures this places on firms and national economies to adapt, has been driven by the economic integration of Europe and at the same time has fuelled attempts to deepen cooperation in Europe. The interactive, even synergistic relationship between integration and globalisation has had a profound impact on the German model of political economy. Although the effects have become more visible since 1990, this external source of change has been a fact of life in Germany since the later period of the Bonn Republic.

Growing awareness and concern in Germany about the changing global economic environment manifested itself as early as the mid-1980s and shaped debates about domestic reform as well as the country's approach to Europe. This is especially visible in the debate about Germany as a viable location for production (*Standort Deutschland*). Conservative political parties and their supporters in the business community questioned whether the country, which had always qualified as a high-cost production location, could carry on with old habits under radically changed circumstances. *Standort Deutschland* was becoming an inhospitable place in Europe and, indeed, the global economy: it had the highest wages, the shortest work week, the most vacation days, the highest degree of job protection, the most burdensome business taxation system, the most uncompromising environmental regulations, and so on.

Germany's full-blooded support for the Single European Act in 1987 sprang from a desire to build on and promote the already impressive competitiveness of German export industry. The completion of the internal market, combined with a commitment to liberalise the financial services and banking sector, set in motion a gradual transformation of the broader economic context in which the German model of political economy operated. The Treaty on European Union (Maastricht), signed in 1992 and implemented in 1993, further accelerated these impulses for change. German support for the single currency stemmed from geopolitical considerations rather than from rational economic interest, but the end effect was to initiate direct legal-institutional and indirect market changes to the traditional Modell Deutschland.

The greatest impact of globalisation and European integration on the traditional German model of political economy is to be found in the structure and responsibilities of the state in the realm of monetary fiscal policy; these changes can be linked directly to the Treaty on European

Union and the commitment contained therein to the single currency. The creation of the European Central Bank (ECB), and the parallel demotion of the Bundesbank, means that primary policy responsibility for monetary and currency matters now resides beyond the borders of the Federal Republic. The role carved out for the ECB by the EU treaty framework is closely modelled on the Bundesbank template, at the German government's insistence. The ECB's main focus is price stability, and it was intentionally shielded from the kind of direct political influence that was typical of central banking arrangements in many parts of Europe at the time, including France and Italy. And the historical record of ECB management of the eurozone since 2000 generally conforms to the intentions and hopes of the designers of the single currency; price stability and a preference for low rates of inflation (as opposed to growth or full employment) represent the first priorities of the institution.

Although a formal-legal change, the transfer of central bank authority from the national to the European level has not had a dramatic impact on the functioning of the German model – at least not yet. The potential is there, however. In the first place, the Bundesbank played an important role in setting expectations for firms (pricing and wage/benefit costs) and for trade unions (collective bargaining objectives) through its choice of monetary targets and interest rate decisions; experts attributed a vital role to it in terms of establishing a climate of restraint and longer-term planning horizons that had a discernible impact on labour-management relations nationwide. Although the ECB pursues a similar set of objectives to the Bundesbank, its reference points, attached as they are to the entire eurozone, are much broader and much more varied than the Bundesbank's, and so its decisions are further removed from the decision horizons of German capital and labour. To be sure, wage and benefit settlements have been characterised by restraint during the post-1990 period, but this is attributable to the uncertain and somewhat stagnant economic performance of the German economy, and not to ECB signalling. What might happen if and when expansionary times return is an open question.

In the second place, the ECB, despite its status of independence, has been drawn into political debates much more directly than the Bundesbank ever was during the heyday of the Bonn Republic. Especially since the onset of the international financial crisis in 2008, which soon metastasised into a sovereign debt crisis throughout the European periphery, the ECB has moved to the centre of a bitter struggle among EU members over its proper role and instrumentarium. Those who would elevate growth and employment objectives to first-order priorities of the European Union have advocated far-reaching changes to the ECB, hoping to move the institution more in the direction of proactive central banks like the US Federal Reserve. This initiative, which includes enabling the ECB to issue Eurobonds, has been vigorously opposed by the government, opposition parties, and economic interest groups in Germany.

Less definite, though no less important changes resulting from globalisation and European integration can be identified in the structure and orientation of the financial/banking sector. Although it would be a complete exaggeration to say that Germany's system of 'patient capital', anchored by powerful universal banks and supported by a dense network of 'house banks' closely tied to German small and medium-sized enterprises, has been dissolved, the fact is that financial market liberalisation, ushered in by the Single European Act, has left an imprint. Germany's big three universal banks have become much more internationally oriented, which has diminished somewhat their capacity to 'organise' capital through the interlocking directorships so prevalent during the days of the Bonn Republic. On the other side of the table, large firms have substantially diversified their sources of long-term finance, moving away from the nearly exclusive reliance on house banks. The picture at the lower end of the size scale exhibits much more continuity with the basic contours of the Bonn Republic template. Overall, though, the industry-finance nexus has both internationalised and become less oriented to the longer-term horizons that promoted the classic German patient capital (Deeg 2010; Jackson and Deeg 2012).

German unification

The path to German unification is by now a well-known tale. For many living in the east, it is a story of arrogance and hubris. For many in the west, it is a story of good intentions and disastrous miscalculations. More than 20 years after the fact, one could describe the project as a qualified success, but one that resulted in a very different country. Perhaps nowhere is this impact more apparent than in the institutions and operations of the political economy. And there is no small amount of irony in this outcome – the manner in which the two Germanies were unified economically was driven by absolute faith and confidence in the power of the Bonn Republic's Modell Deutschland, and yet the end result entailed significant departures from the original model.

The Kohl Government, rejecting calls from the opposition Social Democrats, academic economists, business associations, and even government agencies like the Bundesbank for a gradual, cautious approach to unification, opted for a policy of rapid institutional transfer, based on complete faith in the principles of the social market economy and the proven track record of the West German political, social, and economic model. This supreme confidence extended to the integration of the new parts of Germany into the broader European market and regulatory framework. Almost immediately after its implementation in 1990, however, Bonn's policy of institutional transfer generated massive social and economic problems for the new Länder and for unified Germany. As Eastern German export markets in eastern Europe and the Soviet Union collapsed, the region's industrial base imploded, generating mass unemployment and necessitating massive transfers, through the social welfare system and through intergovernmental channels, to prop up the faltering new states of a unified Germany. The privatisation of East German industry, which had been entrusted to the Treuhandanstalt, a new parapublic agency, sputtered, requiring the West German state to begin supporting nonviable enterprises in order to stave off a complete collapse in the east. It soon became clear that the mounting problems in the new Federal states would also require a more lenient approach in Brussels.

The process by which unification challenged and in key respects transformed the German model makes for an absorbing narrative, but one that would take us well beyond the confines of this chapter. The outcomes of this process are clear, even if some of them are not yet finalised. The most significant changes are to be found in the realm of ideas, in the state sector, and in the labour market.

The most obvious casualty of German unification is the doctrine of the social market economy. The Kohl Government, backed by the coalition parties and a bevy of respectable policy analysts and academic economists, justified the rapid and uncompromising transfer of western German institutions, practices, and norms to the new Federal states in terms of social market orthodoxy. Reversing the effects of 40 years of state socialism rested on the application of a tried and true system of ideas and institutions. The main thrust of government policy was to introduce the market, and to be prepared to cushion its negative effects through social policy and, where necessary, targeted and temporary state intervention. As the evidence soon began to mount that the treatment was not working, and in fact appeared to be making matters worse, support for these tenets of the social market economy began to waiver.

The undermining of faith in SME principles was an inherently political process. Eastern German interests, frustrated by the government's failure to deliver on the promise of adherence to social market orthodoxy, allied with sceptics in the west to question many of the established truths of the postwar political economy in West Germany, forcing the government into an improvisational mode. Motivated by differing agendas but united in their criticism of the traditional German model, they mounted a significant challenge to the consensus in Germany underpinning the domestic model of political economy.

The challenge to social market orthodoxy has not resulted in the demise of the doctrine. If one were to ask a government official or an academic economist about the philosophy that guides the operations of the German economy, he or she would reply, '*Soziale Marktwirtschaft!*' The empirical referents of that term in 2014, however, are substantively different from those that existed even 30 years ago.

What is meant by that? In a nutshell, German government officials were compelled to act in ways that stretched the implicit balance between 'market' and 'social' well beyond established parameters. Examples are legion. The Treuhandanstalt, rather than liquidate when no buyers were to be found, was forced time and again to prop up and sustain large, inefficient enterprises to preserve jobs and sustain faltering local and regional economies (Fischer, Hax, and Schneider 1995). German officials in Brussels increasingly sought exemptions and even outright changes in EU policies to cushion the effects on the eastern German region, even if this meant departing from long-established positions adopted during the Bonn Republic (Anderson 1999). Although government officials took great pains to square these interventionist impulses with social market orthodoxy, the fact is that by the end of the first decade of unification, the range of acceptable state roles and the balance between 'the market' and 'the social' embraced by the *soziale Marktwirtschaft* had expanded dramatically.

The labour market in the Berlin Republic also bears signs of profound change that represent significant departures from the postwar Modell Deutschland. Some of these changes have come about as the result of changes in government policy sparked by the *Standort* debate. Concerns about the government's expansive fiscal policies after unification risked undermining the broader parameters that made Germany such an attractive place to do business – that is, a sound budgetary policy, a strong currency, and a low inflation rate. Business interests in particular hoped to use unification as an occasion to force policymakers to undertake a major reappraisal of state regulatory and taxation policy, as well as social policy. The result: a series of government reforms of the labour market – specifically, the Schröder Government's Agenda 2010 initiative, at the centre of which were the Hartz I–IV reform proposals. These reforms bundled social insurance and unemployment benefits and tied their receipt more directly to the search for and the willingness to accept work, and sought to create a set of new employment programmes oriented towards the promotion of competition and incentivising entrepreneurship (Czada 2005: 175–8). The objective was to create a more flexible and responsive labour market, one theoretically more open to part-time and low-wage earners hovering at or near the poverty/ unemployment line. The reforms were hugely controversial within organised labour and left-wing political circles; many viewed the Schroeder Government's initiative as a betrayal not only of social democratic principles, but of the common understanding of social market economy principles. The Hartz reforms in particular have been directly tied to growing inequality in Germany, and feed the perception of a growing 'dualism' in the new German economy.

Industrial relations sit at the core of the labour-capital nexus. Like other elements of the German model, there is much here that is recognisable in the Berlin Republic. Vocational training is structured and operates much as it did during the days of the Bonn Republic. Works councils and co-determination remain anchored in German law and function much as they did during the years of the Bonn Republic, although it is fair to say that during difficult times, when unemployment was high and corporate threats of job exports and plant closures rang true, these mainstay institutions of worker inclusion came in for increasing criticism within trade union and leftist circles for playing a more accommodationist role within firms, even heralding the demise of organised capitalism (Beyer and Höpner 2003). Although it would be an overstatement to say that these institutions now represent a locus of company unionism, the fact is that during the course of the 1990s firm-level 'pacts' and other enterprise-level agreements, in which worker representatives agreed to worker concessions on wages and other matters in exchange for job guarantees, became quite common. Although it is unlikely that unification caused these changes, the incorporation of the former German Democratic Republic certainly contributed to them, both by worsening the general economic performance of the overall German economy and by adding employer and especially worker mentalities, fostered by decades of top-down state socialism, that encouraged a more enterprise-centred approach to labour-management relations.

The framework of collective bargaining has also survived into the Berlin Republic, but its reach is now less extensive. Some of this has to do with a weakening of labour – whereas unionisation rates during the heyday of Modell Deutschland hovered between 30 and 35 per cent, today's German labour force is only 20 per cent unionised. On the other side of the table, employer associations now encompass fewer members, as firms, especially in eastern Germany but also in the west, have left the associations to forge collective bargaining agreements with labour on their own. So by definition the coverage of collective bargaining agreements has diminished as the organisational reach of both capital and labour has shrunk.

The decline in coverage by the traditional institutions of Modell Deutschland associated with the capital-labour nexus has resulted from multiple and reinforcing pressures: increasingly global competition, the completion and expansion of the European market, the lingering recessionary environment, and the social and economic consequences of unification. The latter's fingerprints are especially prominent; whereas coverage of both works councils and collective bargaining agreements in the original Federal states of Germany declined from 83 per cent in 1995 to approximately 60 per cent in 2011, over the same period coverage in eastern Germany dropped to 50 per cent (Silvia 2013). This has led some experts to describe the German economy in terms of dualism, characterised by a still sizeable but inexorably shrinking sector in which conditions prevailing during the Bonn Republic still hold, and a growing sector in which weak or unorganised labour contends with firms on terms reminiscent of liberal market economies (Deeg 2010).

Conclusion

If the question is simply, 'Does a distinctively German model of political economy still exist?', then the answer is 'yes'. Down to the present day, the Federal Republic of Germany has retained a distinctive mix of institutions, actors, and processes that exist and operate on the basis of a distinctive set of norms, values, and principles. And yet, this is not the Modell Deutschland of old. The theory and reality of the social market economy have diverged under the strains of unification. The social partners that animated the model – labour and capital – have lost members, and consequently enjoy a more limited reach and possess fewer means to drive the system, either on their own or by acting together. The state has found itself called upon to do more with less, and has found many of its responsibilities and associated authority unbundled and packed off to Brussels. To the extent that the traditional Modell Deutschland exists, it is a shrunken version of itself, existing alongside a growing and separate political economy that bears the imprint of a long process of deregulation and liberalisation. Dualism seems to be a lasting legacy of the post-1989 transition. One must be cautious in connecting these changes in the make-up and constitution of the Berlin Republic's model of political economy with performance. No advanced industrial economy is doing better than its Cold War incarnation. That said, in terms of the standard measures of economic performance, which include GDP growth rates, unemployment, and inflation, the German economy today is outperforming many if not all of its fellow EU members, to say nothing of the broader class of OECD members. Relative to others, Germany is doing well.

However, all this has come at a price. Internally, respectable growth and better-than-average unemployment and inflation have come at the price of growing inequality, which carries at least the potential for social conflict. Externally, relative German economic success, which is symbolised most visibly in the growing export surplus that Germany posts, has come at the price of the support and respect of Germany's EU partners. Here there is not only the potential for conflict – there is conflict. And the risk is that the success of the German model, which during the Bonn Republic years was viewed both inside and outside Germany as compatible with, and in some sense central to, European success, could come to be seen as contrary to the EU's economic prospects. That would spell disaster for Germany and for Europe.

Notes

1   'World from Berlin: Germany No Longer a Role Model for Europe', *Spiegel Online*, 28 November 2013. Available online at www.spiegel.de/international/germany/0,1518,936162,00.html (accessed 15 December 2013); N.D. Schwartz, 'Where Factory Apprenticeship is Latest Model from Germany', *New York Times*, 30 November 2013. Available online at www.nytimes.com/2013/12/01/business/where-factory-apprenticeship-is-latest-model-from-germany.html (accessed 15 December 2013).
2   In 2001 the DIHT was renamed the Deutscher Industrie- und Handelskammertag (DIHK).
3   Source: OECD.StatExtracts. Available online at http://stats.oecd.org/index.aspx?datasetcode=MEI_TRD# (accessed 15 December 2013).

Bibliography

Allen, C. (2010) 'Ideas, Institutions, and Organised Capitalism: The German Model of Political Economy Twenty Years after Unification', in J. Anderson and E. Langenbacher (eds) *From the Bonn to the Berlin Republic*, New York: Berghahn Books.
Anderson, J. (1999) *German Unification and the Union of Europe*, New York: Cambridge University Press.
Anderson, J. and Langenbacher, E. (eds) (2010) *From the Bonn to the Berlin Republic: Germany at the Twentieth Anniversary of Unification*, New York: Berghahn Books.
Beyer, J. and Höpner, M. (2003) 'The Disintegration of Organised Capitalism: German Corporate Governance in the 1990s', *West European Politics*, 26(4): 179–98.
Culpepper, P. (2000) *The German Skills Machine*, New York: Berghahn Books.
Czada, R. (2005) 'Social Policy: Crisis and Transformation', in S. Green and W. Paterson (eds) *Governance in Contemporary Germany: The Semisovereign State Revisited*, New York: Cambridge University Press, 165–89.
Deeg, R. (2010) 'Institutional Change in Financial Systems', in G. Morgan, J. Campbell, C. Crouch, O.K. Pedersen, and R. Whitley (eds) *Oxford Handbook of Comparative Institutional Analysis*, Oxford: Oxford University Press.
Fischer, W., Hax, H., and Schneider, K.-H. (eds) (1995) *Treuhandanstalt: The Impossible Challenge*, Hoboken, NJ: Wiley.
Gerschenkron, A. (1965) *Economic Backwardness in Historical Perspective*, New York and London: Praeger Press.
Goodman, J. (1992) *Monetary Sovereignty: The Politics of Central Banking in Western Europe*, Ithaca: Cornell University Press.
Gourevitch, P., Martin, A., Ross, G., Allen, C., Bornstein, S., and Markovits, A. (1984) *Unions and Economic Crisis: Britain, West Germany, and Sweden*, New York: Allen & Unwin.
Green, S. and Paterson, W. (eds) (2005) *Governance in Contemporary Germany: The Semisovereign State Revisited*, New York: Cambridge University Press.
Hall, P. (1986) *Governing the Economy*, New York: Oxford University Press.
Hall, P. and Soskice, D. (eds) (2001) *Varieties of Capitalism*, New York: Oxford University Press.

Jackson, G. and Deeg, R. (2012) 'The Long-Term Trajectories of Institutional Change in European Capitalism', *Journal of European Public Policy*, 19(8): 1109–25.

Katzenstein, P. (1987) *Policy and Politics in West Germany: The Growth of a Semisovereign State*, Philadelphia: Temple University Press.

Müller-Armack, A. (1948) *Wirtschaftslenkung und Marktwirtschaft*, Hamburg: Verlag für Wirtschaft und Sozialpolitik.

Ragin, C. (1992) *What is a Case: Exploring the Foundations of Social Inquiry*, New York: Cambridge University Press.

Shonfield, A. (1965) *Modern Capitalism*, New York and London: Oxford University Press.

Silvia, S. (2013) *Holding the Shop Together: German Industrial Relations in the Postwar Era*, Cornell University Press.

Part II

The Berlin Republic

6

The political and constitutional order

Eric Langenbacher

Few countries have had such starkly different political experiences before and after a significant historical juncture. Before 1949, high levels of instability and dysfunction characterised modern Germany. Depending on how one counts, there have been between five and seven regimes on German soil over the century and a half since unification in 1870–71: the monarchical, decentralised, yet Prussian-dominated German Empire from 1871 to 1919; a military dictatorship during World War I; the fissiparous, almost anarchic Weimar Republic from 1919 to 1933; the totalitarian Third Reich from 1933 to 1945; foreign military occupation from 1945 to 1949 (with continued Allied supervision until 1990); and the period of division from 1949 to 1990 when there was a communist dictatorship in East Germany (the German Democratic Republic or GDR)[1] and a liberal democracy in West Germany (the Federal Republic of Germany or FRG). Moreover, most commentators now differentiate between the 'old' or 'Bonn' Federal Republic, named after the city on the Rhine that was the (provisional) capital after 1949, and the 'Berlin' Republic, so-called since the main political and administrative institutions moved back to Berlin in 1999.[2]

Until well into the postwar era, seemingly irresolvable tensions existed with respect to the boundaries of 'Germany', notions of belonging and citizenship, the nature of government and the economy, and the role of religion. Deep divisions and disputes persisted among ideologies, religions, majorities and minorities, regions, and classes – all in the context of rapid economic growth, industrialisation, and cultural change, as well as rising tensions with other European and colonial powers. The world spoke fearfully of 'the German question', which revolved fundamentally around the country's apparent inability to create sustainable borders, political institutions, and collective identities that could prevent and resolve conflict domestically and internationally (Ritter 1965; Dahrendorf 1967; Banchoff 1999).

The post-1949 Federal Republic of Germany, by contrast, has been quite successful. Early on it became a stable, high quality democracy with excellent policy outcomes (Verba 1965; Conradt 1980; Baker *et al.* 1981; Bernhard 2001). The country has ranked at or near the top on almost all governance and quality of life indicators for decades – per capita income, infrastructure, control of corruption, regulatory quality, life expectancy, absence of violence, and so on (Langenbacher 2010).[3] It has proved sufficiently adept at resolving conflict and at integrating a variety of disparate groups into society and the polity – Protestants and Catholics, rich and poor, indigenous and refugees (expellees), Easterners and Westerners, as well as those with a migration background, albeit still only partially and problematically (see Chapter 12). The political system has facilitated outstanding economic performance over the long haul (with the exception of the 1995–2005 decade), a high degree of social justice, international reconciliation, and peace (Gardner Feldman 2012), regional integration (especially the European Union and currency union), and, more recently, a progressive environmental policy. The citizenry has internalised democratic values and behaviours (Dalton 2006). With almost 65 years behind it, the Federal Republic has already exceeded the life of the Empire by just under 20 years and is less than a decade away from outlasting the entire 1871–1945 period. What, then, are the political and institutional components behind postwar Germany's transformation?

Constitutional foundations

The caesura of 1945 has often been called *Stunde Null* (zero hour), when Germans started afresh. Despite the resilience of this belief, there were marked continuities with the past – evident, for example, in the influence of earlier constitutions (1849, 1871, 1919) on the post-1949 political order (Hucko 1987). But the founders of the Federal Republic made a conscious effort to learn from past mistakes and to create structures that would preclude a repetition of the disastrous early 20th century (Moses 2007). Bonn would not be Weimar (Allemann 1956). There would be no more easily manipulated emergency powers, overly permissive proportional representation, unstable governments, or an executive divided into a president and chancellor. Moreover, it was expected that good institutions and solid economic and policy performance would eventually transform previously dysfunctional values – especially amongst the younger generations socialised under the new circumstances – into diffuse support for the liberal democratic order (Sa'adah 1998).

The western zones of occupation, which eventually became the Federal Republic, were also subject to unique conditions insofar as foreign occupation powers, particularly the US (Britain and France to a lesser extent) partially influenced the institutional structures (Jacoby 2000; Bernhard 2005). It has been argued, for example, that American authorities wanted a decentralised system, similar to that of the USA. Yet Germans always had such institutions until the Third Reich and this was the preference of most of the founders – democratically elected politicians from the already reconstructed Federal states, called *Länder* (Peterson 1978). Influential individuals like Konrad Adenauer, Theodor Heuss, and Carlo Schmid who negotiated the Basic Law or *Grundgesetz* at the Parliamentary Council (Parlamentarischer Rat) in 1948 were distinguished politicians or academics during the Weimar Republic. Whatever the specific influence of the occupation powers on these foundational decisions was, the western Allies were important guarantors of acceptable institutional outcomes and, crucially, ensured a welcoming international environment in which West Germany could thrive.

The constitutional foundation of the Federal Republic is the Basic Law, originally promulgated in 1949, but amended frequently since.[4] This was not a *Verfassung* (constitution) per se because it was intended only as a provisional document for the part of postwar Germany that became the Federal Republic. It was to be valid only until formal reunification was achieved, at which point the entire German nation would formulate an appropriate constitution (Art. 146).[5] Importantly, Article 23 allowed for the accession of other Länder and was used by the Saarland in 1957 and, much later, the five Länder of East Germany in 1990 to join the Federal Republic.[6] At the time of reunification, a debate swirled over the possibility of writing a new constitution. But, despite protestations mainly from the Left and from East Germans, a political decision was made to stick with the time-tested Basic Law.

The founders attempted to address the past in five main ways. First, the Basic Law explicitly enshrines civil, political, and human rights, as well the fundamental liberal democratic character of the political system. Articles 1–19 outline these rights (freedom of religion, assembly, property rights, and so on) and Article 20 asserts the federal,[7] social, and republican form of government. These and other core provisions are non-amendable – enshrined in a so-called eternity clause (Art. 79, §3). For example, Article 1 (§1) states that 'The dignity of man is inviolable. To respect and protect it is the duty of all state authority'; and then 'The German people therefore acknowledge inviolable and inalienable human rights as the basis of every community, of peace and of justice in the world' (§2). Other measures include the abolition of capital punishment (Art. 102), the prohibition of extraordinary courts, which had been abused by the Nazis, and a generous right to political asylum (Art. 16a) – although this was amended in 1992.[8] Probably reflective of the strength of conservative and particularly Catholic founders, there are explicit provisions protecting families, children, and marriage (Art. 6). Such conservative provisions became contentious in subsequent decades, especially regarding abortion rights.

Second, the constitutional order is permeated by an ethos deemed *wehrhafte* or *streitbare Demokratie*, best translated as defensive or militant democracy, which led to the establishment of procedures allowing the system to defend itself from enemies. A series of state and Federal offices (*Verfassungsschutz*) monitor potential threats, and mechanisms are in place to ban social groups and political parties for unconstitutional (*verfassungswidrig*) behaviour (Art. 9 and Art. 21, §2). The Constitutional Court, upon the government's request, has banned two parties – the neo-Nazi Socialist Reich Party in 1952 and the Communist Party in 1956.[9] The civil rights of individuals deemed hostile to the constitution can be restricted, and it is possible to bar such individuals from employment in the civil service. Moreover, each citizen has the right as a last resort to resist others trying to destroy the constitutional order. All of these provisions were originally (and are still) directed at the threat of neo-Nazism, but there have also been controversies over the years regarding left-wing radicals, East German former communists, and Islamist terrorists. Although not technically constitutional, mention should also be made of bans on Nazi symbols like the swastika and behaviours like the 'Hitler salute' (Strafgesetzbuch 96a), restrictions on access to materials such as Hitler's book, *Mein Kampf*, and the criminalisation of Holocaust denial.

Third, although not as explicit as in the US constitution, a division of power with checks and balances was created. Competences are divided between the national (the *Bund* or federation) and regional (the *Land* or Federal state) levels of government. The centre makes overarching decisions, but the vast majority of implementation takes place at the regional or local levels with a degree of discretion. For example, of the approximately 4.6 million people working for governments in 2012, only about 11 per cent were employed federally (with a further 8 per cent for the social security system) versus 51 per cent at the regional and 30 per cent at the local level.[10] Two parliamentary chambers are involved in the legislative process, with the Bundesrat safeguarding and defending the interests of the Länder (see below for details). The country is also a committed *Rechtsstaat* (state based on the rule of law) encompassing an independent judicial system (Art. 97) with a powerful and activist Constitutional Court (*Bundesverfassungsgericht*) located in Karlsruhe that provides additional oversight, balancing, and adjudication of disputes among institutions and levels of government (*Organstreit*) (Kommers and Miller 2012).

Looking to the international realm, Article 24 states that the Federal government may 'transfer sovereign powers to international institutions' and Article 25 asserts that 'general rules of international law shall be an integral part of Federal law'. Such provisions facilitated the creation and strengthening of the European Union and the transfer of many sovereign powers to the supranational level. As this process has accelerated in the decades since reunification, much controversy has arisen and has been refereed by the Constitutional Court. Moreover, Article 26 (§1) declares aggressive war unconstitutional: 'Acts tending to and undertaken with intent to disturb the peaceful relations between nations, especially to prepare for a war of aggression, shall be unconstitutional. They shall be made a criminal offence'. An army is allowed for 'defensive purposes' but can be deployed only 'to the extent expressly permitted by the Basic Law' (Art. 87a). This rather ambiguous formulation was long understood to mean that deployments were restricted to the NATO area (fulfilling treaty obligations); but the formulation was contentiously reinterpreted after reunification to allow for participation in combat operations outside of the countries belonging to the NATO alliance, for example against Serbia in 1999 (Kommers and Miller 2012: 201–5; see also Chapters 25 and 26). The Federal Republic also renounced the development, possession, and use of chemical, nuclear, and biological weapons as part of the process of joining NATO in 1955,[11] but not the production or international sale of weapon components.

Finally, unlike many other constitutions, Article 21 (§1) explicitly emphasises the key role and internal structures of political parties: 'Political parties shall participate in the formation of the political will of the people. They may be freely established. Their internal organisation must conform to democratic principles. They must publicly account for their assets and for the sources and use of their funds'. A generous system of public financing supports the liberal democratic system, including funds for parties, the influential party-affiliated foundations like the Christian Democrats' (CDU) Konrad-Adenauer-Stiftung and the Social Democrats' (SPD) Friedrich-Ebert-Stiftung, political education (Bundeszentrale für politische Bildung), and election campaigns. In 2012, for example, approximately €150 million was allotted just to the parties.[12] Although such largesse has been justified as essential to the greater democratic good and to minimise special interests' 'capture' of parties, there have nonetheless been numerous campaign donation and finance scandals over the years.[13]

Political institutions

The Federal Republic of Germany is a parliamentary democracy presided over by an indirectly elected president as head of state. This individual is the formal representative, symbolic leader, or conscience of the country, without any real political influence. Actual power lies with the government and bicameral legislature.[14] The more powerful lower house is the Bundestag (Federal Diet), which consists of at least 598 members. The government – led by the chancellor (akin to a prime minister) and currently consisting of 16 cabinet portfolios – is formed from and must maintain the support or confidence of a party or parties that constitute a majority of Bundestag deputies. Half of the members are elected through single member plurality from small, territorially compact electoral districts (Wahlkreise). The other half are elected from closed regional party lists (Landeslisten) based on national vote totals using the Sainte-Laguë/Schepers method of proportional representation (PR). This system, innovative at the time of its inception, is alternately called a 'mixed' electoral system, personalised proportional representation, 'districts plus', or mixed member proportional.[15]

Eligible voters are determined according to the so-called aktives Wahlrecht – currently all citizens over the age of 18 (reduced from 21 in 1970).[16] Two votes are simultaneously recorded on election day (always a Sunday); the first vote (Erststimme) is for a territorial representative, whereas the second vote (Zweitstimme) is for a party, specifically, a party's regional list. The second vote is the one that ultimately determines parties' strength because national vote totals are tallied and the number of representatives (mandates) for each party is allocated in each of the Länder based on this total. Each Land gets a number of constituencies (*Direktmandate*) in proportion to its population, ranging from two in Bremen to 64 in North Rhine-Westphalia, and then an equal number of PR mandates. Seats already won based on the first vote are deducted from the theoretical number of total mandates a party would win based on a perfectly proportional allocation.

Several caveats exist. First, there is a national electoral threshold of 5 per cent – only parties that surmount this figure are eligible for the seat allocation process at the Land level. The threshold has been justified as a means to combat small, extremist parties and to facilitate the formation of larger, cross-cleavage, catch-all parties. Second, the threshold does not apply if at least three territorial constituencies are won through the first vote. If this pertains, the party is eligible for a corresponding proportion of seats based on the second vote total. This happened to the former communist PDS in 1994 when it won four direct mandates and thus received about 4.4 per cent of the overall seats based on its national vote share. Third, parties keep any direct mandates won even if the electoral threshold/three constituency minimum is not reached. The PDS received two such seats in 2002. Finally, sometimes parties win more territorial constituencies in a Land than they are entitled to, based on their second vote share. These are called over-hanging mandates (*Überhangmandate*). If this occurs, the party keeps the 'extra' seats and the size of the Bundestag is increased accordingly beyond the minimum of 598.[17] In 2002 there were five, in 2005 there were 16, and in 2009 there were 24, so the Bundestag was increased to a total size of 603, 614, and 622 seats.

All of this changed with the 2013 Bundestag election. In 2008 the Constitutional Court ruled that the electoral law was unconstitutional because smaller parties were disadvantaged and due to a phenomenon called 'negative voting weight' (*negatives Stimmgewicht*), which means that it is theoretically possible that in situations where overhanging mandates have been awarded a citizen's second vote could actually reduce the overall number of seats the party receives. A new electoral law came into effect in 2013 that limits the number of overhanging mandates to 15 and creates 'compensatory mandates' (*Ausgleichsmandate*) so that parties' vote and seat shares better correspond. There were concerns that the new law would substantially increase the size of the parliament; some estimated that the Bundestag would exceed 700 members, which would make it one of the largest (and most expensive) parliaments in the world.[18] It was also predicted that the changes would benefit smaller parties because the catch-all CDU and SPD won virtually all overhanging mandates due to ticket splitting,[19] something which had increased markedly in recent elections (Conradt and Langenbacher 2013: 195–6). In the end, however, the impact of the new electoral law was moderate. There were five overhanging mandates and 28 compensatory mandates creating a Bundestag of 631 deputies, just nine more than the last. Interestingly, the new system did not particularly benefit the smaller parties, partly because voters and parties shifted their behaviour in light of the new incentive structure, reducing the amount of ticket splitting and boosting the larger parties' share of the all-important second vote.

Even though one of the main intentions behind the new electoral law was to increase proportionality, other factors still act as impediments – especially the 5 per cent threshold. For example, 6 per cent of the second votes went to parties beneath the threshold in 2009; in 2013 the figure was a whopping 15.7 per cent.[20] There are now calls to reduce or eliminate this electoral threshold. In any case, Bundestag election results have been rather proportional, with a least squares index score of 4.61 in 2002, 2.16 in 2005 and 3.40 in 2009, but rising to a rather high 7.83 in 2013 (Gallagher 2014: 14).[21]

A moderate multiparty system has long characterised the Federal Republic (see Chapter 7), with an effective number of parties based on seats of 2.80 in 2002, 3.44 in 2005, and 3.97 in 2009, but decreasing to 2.80 in 2013 (Gallagher 2014: 42). After the first few parliamentary elections (in 1949, 1953, and 1957),[22] only three parties – the conservative Christian Democratic Union/Christian Social Union (CDU/CSU),[23] centre-left Social Democratic Party (SPD), and classically liberal Free Democrats (FDP) – gained representation. In the 1980s the new left/environmental Greens entered the Bundestag, followed by the former communist Party of Democratic Socialism (PDS, which became The Left – *Die Linke* – in 2007) in the 1990s. The FDP lost its parliamentary representation in 2013 for the first time since the foundation of the Federal Republic, and its future is very much in question. The two 'elephants', the CDU and SPD, have dominated the postwar party system. Every chancellor has come from either the Christian Democrats (five of eight chancellors for 45 years as of 2014) or the Social Democrats (three of eight chancellors for 20 years). Nevertheless, their combined share of the vote has been declining since the 1990s, although this rebounded in 2013 to 67.2 per cent (from 56.8 per cent in 2009). The 5 per cent threshold does not constitute an insurmountable barrier to new entrants. In addition to the successful Greens and PDS/Left party, several right-radical parties have come very close to it in earlier decades. More recently, the Pirate Party and anti-euro Alternative for Germany (AfD) gained support, although the Pirates slumped in 2013, achieving only 2.2 per cent, and, despite a late surge, the AfD managed only 4.7 per cent. Coalition governments have been the norm. Only once (1957–61) was there a single-party majority government,[24] although Angela Merkel came very close in 2013 (Table 6.1 provides an overview of postwar German governments).

Mention should be made of the dynamics within the cabinet and between the cabinet and legislature. The Federal Republic has often been classified as a *Kanzlerdemokratie* with especial

Table 6.1 The governments of the Federal Republic of Germany

	Electoral period	Parties	Chancellor	Bundestag majority
1	1949–1953	CDU/CSU-FDP*	Konrad Adenauer (CDU)	208/402
2	1953–1957	CDU/CSU-FDP**		285/487
3	1957–1961	CDU/CSU*		287/497
4	1961–1963	CDU/CSU-FDP		309/499
	1963–1965	CDU/CSU-FDP	Ludwig Erhard (CDU)	
5	1965–1966	CDU/CSU-FDP		294/496
	1966–1969	CDU/CSU-SPD	Kurt Georg Kiesinger (CDU)	447/496
6	1969–1972	SPD-FDP	Willy Brandt (SPD)	254/496
7	1972–1974	SPD-FDP		271/496
	1974–1976	SPD-FDP	Helmut Schmidt (SPD)	
8	1976–1980	SPD-FDP		253/496
9	1980–1982	SPD-FDP		271/497
	1982–1983	CDU/CSU-FDP	Helmut Kohl (CDU)	279/497
10	1983–1987	CDU/CSU-FDP		278/498
11	1987–1990	CDU/CSU-FDP		269/497
12	1990–1994	CDU/CSU-FDP		398/662
13	1994–1998	CDU/CSU-FDP		341/672
14	1998–2002	SPD-Green	Gerhard Schröder (SPD)	342/669
15	2002–2005	SPD-Green		306/603
16	2005–2009	CDU/CSU-SPD	Angela Merkel (CDU)	448/614
17	2009–2013	CDU/CSU-FDP		332/622
18	2013–	CDU/CSU-SPD		504/631

* Plus German Party (DP)
** Plus DP and an expellee grouping (GB/BHE)

powers vested in the chancellor, the head of government (Niclauß 2004). These include the right to set the direction of government policy (*Richtlinienkompetenz*), sole selection of ministers, and oversight of the bureaucracy. The chancellor calls votes of confidence and can be removed by the opposition only through a constructive vote of non-confidence. The opposition parties must have an alternative government waiting in the wings with a high likelihood of gaining majority support in the Bundestag. This procedure has achieved its aim of minimising governmental instability, which plagued the Weimar Republic and affects parliamentary systems like Italy's. In fact, it has only been used twice – in 1972 (unsuccessfully against Willy Brandt) and in 1982 (successfully against Helmut Schmidt and in favour of Helmut Kohl). In reality, there is more flexibility with such procedures, most notably with Gerhard Schröder using a more conventional non-confidence vote in 2005 to prompt early elections.

In short, the German chancellor dominates the cabinet, in line with an international trend towards what many political scientists describe as the presidentialisation of parliamentary systems (Poguntke and Webb 2005). Chancellors have additional resources that increase their power – the ministry-level Chancellor's Office (Kanzerlamt), access to intelligence (the Bundesnach-richtendienst or BND), control over information through the government's press office (Presseamt), and so on. Because of the parliamentary nature of German democracy, parties have strong internal discipline, so deputies belonging to the majority parties toe the government line. Thus, the chancellor dominates the Bundestag as well.

But this is not a classical majoritarian system in which a 50 + 1 majority can push a partisan agenda through the policy-making process with little regard for the opposition or other minorities (as is often the case in Westminster parliamentary democracies). Coalitions alone make this unlikely. Opposition parties also have numerous means to influence policy and exert over-sight through the powerful committee structure of the Bundestag (*Ausschüsse*), questions posed to the government orally or in writing (*kleine Anfragen*), the Bundesrat, different levels of govern-ment including the supranational (European Union), and the Constitutional Court. Indeed, Germany is a quintessential example of Arend Lijphart's 'consensus democracy' in which as large a majority as possible is achieved, giving numerous stakeholders influence (Lijphart 2012). Alternatively, the country has been classified as a 'grand coalition' or 'semi-sovereign' state (Schmitt 1996; Katzenstein 1987).

The second or upper house is called the Bundesrat (Federal Council) and represents the 16 constituent states, the Länder. Such a chamber has a long history in German political systems, stretching back to the North German Confederation and the Empire (although it was renamed the Reichsrat under the Weimar Republic). The number of votes allocated to each Land ranges from three to six, based on its population size, for a total of 69 votes. Smaller states are consciously overrepresented so that they cannot be steamrollered by the states with larger populations. Members of the Bundesrat are neither directly elected nor permanent, but rather represent a Land's incumbent government. The Bundesrat (like the US Senate) has long ceased solely to represent states' interests and has become a partisan chamber like the Bundestag. The political composition of the Bundesrat can shift after any regional election, most of which are not aligned with Federal elections, creating ever changing and more complex alignments that the government has to negotiate. Given the greater variability of coalitions at the Land level (not just party combinations but differing junior and senior partners), the number of state governments that correspond to the national coalition government can be quite low.

Even though the Bundestag is the more powerful of the two chambers – the government/cabinet does not have to retain the confidence of the Bundesrat and the vast majority of laws originate in the government/Bundestag – the Bundesrat has the right to approve any law that affects the states. As a large majority of legislation impacts the Länder in some manner, the number of laws on which the Bundesrat could vote has increased tremendously over the decades, complicating and slowing down the legislative process. The governing coalition frequently has not commanded majority support in the Bundesrat, and most legislation has faced hurdles here, often resulting in gridlock. Lijphart classifies Germany as a system with strong bicameralism like the US – both symmetrical (similar powers) and incongruent (different methods of election and overrepresentation of minorities, here meaning the demographically smaller Länder) (Lijphart 2012: 199).

Federalism

Germany has a long tradition of decentralised governance (Gunlicks 2003; Ziblatt 2006). The contemporary Federal Republic is composed of 10 Länder from the 'old' Federal Republic or West Germany and five 'new' Länder from the former East Germany as well as Berlin, which had a unique status during the period of division.[25] Three Länder are city-states: Berlin, Hamburg, and Bremen. The populations vary considerably from small Länder such as the Saarland, Mecklenburg-West Pomerania, or Thuringia to much larger states like North Rhine-Westphalia, Bavaria, and Baden-Württemberg (see Table 6.2). The division of powers and interactions between the federation and the states (*Politikverflechtung*) is one of the most important dynamics in Germany's cooperative or interlocking federalism. One of the characteristics that distinguishes Germany from other federations is its 'coordination' by the centre: there is a marked degree of standardisation (tax rates, welfare benefits) from the centre, with implementation taking place at the regional or local level.

Länder prerogatives are ensured in three ways: first, through delineated powers (education, police and internal security, administration of justice, supervision of the mass communications media); second, through their responsibility for the administration of Federal law, including the collection of most taxes and, since 2006, the power to adopt their own regulations for the implementation of some Federal laws; and third, through their representation in the Bundesrat. From 1969 to 2006 the states were also equal participants with the Federal government in certain 'joint tasks' outlined by the Basic Law (Art. 91a and 91b): higher education, regional economic planning and development, agricultural structure, and coastal protection. In 2006, as part of the federalism reform discussed in more detail below, these joint tasks were reduced to regional economic development, agriculture, and coastal protection. Thus, in addition to reserved powers, the Länder have either direct or indirect influence on all national legislation. There are only a few areas, such as defence and foreign affairs, where the national government does not have to consider the views of the states in either the making or the implementation of policy. A series of constitutional amendments passed in 1994 was designed to ensure state influence at the European level. The states want the national government to respect their authority and prerogatives when negotiating in the European Union, and the Länder have offices in Brussels (as well as in Berlin) to pursue their interests.

The Basic Law stipulates that the 'constitutional order in the Länder [should] conform to the principles of republican, democratic, and social government based on the rule of law' (Art. 28, §1). All states have unicameral legislatures with an executive consisting of a minister-president (*Ministerpräsident*) and cabinet responsible to it. State-level cabinets are usually composed of eight to 12 ministers with portfolios such as finance, education, health, justice, and internal affairs. All but three states have adopted the mixed electoral system.[26] Coalition governments have therefore been as common at the regional as at the national level, albeit with more creative variations (e.g. CDU-Green, SPD-PDS/Left, Green-SPD). Although the party systems essentially mirror the national level, some regionally specific parties or protest movements have become

Table 6.2 The German Länder

	Capital	Population (millions, 2011)	Bundesrat votes	Per capita GDP € (2012)	Horizontal payments (million €, 2011)
North Rhine-Westphalia	Düsseldorf	17.8	6	32,631	224
Bavaria	Munich	12.6	6	36,865	−3,663
Baden-Württemberg	Stuttgart	10.8	6	36,019	−1,779
Lower Saxony	Hanover	7.9	6	29,032	204
Hesse	Wiesbaden	6.1	5	37,656	−1,804
Saxony	Dresden	4.1	4	23,400	918
Rhineland-Palatinate	Mainz	4.0	4	29,431	234
Berlin	–	3.5	4	29,455	3,043
Schleswig-Holstein	Kiel	2.8	4	27,220	115
Brandenburg	Potsdam	2.5	4	23,179	440
Saxony-Anhalt	Magdeburg	2.3	4	22,933	540
Thuringia	Erfurt	2.2	4	22,241	527
Hamburg	–	1.8	3	53,019	−62
Mecklenburg-West Pomerania	Schwerin	1.6	3	22,620	429
Saarland	Saarbrücken	1.0	3	31,364	120
Bremen	–	0.7	3	41,897	516
Germany	Berlin	81.8	69	32,281	–

Sources: http://www.statistik-portal.de/Statistik-Portal/en/en_jb01_jahrtab1.asp; http://de.statista.com/statistik/daten/studie/73061/umfrage/bundeslaender-im-vergleich—-bruttoinlandsprodukt/; https://www.destatis.de/DE/Publikationen/StatistischesJahrbuch/StatistischesJahrbuch2012.pdf?__blob=publicationFile (all accessed 14 August 2013).

influential at different points in time, such as the Statt party in Hamburg in the 1990s or the Freie Wähler in Bavaria in the 2000s. The PDS/Left Party has been a strong regional force in eastern Germany, and several right-radical parties have made it into state legislatures, including the Republikaner in Baden-Württemberg in 1992 and the Nationaldemokratische Partei Deutschlands (NPD) in Saxony in the 2000s. The Länder have also proved to be important for new parties like the Greens to build political support and as a training ground for national politicians: four of the Republic's eight chancellors (Kiesinger, Brandt, Kohl, and Schröder) and three of 12 Federal presidents (von Weizsäcker, Rau, and Wulff) were previously state chief executives.

Although the national government has almost sole responsibility for defence, policing is primarily a state function. In the area of social welfare, the national government spends about four times as much as the states, albeit often through semi-public institutions. Education (including universities) has been the prerogative of the states, and it constitutes about one third of all state expenditures. Both levels also transfer funds to other levels of government. For example, approximately one third of local revenue comes from the Länder budgets. The grants of the Federal government (about 10 per cent of expenditure) go largely to the states, but local communities are also the recipients of some funds.

Importantly, the Basic Law commits the Federal Republic to maintain 'equivalent living conditions' (Art. 72, §2) across the Länder. Given different levels of economic development, this can be achieved only by Federal transfers and revenue sharing. The goal is parity of per capita governmental revenues, not equality of personal incomes: each state should have similar per capita funding for schools, roads, hospitals, environmental protection, and other infrastructure responsibilities. This requirement makes financial relations between the states and the Federal government complex and, in addition to sharing common tax revenues, involves two mechanisms. The first is vertical equalisation (Federal payments to poorer states). In 2010, for example, the Federal government paid approximately €12 billion to the 12 'poor' states to bring their level of public expenditure up to 95 per cent of the national average (Statistisches Jahrbuch 2011: 571). Many of these funds have come from the 'solidarity surcharge' on income taxes earmarked for eastern Germany. A second solidarity pact agreed in 2001 will send approximately €150 billion to the five new states from 2005–20, after which time exceptional transfers will cease. The second mechanism is horizontal equalisation (payments to poorer states by richer ones). In 2012 four states – Bavaria, Baden-Württemberg, Hamburg, and Hesse – contributed about €7.3 billion to the others (Statistisches Jahrbuch 2012: 257); and 3) intergovernmental grants and subsidies for various special and joint projects, as well as Federal payments to the states to defray the costs of administering Federal law.

Donor states, especially Bavaria and Baden-Württemberg, have long been dissatisfied with the system of horizontal transfers and argue that it penalises them for their efficient administration by giving their citizens' euros to the poorer, allegedly spendthrift, states. The 'rich' states also complain that they have to contribute so much of their revenues that at the end of the process, when Federal vertical transfers are included, they are worse off than the poorer states that the system is designed to help. Since unification, the vast majority of such funds have flowed from west to east, although a south to north transfer also continues.[27] It has proved difficult to change this system in light of the constitutional guarantee and high levels of public support.

Although the Federal government receives about 45 per cent of all tax revenues, in 2010 it was responsible for only about 42 per cent of all public expenditure, including national defence, whereas the states accounted for 36 per cent and local government for about 22 per cent (Statistisches Jahrbuch 2011: 563). The states and local communities, on the other hand, spend more than they receive in taxes, with the Federal government making up most of the difference. This financial leverage has enabled the national government to achieve some coordination in areas such as education, regional economic development, and social welfare programmes. The states, however, have steadily struggled for a larger piece of the tax pie and hence greater independence from the national government. At present, the states receive about a third of the largest source of tax revenue, the individual and corporate income tax (currently 48 per cent goes to Berlin, 34 per cent to the states, 12 per cent to the cities, and the remainder to the European Union). Since 1995, the states' share of the second-largest source of revenue, value-added tax, has increased from 37 per cent to 44 per cent. The Federal government receives about 95 per cent of its income from taxes, but taxes account for only 70 per cent of Land revenues (Rudzio 2011: 337). The difference of 25 per cent can be construed as the margin of Land dependency on the national government. Neither side has been fully satisfied with this state of affairs, so the struggle over the distribution of tax revenues and burden sharing will continue.

Overall, German federalism has worked well since 1949. Public opinion is quite supportive, and many individuals have developed strong regional identities. Nevertheless, various tensions and problems persist. The Länder have jealously guarded their independence and have opposed many long-overdue administrative reforms, fearing a loss of power and funds. In the 'joint projects' dealing with higher education, regional economic development, and health care, for example, they opposed giving the national government any significant coordinating authority, eventually conceding it only as a planning function. They have also opposed increased authority for the national government on questions of water and air pollution. A weakness of the Federal system became clear in the inability of the police to end quickly the wave of left-wing terrorism (perpetrated primarily by the Red Army Faction or RAF) from the 1970s to 1990s, and more recently to stop the neo-Nazi National Socialist Underground, which murdered 10 individuals between 2000 and 2007. Terrorism and organised crime are likewise national problems, but the structure of law enforcement – largely as a consequence of experiences with the Nazi police state – is highly decentralised and for that reason often ineffective. Finally, by insisting on a greater role in the European Union, the Länder have reduced the country's capacity to speak with a unified voice. Before committing Germany to any major initiative, the national government must consult with the states.

Recent developments

The system continues to evolve in light of ongoing financial constraints, demographic change, regional integration, globalisation, and so on. This concluding section will look at two of the most important topics since unification in 1990: federalism reform and the role of the Constitutional Court.

It is difficult to do justice in one chapter to the political and constitutional order of a complex polity such as the Federal Republic and of course, much more could be mentioned. For example, German foreign policy has involved dramatic changes in the status of the Bundeswehr (armed forces), including the abolition of conscription in 2011. The divisive issue of its deployment abroad (out of the NATO area) was buttressed by a Constitutional Court ruling in 1994, which also stipulated the necessity of parliamentary votes endorsing deployments (see Chapters 25 and 26). Abortion has also been contentious in light of the Basic Law's provisions regarding the sanctity of human life, as well as of the continued influence of the Catholic Church. East Germany had a much less restrictive law, so the early 1990s witnessed legislative efforts to reconcile the differences. This process was complicated by Constitutional Court rulings that left the 1970s West German legislation essentially in place – allowing abortion in the first trimester, with allowances based on medical necessity afterwards, after a three-day waiting period and compulsory counselling (Ferree 2002). Ethnicity-based (*ius sanguinis*) citizenship laws dating from the Empire were also partially changed in 1999–2000 to accommodate citizenship based on birth (*ius soli*), potentially affecting the almost 20 per cent of the population 'with a migration background' (see Chapters 8 and 12). Included in the reform were easier naturalisation procedures and the acceptance of dual citizenship until the age of 25 (Howard 2009). As regional integration gained steam in the 1990s and beyond – the Maastricht Treaty in 1992–3, the common currency, and the Lisbon Treaty of 2009 – a new set of challenges presented themselves. For example, much effort has been expended to implement European directives and laws; estimates are that between 40 and 80 per cent of all recent laws have originated at the EU level.[28] Moreover, the problems and proposed solutions that have arisen thanks to the post-2008 euro crisis – bailouts to countries like Greece, joint eurobond proposals, common banking regulation, and greater EU/European Central Bank control over member states' finances – have caused friction (see Chapters 21 and 22).

Federalism reform

The ability and increasing willingness of the Länder to block national legislation prompted calls for a drastic overhaul of the Federal system.[29] To address these and other problems of federalism (e.g. overlapping jurisdiction, multiplication of functions) and to respond to growing criticism that federalism was in part responsible for policy gridlock, a Reform Commission was convened in 2003. By 2006 both parliamentary chambers had approved the reform package, involving more than 40 constitutional amendments. The changes were intended to streamline the legislative process by reducing the proportion of bills that the Bundesrat can veto from over 60 per cent to less than 30 per cent. Some research doubts that this reduction will occur and estimates that the proportion of bills still going through the Bundesrat will hover around 50 per cent (Burkhart *et al.* 2008). In exchange, the states gained flexibility in how they implement national legislation and greater autonomy in a number of policy areas, most notably education, care for the elderly, pay for public employees, and store-closing hours. The states now have sole responsibility in education, including higher education, which includes whether or not they charge tuition fees.[30] Länder also can deviate from Federal norms in certain environmental policy areas. Thus, there is now less uniformity and somewhat more diversity in the federation. In addition, states' rights in addressing European questions have been reduced, so that during negotiations at the European Union the states now participate only if the issues involve education, culture, or television and radio.

Yet giving the Länder more autonomy means little without corresponding taxation powers. Under the existing system the income of the states depends entirely on decisions made at the Federal level, albeit with considerable input via the Bundesrat. Thus, while the first phase of federalism reform agreed on a clearer definition of state and Federal authority, including a reduction in the issue areas where the states have a veto, it did not address the more important question of how revenues are to be raised and distributed between the states and Federal government. Powers that were transferred totally to the states – that is, those surrendered by the Federal government – were relatively minor and inexpensive.

A second Federalism Reform Commission between 2007 and 2009 attempted to address those lingering issues. The biggest changes involved the passage of a Federal balanced budget amendment in 2009, the creation of a Stability Council comprising the Federal ministers of finance and economy and the 16 Länder ministers of finance, and the requirement that the Federal (by 2015) and state governments (by 2019) balance their budgets without taking on more debt. In future only the Federal government will be allowed to take on more debt, but this cannot exceed 0.35 per cent of GDP. Particularly indebted states (Berlin, Bremen, Saarland, Saxony-Anhalt, and Schleswig-Holstein) have been given extra funds to balance their budgets by 2019. There was no agreement on providing more regional control over taxes, and the rigid limits on debt and balancing budgets will constrain the Länder even more. The new strictures have also caused Länder increasingly to shirk financial responsibilities and burden-sharing. Indeed, many predict that the 'debt brake', coupled with rising pension and infrastructure costs, will inevitably necessitate further, recentralising structural reform.[31] Finally, the Commission considered the amalgamation of existing Länder as a way of reducing administrative costs – to no avail.

The Constitutional Court

Behind almost all of the recent public policy controversies and institutional changes has been the Constitutional Court. Always an influential force, the decades since unification have witnessed even more power accruing to this actor – a trend observed more generally across advanced democratic systems from the US to Japan to the European Union. There are multiple causes behind this development, including political cowardice. It is often easier for elected politicians to 'let the courts decide' than to take a position on a controversial issue, or to use the courts as political cover. Furthermore, an increasing number of rights-based claims have had to be adjudicated, a situation exacerbated by the increasing legal complexity of modern life.

The German Constitutional Court has the power of judicial review, but diverges from other supreme and constitutional courts in several important ways. The Bundestag and Bundesrat each select half of the 16 judges, and each judge has a non-renewable term of 12 years with mandatory retirement at the age of 68. The Court is divided into two eight-member senates with mutually exclusive personnel and jurisdiction, and each senate is further divided into three three-member chambers (Kommers and Miller 2012: 18–22). The Court is not a regular appellate court because other dedicated courts, such as the Bundesgerichtshof for civil and criminal matters or the Bundesfinanzhof for taxation issues, act as courts of last resort in their respective and clearly delineated fields of law. The Constitutional Court also has comparatively open access. Where the US Supreme Court (for example) has only *ex post facto* review, in Germany certain groups such as Federal and state governments or one quarter of Bundestag members can ask for abstract judicial review before a law is implemented. Moreover, through a so-called constitutional complaint, individual citizens can request Court action. Over 130,000 such complaints have been submitted in the decades since the Court's establishment (Kommers and Miller 2012: 31), even though the success rate is in the low single digits. Especially because of this procedure, the Court maintains very high levels of public support – higher than almost any other state institution.

In addition to the many solely domestic issues on which the Court has made ultimate decisions (including abortion, privacy rights, the electoral law, and financial transfers among states) Europe-related issues have become central, In fact, the Court has become a key national and international arbiter: in several instances Constitutional Court approval has been the final Europe-wide hurdle for the ratification of various treaties. Although it traditionally interprets the Basic Law as compatible with the European integration process – that is, transferring sovereign powers to supranational entities – the Court has taken a more restrictive attitude in recent years. It has increasingly emphasised the importance of democratic legitimation and German sovereignty, while criticising the extent of integration and insufficient democratic oversight at the supra-national level.

In 1993 the Constitutional Court found that the Maastricht Treaty, which paved the way for European Monetary Union, was constitutional. But it also asserted its power to decide whether a European initiative is compatible with the Basic Law and hinted that a fully federal Europe would probably not be. In 1998 the court ruled that Germany's entrance into the European Monetary Union was constitutional, but reminded the government and parliament of their duties to ensure monetary stability, as well as of the 'no bailout clause' of the Maastricht Treaty.

Then, in one of the most important decisions in its history, the court ruled that implementation of the Lisbon Treaty could take place only if supplemental legislation was passed (Kommers and Miller 2012: 345–52). The Court essentially ruled that the treaty would be constitutional only with legislation that would allow the states, through the Bundesrat and Bundestag, to give direction to the national government's representatives in the European Council. In its decision the Court was concerned that decisions at European Union level could violate Germany's constitution, especially its federalism provisions and extensive human and civil rights guarantees. It was also critical of the 'democratic deficit' at EU level and outlined the policy areas, including fiscal policy, that ought to remain at the national level. The supplemental legislation, which was passed at a special session just prior to the 2009 Bundestag election, created an 'emergency brake' on the national government's representatives to the EU, so that before the government makes concessions in Brussels, the Bundesrat and Bundestag can essentially exercise a veto. Since the government dominates the Bundestag, it is really the Bundesrat that is empowered. The decision was sharply criticised. The word 'sovereign' is not used at all in the Basic Law, but this decision used it 33 times. Critics argued that the Basic Law clearly commits Germany to a united Europe, a position supported by the Court's own past precedents. The Court empowered itself by signalling its intention to monitor closely the European integration process and to interpret the pro-integration thrust of the Basic Law in a more constrained manner.

The Court was also at the centre of the constitutional debate surrounding the efforts to save the euro and the troubled economies of southern Europe through various bailouts and the establishment of a European stability mechanism (ESM). While these measures passed both chambers of parliament by a two-thirds majority, which is required for constitutional amendments, opponents of the legislation challenged their constitutionality. Once again, the issue was whether too much German sovereignty was being transferred to non-elected European officials and institutions. The Court asked whether democracy itself was being weakened by the Merkel Government's efforts to save the euro and perhaps the entire European Union. The Court issued its final decision in September 2012, upholding the legality of the ESM but reiterating the necessity for prior Bundestag approval.

Conclusion

This chapter has endeavoured to provide an overview of contemporary Germany's constitutional and political order. Overall, the Federal Republic has exhibited exemplary performance and has solved the worrying 'German question' that haunted Europe and the world in the 19th and 20th centuries. Many of its institutions and practices – for example, the 'mixed' electoral system, the central bank (Bundesbank), and the Constitutional Court – have been emulated by other countries. Its social protections, environmental policies, vocational training,[32] and infrastructure, as well as its fiscal and monetary rectitude, are lauded by international elites across the political spectrum. International public opinion mirrors such positive assessments. According to one well-known poll, Germany has been the most liked or respected country worldwide for several years, with 59 per cent believing that the country has mainly positive influence in the world.[33]

Yet from the inside, Germans are and have been deeply critical of the Federal Republic, its performance, and its political institutions. Many chafed at the continuing presence and influence of former Nazis after 1945 (Jarausch 2006), at suboptimal efforts to come to terms with the Nazi past (Giordano 1987), and, more generally, at the conservative 'restorationist' aspects of the postwar order. Policy paralysis has often resulted from the interaction between the numerous decision-making institutions and levels of government, sometimes referred to as a 'joint decision trap' (Scharpf 1988). National and international policy has been affected by the Federal government's solicitousness towards regional concerns in the run-up to Länder elections, with the ever-present possibility of shifting support for the government in the Bundesrat. For example, the Merkel Government's decisions in 2011 not to support NATO intervention in Libya and to transition away from nuclear power were largely motivated by concerns about losing power in the state of Baden-Württemberg (Erlanger and Dempsey 2011). The plight of working Germans has arguably deteriorated in recent years, and challenges persist in achieving just outcomes for eastern Germans, for individuals with a migration background, and for women (Anderson and Langenbacher 2010); the east–west divide still festers (see Chapters 9 and 10), the much heralded infrastructure (especially in the west) has been neglected, and economic hurdles loom as the population ages and shrinks (see Chapter 17).

Moreover, as Germany has recently gained power in Europe and beyond, it continues to be a 'reluctant hegemon' (Paterson 2011; see also Chapters 20 and 21). Some have noted a kind of 'solidarity fatigue' among many Germans, who were first asked to send a fortune to rebuild east Germany and are now being asked to do the same for the 'peripheral economies' of southern Europe. Such attitudes, which have greatly affected the Merkel Government's policies, coupled with an underdeveloped strategic culture (*The Economist* 2013)[34] have been widely criticised for producing insufficient or poor leadership during the euro crisis.

While an overly rosy picture of the Federal Republic should be avoided, overall and from a long-term perspective the positive clearly outweighs the negative. Nevertheless, the system cannot stand still if the policy and leadership challenges of the present and future are to be confronted. There are grounds for cautious optimism. In contrast to many other countries – not least the US – the Federal Republic has proven adept at embracing difficult constitutional, institutional, and policy changes: federalism reforms, tax increases, bailouts of troubled peripheral economies, and the Hartz IV/Agenda 2010 labour market and economic reforms,[35] to mention just a few examples. This ability to self-correct, an underappreciated attribute of the German Federal system, is perhaps its most positive and resonant achievement of all.

Notes

1 This chapter does not deal with the institutions, dynamics, or lingering legacies of East Germany. For insightful treatment of that system see Fulbrook 1992 and Maier 1997. An excellent resource for modern German history more generally is Walser Smith 2011.

2 The close 337 to 320 vote in favour of moving the capital back to Berlin took place in 1991. The original plan was to split functions between the two cities – for example, the Bundesrat was supposed to stay in Bonn. Even today six ministries have their main headquarters in Bonn, which also benefited from the relocation of other Federal offices. Bonn still employs 7,000 civil servants to Berlin's 11,000, but, as with the Bundesrat, the pull of Berlin seems inexorable. For example, the Ministry of Defence recently announced plans to centralise operations in Berlin. See www1.wdr.de/themen/politik/bonnberlin100.html; www1.wdr.de/themen/politik/bonnberlin114.html (accessed 15 August 2013).

3 See, among others, the World Bank's World Governance Indicators, available at http://info.worldbank.org/governance/wgi/index.aspx#home; Transparency International's Corruption Perception Index, available at www.transparency.org/research/cpi/overview; or the Economist Intelligence Unit's Democracy Index, available at www.eiu.com/public/thankyou_download.aspx?activity=download&campaignid=DemocracyIndex12 (accessed 17 August 2013).

4 Amendments (Art. 79) are relatively easy to pass, requiring a two-thirds majority vote in both the Bundestag and the Bundesrat. Referendums are not needed for ratification and have never been used nationally in the Federal Republic, a choice justified due to abuse of plebiscitarian methods by the Nazis.

5 All references to the Basic Law come from the Bundestag's official English translation, available at https://www.btg-bestellservice.de/pdf/80201000.pdf. See also the special issue of *Aus Politik und Zeitgeschichte*, available at www.bpb.de/apuz/32014/60-jahre-grundgesetz (accessed 16 August 2013).

6 The GDR abolished the Länder on its territory in 1952 and replaced them by 14 centrally administered districts (*Bezirke*) plus East Berlin. The states were reconstructed in 1990 as part of the formal reunification process. East and West Berlin were reunited and also entered the federation as a Land. Article 23 was amended after reunification as no other territories will be allowed to accede.

7 Nothing prohibits the amalgamation and/or separation of the Länder. Baden and Württemberg were joined together in 1952 after a referendum. Another referendum rejected the union of Brandenburg with Berlin in 1996.

8 After the fall of the Iron Curtain and the outbreak of violence in the former Yugoslavia, Germany witnessed a sharp increase in asylum claims to over 400,000 in 1992 – about 70 per cent of the EU total that year. The article was amended to prohibit asylum claims from individuals entering from EU member states or other vetted third countries (Hailbronner 1994).

9 There were also unsuccessful attempts to ban the right-radical NPD in 2001–03 and again in 2012–13.

10 See www.destatis.de/DE/ZahlenFakten/GesellschaftStaat/OeffentlicheFinanzenSteuern/OeffentlicherDienst/Personal/Tabellen/Aufgaben.html (accessed 14 August 2013).

11 This was done through a protocol to the Treaty of Brussels and later the War Weapons Control Act, an implementing law (*Ausführungsgesetz*) to Article 26 (§2) of the Basic Law, as well as other international treaties.

12 See www.bundestag.de/bundestag/parteienfinanzierung/festsetz_staatl_mittel/finanz_12.pdf (accessed 15 August 2013).

13 See www.spiegel.de/politik/deutschland/cdu-spendenaffaere-schaeuble-war-mittaeter-a-59401.html (accessed 13 August 2013).

14 At the time of writing, Joachim Gauck is the president (since 2012) and Angela Merkel is the chancellor or head of government (since 2005).

15 See www.fairvote.org/how-districts-plus-has-worked-for-german-elections#.UgkpjNzD_cs (accessed 14 August 2013).

16 There is a movement to reduce this to 16, as in some other countries and at several local levels. See www.machs-ab-16.de/waehlen-ab-16 (accessed 14 August 2013).

17 The size of the Bundestag was increased to a minimum of 496 in 1964 and 656 in 1990 to accommodate eastern German voters. Throughout the years of division, West Berlin was not a formal Land, but sent a delegation of 22 full voting members to the Bundestag. Concerns that the body had become too large led to a reduction to 598 in 1998 (in force for the 2002 elections).

18 Political scientists have long argued that the ideal size of a parliament is the cubic root of the country's population, which in Germany would be about 434 members (Taagepera and Shugart 1989).

19 Of the 97 such mandates between 1949 and 2009, the CDU won 61 per cent and the SPD 35 per cent.

20 One of the most dramatic outcomes of the September 2013 election was that the Liberals (FDP), with 4.8 per cent, did not surmount the electoral threshold. See www.bundeswahlleiter.de/de/bundestagswahlen/BTW_BUND_13/ergebnisse/bundesergebnisse/ (accessed 2 October 2013).

21 The score ranges from 0 (perfect vote–seat correspondence) to 100. Gallagher treats the CDU and CSU as separate parties and excludes the 'other' category. Under the alternate assumptions, the scores are higher. The effective number of party calculations reported here treats the CDU/CSU as one party.

22 The first postwar elections witnessed several smaller parties such as the German Party (DP) or Bavarian Party gaining representation – winning 80/402 seats (20 per cent) in 1949; 45/509 (9 per cent) in 1953, 18/519 (3.5 per cent) in 1957, and then nothing after that. Seat totals here include West Berlin deputies.

23 The relationship between the CDU and CSU has always been unique. The CSU is a formally independent party that operates only in Bavaria with the CDU competing in all other Länder. The two parties are in a perpetual national alliance and are referred to as the CDU/CSU or the 'Union'.

24 But even this designation is complicated by the quasi-independent, more conservative/populist, and often difficult CSU, as well as the existence of the German Party, which was, in any case, soon defunct.

25 Germany also has a robust system of local governments where there is much more variation with regard to the power of the executive, the electoral system utilised, and the amount of direct democratic input allowed (Naßmacher and Naßmacher 2007).

26 Saarland uses straight PR with closed lists; Hamburg and Bremen use PR with open lists. See www.wahlrecht.de/landtage/index.htm (accessed 17 August 2013).

27 In 2012 Bavarian Minister President Horst Seehofer even threatened to take the issue to the Constitutional Court, despite the court upholding the system in 1992 and 2006. Interestingly, Bavaria was a beneficiary of horizontal transfers until the mid-1980s.

28 See http://blogs.lse.ac.uk/europpblog/2012/06/13/europeanisation-of-public-policy/ (accessed 15 August 2013).

29 One of the main impetuses behind these efforts was the weak economy and the inability of the Kohl Government to pass its pro-business tax reform legislation in 1997. In 2000 the Red-Green coalition also faced difficulties passing its own tax reform.

30 Yet the Federal government still (co-)finances many research programmes such as, from 2006, the Excellence Initiative to foster world-class research universities.

31 See 'Finanzpolitik: Himmel hilf', *Der Spiegel*, 34/2013.

32 Even US President Obama lauded Germany's vocational training system in his 2013 State of the Union Address. Online. Available at www.whitehouse.gov/state-of-the-union-2013#webform (accessed 17 August 2013).

33 See www.worldpublicopinion.org/pipa/2013%20Country%20Rating%20Poll.pdf (accessed 17 August 2013); 15 per cent stated that the country has mainly negative influence.

34 Strategic culture refers to the assumptions, norms, beliefs, and traditions that structure a country's foreign policy. The criticisms are that postwar German elites have eschewed developing such a culture to the detriment of long-term continuity, coherence, and predictability and that the country lacks the intellectual and policy infrastructure to plan successfully.

35 The Hartz IV reforms were a series of labour market reforms passed in 2003 that reduced the length and level of benefits for the unemployed and restructured/decentralised the bureaucracy that administers such payments. The Agenda 2010 of Schröder's Government involved the Hartz reforms, as well as lower income taxes, cuts to pensions, and reductions in certain medical benefits. All of these reforms were intended to increase the competitiveness of the German economy and improve public finances. Although many analysts assert that these reforms are responsible for the good economic performance currently, others blame these policy changes for the rise in poverty and income inequality over the last decade.

Bibliography

Allemann, F.R. (1956) *Bonn ist Nicht Weimar*, Cologne: Kiepenheuer & Witsch.

Anderson, J.J. and Langenbacher, E. (eds) (2010) *From the Bonn to the Berlin Republic: Germany at the Twentieth Anniversary of Unification*, New York: Berghahn Books.

Baker, K., Dalton, R.J., and Hildebrandt, K. (1981) *Germany Transformed: Political Culture and the New Politics*, Cambridge: Harvard University Press.

Banchoff, T.F. (1999) *The German Problem Transformed: Institutions, Politics, and Foreign Policy, 1945–1995*, Ann Arbor: University of Michigan Press.

Bernhard, M. (2001) 'Democratization in Germany: A Reappraisal', *Comparative Politics*, 33: 379–400.

Bernhard, M. (2005) *Institutions and the Fate of Democracy: Germany and Poland in the Twentieth Century*, Pittsburgh: University of Pittsburgh Press.

Burkhart, S., Manow, P., and Ziblatt, D. (2008) 'A More Efficient and Accountable Federalism? An Analysis of the Consequences of Germany's 2006 Constitutional Reform', *German Politics*, 17: 522–40.

Conradt, D.P. (1980) 'Changing German Political Culture', in G. Almond and S. Verba (eds) *The Civic Culture Revisited*, Boston: Little, Brown: 212–72.

Conradt, D.P. and Langenbacher, E. (2013) *The German Polity*, 10th edn, Lanham: Rowman and Littlefield.

Dahrendorf, R. (1967) *Society and Democracy in Germany*, New York: Doubleday.

Dalton, R.J. (2006) *Citizen Politics: Public Opinion and Political Parties in Advanced Industrial Democracies*, Washington: CQ Press.

The Economist (2013) 'Special Report: Germany', 15 June.

Erlanger, S. and Dempsey, J. (2011) 'Germany Steps Away From European Unity', *New York Times*, 23 March. Online. Available at www.nytimes.com/2011/03/24/world/europe/24germany.html?pagewanted=all&_r=0 (accessed 17 August 2013).

Ferree, M.M. (2002) *Shaping Abortion Discourse: Democracy and the Public Sphere in Germany and the United States*, New York: Cambridge University Press.

Fulbrook, M. (1992) *The Divided Nation: A History of Germany, 1918–1990*, New York: Oxford University Press.

Gallagher, M. (2014) Election Indices Dataset. Online. Available at www.tcd.ie./Political_Science/staff/michael_gallagher/ElSystems/index.php (accessed 29 August 2014).

Gardner Feldman, L. (2012) *Germany's Foreign Policy of Reconciliation: From Enmity to Amity*, Lanham: Rowman and Littlefield.

Giordano, R. (1987) *Die zweite Schuld oder Von der Last Deutscher zu sein*, Hamburg: Rasch und Röhring.

Gunlicks, A. (2003) *The Länder and German Federalism*, New York: Palgrave Macmillan.

Hailbronner, K. (1994) 'Asylum Law Reform in the German Constitution', *American University International Law Review*, 9: 159–79.

Howard, M.M. (2009) *The Politics of Citizenship in Europe*, New York: Cambridge University Press.

Hucko, E.M. (ed.) (1987) *The Democratic Tradition: Four German Constitutions*, New York: Berg.

Jacoby, W. (2000) *Imitation and Politics: Redesigning Germany*, Ithaca: Cornell University Press.

Jarausch, K.H. (2006) *After Hitler: Recivilizing Germans, 1945–1995*, trans. B. Hunziker, New York: Oxford University Press.

Katzenstein, P.J. (1987) *Policy and Politics in West Germany: The Growth of a Semisovereign State*, Philadelphia: Temple University Press.

Kommers, D.A. and Miller, R.A. (2012) *The Constitutional Jurisprudence of the Federal Republic of Germany*, 3rd edn, Durham, NC: Duke University Press.

Langenbacher, E. (2010) 'Conclusion: The Germans Must Have Done Something Right', in J.J. Anderson and E. Langenbacher (eds) *From the Bonn to the Berlin Republic: Germany at the Twentieth Anniversary of Unification*, New York: Berghahn Books: 397–413.

Lijphart, A. (2012) *Patterns of Democracy: Government Forms and Performance in Thirty-Six Countries*, 2nd edn, New Haven: Yale University Press.

Maier, C.S. (1997) *Dissolution: The Crisis of Communism and the End of East Germany*, Princeton: Princeton University Press.

Moses, A.D. (2007) *German Intellectuals and the Nazi Past*, New York: Cambridge University Press.

Naßmacher, H. and Naßmacher, K.-H. (2007) *Kommunalpolitik in Deutschland*, 2nd edn. Wiesbaden: Verlag für Sozialwissenschaften.

Niclauß, K. (2004) *Kanzlerdemokratie: Regierungsführung von Konrad Adenauer bis Gerhard Schröder*, Paderborn: Schöningh.

Paterson, W.E. (2011) 'The Reluctant Hegemon? Germany Moves Centre Stage in the European Union', *JCMS: Journal of Common Market Studies*, 49: 57–75.

Peterson, E.N. (1978) *The American Occupation of Germany: Retreat to Victory*, Detroit: Wayne State University Press.

Poguntke, T. and Webb, P. (eds) (2005) *The Presidentialization of Politics: A Comparative Study of Modern Democracies*, New York: Oxford University Press.

Ritter, G. (1965) *The German Problem: Basic Questions of German Political Life, Past and Present*, Columbus: Ohio State University Press.

Rudzio, W. (2011) *Das politische System der Bundesrepublik Deutschland*, Wiesbaden: Verlag für Sozialwissenschaften.

Sa'adah, A. (1998) *Germany's Second Chance: Trust, Justice, and Democratization*, Cambridge: Harvard University Press.

Scharpf, F.W. (1988) 'The Joint-Decision Trap: Lessons from German Federalism and European Integration', *Public Administration*, 66: 239–78.

Schmitt, M.G. (1996) 'Germany: The Grand Coalition State', in J.M. Colomer (ed.) *Political Institutions in Europe*, London: Routledge: 62–98.

Statistisches Jahrbuch (2011), Wiesbaden: Statistisches Bundesamt. Online. Available at https://www.destatis.de/DE/Publikationen/StatistischesJahrbuch/FinanzenSteuern.pdf?__blob=publicationFile (accessed 17 August 2013).

Statistisches Jahrbuch (2012), Wiesbaden: Statistisches Bundesamt. Online. Available at https://www.destatis.de/DE/Publikationen/StatistischesJahrbuch/StatistischesJahrbuch2012.pdf?__blob=publicationFile (accessed 14 August 2013).

Taagepera, R. and Shugart, M.S. (1989) 'Designing Electoral Systems', *Electoral Studies*, 8: 49–58.

Verba, S. (1965) 'Germany: the Remaking of Political Culture', in L.W. Pye and S. Verba (eds) *Political Culture and Political Development*, Princeton: Princeton University Press: 130–70.

Walser Smith, H. (ed.) (2011) *The Oxford Handbook of Modern German History*, New York: Oxford University Press.

Ziblatt, D. (2006) *Structuring the State: The Formation of Italy and Germany and the Puzzle of Federalism*, Princeton: Princeton University Press.

7

Party politics and electoral behaviour

Thomas Saalfeld and Harald Schoen

A political party can be defined as 'any group, however loosely organised, seeking to elect governmental officeholders under a given label' (Epstein 1979: 9). Building on Key's (1964: 164) fundamental distinction and Katz's and Mair's (2002: 113) modifications, this chapter describes and analyses the interaction of German voters and party elites at three distinct levels: the 'party-in-the-electorate', the 'party-in-the-government' (Key) or 'party in public office' (as Katz and Mair put it), and the party organisation outside the legislature, particularly the 'party on the ground' (Katz and Mair 2002). Our analysis focuses on individual parties and also covers the party system as 'the *system of interactions* resulting from inter-party competition' (Sartori 1976: 44, emphasis in the original). We will aim to track important continuities in, and changes to, voting behaviour in respect of the main German parties individually and of the party system as a whole, concentrating on the period since unification in 1990. Drawing on a number of theoretical perspectives, including theories of electoral change, theories of organisational reform in political parties (in response to electoral change), and coalition politics at the governmental level, we will develop our argument as follows: after introducing the main parties and analysing continuities and change in voting behaviour and party membership, we will analyse how political parties have responded to the growing levels of political uncertainty in organisational terms and will seek to address the seemingly paradoxical question why Germany's party system has remained relatively stable at the governmental level (the party in public office), while parties in the electorate and parties as organisations have become far more fluid and vulnerable. (On the electoral system in Germany, including proportional representation and the statutory minimum of 5 per cent of the national vote a party should achieve to be represented in the Bundestag, see Chapter 6.)

'Dramatis Personae': the parties

Six parties were represented in the German parliament or Bundestag between the first election after unification and the general election of 2013. They are the main 'actors' on the stage of the Bundestag. We will briefly characterise the main parties and their challengers, starting with the parties of the centre-right and right (for some further short portraits and further information see Hornsteiner and Saalfeld 2014).

The leading parties on the centre-right are the *Christian Democrats*, the CDU (Christian Democratic Union) and the CSU (Christian Socialist Union), the CDU's sister party in the Federal state of Bavaria. Both parties have been consistent advocates of the German model of a social market economy (see Chapters 5 and 22) and of Germany's membership of NATO, and have shown a commitment to the process of European integration. Business friendly in their economic policies, they have always had an organised trade union wing amongst their membership. The ideological differences between the two parties are small, although the Bavarian CSU has always tended to be slightly more conservative on law and order and issues of social morality (Bräuninger and Debus 2012). Both parties draw their electoral support from across the entire spectrum of the citizenry, with a certain overrepresentation amongst practising Christians and middle-class voters. The sister parties have led national governments between 1949 and 1969, between 1982 and 1998, and from 2005 to the present day.

For much of the time between 1949 and 2013, the liberal *Free Democratic Party* (FDP) was the CDU/CSU's 'natural' partner in government coalitions. Exceptionally, between 1969 and 1982, the Liberals formed a coalition with the SPD and positioned themselves as a pivotal party between the two major parties (Pappi 1984). Ideologically, the FDP has always been a strong advocate of free enterprise and small government. From the late 1960s and early 1970s, it also became a party strongly associated with the process of détente and reconciliation with Germany's central and eastern European neighbours. But with 4.8 per cent in the 2013 election, it failed to reach the statutory minimum of 5 per cent of the national vote necessary to be represented in the Bundestag. For the first time since 1949, the FDP was not represented in parliament.

In 2013 the *Alternative for Germany* (AfD) emerged as a competitor to the centre-right parties. It was founded in February 2013 by a group of disaffected CDU members critical of the party leadership's policy during the eurozone crisis, a policy that was broadly supported by all Bundestag parties except The Left (Die Linke, see below). The core demand in the AfD's 2013 manifesto was Germany's withdrawal from the euro and a return to national currencies. Other policy areas were less developed. In the election of 2013, the AfD narrowly failed to achieve the 5 per cent threshold, winning 4.7 per cent of the national vote. This was a remarkable result only months after its establishment. The party's support was particularly strong in the eastern German states, where it gained support from around 5.8 per cent of voters.

The *Social Democratic Party* (SPD) has since 1949 been the largest party left of the political centre. It has a social democratic programme that accepts the social market economy but simultaneously advocates an active role for the government to ensure a degree of social equality and cohesion. It has participated in coalition governments with the CDU/CSU, in 1966–9, in 2005–09, and since 2013; with the FDP, in 1969–82; and with the Greens, in 1998–2005. The 1998–2005 SPD-Green coalition under Chancellor Gerhard Schröder initiated major reforms to labour market policy, social benefits, and pensions, which were deeply unpopular with some of the party's activists and core voters and severely depressed electoral support after 2005.

The *Green Party* was founded in the 1970s as a broad and relatively disparate coalition of pacifists, environmentalists, feminists, left-libertarians, and other social movement organisations. It developed into a modern democratic centre-left party with a strong focus on questions of environmental policy. In the 1983 Bundestag election, it polled more than 5 per cent of the vote for the first time and has been represented in the Bundestag ever since. At the national level, the Greens governed in a coalition with the SPD between 1998 and 2005. Very much an outsider during the 1980s and much of the 1990s, the party is now seen as a potential coalition partner for both the SPD and the CDU/CSU at the national as well as the regional and municipal levels. Its coalition formed with the CDU in Hesse in December 2013 is seen as a strong indication of the Greens expanding their strategic options, also at the national level.

The Left (Die Linke) was established in 2007 through a merger of The Left Party/PDS (Linkspartei.PDS), formerly the Party of Democratic Socialism (Partei des Demokratischen Sozialismus, PDS), and the Electoral Alternative for Labour and Social Justice (WASG). The PDS had been the successor organisation of the SED (Socialist Unity Party), the ruling party in the German Democratic Republic, which was disbanded in 1989–90.[1] The WASG was a party founded by trade unionists and former Social Democrats in January 2005 in opposition to Federal Chancellor Gerhard Schröder's reforms to labour market policy, unemployment benefit, social insurance, and pensions, known as the Hartz IV reforms. The merger to form The Left did not resolve intra-party tensions between pragmatic factions (mostly from the east) and more radical factions (mostly from the west).

The 'audience': voting behaviour in unified Germany

Sticking to our metaphor of a theatrical performance, the voters may be seen as the audience choosing their favourite act at the end of a show. The behaviour of voters has undergone significant changes since German unification in 1990. These changes concern their participation, the way they make their choices, and the social and political drivers underpinning their choices. It has proven useful to conceive of vote choice as resulting from the interplay of voter attitudes and expectations on the one hand, and the choices offered by political parties on the other (Campbell et al. 1960; Key 1966). As far as the voters are concerned, short-term, occasionally quite fickle forces affecting choices at the ballot box can be distinguished from more stable longer-term forces. The former include evaluations of the political leaders and issues of the day. The latter include relatively stable psychological attachments to political parties that operate like a psychological and cognitive 'filter' affecting short-term attitudes and political behaviour in favour of a party (Campbell et al. 1960; Bartels 2002; Lodge and Taber 2013). In addition, voters' general policy preferences tend to be more stable and less dependent on short-term factors. While long-term factors lend stability to political attitudes and behaviour, short-term factors such as changing candidates, new policy proposals, and issues on which parties focus in their electoral campaigns account for changes in vote choice. Campaigns define the menu from which voters, relying on long- and short-term attitudes, choose. In this sense, 'the voice of the people is but an echo', as V.O. Key (1966: 2) famously put it.

German unification led to significant changes in both longer-term and short-term factors. Some of the short-term factors are easy to identify: unification transformed the policy agenda, and a whole array of new policy problems affected the responses of political parties not only in the domestic arena (the question of re-integrating the eastern states economically and socially, for example) but also in Germany's international environment. In addition, research has identified changes in the longer-term factors. These changes had started before unification but were accelerated by it. Long-standing partisan attachments, often rooted in the voters' social backgrounds and in traditional social cleavages (Lipset and Rokkan 1967), had started to decline in western Germany since the late 1970s. Like other advanced democracies (Dalton and Wattenberg 2000), West Germany had begun to experience a process of partisan dealignment before unification. Aggregate levels of partisan attachment were reduced further by the fact that former East Germans were less likely to identify with political parties due to their own experience with the notion of 'party' during the SED's dictatorship in the German Democratic Republic (GDR) between 1949 and 1989 and their lack of attachment to the essentially western German parties dominating electoral politics after unification. Thus, unification increased the overall proportion of independents in the German electorate, although even today a majority of German voters hold partisan loyalties (Schoen and Weins 2005; Arzheimer 2006). Independent voters are more likely to abstain in elections, to make up their minds late in the election campaigns, and to switch parties from one election to the next. As the potential for electoral volatility has increased, party leaders have had stronger incentives to be responsive to voter demands and to compete for votes more intensely than in the past, when they could rely on a larger proportion of loyal core voters. Moreover, the electorate has become more heterogeneous in terms of the range of policy preferences. East Germans differ from West Germans in their values and policy orientations. As some kind of legacy, pro-socialist preferences are more pronounced and pro-Western views in foreign policy less pronounced in the east (Arzheimer and Falter 2013). In short, unification has thoroughly reshaped the environment for electoral competition.

As the top row in Table 7.1 records, electoral turnout rates varied between approximately 70 and 80 per cent between 1990 and 2013. The bottom part of Table 7.1 reveals some crucial west–east differences. The penultimate line demonstrates that turnout rates in the west have exceeded those in the east (the so-called *neue Bundesländer* or new Federal states) by between 3 and 8 percentage points in each election since 1990. This difference is likely to reflect the aforementioned differences in political predispositions. Irrespective of geographic differences, turnout in Federal elections has declined across the entire country since the early 1990s. Whereas turnout rates approached 80 per cent until 2005, they dropped to roughly 70 per cent in the 2009 and 2013 general elections. Not only have turnout rates varied between western and eastern Germany, the drop has been particularly pronounced in certain sociodemographic groups, that is, amongst low-status and poorly educated citizens (Schäfer 2011). Although German turnout rates are still not lower than those in comparable European democracies (Mair 2002; Steinbrecher *et al.* 2007), the development has led some scholars to consider compulsory voting (Schäfer 2011).

Eastern and western Germany differ not only in turnout, but also in terms of election outcomes. The bottom row of Table 7.1 shows the substantial west–east differences in party

Table 7.1 Results of the German federal elections, 1990–2013

	1990	1994	1998	2002	2005	2009	2013
Turnout (per cent)	77.8	79.0	82.2	79.1	77.7	70.8	71.5
CDU/CSU	43.8	41.4	35.1	38.5	35.2	33.8	41.5
SPD	33.5	36.4	40.9	38.5	34.2	23.0	25.7
FDP	11.0	6.9	6.2	7.4	9.8	14.6	4.8
Linke/PDS	2.4	4.4	5.1	4.0	8.7	11.9	8.6
Greens	5.1	7.3	6.7	8.6	8.1	10.7	8.4
AfD	–	–	–	–	–	–	4.7
Other	4.3	3.6	5.9	3.0	4.0	6.0	6.3
Volatility*	–	7.2	7.6	6.5	8.1	12.6	15.4
Fractionalisation**	0.32	0.32	0.30	0.31	0.27	0.22	0.26
West-East Differences							
Turnout***	4.1	7.9	2.8	7.8	4.2	7.5	4.8
Party shares****	14.5	18.8	23.8	18.4	22.7	20.5	19.8

* Volatility is the sum of differences in party shares between elections in t and t+1. To avoid counting shifts in electoral support twice the sum is divided by two (Pedersen 1979).
** Fractionalisation is the sum of the squared party shares in a given election (Laakso and Taagepera 1979).
*** This difference is calculated by subtracting east German turnout from west German turnout.
**** The difference in party shares is calculated analogously to electoral volatility.

Note: Treating smaller parties as the single category 'others' in the table above leads to conservative estimates of volatility, fractionalisation, and regional differences.

shares. Remarkably, this difference has not begun to decrease since 1990, reflecting, first and foremost, the much larger electoral support for the PDS (until 2005), The Left Party/PDS (2005–07), and its successor, The Left (since 2007), in eastern Germany. This east–west difference was not diminished after The Left Party/PDS's merger with the WASG (Schoen and Falter 2005). As a kind of mirror image of the strong electoral performance of The Left and its predecessor parties in the east, the remaining main parties have, in most elections, been considerably more successful in western Germany.

Before 1983, Germany's party system was often described as a 'two-and-a-half party system'. When the Greens overcame the 5 per cent threshold for the first time in 1983, the system was referred to as a 'two-block system' with the CDU/CSU and the FDP to the right of the political centre and the SPD and Greens to its left (Saalfeld 2005). The underlying trend towards a more fractionalised party system has become more pronounced since 2000 (e.g. Niedermayer 2011) and can be tracked in the results for the political parties in general elections (table 7.1). In the three general elections of the 1990s, at least one of the two major parties, the CDU/CSU or the SPD, gained more than 40 per cent of the votes. Between them, the two major parties tended to attract some 75 to 80 per cent. The three smaller parties represented in the Bundestag – the FDP, the Greens, and the PDS – received some 15 to 20 per cent in aggregate. In the three general elections after 2000, electoral support for the CDU/CSU and SPD dropped considerably. In 2005 their combined vote amounted to less than 70 per cent. In 2009 it dropped to less than 57 per cent. Electoral support for the Social Democrats eroded precipitously from some 40 per cent in 1998 to approximately 25 per cent in 2009 and 2013. There is now an asymmetry between the SPD and the CDU/CSU, as the latter appears to have recovered, at least momentarily, from its previous electoral decline.

While support for the traditional catch-all parties declined, the proportion of votes cast for smaller parties increased. In the 2005 and 2009 elections, the electoral strength of the three small parties in the Bundestag increased by sizeable margins. In the 2013 election, the trend towards increased electoral fractionalisation continued as the new, anti-euro party Alternative für Deutschland (AfD) narrowly failed to achieve the 5 per cent minimum. These changes in voting behaviour have had considerable effects on the process of government formation. Since 2005 the traditional two-party coalitions consisting of one of the major and one of the smaller parties have become difficult or even impossible to form. Between 2005 and 2009 and since 2013, so-called 'grand coalitions' of the two major parties have formed the government, an arrangement that was previously a rarity (between 1949 and 2005 a 'grand coalition' had only once been created in the Federal Republic, in 1966–9). In addition, parties have begun to consider hitherto unusual three-party coalitions, some of which (e.g. coalitions of the Christian Democrats and Greens) would cross the traditional boundaries between the centre-left and centre-right 'camps'.

This trend towards a more fractionalised party system at the electoral level has been accompanied by a considerable, and increasing, level of electoral volatility. Volatility can be measured at the aggregate level of the party system as an index (the Pedersen index, named after its creator, Mogens Pedersen; see Pedersen 1979) that sums up all gains and losses of the competing parties and divides this sum by two. It provides a rough indication of net changes in party strengths. Volatility can also be measured at the level of the individual voters, indicating how many voters switch their vote choice from one election to the next. In the 1990s, net aggregate volatility equalled approximately seven percentage points, indicating a relatively moderate electoral turnover from one election to the next. Between the elections of 2005 and 2009, however, aggregate volatility increased rapidly, and in 2013 it reached an all-time high unmatched since the founding period of the Federal Republic between 1949 and 1957. That means that the result of an election can no longer be predicted from the result of preceding elections with the kind of accuracy that was possible for most elections after the late 1950s.

The increase in net aggregate volatility is accompanied by changes suggesting higher levels of inter-election volatility in individual-level voting behaviour. Whereas before 1990 only around 10 per cent of voters switched parties from one election to the next, the proportion of 'party switchers' increased to at least 30 per cent in the 2009 election (Schoen 2003: 130–51; Weßels 2011: 47). In addition, there is a considerable number of voters switching from abstention in one election to voting for a party in the next and then back to abstention (Rattinger and Schoen 2009). From this perspective, the low levels of turnout and the high levels of volatility in the 2009 and 2013 elections are correlated. It is worth noting that turnout is even lower and volatility considerably higher than at the Federal level when it comes to so-called 'second-order elections' at the regional, local, or European levels (Steinbrecher et al. 2007). In a nutshell, continuity in election outcomes in Germany has declined, leading to growing uncertainty for parties and regarding government formation.

And voters have become more volatile in the run-up to elections, although not to the same extent as previously thought (Plischke 2014). A considerable number of voters waver and change voting intentions during election campaigns. The share of voters who make their voting decision immediately before, or on, election day has increased, adding a degree of uncertainty to survey-based forecasts. At the same time as participation in elections has ceased to be considered a citizen's duty for many Germans, some voters not only consider a broader range of parties than in the past, but also waver between abstention and voting for a party. As a result, there is considerable potential for campaign efforts and unforeseen events during the campaigns to affect individual voting behaviour and election outcomes.

Increases in inter- and intra-election volatility sit well with the notion that (loosening) longer-term partisan ties have given way to an increasing influence of short-term factors. In an era of personalised campaigning and media attention, the increasing impact of variables capturing 'candidate orientations' on vote choice seems a plausible consequence. The evidence, however, is far from supporting this expectation unequivocally. To be sure, candidates play an important role in campaigns. The US-style televised debates between chancellor candidates that have featured in German election campaigns since 2002 are a case in point. Attitudes towards candidates (for the chancellorship) have certainly been shown to affect individual vote choice (Ohr et al. 2013; Wagner 2011); but the evidence suggests that the impact of candidate evaluations on individual-level vote choice and aggregate election outcomes is not overwhelming, and is by and large confined to independents (Brettschneider 2002; Ohr et al. 2013). What is more, there is little evidence of a steady increase in candidate effects in unified Germany. Rather, the evidence is more in line with the notion that the weight of voters' evaluations of candidates, and the impact of such evaluations on a party's success, varies in response to election-specific factors (Ohr et al. 2013; Schoen 2011).

Another hypothesis might be that voters' issue orientations (how they see the parties' positions and competencies on particular issues) are filling the void left by loosening partisan ties. Political issues and policy pledges (e.g. in party manifestos) play a considerable role in campaigns and do affect voting behaviour, whether for symbolic or for instrumental reasons (Sears et al. 1979). The election of 2002 provided some good illustrations of the potentially decisive role of certain policy issues. Schröder attracted many votes by having himself portrayed as an effective crisis manager following the Elbe flood disaster and by opposing the participation of German troops in the war against Iraq (Schoen 2004; Bechtel and Hainmueller 2011). In a negative effect, the liberal reforms of the German welfare state that Chancellor Schröder initiated after that election of 2002 led to the formation and electoral success of The Left Party (Schoen and Falter 2005).

This anti-welfare state reform is likely to have contributed to the electoral decline of the SPD since 2005. Despite anecdotal evidence, it cannot be taken for granted that even far-reaching policy changes play a role in voting behaviour, however. Two examples suffice to illustrate this point. Whereas German troops were not sent abroad for military missions before unification, unified Germany has witnessed considerable policy change in the field of military engagement e.g. participation in the war in Kosovo in 1999 and in the war in Afghanistan in the aftermath of the terrorist attacks on 9/11 (see Chapters 25 and 26). Yet neither mission affected voting behaviour or election outcomes significantly (Schoen 2010, 2011). Moreover, as a member of the European Monetary Union (EMU), Germany replaced the German mark with the euro. Given the significance of the mark as a symbol of national pride, replacing the national currency with a common European currency could have been expected to be a vote loser. As a matter of fact, the replacement of the mark by the euro as well as the introduction of and major changes to the European Monetary Union affected voting behaviour and electoral outcomes in Federal and European elections moderately at most (see Pappi and Thurner 2000). The reason for these findings is simple: these policy changes had the support of all mainstream parties, meaning that voters had little choice on euro-related issues at election time. Nonetheless, the electoral success of The Left in response to Schröder's Hartz reforms and of the anti-euro AfD in 2013 suggests that there are limitations to a strategy of depoliticising important political issues. It remains to be seen whether this and other issues will affect vote choice in future elections.

Policy changes have also affected the relationship between voting behaviour and social divisions. Traditionally, the CDU/CSU was the choice of (Catholic) Christian voters whereas the SPD was the preferred party of (unionised) workers and the less well-to-do. The latter alignment has weakened over the years – and has now finally been transformed. In response to the Hartz reforms, The Left managed to gain increasing support amongst those social groups that were formerly core supporters of the SPD (Elff and Roßteutscher 2011). Although the electoral affinity of Christians and the CDU/CSU has turned out to be more robust, it also appears to respond to short-term factors such as candidates and policy decisions (Elff and Roßteutscher 2011). As a result, voting behaviour is still related to social divisions, but the nature of the relationship has changed. To a certain extent, traditional affinities have given way to new alliances (see also Müller and Klein 2012). With regard to social divisions and voting behaviour, short-term forces have become more important at the expense of long-term attachments, thereby rendering the relationship less robust and more vulnerable (Schoen 2005).

Given the trend towards a more fractionalised party system and more volatility, forming coalition governments after an election has become both riskier and more complicated for political parties. It is no longer guaranteed that traditional ideologically coherent two-party coalitions will be viable; and (unlike in Austria) grand coalitions are not considered acceptable over longer periods. So, parties (have to) consider new types of coalitions. For voters, it thus becomes less predictable which coalition government will be formed after an election and how their vote for a specific party may influence government formation. In effect, making electoral decisions is likely to become more complicated for voters because they may have to consider coalition preferences and the viability of various coalitions (Bytzek 2013). Moreover, if voters deliberately take coalitions into account when deciding for whom to vote, they may feel disappointed when parties form coalitions their voters do not like. As a result, the trend towards a more fractionalised party system has repercussions for individual-level voting behaviour and the interplay between parties and voters.

In sum, voting behaviour in unified Germany has undergone considerable changes. The process of partisan dealignment has not yet come to an end – there are no signs of a realignment. As a result, electoral participation and voting behaviour are less predictable. This provides parties with strong incentives for intense campaigns, and has led to considerable shifts in the party system. The first shifts took place between the traditional parties represented in the Bundestag; more recently, new political entrepreneurs such as the founders of the AfD appear to be attracting votes from dissatisfied citizens. The decreasing predictability and the increasing fluidity of voting behaviour are thus likely to have repercussions for the party system. In the end, these developments may change the rules of the game for political parties and the interplay of parties and voters in Germany.

Shrinking membership organisations

The Social and the Christian Democrats have traditionally relied on large membership organisations for the recruitment and training of their leadership personnel, including their candidates for electoral contests (Klein *et al.* 2011). This continued to be the case after 1990. And although political parties have increasingly made use of professional agencies in their electoral campaigns (Katz and Mair 2002), their members on the ground are still considered to be a crucial resource in fighting campaigns, both in terms of manpower and to maintain a credible presence across the country. Nevertheless, studies of party membership decline since 1990 observe the growing fluidity and unpredictability of voting behaviour since 1990.

In the mid–1970s, all three major German parties – the Christian Democratic parties (CDU and CSU) as well as the Social Democrats (SPD) – maintained extensive membership organisations. In 1976 and 1977 the SPD had over a million members on the territory of the 'old' Federal Republic. Its membership has steadily declined since, a decline that has accelerated since the late 1990s. By the end of 2012, the SPD's membership had halved to approximately 477,000. The Christian Democrats' membership continued to grow between the mid–1970s and the early 1980s, but then also began to decline. Unlike the SPD, the CDU's membership benefited from German unification. The party had had a 'sister' organisation in the German Democratic Republic, and the Christian Democrats' membership therefore received a certain boost following unification; but it, too, has declined since. At the end of 2012, the CDU had approximately 476,000 members, with almost 148,000 in the CSU. Nevertheless, the rate of decline experienced by the Christian Democrats has been lower than for the SPD.

Figure 7.1 expresses the Bundestag parties' aggregate membership as a percentage of the population eligible to join a party (all residents, irrespective of citizenship, of 16 years of age or older). The bars in the diagram illustrate that aggregate party membership has nearly halved between 1990 and the end of 2011: in 1990 approximately 3.65 per cent of all German residents were members of a mainstream party (CDU, SPD, CSU, FDP, Greens, or PDS). By the end of 2011, this percentage had dropped to 1.86 (with The Left replacing the PDS).

This decline has had important practical consequences. The smaller parties have never been able to rely on their activists as strongly as the larger parties when it comes to fighting countrywide electoral campaigns. Their presence on the ground has always been relatively weak, especially in the larger, less densely populated area of the northeast such as the rural parts of Lower Saxony, Mecklenburg-West Pomerania, and Brandenburg. Although the SPD and CDU/CSU are still able to draw on a relatively dense network of activists in the larger western German states (especially Baden-Württemberg, Bavaria, Hesse, and North Rhine-Westphalia) and the city states of Berlin, Hamburg, and Bremen (Niedermayer 2012), their presence in other areas, especially in eastern Germany, has become less extensive. In such regions, even the larger parties cannot rely on their local associations to run campaigns and show a credible presence. In these areas, in particular, the parties have moved more closely towards the ideal-typical model of so-called 'electoral-professional' parties (Panebianco 1988), a type of organisation that tends

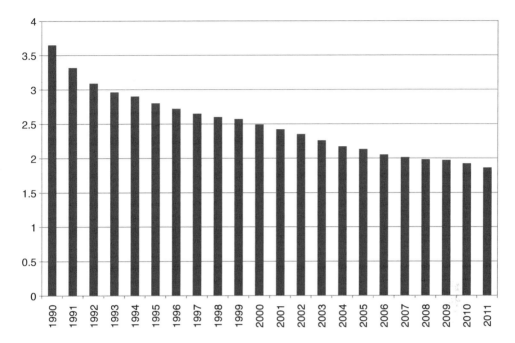

Figure 7.1 Membership of the German mainstream parties as percentage of eligible persons over the age of 16, 1990–2011

Source: authors' own analysis. Data extracted from Niedermayer (2013: 3).

Note: Parties included are: CDU, SPD, CSU, FDP, Greens, PDS/Left Party/The Left

to rely less on its membership organisation on the ground than on professional agencies outside the party for campaigning purposes. In particular, the electoral-professional party depends heavily on the public trust enjoyed by party leaders and the funds and expertise that can be accessed by their representatives in the national or regional parliaments (Grabow 2000).

A number of parties have sought to respond to the loss of membership on the ground by modernising their organisations. In the main, these reforms have been intended to increase the attractiveness of party membership by strengthening the powers of grassroots members within the parties. In some cases, parties have sought to enhance their attractiveness by opening up policy debates to non-members, or encouraging looser forms of association below the level of formal membership. Such reforms have taken place in all parties, albeit to varying degrees. In the CDU, organisational changes in the early 2000s led to an increasing involvement of party members in candidate selection, and to a lesser extent in leadership selection. The CDU's grassroots members, however, still have relatively little say in policy decisions, which remain the prerogative of formal party associations and representative party organs (Turner 2013: 127). Other parties have gone further. Three examples of manifesto formation prior to the election of 2013 illustrate these developments.

The FDP has used web-based platforms for programme discussion since 2002. For its 2013 manifesto, the party introduced an internet-based tool to make its draft manifesto available for public discussion. Registered users (members and non-members alike) were invited to suggest amendments, and the move had considerable public resonance. Also, intra-party groups within the FDP have become more likely to force membership ballots on substantive policy issues on to the agenda. The FDP's 2011 membership ballot on a proposal rejecting the European stability mechanism (ESM) ended with a narrow victory for the party leadership, which opposed the proposal, but is an example of growing membership involvement (Hornsteiner and Saalfeld 2014).

The SPD, too, has strengthened the voice of non-members as well as members in its procedures. In its organisational reform of 2011, the party lowered the threshold for groups seeking ballots of the entire membership for leadership elections and important policy decisions. In the run-up to the 2013 election, the SPD launched a 'citizens' dialogue' (*Bürgerdialog*), in which the party called on the public to propose policy reforms. Although the manifesto was ultimately adopted by a conference of party delegates in April 2013, the strategy of increasing participation was designed to reach out beyond traditional party members. A further example of the increased emphasis on meaningful membership participation is the SPD's membership ballot on the coalition agreement negotiated with the Christian Democrats in 2013 (Hornsteiner and Saalfeld 2014).

For the Green Party, direct grassroots participation and a high level of leadership accountability have traditionally been characteristic organisational features. In the run-up to the 2013 election, the party held a membership ballot on the choice of national lead candidates (one female, one male) for the election. In a highly competitive election, party members chose two candidates from a pool of 15 contenders. In the same election, the party's leadership involved grassroots members closely in the process of manifesto writing. The members' votes led to unexpected results both in manifesto formulation and the leadership elections (Hornsteiner and Saalfeld 2014).

The extent and intensity of intra-party debates over candidates and policy demonstrated a 'thirst' for meaningful participation at the parties' grassroots and suggests that the parties' reforms have been at least partially successful in tackling the trend towards membership apathy.

Stable parties in elected office

Despite considerable changes in the electoral environment and memberships of political parties, the 'party in government' at the parliamentary level has remained surprisingly unaffected: despite a complex political space, with many risks for coalition formation, cabinet stability has remained remarkably high since the early 1970s. The refragmentation of the party system in the country and in parliament has not jeopardised stability. Despite considerable economic shocks (such as the banking crisis of 2008–09 and the subsequent sovereign debt crisis in the eurozone) and growing electoral volatility, governments have remained stable, not least due to the stability of the parties in public office: in the Bundestag, parties have shown a high degree of unity, with no significant splits or breakaways at the parliamentary level. All cabinets since 1983 save one (the second Schröder cabinet in 2002–05) have served out their full four-year terms in government. This is in stark contrast to the simultaneous experience of considerable cabinet instability in other European multiparty systems (Saalfeld 2013: 65).

How can we explain this discrepancy between growing fluidity at the electoral and membership level, on the one hand, and continuing stability at the parliamentary and governmental level, on the other? Katz and Mair (1995) offer an influential explanation, arguing that many European parties have compensated for their weakening ties with voters and civil society by partially suspending competition and by jointly appropriating more and more state funds such as public subsidies in a 'cartel' of established parties. Despite some differences in emphasis, this answer is partly compatible with Panebianco's (1988) claim that we have witnessed a rise of the 'electoral-professional party' as a model of party organisation, whereby political life within the party is strongly dominated by a professional leadership in the governmental sphere, supported by professional agencies rather than rank-and-file members.

There is some support for Katz's and Mair's argument if we consider the public funding parliamentary parties receive in Germany. In January 2010, for example, the five parliamentary parties in the Bundestag were able to employ a total of 870 staff from public funds, 397 of whom occupied university degree-level positions. The total amount of funding available to the legislative parties in that year was over €78.7 million. This was in addition to the 4,209 publicly funded staff members employed by members individually, and has allowed the parliamentary leadership and the 'party in public office' to maintain a certain degree of autonomy from the more volatile voters, the (declining number of) extra-parliamentary activists, and collateral interest groups such as trades unions or church-based organisations (Hassel and Trampusch 2006).

In addition to organisational and institutional arguments, the so-called 'median-voter theorem' points to a further, strategic reason for the continued strength of the major parties. This theorem cannot be explained fully in this chapter (for a brief non-technical explanation see Hornsteiner and Saalfeld 2014; for a fuller treatment with regard to coalition governments see Laver and Shepsle 1996). Nevertheless, the key idea is intuitively plausible: large and cohesive political parties occupying the centre ground of the political spectrum across the main dimensions of policy conflict are in a particularly influential position when it comes to coalition formation. Because of their political centrality, they are more likely than extreme parties to be included in government coalitions. Most important, they are in a strong bargaining position, because they tend to be able to choose between competing coalition partners to their left and to their right. Since all new contenders in the Bundestag have appeared on the ideological extremes (the Greens in 1983, the PDS in 1990, and The Left in 2009), one of the established centrist parties has always remained in this strong bargaining position. Despite the changes in the party system and growing fluidity at the electoral level, therefore, one of the established parties has thus far always controlled the parliamentary median. Hence, although electoral support for the main parties has eroded, and although voters have become more volatile, the main parties have retained as much power over policy as in times when they had in excess of 45 per cent of the vote (Lees 2013; Hornsteiner and Saalfeld 2014).

Conclusions

The German party system has experienced considerable change since the 1990s. Voters have become more critical and volatile. As a result, the party system has become more fragmented and fluid. Not only has the parties' electoral base eroded, but so has their membership. These developments in the 'party-in-the-electorate' and the 'party on the ground' have resulted largely from economic and social changes in the environment of political parties (see Dalton and Wattenberg 2000). Inglehart (1997) and others have demonstrated that this is not a German peculiarity. Crucially for this chapter, political parties have responded to these trends in at least four ways. First, they have compensated for their more uncertain electoral and organisational environment by accessing state funds in line with the cartel-party thesis advanced by Katz and Mair (1995). This has effectively strengthened the party in public office at the expense of the party as organisation. Second, they have built up more professional campaign organisations, as electoral campaigns have become more decisive for electoral outcomes. Third, they have become more sophisticated strategic players in the policy space that constitutes the battleground for party competition in German politics. Finally, some parties have opened up their organisations to non-members and have enhanced opportunities for membership participation within their organisations.

While greater volatility, in particular, has increased the political uncertainty for Germany's party leaders, this may be an attractive development from a normative perspective: more than in the past, voters are actually choosing, and calling government parties to account for their performance. The 1998 election was the first postwar election where the voters' choices led to a complete change of government parties (rather than a change in government through changing post-electoral choices of coalition arrangements by party leaders). The electoral losses suffered by the SPD in 2005 and 2009 were in direct response to the party's involvement in unpopular welfare reforms during the preceding parliaments. The FDP's ejection from the Bundestag in 2013 also demonstrates this increased level of electoral accountability for (perceived or real) poor performance in government. As a result, very long episodes of stable government by the same parties (such as Adenauer's various coalitions dominated by the CDU/CSU between 1949 and 1963, or Kohl's reign at the helm of a CDU/CSU-FDP coalition in 1982–98) are less likely to occur. With the exception of the 1990, 1994, and 2002 elections, the party composition of the German government has changed after each of the seven general elections since unification. In short, alternation in government has increased.

However, this new fluidity does not come without electoral and organisational risks to the parties. In particular, coalition formation between the parties has become more difficult. It is likely that the national parties will follow patterns explored at the regional and local levels, where coalitions across the traditional divide between centre-right and centre-left have become more common in recent years. These may include coalitions between the SPD and The Left at the national level, an option ruled out by the Social Democrats between 1990 and 2013. They may also include coalitions between the Christian Democrats and the Greens. A CDU-Green coalition failed in the state of Hamburg in 2010 but was formed again in Hesse in 2013, in an event widely perceived as a test case for a future national coalition. Such new coalitions will not be without costs, however: they may lead to more controversies within the parties, and they may contribute to severe electoral penalties in situations where parties lose credibility due to costly coalition agreements.

Note

1   In the transitional period of 1989–90 the party was known as SED-PDS. In 1990 the SED-PDS experienced an almost complete change of leadership and was renamed PDS. The PDS, in turn, was renamed Linkspartei.PDS in 2005.

Bibliography

Arzheimer, K. (2006) '"Dead Men Walking?" Party Identification in Germany, 1977–2002', *Electoral Studies*, 25: 791–807.

Arzheimer, K. and Falter, J.W. (2013) 'Versöhnen statt spalten? Das Ergebnis der Bundestagswahl 2009 und die Rolle der PDS/Linkspartei in Ost-West-Perspektive', in B. Weßels, H. Schoen, and O.W. Gabriel (eds) *Wahlen und Wähler. Analysen aus Anlass der Bundestagswahl 2009*, Wiesbaden: VS Verlag für Sozialwissenschaften, 118–50.

Bartels, L. (2002) 'Beyond the running tally: partisan bias in political perceptions', *Political Behavior*, 24(2): 117–50.

Bechtel, M.M. and Hainmueller J. (2011) 'How Lasting is Voter Gratitude? An Analysis of the Short- and Long-Term Electoral Returns of Beneficial Policy', *American Journal of Political Science*, 55(4): 852–68.

Bräuninger, T. and Debus, M. (2012) *Parteienwettbewerb in den deutschen Bundesländern*, Wiesbaden: Springer VS.

Brettschneider, F. (2002) *Spitzenkandidaten und Wahlerfolg – Personalisierung, Kompetenz, Parteien: Ein internationaler Vergleich*, Wiesbaden: Westdeutscher Verlag.

Bytzek, E. (2013) 'Koalitionspräferenzen, Koalitionswahl und Regierungsbildung', in B. Weßels, H. Schoen, and O.W. Gabriel (eds) *Wahlen und Wähler: Analysen aus Anlass der Bundestagswahl 2009*, Wiesbaden: VS Verlag für Sozialwissenschaften, 231–46.

Bytzek, E. and Roßteutscher, S. (eds) (2011) *Der unbekannte Wähler: Mythen und Fakten über das Wahlverhalten der Deutschen*, Frankfurt a.m.: Campus.

Campbell, A., Converse, P.E., Miller, W.E., and Stokes, D.E. (1960) *The American Voter*, New York: Wiley.

Dalton, R.J. and Wattenberg, M.P. (eds) (2000) *Parties without Partisans: Political Change in Advanced Industrial Democracies*, Oxford: Oxford University Press.

Elff, M. and Roßteutscher, S. (2011) 'Stability or Decline? Class, Religion and the Vote in Germany', *German Politics*, 20(1): 107–27.

Epstein, L. (1979) *Political Parties in Western Democracies*, New Brunswick, NJ: Transaction Publishers.

Grabow, K. (2000) *Abschied von der Massenpartei: Die Entwicklung der Organisationsmuster von SPD und CDU seit der Deutschen Vereinigung*, Wiesbaden: Deutscher Universitäts-Verlag.

Hassel, A. and Trampusch, C. (2006) 'Verbände und Parteien: Die Dynamik von Parteikonflikten und die Erosion des Korporatismus', in J. Beckert, B. Ebbinghaus, A. Hassel, and P. Manow (eds) *Transformationen des Kapitalismus: Festschrift für Wolfgang Streeck zum sechzigsten Geburtstag*, Frankfurt a.m.: Campus, 111–32.

Hornsteiner, M. and Saalfeld, T. (2014) 'Parties and Party System', in S. Padgett, W.E. Paterson, and R. Zohlnhöfer (eds) *Developments in German Politics 4*, Basingstoke: Palgrave Macmillan.

Inglehart, R (1997) *Modernization and Postmodernization. Cultural, Economic, and Political Change in 43 Societies*, Princeton: Princeton University Press.

Katz, R.S. and Mair, P. (1995) 'Changing Models of Party Organization and Party Democracy. The Emergence of the Cartel Party', *Party Politics*, 1(1): 5–28.

Katz, R.S. and Mair, P. (2002) 'The Ascendancy of the Party in Public Office: Party Organizational Change in Twentieth-Century Democracies', in R. Gunther, J. Montero, and J. Kinz. (eds) *Political Parties: Old Concepts and New Challenges*, Oxford: Oxford University Press, 113–35.

Key, V.O. (1964) *Politics, Parties and Pressure Groups*, 5th edn, New York: Crowell.

Key, V.O. (1966) *The Responsible Electorate: Rationality in Presidential Voting, 1936–1960*, Cambridge: Harvard University Press.

Klein, M., von Alemann, U., and Spier, T. (2011) 'Warum brauchen Parteien Mitglieder?', in T. Spier, M. Klein, U. von Alemann, H. Hoffmann, A. Laux, A. Nonnenmacher, and K. Rohrbach (eds), *Parteimitglieder in Deutschland*, Wiesbaden: VS Verlag für Sozialwissenschaften, 19–30.

Laakso, M. and Taagepera, R. (1979) 'The "Effective" Number of Parties: A Measure with Application to West Europe', *Comparative Political Studies*, 12(1): 3–27.

Laver, M. and Shepsle, K. (1996) *Making and Breaking Governments: Cabinets and Legislatures in Parliamentary Democracies*, Cambridge: Cambridge University Press.

Lees, C. (2013) 'Christian Democracy is Dead: Long Live the Union Parties: Explaining CDU/CSU Dominance within the German Party System', *German Politics* 22(1–2): 64–81.

Lipset, S.M. and Rokkan, S. (1967) 'Cleavage Structures, Party Systems, and Voter Alignments: An Introduction', in S.M. Lipset and S. Rokkan (eds) *Party Systems and Voter Alignments: Cross-National Perspectives*, London: The Free Press.

Lodge, M. and Taber, C.S. (2013) *The Rationalizing Voter*, Cambridge: Cambridge University Press.

Mair, P. (2002) 'In the Aggregate: Mass Electoral Behaviour in Western Europe, 1950–2000', in H. Keman (ed.) *Comparative Democratic Politics*, London: SAGE, 122–42.

Müller, W. and Klein, M. (2012) 'Die Klassenbasis in der Parteipräferenz des deutschen Wählers: Erosion oder Wandel?', in R. Schmitt-Beck (ed.) *Wählen in Deutschland*, PVS-Sonderheft 45, Baden-Baden: Nomos, 85–110.

Niedermayer, O. (2011) 'Das deutsche Parteiensystem nach der Bundestagswahl 2009', in O. Niedermayer (ed.) *Die Parteien nach der Bundestagswahl 2009*, Wiesbaden: VS Verlag für Sozialwissenschaften, 7–35.

Niedermayer, O. (2012) 'Parteimitgliedschaften im Jahre 2011', *Zeitschrift für Parlamentsfragen*, 43(2): 389–407.

Niedermayer, O. (2013) *Parteimitglieder in Deutschland: Version 2013*, Arbeitshefte aus dem Otto-Stammer-Zentrum, 20, Berlin: Freie Universität Berlin.

Ohr, D., Klein, M., and Rosar, U. (2013) 'Bewertungen der Kanzlerkandidaten und Wahlentscheidung bei der Bundestagswahl 2009', in B. Weßels, H. Schoen, and O. W. Gabriel (eds) *Wahlen und Wähler: Analysen aus Anlass der Bundestagswahl 2009*, Wiesbaden: VS Verlag für Sozialwissenschaften, 206–30.

Panebianco, A. (1988) *Political Parties: Organization and Power*, Cambridge: Cambridge University Press.

Pappi, F.U. (1984) 'The West German Party System', *West European Politics*, 7(4): 7–26.

Pappi, F.U. and Thurner, P. (2000) 'Die deutschen Wähler und der Euro: Auswirkungen auf die Bundestagswahl 1998?', *Politische Vierteljahresschrift*, 41: 435–65.

Pedersen, M.N. (1979) 'The Dynamics of European Party Systems: Changing Patterns of Electoral Volatility', *European Journal of Political Research*, 7: 1–26.

Plischke, T. (2014) *Wann Wähler entscheiden: Abläufe von Entscheidungsprozessen und der Zeitpunkt der Wahlentscheidung*, Baden-Baden: Nomos.

Rattinger, H. and Schoen, H. (2009) 'Ein Schritt vorwärts und zwei zurück? Stabiles und wechselndes Wahlverhalten bei den Bundestagswahlen 1994 bis 2005', in O.W. Gabriel, B. Weßels, and J. W. Falter (eds) *Wahlen und Wähler. Analysen aus Anlass der Bundestagswahl 2005*, Wiesbaden: VS Verlag für Sozialwissenschaften, 78–103.

Saalfeld, T. (2005) 'Political Parties', in S. Green and W.E. Paterson (eds) *Governance in Contemporary Germany: The Semisovereign State Revisited*, Cambridge: Cambridge University Press, 46–77.

Saalfeld, T. (2013) 'Economic Performance, Political Institutions and Cabinet Durability in 28 European Parliamentary Democracies, 1945–2011', in W.C. Müller and H.-M. Narud (eds) *Party Governance and Party Democracy*, New York: Springer, 51–79.

Sartori, G. (1976) *Parties and party systems: A framework for analysis*, Cambridge: Cambridge University Press.

Schäfer, A. (2011) 'Der Nichtwähler als Durchschnittsbürger: Ist die sinkende Wahlbeteiligung eine Gefahr für die Demokratie?' in E. Bytzek and S. Roßteutscher (eds) *Der unbekannte Wähler: Mythen und Fakten über das Wahlverhalten der Deutschen*, Frankfurt a.m.: Campus, 133–54.

Schmitt-Beck, R. (ed.) (2011) *Wählen in Deutschland*, PVS-Sonderheft 45, Baden-Baden: Nomos.

Schoen, H. (2003) *Wählerwandel und Wechselwahl: Eine vergleichende Untersuchung*, Wiesbaden: Westdeutscher Verlag.

Schoen, H. (2004) 'Der Kanzler, zwei Sommerthemen und ein Foto-Finish. Priming-Effekte bei der Bundestagswahl 2002', in F. Brettschneider, J. van Deth, and E. Roller (eds) *Die Bundestagswahl 2002: Analysen der Wahlergebnisse und des Wahlkampfes*, Wiesbaden: Westdeutscher Verlag, 23–50.

Schoen, H. (2005) 'Soziologische Ansätze in der empirischen Wahlforschung', in J.W. Falter and H. Schoen (eds) *Handbuch Wahlforschung*, Wiesbaden: VS Verlag für Sozialwissenschaften, 135–85.

Schoen, H. (2010) 'Ein Bericht von der Heimatfront. Bürger, Politiker und der Afghanistaneinsatz der Bundeswehr', *Politische Vierteljahresschrift*, 51: 395–408.

Schoen, H. (2011) 'Two Indicators, One Conclusion: On the Public Salience of Foreign Affairs in Pre- and Post-Unification Germany', in K. Oppermann and H. Viehrig (eds) *Issue Salience in International Politics*, New York: Routledge, 23–38.

Schoen, H. and Falter, J.W. (2005) 'Die Linkspartei und ihre Wähler', *Aus Politik und Zeitgeschichte*, B/51–2: 33–40.

Schoen, H. and Weins, C. (2005) 'Der sozialpsychologische Ansatz zur Erklärung von Wahlverhalten', in J.W. Falter and H. Schoen (eds) *Handbuch Wahlforschung*, Wiesbaden: VS Verlag für Sozialwissenschaften, 187–242.

Sears, D.O., Hensler, C.P., and Speer, L.K. (1979) 'Whites' Opposition to "Busing": Self-Interest or Symbolic Politics?' *American Political Science Review*, 73: 369–84.

Steinbrecher, M., Huber, S., and Rattinger, H. (2007) *Turnout in Germany: Citizen Participation in State, Federal, and European Elections since 1979*, Baden-Baden: Nomos.

Turner, E. (2013) 'The CDU and Party Organisational Change', *German Politics*, 22(1–2): 114–33.

Wagner, A. (2011) 'Die Personalisierung der Politik: Entscheiden Spitzenkandidaten Wahlen?' in E. Bytzek and S. Roßteutscher (eds) *Der unbekannte Wähler: Mythen und Fakten über das Wahlverhalten der Deutschen*, Frankfurt a.m.: Campus, 81–97.

Wagner, A. and Weßels, B. (2012) 'Kanzlerkandidaten – Wie beeinflussen sie die Wahlentscheidung?' in R. Schmitt-Beck (ed.) *Wählen in Deutschland*, PVS-Sonderheft 45, Baden-Baden: Nomos, 345–70.

Weßels, B. (2011) 'Schwankende Wähler: Gefährden Wechselwähler die Demokratie?' in E. Bytzek and S. Roßteutscher (eds) *Der unbekannte Wähler: Mythen und Fakten über das Wahlverhalten der Deutschen*, Frankfurt a.m.: Campus, 43–57.

Weßels, B., Schoen, H., and Gabriel, O.W. (eds) (2013) *Wahlen und Wähler: Analysen aus Anlass der Bundestagswahl 2009*, Wiesbaden: VS Verlag für Sozialwissenschaften.

8

Citizenship

Helen Williams

The partition of Germany following World War II, combined with the historical movement of ethnic Germans and the frequent changes to Germany's borders in the preceding century, led to a configuration of citizenship in Germany that diverged significantly from European norms. Until 2000, Germany had no provisions for acquisition of German nationality by birth on German soil (*ius soli*), while most European countries at least had provisions for double *ius soli*, whereby a child born to non-national parents also born in the country would have access to that country's nationality, effectively granting citizenship automatically to third-generation immigrants.[1] German citizenship, by contrast, was inherited almost exclusively through the bloodline (*ius sanguinis*). Historically, Germany has been a country of emigration, and there is a clear trend for countries that are net exporters of migrants to regulate nationality through *ius sanguinis* (Koslowski 2000).[2] However, this does not explain Germany's avoidance of naturalisation and *ius soli* citizenship.

Naturalisation of postwar immigrants was until 2000 the exception rather than the norm, with naturalisation being granted only after extensive criteria had been met and then at the discretion of the authorities. High barriers to naturalisation were augmented by a ban on dual nationality for naturalisation candidates, requiring applicants to give up their current nationality in order to acquire German nationality. That created conflicts with property and travel rights for Germany's immigrant population: for example, if Turkish immigrants in Germany gave up their Turkish nationality they faced being banned from inheriting in Turkey and also needing a visa to visit extended family there. On the other hand, children born to parents with two nationalities were allowed to keep both throughout their lives.

Germany's wider self-conception has been *not* as a country of immigration, despite its postwar policy of recruiting foreign workers (see Chapter 12). That continued denial, alongside steady immigration and very favourable citizenship policies towards ethnic Germans, has been a hallmark of Germany's historical outlier status.[3] But since the unification of the Federal Republic of Germany (FRG) with the German Democratic Republic (GDR) in 1989, the emerging 'Berlin Republic' has embarked on a general process of normalisation, leading to widespread policy convergence with European norms.

This chapter first tracks the evolution of the status of ethnic Germans, addressing the legal framework, the statistical trends for ethnic German repatriation, and the gradual curtailment of privileges. It then addresses the situation of non-Germans within Germany's borders, detailing the liberalisation of citizenship policy that has led to higher levels of naturalisation. The final section explores how these changes show Germany adjusting to European norms in order to bring its policies into line with convention requirements, especially those of the European Convention on Nationality.

Ethnic Germans

Since 1990, German nationality law has changed considerably, with increasing liberalisation of the regulations for non-ethnic German foreigners and restrictions on repatriating Germans. This chapter deals first with the repatriates, presenting the laws and regulations concerning their return and tracking the changes and statistical developments in the repatriation of ethnic Germans. This is followed by a discussion of the changing position of non-ethnic German foreigners in German law. The shifts in both cases show a tendency towards conformity to European norms concerning national membership, though Germany's continued (formal) rejection of dual nationality remains perhaps the greatest hurdle to the incorporation of its longstanding immigrant populations and will likely continue to be a point of contention for some years to come.

The legal framework

Ethnic Germans have historically held a privileged status in German immigration and nationality law. During the division of Germany from 1949 to 1989, membership in the Federal Republic of Germany (FRG) was defined on the basis of the 1913 Reichs- und Staatsangehörigkeitsgesetz (RStAG) and Article 116 of the Basic Law, the German constitution. The Federal Expellees Act (Bundesvertriebenengesetz, BVFG) of 1953 included generous provisions for ethnic Germans who found themselves outside the postwar borders of Germany, while Austrians were granted privileged access to German nationality until 1956 (Hailbronner 2012: 2; Makarov 1956: 744). The RStAG also functioned as a political statement, with the aim of undermining the legitimacy and separation of the GDR, by including East Germans in its definition of membership (Green 2001: 85–6, 2003: 233). The primary means of access to German nationality in the 1913 law was descent-based *ius sanguinis*; it made no allowances for acquisition of German nationality by *ius soli*, and acquisition by *ius domicilii* (nationality by residence) was exceptional and granted on the basis of the benefit to Germany. Given Germany's history as an emigrant nation (Ette and Sauer 2010; Gosewinkel 2008; Koslowski 2000) and the estimated 14 million ethnic Germans caught outside the postwar borders of the FRG (Bundesministerium für Vertriebene 1967), the long adherence to blood-based nationality is logical, though it does not explain the preclusion of any other forms of acquisition of nationality.

The continued privileged status of ethnic Germans in the FRG stems at least partially from the postwar division of Germany and was reinforced in response to the German Democratic Republic's implementation of its own citizenship law (Staatsbürgerschaftsgesetz) in 1967, which established a separate citizenship for East Germans (Hailbronner 2012: 2). The FRG's response to this was to insist on a single German nationality, as enshrined in the 1913 RStAG and decisions of the Federal Constitutional Court (Hailbronner 2012: 2). This legal framework allowed the FRG to claim any Germans arriving from the Soviet bloc as German nationals who were taking up their German nationality rather than as immigrants subject to control and able to access naturalisation by exception only (Hailbronner 1981: 712–13; Klein 1983: 2289; Vedder 2003: 11ff.).

The continued separation of Germany and inclusion of expellees and East Germans in West German law made fundamental changes to the legal basis of membership in the FRG politically unfathomable until unification (Green 2003: 233). The reunification of Germany on 3 October 1990 and the resulting application of German nationality to East Germans meant that the remaining populations affected by these regulations were the ethnic Germans in other Soviet bloc countries. The combination of growing recognition of the problems posed by the long-resident non–ethnic German populations without rights, on the one hand, and the easing of movement out of the Soviet bloc in the early 1990s, on the other, led to increasing discussions about the continued privileged status of ethnic Germans compared with other immigrant groups (Dancygier 2010; Senders 2000; Wolff 2000; Zank 1998).

Ethnic Germans and their spouses and descendants continued to enjoy facilitated naturalisation under Article 116 of the Basic Law and the Expellees Act, which allowed claims on the basis of admission to the territory defined by the German borders of 31 December 1937 (Hailbronner 2012: 4). As a consequence of this legal structure, almost 72 per cent of naturalisations in the early 1990s involved ethnic Germans, though this had dropped starkly by 1999 to slightly over 42 per cent (Bundesverwaltungsamt 2012). Following the implementation of the Staatsangehörigkeitsgesetz in 2000, expellees were no longer included in the naturalisation statistics, as they automatically became German upon presentation of their repatriation certificate in Germany, in line with changes implemented on 1 August 1999 (BAMF 2006: 156).

Ethnic Germans in numbers

Between 1950 and 2011, more than 4.5 million ethnic Germans and their family members arrived in Germany (Bundesministerium des Innern 2005: 7; Bundesverwaltungsamt 2012). Peak ethnic German immigration occurred in 1990, with 397,073 immigrants arriving with this status; this was followed by a sharp drop (Figure 8.1). The sudden increase can be attributed to the greater ease of movement following the collapse of the Soviet bloc, when mass repatriations occurred across eastern Europe. The subsequent fall in ethnic German immigration can be explained through a combination of factors: those with the closest links to Germany had already repatriated; and the hurdles for repatriation have risen as the proportion of secondary immigrants has risen. The German government estimates that there are around two million ethnic Germans still living in former Soviet bloc countries, with the largest population in Russia (Andersen and Woyke 2003). Given that two decades have elapsed during which these populations could have exercised their right to return to Germany, it would appear that they have little interest in doing so.

Until 1999, when ethnic Germans automatically became German upon presentation of a valid repatriation certificate in the FRG, they were included in the federal naturalisation statistics. Between 1980 and 1999, naturalisations of ethnic Germans comprised 70 per cent of all naturalisations in Germany (Figure 8.2). This figure began to change following changes to naturalisation laws that accompanied the fall in ethnic German immigration.

The curtailment of Aussiedler privileges

The privileged status of the ethnic German diaspora has come under increasing scrutiny since the reunification of Germany in 1990. Germans repatriating after World War II were initially received with open arms and offered liberal access to the welfare state and integration assistance: they were paid a lump sum to assist in their initial settlement, were immediately allowed to draw unemployment benefits, and had access to the full pension system (Bade and Oltmer 2003;

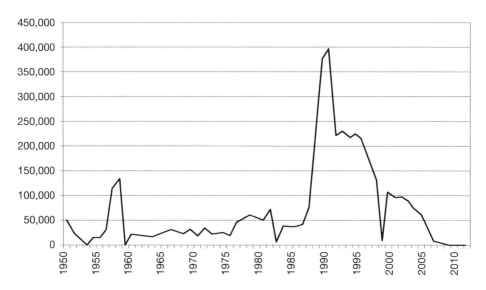

Figure 8.1 (Spät)aussiedler[4] arriving in Germany, 1950–2011. Bundesverwaltungsamt 2012

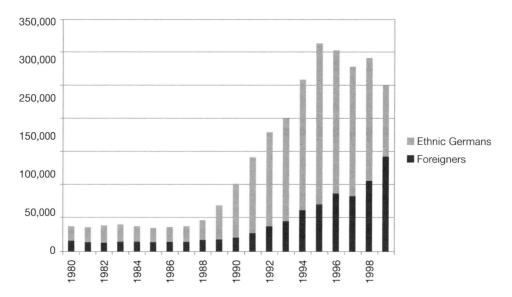

Figure 8.2 Naturalisations 1980–99, ethnic Germans vs other foreigners. Statistisches
Bundesamt 2012; own calculations

Schneider 2005). From 1976, the FRG established a dedicated integration programme for
Aussiedler to promote quick integration. Through this programme, they received widespread
assistance, including heavily subsidised language courses, also for pensioners and housewives;
loans with reduced interest rates to assist them in setting up a household; facilitated recognition
of test results and qualifications from their home countries; and assistance in finding work,
including access to retraining opportunities (Bade and Oltmer 2003; Schneider 2005). This liberal
system was largely uncontested during the Cold War, as the numbers of *Aussiedler* were

relatively low, and larger proportions of the accompanying family members were ethnic Germans themselves and integrated fairly unproblematically into West German society. The generous provisions must also be placed in the context of the ideological conflict of the Cold War, when those fleeing oppression in the East were embraced by the West as proof of the ideological superiority of anti-communism. From this perspective, the legal status of Germans behind the Iron Curtain was less a matter of ethnicity and more a practical way of enshrining ideology in law (Klekowski von Koppenfels 2002). This argument is supported by the fact that facilitated naturalisation was not available to ethnic German populations in Africa and the Americas (Klekowski von Koppenfels, 2002: 12) and that the special provisions have been slowly dismantled since the end of the Cold War (Hailbronner 2012).

The stark rise in repatriations after 1989 made the heavily subsidised repatriation assistance unwieldy. In response, Germany began to implement restrictions on ethnic German immigration. With the 1990 Aussiedleraufnahmegesetz, Germany began to require expellees to apply for leave to repatriate from their home country and demanded proof of German language ability as evidence of their identification as ethnic Germans (Green 2003: 234; Hailbronner 2012: 25). In a further effort to limit the indefinite continuation of ethnic German repatriation, those born from 1993 onwards must meet all of the entry requirements for older expellees and must prove that they are disadvantaged in their country because of their German identity (Green 2003: 235).

A growing body of research has identified persistent and severe integration problems amongst these populations, especially for secondary migrants, and integration measures consistently show that ethnic Germans face the same integration problems as other immigrant populations (Bade and Oltmer 2003; Dietz 1997; Dietz and Hilkes 1994; Talke 2011; Vogelgesang 2008). In response to the decreasing proportion of primary ethnic German immigration and recognition of integration issues, regulations for ethnic German immigration have been steadily tightened. This began with the institution of an annual quota of 255,000 in 1993; this was reduced to 100,000 in 2000, though numbers have naturally remained below the quota and have continued to fall in the past decade. A pre-entry German language test was introduced in 2000 as part of the Nationality Act, and the entitlement to naturalisation upon admission to German territory was abolished at the same time as the quota was lowered (Hailbronner 2012: 18).

The increasing proportion of non-ethnic German family members immigrating with a repatriating relative led to growing problems with integration that had not been noticeable in the earlier years of ethnic German immigration, when the majority of family members were ethnic Germans themselves: between 1994 and 2006, the proportion of non-ethnic German family members as a proportion of total ethnic German migration rose from 29.1 per cent to 62.4 per cent (BAMF 2006: 246). Non-ethnic German relatives struggled to meet the new pre-entry language requirement brought in as part of the Immigration Act of 2004, resulting in a marked drop in arrivals. Applications for immigration as ethnic Germans and family members became distinctly less successful, with a drop from around two-thirds to only one-eighth acceptance after the introduction of the new restrictions (BAMF 2006: 51). The numbers in 2006 dropped to the lowest levels since the FRG began to accept ethnic German repatriation in 1950 (BAMF 2006: 51). Estimates of the size of the remaining ethnic German population in various Soviet bloc countries are unreliable, ranging from 800,000 (BAMF 2006) to two million (Andersen and Woyke 2003). Despite the variation, the numbers indicate that a majority of the ethnic Germans in the Soviet bloc did indeed repatriate to Germany, and the majority of those remaining outside Germany cannot fulfil the language requirement (BAMF 2006: 54). Furthermore, after the 2005 eastward expansion of the EU, many people who might be classed as ethnic Germans became EU citizens, making it unlikely that they would need to claim German repatriate status, especially after the removal of restrictions to freedom of movement in 2012.

Foreigners

This section looks at the situation of non-Germans within the borders of the Federal Republic. Like the previous section, it discusses first the legal regulations concerning their status and then the number of people affected by these policies and the changes to naturalisation trends as a result of policy changes.

The legal framework

Between the establishment of the West German government in 1949 and unification in 1990, immigration and nationality laws were constant, with only one piece of legislation passed concerning non-ethnic Germans, the Ausländergesetz (AuslG, Foreigners Law) of 1965 (Green 2003: 232).[5] During the postwar period, discussions focused on the status of ethnic Germans and the ongoing ramifications of the division of Germany, as discussed above. The primary purpose of the German nationality regulations chosen in the postwar environment was to establish a mode of recognition of membership of the German nation even for those who found themselves outside the newly drawn borders of the FRG in 1949. This included explicit provisions to incorporate the large ethnic German populations resident in Soviet bloc countries as well as the explicit attempt to undermine the GDR through non-recognition of its proclaimed separate citizenship as announced in the East German Staatsbürgerschaftsgesetz of 1967. Such an ethno-centric definition of German nationality was not entirely surprising in the prevailing political environment and in view of Germany's historical status as a country of net emigration (more Germans leaving the country than foreigners arriving) rather than a country of net immigration (more foreigners arriving than Germans leaving the country) (Bade 1980, 1995).

This pattern of general continuity was considerably disrupted following unification, with major legal changes passed in 1990, 1993, 1999, 2004, and 2008, as the problem of the division of Germany disappeared and the FRG began to grapple with the status of its long-resident foreign populations, many of which had been established by Germany's postwar guestworker recruitment policies. As a result of those policies, EU freedom of movement, and post-unification migration from poorer countries, Germany has been a country of net migration during 47 of the years between 1954 and 2010 (BiB 2012). At the time of reunification, German law allowed for acquisition of nationality only through birth to a German parent (*ius sanguinis*) and did not include provision for regular access to citizenship by naturalisation on the basis of residence (*ius domicilii*). Although naturalisation did exist, it was always by discretion of the state and with very heavy conditions, including 15 years' residence in Germany and prohibitive costs. Such restrictions on access to German nationality had created a large, long-resident foreign population without access to full rights, especially voting.

Following a series of attempts by German Länder to try to address the lack of rights of these denizens, the Bundestag passed the first reform in 1990 to facilitate acquisition of German nationality by foreigners between the ages of 16 and 23. Under the changes, they had to give up their previous nationality, to have lived in Germany 'permanently and lawfully' for eight years, to have attended a German school for at least six years, and to have no criminal convictions. The 1990 law also simplified naturalisation for other foreigners who had lived in Germany for 15 years, gave up their previous nationality, had no criminal convictions, and could show that they were able to earn a living. Perhaps the most important aspect of these changes was that if the applicant met the conditions naturalisation was to be granted 'as a rule', which severely limited the exercise of administrative discretion; this reversed the previous system, whereby naturalisation was by discretion only. The change was reinforced in the 1993 act, which established a right to naturalisation when the applicant fulfilled the criteria. Furthermore, although both legal changes formally required the renunciation of previous nationality, the number of exceptions granted led to a steady increase in naturalisations of the non-ethnic German foreign population (Hagedorn 1998: 28; figure 8.3). The naturalisation rate – the number of naturalisations as a proportion of the foreign population as a whole – rose from an average of 0.33 per cent in the 1980s to 1.12 per cent in 1997. However, although this represented a vast increase, it was still far below the rates in countries like the UK, and Germany's foreign population remained stubbornly at around 9 per cent of the national population.

By the late 1990s, many of Germany's foreigners had been present in the country for decades. At the end of 1997, half of all foreigners in Germany had been resident there for more than a decade, and nearly a third had been resident for two decades or more (Hailbronner 2012: 3); by the end of 2011, more than two thirds of foreigners had been living in Germany for over a decade (Bundeszentrale für politische Bildung 2012). By the end of 1997, more than one in five 'foreigners' had even been born in Germany, but they were still classified as foreign nationals because of the lack of provision in German law for birthplace-based (*ius soli*) citizenship (Hailbronner 2012: 3).

The pressures created by these demographics, ongoing discussions within and between political parties throughout the 1990s,[6] and a change in the Federal government to a politically liberal SPD-Green coalition in 1998 under Chancellor Schröder led to the creation of an entirely new legal framework in the Nationality Act (Staatsangehörigkeitsgesetz, StAG) of 1999, implemented on 1 January 2000. Draft proposals originally included wider provisions of *ius soli* nationality acquisition and greater tolerance of dual nationality, but power shifts towards the Christian Union parties in the upper house of the Federal legislature led to a watering down of these proposals. The final version of the act introduced provisions for acquisition of German nationality by *ius soli* for the first time; this enabled children to be granted German nationality at birth when born to a foreign national parent who had been habitually resident in Germany for eight years and was in possession of a 'secure' residence permit for three years before the birth. A transitional clause allowed children up to the age of 10 to opt into the new rules if at least one parent had fulfilled the conditions at the time of their birth, in order not to disadvantage children born in the years preceding the reform.

The catch of this *ius soli* provision was a messy compromise known as the *Optionsmodell*, which effectively permitted dual nationality to these children until the age of 18; between the ages of 18 and 23, they formally had to declare their intention to retain either their German nationality or their other nationality. This compromise led critics to argue that it was incompatible with the Basic Law. The SPD made the abolition of the optional model and the enshrinement of double *ius soli* a core part of the coalition agreement for the grand coalition formed following the 2013 election (CDU, CSU, and SPD 2013: 105), coinciding with the coming of age of the first generation of children affected by the *Optionsmodell*. This promise was fulfilled swiftly in the Second Nationality Act of 2014. This act avoids problems of ignorance of the regulation and pressure from families to retain foreign nationality, though a government report had indicated the majority of *Optionsmodell* children intended to keep German nationality (Weinmann *et al.* 2012).

The StAG reforms were accompanied by a formal renunciation of the succinctly named 1963 Convention on the Reduction of Cases of Multiple Nationality and Military Obligations in Cases of Multiple Nationality; this was followed in 2002 by Germany signing the European Convention on Nationality (ECN), which included a commitment to lower hurdles for naturalisation and acceptance of dual nationality at birth for children of multinational marriages. Germany's acceptance of the new convention wording regarding dual nationality constitutes a further step towards normalisation of German nationality law by bringing it into line with the modern European norms. Germany signed the treaty with a reservation for the *Optionsmodell*, however, which does not conform to some of the convention requirements.

The StAG reform also made further changes to the naturalisation requirements for adults, decreasing the minimum residence period from 15 to eight years, introducing an oath of loyalty to the German Basic Law, and expanding the number of situations in which dual nationality would be accepted; previous regulations requiring proof of the ability to earn a living, absence of criminal convictions, and renunciation of previous nationality continued to apply. Besides cementing the change in philosophy that had begun in the earlier reforms towards acquisition of German nationality by non-ethnic Germans, the StAG constituted a further step towards normalisation of German nationality policy by limiting acquisition by descent for Germans born abroad: German nationals born abroad after 31 December 1999 and with their habitual residence abroad will no longer be able to pass on German nationality to a child unless the child would otherwise be stateless. Although unlikely to affect large numbers of future children, this signals an important shift in the definition of German membership.

The 2000 reforms were intended to be followed quickly by a second bill to deal further with ethnic Germans and comprehensive changes to migration policy. The second act was introduced soon after the StAG had been implemented and made its way through both houses, but it was passed in the Bundesrat only through a controversial interpretation of procedure in tallying the final vote. The opposition Christian Union parties took legal action to block the law's implementation. Eventually, after intervention by the German president, the act was declared invalid. A Federal election then followed, causing further shifts in power, and the act had to be re-introduced to the new parliament in 2004. As a consequence, the final Immigration Act (Zuwanderungsgesetz, ZuG) was not as liberal as the parties of the left had originally intended, although it did still constitute a further reform.

Following the initial steps of the StAG reforms, the ZuG dealt with the further integration of Germany's foreign population and sought to formalise and homogenise the integration and naturalisation process, which had varied greatly across the different Länder. The 2004 act, implemented in 2005, set formal requirements for mastering the German language and introduced an integration course, successful completion of which would reduce the required residence period for naturalisation from eight years to seven. The circumstances in which exemptions from the naturalisation requirements could be granted were expanded. However, the conditions under which children born in Germany to foreign parents would be granted German nationality by *ius soli* were restricted by requiring one of the parents to hold a permanent residence permit rather than a 'secure' residence permit. The conditions for obtaining a permanent residence permit require a relatively high degree of parental integration, thereby reducing the number of cases in which *ius soli* is applied. Disagreements over ethnic Germans and toleration of dual nationality continued between the left and the right. The far-reaching reforms originally envisaged for the Immigration Act failed to pass both houses due to the balance of power following the 2003 Federal election, leaving many issues unresolved.

The next round of changes followed in 2007, under Chancellor Merkel's leadership of a CDU/CSU/SPD grand coalition. The reforms were attached in the form of 24 amendments to a bill implementing a series of EU directives. These amendments further regularised and defined integration for the purpose of naturalisation and constituted a mixture of liberalisations and restrictions to naturalisation requirements. The level of mastery of the German language was set at B1 on the Common European Framework of References for Languages;[7] a provision was also made to reduce the residence requirement by a further year for those showing exceptional linguistic competence, potentially decreasing the required residence period to six years.

The clear definition of the language requirement homogenised the diverse interpretations of the various Federal states or Länder regarding required levels of German, which had led to naturalisation being considerably easier in some states than in others. A naturalisation exam and a citizenship oath were introduced, and the levels of fines or days in jail that could be excluded from the criminal convictions requirement were halved. Like the formalisation of language requirements, the requirement of the naturalisation exam has the potential to be either liberal or restrictive, depending upon implementation. In practice, 99 per cent of applicants have passed the naturalisation exam (Wöhrle 2009), which is considerably higher than the 71 per cent pass rate for the British integration exam (Wray 2010), for example.

Non-Germans in numbers

In response to Germany's legal changes during the past two decades, naturalisations have increased substantially, but they still remain at significantly lower levels than in other western European countries. Long-resident foreigners still show little interest in naturalising: in 2011 only one out of every 45 foreigners who qualified for naturalisation in Germany became a German national, equating to a naturalisation rate of 2.3 per cent (Hailbronner 2012: 24). The highest levels of non-*Aussiedler* naturalisations occurred in 2000, following the implementation of the 1999 reforms; naturalisations now stand at the same levels as in the late 1990s (Figure 8.3).

Here, though, simple naturalisation rates can be misleading, as for the past two decades EU citizens have constituted between a quarter and a third of the total foreign population in Germany.[8] There is little incentive for naturalisation for EU citizens, and this is reflected in the consistently low levels of naturalisation, generally between 0.6 and 0.7 per cent. However, even with EU citizens excluded from the calculation, naturalisation rates of non-EU foreigners have remained stubbornly below 2.5 per cent, with rates below 2 per cent each year between 2007 and 2011, the latest year for which statistics are available. The continued lack of interest in naturalisation is also perplexing given the long residency of much of Germany's foreign population: in 2011, the *average* length of residence of Germany's foreigners was 19 years, and nearly three quarters had lived in Germany for eight years or more, thus fulfilling the minimum

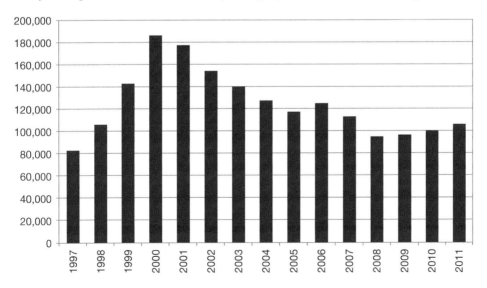

Figure 8.3 Naturalisations in Germany, 1997–2011. Statistisches Bundesamt 2012

residence requirement for naturalisation (Statistisches Bundesamt 2011: table 9). There are several explanations for the sustained lack of interest in naturalisation, despite the reforms enacted since 1990: Germany's continued (official) rejection of dual nationality; the increased requirements for naturalisation over the past decade; and the perpetuation of a perception of Germany as a country unwelcoming to foreigners. We will deal with each of these points in turn.

Germany's sustained rejection of dual nationality is, without doubt, a great obstacle to achieving higher levels of naturalisation, with many foreigners citing this as a reason for not applying (Sauer 2013; Weinmann *et al.* 2012). However, other research shows that a sizeable portion of the foreign community would not elect to naturalise even if applicants could keep their previous nationality: a survey by the German charity Caritas asked foreigners who expressed an intention not to naturalise, 'Would you naturalise if dual nationality were possible?', to which 63 per cent of respondents replied in the negative (Deutscher Caritasverband 2008: 20). The same survey found that 64 per cent of respondents as a whole were 'probably' or 'definitely' not interested in naturalising (Deutscher Caritasverband 2008: 19). The Federal government has begun to explore these objections itself, with a 2012 study issued by the BAMF concluding that the main argument against naturalisation, cited by more than 50 per cent of respondents, was the loss of their current nationality (Weinmann *et al.* 2012: 40). Besides such counterfactual polls and reports, Federal statistics show that, although dual nationality continues to be formally rejected, in practice applicants are now permitted to retain their former nationality in a majority of cases, a trend that shows a steady upward pattern (Figure 8.4). Although this pattern shows no signs of reversal, the formal rejection of dual nationality is still likely to affect foreigners' willingness to apply for naturalisation because, although the chances of success are good, the retention of their former nationality is far from a certainty. In fact, the ability of applicants for naturalisation to secure multiple citizenship varies widely according to nationality: Turks, who constitute the largest foreign population in Germany, were permitted to retain their Turkish nationality in only 27.7 per cent of cases in 2010, compared with an overall acceptance rate of 53.1 per cent (Statistisches Bundesamt 2011: 85).

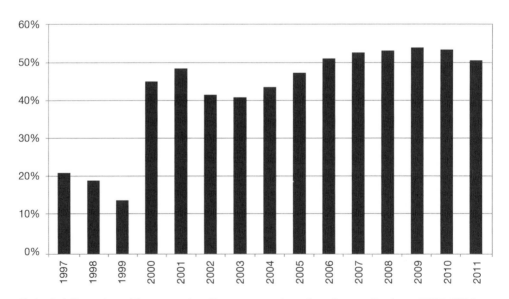

Figure 8.4 Retention of former nationality as proportion of total naturalisations, 1997–2011. Statistisches Bundesamt 2011

Associated with the rejection of dual nationality is the continued perception of Germany as unwelcoming to foreigners, which is reinforced by right-wing extremism, continued public debates about *Leitkultur*,[9] and the implicit rejection of multiculturalism and judgments about the nature of loyalty underlying Germany's and Germans' position on dual nationality. In addition to polls of foreigners themselves about their feelings towards dual nationality and how this might affect their interest in naturalisation, there are polls of Germans' willingness to accept multiple nationalities as a formal policy. In such surveys, respondents tend overwhelmingly to reject the possibility of permitting foreigners to keep their previous nationality when naturalising (Bertelsmann Stiftung 2012; Terwey and Baltzer 2011: 109; Wasmer and Koch 2000: 262).

Normalisation at the European level

We have now established that Germany's treatment of ethnic Germans and foreigners in its nationality law has changed drastically since 1990, and we have hinted at the normalisation of its nationality policies. Given that normalisation can be a moving target, 'normal' needs a measureable definition. First, Germany should be compared with similar peers – in this case, other European countries in the so-called 'second phase' of immigration (de Hart and van Oers 2006: 317), that is, states with an established, stable immigrant community. This second phase is typified by 'de-ethnicising citizenship' in three main ways: lowering naturalisation requirements for first-generation immigrants; easing access to nationality for second-generation immigrants by creating provisions for *ius soli*; and accepting multiple nationality (Joppke 2003).

In this peer assessment, Germany now conforms to two of the three criteria, and it has made informal progress towards implementation of the third. Although Germany's *ius soli* provisions are limited, so are those of its peers: Ireland was the last European state to abolish pure *ius soli* in 2004; all *ius soli* provisions are conditional. Germany's residence requirements for naturalisation now conform solidly with the norms enshrined in the European Convention on Nationality. Germany's other requirements for naturalisation reflect general European trends: while only five out of 32[10] European states required a formal language test in 1998, 19 did by 2010, with another seven requiring an informal test (Bauböck and Honohan 2010). Integration tests have also become more common, with over half of these countries having implemented them by 2010 (Bauböck and Honohan 2010), while several of the countries without civic knowledge tests are considering introducing them. Germany's naturalisation fees are roughly average and are significantly lower than those of historic countries of immigration such as the UK. Acceptance of multiple nationality is the norm in a majority of European states, but Germany is certainly not an outlier in this area, and its widespread exceptions make it more liberal than several other European countries. Finally, Germany's de-ethnicisation has also occurred through the gradual curtailment of privileges of ethnic Germans outside Germany's postwar borders. All of these indicators show that Germany has normalised its naturalisation policy. The debates and struggles it now faces are common to many of its peers.

Conclusion

This chapter has provided an overview of the normalisation of German citizenship policy through the de-ethnicisation of citizenship. In Germany's case, de-ethnicisation has required both the curtailment of historical privileges granted to ethnic Germans outside its borders and the facilitation of access to citizenship for non-Germans living within its borders. The latter has occurred through the provision of territorial citizenship for the first time as well as through the relaxation of naturalisation requirements. Though Germany still has a significant long-term resident foreign population and still officially rejects dual nationality, it has moved steadily towards conformity with the norms of its European peers. Although there is evidence that even Christian Democrats are moving towards accepting dual nationality, it remains to be seen whether the policy will be amended in coming years. While the Christian Union parities swiftly fulfilled their coalition promise with regards to the abolition of the *Optionsmodell*, there is continued strong resistance to accepting dual nationality for naturalisation applications during the 18th parliament. This policy continues disproportionately to affect the large Turkish community in Germany, many of whom have been resident in Germany for decades – or even born there; and this continues to pose problems for democratic participation. Yet the successful abolition of the *Optionsmodell* represents another step towards normalisation that many commentators did not expect to come so soon.

Notes

1 In order to qualify, at least one parent needs to have been born in Germany and to hold permanent residency status.
2 The major exceptions to this trend are the UK and Ireland, which both have a strong tradition of *ius soli*, though again for reasons related to the history of the British Empire.
3 'Ethnic German' is notoriously difficult to define. Traditionally, it refers to people with a German cultural background, including being native German speakers. For various historical reasons, especially as a result of pogroms and Catherine the Great's invitation to Germans to resettle to the Russian Empire, Germany developed a large diaspora community, though there was always a certain level of inter-marriage with the local populations. Thus, 'ethnic' Germans are more to be identified through culture than a shared genetic heritage.
4 *Aussiedler*, literally 'outsettler' is variously translated as ethnic German, refugee, emigrant, and repatriate, depending on the source. *Aussiedler* refers to those classed as ethnic Germans who repatriated to the FRG through the end of 1992; *Spätaussiedler* refers to those who repatriated after 1992. The terminology is reflective of a general change in the composition of the repatriates, as post-1992 repatriations included much larger proportions of non-ethnic German family members.
5 For a fuller discussion of the legal development during this period see Hailbronner 2012 and Hailbronner Renner 2010.
6 See Hailbronner 2012 for an extensive list of references to different proposals.
7 B1 proficiency means that the person can operate independently in the language in routine circum-stances, can understand the main points on everyday topics from a native speaker, and can write at a basic level on specific topics (Council of Europe 2001).
8 This is calculated using EU15 citizens until 2004, then EU25 (2004–06) and EU27 (2006–13) citizens.
9 *Leitkultur* has been translated as leading or guiding culture and is embedded in debates about immigrant integration and assimilation. It has been used to express sometimes contradictory ideas, from promoting full assimilation, whereby immigrants should completely immerse themselves in German culture, to a more multicultural construct, whereby immigrants are simply expected to subscribe to a core set of liberal democratic values (the leading culture) but are otherwise free to pursue a more multicultural model of integration.
10 The 32 states are the EU27 plus Croatia, Iceland, Norway, Moldova, and Turkey, which were profiled in 2010 by the EU Citizenship Observatory.

Bibliography

Andersen, U. and Woyke, W. (2003) 'Auslandsdeutsche', in U. Andersen and W. Woyke (eds) *Handwörterbuch des politischen Systems der Bundesrepublik Deutschland*, Opladen: Leske + Budrich.
Bade, K.J. (1980) 'German Emigration to the United States and continental immigration to Germany in the late nineteenth and early twentieth centuries', *Central European History*, 13(4): 348–77.
Bade, K.J. (1995) 'From emigration to immigration: The German experience in the nineteenth and twentieth centuries', *Central European History*, 28(4): 507–35.
Bade, K.J. and Oltmer, J. (eds) (2003) *Aussiedler: deutsche Einwanderer aus Osteuropa*, Göttingen: V&R Unipress.
BAMF (2006) *Migrationsbericht*, Berlin: Bundesministerium des Innern.

Bauböck, R. and Honohan, I. (2010) 'Access to citizenship in Europe: Birthright and naturalisation', paper presented at EUDO Dissemination Conference, Brussels, 18–19 November 2010. Slides available at www.eui.eu/Projects/EUDO/Documents/12–06-BauboeckandHonohanpresentations.pdf (accessed 3 January 2014).

Bertelsmann Stiftung (2012) 'Deutsche hin- und hergerissen in Haltung zur Zuwanderung'. Online. Available at www.bertelsmann-stiftung.de/cps/rde/xchg/bst/hs.xsl/nachrichten_114652.htm (accessed 11 January 2013).

Bundesinstitut für Bevölkerungsforschung (BiB) (2012) *Zu- und Abwanderung von Ausländern*, Wiesbaden: Bundesinstitut für Bevölkerungsforschung. Online. Available at www.bib-demografie.de/DE/ZahlenundFakten/Wanderungen/Abbildungen/aussenwanderung.html?nn=3071818 (accessed 3 January 2014).

Bundesministerium des Innern (2005) *InfoDienst: Deutsche Aussiedler*, November, Berlin: BMI.

Bundesministerium für Vertriebene, Flüchtlinge und Kriegsgeschädigte (1967) *Dokumentation der Vertreibung der Deutschen aus Ost-Mitteleuropa*, 9th edn, Bonn: Bundesministerium für Vertriebene, Flüchtlinge und Kriegsgeschädigte.

Bundesverwaltungsamt (2012) *Statistik zum Aussiedleraufnahmeverfahren*, Cologne: BVA.

Bundeszentrale für politische Bildung (2012) 'Ausländische Bevölkerung nach Aufenthaltsdauer'. Online. Available at www.bpb.de/nachschlagen/zahlen-und-fakten/soziale-situation-in-deutschland/61628/aufenthaltsdauer (accessed 12 January 2013).

CDU, CSU, and SPD (2013) 'Deutschlands Zukunft gestalten: Koalitionsvertrag zwischen CDU, CSU und SPD'. Online. Available at https://www.cdu.de/sites/default/files/media/dokumente/koalitionsvertrag.pdf (accessed 3 January 2014).

Council of Europe (2001) 'Common European Framework of Reference for Languages: Learning, teaching, assessment'. Online. Available at www.coe.int/t/dg4/education/elp/elp-reg/Source/Key_reference/Overview_CEFRscales_EN.pdf (accessed 3 January 2013).

Dancygier, R.M. (2010) *Immigration and Conflict in Europe*, Cambridge: Cambridge University Press.

de Hart, B. and van Oers, R. (2006) 'European trends in nationality law' in R. Bauböck *et al.* (eds) *Acquisition and Loss of Nationality: Policies and Trends in 15 European States*, Amsterdam: Amsterdam University Press, 317–58.

Deutscher Caritasverband (2008) *Quantifizierung Migranten-Milieus: Repräsentativuntersuchung der Lebenswelten von Menschen mit Migrationshintergrund in Deutschland*, Heidelberg: Deutscher Caritasverband.

Dietz, B. (1997) *Jugendliche Aussiedler: Ausreise, Aufnahme, Integration*, Berlin: Arno Spitz.

Dietz, B. and Hilkes, P. (1994) *Integriert oder isoliert? Zur Situation russlanddeutscher Aussiedler in der Bundesrepublik Deutschland*, Munich: Olzog.

Ette, A. and Sauer, L. (2010) *Auswanderung aus Deutschland: Daten und Analysen zur internationalen Migration deutscher Staatsbürger*, Wiesbaden: Verlag für Sozialwissenschaften.

Gosewinkel, D. (2008) 'Citizenship in Germany and France at the turn of the twentieth century: some new observations on an old comparison' in G. Eley and J. Palmowski (eds) *Citizenship and National Identity in Twentieth-Century Germany*, Stanford, CA: Stanford University Press, 27–39.

Green, S.O. (2001) 'Immigration, asylum and citizenship in Germany: The impact of unification and the Berlin Republic', *West European Politics*, 24(4): 82–104.

Green, S.O. (2003) 'Towards an open society? Citizenship and immigration', in S. Padgett, W.E. Paterson, and G. Smith (eds) *Developments in German Politics 3*, 3rd edn, Basingstoke: Palgrave Macmillan, 227–47.

Hagedorn, H. (1998) 'Einbürgerungen in Deutschland und Frankreich', in D. Thränhardt (ed.) *Einwanderung und Einbürgerung in Deutschland: Jahrbuch Migration*, Münster: LIT.

Hailbronner, K. (1981) 'Deutsche Staatsangehörigkeit und DDR-Staatsbürgerschaft', *Juristische Schulung*, 10: 712–18.

Hailbronner, K. (2012) *Country Report: Germany*, October, Florence: EUDO Citizenship Observatory.

Hailbronner, K. and Renner, G. (2010) *Staatsangehörigkeitsrecht*, 5th edn, Munich: Beck.

Joppke, C. (2003) 'Citizenship between de- and re-ethnicization (I)', *Archives européennes de sociologies*, 44: 429–58.

Klein, E. (1983) 'DDR-Staatsbürgerschaftserwerb und deutsche Staatsangehörigkeit', *Neue juristische Wochenschrift*, 41: 2289–92.

Klekowski von Koppenfels, A. (2002) 'Politically minded: The case of Aussiedler as an ideologically defined category', *Sozialwissenschaftlicher Fachinformationsdienst: Migration und ethnische Minderheiten*, 1–28.

Koslowski, R. (2000) *Migrants and Citizens: Demographic Change in the European State System*, London: Cornell University Press.

Makarov, A.N. (1956) 'Das Gesetz über die deutsch-österreichische Staatsangehörigkeit', *Juristenzeitung*, 23: 744–9.

Sauer, M. (2013) *Einbürgerungsverhalten türkeistämmiger Migrantinnen und Migranten in Nordrhein-Westfalen*, Essen: Stiftung Zentrum für Türkeistudien und Integrationsforschung.

Schneider, J. (2005) 'Aussiedler: Integration', Bundeszentrale für politische Bildung. Online. Available at www.bpb.de/gesellschaft/migration/dossier-migration/56404/integration?p=all (accessed 28 December 2012).

Senders, S. (2000) '*Jus sanguinis* or *jus mimesis*? Rethinking "ethnic German" repatriation', in D. Rock and S. Wolff (eds) *Coming Home to Germany? The Integration of Ethnic Germans from Central and Eastern Europe in the Federal Republic Since 1945*, Oxford: Berghahn Books, 87–101.

Statistisches Bundesamt (2011) *Bevölkerung und Erwerbstätigkeit – Einbürgerungen 2010*, Wiesbaden: Statistisches Bundesamt.

Statistisches Bundesamt (2012) *Einbürgerungsstatistik*, Wiesbaden: Statistisches Bundesamt.

Talke, M. (2011) '*(Spät)Aussiedler*: From Germans to Immigrants', *Nationalism and Ethnic Politics*, 17(2): 161–81.

Terwey, M. and Baltzer, S. (2011) 'ALLBUS 2006 – Variable Report', *GESIS Variable Reports*, 3.

Vedder, C. (2003) 'Kommentierung zu Art. 116 GG', in I. von Münch and P. Kunig (eds) *Grundgesetz Kommentar*, Munich: C.H. Beck.

Vogelgesang, W. (2008) *Jugendliche Aussiedler: Zwischen Entwurzelung, Ausgrenzung und Integration*. Weinheim: Juventa.

Wasmer, M. and Koch, A. (2000) 'Ausländer als Bürger 2. Klasse?: Einstellungen zur rechtlichen Gleichstellung von Ausländern', in R. Alba, P. Schmidt, and M. Wasmer (eds) *Deutsche und Ausländer: Freunde, Fremde oder Feinde? Empirische Befunde und theoretische Erklärungen*, Wiesbaden: Westdeutscher Verlag, 255–93.

Weinmann, M., Becher, I., and Babka von Gostomski, C. (2012) *Einbürgerungsverhalten von Ausländerinnen und Ausländern in Deutschland sowie Erkenntnisse zu Optionspflichtigen: Ergebnisse der BAMF-Einbürgerungsstudie 2011*, Berlin: Bundesamt für Migration und Flüchtlinge.

Wöhrle, C. (2009) 'Deutschland: Einbürgerungstest wird fast immer bestanden', *Migration und Bevölkerung*, 1 January. Online. Available at www.bpb.de/gesellschaft/migration/newsletter/57229/deutschland-einbuergerungstest-wird-fast-immer-bestanden (accessed 1 December 2013).

Wolff, S. (2000) 'Coming home to Germany? Ethnic German migrants in the Federal Republic after 1945', in D. Rock and S. Wolff (eds) *Coming Home to Germany? The Integration of Ethnic Germans from Central and Eastern Europe in the Federal Republic Since 1945*, Oxford: Berghahn Books, 221–7.

Wray, H. (2010) 'United Kingdom: 29.1 percent of migrants taking the citizenship test fail', EUDO Citizenship Observatory, Florence. Online. Available at http://eudo-citizenship.eu/citizenship-news/314-uk-291-percent-of-migrants-taking-the-citizenship-test-fail- (accessed 1 September 2010).

Zank, W. (1998) *The German Melting-Pot: Multiculturality in Historical Perspective*, Basingstoke: Palgrave Macmillan.

9

Social wellbeing and democracy

Patricia Hogwood

This chapter investigates the economic and cultural foundations of wellbeing in the Berlin Republic and assesses the role of objective and subjective wellbeing in social and political life. It finds that although Germany enjoys the economic prerequisites for generally high levels of individual and social wellbeing, certain individuals and groups of Germans struggle to realise their life potential, either because of material constraints or because of subjective constraints relating to social tensions and cultural perceptions.[1] These constraints include a deep-seated 'materialist-pessimist' cultural outlook; ongoing tensions relating to the unification of the Federal Republic of Germany (FRG) with the German Democratic Republic (GDR) in 1990; and a new public discourse of austerity arising out of government responses to an overloaded welfare system and the European financial crisis.

It has long been recognised that individual and societal wellbeing is significant for the health of a democracy (Veenhoven 1991; Tov and Diener 2009). Nations that enjoy high levels of citizen wellbeing also tend to demonstrate high levels of citizen trust in the system and positive attitudes towards democratic values. The greater the levels of citizens' 'affect' (positive emotional orientation) towards the regime and the higher their confidence in governments' responsiveness, the more stable the system is expected to be. This stabilising potential has even greater salience for transition democracies, where citizens are likely to experience financial hardships and social dislocation while the new regime is consolidated (Berg and Veenhoven 2010: 187). Itself a transition democracy after World War II, the FRG has always been keenly aware of the potential fragility of democratic governance. In 1990 it faced the unique challenge of cementing social cohesion in a united Germany that now incorporated citizens of the former GDR. In the early 1990s German unification represented a unique path to post-socialist transition for these east German citizens. Their values had been framed within a socialist state system that stood in direct ideological opposition to their new home state. Socialised over the previous 40 years in a system founded on egalitarian principles, they now had to learn life satisfaction in one predicated on libertarian principles, and characterised by late-capitalist structures and modes of social participation.

In the academic arena, wellbeing research has emerged as an interdisciplinary field, elaborated largely within the fields of behavioural psychology and behavioural economics. Wellbeing is an intangible and complex human phenomenon that cannot readily be quantified. In psychology, interest in wellbeing has focused on its subjective components. Leading authors in the field have included Diener (1984; Diener *et al.* 1999) and Kahneman (Kahneman, Diener and Schwarz 1999). For economists, the challenge has been to capture the bounded rationality of the pursuit of wellbeing, to assess its social, cognitive and emotional factors, and to evaluate its implications for economic development and economic policy. Key economists in the development of wellbeing research have included Easterlin (2002), Frey and Stutzer (2002), Bruni and Porta (2005), and Helliwell (2002). Within the discipline of politics, starting with Bentham (1789), interest in wellbeing has traditionally been the concern of normative theory, concerned with ways in which governments can provide a good life for their citizens. Since the 1960s, behaviouralists have viewed wellbeing as the inevitable outcome of good governance, and have been more interested in the processes by which a healthy relationship might be achieved between citizens and their regime than in the nature and extent of wellbeing in itself. It is only recently that interdisciplinary research has attempted to apply lessons on wellbeing from psychology and economics more explicitly to problems of globalisation, political authority, political legitimation, and public policy (see e.g. Helliwell 2002; Diener *et al.* 2009; Xefteris 2012).

Governments and academics alike are interested in the interplay between different dimensions of wellbeing and their implications for democratic society. Governments try to ensure that citizens enjoy a satisfactory level of material security. A range of objective conditions helps to shape an individual's life chances and satisfaction, including family, living conditions, employment, health, and income. Beyond objective wellbeing, citizens should also have the opportunity for self-fulfilment and the chance to participate fully in social life (Göbel *et al.* 2011: 377). Subjective wellbeing concerns the way in which individuals perceive and evaluate their place in life: whether they are happy or unhappy with the conditions that frame their life and with the opportunities open to them. Satisfactory objective living conditions help to promote, but are not in themselves a sufficient condition of, subjective wellbeing. Experts are also interested in the way in which individuals perceive and evaluate their common society and their place in it. Such evaluations of individual and collective wellbeing are now commonly used as barometers of government and regime performance.

It is widely accepted that perceptions of subjective wellbeing are relative rather than absolute. Nobody can deny that in comparison with other parts of the world, the population in Germany is very well off in terms of economic and physical security. However, individuals tend to compare their lot with others in their own community, rather than elsewhere. Physical proximity allows comparisons to be drawn with family, friends, neighbours, and colleagues. Intercultural collective references and access to news media allow people to reflect on their circumstances in a wider, national context. The less immediate the context in which an individual judges his or her own situation, the less likely it is to have a definitive impact on that judgment. For that reason, this chapter focuses on how Germans compare themselves with other Germans. European data are used solely to provide an analytical context for the evaluation of Germans' wellbeing.

Wellbeing research in Germany

The FRG has conducted its own surveys on citizen wellbeing since 1978 (Glatzer and Bös 1998: 172; Noll and Weick 2010a: 87, note 1), primarily to determine levels of citizen affect towards the regime and its institutions. German unification added a new dimension to these surveys as experts tried to ascertain how east Germans were adjusting to liberal democracy and also the extent of social conflict between east and west Germans. Comparisons of east and west German responses to opinion research have offered observers a window on the ongoing process of social integration of the two German communities. Comprehensive survey research is now conducted at national and international level to determine how citizens' lives are changing and how they feel about this change. The development of more sophisticated measures and the pooling of data through organisations such as the Organisation for Economic Cooperation and Development (OECD) and the European Union (EU) mean that researchers have numerous resources at their disposal in developing a multifaceted understanding of wellbeing in Germany. Over the last two decades, German governments have faced unprecedented resource constraints arising from both external and internal pressures. These include the costs following from German unification; the impact of globalisation on Germany's economic model; an ageing population; and the crisis in the eurozone. Policy options for dealing with these developments may challenge some of the fundamental assumptions German citizens have held about the role of their government as a service provider. In particular, experts are keen to assess Germans' adjustment to new modes of employment, service, and welfare provision. By the end of the 20th century, the postwar 'classic' pattern of full-time, permanent employment was giving way to more flexible employment patterns that better serve the globalised economy. While employees may themselves derive some benefit from the restructuring, it harbours potential disadvantages, such as short hours, short-term contracts, lack of a clear career structure and employment insecurity.

In common with other major European countries, there has recently been a shift in emphasis in the way in which German governments are using survey research on wellbeing to inform their relationship with their citizens. As before, wellbeing data is used to inform electoral campaigns and policy development. However, there is a new emphasis on managing citizens' expectations. Germany is faced with a need to scale down its welfare spending. In the longer term, the country must reduce citizens' dependency on government as a source of wellbeing while maintaining individuals' contribution to democratic, economic, and social life. One initiative has been an attempt by government to manipulate the political discourse on wellbeing. Inspired by the report of the Stiglitz-Sen-Fitoussi Commission (2009), the German Federal parliament appointed a Commission of Inquiry on Growth, Wellbeing and the Quality of Life,[2] which reported in May 2013. Amongst other things, it investigated alternatives to objective explanators of wellbeing, including claims that there may not be a straightforward correlation between increases in objective living standards and levels of subjective wellbeing (the Easterlin paradox[3]). A more diffuse approach to managing expectations can be seen in the promotion of a general discourse of austerity that has come to characterise political debate in Germany.

Profiling German wellbeing: the Germans as 'materialist pessimists'

Recent OECD figures (in 2010) suggest that, at around 6.7 overall,[4] Germans' life satisfaction is close to the OECD average. However, they confirmed the Easterlin paradox in that, generally, life satisfaction demonstrates a weak correlation to *per capita* income (OECD 2011: 270–1). EU statistics confirm that, in terms of their objective living standards, Germans perhaps ought to be happier. The German standard of living corresponds quite closely to the average for the EU15. However, in a comparison of subjective evaluations across all EU member states, Germans tend to see themselves as worse off than the average European. Germans are relatively happy with their lives in the private sphere. It is the public sphere that triggers pessimism, particularly where respondents are asked to evaluate their current personal situation in relation to a past point in time, or expectations for a future point in time (Habich and Noll 2009: 44–5). Not only do the Germans have a gloomy perspective on life, they also emerge as a nation driven by material satisfaction. A European comparison reveals that household income exerts an unusually strong influence not only on east Germans' but also on west Germans' subjective well-being. Whereas this finding is quite typical for citizens of transition economies such as eastern Germany, in the west German context it confounds expectations that once a satisfactory level of material security has been attained, people tend to look to other, 'post-materialist' values in achieving a fulfilled and happy life. In both west and east Germany, household income has an impact on subjective wellbeing more typical of a central or eastern European (CEE) country than an EU15 country (Noll and Weick 2010b: 8). From a rationalist perspective, Habich and Noll have characterised the Germans as 'realistic pessimists'. They and others suggest that German pessimism is based on recent experience of stagnating real income levels, high unemployment, and rational comparisons with rising standards of living in other European countries (Habich and Noll 2009: 45; Noll and Weick 2010a: 77, 2010b: 6, 8–9).

As we will see, for certain sectors of society there is evidence to support the claim that perceptions of wellbeing incorporate a rational response to constraints on standards of living. However, given that individuals tend to frame their social expectations within a proximate and tangible frame of reference, it is unlikely that rational comparisons with other Europeans play a key role in Germans' subjective wellbeing (Schöneck et al. 2011: 2). Moreover, whereas both cognitive and affective processes are involved in determining individuals' subjective wellbeing (Glatzer and Zapf 1984; Diener et al. 1999), it is the affective component that tends to dominate in overall evaluations of subjective wellbeing (Veenhoven 2010). This suggests that cultural explanations for German pessimism and materialism are at least as important as rational explanations. By a cultural logic, Germans might be characterised as 'materialist-pessimists' (Hogwood 2011). Germans have a deep-rooted cultural relationship with pessimism. Historically, pessimism and sadness have not always been perceived as pathological states. An evolving cultural discourse of melancholy has at times elevated the experience of sadness to an enviable and valued condition, particularly during the Renaissance, when it was associated with creative genius. Since World War II, in common with other western postindustrial societies, Germany has increasingly subscribed to a norm of happiness and has correspondingly pathologised sadness (Cosgrove 2012: 2–6). Nevertheless, in its cultural resonance, pessimism still enjoys a measure of dignity in Germany. Materialism has been prominent in the FRG's normative values since World War II. In the context of the physical devastation and moral bankruptcy experienced in Germany in the aftermath of the war, the 1950s 'economic miracle' effectively substituted for a debased national identity as a positive focus for collective pride. In the early 1950s Helmut Schelsky coined the phrase 'nivellierte Mittelstandsgesellschaft' (levelled middle-class society) to describe the way in which West German society was evolving (Schelsky 1953). The unprecedented social mobility of the early postwar period was producing a society in which a new, broad-based middle class was coming to dominate the values and attitudes of the new FRG, as well as its workforce. This broad middle class identified strongly with materialist values and rooted them in the postwar cultural landscape. Wealth was proudly displayed through the ostentatious consumption of luxury goods. For much of the postwar period, the successful German economic model continued to deliver high levels of economic security and prosperity. German society was associated with low levels of social inequality, security of employment and social status, comfortable living standards, and confidence in the potential for upward mobility. As discussed below, although this confidence began to crumble in the 1980s, the value of materialism was upheld and would be carried over and enhanced in the social discourse through the processes of German unification (Giesen 1993: 248–55). The prominence of the materialist discourse suggests that Germans' subjective linkage of household income with wellbeing may be more affective than cognitive.

Current indicators of wellbeing in Germany

Taken at face value, Germany appears to be a relatively cohesive and equal society. However, current indicators suggest that three cohorts are vulnerable to lower than average levels of wellbeing. These comprise a diverse group of the most vulnerable in society; east Germans; and the 'middle' middle class. Of these, the relative subjective illbeing of society's most vulnerable is most readily linked to the material impacts of the current economic downturn and economic liberalisation. This group is distinguished by incomes so low as to threaten material deprivation and social marginalisation. The relative illbeing of east Germans is more complex because it also involves deep-rooted constructs of consumerism and east–west relations. Of all the vulnerable cohorts, it is the 'middle' middle classes that appear to have been most negatively affected by a new discourse of austerity in Germany.

The most vulnerable

There is a widely accepted assumption that, in a democratic society, individual and collective wellbeing is predicated on equality of access to social and economic goods. It follows that high levels of social cohesion are indicative of a happy, and therefore healthy, society. The EU's statistical service Eurostat uses standard structural indicators to assess levels of social cohesion in participating member states. These include indicators of income, poverty, social inclusion, and living conditions.[5] The S80/S20 ratio demonstrates the inequality of income distribution in its member states.[6] In 2010 the EU member states were characterised by relatively wide and largely stable inequalities in income distribution: on average the income of the wealthiest 20 per cent of the population was five times that of the poorest 20 per cent (an S80/S20 ratio of 5.0 for the EU27). In these terms, German society does not differ radically from comparable European countries. In 2010 Germany's S80/S20 ratio was 4.5, falling between that of the Netherlands (3.8), and France (4.6) and the UK (5.6) (DeStatis 2012a).

Nevertheless, this still points to relatively high levels of income inequality in Germany and suggests that certain individuals and groups may be at risk of social exclusion. Within the EU, risk of social exclusion is attributed to individuals experiencing at least one of three key conditions: risk of poverty; severe material deprivation; or belonging to a household characterised by 'very low work intensity'. The 'risk-of-poverty' indicator and the 'very-low-work-intensity' indicator are material and relative. Individuals are considered to be at risk of poverty if their net income falls below 60 per cent of the median of the member state in question.[7] In Germany, this applied to those with a monthly income of less than €952 in 2010. The designation 'very low work intensity' is applied to households whose adult members work less than 20 per cent of their joint capacity.[8] The indicator 'severe material deprivation' is a subjective measure derived from respondents' self-assessment on the basis of nine measures of deprivation.[9]

Between 2005 and 2009, Germany experienced a sharp rise in the percentage of its population at risk of poverty and social exclusion, from 18.4 per cent to 20 per cent. One factor accounting for this was the relatively high proportion of very low work intensity households in Germany. Since 2009 this cohort has remained stable. In 2011, 19.9 per cent (some 16 million people) in Germany were facing poverty or social exclusion. These findings rank Germany's risk rating slightly higher than those of the neighbouring Netherlands (15.7 per cent) and France (19.3 per cent), but lower than that of the UK (22.7 per cent) (DeStatis 2012a). Of this cohort, 15.8 per cent were at risk of poverty; 5.3 per cent, by their own reckoning, were experiencing severe material deprivation; and 11.1 per cent were living in a household whose members' work intensity was very low in relation to their potential. Overall then, one in five in Germany find themselves constrained by their material circumstances in engaging with normal patterns of social engagement. Within this group of the socially marginalised, there was relatively little differentiation by gender and age. However, women were slightly more at risk than men (21.3 per cent compared with 18.5 per cent). In age terms, the over-65s (15.3 per cent) were the least likely to fall into this cohort and those aged between 18 and 64 (21.3 per cent) faced the highest risk. Women between the ages of 18 and 64 scored the highest levels across the board (22.4 per cent) on poverty and social exclusion indicators (DeStatis 2012b).

However, this overview masks a degree of social polarisation that becomes evident once differences in household are factored in for those at risk of poverty. For example, pensioners (the over-65s) living alone are at a substantially higher risk of poverty than the general population in Germany (24.1 per cent compared with 15.8 per cent). Two highly vulnerable groups stand out, though: the under-65s living alone (36.1 per cent) and single parents and their dependent children (37.1 per cent) (DeStatis 2012c; see also Grabka et al. 2012). Well over a third of individuals in these categories face material hardship, financial insecurity, and social marginalisation. Even those in employment may face difficulties in meeting household expenses from the often low-paid or casual labour opportunities open to them. The situation of these groups emerges as even more precarious when other information is taken into consideration. For example, in 2010 a high proportion (63.3 per cent) of single parents felt that their accommodation was substandard, reporting problems of damp, of restricted daylight, or of noise disturbance. Further, 26.8 per cent of the group of single parents at risk of poverty revealed that they were falling behind with essential payments on items such as rent, utility bills, and credit cards (DeStatis 2012a).

Perceptions of imminent social risk – that is, the fear of slipping into poverty and deprivation – seem to be limited to lower income and status groups in German society. Indeed, objective indicators suggest that this is an entirely rational fear, grounded in situations of material insecurity for those concerned. The higher up the social and income ladder Germans are placed, the less likely they are to be troubled by fears of a short-term change for the worse in their fortunes. Irrespective of how one evaluates one's own financial and social security, though, the issue of social polarisation has recently risen to the top of the agenda of public concern in Germany. In 2010, when asked to rate their concerns about a range of social tensions, respondents identified the gap between rich and poor as by far the most significant. East Germans, with their socialist, egalitarian heritage, had already been attuned to social injustice in the FRG, and their perceptions of this problem rose only marginally between 1998 and 2010, from 73 per cent to 76 per cent. However, awareness amongst west Germans of a rich–poor divide has soared over the same time period, from 54 per cent in 1998 to 76 per cent in 2010 (Göbel et al. 2011: 383).

East Germans

East Germans' perceptions of illbeing also appear to be grounded partly in objective reality, but in this cohort they are shaped by political and cultural discourses that go beyond current material indicators. Experiences of postwar state rivalry and the construction of the unification project in material terms have had a lasting impact on how east Germans understand and evaluate happiness (Hogwood 2011: 150). During the Cold War years, the rival East and West German states engaged in overt competition as providers of social security for their citizens. The FRG rapidly established itself as a benchmark for East Germans' troubled relationship with consumerism, in which a disapproval of Western capitalist decadence was mixed with a desire for a share of the luxury consumer goods enjoyed by their West German neighbours (Hogwood 2002: 55, 2012: 4). This politicisation of consumerism was compounded by the way in which German unification (1989–90) was legitimised and pursued by West German government elites (Hogwood 2011: 149–50). FRG Chancellor Helmut Kohl used the theme of material progress overtly and instrumentally to win over popular opinion for unification in East Germany. The unification project was constructed in material terms, under which economic success was portrayed as the key means of future social integration of east and west Germans (Offe 1996: 139, table 7.1). Until the recent interest in new conceptualisations of wellbeing, successive governments have interpreted the ongoing inner unity project largely as one of a convergence of living standards, measurable by economic indicators.

These developments have influenced wellbeing in east Germany in a number of ways. Even within the German 'materialist-pessimist' cultural outlook, objective economic indicators have proved an unusually strong determinant of subjective wellbeing for east Germans. Significantly, it is not their material standards of living per se that make east Germans unhappy, but rather comparisons of objective economic wellbeing with a west German benchmark. As the Easterlin paradox suggests, it is relative, rather than absolute income that matters most for an individual's life evaluations. People are generally happier if they feel at least as well off as those in their reference group. Since the postwar economic boom of the 1950s, east Germans have compared their lot with west Germans rather than with the objectively more readily comparable lives of citizens in CEE states. In east Germany, the unification process promoted unrealistically high expectations of a rapid improvement in individual prosperity and lifestyle to match the west German standard. These factors have combined to depress potential levels of wellbeing in east Germany.

Together with the restricted timeframe for the international diplomatic resolution of German unification, the prominence of material factors in the unification discourse stifled any meaningful debate at the time about the future of German democracy. This has had a fundamental impact on inner-German relations – and, by extension, on east German wellbeing – in united Germany. On German unification in 1990, the population of the former GDR was drawn into the pre-existing political, legal, and economic structures of a territorially expanded FRG. With this, the post-authoritarian democratisation of the former GDR was taken as formally accomplished. Only marginal elements of the socialist political heritage were recognised in the post-unification constitutional revision of the FRG's Basic Law (Grundgesetz), which effectively served to uphold the constitutional status quo. At a material level, the FRG's handling of east Germany's post-socialist economic transition undoubtedly ensured a far more stable and comfortable transition experience than that endured by neighbouring CEE citizens. However, the sense of political disempowerment associated with the entrenchment of asymmetric east–west power relations left many east Germans with a sense of being second-class citizens.

In practice, the post-unification equalisation of living standards promised by successive German governments has proved difficult to realise. In objective terms, there is still a significant discrepancy between the living standards of east and west Germans. In 2009, the rate of unemployment in the western Federal states or *Länder* lay at 6.4 per cent compared with 12.6 per cent in the eastern Länder, while the average employment income in the east lay just short of 77 per cent of that in the west. Even factoring in tax breaks and supplementary benefits such as pensions and child benefit payments, east Germans' disposable income amounted on average to just over 78 per cent of the west German level (Statistisches Bundesamt 2010). Since 2005, just short of 20 per cent of east Germans have been considered at risk of poverty, compared with around 14 per cent of west Germans. Moreover, although levels of income inequality in

Germany overall may have peaked, for east Germany there are still signs that the poor are getting poorer in terms of disposable income (Grabka *et al.* 2012). A higher risk of poverty for east Germans is unsurprising, given that east Germans are more likely than west Germans to be unemployed or to earn a lower wage. It is not yet known whether inclusion in this at-risk group is transitory or whether east German households in this category are effectively stuck in a poverty trap.

For east Germans, the first decade of unification was marred by a crisis of subjective illbeing. The dislocation of unification was initially expressed in feelings of helplessness and low levels of confidence and self-worth. Levels of satisfaction with material circumstances such as work, household income, and standard of living – and levels of wellbeing overall – gradually recovered. Since the mid to late 1990s, these measures of east German wellbeing have tracked the west German profile without quite attaining west German levels. Overall levels of wellbeing currently fall short of west German levels by around 0.4, at 6.5 to west Germans' 6.9 (Göbel *et al.* 2011: 377). The east German wellbeing profile can be characterised as one of 'stalled approximation' with west Germany (Hogwood 2011: 150–2).

The twin characteristics of materialism and pessimism feature particularly strongly in east Germans' subjective wellbeing. The persistence of the west German reference culture in framing east Germans' expectations suggests that their relative dissatisfaction is linked primarily to conflictual collective identities. Opinion research shows that, 20 years after unification, there is still an entrenched public perception of separate and competing 'eastern' and 'western' interests in Germany,[10] but the tension is much more keenly felt by east Germans than by west Germans. In 2011 a group of Germans were asked to compare their own material standard of living with that of the average German. Of the group who had been living in the GDR in 1990 (designated for the purposes of the study as 'east Germans'), 42 per cent judged that their standard of living was either 'worse' or 'much worse' than that of the average German. In comparison, only 10.7 per cent of the west Germans opted for these two categories. East Germans' pessimistic outlook on their own wellbeing extended to evaluations of change in their individual standard of living compared with their situation 10 years previously (here and following, see Schöneck *et al.* 2011: 4–7). Almost twice as many of the east German respondents (41.5 per cent compared with 24.4 per cent of the west Germans) judged that their current standard of living was 'worse' or 'much worse' than 10 years before. Further, a quarter of the east Germans reported that they had not attained the standard of living they had previously hoped for, compared with only 12.7 per cent of the west Germans. Again, twice as many east as west Germans (20.4 per cent compared with 11.1 per cent) feared that they might face financial hardship over the coming year. East Germans' evaluation of their position in society (and, by extension, of social justice) also tended to a more pessimistic view than that of west Germans. Since unification, east and west Germans have been polled on a regular basis on whether they believe they are getting their fair share of the country's prosperity in relation to others. Since 1992, west German responses have remained stable, with around 65 per cent believing that they were enjoying their fair share or more of the country's prosperity. Over the same period, only 29 per cent of east Germans responded positively. The most recent figures show that 60 per cent of west Germans compared with 32 per cent of east Germans believe that they are getting their fair share or more (Scheuer 2011: 388–9).

These findings might in part be explained by the persistence in objective differences in the material standards of living enjoyed by east and west Germans respectively. However, research has confirmed that, also for east Germans, it is relative rather than absolute income that is significant for life happiness (Easterlin and Plagnol 2008). With this insight, the findings take on a cultural relevance. They illustrate the way in which expectations framed under circumstances many years in the past may continue to exert a powerful impact on perceptions of wellbeing in the present. In this case, east Germans' expectations, cemented through a western reference culture that originated during the Cold War years of German division, have incorporated understandings of a structural superiority of western living standards over those in the east. In consequence, there is a lasting perception that west German standards of living are inherently unreachable (Hogwood 2011: 156). This suggests that differences in subjective wellbeing between east and west Germans persist not primarily because of slow progress on the convergence of objective living standards but because of a failure to address the sense of material inferiority vis-à-vis West Germans instilled in East Germans during the Cold War years. By extension, in the context of the materially determined cultural outlook and consumer society in the FRG, a sense of material inferiority equates with a sense of social inferiority. In expressing dissatisfaction, east Germans are articulating an affective as well as a rational response to material indicators of status and inclusion in their social environment.

In spite of their more acute awareness of east–west difference, east Germans are just as likely as west Germans to feel a bond with the 'other' Germans. When asked to take a stance on the statement: 'The citizens of the other part of Germany are in many ways more foreign to me than those in other countries', east–west responses virtually mirrored each other. Only around a fifth of respondents tended to agree or agreed fully with the idea that the 'other' Germans were 'more foreign'. The other four fifths tended to disagree or disagreed fully (Terwey et al. 2009: 335). This suggests that the tensions that persist in inner-German relations can be described as 'sibling rivalries' rather than as a more fundamental conflict (Hogwood 2011: 153).

The 'middle' middle class

As we have seen in the context of east–west subjective wellbeing, individual evaluations of past circumstances in relation to the present can reveal a great deal about underlying collective perspectives on society. In a similar way, subjective evaluations of an individual's future prospects in life can give an insight both into cultural predispositions and into the overall levels of collective confidence in current and future government performance. Opinion research into individual levels of optimism or pessimism demonstrates how members of the public perceive the resilience and dynamism of their society. At an individual level, lack of confidence in the future may sap social dynamism. For example, in an uncertain labour market, individuals might choose to avoid the financial risk of further education or vocational training, thereby restricting their own future social mobility and potential individual contribution to social and economic life. For policymakers, negative evaluations of future prospects might indicate growing voter frustration with the government in office that might influence the next election; or a falling consumer confidence that might have a negative impact on the economy.

It is the perceptions of the 'middle' middle class that give the clearest indication of the tensions arising out of economic uncertainties and new social challenges in German society. For the greater part of the postwar period, the German middle class held little interest for academics. They were considered unproblematic: the epitome of stability, the bulwark of the democratic system, and the main driver of upward social mobility. With the economic upturn in (West) Germany in the 1950s, confidence in increasing prosperity and collective upward mobility became fundamental tenets of the middle class. However, since the new millennium, fuelled by the financial and economic crisis of 2008–09 and the ongoing eurozone crisis, concerns about employment insecurity and social marginalisation have become increasingly common. Particularly vulnerable to these developments, the middle class in Germany has been dubbed a new 'zone of status anxiety' (Schöneck *et al.* 2011: 1, 4; also Lengfeld and Hirschle 2009; Mau 2012). This represents a seismic shift in the subjective outlook of the social mainstream and poses a fundamental challenge to the postwar model of German society. Unsurprisingly, there has been a prominent focus on middle-class status anxiety and downward social mobility in recent national debate on precarious employment and marginalisation (see e.g. Burzan 2008).

Defined in terms of income distribution, the middle class in Germany is by far the most significant group, comprising around 62 per cent of the population at the time of unification. The new millennium brought a period of economic stagnation and the middle income group underwent a rapid contraction, from 62 per cent in 2000 to 54 per cent in 2006. The shrinking of the middle class was accompanied by internal polarisation marked by simultaneous upward and downward mobility. However, the most noticeable trend within the middle class was a downward drift to the lower-income margins. In real terms, middle-class individuals at the lower-income margins now faced slipping into the group in German society at risk of poverty. This trend might in part be attributable to the relatively high rate of unemployment of the early 2000s. However, it was underpinned by more fundamental structural changes in employment patterns, particularly the reduction of full-time employment in favour of lower-work-intensity employment; and social change, such as the breakdown of the nuclear family and the rise in single-parent households (Grabka and Frick 2008: 103–05).

These changes appear to have launched a lasting crisis of confidence within the middle class. Of this group, the lower-income band of the middle class is most likely to suffer anxiety over imminent risk of falling into financial difficulties. Objective indicators show that these fears are not unwarranted. However, concerns about longer-term prosperity are expressed not only by the lower-income groups but by middle-class respondents across the board, particularly those in the middle income band (the 'middle' middle class) (Schöneck *et al.* 2011). Evidence appears to suggest that members of the 'middle' middle class do not fear restrictions in income *per se* – which in many cases would not threaten poverty – but an accompanying threat to their social position. In 2005 a record 26 per cent of the middle class claimed that they were 'very worried' about their financial situation. Even with the beginnings of an economic recovery, there was little sign of a return in confidence (Grabka and Frick 2008: 106–07). Subjective indicators of wellbeing reveal a complex interdependency between material security and social status amongst the middle classes in Germany. When respondents were asked to compare their material standard of living with that of the average German citizen, 58.4 per cent – a group approximating to the size of Germany's middle class – responded that they were roughly as well off as the average. However, long-term expectations of downward social mobility have become increasingly prominent. A third of middle-class respondents (33.5 per cent) now anticipate that they will not be able to maintain their current standard of living in old age. Almost as many (over 30 per cent) believe that their children's generation is likely to experience downward social mobility (Schöneck *et al.* 2011: 4–6). Particularly respondents from the 'middle' middle class express an exaggerated fear of downward social mobility in relation to their objective standard of living and objective indicators of social mobility. The twin traits of materialism and pessimism are evident in these findings. The assertion of being as good as others in material terms combined with heightened risk perceptions of future prosperity suggest that the middle class is a group for whom social status and social engagement are very strongly associated with material factors. It has been argued that the 'respectable employees' of the middle class are particularly hard hit in conditions of social uncertainty because their heightened sense of social responsibility and pronounced work ethic may restrict their potential for flexibility (Vester 2006: 273, cited in Burzan 2008: 11).

Future wellbeing in Germany

In terms of wellbeing at least, Germany demonstrates the hallmarks of a 'normal' European polity. Overall, Germans' life satisfaction comes close to the European average, and the country's level of social cohesion does not stand out in any way. However, these general indicators fail to convey the complex processes and relationships involved in the construction of individual and collective wellbeing in Germany. Since World War II, European governments have relied on increasing economic growth and prosperity to promote a vital, socially mobile society and to provide welfare support for those in need. In the face of long-term resource constraints, they are now exploring new ways of promoting citizen wellbeing. German governments have traditionally viewed the equalisation of living standards across the FRG as the route to social cohesion. Now, in addition to 'buying' citizen wellbeing, they are looking at the potential for alternative subjective constructions of wellbeing in society.

The findings of this chapter highlight some of the difficulties they may face in decoupling subjective perceptions of wellbeing from material prosperity. Overall, the Germans emerge as a nation of 'materialist-pessimists'. Germans' understanding of wellbeing is heavily dependent on their material standard of living. The most vulnerable and the lower-income groups within the middle class associate their worsening economic prospects with marginalisation in a society that once prided itself on its openness and equality. This group's subjective perceptions of illbeing are tied to actual experiences of material hardship. In order to secure higher levels of wellbeing for the most vulnerable and the low earners, there is no alternative for German governments but to address the objective causes and consequences of poverty and deprivation. For east Germans, attachment to objective standards of living is coloured by cultural understandings that go back to the Cold War division. Deep-rooted perceptions of inequality with west Germans continue to fuel a pessimistic outlook and heightened perceptions of cultural and social conflict along an east–west divide. Continued government efforts to secure equal standards of living for west and east Germans alike may help to mollify east Germans; but the root of the illbeing experienced by east Germans is one of perceived political inequality. For the core middle class, the association of material prosperity with wellbeing is elemental in that it validates their individual and collective identity. The discourse of austerity accompanying the European financial crises of the 21st century has served only to heighten middle-class anxieties, even in cases where a reduction in living standards would not carry with it any real threat of poverty. Governments' challenge here is to develop a new social model that supports this core middle class, with its fixed ideas and aspirations of career path and material rewards, in what may prove to be a difficult adjustment to new economic realities.

Notes

1 It is widely recognised that an individual's personality or emotional predisposition also exerts a strong influence on his or her subjective wellbeing. However, in this chapter attention is restricted to structural and cultural influences on German wellbeing.
2 For an English-language summary of the findings of the Commission on 'Wachstum, Wohlstand, Lebensqualität – Wege zu nachhaltigem Wirtschaften und gesellschaftlichem Fortschritt in der sozialen Marktwirtschaft', see www.bpb.de/shop/buecher/schriftenreihe/175745/schlussbericht-der-enquete-43kommission (accessed 9 September 2014).
3 The Easterlin paradox argues that an increase in personal income leads to an increase in an individual's subjective wellbeing, but that a rise in a country's average income does not produce a correspondingly higher average subjective wellbeing for that country.
4 The indicator is based on the 'Cantril ladder', which asks respondents to rate their choices from the worst (0) to the best (10) possible.

5 Germany has contributed since 2005 to the European Union's dataset EU-SILC (European Union Statistics on Income and Living Conditions) on income, poverty, social exclusion, and living conditions. For full details of the current findings see http://epp.eurostat.ec.europa.eu/portal/page/portal/income_social_inclusion_living_conditions/data/main_tables (accessed 14 April 2013). The most recent results for Germany can be found in DeStatis 2012a.

6 The income quintile share ratio or S80/S20 ratio is a measure of the inequality of income distribution. On the basis of equivalised disposable incomes, it is calculated as the ratio of total income received by the 20 per cent of the population with the highest income (the top quintile) to that received by the 20 per cent of the population with the lowest income (the bottom quintile). For further information, see http://epp.eurostat.ec.europa.eu/statistics_explained/index.php/Glossary:Income_quintile_share_ratio (accessed 9 September 2014).

7 The at-risk-of-poverty threshold is set at 60 per cent of the national median equivalised disposable income. For further information, see http://epp.eurostat.ec.europa.eu/statistics_explained/index.php/Glossary:At-risk-of-poverty_rate (accessed 9 September 2014).

8 In EU statistics the term 'work intensity' refers to the ratio between the number of months that household members of working age (aged 18–59, excluding students aged 18–24) worked during the income reference year, and the total number of months that could theoretically have been worked by the same household members. For further information, see http://epp.eurostat.ec.europa.eu/statistics_explained/index.php/Glossary:Persons_living_in_households_with_low_work_intensity (accessed 9 September 2014).

9 These comprise difficulties in paying rent or utility bills on time; affording adequate heating in the home; paying unanticipated expenses; affording a nutritious meal (with meat, fish, or vegetarian protein) every other day; and affording an annual week's holiday away from home; and inability to afford a household car, washing machine, colour television, or telephone.

10 This holds whether survey questions are designed so as to pit western and eastern interests against one another or whether they are framed solely in terms of either western or eastern interests.

Bibliography

Bentham, J. (1789) *An Introduction to the Principles of Morals and Legislation*, reissued by J. Burns and H.L.A. Hart (eds) (1996), Oxford: Clarendon Press.

Berg, M. and Veenhoven, R. (2010) 'Income inequality and happiness in 119 Nations: In search for an optimum that does not appear to exist', in B. Greve (2010) (ed.) *Happiness and Social Policy in Europe*, Cheltenham: Edward Elgar, 174–94.

Bruni, L. and Porta, P.L. (2005) *Economics and Happiness: Framing the Analysis*, Oxford: Oxford University Press.

Burzan, N. (2008) 'Die Absteiger: Angst und Verunsicherung in der Mitte der Gesellschaft', *Aus Politik und Zeitgeschichte*, 33(34): 6–12.

Cosgrove, M. (2012) 'Introduction: sadness and melancholy in German-language literature from the seventeenth century to the present: an overview', in M. Cosgrove and A. Richards (eds) *Edinburgh German Yearbook 6: Sadness and Melancholy*, New York: Camden House, 1–18.

DeStatis (Statistisches Bundesamt) (2012a) *Leben in Europa (EU-SILC). Einkommen und Lebensbedingungen in Deutschland und der Europäischen Union*, Wiesbaden: Statistisches Bundesamt, 14 December 2012.

DeStatis (2012b) 'Jede/r Fünfte in Deutschland von Armut oder sozialer Ausgrenzung betroffen', press release 369/12, 23 October 2012. Online. Available at https://www.destatis.de/DE/PresseService/Presse/Pressemitteilungen/2012/10/PD12_369_634.html (accessed 14 April 2013).

DeStatis (2012c) '15.8 per cent der Bevölkerung waren 2010 armutsgefährdet', press release 362/12, 17 October 2012. Online. Available at https://www.destatis.de/DE/PresseService/Presse/Pressemitteilungen/2013/03/PD13_121_634.html (accessed 14 April 2013).

Diener, E. (1984) 'Subjective well-being', *Psychological Bulletin*, 93(3): 542–75.

Diener, E., Lucas, R.E., Schimmack, U., and Helliwell, J. (2009) *Well-Being for Public Policy*, Oxford: Oxford University Press.

Diener, E., Suh, E.M., Lucas, R.E., and Smith, H.E. (1999) 'Subjective well-being: Three decades of progress', *Psychological Bulletin*, 125(2): 276–302.

Easterlin, R.A. (2002) *Happiness in Economics*, Cheltenham: Edward Elgar.

Easterlin, R.A. and Plagnol, A.C. (2008) 'Life satisfaction and economic conditions in East and West Germany pre- and post-Unification', *Journal of Economic Behavior and Organization*, 68(3–4): 433–44.

Frey, B.S. and Stutzer, A. (2002) *Happiness and Economics: How the Economy and Institutions Affect Human Well-Being*, Princeton: Princeton University Press.

Giesen, B. (1993) *Die Intellektuellen und die Nation: Eine deutsche Achsenzeit*, Frankfurt a.m.: Suhrkamp.

Glatzer, W. and Bös, M. (1998) 'Subjective attendants of unification and transformation in Germany', *Social Indicators Research*, 43: 171–96.

Glatzer, W. and Zapf, W. (eds) (1984) *Lebensqualität in der Bundesrepublik. Objektive Lebensbedingungen und subjektives Wohlbefinden*, Frankfurt a.m.: Campus.

Göbel, J., Habich, R., and Krause, P. (2011) 'Subjektives Wohlbefinden', in Statistisches Bundesamt (DeStatis) and Wissenschaftszentrum Berlin für Sozialforschung (WZB) *Datenreport 2011. Ein Sozialbericht für die Bundesrepublik Deutschland*, Bonn: Bundeszentrale für politische Bildung, chapter 15.1: 377–84.

Grabka, M.M. and Frick, J.R. (2008) 'Schrumpfende Mittelschicht – Anzeichen einer dauerhaften Polarisierung der verfügbaren Einkommen?' *DIW Wochenbericht*, 75(10): 101–08.

Grabka, M.M., Goebel, J., and Schupp, J. (2012) 'Höhepunkt der Einkommensungleichheit in Deutschland überschritten?' *DIW Wochenbericht*, 79(43): 3–15.

Habich, R. and Noll, H.-H. (2009) 'Realistische Pessimisten. Deutsche sind mit vielen Lebensumständen unzufriedener als ihre Nachbarn', *WZB-Mitteilungen*, 123: 44–5.

Helliwell, J.F. (2002) *Globalization and Well-Being*, Vancouver: UBC Press.

Helliwell, J.F., Layard, R., and Sachs, J. (eds) (2012) *World Happiness Report*, New York: The Earth Institute, Columbia University.

Hogwood, P. (2002) '"Red is for Love . . .": Citizens as consumers in East Germany', in J. Grix and P. Cooke (eds) *East German Distinctiveness in a Unified Germany*, Edgbaston: University of Birmingham, 45–60.

Hogwood, P. (2011) '"How happy are you . . .?" Subjective well-being in East Germany twenty years after unification', *Politics*, 31(3): 148–58.

Hogwood, P. (2012) 'Political (re)learning and consumer culture in post-GDR society', *German Politics*, 21(1): 1–16.

Kahneman, D., Diener, E., and Schwarz, N. (1999) *Well-Being: The Foundations of Hedonic Psychology*, New York: Russell Sage Foundation.

Lengfeld, H. and Hirschle, J. (2009) 'Die Angst der Mittelschicht vor dem sozialem Abstieg: Eine Längsschnittanalyse 1984–2007', *Zeitschrift für Soziologie*, 38(5): 379–98.

Mau, S. (2012) *Lebenschancen: Wohin driftet die Mittelschicht?* Berlin: Suhrkamp.

Noll, H.-H. and Weick, S. (2010a) 'Subjective well-being in Germany: Evolutions, determinants and policy implications', in B. Greve (ed.) (2010) *Happiness and Social Policy in Europe*, Cheltenham: Edward Elgar, 69–88.

Noll, H.-H. and Weick, S. (2010b) 'Materielle Lebensbedingungen prägen Lebenszufriedenheit in Deutschland stärker als in anderen Ländern: Analysen zum subjektiven Wohlbefinden', *Informationsdienst Soziale Indikatoren*, ISI 44, GESIS, August 2010, 5–10.

OECD (2011) *How's Life? Measuring Well-Being*. Online. Available at www.oecd-ilibrary.org/economics/how-s-life_9789264121164-en (accessed 14 April 2013).

Offe, C. (1996) *Varieties of Transition: The East European and East German Experience*, Cambridge, MA: MIT Press.

Schelsky, H. (1953) *Wandlungen der deutschen Familie in der Gegenwart: Darstellung und Deutung einer empirisch-soziologischen Tatbestandsaufnahme*, Dortmund: Ardey.

Scheuer, A. (2011) 'Wertorientierungen, Ansprüche und Erwartungen', in Statistisches Bundesamt (DeStatis) and Wissenschaftszentrum Berlin für Sozialforschung (WZB) (2011) *Datenreport 2011: Ein Sozialbericht für die Bundesrepublik Deutschland*, Bonn: Bundeszentrale für politische Bildung, chapter 15.2: 385–92.

Schöneck, N.M., Mau, S., and Schupp, J. (2011) *Gefühlte Unsicherheit – Deprivationsängste und Abstiegssorgen der Bevölkerung in Deutschland* (SOEP Papers on Multidisciplinary Panel Data research no. 428), Berlin: DIW.

Statistisches Bundesamt (2010) *20 Jahre Deutsche Einheit, Wunsch oder Wirklichkeit?* Wiesbaden: Statistisches Bundesamt. Online. Available at https://www.destatis.de/DE/Publikationen/StatistischesJahrbuch/DeutscheEinheit.html (accessed 14 April 2013).

Stiglitz, J.E., Sen, A., and Fitoussi, J-P. (2009) *Report by the Commission on the Measurement of Economic Performance and Social Progress*. Online. Available at www.stiglitz-sen-fitoussi.fr (accessed 14 April 2013).

Terwey, M., Bens, A., Baumann, H., and Baltzer, S. (2009) (first published 2007) *Elektronisches Datenhandbuch, integrierter Datensatz und Surveydeskription ALLBUS 2006*, ZA-Nr. 4500, Cologne and Mannheim: GESIS. Online. Available at https://social-survey.gesis.org/ (accessed 14 April 2013).

Tov, W. and Diener, E. (2009) 'The well-being of nations. Linking together trust, cooperation and democracy', in E. Diener (ed.) *The Science of Well-Being: The Collected Works of Ed Diener*, Dordrecht: Springer, 155–73.

Veenhoven, R. (1991) 'Questions on happiness: Classical topics, modern answers, blind spots', in F. Strack, M. Argyle, and N. Schwartz (eds) *Subjective Wellbeing. An Interdisciplinary Perspective*, Oxford: Pergamon Press, 7–26.

Veenhoven, R. (2010) 'How universal is happiness?' in E. Diener, J. Helliwell, and D. Kahneman (eds) *International Differences in Well-Being*, New York: Oxford University Press.

Vester, M. (2006) 'Der Kampf um soziale Gerechtigkeit: Zumutungen und Bewältigungsstrategien in der Krise des deutschen Sozialmodells', in H. Bude and A. Willisch (eds) *Das Problem der Exklusion*, Hamburg: Hamburger Edition, 243–92.

Xefteris, D. (2012) 'Formalizing happiness', *Journal of Happiness Studies*, 13: 291–311.

10

Being East German in the Berlin Republic

Laurence McFalls with Alexandra Hausstein[1]

'Artikel 23 – Kein Anschluss unter dieser Nummer' (Article 23 – no connection/annexation at this number). Back in 1990, with this telephonic play on words, left-leaning Germans, mostly from the East but also from the West, criticised the use of Article 23 of the Federal Republic's Basic Law to expedite the incorporation of the newly formed Federal states or *Länder* on the territory of the defunct German Democratic Republic (GDR) into the Federal Republic. After all, Article 146, they rightly pointed out, foresaw reunification along with Germany's return to fully sovereign status and prescribed the replacement of the provisional Basic Law with a permanent constitution to be adopted freely by the entire German people. Mainstream politicians, pundits, and professors in the West, aside from invoking the need for a quick unification process in light of the international context of instability (in the Soviet Union in particular), generally opined that the Basic Law had proven historically and uniquely successful in guaranteeing the Federal Republic a stable liberal democratic constitutional order and therefore did not require replacing. They assumed that the failure of the GDR due to its apparently obvious lack of popular legitimacy meant that the eastern German minority would not be bringing in any new or alternative expectations or ideas for an all-German constitutional order.

Even at the more informal level of political culture, western Germans did not expect easterners to contribute any democratic values, despite their experience as the authors of Germany's only successful democratic revolution (and a peaceful one at that). If anything, it was assumed, they would require democratic re-education within the systematically transferred framework of the Federal Republic's provisional constitutional order. While Jürgen Habermas labelled the collapse of communism a 'nachholende [catch-up] Revolution' (Habermas 1990), the well-known political scientist Kurt Sontheimer (1990: 87) wrote that East German political culture would not be a factor 'that could independently influence the political culture of the Federal Republic'; instead, the revolution had 'left behind a political and intellectual vacuum that [would] now be progressively filled from the West'. Such self-satisfied western arguments resurfaced the following year during the so-called capital city debate (*Hauptstadtdebatte*) in the Bundestag, which led to a narrow vote in favour of moving unified Germany's seat of government from Bonn to Berlin. The proponents of Bonn invoked the if-it-ain't-broke-don't-fix-it argument, claiming that Bonn's quiet provincialism had played a key role in fostering the Federal Republic's pacific, Atlanticist, pro-European democratic culture, whereas Berlin backers argued that precisely because the democratic credentials of the Bonn Republic were so well grounded, something as cosmetic as a move to Berlin could not shake them. Berlin would be neither Weimar nor even Bonn plus Pankow: Berlin would be Bonn – with a bit of harmless historical memory and metropolitan flair thrown in.

Few Germans now remember Article 146 and its promise of a democratic constitution for a sovereign reunited Germany, but most intuitively recognise or speak of the Berlin Republic as something qualitatively different from the old Bonn Republic. Institutionally very little has changed. By the late 1990s, the institutional logic of the old Federal Republic had made politicians and voters in the new Länder behave much like those in the west, even if the relative success of successor parties to the communist SED (Socialist Unity Party) in their various manifestations has left some local colour (Yoder 1999; Davidson-Schmich 2006; and see Chapter 7). At the level of political culture, however, Germany qua the Berlin Republic has changed dramatically – at least if we understand political culture in the broad anthropological sense (as opposed to the narrower one of opinion pollsters, who tell us that democratic attitudes and values remain well implanted, generally stable, and broadly similar between east and west; see Petersen 2011). In this chapter, I shall examine the politically relevant cultural transformations in the Berlin Republic through: (a) a review of ethnographic and other social scientific studies of German (political) culture, with particular reference to the eastern context and to the questions of cultural rapprochement and rupture; (b) my own observations as a North American political scientist who has followed some 200 ordinary eastern Germans' adaptations to their new polity and society since 1990; and (c) a theoretical reflection on the new forms of subjectivity and power within Germany, forms that suggest that eastern Germans after the great experiment of unification may stand at the vanguard of the contemporary neoliberal order. I shall argue that, despite political and institutional continuities with the old Federal Republic, the Berlin Republic has brought a radical social and cultural break not only in the life histories of East Germans but for Germany and Europe as a whole.

The ethnography and social science of unification

In the early 1990s, when culture clashes between 'Ossis' and 'Wessis' (as former East and former West Germans now called each other) cast doubt not only on whether, in Willy Brandt's words, 'what belonged together was growing together' ('was zusammengehört, wächst zusammen'; Garton Ash 2001) but on whether the 'two Germanies' even belonged together, an American political scientist proposed considering East Germans an ethnic minority in reunited Germany (Howard 1995). At the Berlin conference where he defended his thesis, few of even the most embittered East Germans and none of the West Germans present were willing to entertain the idea. Some 15 years later, in April 2010, a Stuttgart labour court ruled that East Germans did not constitute an ethnic group within German society. The decision put an end to the claim of an East German accountant who had sued a West German company, which had chosen not to hire her on the grounds that she was an 'Ossi' (the company had neglected to erase a remark to this effect in the papers sent back to the unsuccessful candidate). If the court had considered East Germans an ethnic group, the plaintiff's claim might have been successful, as the case could have been judged as a violation of the General Equal Treatment Act (Allgemeines Gleichbehandlungsgesetz or AGG). In the media stir that followed, several anthropologists were asked for a statement and, of course, they disagreed on the case. Yet that they, like the court, took the case seriously indicates that the question is still open: do the East Germans have a particular collective identity/ethnicity that distinguishes them from the West Germans? No, said anthropologist Wolfgang Kaschuba (Prase 2010), 50 years of common experiences as citizens of the German Democratic Republic were not sufficient to create an ethnic identity. Yes, said anthropologist Thomas Bierschenk (2010), the East Germans have developed their own cultural particularities that distinguish them from West Germans.[2] Twenty years after the fall of the Berlin Wall and the accession of the former GDR to the Federal Republic of Germany, these issues obviously still mattered and raised the question whether the gap between East and West had closed in favour of a common German cultural identity.

Much has been written on the processes of not only the political, but also the social, cultural, and mental transformation of the new Federal states (*neue Länder*) in the wake of reunification. My own research on these processes has included an ongoing panel study that began in 1990 with biographical interviews of 202 randomly selected 'ordinary' eastern Germans. Despite significant attrition over the decades since, the continuity of my sample has allowed me to track the dynamics of cultural change. Before presenting some of my findings, however, I would like to provide a non-exhaustive overview of the state of research on culture and identity in eastern Germany since unification. The Federal Ministry of the Interior (Bundesministerium des Innern), for example, publishes an annual analysis of the advances and the status of German unification. In 2009 the Federal Ministry of Transport, Building, and Urban Development (Bundesministerium für Verkehr, Bau und Stadtentwicklung) launched a study of the perception and interpretation of German unification, basing its conclusions on studies in social sciences, politics, media, surveys, polls, and a cyberconference with 230 participants (Innovationsverbund Ostdeutschlandforschung 2009). Beyond such governmental evaluations, several joint research projects (such as the collaborative research centre SFB 580 at the universities of Jena and Halle) have studied the transformation processes in the eastern German Länder.[3] Media reports on surveys by the Emnid and Allensbach polling firms regularly stir up dust (e.g. the recent Emnid survey on behalf of the Federal Government that showed that most East Germans have a positive image of the GDR). The Innovationsverbund Ostdeutschlandforschung founded in 2005 (Innovation Network East Germany Research; www.ostdeutschlandforschung.net; Busch and Land 2006) provides a platform for young researchers with an interest in East German issues. Among the publications in sociology, psychology (Silbereisen *et al.* 2006), communication studies, economics, political sciences, history, and anthropology, qualitative and quantitative studies or second-hand analyses of empirical research abound.[4]

Ethnographic studies that inquire into the perceptions and representations of the transformation process in the life world of East German society remain scarce. Some autobiographical accounts from mostly East German writers provide – rather subjective – insight (Bisky 2005; Franck 2009; Maron 2010; Rusch 2009; Wolf 2010). Most autobiographical writings describe experiences in the former GDR, but stop short of discussing what it means to be East German in unified Germany (Bisky 2004; Hensel 2004; Rusch 2003). Only slowly have autobiographical writings on East German life in the 1990s appeared on the book market (Hacker *et al.* 2012; Hünniger 2011; Ide 2007; networking initiative www.dritte-generation-ost.de). Several writers and researchers have written political essays but without systematic empirical evidence or a clear research methodology (Ahbe 2005; Engler 1999; Engler 2002; Kollmorgen 2005; Wagner 2006). Some non-scientific, satirical reports of the experiences of West Germans in East Germany can be a fun read but again do not live up to scholarly standards (von Uslar 2010; Sonneborn and Coerper 2010);[5] and some accounts of the professional experiences of West Germans in East Germany read as if an international organisation had sent the authors to some wildly exotic country (Endlich 1999; Wolff 2012). Ethnographic studies were conducted early on until the late 1990s (Bittner 1998; Müller 2002), some by foreign researchers. Among the most interesting is the study of a Thuringian village in the restricted western border zone undertaken by Daphne Berdahl in the early and late 1990s (Berdahl 1999a). Despite the particularities of her case and her informants' retrospective accounts of the past, Berdahl's classic ethnography teases out the textures and ambivalences of daily life under authoritarian rule and during the often traumatic transformations of unification.

In addition to ethnographies, a vast social scientific literature on the transformation process in the new Länder offers analyses not only of the probabilities and improbabilities of unification in the social and cultural sphere, but also of the impact of social transformations on the psychosocial sphere (identity ruptures and their mending, the emergence of nostalgia or 'Ostalgie' and of distrust, fear); of the devaluation of old and the development of new competencies, skills, and coping strategies; of social innovations; of the formation of a collective memory, or of the culture of remembering and commemorating the GDR; and last but not least of public and private representations and stereotypes of East German reality in media discourses, political discourses, and private conversations.

This chapter cannot even begin to offer a systematic review of the research on East German social change under the Berlin Republic (nor can it consider the more subtle, almost imperceptible but nonetheless real changes that affected West German society). The research points to a social landscape in the East that has been changing so rapidly and with such drastic shifts, alterations, and displacements that in some regions East Germans must be seen as struggling to survive in the midst of abiding uncertainty. A 'failed state' had bestowed devalued social and cultural capital on its former citizens, and unification demanded a quick adaptation in learning new skills, competencies, tastes, and behaviour for a desired upward social mobility; but East Germans in most cases do not show failed individual biographies, nor could the East German population as a whole be considered a failure in the new system. On the contrary, 20 years after the accession of the GDR to the Federal Republic, eastern Germans enjoy a comparably high living standard and share similar values, tastes, and behaviours with western Germans. Still, there is a culture of remembering the GDR, as positive perceptions of the GDR and identifications as East Germans prevail: self-labelling as East Germans (*Ostdeutsche*) has replaced the 'former citizens of the GDR' (*ehemalige DDR-Bürger*) that was common through the 1990s. In this chapter I therefore use the designation East German to describe citizens of the Berlin Republic who were once citizens of the GDR.

This persistent mode of remembering the past is even more striking now that East Germans seem to have arrived fully in the post-Fordist, post-industrialist consumer culture of late capitalism.[6] The culture of the GDR lives on in the collective memory of eastern Germans as a counterculture to the present, as a culture of an idealised past, as a memory play, but it does not materialise in the present. GDR material culture ceased to exist in the early 1990s, when former East German production finally petered out and East German products were no longer available in the supermarkets and shops. Only a few brands continue to exist and almost exclusively East Germans consume these. Some engage in practices of re-enactment of an imagined GDR past using fragments of East German culture – consumer goods, clothes, music – to perform, publicly or privately, acts of mourning, shame, or pride (Hodgin and Pearce 2012; Rechtien and Tate 2011; Neller 2006; Clarke and Wölfel 2011; Saunders and Pinfold 2012).

East German material culture as an expression of identity constitutes a special case in contemporary capitalism, not only because of its pre-history from 1945 to 1990 but also because of the unique way it has been exposed to transformative social processes in the last 20 years. Those have taken place at much higher speed than elsewhere in Western Europe or in the post-communist East. During the last 20 years, East Germans were first exposed to a post-socialist transformation, and then (while still in the midst of radical restructuring) were hit by the next wave of social transformation. Deindustrialisation and the rise of service industries, unemployment, labour migration, the demographic challenges of an ageing society, and recurrent financial crises followed quickly upon reunification. Whereas the post-socialist transformation was limited to the eastern part of Germany, the transition from an industrialist, Fordist economy to a post-industrialist, post-Fordist economy concerns the whole Western world. In the West German Länder this process has been evolving since the late 1970s, but the East German Länder experienced the change much more immediately and with hardly any preparation, falling from the promised heavens of 'soziale Marktwirtschaft' (social market economy) and 'blühende Landschaften' (blooming landscapes) into the purgatory of neoliberal political economy. These two transitional processes brought about not only political and economic change, but upheaval and a marked diversification of East German society due to different experiences of the unification process (according to gender, generation, and region) and the development of different coping strategies as well as different levels of adaptation to the new system.

As decades of individual life arrangements became devalued after the Berlin Wall fell, biographical scripts were revised in response to the demands of a life in the shadow of growing uncertainty. In these scripts, labour and consumption play a significant role. Even though they can be considered essential values of high modernity, they were of importance in the GDR, too, and continue to be in late modern unified Germany. The destruction of its industry and the abolition of jobs and related social networks hit East Germany especially hard, not only because a 'right to work' had been inscribed in the GDR constitution, but also because professional life in the GDR had been the most important source of collective identity and interests, and quintessential to the notion of equality. In a society with almost zero official unemployment, to be actually unemployed, or rather not to work, was considered a sign of complete personal failure or social self-exclusion. To receive social welfare today is not a personal failure, since in some regions up to half of the population depends on welfare benefits. Ethnographic studies show that being a recipient of the welfare payments now called 'Hartz IV' and being unemployed does not mean that people do not work. Incidental earnings through illicit employment and multiple jobs are increasing. As the welfare state itself transforms, increasing labour migration, precarious living conditions, changing jobs, and phases of unemployment become the normal lot for substantial parts of the middle class, too. The research project *ÜberLeben* (Bude 2011a) as well as observations in Brandenburg by the journalist/author Moritz von Uslar (2010) confirm the importance of these transformations. While these transformations affect Germany as a whole, they are especially pertinent for peripheral towns and villages in East Germany. There, they require individuals to develop new attitudes and behaviours relative to their health and bodies, to their physical environment, to their social networks, to time management, and to communicative skills both as coping strategies and as markers for a proactive attitude towards life under conditions of constant uncertainty (Bude and Lantermann 2010). Von Uslar vividly describes the polished, even overblown appearances of Brandenburg's small-town citizens: the metrosexual men, the stylish 'Proll-Fighter' (proletarian fighters), their tidy cars and apartments, their socialising in pubs, boxing clubs, in front of the dairy bar, their hyperactive manner of speech ('Top-Speed-Labern'). East Germans on Hartz IV welfare support receive it only temporarily, therefore they do not see themselves as typical welfare recipients: 'Somehow we manage to get our money. We are Ossis, you see, we are smart at making money' ('Unser Geld kriegen wir immer irgendwie ran. Wir sind Ossis, verstehst du, wir sind tüchtig mit Geldmachen'; Von Uslar 2010: 107). And they reject the label of the lamenting East German stereotypical to some in the West: 'Whining? Not us' ('Jammern ist mit uns nicht'; von Uslar 2010: 108).

Under post-industrial conditions, consumption and the ability to consume replaces the world of work in building community, enabling socialising, and mastering social and communicative networks. Consumption and the acquisition of status markers in the form of material goods were important in East Germany, despite or precisely because of its economy of scarcity. What changed after unification was not the need for strategies for handling scarcity then and precarity now, but the consumer skill set. Previously that involved using social networks – within the GDR or beyond its borders to the West – to procure whatever the market did not offer; today those skills include finding deals, comparing prices, and making consumer decisions in the face of an overwhelming diversity of goods and insufficient monetary means to procure them. The challenge today is to develop a taste and to consume coherently according to one's self-positioning in a certain milieu. The researchers on the project *ÜberLeben* describe how discount markets, among the very first flowers of the 'blooming landscapes' of the new Länder, became the local crossroads for communication for a population that quickly made consumption part of its daily agenda and for which consumption evolved into a strategy of social integration where unemployment had caused disintegration. In such circumstances, even being a 'Nazi' can be a matter of style rather than a political attitude (Bude 2011a). The mode of consumption occupies not only the social sphere of networks and communication, but reaches into the private sphere of sex (consumed over the internet), especially in regions where young women emigrated and left behind an overpopulation of unemployed, angry young men. The degree of integration into the labour market and the different ability to consume differentiates eastern German society along the lines of age, gender, generation, and region.

Experiencing the twofold process of internal post-socialist and global post-Fordist transformations, East Germany was and still is the 'Lab East Germany': a site of experimentation and avant-garde for social innovation (Martens 2010; Engler 2002). Some innovations, especially in urban planning, stand out positively, such as Leinefelde, a restructured cityscape where socialist concrete high-rise buildings were transformed into an ultramodern architecture (Kil 2008). Under late capitalism, eastern Germans seem to have taken on the role of the avant-garde quite easily, even though West Germany's Christian Democratic Party (CDU) won the first free elections in the GDR with a recycled slogan from the 1950s: 'Keine Experimente' (no experiments). Social innovations, however, are taking place under present conditions of deindustrialisation, decline of the welfare state, capital flight, and a shortage of public funds, particularly under the most recent policies of austerity. The term 'avant-garde' should therefore be read as a euphemism for new coping strategies in the face of declining and shrinking opportunities that sooner or later will affect the West, too (Hein 2004). The difficulties and the many failures of the transformation process in East Germany must certainly be viewed in the context of considerable challenges for the Western industrialist nations as a whole.

Contrary to the literature published in the 1990s and 2000s that discussed the losses and costs of German unification for the eastern German Länder (especially perpetual inequality between East and West regarding economic power, level of prosperity, allowances and benefits, environmental issues, emigration, unemployment, demographic decline, and shrinking cities), recent social science literature looks at the signs of upward mobility, the return of East German migrant labourers to their home towns, successful coping strategies that build on transfers, and social innovations in times of uncertainty and scarcity. Innovations are evident in the fields of cultural policy, recultivation of landscapes, energy policies, urban planning, and restructuring (Bauer-Volke and Dietzsch 2003).

The example of East German transformation, both post-socialist and post-Fordist, is unique as it evolves within a discourse on 'being East German' and refers to a collective identity of East Germans. As sociologist Heinz Bude (2011a) argues on the basis of his field work in Wittenberge, East Germany does not exist any longer, but being East German is still an emotional and political reality. It is a reality that is constructed with reference and in contradistinction to the West Germans. Moritz von Uslar (2010) experienced this when, in what was supposed to be a friendly sparring match, his East German opponent beat him black and blue and in the end called him a 'western pig' ('Westsau'). This sense of belonging, though based on a common heritage, expresses itself variously. Bude analyses different strategies of distorting or confirming East German identity: total distortion or making oneself unrecognisable (as modelled by Angela Merkel); dosed distortion (television presenter Maybritt Illner); and open, deliberate provocation (the writer Heiner Müller). Paradoxically, even concealing an eastern identity, as opposed to playing it up strategically or provocatively, reaffirms that identity: Merkel's neutral blandness inevitably prompts reminders of her eastern origins (Bude 2011b). Speaking about a collective identity as East Germans therefore does not necessarily refer to social homogeneity or to a common East German subculture. Rather, as the transition process has come to an end, multiple ways of remembering the GDR and of coping differently with a new system have emerged.

It is precisely the invocation of an East German 'we' that caused anger, especially among East Germans, when Jana Hensel's book *After the Wall* (*Zonenkinder*) was published and catapulted to the top of the German bestseller list in 2002. Her literary account of life in the GDR was accused of being an uncritical narrative of the triviality of daily life in the GDR, which ignored that the GDR was an *Unrechtsstaat*: a state without rule of law. Reactions to movies like the telenovelas *Weissensee* and *Deckname Luna* (codename Luna) and to the film version of Uwe Tellkamp's novel *Der Turm (The Tower)* (Tellkamp 2008) caused similarly strong and diverse reactions: some East Germans applauded these representations, some consumed them as stories of their distant past, some criticised them, and others refused to watch them at all on the grounds that they were just more stories about the GDR written by West German scriptwriters and performed with West German actors. The pan-German mediatisation of the East German past and the fall of the Berlin Wall, largely controlled by West German authors, editors, or film industries, can be blamed for obstructing a public, diverse culture of remembrance particular to the East Germans, and is also making it harder to tackle the challenges of East Germans' post-unification experiences from a social anthropological perspective. According to Jana Hensel, the East has become 'foreign matter,' an exoticised subject in unified Germany, without its own public voice, judged and described by West German standards and categories, and by the West German media. The East German is thus characterised by voicelessness and invisibility (Hensel 2010). East Germans who have made a successful transition into the new system tend to deny their origins, migrants to the West[7] to remain silent about their provenance and overperform their adaptation by distorting their East German identities.

There is no literary or documentary account of the experiences of East Germans in the unified Germany. Those experiences are unique to East Germany, and the impossibility of authentically portraying and representing them in the context of an enforced West German view on things ('aufgezwungener fremder Blick') causes a certain kind of melancholia among East Germans, often dismissed as kitschy nostalgia (Hensel 2009a). That many have successfully survived the breakdown of the state and compensated the loss of status and deficiencies or differences in education, institutional knowledge, competencies, and habitus does not mean that there is not also a culture of evoking the East German past that involves pessimism, resignation, depoliticisation, and a general critique of capitalism.

A small dose of nostalgia and counter-discourse[8] regarding the hegemonic representations of the East German past is tolerated in reunified Germany, if not encouraged. On occasions like anniversaries (of German unification, for example), publications swamp the book market. They include literature of remembrance (Franck 2009), but hardly any political essays that present a specific East German identity as a central theme (Hensel 2009b; Maron 2010). These books and their topics no longer cause controversies. They reflect a political atmosphere of constructive debate in the Western political system with its culture of consumption and labour relations. In the eastern Länder there is no latent desire to challenge the *status quo* of democratic liberal capitalism from a socialist perspective. The real counterculture that severely challenges the system was and still is the politics and culture of the far right. In the context of high rates of unemployment, of limited career prospects, and of unstable identity due to the rapid succession of social transformations, radical right-wing gangs have carved out no-go areas: so-called zones of fear (*Angstzonen*) and lawless spaces (*rechtsfreie Räume*). Since the beginning of the 2000s, however, these zones have grown rarer.[9] Thus in 2006, in preparation for the soccer world cup in Berlin, the publication of a map indicating these areas was considered but then dropped as no longer really necessary. Still, the lure of the radical remains attractive in the East, if only as a provocation.

Being East German does not only mean a commonality in experiences of the GDR as political and social system, but in current discourses refers to a common tacit knowledge concerning East German material and immaterial culture, language, humour, and symbolic systems. Social change in eastern Germany has not led to more homogeneity in common experiences of the present and common evaluations of the past. On the contrary, it has caused a fragmentation and differentiation of East German society along the lines of generations, classes, regional origins, and gender. The activation of a sense of belonging as East German and the phenomenon of 'ostalgia' (*Ostalgie*) appears in different social settings, fulfils different social functions, and is related to different emotions and sentiments – mourning, withdrawal, justification for failure, and longing for an imagined past, but also pride, avantgardism, and ironically evoking the past as a celebration of faded youth culture (Ahbe 2005).

Thus remembering the GDR can take the form of consumption (buying East German consumer goods for different reasons), ironic play, or persistence in valuing the personal past against a West German hegemonic discourse of representing and remembering the GDR. It is a strategy of inclusion and integration by refusing to totally devalue one's own biography or to present oneself as a failed person who cannot offer anything valuable to the present society. 'Es war nicht alles schlecht' (not everything was bad) is the key expression of this sentiment. It can be used on a sliding scale between irony and seriousness, but only an East German is allowed to use it. The East German past is enacted by using elements of material culture (goods, food, clothes), and *Ostalgie* carries a certain pride in consumer goods as the product of the work of one's own hands in recollection of times when the workplace was the central site for social life (Berdahl 1999b). With the passage of time, though, the revival and reproduction of consumer goods as material culture and part of East German identity becomes less and less significant. *Ostalgie* refers primarily not to an idealisation of innovative life practices in times of scarcity but rather to an idealisation of a form of *Vergemeinschaftung* (communalisation) in contradistinction to West German society, where individualisation is the dominant strategy of resistance to totalising *Vergesellschaftung* (societalisation).

Even though detailed evaluations of the GDR may differ, the overall perception of the GDR among East Germans remains positive, even 20 years after the fall of the Berlin Wall. Several empirical studies come to this conclusion, for example the longitudinal study of Saxony from 1987 to 2007 (Berth *et al.* 2009),[10] the Emnid survey of 2009 (Petersen 2011),[11] and the Allensbach survey of 2009 (*Die Zeit* 2009).[12] The positive image of the GDR is not limited to social welfare, education, and medical care, but refers first and foremost to aspects of social life like social cohesion, solidarity, and cooperation, even among young East Germans who do not have concrete experiences or memory of the GDR. Cultural standards, communication patterns, and role models continue to exist despite colossal social changes. And the debate about whether the GDR was a state not based on the rule of law (*Unrechtsstaat*) shows that perceptions differ according to personal experiences with the system. Most young eastern Germans express uncertainty about the dictatorial nature of the GDR, probably out of loyalty towards their parents and their parents' remembrance of the past. Because the state was such a strong part of the parents' identity, it is difficult for them and for their children to distinguish their personal or family history from their collective past as citizens of the GDR, so that East Germans feel compelled not to condemn the GDR past as easily as their western compatriots do. Nevertheless, the surveys mentioned indicate that unification itself and the fall of the Berlin Wall are perceived as positive events in both east and west despite enduring differences in mentality, language, and religious attitudes (Petersen 2010). The Germans thus seem to be able to live with their differences, or at least do not want to put them on the agenda any more.

(Auto)biographical testimonies

My own research into life in the Berlin Republic's east as a North American who has followed the life stories of some 200 East Germans since 1990 largely concurs with the general cultural and social scientific findings sketched out so far. Indeed, it informed the preceding summary and in some ways contributed to those scientific discussions and debates. The results of my oral history project (McFalls 1995, 1999a, 1999b, 2001, 2002a, 2002b) caused some surprise in the late 1990s when I argued that the cultural unification process was already complete. Contrary to the then-dominant social scientific view that the long-lasting effects of socialisation in the GDR meant that cultural unification would take generations, I contended, on the basis of a third round of interviews with my random sample of ordinary East Germans, that they had undergone a radical metamorphosis of the most fundamental anthropological categories of their life world. Their understanding of and attitudes to their own bodies, to their fellow humans, to time, and to space, all of which categories had shaped their experiences in a manner consistent with 'real existing' socialism, had become coherent with the exigencies of life in a late capitalist consumer society. I argued, moreover, that this rapprochement with the norms and attitudes of West Germans had gone largely unnoticed precisely because the mechanism of change had lain in the cultural clashes of the 1990s that had suggested irreconcilable differences between 'Ossis' and 'Wessis'. This symbolic sparring, which I theorised in Gramscian terms as the dialogic moment of hegemonic subordination, had incited East Germans to surpass the westerners in their performance of norms they ostensibly attacked, be they of body image, labour flexibility, conspicuous consumption, or mobility.

To be sure, cultural differences between east and west persisted well into the 2000s and persist up to the present. As the social scientific literature I have summarised indicates, however, the dramatic upheavals and differentiation in East German society over the past generation make it difficult to speak of a common East German culture, except in the realm of collective memory of an increasingly fictionalised GDR past and its intergenerational transmission – in positive terms to children born in the now–not-so-new Länder and in negative terms, if at all, to children born into otherwise entirely similar lifestyles in the 'old' Länder. As I found in a new round of interviews with some of my East German subjects in 2012, the retreat of marked cultural differences into the realm of memory – individual and collective – does not reduce it to 'mere' folklore. Collective memory and officially commemorated public memory carry high political stakes not only because hegemonic representations of the past have (dis)enfranchising effects in struggles over collective goods but because memory itself has become big business, particularly in places like Berlin, Leipzig, or Dresden.

In a dozen interviews conducted in 2012, I found my interlocutors simultaneously ready to withdraw into private thoughts and to fall into public stereotypes. That is, inasmuch as they still cherish past values, they have given up on defending them publicly, or, alternatively, they do not hesitate to resort to stereotypes propagated in the media. A woman from a small town near Jena, who in 1991 had told me how her disgust with public deceit had motivated her to take an active role in the citizen movements of 1989 and during the transition years in unified Germany, now felt just as angry with public hypocrisy but no longer wished to seek justice for past or present wrongs, saying, 'Each of us must make peace with ourselves' ('Jeder muss alleine seinen eigenen Weg finden'). When I showed her the video clips excerpted from a previous interview with her that, like those of 60 of my other research subjects, had been built into a museum exhibit on GDR history, she found the clips reductionist but said that she would not want to bring too much nuance into the public discourse. Another interviewee whom I accompanied to the museum exhibit so that she could see how her own testimonials had been incorporated was quick to concur with the master narrative of oppression and resistance that the exhibit necessarily entailed. What is more, she fell into familiar tropes that the narrative structure of the exhibit suggested, repeating stories that seemed to respond to expectations of what the GDR had been like. Certain visual artefacts, however, spurred memories that strayed from the beaten path of common post-unification discourses. This experience of finding my interview partners unwilling or unable to articulate private memories beyond public memory within the narrative framework of both the biographical interview and the public commemoration encouraged me to develop new research methods drawing on visual and other sensory cues in order to investigate the subjective place of the past in present East German culture.

From past imperfect to future conditional

East Germans may not constitute an ethnic minority within unified Germany. They may not even constitute a distinct community of memory, for in a sense the memory of the GDR, just like that of Nazi Germany, lies at the heart of the entire Berlin Republic, east and west. The city-state of Berlin, the Federal capital, resembles almost immediately for any visitor a *lieux de mémoire* theme park. Visitors cannot escape the past, rather they wallow in it, as they putt-putt-putt around the Holocaust Memorial in a stinking vintage 'Trabi', contemplate the photo exhibit on the Reichstag fire inside Norman Foster's transparent dome, sing karaoke in the former no-man's-land of Mauerpark, or run to admire the East Side Gallery before foreign investors build luxury condominiums in the former death strip to cater to the macabre-chic tastes of global elites seeking a pied-à-terre in Europe's unofficial capital. In Berlin, the slippery slope running from historicisation to memorialisation to commercialisation and on to trivialisation is particularly steep, lending salience to Perry Anderson's (2004) critique of Pierre Nora's (1984) concept of the *lieu de mémoire*. Whereas Nora himself recognised the danger that memorialisation could crowd out actual active memory, Anderson denounced historians' recent preoccupation with social practices and concrete places of memory not only as faddish and uncritical but as a specifically neoliberal ploy to turn history into a consumer good and to fabricate consensuses that evacuate politics from history and history from politics.

Indeed, it is possible to read Berlin qua *lieu de mémoire* as a metonymy for the Berlin Republic's retreat from history; that is, as a depoliticising neoliberal strategy for disarming criticism of the market-driven present and for foreclosing alternatives. Just as Berlin has transformed its horrific history into a highly marketable present, so too has the Berlin Republic succeeded in neutralising Germany's imperfect past and turning the country into Europe's conditional future. This premise no doubt appears paradoxical in light of postwar Germany's reputation as an international role model for confronting if not mastering an 'unmasterable past' (Maier 1998). Following Michel Foucault's remarkable analysis of the postwar German political economy (Foucault 2004), however, I contend that the Berlin Republic has completed and perfected the Bonn Republic's neoliberal break with the past, not only making German conditionality into Europe's new govern-mentality but concomitantly introducing new forms of subjectivity for which East Germans have served as the experimental vanguard.

In 1979 Foucault devoted more than four weeks of his annual lecture course at the Collège de France, published as *Naissance de la biopolitique* (Foucault 2004), to a critical analysis of German ordoliberalism and its policy translation into the postwar Federal Republic's *soziale Marktwirtschaft*. Foucault's rare scholarly incursion into contemporary political economy was motivated both by his genealogical interest in liberal theory's 'statophobia' (fear of state authority) and by France's initial reorientation, in the context of the economic crisis of the 1970s, of its traditionally statist, or *dirigiste*, economic policy towards the alternative model of its largest trade partner, West Germany. I cannot go into greater detail here (compare McFalls and Pandolfi 2014), but suffice to say that Foucault's analysis of the West German *Wirtschaftswunder* offers original insights into 'miracle-worker' Ludwig Erhard's 1948 currency reform and subsequent implementation of a 'social market economy' roughly in line with interwar ordoliberal economic theory. Foucault summarises his assessment: 'Germany's real miracle is to have made the jurisdiction of the state derive from the veridiction of the market' (Foucault 2004: 96). That is, Foucault goes beyond the usual claims that the Federal Republic's political legitimacy depended on its economic performance, or that the economic miracle coupled with the myth of *Stunde Null* (hour zero: the idea that the destruction of war gave Germany a fresh start) absolved West Germany of war guilt. He affirms instead that the Nazi state's absolute discrediting of a juridical/legal/constitutional foundation of political authority necessitated the introduction of a new form of political reason (or 'governmentality') in historical rupture with previous German states and based exclusively on the empirical truth regime of the market. Thus, the 'social market economy' does not refer to a political tempering of market effects on social relations, or to their decommodification, but rather to a complete subordination of social relations to the perpetuation of a competitive free market. The Bonn Republic thus became the first truly neoliberal state in the sense that neoliberal governmentality does not dismantle the state to let markets spontaneously thrive but uses and legitimises a new state authority, without regard for historical or cultural continuities, to mould social relations and individuals into competitive market forces.

In a brief comment on the GDR in one of his 1979 lectures, Foucault offers insight into the political logic of postwar East Germany when he remarks that state socialism cannot survive for long because it lacks its own form of governmental reason and must revert either to authoritarian reason of state or collapse under the weight of market veridiction (Foucault 2004). Foucault's unprepared lecture comments prove even more prescient when he notes that debates on socialism revolve around its authenticity, or truth to founding principles or doctrinal texts, whereas liberalism is judged not by its inherent truth but by its efficacy in conformity with the independent, empirical truth of the marketplace. Foucault's observations implicitly foresee the form that the collapse of state socialism took in the GDR in particular. Whereas the critical dissident movement, whether on the margins of the party or in the citizens' movements (*Bürgerbewegungen*), decried the regime's betrayal of socialist principles, the bulk of the population ultimately succumbed to the logic of the market. To be sure, the substantive causes of the mass mobilisations that brought down the GDR were multiple, complex, and not primarily material (McFalls 1995). Still, the form that the popular revolution took was neoliberal in the sense that the movement lacked ideological leadership as well as content, and its targets and goals were largely impersonal and institutional as East Germans primarily sought freedom of movement and access to convertible hard currency – 'if the D-Mark does not come to us, we'll go to it (kommt die D-Mark nicht zu uns, gehen wir zu ihr)'. The key slogan of 1989 – 'Wir sind das Volk' (we are the people) – was a perfect empty signifier, revolutionary form without content, a mechanism for social exchange where each can find her or his own, as in the marketplace.

Born of the Bonn Republic and the unidealistic revolution in the GDR, the Berlin Republic has brought German neoliberalism to full fruition, and not just in Foucauldian theory. The empirical post-unification life experiences of ordinary East Germans suggest that they are indeed in the vanguard of emergent forms of subjectivity in line with neoliberal market govern-mentality. As we saw in the review of ethnographic and social scientific observations of life in the new Länder, East Germans have had constantly to redefine themselves in a context of radical uncertainty, mobility, dismantling of the welfare state, and perpetual crises of deindustrialisation, globalisation, tertiarisation, and financialisation. They have had to learn to retool, retrain, and recast themselves on the labour market and to redefine and to re-remember themselves on the consumer market. They have had to become, as Foucault anticipated, entrepreneurs of the self. Whereas the modern subject of classic as well as welfare-state liberalism enjoyed a transcendent essence as a universalist bearer of reason and rights, and an immanent essence as a socially and historically contingent bearer of particular interests (Dillon and Reid 2009), the neoliberal – or perhaps even post-liberal (McFalls and Pandolfi 2012) – subject must constantly (re)construct her- or himself as a simulacrum, to position him- or herself in unstable labour and consumer markets.

East Germans are, of course, not the only contemporary neoliberal simulated subjects to define their lives through the constant marketing of their selves (we need think only of our own virtualised life-forms to recognise the both tragic and trivial nature of the East German experience of the present). East Germans, however, do have the privilege of being among the first in Europe to experience the remaking of their lives according to the neoliberal model made in Germany. On the one hand, the lifestyles of those in (parts of) east Berlin, Leipzig, and Dresden who, for the time being, have managed to plug themselves into world-class, high-performance, productive but mostly artistic and service industries have become the envy of the well-connected (in all senses of the word) in Düsseldorf, Munich, and Stuttgart, as young *Schwaben* ('Swabians', as the locals indiscriminately describe well-heeled migrants from the West) flock to inhabit hip urban centres in the east. On the other hand, the equally improvised, adaptive, but less fortunate lifestyles of those in the east who have not moved upmarket have migrated west: the discount supermarket and the street-side beer kiosk are no longer the preserves of the 'Ossi' losers of unification. Hartz IV welfare recipients and so-called one-euro jobholders (i.e. those with temporary, part-time subsidised jobs) in North Rhine-Westphalia and in the backwaters of all the Länder share the same habitus. The tattooed, tanned, shaven-headed 'Proll-Fighter' whom von Uslar describes can prowl the streets of Idar-Oberstein in Rhineland-Palatinate as easily as those of Oberhavel in Brandenburg.

The details of the social and cultural costs and consequences of the 'Agenda 2010' reforms, which in the approving neoliberal assessment of *The Economist* transformed Germany from Europe's 'sick man' into its role model (Siegele 2004), go beyond the scope of this chapter. Suffice it to say that the reduction of welfare benefits and of labour costs brought on by the nominally Social Democratic Government of Gerhard Schröder in 2003 not only set up Germany to profit most from the European single currency and to dictate the terms of reform in response to the financial and fiscal crisis that the euro subsequently prompted (Giesen 2012): they also generalised the market flexibility and associated lifestyles that had emerged from the laboratory of socio-economic transformation in the new Länder. Insofar as the German neoliberal model can thrive on a continental scale, the East German life experiences described here may well prove premonitory.

Notes

1 I wish to thank Dr Alexandra Hausstein for her assistance with the research and writing of this chapter's review of the relevant literature.
2 Bierschenk argues that East Germans have an ethnic identity because they create boundaries between themselves and the West Germans (and vice versa). A symbolic delimitation combined with specific practices (*Jugendweihe*) and cultivation of material culture (*Ostprodukte*) results in a collective identity as East Germans that is further fuelled by inequality and lack of recognition.
3 Research results are available at www.sfb580.uni-jena.de and, for a broader audience, at the knowledge portal 'German Unification' at www.bpb.de/themen/FXJA2R,0,Lange_Wege_der_Deutschen_Einheit.html.
4 A comprehensive collection of bibliographical information on literature published on the topic is available; see Wilde and Mallock 2009.
5 Sonneborn and Coerper's (2010) laconic summary of their findings is that there are two types of Ossis: the younger ones ('Die DDR hat es nie gegeben und sie war besser'); and the older Ossis ('Ich war DDR und ich bleibe DDR. Ich kann mit diesem Staat nichts anfangen').
6 We distinguish between post-Fordism and post-industrialism since Fordism refers to standardised mass production and consumption and since industrialism can be post-Fordist with flexible, vertically disintegrated production of specialised consumer goods.
7 Toralf Staud proposes that we view the East Germans as migrants to the West, which could explain the gap between the West German expectations for assimilation and the East German willingness to integrate (Staud 2003).
8 Such as the following identified by the project SFB 580: GDR nostalgia, the price of unification, shrinking processes, unjust state, social justice, unification as experiment.
9 Also according to von Uslar's informants: 'Der Reporter verstand, dass es nahelag, jene Zeiten, in denen es Angst und Gewalt auf den Strassen von Oberhavel gegeben hatte, heute als Abenteuer-, als Helden-, als Angebergeschichte zu erzählen. Jene eisenharten Nazizeiten, die es in Oberhavel offenbar echt gegeben hatte, durften heute aber nicht als Heldengeschichte erzählt werden. Das wäre dumm, falsch, unerträglich, das wäre widerlich gewesen' (Von Uslar 2010: 344).
10 Positive perception of the GDR refers to medical care, youth work, education and training, social welfare, security, child care, and social justice. The positive evaluation of the present system is restricted to personal freedom, democratic participation, and the housing situation.
11 'Ostdeutsche haben positives DDR-Bild', in *Die Zeit*, 26 June 2009; 49 per cent of East Germans said that the GDR had more positive than negative aspects.
12 Survey findings show that the Germans are predominantly optimistic regarding the process of unification. Also, the feeling of being second-class citizens has diminished in recent years (Petersen 2011).

Bibliography

Ahbe, T. (2005) *Ostalgie: Umgang mit der DDR-Vergangenheit in den 1990er Jahren*, Erfurt: Landeszentrale für politische Bildung.
Anderson, P. (2004) *La pensée tiède*, Paris: Seuil.
Bauer-Volke, K. and Dietzsch, I. (eds) (2003) *Labor Ostdeutschland. Kulturelle Praxis im gesellschaftlichen Wandel*, Halle/Saale: Kulturstiftung des Bundes.
Berdahl, D. (1999a) *Where the world ended. Re-unification and Identity in the German Borderland*, Berkeley: University of California Press.
Berdahl, D. (1999b) '(N)Ostalgie' for the present: Memory, longing, and East German things', *Ethnos*, 64: 192–211. Online. Available at http://diasporiclivesofobjects2012.files.wordpress.com/2012/01/east-german-objects-nostaligia.pdf (accessed 3 April 2013).
Berth, H., Förster, P., Brähler, E. and Stöbel-Richter, Y. (2007) *Einheitslust und Einheitsfrust. Junge Ostdeutsche auf dem Weg vom DDR- zum Bundesbürger. Eine sozialwissenschaftliche Längsschnittstudie von 1987–2006*, Gießen: Psychosozial-Verlag.
Berth, H., Förster, P., Brähler, E., Balck, F. and Stöbel-Richter, Y. (2009) '"Vorwärts und nicht vergessen": Wie bewerten junge Ostdeutsche 20 Jahre nach dem Mauerfall die DDR?' *psychosozial*, 117: 37–46. Online. Available at www.wiedervereinigung.de/sls/PDF/fokusberatung2010.pdf (accessed 3 April 2013).

Bierschenk, T. (2010) 'Das „Wir"-Gefühl der Ostdeutschen', *Stern,* 23 April 2010. Online. Available at www.stern.de/panorama/ethnologe-widerspricht-ossi-urteil-das-wir-gefuehl-der-ostdeutschen-1561003. html (accessed 3 April 2013).

Bisky, J. (2004) *Geboren am 13. August – der Sozialismus und ich*, Berlin: Rowohlt Verlag.

Bisky, J. (2005) *Die deutsche Frage. Warum die Einheit unser Land gefährdet*, Berlin: Rowohlt Verlag.

Bittner, B. (1998) *Kolonien des Eigensinns: Ethnografie einer ostdeutschen Industrieregion*, Frankfurt a.m.: Campus.

Bude, H. (2011a) 'Ein natürliches Experiment' in H. Bude, T. Medicus, and A. Willisch (eds) *ÜberLeben im Umbruch. Am Beispiel Wittenberge: Ansichten einer fragmentierten Gesellschaft*, Hamburg: Hamburger Edition 13–30.

Bude, H. (2011b) 'Vom Ostdeutschen Glauben, mehr zu wissen', *Die Zeit*, 4 August. Online. Available at www.zeit.de/gesellschaft/zeitgeschehen/2011–08/heinz-bude-interview (accessed 3 April 2013).

Bude, H. and Lantermann, E.-D. (2010) 'Vertrauen, Kompetenzen und gesellschaftliche Exklusion in prekären Zeiten', *Positionen*, 1: 2–8. Online. Available at www.uni-kassel.de/upress/online/Open Access/978–3-89958–499–8.OpenAccess.pdf (accessed 3 April 2013).

Busch, U. and Land, R. (2006) 'Zur Lage in Ostdeutschland', special issue *Berliner Debatte Initial*, 17(5): 2–96. Online. Available at www.rla-texte.de/texte/4%20Ostdeutschland/2006–5%20Bericht%20 gesamt.pdf (accessed 3 April 2013).

Clarke, D. and Wölfel, U. (eds) (2011) *Remembering the German Democratic Republic: Divided Memory in a United Germany,* Basingstoke, New York: Palgrave Macmillan.

Davidson-Schmich, L. (2006) *Becoming Party Politicians: Eastern German State Legislators in the Decade Following Democratization*, Notre Dame, IN: University of Notre Dame Press.

Deckname Luna (2012) [TV film] Directed by U. Wieland. Germany: FSK 12.

Die Zeit (2009) 'Ostdeutsche haben positives DDR-Bild,' 26 June.

Dillon, G. and Reid, J. (2009) *The Liberal Way of War: Killing to Make Life Live*, London: Routledge.

Endlich, L. (1999) *NeuLand. Ganz einfache Geschichten*, Berlin: Transit Verlag.

Engler, W. (1999) *Die Ostdeutschen. Kunde von einem verlorenen Land*, Berlin: Aufbau-Verlag.

Engler, W. (2002) *Die Ostdeutschen als Avantgarde*, Berlin: Aufbau-Verlag.

Foucault, M. (2004) *Naissance de la biopolitique*, Paris: Seuil/Gallimard.

Franck, J. (ed.) (2009) *Grenzübergänge. Autoren aus Ost und West erinnern sich*, Frankfurt a.m.: S. Fischer.

Garton Ash, T. (2001) *Wächst zusammen, was zusammen gehört?* Bundeskanzler-Willy Brandt-Stiftung, Schriftenreihe, 8, Berlin: Bundeskanzler-Willy Brandt-Stiftung.

Giesen, K.-G. (2012) 'L' "Agenda 2020" pour l'Europe', *Le Devoir*, 30 December, B5.

Habermas, J. (1990) *Die nachholende Revolution*, Frankfurt a.m.: Suhrkamp.

Hacker, M., Maiwald, S., and Staemmler, J. (eds) (2012) *Dritte Generation Ost: Wer wir sind, was wir wollen*, Berlin: Ch. Links Verlag.

Hauschild, T. (ed.) (2002) *Inspecting Germany: Internationale Deutschland-Ethnographie der Gegenwart* (Forum europäische Ethnologie, vol. 1), Münster: LIT Verlag.

Hein, C. (2004) 'Dritte Welt überall: Ostdeutschland als Avantgarde der Globalisierung . . .', *Die Zeit*, 30 September. Online. Available www.zeit.de/2004/41/Blick_auf_Ostd_ (accessed 3 April 2013).

Hensel, J. (2004) *Zonenkinder*, Berlin: Rowohlt Verlag; Eng. trans. (2004) *After the Wall*, New York: Public Affairs.

Hensel, J. (2009a) 'Der fremde Blick', *Der Spiegel*, 46/2009, 9 November, 134–5. Online. Available at www.spiegel.de/spiegel/print/d-67682732.html (accessed 3 April 2013).

Hensel, J. (2009b) *Achtung Zone*, Munich: Piper Verlag.

Hensel, J. (2010) 'Wir sind anders', *Die Zeit*, 28 September. Online. Available at www.zeit.de/2010/ 39/Osten-Medien (accessed 3 April 2013).

Hodgin, N. and Pearce, C. (eds) (2012) *The GDR Remembered: Representations of the East German State since 1989*, Rochester, NY: Camden House.

Holtmann, E. (2009) 'Signaturen des Übergangs', in A. Wilde and W. Mallock (eds) *Wende und Wandel in Ostdeutschland – 20 Jahre nach dem Mauerfall*, Bonn: GESIS – Leibniz-Institut für Sozialwissenschaften, 9–16. Online. Available at www.gesis.org/fileadmin/upload/dienstleistung/fachinformationen/ recherche_spezial/RS_09_10_-_Wende_Wandel_Ostdeutschland.pdf (accessed 3 April 2013).

Howard, M. (1995) 'An East German Ethnicity? Understanding the New Division of Unified Germany', *German Politics and Society,* 13(4): 49–70.

Hünniger, A.H. (2011) *Das Paradies. Meine Jugend nach der Mauer*, Stuttgart: Tropen-Verlag.

Ide, R. (2007) *Geteilte Träume: Meine Eltern, die Wende und ich*, Munich: Luchterhand.

Innovationsverbund Ostdeutschlandforschung (2009), on behalf of the Bundesministerium für Verkehr, Bau und Stadtentwicklung, *Wahrnehmung und Bewertung der deutschen Einheit*. Online. Available at www.unsere-deutsche-einheit.de (accessed 1 June 2013).

Kil, W. (2008) *Das Wunder von Leinefelde: Eine Stadt erfindet sich neu*, Dresden: Sandstein Kommunikation.

Kollmorgen, R. (2005) *Ostdeutschland. Beobachtungen einer Übergangs- und Teilgesellschaft*, Wiesbaden: VS Verlag.

Kollmorgen, R., Koch, F.T. and Dienel, H.-L. (2011) *Diskurse der deutschen Einheit*, Wiesbaden: VS Verlag.

Maier, C. (1998) *The Unmasterable Past: History, Holocaust and German National Identity*, 2nd edn, Cambridge, MA: Harvard University Press.

Maron, M. (2010) *Zwei Brüder. Gedanken zur Einheit 1989–2009*, Frankfurt a.m.: S. Fischer.

Martens, B. (2010) 'Die Einigung als Experiment', Bundeszentrale für politische Bildung, 30 March. Online. Available at www.bpb.de/geschichte/deutsche-einheit/lange-wege-der-deutschen-einheit/47589/einigung-als-experiment?p=all (accessed 28 March 2013).

McFalls, L. (1995) *Communism's Collapse, Democracy's Demise? The Cultural Context and Consequences of the East Germans' Revolution*, New York and Basingstoke: New York University Press and Macmillan.

McFalls, L. (1999a) 'Nationale Einheit und kultureller Widerspruch: die deutsche Einheit vor dem Hintergrund der drohenden Spaltung Kanadas', *Berliner Debatte Initial*, 10(4): 157–64.

McFalls, L. (1999b) 'Eastern Germany Transformed: From Real Existing Socialist to Late Modern Capitalist Culture', *German Politics and Society*, 17(2): 1–24.

McFalls, L. (2001) 'Die kulturelle Vereinigung Deutschlands', *Aus Politik und Zeitgeschichte*, 11(9): 23–9.

McFalls, L. (2002a) 'Die Verwandlung: Ostdeutsche politische und Alltagskultur vom real-existierenden Sozialismus zur postmodernen kapitalistischen Konsumkultur', in H. Timmermann (ed.) *Deutsche Fragen: von der Teilung zur Einheit*, Berlin: Duncker & Humblot: 541–60.

McFalls, L. (2002b) 'Political Culture and Political Change in Eastern Germany: Theoretical Alternatives', *German Politics and Society*, 63(20): 75–92.

McFalls, L. and Pandolfi, M. (2012) 'Post-Liberalism', *Academic Foresights*, 5.

McFalls, L. and Pandolfi, M. (2014) 'Therapeusis and Parrhesia', in J. Faubion (ed.) *Foucault Now*, New York: Polity Press.

Müller, B. (2002) *Die Entzauberung der Marktwirtschaft: Ethnologische Erkundungen in ostdeutschen Betrieben*, Frankfurt a.m.: Campus.

Neller, K. (2006) *DDR-Nostalgie*, Wiesbaden: VS Verlag für Sozialwissenschaften.

Nora, P. (1984) *Les lieux de mémoire I*, Paris: Gallimard.

Petersen, T. (2010) 'Blühende Landschaften', *Frankfurter Allgemeine Zeitung*, 22 September. Online. Available at www.faz.net/aktuell/politik/inland/allensbach-umfrage-zur-deutschen-einheit-bluehende-landschaften-11040029.html (accessed 3 April 2013).

Petersen, T. (2011) 'Auch die "Mauer in den Köpfen" fällt', *Frankfurter Allgemeine Zeitung*, 25 September 2011. Online. Available at www.faz.net/themenarchiv/2.1278/allensbach-analyse-auch-die-mauer-in-den-koepfen-faellt-1885202.html (accessed 3 April 2013).

Prase, E. (2010) 'Die Minus-Menschen aus dem Osten', *Freie Presse*, 15 April. Online. Available at www.freiepresse.de/NACHRICHTEN/TOP-THEMA/Die-Minus-Menschen-aus-dem-Osten-artikel7355195.php (accessed 3 April 2013).

Rechtien, R. and Tate, D. (eds) (2011) *Twenty Years On: Competing Memories of the GDR in Postunification German Culture*, Rochester, NY: Camden House.

Rusch, C. (2003) *Meine freie deutsche Jugend*, Frankfurt a.m.: S. Fischer.

Rusch, C. (2009) *Aufbau Ost: Unterwegs zwischen Zinnowitz und Zwickau*, Frankfurt a.m.: S. Fischer.

Saunders, A. and Pinfold, D. (eds) (2012) *Remembering and Rethinking the DGR: Multiple Perspectives and Plural Authenticities*, Basingstoke, New York: Palgrave Macmillan.

Siegele, L. (2004) 'Germany on the Mend', *The Economist*, 17 November. Online. Available at www.economist.com/node/3352024 (accessed 3 April 2013).

Silbereisen, R.K., Pinquart, M., Reitzle, M., Tomasik, M.J., Fabel, K., and Grümer, S. (2006) 'Psychosocial resources and coping with social change', *SFB 580 Mitteilungen*, vol. 19. Online. Available at www.sfb580.uni-jena.de/typo3/uploads/tx_publicationlist/sfb_580_silbereisen_5.pdf (accessed 3 April 2013).

Sonneborn, M. and Coerper, A. (2010) *Heimatkunde: Eine Expedition in die Zone*, Berlin: Ullstein Verlag.

Sontheimer, K. (1990) *Deutschlands politische Kultur*, Munich: Piper.

Staud, T. (2003) 'Ossis sind Türken', *Die Zeit*, 2 October. Online. Available at www.zeit.de/2003/41/Einwanderer (accessed 3 April 2013).

Tellkamp, U. (2008) *Der Turm: Geschichte aus einem versunkenen Land*, Frankfurt a.m.: Suhrkamp Verlag.

Von Uslar, M. (2010) *Deutschboden. Eine teilnehmende Beobachtung*, Cologne: Kiepenheuer & Witsch.

Wagner, W. (2006) *Kulturschock Deutschland – revisited*, Hamburg: Europäische Verlagsanstalt. Online. Available at www.fh-erfurt.de/soz/fileadmin/SO/Dokumente/Lehrende/Wagner_Wolf_Prof_Dr/Publikationen/Kulturschock_Deutschland_2005.pdf (accessed 3 April 2013).

Weissensee (2010) [TV series] Directed by F. Fromm. Germany: Das Erste.

Wilde, A. and Mallock, W. (2009) *Wende und Wandel in Ostdeutschland – 20 Jahre nach dem Mauerfall*, Bonn: GESIS – Leibniz-Institut für Sozialwissenschaften. Online. Available at www.gesis.org/sowiport/fileadmin/user_upload/pdf_recherche_spezial/rs_09_10_wende_wandel_ostdeutschland.pdf (accessed 3 April 2013).

Wolf, C. (2010) *Die Stadt der Engel oder The Overcoat of Dr. Freud*, Berlin: Suhrkamp Verlag.

Wolff, C. (2012) *Osterweiterung – Leben im neuen Deutschland*, Berlin: Evangelische Verlagsanstalt.

Yoder, J. (1999) *From East Germans to Germans? The New Postcommunist Elites*, Durham, NC: Duke University Press.

Zapf, W. (1992) 'Die Transformation in der ehemaligen DDR und die soziologische Theorie der Modernisierung', Max Planck Institut für Gesellschaftsforschung, *MPIFG Discussion Paper*, 92(4). Online. Available at www.mpifg.de/pu/mpifg_dp/dp92-4.pdf (accessed 3 April 2013).

11

Visual culture

Memory work and arts of the present

Andrew Webber

This chapter addresses key developments in the visual culture of Germany since the establishment of the unified Germany as what came to be called the Berlin Republic. The shifting of the governmental structures of Germany back to its old capital, with the new Federal Republic taking the place of both the West German 'Bonn Republic' and the GDR, was a contentious matter. Most famously, Jürgen Habermas, the doyen of German social and political thinking, entered into the debate to question the foundations of this new republic in the collection of interviews and political writings published in 1997 as *Die Normalität einer Berliner Republik* (translated as *A Berlin Republic: Writings on Germany*, 1998). The English translation loses the ironically inflected 'normality' that is attributed to the Berlin Republic here, as a country that for Habermas provides a compelling case against established normative ideas of nationhood in an age of globalisation and after the terrible state-sponsored crimes of the 20th century. For Habermas, the reconstitution of Germany on the basis of an old nation-state model with an underpinning of ethnic identity is both inadequate and dangerous. We might think of it in the visual cultural form of Thomas Schütte's patinated bronze sculpture, *Vater Staat* (Father State, 2010): an overbearing patriarchal figure but with his hands bound in his coat.

Habermas calls instead for a norm of civil society based upon 'constitutional patriotism': commitment to the governmental principles of a postnational, liberal democratic republic with an open political public sphere enlivened and ensured by 'communicative action'. This, then, is the challenge that Habermas lays down for the polity of the Berlin Republic and its claims to normalcy. The argument of this chapter will be that the aspirations and tensions that characterise the epochal shift of social and political structures after unification are registered in particularly telling ways in the visual culture of the new republic, a culture that tends to participate actively in the political public sphere.

The term 'visual culture' is in need of some definition here. Over the last 20 years, scholars have identified first a 'pictorial turn' in the study of culture, and then a broader 'visual turn'. These moves mark the recognition that visual objects, and the operation of visuality in cultural production and consumption, demand their place alongside the study of texts and the operations of writing and reading, or indeed – following the linguistic turn – of language also in its non-textual forms. In many respects, the visual turn has transferred the critical language of the linguistic turn to the visual field, to the optical workings and effects of culture. It is a shift that has not least been enabled by the attention to the function of performativity in linguistic culture, and its resonance for the event character of visual culture, for how it takes effect or is enacted. That visual culture frequently also incorporates language, as sound or text, should be noted here. Indeed, much of the attention given to visual culture in recent years has focused on the relationships between the visual and other sense systems, not least in discussion of the haptic – the nexus of vision and touch. At the same time, the turn to visual culture has been accompanied by a new concern for cultural space (following the 'spatial turn') and the structures and dynamics of its organisation (following the 'topographical turn').

This cumulative sequence of turns indicates that how and where cultural artefacts and events are shown and seen is of fundamental importance for our understanding of how culture works. At the same time, a crucial matter is how looking is brought into play by visual cultural objects, exposing the character of the 'visual event' as 'performing acts of seeing' (Bal 2003: 9, 11). Plato – in his famous allegory of the cave with its projected shadows – inaugurated an attitude of distrust towards the image, wanting to exclude its seductively imitative effects from his Republic (Mirzoeff 1999: 9). How, then, might the role of images be understood as an inclusive part of the Berlin Republic? And how do they enable acts of seeing to be performed? Are the varied effects of image making in visual culture to be cast on the side of the illusory shadows for enchained viewing subjects in Plato's cave, or can some, at least, be seen in a more positive, critical light? Of course, German visual culture in the 20th century has a particular historical charge, having produced a dark set of dominant shadow images during the National Socialist period and its aftermath. This has provoked the need amongst visual artists to work against the background of that historical catalogue. We could think, for instance, of Anselm Kiefer's 1969 *Besetzungen* (Occupations) project, where the artist photographed himself giving the Nazi salute in various European locations. This kind of provocative counter-occupation is one way in which the German catalogue of images can be resignified. We will consider here what has become of that legacy in the last two decades, and how to place it between the complacent claims of normalcy that Habermas warns against and the work of critical revision or resistance.

In keeping with the principles of visual cultural studies as an (inherently transdisciplinary) academic discipline, visual culture will be construed here in a rather broad, though necessarily not comprehensive sense. It will encompass architecture, museum displays, public spectacle, and film, as well as the visual arts proper (painting, sculpture, photography, mixed-media works, and performance work). Examples will include canonical visual cultural objects, events, and practitioners, alongside less familiar ones; and they will move between gallery-based work and that which is sited – or takes place – in other spaces or arenas. The abiding concern of the chapter will be to show how German visual culture of the last two decades projects forms of historical double-vision, with one eye on the breaks and divisions of the past and one looking for present and future perspectives. Berlin – as the renovated capital of the new Germany and the privileged stage for its enactments of political and cultural identity – will be the central focus. Attention will be given both to the more official forms of image making on the part of the nation and its capital and to more counter-cultural trends. At the same time, the chapter will recognise that German visual culture may take place outside the borders of the nation, or indeed within them but as undertaken by non-nationals, especially in Berlin, which is perhaps the leading contemporary international centre in this field. The account given here will thus range from expressly national forms of visual culture to more postnational ones, encompassing a range of tendencies from the transnational to the subnational and the para- or antinational.

Pictures on the Wall

The events of the autumn of 1989 in Berlin provided one of the most potent spectacles in recent global history. In many respects, the *Wende*, the historical 'turn' that prepared the ground for the Berlin Republic, went hand in hand with a kind of visual turn on the part of Germany. It had its primary impact in visual mediation, with the scenes of the 'fall of the Wall' broadcast around the world as perhaps the ultimate television event of the late 20th century. It was spectacle of a political-historical kind, but also a visual cultural happening, performed for global audiences. For the purposes of this televisual spectacle, the Wall and the historical architectural features that surrounded its focal site (the Reichstag and the Brandenburg Gate) presented a powerfully telegenic scenography for the representation of breaking down of barriers between the two cultures of the divided Germany and of the Cold War blocs at large.

The Wall was already an object of visual culture while it functioned as a barrier between East and West Berlin – in particular, a canvas for graphic art on its western side (Figure 11.1). With impromptu works from amateur 'smearers' and staged interventions from international star artists such as Keith Haring, the Wall became the most extensive piece of collaborative visual culture on the globe. What Wall photographer Hermann Waldenburg (1990:14) has called a panopticon, a total apparatus of state surveillance, was repurposed as a kind of universal spectacle (panoptical, that is, in a more benign sense). It created an overload of visual culture on one side of the Wall against the visual cultural vacuum on the blank GDR side, which, so Waldenburg speculates, could only lead to implosion. The heroic language of his account, looking back in

Figure 11.1 The East Side Gallery, Spreeufer, Berlin
Photograph by the author, 2007

1990 upon the Wall art of the 1980s and suggesting that it might be '*the* outstanding artistic phenomenon' of that decade (Waldenburg 1990: 13), is cast in an ironic light by the current stand-off between protestors and municipally supported property developers over the integrity of the painted remains of the Wall on the banks of the Spree dubbed the East Side Gallery. The Wall-as-gallery now has a memorial function, but perhaps devoted less to the violence of division than to the place of urban anti-art as a form of popular possession in a city increasingly driven by the global forces of capital development.

At the time of its fall, the Wall also served as an object of, and framework for, visual cultural spectacle. A particular example would be Jürgen Böttcher's film *Die Mauer* (*The Wall*, 1990). As an artist working in the GDR and subject to the strictures of its cultural regime, Böttcher experienced the Wall as a provocation, a commanding visual object that was also taboo for visual cultural representation. After it was breached, he set about making his film on and around it. The documentary work of the film involved a visual reckoning both with the broader *Geschichtsraum* or historical space of this site and with the optical regime of the Wall during the GDR years (Böttcher 1991). The film adapts the techniques of *Übermalung* or over-painting that he had deployed in his earlier career, under the name Strawalde, by applying historical film images to the Wall as screen and creating a critical *mise-en-abyme* through its projection of film within film. The film takes the recalcitrant, but now crumbling, materiality of the Wall as its substrate, projecting an allegorical image of Berlin's fractured history through this ultimate visual symbol of that fracture. As one reviewer put it, the superimpositions of historical image in Böttcher's film created forms of *Denkbilder* – images for thinking – in their working together of materiality and meaning, transience and persistence.[1] Böttcher's *Mauer* can be understood as a kind of revision of the shadow projections of Plato's cave, encouraging a contemplation of images on the Wall, but one that activates the viewer as a critical subject of history. At its best, the same can be said of the mural art that has sprung up on fire-walls across Berlin in recent years, working in the graffiti tradition of the Wall artists and encouraging a popular engagement with the local environment (Figure 11.2).

While the Wall acted as a spectacular, elongated screen or canvas for visual cultural work of various kinds, the architecture of Berlin more broadly has also been the object of such work in its processing as centre of the new republic. The treatment of two monumental buildings, governmental palaces of different kinds, designed not least for their visual cultural impact, will serve as examples here. As the Wall fell, so the Reichstag was made available for refitting at one end of Unter den Linden, on the Platz der Republik. And the 'Palace of the Republic', also known as Erich's *Lampenladen* (the 'lamp shop' of GDR leader Erich Honecker), was set for decommissioning at its other end. The heavy stone frame of the Wilhelmine Reichstag, ravaged by war and neglect, was in waiting to become the parliament of the new republic, while the mirror-glass light-box of the Palace of the Republic, which had taken the place of the demolished imperial Stadtschloss or City Palace, stood as an imposing monument to the self-projection of the GDR as a regime of modernity. As sites of memory, saturated with ideology and historical happening, the Reichstag, dedicated by the inscription on its façade to the German people ('Dem deutschen Volke'), and the GDR's 'people's palace', also the seat of its 'People's Chamber' (Volkskammer), were prime objects for the treatment of visual culture on a mass popular scale.

While the Reichstag was dedicated to the German people, its appropriation for perhaps the most spectacular visual cultural event of the late 20th century was also an act of inter-nationalisation. Christo had not been able to realise his 1970s project for a wrapped fence to run the length of the Wall, but in 1995 he and his collaborator Jeanne-Claude achieved a parallel project: the wrapping of the Reichstag. The project had first emerged in 1971, on the 10th

Figure 11.2 Graffiti mural by Blu, Cuvrystraße/Schlesische Straße, Berlin
Photograph by the author, 2007

anniversary of the building of the Wall, but was held back by the fear that it would be a provocation to East Germany. The decision in 1991 to move the seat of government of the new republic from Bonn to Berlin and to transform the Reichstag into its parliament made the – still controversial – intervention possible as a prelude to the reconstruction. Following approval by a vote of the Bonn parliament, the Reichstag was duly wrapped in vertical sheets of canvas, bound by blue polypropylene cords, and became an enormously successful popular spectacle. If this had taken place before the fall of the Wall, it could only have been understood as a representation of democracy under wraps or in phantom form, a challenge in particular to the nominal democratic status of the GDR. It now became an image of a more ritual kind, a shrouding that was making ready for the revelatory unwrapping of the new democratic settlement of the Berlin Republic. In common with much of the public art, both officially commissioned and unofficial, that would follow in the Berlin Republic's capital, it was a fundamentally transitory intervention, with the character of an event. As Christo describes it, it was designed to question the 'immortality of art' through a monumental but fundamentally nomadic act of visitation, incorporating a gesture of the work's 'self-extinction', and yet thereby to confirm the ultimate resilience of democratic convictions and institutions (Baal–Teshuva 1995: 86). The temporary work was accordingly received as a kind of visual cultural festival for the new German polity and for international visitors to it. As a monumental tent, with free access enabling gathering around its spectacular exterior, it created the conditions for huge crowds to participate in its event character and in collective (also photographic) ownership of that event.

While the Reichstag was being reconstructed, with a new dome by Norman Foster for viewing both the workings of democratic government within and the evolving cityscape of Berlin without, another monumental building took centre stage in artistic and public discussion around the interaction of architecture, visual culture at large, and politics. Debates over the retention or replacement of the Palace of the Republic constituted a *cause célèbre* of civic – and, by extension, national – cultural politics at the centre of the Berlin Republic. Broadly, the debate was split between right and left, with conservative opinion embracing the demolition of the Palace and the restitution of the Stadtschloss, while left-leaning commentators and activists favoured the preservation of this GDR site of memory at the heart of the reconstructed imperial middle of Berlin. One particularly theatrical intervention came in 2006, when the fate of the Palace was already sealed, from Claus Peymann, director of the Berliner Ensemble theatre. He drew much media attention when he made the carnivalesque proposal that the dismantled Palace be shipped along the Spree to the Schiffbauerdamm quay and rebuilt on the square at Am Zirkus (nicely named for the purpose). Peymann thus proposed the creation of a 'centre of nostalgia' or a 'Wailing Wall' for the GDR,[2] setting the Palace alongside the Brechtian Berliner Ensemble, the East Berlin palace of popular entertainment – the Friedrichstadtpalast, and the transit hall of the Friedrichstraße station, known as the 'palace of tears' (*Tränenpalast*). But if this spectacle of removal and reconstruction in a new arrangement of GDR palaces never came to be, the Palace nonetheless became the arena for a series of works within, around, and about it, exploring the specificity of this site of relatively recent memory.

From the beginning of its unhappy post-*Wende* afterlife, the Palace was a site for visual cultural dissent. As early as March 1990, when it had been given over to music and travesty shows, a group of alternative artists undertook an occupation of the building, protesting against its commercial exploitation under the banner 'Der Palast ist besetzt' ('The Palace is occupied'). In subsequent years, after its closure for the removal of asbestos, its semi-derelict exterior, with the state emblem of the GDR removed, became an object of melancholically inflected treatments from without, as by the French photographer and performance artist Sophie Calle and the Berlin-based British image- and filmmaker Tacita Dean (see also Webber 2008: 69). Photographer Thomas Florschuetz and writer Durs Grünbein collaborated on a book of images of the Palace in the process of its dismantling, interspersed with Berlin poems, which, if not nostalgic for the building and the ideology that occupied it, nonetheless creates what might be called a melancholia effect through the ruined state of its object. Grünbein notes that the building with 'the Platonic name' Palace of the Republic will be long outlived by the remains of ancient buildings in the nearby museums (Holfelder 2008: 186). In a more light-footed mode, Stefanie Bürkle, much of whose recent work has been devoted to what she calls the 'scenographies' of architectural dismantling, reconstruction, and mock-up in the New Berlin (see Bürkle 2009), made wallpaper carrying the pattern of the building's exterior, which was then hung in the offices of leading cultural and political figures (see Bürkle 2007: 134–49). Thus the iconically obsolete palatial exterior was converted into cladding for interiors and became the background for the staging of workplace photographic portraits of the figures in question.

Both the exterior and the stripped interior of the palace were also given over to event-based visual cultural interventions in the period of so-called *Zwischennutzung*, or interim usage, between 2003 and 2005, with the Palace dubbed the 'Volkspalast', or People's Palace, for the purpose. Through the successive projects, the condemned Palace became less a site of memory or indeed nostalgia for the GDR than, as Moritz Holfelder (2008: 100) puts it, a 'laboratory' for a communal, future republic. Internal events included a staged adaptation of Döblin's classic Weimar period novel *Berlin Alexanderplatz* by Franz Castorf and the Volksbühne company;

a choreographic discussion with the space by Sasha Waltz's dance ensemble (*Dialoge 04*); and the construction of an interactive installation, the *Fassadenrepublik* or *Republic of Facades*, by the artistic collective raumlabor berlin and the Peanutz Architects, with the public navigating their way round a flooded interior on rubber dinghies and making planning decisions with immediate impact for the architecture of the mock republic. Drawing on Cedric Price's classic concept for a Fun Palace (1961), the building was repurposed for visual culture in the mode of communicative happening and process. The 'fun' here was in the nature of critical questioning. In January 2005, Norwegian artist Lars Ramberg mounted the word *ZWEIFEL* (doubt), in enormous light-box letters on top of the Palace and thereby marked out the programmatic challenge of the interim usage: casting doubt on the political settlement of the new republic and its visual cultural self-presentation. Ramberg's intervention marked out the Palast der Republik as an allegorical Palace of Doubt, with questioning taking the place of ideological belief in a republic that he saw as characterised by the virtue of doubt in its public political discourse (Holfelder 2008: 197).

In the following year, the demolition of the Palace became a time-based spectacle in itself, with the installation of an observation platform and a documentary webcam recording the process from the roof of the nearby German Historical Museum. While the spectacular post-*Wende* building frenzy around the Potsdamer Platz and elsewhere had been packaged with the slogan 'Baustelle als Schaustelle' (building site as viewing site, or sight), the *Palastschaustelle* presented the reduction of a site of memory to a sightless condition. Following the pun used by a 2007 exhibition on 'private memories and public discussion' around the Palast der Republik (Schug 2007), the Palace was now 'der geSchlossene Palast',[3] at once 'closed' and 'Castled' or 'Palaced'. What will be made of the spectacle of the reconstruction of the Stadtschloss as monumental simulacrum of a lost site of memory remains to be seen. Anyone recalling Ramberg's DOUBT writ large on the top of the Palace might well view the reconstruction as the crowning example of façadism: a 'Potemkin Castle', as Grünbein suggests (see Holfelder 2008: 187), or the epitome of what Janet Ward (2006) has called the 'Las Vegasisation', the commercial self-simulation, of post-*Wende* Berlin.

Body works

As the refashioning of buildings carries particular weight in the visual cultural field, so does the reworking of the body. If 20th-century German visual culture had a back-catalogue of shadow images, then these are not least images of the body, in particular the body as staged *in situ*. We might think of the seductive, specular performances of Riefenstahl's films: images of bright, muscular vitality, but cast retrospectively in darkness by the deathly body-pictures that would follow as their shadows. Kiefer's enactments in *Besetzungen* can be understood as attempts to expose and exorcise those images and their occupation of representational space on both national and international levels. How, then, has the body been treated in the visual culture of the Berlin Republic, and what relationship does this have to the enablement of an open and, following Habermas, communicatively active body politic? The interventions range from strategic representations of physical absence to provocative, if not obscene, enactments of presence.

The absenteeism of the body that is a significant strand in the visual culture of this period is a corollary of the shadow images of National Socialist Germany. It applies in particular to memorial culture and to what James Young (1992) called the counter-monumental, a tendency that predates the Berlin Republic and has come to dominate public memorial practice in Germany since the *Wende*. Examples of this practice, which involves more or less performative

Figure 11.3 Karl Biedermann, *Der verlassene Raum* (The Abandoned Room/Space, 1996), with words by Nelly Sachs, Koppenplatz, Berlin

Photograph by the author, 2007

presentations of disappearance, are legion, both in Berlin and across the Republic. Perhaps the best known are those by sculptor Jochen Gerz. One with particular impact is *2146 Steine: Mahnmal gegen Rassismus* (2146 stones: memorial against racism, 1990–3), where the names of the Jewish cemeteries that existed in Germany before the Holocaust were inscribed on the underside of stones in the space in front of the Schloss in Saarbrücken, seat of the Saarland's regional government. This led to the square being renamed the Platz des unsichtbaren Mahnmals or Square of the Invisible Memorial, marking the work of public visual culture *in absentia*. As with Gerz's other interventions in public space, bodies – here the bodies of the dead that are metonymically represented by the hidden names of the cemeteries – are what is most invisible in the work.

Similar types of representational logic apply to some of the principal memorials of the capital, works of abandonment or evacuation of embodied existence – Biedermann's *Der verlassene Raum* (The Abandoned Room/Space, 1996), Ullman's *Bibliothek* (Library, 1995), or Eisenmann's monumental *Monument for the Murdered Jews of Europe* (*Denkmal für die ermordeten Juden Europas*), completed in 2005. Here, too, the logic is metonymic. The first, in the old Jewish area of the Scheunenviertel, depicts domestic furniture abandoned by those who used it (Figure 11.3). The second – on the Bebelplatz, scene of the book burning in 1933 – represents a removal of books from the empty underground shelves visible through a pane of glass in the square. The human absence that is signified, at one remove, by the missing books is indicated in the inscription on the plaque for the memorial of lines from Heine's *Almansor* (1821):

Das war ein Vorspiel nur, dort
wo man Bücher verbrennt,
verbrennt man am Ende auch Menschen.

(That was but a prelude, in the place where books are burnt, people too will be burned
in the end [my translation])

The third appears to approximate to a set of stylised sarcophagi, but in blocks that exclude
the possibility of incorporating the bodies of those who are commemorated. If these are described
as stelae, they are monumentally devoid of any effigy or inscription that would relate them to
the bodies of the dead. What these counter-monuments – whether invisible (Gerz), barely visible
(Ullman), or insistently but blankly visible (Eisenmann) – have in common is reduction towards
a degree zero of visual culture. Like the voids of Libeskind's Berlin Jewish Museum, the memory
work they do is of a strategically negative or absent kind, requiring work – embodied work of
communicative action – on the part of the polity that hosts them. Spectators or visitors, who
pass by or through these works, temporarily inhabiting their space, are required to project their
own bodily presence into a form of virtual cohabitation with the missing bodies commemorated
by them.

A final example of this visual elision of the German historical body in its most extreme form
takes us back to the Reichstag in its reconstructed shape as governmental palace of the Berlin
Republic. In the west foyer of the Reichstag building hangs Gerhard Richter's *Schwarz Rot
Gold* (Black Red Gold, 1998). The piece is made up of three slim, rectangular blocks of colour,
hung in a vertical strip from black down to gold. The colours approximate to but are not tonally
identical with those of the flag of the Federal Republic in the form that can be seen, for instance,
flying over the building. Each of the blocks is made of two panels, painted behind glass, thus
introducing seams into the dismantled projection of the flag, perhaps representing the melding
of two black, red, and gold flags (the flag of the GDR, where Richter grew up, was also of
course in those colours). The work is characteristic of one tendency in Richter's work: the
abstraction of painting to rectangles of barely modulated colour (as in his grey mirror paintings).
But one of the studies for the work also reveals a radical counter-image, which is more in keeping
with the sort of hybrid photo-painting for which Richter is best known. His original concept
for the monumental fresco was for a vertical strip, as if frames from a black-and-white film, of
four painted images of concentration camp scenes, drawn from photographic sources. These
shadow images, deemed inappropriate for the emblematic foyer work, are radically sublimated
in *Schwarz Rot Gold*; it is only in the light of knowledge that an informed viewer might bring
to the work, whether of its genesis or of Richter's broader portfolio, that they might be unfolded
by the abstracted flag.

If Richter's work has gravitated between images of bodily extremity, breaking taboos of
shame (drawing on pornography as well as the Holocaust), and radical abstraction or sublimation,
this split might be seen as a characteristic one for contemporary German visual culture. The
final turn in this section takes its cue from that always potentially grotesque disjuncture, making
a move from the high art of perhaps the world's greatest living painter to another level of visual
culture altogether. The body as displayed *post mortem* (we might think of Richter's *18 October
1977* series, based upon press photographs of dead members of the RAF group) takes a differently
obscene form in one of the most spectacular phenomena of German visual culture in the last
20 years: the *Körperwelten* or *Body Worlds* of Gunther von Hagens.[4] The provocation of von
Hagens's exhibitions of plastinated human and other anatomies, their skin flayed so that they
are stripped in obscene exposure, undoubtedly has a particularly German implication to it. Von

Hagens appears as styled between an experimental doctor or scientist without scruple and an idiosyncratic artist after the shamanic model of Joseph Beuys. But while Beuys's assemblages and vitrine pieces represented the corporeal extremity of the Second World War and the Holocaust in metonymic forms and materials (in particular, through felt and fat), von Hagens's anatomical shows seem to claim an impossible normality for his drastic form of body works. *Body Worlds* is presented as a contribution to the project of Enlightenment, a project to which Germany contributed so much in its 18th-century heyday, but it also taps into an obscene possibility that the 'Germanness' of the show and its impresario add a lugubrious or prurient appeal to the event.

Photographic snapshots

Gerhard Richter is in important respects a photographic artist: a compulsive collector of personal snapshots and of photographs from the public domain, both historic and everyday, and a reworker of that atlas of photographic images in his paintings. In his work, photography reveals its particular political – and also ethical – dimension as a medium particularly associated with historical evidence. If the works of a postwar generation of painters – Richter himself, Anselm Kiefer, Georg Baselitz, Wolf Vostell, and others – have placed Germany at the forefront of international developments in that medium, the same can be said of the photographic works of German artists and artists working in Germany since the *Wende*. Here, too, a crux of the work is the relationship between the bodily (following the paradigm of portrait – also group portrait – photography) and architectural frames or other spatial effects of mise-en-scène (following the paradigms of landscape/cityscape or interior photography). Richter's hybrid photo-paintings might seem to expose an exhaustion of the two media in question in an age that is both 'post-painterly' (as coined by Clement Greenberg) and 'post-photographic'. For photography, in particular, the reality index of the analogue process (taken to record that which lies before the camera) has been superseded by the advanced editorial treatments of the digital. On the face of it, this might seem to take photography away from its established political function as a medium engaged with the actual conditions of identity and society. However, as Fiona Summers points out, the post-photographic condition of contemporary visual culture should not be taken for granted. The analogue may be aligned with 'an indexical relation to the world' and the digital with 'visions of alternative worlds' with hyper-real appearance (Summers 2012: 447), but these distinctions are not straightforward either for current practice or historically. Richter's intermedial inventions are but one form of the visual cultural power that the 19th-century medium has retained in its contemporary reworkings. Another would be the *jpegs* series by Thomas Ruff, where such photographic 'events' as 9/11 or images of supposed 'weapons of mass destruction' bases in Iraq are digitally manipulated in order to question their status as spectacle or evidence. Even as it marks its own artifice and evidential unreliability, in association with the technical shift from the camera lens to the computer screen, photography has burgeoned as a compelling element of German visual culture in the last two decades.

We might start by considering a leading American photographer who lived in Berlin for the first three years of the Berlin Republic and made a significant contribution to the visual cultural record of those years. Nan Goldin, best known for her frank images of friends and lovers, worked in Berlin and helped define the city's artistic underground from 1991. Her works are caught between a provocatively intimate sense of bodily presence in individual or group portrait work and its absence in her photographs of domestic spaces demonstratively empty of occupants. While the portraits work to celebrate the pleasures of the body in more or less explicit ways, the empty interiors appear to mark the transience of the corporeal presence that has inhabited them. The community, or 'family', that Goldin portrays was ravaged by AIDS, and the album or slide-show (a preferred form for her work) also represents the loss of lives in the underground scene. The treatment both of bodies and of scenes without bodies develops a form of visuality that is also haptic in effect, a physical presentation that makes contact with the viewer, breaching conventions of shame.

We can see this in one of Goldin's less drastically exposing portraits, *Siobhan with a cigarette, Berlin 1994*, an image where the time and place of the title is not simply an arbitrary marker, but makes a claim for lived experience in that place at that time. In this portrait of her lover, she adopts a restrained, demure technique that nonetheless exposes the subject, puts her forward in photographic space, in a more subtle sense. Thus, the hand with the cigarette is held forward, its line echoed by that of the fragment of furniture in one corner of the image, with the ash and the slight wisp of smoke proffered as indices of the time-based medium. As Mirzoeff (1999: 83–4) describes it, the image evokes both the neo-classical portrait and the stereoscope. We could add that it references the Weimar style of *Neue Sachlichkeit* (New Objectivity/Sobriety), as a high point in the modern German visual cultural tradition. This photographic treatment of the body incorporates avatars of the medium of photography and styles from its history, while also looking to the digital in its hyper-real challenge to the logic of two-dimensional representation. It is an image that is at once photographic, pre-photographic, and already post-photographic, capturing and exposing the body in the representational force field between those modes.

Goldin's portraits and interiors can be seen as aligned with two key categories in photography by Germans and/or made in Germany since the early 1990s. A third would be exteriors, or the portraiture of architectural structures and landscapes, which is informed in particular by the monumental documentary photography of Hilla and Bernd Becher. Internationally recognised contemporary German photographers such as Candida Höfer, Andreas Gursky, Thomas Struth, and Thomas Ruff emerged from what has come to be known as the Becher School, with its typological approach to photography of industrial and post-industrial structures and scenes. While many of the leading photographic artists work across the boundaries between the categories of portrait, interior and exterior, a set of practitioners can be taken here as exemplary for each. What they have in common is the exploration of Bal's 'visual event': the disposition of acts of viewing both of the image and within it.

Examples of the intimate portrait include work by the London-based Wolfgang Tillmans, who develops a queer aesthetic related to Goldin's, or the feminist work of Rosemarie Trockel. Tillmans's body images are closely linked to and often combine with his work on materials and interiors, with an attention to different forms of skin, actual and metaphorical. Trockel, too, shows her concern for skin as a medium for photographic work in the work used to publicise her 2013 show 'A Cosmos' at London's Serpentine Gallery: *Prime-Age* (2012). In what is apparently an allegory of a prime age that may be personal or epochal, the exquisitely decorative artwork of the tattoos on the no less exquisite, androgynous body performs a similar function to the artist's use of knitted cladding in other mixed-media work. The tattoos partially cover the body and also represent it as a medium for showing, a corollary of canvas or photographic paper, while in themselves mediating the showing of the body as photographic object. In the work of both Tillmans and Trockel, the portrait photograph is an exercise in intermedial representation, with a concern for the body as object of mise-en-scène. And the individual body images are always in a relationship to other works in the montage or collage space of the exhibition interior.

The interior – including the gallery interior – as visual cultural object has a particular function in the photographic work of Candida Höfer, Thomas Struth, and Thomas Demand. Although both Höfer and Struth have also worked on external views of buildings, in allegiance to the Becher School, they are best known for their shots of elaborate interior scenes, with or without people. Höfer's work has generally focused on institutional interiors, ranging from the enfolded ornament of baroque churches and opera houses to more minimal, modernist spaces. Her particular interest lies in spaces of knowledge, such as libraries, museums, and lecture theatres; and she finds that it is when evacuated of human presence that they reveal most about 'what people do in these spaces – and what these spaces do to them' (Höfer 2013). Thus her Dresden series includes interiors from institutions that are devoted to the study of human life but apparently devoid of its traces: the shots of the German Hygiene Museum (2000) present an absence of human subjects or material in a study of cleanliness of space and line; and those of the Ethno-graphical Museum (1999–2000) also remove the evidence of people, or peoples, from the frame (as ironically highlighted by the monumental forms of caryatids). Struth, on the other hand, characteristically treats his interiors as forms of group portrait. He is perhaps best known for works that show viewers around exhibits in galleries or museums, thus creating an effect of *mise-en-abyme*: a viewing of acts of viewing. An example would be his medium-scale shots of rooms in Berlin's Pergamon Museum (2001), where viewers are cast in staged clusters around the – often broken – bodily and architectural forms of archaeological exhibits. Like Höfer, he takes an interest in organised spaces of viewing, but there is also a contingently distributed character to the human acts of looking that he captures. Thomas Demand, in the scenes that he mocks up for his works, adopts a more radical approach to the exposure of the interior as viewing space. He creates spaces that typically appear to be after-the-event reconstructions of scenes of crime or other acts, often anonymous in character and devoid of human presence. Thus, his 1994 scenographic work, *Raum* (Room/Space) shows an office that has been wrecked through some unattributed drastic intervention. The viewer is unlikely to know that the image is taken from a studio reconstruction of a photograph of the scene in Hitler's HQ in East Prussia after Von Stauffenberg's assassination attempt in July 1944. Demand's works appear to present the uncanny counter-image of the organised institutional spaces of Höfer and Struth. He achieves similar levels of pictorial precision (also in the elaborate artefact of the mock-up), but – in images such as *Raum* – exposes disorder, at personal and political levels, in the conditions of the interior.

While Demand's *Raum* is readable at once as a representation of a room and as a more abstract study of space in an enclosed form, Andreas Gursky has established himself as a preeminent photographer of the spatial – and, in particular, of German spaces – on an epically expansive scale. The missing body of Demand's 'crime scenes' or the missing bodies of Höfer's institutional interiors also feature as an absent or semi-absent presence in some of Gursky's best-known landscape images. In works such as *Rhein II* (1999), with its lateral lines working as a set of receding horizons, or the bird's-eye view of Brandenburg asparagus fields in *Beelitz* (2007), with its gridded horizontal lines of earth occasionally interrupted by minute, foreshortened workers, there is a lack, or radical reduction, of human figures to provide scale. Natural or cultivated expanse thus appears as abstracted, without measure. And where the human does feature, it is frequently in forms of spectacular massing, as in his photograph of the Berlin *Loveparade* (2001), where it is subject to a similar kind of epic abstraction. Accordingly, when Gursky presents an internal view of the *Bundestag* (1998), the representatives of the German people appear in a constellation of more or less indistinct figures, segmented laterally by window frames, as if repeating the division of elements in the *Rhein* landscape. It remains uncertain whether the visual tricks played by the image are the product of the building's architecture or of the sort of digital manipulation that Gursky standardly applies in his (post-)photographic work. The image accordingly asks questions about what the transparency of view enabled by Foster's glass dome reveals of political representation and responsibility in the nerve centre of the Berlin Republic.[5]

New normality?

We should perhaps conclude by returning to the cautionary note in Habermas's questioning of what it might mean to see the Germany of the Berlin Republic as normal. The spaces and forms of visual culture in contemporary Germany cannot be 'normal' in their relation to questions of national identity and history. We see this in the disruption of the abandoned room/space of Biedermann's memorial sculpture to the abandoned Jews of National Socialist Berlin or of the room/space of Demand's *Raum*, marking the 50th anniversary of an anything but normal event in an anything but normal space. At the same time, the examples given here should have made clear that German visual culture is not circumscribed by the contours of those national shadow images. Thus the project by Alexander Laner selected for Munich's 2013 version of the fourth plinth, translated from London, was for a domestic space to be created within the plinth itself and inhabited by a series of lodgers, in an unconventional form of quotidian normality. The political establishment of the Berlin Republic certainly feels bound to make the nation look again at the shadow images, not least in its commissioning of public memorials, and artists do the same of their own accord, often in more subtle ways. But the visual cultural shape of things as projected out of and into Germany is more complicated, being reducible neither to the aftermath of those historical acts nor to the borders of the contemporary nation. Thus the kinds of variety of object and practice that we have seen in the case of photography could also be shown in other areas of visual cultural activity, in both 'high' and more popular forms.

In the domain of performance art, there is the Wuppertal Dance Theatre of the late Pina Bausch or the work of Sasha Waltz, whose *Dialoge 09* inaugurated the Neues Museum in Berlin after its reopening in a shape at once old and new. Bausch's work is both an eminent product of a German tradition and avowedly internationalist, with practitioners and performance concepts drawn from across the world. Waltz's choreographic dialogues with the institutional spaces of the Berlin Republic, from the obsolete GDR Palace to the renovated New Museum, are also explorations of how relationships between the embodied practices of living and the ideologically and culturally freighted spaces of the republic can be seen. At the other end of the cultural scale are the mass spectacles of street entertainment, from the TV screenings of football and other events on the 'fan mile' at the Brandenburg Gate, to the Love Parade, or the Berlin performance of the giant marionettes of the Royal de Luxe company marking the 20th anniversary of the fall of the Wall in 2009. Taking their cue from the celebrations of the *Wende*, all of these events – at once politically managed and crowd sourced, mobilised by collective participation – have contributed to what might be viewed as a certain 'normalisation' of popular visual culture in the Berlin Republic. And they have done so precisely in so far as they presented such powerful exceptions to prevailing notions of the national norm.

In the sphere of film, too, German visual culture is at once still shaped in national terms in certain respects and yet not confined by this (see Chapter 19). As photographers of Germany and in Germany find new modes of expression in the 'post-photographic' era, so do filmmakers in the 'post-cinematic'. The international mainstream image of German film is still substantially defined by markedly national scenarios, from Eichinger's *Downfall* (*Der Untergang*, 2004) to von Donnersmarck's *The Lives of Others* (*Das Leben der Anderen*, 2006). But its contours, both in the popular form of genre films and in more art house productions, are increasingly diverse and hybridised – also across genre boundaries – as, for instance, in the transnational films of Fatih Akin. Norms of national cinematic representation are thus being revised. Perhaps the most distinctive trend in German cinema of the last two decades has been the restrained narrative films of the so-called Berliner Schule, or Berlin School, with directors such as Angela Shanelec, Thomas Arslan, Valeska Grisebach, and Christian Petzold. It is a loosely configured school of filmmaking that seems to have been named for the Berlin Republic, producing works that are for the most part concerned with the modalities of everyday living in that republic and investigating its claims for a new normality, but also reaching beyond the German case to the wider conditions of contemporary life.

What is clear is that any notion of normality needs to be qualified carefully here, understood as a field of contesting normative and counter-normative positions. In their collaborative work around the Palace of the Republic, Grünbein and Florschuetz invoked contradictory forms of visual cultural normality: the attempts of the oppressive GDR regime to present itself as 'normal' through this building (Grünbein in Holfelder 2008: 185) and the replacement of one palace by another as part of a 'normal' historical process (Florschuetz in Holfelder 2008: 201). Such competing norms of social and political life are at once represented, fashioned, and resisted by the methods of visual culture, both official and unofficial or dissident. The final word on this might go to Gerhard Richter, talking about his sense of the inadequacy of the visual cultural means at his disposal for his project of representation as perhaps the master artist of the Berlin Republic. The practitioner of exceptional technical and aesthetic precision describes this impossible congruence of the object and means of representation as 'a perfectly normal state of affairs [. . .] the normal mess if you like' (Richter 1995: 158).

Notes

1   Stefan Reinicke, writing in *Der Freitag*, 7 December 1990 (in Böttcher 1991). The term *Denkbild* is drawn from Walter Benjamin, who uses it to describe images charged with particular dialectical force for analysis.
2   Peymann's intervention was reported, for instance, in the Berlin daily *Das Tagesspiegel*, 17 January 2006. See www.tagesspiegel.de/berlin/peymann-will-den-palast-der-republik-umsetzen/675844.html (accessed 6 March 2013).
3   See www.palastarchiv.de/ (accessed 5 March 2013).
4   For an account of the controversial politics of Von Hagens's work, see McIsaac (2008).
5   The image can be contrasted with Demand's *Parlament* (2009), which reconstructs a site of memory from the Bonn Republic, with the seat of the chancellor – demonstratively empty – behind the dark block of the iconic lectern from the old Bundestag.

Bibliography

Baal-Teshuva, J. (1995) *Christo & Jeanne-Claude*, Cologne: Benedikt Taschen.
Bal, M. (2003) 'Visual Essentialism and the Object of Visual Culture', *Journal of Visual Culture*, 2.1: 5–32.
Böttcher, J. (1991) Brochure no. 2, '21. internationales forum des jungen films, berlin 1991', Berlin: Internationales Forum des Jungen Films/Freunde der Deutschen Kinemathek (no page numbers).
Bürkle, S. (2007) *Home: Sweet: City: 1997–2007*, Berlin: Vice Versa.
Bürkle, S. (2009) 'Architecture as Scenography, the Building Site as Stage', in U. Staiger, H. Steiner, and A.J. Webber (eds) *Memory Culture and the Contemporary City: Building Sites*, Basingstoke: Palgrave Macmillan, pp. 81–90.
Die Mauer (1990) [Film] Jürgen Böttcher. Germany: DEFA-Studio für Dokumentarfilme GmBH.
Florschuetz, T. and Grünbein, D. (2006) *Museumsinsel*, Cologne: Walther König.
Habermas, J. (1998) *A Berlin Republic: Writings on Germany*, trans. S. Rendall, Cambridge: Polity Press.
Höfer, C. (2013) 'My best shot', *The Guardian*, 7 February 2013.
Holfelder, M. (2008) *Palast der Republik: Aufstieg und Fall eines symbolischen Gebäudes*, Berlin: Ch. Links.
McIsaac, P. (2008) 'Worrying about Democratic Values: Body Worlds in German Context, 1995–2004', in C. Jespersen, A. Rodriguez, and J. Starr (eds) *The Anatomy of Body Worlds: Critical Essays on Gunther von Hagens' Plastinated Cadavers*, Jefferson, NC: McFarland, pp. 121–35.
Mirzoeff, N. (1999) *An Introduction to Visual Culture*, London and New York: Routledge.
Richter, G. (1995) *The Daily Practice of Painting*, London: Thames and Hudson.
Schug, Alexander (2007) *Palast der Republik. Politischer Diskurs und private Erinnerung*, Berlin: Berliner Wissenschaftsverlag.

Summers, F. (2012) 'Photography and Visual Culture', in I. Heywood and B. Sandywell (eds) *The Handbook of Visual Culture*, London and New York: Berg, pp. 445–63.

Waldenburg, H. (1990) *Berliner Mauerbilder*, Berlin: Nicolai.

Ward, J. (2006) 'Las Vegas on the Spree: The Americanization of the New Berlin', in G. Finney (ed.) *Visual Culture in Twentieth-Century Germany: Text as Spectacle*, Bloomington and Indianapolis: Indiana University Press, pp. 83–100.

Webber, A.J. (2008) *Berlin in the Twentieth Century: A Cultural Topography*, Cambridge: Cambridge University Press.

Young, J. (1992) 'The Counter-Monument: Memory against itself in Germany Today', in W.J.T. Mitchell (ed.) *Art and the Public Sphere*, Chicago and London: Chicago University Press, pp. 49–78.

Part III

Society and diversity

12

Immigration and integration

Alex Street and Randall Hansen

Immigration has brought significant changes to German society in the postwar period. In this chapter we present evidence on the scope and scale of these changes, and on the changes that German society has wrought upon immigrants and their descendants. Drawing on both historical and comparative evidence, we argue that integration is a process that should be expected to take place on a generational time scale. Data are now becoming available that make it easier to study integration on the generational scale in Germany. We present new evidence that the children of immigrants remain poorer and less educated than native Germans, with little sign of progress over recent decades. The chapter closes with a discussion of reforms that might improve integration outcomes for the country's immigrants and, especially, for their children.

In this chapter we focus mainly on migration to the former West Germany. Like the West, the German Democratic Republic (GDR) became home to German refugees from eastern Europe in the immediate postwar period. Additionally, the GDR recruited migrant workers from communist regimes such as Poland, Hungary, Vietnam, and Mozambique, but only small numbers settled permanently in Germany, with the result that the immigrant–origin population of today's Germany is composed predominantly of people who moved to West Germany, as well as those who arrived after unification in 1990.

Immigration: Expellees, guest workers, and asylum seekers

Expellees

Knowing the history of immigration to Germany is a necessary first step towards understanding how migration has changed German society, and what future changes we should expect. The history of immigration is itself bound up with the country's political history. At the peak of World War II, in the summer of 1944, Germany was home to around 7.7 million forced workers and prisoners of war from other countries (Herbert 2001: 193). Almost all of them left the country or perished as Germany was defeated, but millions more migrants soon arrived, and indeed often took over the same accommodation. By far the largest group were the millions of Germans who fled the Red Army or were expelled by eastern European governments. These refugees included three types of people: those who had lived within the boundaries of pre-World World I and pre-World War II Germany, the Sudeten Germans from Czechoslovakia, and those of ethnic German descent who had lived further east. The first two groups were culturally and linguistically similar to other residents of Germany; the last was a mixed movement, including some who still had close ties to Germany and some who were German only by distant descent. By 1960 the number of Germans who had arrived as refugees – including emigrants from the nominally democratic but in fact authoritarian East Germany – was 13.2 million, or almost one quarter of the total German population (Herbert 2001: 194).

The expellees (*Vertriebene*) were distinctive migrants. On the one hand, they were German citizens, and mostly spoke German. On the other hand, they faced the same kind of native resentment over scarce resources and space that most migrants face. The harsh conditions in bomb-ravaged Germany exacerbated those problems. Until the West German economy stabilised and started to grow rapidly after currency reform in 1948, hunger and deprivation were widespread in the new republic. After this period of hardship, once the West German economy recovered, the refugees and expellees enjoyed some key advantages: language skills, full rights of citizenship, and plentiful employment opportunities in the years of the economic miracle (*Wirtschaftswunder*), which lasted from the early 1950s until 1973, with a brief pause in 1967.

'Guest workers'

As the West German economy grew through the 1950s, even the millions of German expellees were insufficient to meet the demand for labour. Employers, starting in the agricultural sector, pushed the government to facilitate the recruitment of workers from other parts of Europe. The first treaty for this purpose was signed with Italy in 1955, and the first 'guest workers' (*Gastarbeiter*) were employed mainly on farms in southern Germany. Demand increased after the construction of the Berlin Wall in 1961 had put an end to migration from the East, and further agreements were signed with Spain and Greece (1960), Turkey (1961), Morocco (1963), Portugal (1964), Tunisia (1965), and Yugoslavia (1968). Workers were recruited by representatives of the German Labour Ministry (Bundesanstalt für Arbeit) in response to requests from German employers. Much of the work was in heavy industry, especially mining and steel production, in manufacturing, and in construction. Most of the recruits were men between the ages of 20 and 40.

Initially, the guest workers were granted residence permits for one year, during which time they had to remain with the original employer. The permits could be renewed only at the discretion of the Labour Ministry. The idea was that workers would 'rotate' out of the country after two years to be replaced by newcomers. If the rate of economic growth slowed, the plan was that the guest workers would leave. In practice, however, employers found that they preferred to hold on to trained workers. Certain jobs became the preserve of foreign workers, since native Germans could earn more in other sectors of the economy (Herbert 2001: 214). In 1971 the government recognised this trend, granting a five-year residence permit to foreign workers who had already worked in Germany for five years. Beginning in the late 1960s, foreign workers began to bring spouses and children to Germany. As economic conditions deteriorated in the wake of the OPEC oil embargo of 1973, and amid growing concern that the guest workers were no longer playing the role of reserve labour force, but instead competing for employment with native Germans, the government ceased recruitment.

From a technical point of view, the guest worker policy was not, as many people now believe, a failure. Temporary labour was a boon to employers, and in most cases the rotation principle worked. Around two thirds of those who came to Germany for stays of longer than 30 days returned home (Martin 1994). However, given the massive number of arrivals, the one third who stayed translated into a large remaining population. Herbert (2001: 384) records 7.1 million arrivals between 1962 and 1973, and five million departures. Following the migration stop of 1973, which meant that there was only a one-way ticket home, the family members of those who had chosen to stay in Germany came to join them in growing numbers. This pattern was common across Europe; similar dynamics were found in Austria and France and, in the earlier postwar period, in the UK. From the 1970s onwards, the number of foreign residents living in Germany rose steadily: from four million in 1973 to 4.5 million by 1980 and nearly five million by the late 1980s.

The greatest difference between the pre- and post-1973 periods concerned employment. Whereas in 1973 two thirds of the immigrant population were working, by 1980 the figure had fallen to 43 per cent and by 1989 to 35 per cent (Herbert 2001: 233). This trend reflected the combination of falling employment in the heavy industrial and resource extraction sectors where foreigners had been concentrated, and the rising numbers of non-working spouses and children.

Asylum seekers

The next new source of migration to Germany was growing numbers of refugees and applicants for asylum. Numbers rose from less than 10,000 asylum applications in 1975 to over 100,000 in 1980. This was due to conflicts in areas such as eastern Turkey and Afghanistan and also to the fact that many western European countries moved to restrict migration in the 1970s, with the result that applying for asylum became one of the only ways for people to move to the continent.

West Germany was not the only European country to see growing numbers of asylum seekers in the 1970s and 1980s. The German experience was distinctive, however, because Germany was the only country in the world with a constitutionally guaranteed right to asylum. The other signatories to the 1951 UN Convention relating to the status of refugees, and its 1967 Protocol, guaranteed asylum seekers a right to *apply* for asylum, but without a corresponding duty on the part of the state to provide it. Article 16a of the Basic Law or Grundgesetz states that 'Persons persecuted on political grounds shall have the right of asylum.' This clause was adopted against the backdrop of the horrors of National Socialism and some Germans' success in securing asylum from the Nazis abroad. The provision made Germany a relatively easy place to receive asylum. After the fall of the Berlin Wall the number of applicants shot up in the early 1990s, reaching nearly half a million in 1992, due to arrivals from eastern Europe and, above all, the outbreak of war in Yugoslavia.

The wave of asylum seekers arrived at exactly the moment when Germany faced a different mass influx: hundreds of thousands of 'ethnic German' migrants (*Aussiedler*) who had been stuck behind the Iron Curtain also moved to Germany. In 1989, 380,000 arrived, followed by 400,000 in 1990 (Klekowski von Koppenfels 2003: 16). The *Aussiedler* were, formally, citizens rather than immigrants. Article 116 of the Basic Law and the 1953 Expellee and Refugee Law gave German citizenship to citizens and refugees within Germany's 1937 borders, to German expellees, and to those stripped of German citizenship from 1933 to 1945 (the last group included Jews and political opponents of the Nazi regime; see Rock and Wolff 2002: 103; Klekowski von Koppenfels 2003: 4). During the Cold War, the West German government continued to regard these people as German citizens. This policy was adopted in part out of recognition that Germans in eastern Europe and the USSR had been harshly treated in the aftermath of World War II, but also in order to support the argument that West Germany was the sole legitimate state of the German people. Granting a right to citizenship to ethnic Germans in the east had been largely theoretical while the Cold War continued, but suddenly entailed welcoming large numbers of migrants with ethnic German ancestry – not all of whom spoke German – after the Berlin Wall fell. For several years in the early 1990s, net migration to Germany exceeded 300,000 per year, a product of family migration, asylum seekers, and the arrival of ethnic Germans. The German government made efforts to reduce all three.

Following the great upsurge in asylum applications in the early 1990s, the German government, led by Chancellor Helmut Kohl, moved to restrict those movements by negotiating an amendment to the constitution. The amendment limited the right to asylum by stating that people who passed through 'safe third countries' before reaching Germany should apply in those countries, rather than in Germany. The list of safe countries was soon defined to include all of those bordering Germany. The Kohl Government also gradually restricted the class of 'ethnic Germans', by requiring evidence of persecution in the case of migrants from certain countries, by requiring that applicants provide evidence of language ability, and by limiting the number of family members who would also be eligible to migrate. Germany's guest workers benefited from these negotiations: the Social Democrats agreed to the constitutional amendment only on the condition that the government ease nationality requirements. Wolfgang Schäuble, then Interior Minister, guided through a law that granted a right to German citizenship to individuals who had lived in Germany for at least 15 years, with a shorter waiting period (eight years) for those who had gone to school in the country.

The net migration rate fell as a result of these reforms. By the final years of the 20th century, nearly as many Germans were leaving the country as there were foreigners arriving. This state of affairs has continued into the 21st century, with some years even showing negative net migration. Nonetheless, German society has been lastingly altered by recent immigration. The foreign population grew from around five million in 1989 to nearly 7.5 million a decade later, while around three million 'ethnic Germans' arrived during the 1990s. Although the latter group enjoyed immediate citizenship, many Germans viewed them as immigrants (they were often referred to as 'Russians') because many spoke little or no German (Klekowski von Koppenfels 2003).

Family migration

Family immigration is a particularly complex area for several reasons. First, in many countries, family migration accounts for the majority of migrants. Serious efforts to limit the number of immigrants must, therefore, address family migration. Second, governing family migration involves both a control logic and an integration logic. Concerns are frequently expressed that too many members of ethnic minority groups marry spouses from their countries of origin, which encourages home country language use and discourages integration. Third, family migration is often difficult to control because courts and international treaties (e.g. the European Convention on Human Rights, to which Germany is a signatory) view family unification as a human right. The German courts blocked the Federal government's efforts to restrict family reunification in the 1970s, and they have also blocked less ambitious efforts, launched at the state level, to initiate long waiting periods before foreign spouses can move to Germany. Finally, family migration can exaggerate certain features of the immigration system, such as the socio-economic profile of immigrants. Highly educated migrants tend to have spouses who are also highly educated, and to send their children on to higher education. Migrants with fewer skills tend to bring low-skilled family members with them. Of course, some family migrants are able to acquire new skills, but in general family migration tends to perpetuate the educational profile of past migrants, in some cases for decades to come. Insofar as countries aim to attract the most educated workers, this helps to explain why Canada, which selects migrants on the basis of skill, can afford to be relaxed about family migration (at least for the immediate family), while western European countries, which have tended to recruit low–skilled workers, cannot.

Overview of Germany's immigrant population

Table 12.1 provides an overview of the foreign-born population of Germany. Here we focus on immigrants; we turn our attention to the children of immigrants later in the chapter. There are now nearly 11 million people living in Germany who were born in another country. Almost half of them now hold German citizenship, but this figure is driven upwards by the 'ethnic Germans' who make up a large share of migrants from Poland, Romania, Russia, Ukraine, and Kazakhstan. If we exclude these people, the share of migrants who now hold German citizenship falls to 24 per cent. The information in Table 12.1 on length of residence also marks out the ethnic Germans, who arrived mainly in the 1990s, from the former guest workers, who have lived in the country for around twice as long. Indeed, it is worth stressing that many of the foreigners living in Germany have been in the country for a very long time, often 30 years or more. Finally, Table 12.1 also shows the share of the immigrant population at risk of poverty. The poverty line is measured as 60 per cent of the median income, adjusted for household size. The overall poverty rate among immigrants is 27 per cent, compared with 12 per cent for Germans with no recent family history of immigration.

Table 12.1 Descriptive statistics on the foreign-born population of Germany

Country/region of origin	Number of residents	With German citizenship	Mean years residence	Risk of poverty
EU27	3,470,000	40%	24.3	18.4%
• of which Greece	227,000	7%	29.7	24.9%
• of which Italy	425,000	6%	31.9	22.8%
• of which Poland	1,137,000	67%	21.4	17.8%
Other Europe	3,933,000	39%	22	31.9%
• of which Bosnia-Herz.	155,000	12%	23.6	24.6%
• of which Croatia	227,000	10%	30.6	17.7%
• of which Russia	1,004,000	77%	14.8	27.6%
• of which Serbia	185,000	8%	24.8	29.4%
• of which Turkey	1,491,000	23%	27.1	38.2%
• of which Ukraine	233,000	36%	12.8	43%
Africa	350,000	35%	16.3	42%
Americas	276,000	32%	16.8	15%
Middle East and C Asia	1,239,000	75%	15.7	32.5%
• of which Kazakhstan	747,000	93%	15.6	24.6%
S and SE Asia	526,000	33%	16.9	38%
Other	896,000	n/a	n/a	n/a
TOTAL	10,690,000	47%	21.8	26.6%

Source: Statistisches Bundesamt 2012a. *Bevölkerung mit Migrationshintergrund – Ergebnisse des Mikrozensus 2011.*

Integration

The concept of integration is contested. Integration involves immigrants and their descendants becoming part of the society of the country where they live. But in Germany, as elsewhere, there is fierce debate over how this should happen, how far the receiving country must change in order to accommodate newcomers, and which aspects of their culture immigrants and their children should be able to retain. Even when describing how integration actually proceeds, there is no way to be neutral on these questions. It is important, therefore, that we explain how we use the concept of 'integration' in this chapter.

Our view is that, in social domains characterised by scarcity, integration means similarity with mainstream society. For example, integration in the labour market means similar rates of employment for immigrants and natives, in jobs with similar levels of prestige and with similar pay scales. This implies a group-level approach. Just as there will be some individuals with no family history of immigration who struggle to find a job, so we would expect this to be true of some immigrants. But systematically different levels of access to scarce resources would count as evidence of incomplete integration. This understanding of integration in areas such as employment or income appears to be widely shared. Although some native members of societies that receive immigrants may prefer to retain privileged access to scarce resources, most people see this kind of integration in a positive light (Abali 2009).

In domains that do not involve competition over scarce resources, matters are more complex. Consider, for example, religious practice. Integration is complicated in part because the host society typically has multiple religious traditions; there is no single standard for integration. In the absence of direct competition it may be possible for immigrant traditions to coexist with native practices, without creating conflict. Muslims, for instance, could work on Sunday but take Friday off. Nonetheless, the question of integration arises. Organised religions must interact with state institutions that regulate issues such as public holidays, dress codes, the provision of certain kinds of food in schools or prisons, or mandatory participation in sports activities. Questions of integration arise, then, in deciding how the state will treat the minority religion: whether it will be recognised and, if it is recognised, if, when, and how religious requirements will be accommodated. In Germany, for example, some organised religions are recognised as public bodies that can use taxpayers' money to provide services such as care for the elderly (they are *Körperschaften des öffentlichen Rechts*). Should such recognition be extended to Islam and, if not, how can such inequality by faith be justified in a liberal society?

In this chapter our main focus is on processes of integration in terms of similarity in domains such as employment, education, and income. At points we also discuss integration as a process of dispute and accommodation in areas such as language, religion, and cultural practices, although these are issues that are also covered in other chapters of this volume (see Chapters 15 and 18). In order to understand the processes of integration it is important to consider the advantages and disadvantages that each set of migrants to Germany has faced. We focus on five areas: the degree of selection in the immigration process; access to citizenship; expectations regarding settlement; the state of the economy; and language. When scholars describe immigrants as positively or negatively selected, they refer to the idea that immigrants may have skills and characteristics that make them more (positively) or less (negatively) likely to achieve high socio-economic status in the new homeland.

The refugees and expellees who moved to Germany in the late 1940s and the 1950s initially faced great economic hardship, but matters improved rapidly as the postwar 'economic miracle' got under way. These migrants benefited from their ability to speak German. Like guest workers decades later, they harboured illusions of returning to their countries of origin in due course, despite the fact that their integration into German society, to say nothing of the Iron Curtain, made such an outcome highly unlikely. The forced nature of migration meant that migration was not selective, in the sense that people with low levels of skills were just as likely to move as the high-skilled. As a result the newcomers filled a range of economic roles similar to those occupied by native Germans.

The expellees and refugees also benefited from their status as German citizens. As noted above, these immigrant groups formed a large share of the postwar West German population. They were a voting bloc to be courted, and formed a highly influential lobby in the Bund der Vertriebenen (Union of the Expellees). Many were able to obtain work as civil servants, which would not have been possible without German citizenship. In short, a range of factors facilitated the integration of the postwar refugees and expellees into West German society. No data exist that would allow us to measure integration levels among the postwar arrivals and their descendants. Since they were treated as Germans, statistical records do not even allow us to identify these people. The absence of a debate over integration can be taken as evidence that it was not perceived to be a major source of social problems.

The conditions were less conducive to the integration of the guest workers. The economic context was favourable in some ways: not only was work plentiful, but the German trade unions had also insisted, as a condition of supporting the recruitment of foreign workers, that the foreigners would have equal wages and labour rights. The goal of the unions was to prevent employers from using the guest workers to undercut the employment conditions of natives. As a result, foreign workers were well integrated in certain sectors of the German economy. This was not integration in the sense of equality, however. The sectors in which they worked involved physical labour and often low wages, though some jobs – such as in the automobile industry – were relatively well paid. Indeed, the guest workers were deliberately recruited as low-skilled labourers from the poorest and least educated parts of southern Europe and Turkey, in order to carry out physical labour. This was an example *par excellence* of negative selection for educational levels and skills. The prospects for integration dimmed as sectors such as mining and steel production began to decline in the 1970s and 1980s, meaning that such immigrants were shut out of the labour market.

The expectation on the part of both the German government and the guest workers themselves that they would soon return to their countries of origin worked to delay integration. The guest workers were not unique in this regard. Many migrants initially intend to return to the country of origin, and keep their faith in the 'myth of return' even as they become embedded in the labour market and society of their new homeland. In fact, rates of return tend to fall over time, especially once migrants have children and grandchildren in the country of residence (see e.g. Dustmann 2003). Nonetheless, the expectation of impermanence was especially strong in the case of the guest workers, and was actively reinforced by German governments that insisted the country was not a 'country of immigration' (*kein Einwanderungsland*), using financial incentives to encourage return.

Very few of the guest workers spoke German when they arrived, and, in line with the policy of rotation, the state did little to help them learn. The secondary literature contains reports that the children of the guest workers were educated separately and in the languages of their parents' countries of origin, although the details are often lacking. Perhaps of greater impact was the crushing effect of low expectations on the part of both teachers and pupils (Popp 2011). The guest workers were also barred from becoming German citizens. Naturalisation was possible in postwar Germany but required evidence of assimilation, and the presumption was that migrant workers did not qualify. Some of the guest workers married Germans and were able to use this as evidence of assimilation, but the numbers were very small. As a result there was no German equivalent of the view famously uttered by a leading British Conservative Party politician on the country's immigrants: 'Let this party's position be absolutely clear. They are British. They live here. They vote here' (Heseltine 1987). German politicians had little to gain from representing the interests of migrant workers. Some of the guest workers became influential within the trade unions, but in other domains they rarely rose to positions of prominence.

Overall, while the guest workers enjoyed some advantages with respect to labour market integration, on the whole the conditions of their entry were not conducive to integration on equal terms with the German population. Much the same can be said of the family members who moved to join their spouses and parents in Germany. There were some advantages to moving to a country where ethnic communities were already becoming established, providing sources of information on the receiving society for potential incomers and, in some cases, opportunities for employment. But many of those who moved to the country as spouses were not looking for work and thus had relatively few opportunities for interaction with native Germans. As the poverty data in Table 12.1 indicate, the former guest workers have not integrated on terms of equality into German society. Migrants from two important sending countries – Greece and Italy – exhibit higher poverty rates than those who came to Germany from other countries in what is now the European Union. Poverty rates are also two or three times higher among migrants from Turkey and the former Yugoslavia than among native Germans with no family history of immigration. Higher incidence of poverty among Greeks and Italians is noteworthy, since it suggests that arguments attributing poverty among Turkish migrants to either the reluctance of Muslims to integrate, or to racism and Islamophobia, are oversimplifying the matter. It is not only the Turks who have struggled to reach the level of prosperity that is typical among native Germans.

The prospects for the integration of the refugees who came to Germany in growing numbers from the 1980s onwards were arguably more favourable than those for migrant workers. Most refugees accept that the move will be permanent, which encourages integration. Recognised refugees are typically given state aid in settling, and this is also true in Germany. For asylum seekers the situation is more complicated, since they cannot be sure that their applications will succeed. Acceptance rates have fallen dramatically since the 1980s and early 1990s. The economic conditions in the years that have seen relatively many refugees and asylum seekers coming to Germany have been moderately favourable to integration. Few of these people speak German before their arrival, of course, which can delay their integration.

Microcensus data show that migrants from countries that send large numbers of refugees to Germany have widely varying standards of living in Germany. Migrants from African countries are overrepresented among the poorest of the country's residents, whereas migrants from Iran are relatively prosperous. These differences may be linked to the nature of the conflicts that result in political persecution in different parts of the world and in different time periods: refugees and asylum seekers typically arrive with little by way of physical capital, but may have varying skill profiles. Civil wars often displace poor, rural populations, leading to streams of migrants with relatively low human capital; other forms of political oppression may focus on members of social elites who are seen as having the potential to compete for power with incumbents. This can result in streams of migrants who have relatively high levels of education and skills, as, for example, in the case of many Cuban émigrés to the United States (see Borjas 1994). Even skilled refugees often face difficulties having their qualifications recognised in the new country of residence. This has certainly been an issue of contention in Germany, although there is some evidence that the country performs better than its European neighbours in this regard (Will 2012).

Table 12.2 Conditions for integration

Migrant stream	Timing	Conditions for integration
Refugees and expellees	1940s and 1950s	– Citizenship: automatic – Language: almost all migrants already spoke German – Economy: initially very difficult, but soon very good – Selection: range of social backgrounds – Expectations: some hope of return, but unrealistic
Guest workers	1950s to 1970s; then family migrants	– Citizenship: access very difficult – Language: few spoke German before coming, little help – Economy: good for workers in low-wage sectors – Selection: migrants from poor regions had few skills – Expectations: migrants and state planned for return
Refugees	1980s on	– Citizenship: access difficult – Language: few spoke German, but some help on arrival – Economy: low demand for labour, some discrimination – Selection: some very poor, some middle class or elite – Expectations: refugees plan to stay, asylees less certain
Ethnic Germans	1990s	– Citizenship: automatic – Language: some already spoke German – Economy: low demand for labour, qualifications not recognised – Selection: range of social backgrounds – Expectations: most planned to stay

The conditions that brought ethnic German migrants from eastern Europe and the former Soviet Union to West Germany in the 1990s were distinctive. Like the refugees and expellees of the 1940s and 1950s, they were automatically eligible for German citizenship upon arrival, and the expectation on all sides was that migration would be permanent. Indeed, the newcomers received some support from the Bund der Vertriebenen, which lobbied against restrictions on the numbers of new arrivals. However, the migrants who moved to Germany in the 1990s did not form a lobby of their own. The share of people fluent in German was much smaller than in the immediate postwar period, and that has been a barrier to integration. The economic conditions in the mid to late 1990s and the early years of the 21st century were not favourable, since the unemployment rate in Germany was quite high. Census data suggest that ethnic German migrants from the 1990s occupy an intermediate socio–economic position, between native Germans with no family history of migration and most other migrant groups. For example, the poverty rate in this group is 19 per cent, which is higher than the 12 per cent among native Germans, but lower than the rate among naturalised German citizens (23 per cent) or foreign residents (32 per cent; see Statistisches Bundesamt 2012a: 240).

In Table 12.2 we provide a summary of the conditions for integration, as they applied to the most important streams of immigrants to Germany in recent decades.

Integration across generations

Our focus in this chapter so far has been on immigrants in the narrow sense of people born in one country who have moved to live in another. It is reasonable to ask whether immigrants are able to integrate in the sense of adapting to the patterns of behaviour and the living standards of natives. However, full integration is much more likely for the children of immigrants. The so-called immigrant 'second generation' is much more likely to learn the language. Spending many years in the educational system does a great deal to familiarise the children of immigrants with the norms and institutions of the country of residence, as well as providing them with skills and credentials that are fully relevant. The evidence from Germany and many other countries with significant numbers of immigrants is that integration is a process that moves forward during the individual life span but is much more clearly evident across generations (e.g. Alba and Nee 2003; Sürig and Wilmes 2011). To put the point another way, it is much more troubling when we see that the children of immigrants are not integrating, since this suggests either systematic barriers to the full social inclusion of cultural minorities, an enduring reluctance to integrate, or some combination of the two.

One difficulty in studying integration on a generational time scale is that it requires high-quality data collected to ensure comparability over many years. Countries that do not have long histories of experience with mass immigration often lack this kind of data. Belatedly, 50 years after the heyday of the guest worker programme, the German government and German research institutes are now collecting the kind of data that are needed to study integration across generations. The most important source of data is the microcensus (*Mikrozensus*), a yearly survey of 1 per cent of the resident population. The large and representative sample allows high-quality data to be collected even on small segments of the population, including immigrants born in particular countries. Since 2005, the microcensus asks a series of questions that make it possible not only to distinguish between German citizens and foreigners, but also to identify the subset of German citizens who previously held another citizenship, as well as the German-born children of immigrants. The microcensus defines 'people with a migration background' (*Personen mit Migrationshintergrund*) as 'all those who migrated to Germany after 1949, as well as all foreign citizens born in Germany and all of those born in Germany to at least one parent who immigrated or was born in Germany as a foreign citizen' (Statistisches Bundesamt 2012a: 6). Despite the unwieldy terminology, *mit Migrationshintergrund* has become a standard phrase.

Evidence from the microcensus data is published each year in gruelling detail by the Federal Statistical Office, and researchers can also use the original data for their own analyses. The major limitation of these data for the study of integration, however, is that they go back only to the year 2005. We are thus able to study current differences between immigrants and their children, but cannot compare those with the differences that emerged in the 1970s, 1980s, or 1990s.

In order to provide evidence on the progress of integration across generations, we turn to another data source, the German Socio-Economic Panel (SOEP) (Wagner *et al.* 2007). This is an annual survey that follows the same people over the course of their lives. The survey began in 1984 and is ongoing. The panel also aims to follow children who grew up with adults in the survey, even after they move out and form households of their own. Not everyone is able to participate across multiple years, of course. The panel is therefore refreshed with new respondents every few years. In a typical year the survey reaches between 10,000 and 15,000 individuals.

The great advantage of the SOEP data, for our purposes, is the long timeframe. The survey also included, from the very beginning, an over-sample of immigrants from four of the main countries of origin for guest workers: Greece, Italy, Turkey, and the former Yugoslavia. The data are not perfect, of course. Scholars must rely on assumptions about response likelihood, and about the reasons people drop out of the panel, to create weights that give a representative picture of the German population. The smaller sample size results in much less precise estimates than are possible with the microcensus and can preclude subdividing the immigrant–origin population, for example, by country of origin. Finally, the focus on the same people over time implies that these panel data are slow to pick up on changes that arise due to the replacement of cohorts, although this concern is offset by the recruitment of young people into the sample and by the very long time horizon available with the SOEP data. Despite these limitations, we believe that the SOEP provides a valuable source of information on integration and that scholars of immigration and citizenship could make greater use of this resource. In this chapter we focus on three issues: poverty, child poverty, and education.

Figure 12.1 shows trends in poverty rates among immigrants, the offspring of immigrants, and native Germans with no recent family history of immigration. The data run from 1984 to 2009. The poverty line is set at 60 per cent of median household income. Equivalence scales are used to reflect the fact that larger households require more income in order to avoid poverty, but, since some resources are shared, do not require as much extra income as would be needed by a set of individuals living separately.[1] In Figure 12.1, the black points and the connecting line show results for German citizens with no migration background, the light grey points and line show values for immigrants, and the dark grey points and line show the results for the offspring of immigrants. Vertical lines through the estimate for each year show 95 per cent confidence intervals. Because it is not possible to identify the country of origin of all of the parents of the second generation, we do not distinguish between, for example, the offspring of guest workers and the offspring of ethnic German migrants who moved to Germany in the 1990s. All of the analyses of SOEP data in this paper use cross-sectional and longitudinal weights, and standard errors are clustered by household.

The patterns in Figure 12.1 show that, since the early 1980s, the poverty rate among native Germans has consistently been around half the level of the poverty rate among people with a migrant background. We also see that poverty rates among immigrants, and among the offspring of immigrants, have been similar. The figure provides suggestive evidence that, since 2000, the

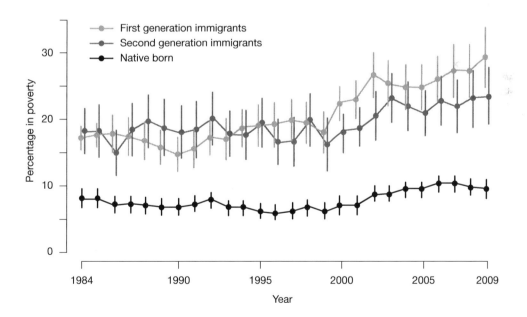

Figure 12.1 Poverty rates in Germany

Note: This figure shows the percentage in poverty (less than 60 per cent of median income, adjusted for household size) among first and second generation immigrants, and native Germans; 95 per cent confidence intervals for the annual estimates are shown with vertical lines. The analysis used longitudinal weights and clustered standard errors by household.

second generation is slightly less likely to be poor than the first generation. However, since confidence intervals overlap for much of this period, the evidence is not conclusive.

We now turn to the issue of child poverty. Living in poverty as a child can have long-term detrimental effects in areas such as education, income, and health. Figure 12.2 presents the poverty rate among children (aged 17 or younger) living in Germany, from 1984 to 2009, again using the SOEP data. The black points, connected by a black trend line, are for children without a migration background, and the dark grey points are for the children of immigrants. Vertical lines through each point estimate show 95 per cent confidence intervals.

All of these children were born and grew up in Germany. Thus, comparing poverty rates between natives and the second generation allows us to see whether children who have much in common – having been born in the same country – are set on different tracks by the experiences of their parents. By studying whether the difference becomes smaller over time, we can also assess whether the impact of parental differences is declining. The results in Figure 12.2 show that child poverty rates are around twice as high among those with a migration background as among those with no such family history. There is no evidence that this difference has been attenuated in the quarter-century since the survey that generated these data was first conducted.

Finally, we turn to educational attainment. Among the most consistent findings in the social sciences is that higher levels of education are associated with many other 'goods', including income, health, and the breadth and depth of one's social networks. Again, we compare the German-born children of immigrants with people born in Germany to parents who were not migrants. Since all of these people grew up in the same country and went through the same educational system, one might expect similar outcomes. Our measure of educational attainment is the percentage of people with the *Abitur*, the qualification obtained at age 18 or 19 that allows Germans to attend university.

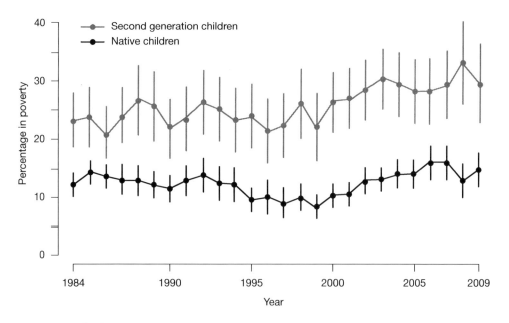

Figure 12.2 Child poverty rates

Note: This figure shows the percentage in poverty (less than 60 per cent of median income, adjusted for household size) among native and second generation children (aged under 17); 95 per cent confidence intervals for the annual estimates are shown with vertical lines. The analysis used longitudinal weights and clustered standard errors by household.

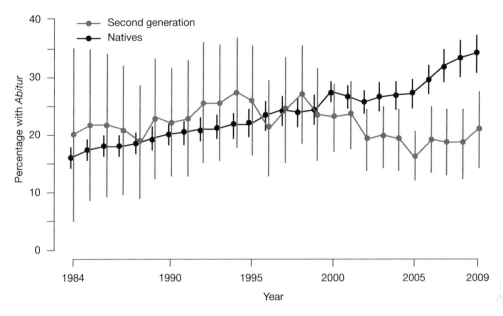

Figure 12.3 Achievement of the *Abitur*

Note: This figure shows the percentage obtaining the *Abitur* among native Germans and second generation immigrants, in the age range of 22–40; 95 per cent confidence intervals for the annual estimates are shown with vertical lines. The analysis used longitudinal weights and clustered standard errors by household.

Figure 12.3 shows results from the study of education. As before, black points and the black trend line show estimates for people without a migration background, and the results for the children of immigrants are displayed in dark grey. We restrict the analysis to people aged 22–40. The lower end of this category is set just above the age when most people complete full-time education, and we use an upper limit because the second generation population is relatively young and we want to compare them with natives who grew up around the same time. This is important because the trend, over time, has been towards a higher proportion of people obtaining the *Abitur*. That trend is evident in the black line, which increases significantly from the early 1980s to 2009. It appears, however, that the children of immigrants have, since the late 1990s, been excluded from this trend. Following a period during which they matched, and indeed exceeded, the rate among natives, the children of migrants have been falling behind.

Policy implications: improving integration outcomes

Concerns over immigrant integration are nothing new in Germany. Indeed, German opinion makers have recently been engaged in heated debates over the perceived 'failure' of integration. A book published by the politician Thilo Sarrazin (2010) provides an instructive example of recent discussions. The book has the title 'Germany does away with itself: how we are gambling our future' (*Deutschland schafft sich ab: Wie wir unser Land aufs Spiel setzen*). It claims that Germany's prosperity is endangered by recent immigrants, especially the guest workers and their children. Sarrazin expresses two concerns. The first is that immigrants and their children have low intelligence, and, due to higher birth rates, will drag down the average intelligence of the population. This claim rests on a misunderstanding of both the relationship between genetics and intelligence, on the one hand, and the effect of birth rates on average IQ, on the other. Indeed, the book recycles long-discredited eugenic arguments from the early 20th century (Gould 1981; Kevles 1999). Second, Sarrazin sees Islam as a source of 'authoritarian, anti-modern, and anti-democratic tendencies' that pose 'a direct threat to our way of life' (Sarrazin 2010: 266; our translation).

Sarrazin's book sold millions of copies and was among the most popular nonfiction works in recent decades. Three factors explain its success. First, it had a populist, scapegoating message: Sarrazin suggests that his readers simply blame Muslims for the complex problems facing German society. Second, Sarrazin tapped into a widespread impression that concerns about migration, particularly among the less educated and less well earning, were insufficiently expressed by a liberal political elite; in this narrow sense, Sarrazin was something of a German Enoch Powell (see Hansen 2000, chapter 8). Third, the book benefited from Sarrazin's reputation as a competent finance minister in the Berlin Senate, which, along with the book's use of statistics, gave it an aura of credibility. The fact that these statistics were used selectively would not be picked up by a lay reader. One noteworthy inaccuracy in the book is the claim that fertility rates among immigrants and their children are much higher than among native Germans. In fact, birth rates have converged surprisingly quickly over recent years. Whereas in 1990 non-citizen women had, on average, 2.1 children, by 2010 the number of children per non-citizen woman had fallen to 1.6 (Statistisches Bundesamt 2012b: 35). The average number of children for female German citizens remained steady at around 1.4 over this time period.

The exaggerated claims about Germany's demise, and about the threat posed by Islam, stand in contrast to evidence from academic research on interactions between Muslims and other residents of Germany, which paint a picture of accommodation and mediated conflict (e.g. Foroutan *et al.* 2010; Haug, Müssig, and Stichs 2009). One feature of the debate over Sarrazin's book, which in itself serves as evidence against his theses, is that immigrants and the children of immigrants, many with roots in predominantly Muslim countries, have been prominent among his critics. We take it as evidence of progress towards integration that these debates are no longer only *about* immigrants, but also feature immigrants as recognised experts in academia and public policy. In all such debates, however, a certain academic caution is in order, as they are ideologically infused on both sides. In all countries, pro-migrant lobbyists exaggerate the benefits of migration, while anti-migration lobbyists exaggerate the costs.

Most scholars agree that education is a crucial domain, perhaps even *the* crucial domain, for improving integration outcomes. Sarrazin (2010: 59) argues that immigrant parents are to blame for not placing sufficient value on their children's education. The evidence in favour of such a claim is limited. There is certainly evidence that the children of immigrants, especially those with origins in countries where migrants were selected from social groups with poor education, are struggling in the German educational system. In Germany and elsewhere, there is empirical and anecdotal evidence that parents' expectations have a powerful influence on children's educational success (e.g. Chen 2001; Fan and Chen 2001; Schmitt 2009). On the other hand, there is evidence that Turkish-Germans, in particular, do value education. A 2011 survey by the Bertelsmann Stiftung suggests that Turkish parents are more likely than native German parents to say they would pay higher taxes for improved schools, and also more confident that a better school system would reduce poverty, unemployment, and criminality (Projektbüro Bildung 2011). Wippermann and Flaig (2009: 11) also draw on survey evidence to characterise German immigrants as 'education optimists', but note that 'structural hurdles, information deficits, and unrealistic expectations' can prevent the optimism from feeding through to qualifications.

Other commentators, including many academics, focus not on parents but on the structure of the German educational system. For example, Kalter, Granato, and Kristen (2011: 258) cite research suggesting that inequality between the second generation and native Germans is due to general mechanisms of social inequality, rather than ethnic background in particular. Schoolchildren in most parts of Germany are placed in academic or vocational tracks between the ages of 10 and 12, based on teacher assessments and consultation with parents. As in most cases of early selection, there is a strong class bias in the choices: middle-class parents tend to set their children on academic tracks, working-class parents on vocational ones. This can serve as a barrier to intergenerational mobility. As Kalter, Granato, and Kristen argue: 'To put it simply, the problems of the second generation are due mainly to the earlier, negatively selected immigration [. . .] and to the peculiarities of German institutions that – independent of immigrant background – tend to perpetuate disadvantages across generations' (2011: 258).

According to this view, promoting the integration of immigrants and their children may require fundamental changes in the educational system in order to enhance social mobility. However, this account appears incomplete. The German educational system has provided middle-class living standards for millions of people who were placed on the vocational track. Vocational training cannot be equated with low income and unrewarding work. The combination of on-the-job training and apprenticeships has produced a steady supply of skilled workers for German employers. According to a recent report, two thirds of young adults without a family history of migration find a place in this 'dual education system', compared to just one third of youth with a migration background (Bundesministerium für Bildung und Forschung 2012: 36). Some recent research suggests that discrimination on the part of teachers and administrators, from the kindergarten to the university, is holding back people with immigrant backgrounds (Antidiskriminierungsstelle des Bundes 2013). An urgent priority for future research is to explain exactly why the children of immigrants are unable to reap the potential benefits of the German education and training system.

Conclusion

Immigrant integration will remain among the most pressing issues facing Germany, for two reasons. First, as we have seen, the country is already home to a large number of immigrants and their descendants. Many have lived in the country for decades, or were even born in Germany – they are not going to leave. As a group they are typically poorer, less well educated, and more vulnerable to economic risks. This chapter presents new evidence that those disadvantages are not attenuating over time or across generations. We should ignore the fearmongers who claim that Germany is doomed, but this systematic inequality is a matter of great social, economic, and political concern.

The second reason that the issue of immigrant integration will stay at the top of the agenda is that Germany is likely to continue to attract significant numbers of immigrants. An ageing society will create demand for migrant labour, and even if immigration from other sources can be curtailed, EU member states seem likely to provide a ready supply. Even in the absence of economic push and pull factors, chains of family migration that have now been established will continue to draw immigrants to Germany. As in the past, many of these immigrants will return to their homelands, but some will settle and will need to find their place in German society.

In recent years public debate over integration has become more intense, and politicians of all parties recognise the need for action. As yet, however, there is little evidence that this will involve deep changes in existing structures such as the educational system. It remains to be seen whether German institutions can be reformed so that they serve all of the country's residents, regardless of background.

Note

1   We use the OECD equivalence scale. This assigns a value of 1 to the first household member, a value of 0.7 to each extra adult, and 0.5 to each child. For example, if 60 per cent of the median monthly income is €1,500, then a single-person household requires at least this amount of income to avoid poverty. A household with two adults would require €1,500 + (0.7 ★ €1,500) = €2,550. A household with two adults and two children would require €1,500 + (0.7 ★ €1,500) + (0.5 ★ €1,500) + (0.5 ★ €1,500) = €4,050 per month.

Bibliography

Abali, O.S. (2009) *German Public Opinion on Immigration and Integration*, Washington: Migration Policy Institute.

Alba, R. and Nee, V. (2003) *Remaking the American Mainstream: Assimilation and Contemporary Immigration*, Cambridge, MA: Harvard University Press.

Antidiskriminierungsstelle des Bundes (2013) *Diskriminierung im Bildungsbereich und im Arbeitsleben*, Berlin: Antidiskriminierungsstelle des Bundes.

Borjas, G.J. (1994) 'The Economics of Immigration', *Journal of Economic Literature*, 32: 1667–1717.

Bundesministerium für Bildung und Forschung (2012) *Berufsbildungsbericht 2012*, Bonn: Bundesministerium für Bildung und Forschung.

Chen, H. (2001) 'Parents' Attitudes and Expectations Regarding Science Education: Comparisons among American, Chinese-American, and Chinese Families', *Adolescence*, 36 (142): 305–13.

Dustmann, C. (2003) 'Children and Return Migration', *Journal of Population Economics*, 16: 815–30.

Fan, X. and Chen, M. (2001) 'Parental Involvement and Students' Academic Achievement: A Meta-Analysis', *Educational Psychology Review*, 13(1): 1–22.

Foroutan, N., Schäfer, K., Canan, C., and Schwarze, B. (2010) *Sarrazins Thesen auf dem Prüfstand: Ein empirischer Gegenentwurf zu Thilo Sarrazins Thesen zu Muslimen in Deutschland*. Online. Available at www.heymat.hu-berlin.de/sarrazin2010/.

Gould, S.J. (1981) *The Mismeasure of Man*, New York: W.W. Norton.

Hansen, R. (2000) *Citizenship and Immigration in Postwar Britain*, Oxford: Oxford University Press.

Haug, S., Müssig, S., and Stichs, A. (2009) *Muslimisches Leben in Deutschland: Im Auftrag der Deutschen Islam Konferenz*, Nuremberg: Bundesanstalt für Migration und Flüchtlinge.

Herbert, U. (2001) *Geschichte der Ausländerpolitik in Deutschland: Saisonarbeiter, Zwangsarbeiter, Gastarbeiter, Flüchtlinge*, Munich: Verlag C.H. Beck.

Heseltine, M. (1987) *Where There's a Will*, London: Bloomsbury.

Kalter, F., Granato, N., and Kristen, C. (2011) 'Die strukturelle Assimilation der zweiten Migranten-generation in Deutschland: Eine Zerlegung gegenwärtiger Trends', in R. Becker (ed.) *Integration durch Bildung: Bildungserwerb von jungen Migranten in Deutschland*, Wiesbaden: VS Verlag für Sozial-wissenschaften.

Kevles, D.J. (1999) *In the Name of Eugenics: Genetics and the Uses of Human Heredity*, Cambridge, MA: Harvard University Press.

Klekowski von Koppenfels, A. (2003) '*Aussiedler* Migration to Germany: Questioning the Importance of Citizenship for Integration', paper prepared for the Alumni Conference, Common Global Responsibility, Working Group 4: Migration Issues, Washington, DC, 6–9 November.

Martin, P.L. (1994) 'Germany: Reluctant Land of Immigration', in W.A. Cornelius, P.L. Martin, and J.F. Hollifield (eds) *Controlling Immigration: A Global Perspective*, Stanford, CA: Stanford University Press, pp. 189–226.

Popp, M. (2011) 'Hässliche Heimat: Der deutsch-türkische Anwalt Mehmet Daimagüler gilt lange als Vorzeigezuwanderer. Nun rechnet der frühere FDP-Mann mit dem Staat und Gesellschaft ab', *Der Spiegel*, 17 October.

Projektbüro Bildung (2011) *Zukunft durch Bildung – Deutschland will's wissen*. Online. Available at www.bildung2011.de (accessed 8 October 2014).

Rock, D. and Wolff, S. (2002) *Coming Home to Germany? The Integration of Ethnic Germans from Central and Eastern Europe in the Federal Republic*, Oxford: Berghahn.

Sarrazin, T. (2010) *Deutschland schafft sich ab: Wie wir unser Land aufs Spiel setzen*, Munich: Deutsche Verlags-Anstalt.

Schmitt, M. (2009) 'Innerfamiliale Beziehungen und Bildungserfolg', *Zeitschrift für Erziehungswissenschaft*, 12: 715–32.

Statistisches Bundesamt (2012a) *Bevölkerung mit Migrationshintergrund: Ergebnisse des Mikrozensus 2011*, Wiesbaden: Statistisches Bundesamt.

Statistisches Bundesamt (2012b) *Statistisches Jahrbuch: Deutschland und Internationales*, Wiesbaden: Statistisches Bundesamt.

Sürig, I. and Wilmes, M. (2011) *Die Integration der zweiten Generation in Deutschland: Ergebnisse der TIES-Studie zur türkischen und jugoslawischen Einwanderung*, Osnabrück: Institut für Migrationsforschung und Interkulturelle Studien.

Wagner, G.G., Frick, J.R., and Schupp, J. (2007) 'The German Socio-Economic Panel Study (SOEP) – Scope, Evolution and Enhancements', *Schmollers Jahrbuck*, 127(1): 139–69.

Will, A.-K. (2012) *Deutsche Integrationsmassnahmen aus der Sicht von Nicht-EU-Bürgern: Die Ergebnisse des Immigrant Citizens Survey für Deutschland*, Berlin: Sachverständigenrat deutscher Stiftungen für Integration und Migration (SVR) GmbH.

Wippermann, C. and Flaig, B.B. (2009) 'Lebenswelten von Migrantinnen und Migranten', *Aus Politik und Zeitgeschichte*, 5: 3–11.

13

Germany as *Kulturnation*

Identity in diversity?

Wilfried van der Will and Rob Burns

The reach of cultural policy

This chapter addresses the nature and structure of contemporary cultural politics in Germany. Cultural politics is a field of political practice rarely analysed by scholars of cultural studies either in Germany or in English-speaking countries.[1] This is surprising, first, because culture, elite and popular, is gaining media attention relative to economics and politics; second, because of the extensive private sponsorship and support from the public purse that culture receives, not to mention the provision for administrative and policymaker posts throughout Germany at local, subregional, regional, state (*Land*), and Federal level; and third, because of the increasing cultural activity at all these levels, where individual, small-group, or grassroots initiatives find material support by the official administration and/or private foundations.

Our way of life is deeply affected by technologies of global communication, but culture as the sum of our lived practices cannot be divorced from its enactment in the specificity of time and space. It does not have to take place within the framework of an administered policy. Culture may be understood as a lived practice by individuals and collectives within accepted cognitive systems such as religions, ideologies, and creeds. It may also be seen as an ensemble of attitudes and habits with which human beings realise and regulate their interaction with others. The geographically variant patterns of persistence and change of customs, beliefs, values, languages, and traditions fascinated Johann Gottfried Herder (1744–1803), whose thought is still regularly referred to in the German debate about culture (see Chapter 2). Although his concept of culture was based on the homogeneity of an ethnically and linguistically unified people, he does allow for transcultural and intercultural inspiration between people from different backgrounds. Like many other nations, Germany today is not only made up of distinct regions but also contains within it minority cultures from many parts of the world. It is therefore a playground for cultural enrichment through the incorporation of diverse traditions, but also a society that needs the management of tensions between diverse cultural manifestations and lifestyles existing in close proximity to one another.

Unlike the feudal-absolutist states of the 18th century (Herder's political environment) or the dictatorships of the 20th, the highly evolved forms of contemporary governance have to strike a delicate balance between neutrally supporting culture and giving it a politically desired direction from above. The democratically legitimated state as a system exercising and controlling power seeks to categorise individual and collective practices, including the arts. To reach an audience, artists must constitute themselves as a social presence. A writer makes use of the printed word as a basic medium to find a public, a dramatist uses the stage, a composer requires soloists and an orchestra, a painter needs canvas and an exhibition space, and so on. Even a liberal and relatively affluent state like contemporary Germany will confront the question which creative activities are to be regarded as beneficial and which are not, which might be eligible for public financial support and which should not. Such decisions take place within a wider constitutional framework. Like the First Amendment in the USA, Article 5 of the constitution of the Federal Republic or Basic Law (Grundgesetz), apart from affirming the right to free expression, explicitly declares: 'There shall be no censorship.' Citizens can therefore have guaranteed freedoms enforced by the courts. Beyond this there is an institutionally distinct structure of cultural administration and policy-making, regionally divided but federally coordinated. Its existence is the de facto recognition that culture is an essential part of the way that German society expresses and understands itself. Private initiatives and patronage bolster cultural pursuits further.

The brief of the cultural administrator in Germany is spatially limited by region and locality. The intentions governing these agents' activities are to be supportive, encouraging, and explorative. In response to the complex contemporary environment in which they operate, those working in the field of culture have to adapt to social change and be aware of the plurality of issues arising within and between different social milieus. For example, there is a marked trend towards secularisation (see Chapter 15). According to long-term research on religious orientation, the percentage of those professing allegiance to the Christian faith has fallen in Germany from over 90 per cent in 1970 to below 60 per cent in 2010 (Forschungsgruppe Weltan-schauungen in Deutschland 2011). Also, the number of citizens with a migration background living in Germany is 7.2 million, with Turks representing the largest grouping. In addition to differences in religious and secular beliefs, there are those of social class, education, and ethnic origin. Such factors raise the question how all these diverse social groups might be made part of a society's self-expression and self-representation. Cultural policy is consciously pursued to allow representations of difference by culturally and/or ethnically distinct communities. At the same time, education, celebratory events, the practice of regional and local customs, festivities, and carnivals are used to strengthen social cohesion.

Despite the abundance and distinctiveness of cultural theories that have been elaborated to date,[2] most share a critique of (post)modern culture as an apparatus for incorporating individuals into existing power structures. Against this generalising assumption, most cultural policymakers would insist that there is enough room left for individuals and groups to generate or absorb meanings autonomously and freely. After all, democratic systems claim to allow for the free expression of diverse lifestyles. Any critical examination of cultural policy must query the extent to which this claim is true and to what extent it may be a delusion. Just as freedom of choice in a consumer society hides the limitations of choice if the market is controlled by monopoly suppliers, so the cultural events on offer may only conspire to keep the population quiet. In ancient Rome, rulers mollified the masses by giving them free bread and circuses in architecturally imposing colosseums. Faced with capitalist societies in the 1930s and 1940s dominated by the concentration of intellectual production in a few monopoly publishing concerns, the influential critical thinker Theodor W. Adorno spoke of a 'culture industry' that practised 'enlightenment as mass deception' (Adorno and Horkheimer 1979: 120). Adorno argued that individuals, trying to escape the drudgery of their lives, immersed themselves in an entertainment culture that robbed them of all sovereign thought. The images of motion pictures and the packaged amuse-ments of the leisure industry only made individuals more easily accept the stereotypical patterns of their existence. By making use of the facilities for aesthetic mass consumption (particularly in advertising, cinema, and illustrated magazines) modern human beings were busy internalising passive behaviour that eroded their self-confidence. Adorno's relentlessly negative analysis, which has produced many echoes in cultural theories to the present day, sought to expose hidden interests in popular culture that resist exposure in public discourse and hence stay hidden to those engulfed by them.

Against an entirely pessimistic reading along these lines it is possible to argue that, partly because of the force of Adorno's influence on younger generations of intellectuals, there is now a continual struggle in public discourse to open up critical spaces. The more cultural theorists warn us of the potential confinement of human perception and creativity by manipulative media, the more these provoke the desire to resist their repressive hold. A democratic society is tested continually for its potential to remain open to oppositional forces. These may express themselves in literature and art, in spontaneous demonstrations, or in collective movements. At the same time, such forces are tested for their readiness to come to terms with existing power structures. Within the contradictory complexities of contemporary life, in which there is no central creed or ideology commanding unquestioned authority, individuals and groups looking for new identities and posing new questions are as endemic as the tendency to accept and conform to the given is widespread. The production of symbolic communication – political rhetoric and everyday language, literature, film, and art – cannot be controlled entirely by established power systems. After all, these are only as permanent as their legitimacy is felt to be acceptable by citizens. Democratic structures may serve as instruments of hidden or overt repression, but remain open to dialectical reversals by subversive or oppositional action. Many cultural theories exhort us to regard any structures in the deployment of power, be they political or cultural, traditional, or newly evolving, as a potential incarceration of human perception and creativity. However, the inspirational life of human beings is apt to test such structures for their rigidity or elasticity. Cultural policy is the attempt to manage this uncertain state of affairs, forever confronted with the basic contradiction of recognising creative freedom while at the same time containing it within the social order.

Cultural federalism: internal and external aspects

Germany is an interesting case study because of its experience of, and exit from, two forms of totalitarianism in which culture was overtly controlled by a mix of centrally directed propaganda and terror. The Basic Law insists on the fundamental rights of citizens and thereby delimits the powers of the state. The second foundational element for contemporary Germany is federalism. After the defeat of the National Socialist regime, the Allied powers allowed the re-establishment of regional German states (Länder), which in turn decided to form the Federal Republic in the west of Germany. These appear at first glance to be shifts of a purely political nature; but there can be little doubt that culture is at the heart of Germany's self-definition. Casting aside any differences in socialisation, mentality, and everyday behaviour that had effectively arisen in the divided Germany before 1989, Article 35, §1 of the German Unification Treaty (31 August 1990) averred that art and culture had provided an element of continuing unity even while two German states existed. The political commitment to culture at all levels of governance is reflected in some detail in the voluminous report of 2007 by a committee of enquiry set up by the German Federal parliament (Bundestag). It categorically asserts: 'Culture is not an ornament. It is the foundation on which our society rests and on which it builds' ('Kultur ist kein Ornament. Sie ist das Fundament, auf dem unsere Gesellschaft steht und auf das sie baut') (Deutscher Bundestag 2007: 4). This report repeated the recommendation first formulated by an earlier commission that culture should be defined in the German constitution as an aim, if not the *raison d'être* of the state (Deutscher Bundestag 2007: 69). There is certainly a sense that the cosmopolitanism that was betrayed by coercive totalitarian regimes ought to be reinstated in the cultural practices of a nation governed as a *Kulturstaat*. However, despite much pleading by representatives of all political parties to have the Basic Law amended, the inscription of culture as an aim of the Federal constitution continues to be resisted in order to avoid any suggestion of cultural centralism, while cultural practice and research into culture are to be expanded.[3]

The development of culture in the Federal Republic is predicated on structural specificities defined by the constitution, which assigns different tasks and responsibilities at three administrative levels: the Federal government, the Länder, and the municipalities. Article 30 of the Grundgesetz stipulates that 'the exercise of governmental powers and the discharge of governmental functions is the task of the Länder, except where otherwise provided for in this Basic Law'. From this unambiguous precept is derived the fundamental identity of the Länder as relatively independent states (*Eigenstaatlichkeit*) and, as an essential facet of that autonomy, their primacy in administering and legislating on cultural matters (*kulturelle Eigengesetzlichkeit*). The latter is commonly referred to as the 'cultural sovereignty' of the Länder (*Kulturhoheit der Länder*), a term regarded by some administrators as infelicitous on account of its associations with the pre-democratic, authoritarian state (*Obrigkeitsstaat*).[4] Nevertheless, the principle that concept embodies is jealously guarded, as the first Federal Commissioner for Culture and the Media, Michael Naumann, discovered when, barely two years after assuming office in 1998, he noted that 'cultural sovereignty' was nowhere to be found in the actual wording of the Basic Law and caused outrage in some quarters with his reference to the 'constitutional folklore' of cultural federalism (Naumann 2000). Although Naumann was technically correct, the term has frequently been deployed by the custodian of the constitution, the Federal Constitutional Court. The Court has repeatedly ruled that the Länder's responsibility for art and culture represents a cornerstone of Germany's Federal system. As the individual constitutions of the Länder make clear, 'sovereignty' in this context betokens not an imperious presiding over culture 'from above' but rather its protection and promotion in the interests of the region's citizens.[5]

As critics had predicted, Naumann resigned shortly after his 'unfortunate witticism' (Geis 2001: 139), an indication of just how fiercely protective the Länder are of their cultural policy prerogative. Even before Naumann entered the fray, Chancellor Gerhard Schröder's decision in 1998 to establish what amounted to a Federal ministry of culture[6] had met with vociferous opposition from the Länder, from all the political parties, and from the cultural pages of the broadsheets. Frank Schirrmacher, the influential literary editor of the *Frankfurter Allgemeine Zeitung*, perceived in this move a regrettable tendency towards 'left-wing Wilhelminism'.[7] In fact, the slide into a 'unitary federal state' (Hesse 1982: 116) had already been detected by some observers in the early 1960s.[8] In contrast to the 'dual' or 'separative federalism' evinced by what is arguably the classic federalist model, developed in the United States, German politicians are committed to a system of 'cooperative federalism' in which the respective cultural responsibilities of the Länder and of central government are clearly demarcated, but without excluding opportunities for fruitful collaboration. There is an acknowledgement on the part of the Länder that (notwithstanding their 'cultural sovereignty') certain tasks properly fall within the remit of the Federal government – for example, the pursuit of foreign cultural policy or the promotion of German cinema internationally. A model of cooperation is provided by the Kulturstiftung der Länder, a foundation established in 1987 with the aim of supporting and preserving nationally and internationally valuable art and culture.[9] For Julian Nida-Rümelin, Naumann's successor, the provision of such support constituted one of two key areas in which the Federal Commissioner for Culture should play a decisive role. The other area he identified as advising the government and liaising with parliament on matters relating to the legislative framework within which culture and cultural policy were to be shaped and developed (Nida-Rümelin 2001: 65).[10]

The efforts of Nida-Rümelin – who was to last even less time in the post than Naumann – to carve out a credible brief for his ministry were seen by the Länder as an attempted redefinition of the compact between national and regional remits in the field of culture and, as such, as something to be resisted. The balance in the division of power in cultural policy had already been disturbed by German unification in 1990, which took place only after the five Länder on the territory of the German Democratic Republic had been re-established so that, in accordance with Article 23 of the Basic Law, they could declare their readiness to join the Federal Republic on 3 October 1990. The new Länder boasted a wealth of artistic and cultural institutions and facilities that had been nurtured as an important heritage by the GDR regime. After 1990, continued funding from central government was justified with reference to Article 35, §1 of the Unification Treaty, which declared:

> Art and culture [. . .] have an indispensable contribution to make in their own right as the Germans cement their unity in a single state on the path to European unification. The status and prestige of a united Germany in the world are predicated not only on its political weight and economic strength but equally on its role as a cultural state.

> (Kunst und Kultur [. . .] leisten im Prozeß der staatlichen Einheit der Deutschen auf dem Weg zur europäischen Einigung einen eigenständigen und unverzichtbaren Beitrag. Stellung und Ansehen eines vereinten Deutschlands in der Welt hängen außer von seinem politischen Gewicht und seiner wirtschaftlichen Leistungskraft ebenso von seiner Bedeutung als Kulturstaat ab.)

Interpreted widely to mean that culture in the new Länder could not be allowed to wither on the vine of 'cultural sovereignty', this so-called 'cultural state clause' (*Kulturstaatsklausel*) entailed a recalibration of cultural federalism. The constitutional expert Peter Häberle (2001: 119) proposed the term 'fiduciary federalism' (*fiduziarischer Föderalismus*) to describe the act of solidarity that the Federal government and the old Länder temporarily had a duty to discharge towards the financially weaker new Länder. The temporary nature of this arrangement was open to question, however, for when the original 'Solidarity Pact'[11] was revised in 2000 it was envisaged that the renewed agreement would run until 2019. Consequently the expanded role played by the Federal government on the cultural policy stage was to be more enduring than had been anticipated initially.

Nowhere was this interventionist role more apparent – or more resented in some quarters – than in the Federal government's support for cultural amenities in Berlin. As one of Germany's three city-states – a status it retained when, in a referendum held in May 1996, the citizens of Brandenburg voted by a large majority against merging their region with the city to form a new Land[12] – Berlin's standing was, of course, irrevocably changed by the decision of the Federal parliament on 20 June 1991 to relocate the legislature and the government to the city and thus, as Bodo Mohrshäuser (1998: 135) subsequently suggested, to make it 'the capital of unification'. In other words, it was recognised that as the new capital of the 'Berlin Republic' the city could restore its importance as a major playground of politics and regain its prestige as the country's shop window on the world only by reconstructing and refurbishing its cultural assets, many of them damaged by war, division, and neglect. Even for a city whose halves had each become accustomed to living well beyond their own financial means, amalgamating and integrating their representative cultural institutions imposed cultural policy obligations far exceeding the budget of a city-state. In addition, there were demands for new cultural institutions, especially museums and memorial sites, to give proper symbolic expression to the capital's political topography. The Federal authorities acknowledged that some cultural facilities in Berlin were charged with a national rather than merely regional mission, and in June 2001 concluded a treaty with the Land authorities, the Hauptstadtkulturvertrag, to support the cultural profile of the capital. The sum involved, in excess of €51 million, was earmarked to finance the Jewish Museum, the Berlin Festival, the House of the Cultures of the World, the Martin Gropius Exhibition Centre, and a part of the estates of the Prussian Cultural Trust. Subsequently an ever greater proportion of Berlin's cultural budget was shouldered by the Federal fiscus rather than the Land government, a show of largesse that did not meet with universal acclaim. As Nida-Rümelin (2001: 72) remarked in 2001, his predecessor as Federal Commissioner for Culture was frequently and at times savagely attacked by the culture ministers of the Länder for focusing his cultural policy too firmly on Berlin and thereby testing the limits of cultural federalism.

Since the early 1990s, another challenge to the 'cultural sovereignty' of the Länder has been posed by increasing harmonisation within the European Union. When announcing the programme of his new government on 10 November 1998, Chancellor Schröder declared that the newly created Commissioner for Culture would primarily 'understand his role as being to represent the interests of German culture on the international stage but above all at the European level' (quoted in Gau and Weber 2001: 271). Essentially this was Schröder's response to the Treaty of Maastricht (1993), the founding document of the EU, which significantly now made explicit reference to the cultural dimension of united Europe's agenda with its proclamation that the community would 'contribute to the flowering of the cultures of the Member States'. In the five paragraphs that constituted Article 128 of the treaty – subsequently to be taken over as Article 151 of the Treaty of Amsterdam (1999) – the attempt was made to put some flesh on the bones of this nebulous aspiration, but in such a way as to reassure those who feared that it presaged the formulation of a common European cultural policy. Thus the first paragraph stated that the community would pursue its goal of developing the cultures of its member states 'while respecting their national and regional diversity and at the same time bringing the common cultural heritage to the fore'. The so-called 'cultural compatibility clause' (*Kulturverträglichkeitsklausel* – §4) committed the EU to take cultural aspects into account in all of its other policy areas, thus relativising the primacy of economics in its decision-making processes. As the ultimate reassurance, the final paragraph spelled out what – to German ears, at any rate – sounded like the 'cultural sovereignty' of the member states: forms of intervention in cultural affairs, which in any case are restricted to measures promoting culture, must take account of the EU's hallowed subsidiarity principle. Resolutions by the EU's ministers of culture can only be passed unanimously and have the status of recommendations, which means that they are not binding on member states. Notwithstanding all these various limitations and qualifications, however, the Länder have remained wary of any efforts at harmonisation in the cultural sphere, which they see as just one of the many threats to their cherished 'cultural sovereignty' and the German model of federalism. At the same time, it is that model which, under the terms of the German constitution, is to be promoted as the basis for supporting the development of the European Union.[13]

It is clear from the argument so far that Germany understands itself as a nation of culture, but, crucially, one predicated on the recognition that culture differs from region to region and must not be centrally steered. Despite some coordination between them, Germany therefore has 16 cultural policies, as many as there are Federal states. The subsequent analysis can concentrate only on selected regions, which have been chosen for the following reasons: Berlin is both the capital and one of Germany's three city-states (the others being Hamburg and Bremen); North Rhine-Westphalia, representing the large territorial states (*Flächenstaaten*) of the old Federal Republic, is the most populous and subregionally divided Land; and Saxony, while representative of the five new Länder, has a constitutionally distinct cultural policy.

Metropolitan cultural policy: Berlin

Germany's self-understanding as a *Kulturstaat* finds its legal reflection in the constitutions of the various German states, including Berlin. Article 20, §2 of its constitution affirms: 'Das Land schützt und fördert das kulturelle Leben'. In the official English translation this becomes a general promise or even an exhortation: 'The *Land* shall protect and promote cultural life'. In the foreword to the 'Report on the Promotion of Culture' of 2011, the serving mayor and his secretary for cultural affairs assert that 'culture moves Berlin' and that the city's 'Senate understands itself as an enabler and promoter of culture' ('Kultur bewegt Berlin [. . .]. Der Senat sieht sich in der Rolle des Ermöglichers und Förderers der Kultur'. Bürgermeister von Berlin 2011: 3). Berlin is without doubt a large and internationally important playground for culture, despite its relatively small size in comparison with some other capital cities. Culture in a very broad sense is accorded a place of honour in the decision-making discourse. The scope of action is defined as encompassing the material support of art and artists, the architectural heritage, cultural participation, education, and diversity; it also includes the 'cultural and creative economy', plus tourism (Bürgermeister von Berlin 2011: 5). The administrators and politicians involved might be described as custodians of cultural capital[14] in that they help preserve the accumulated cultural wealth and adjudicate on the criteria and financial means to augment it. The creative imaginary of the artists whose work the senate is minded to facilitate thus becomes an object of promotion, if not subsidy. Applications for projects or stipends can be made in eight subcategories of funding, from the pictorial arts and sculpture to literature, theatre, and music. Decisions are made by juries chosen from specialists in the field. Some €20 million have been available for disbursement each year since 2010. The senate's total budget for culture is given as €845 million in 2011. It is clear that Berlin is working hard at achieving a new identity that, without denying the Nazi past or its political division under the 'two Germanies' of 1949–90, is substantially predicated on the freedom and creativity of various arts, both traditional and popular, and on cutting-edge research and technology.

The city's international orientation and multi-ethnic population are stressed as signs of cultural richness. The *World Cities Culture Report*, published in 2012 on the initiative of the Mayor of London, acknowledges that 'the reunited Berlin is emerging as one of the creative hubs of Europe. Its "poor but sexy" image has helped attract a vibrant youth culture and a growing high-tech business sector' (BOP Consulting 2012). There is every chance that it will keep its sexiness, but it has to survive on straitened finances and to cope with pressing social problems such as the replacement in several districts of old rented accommodation by modernised owner-occupied apartment houses. The radical scale of this development is new for Berlin, where well into the 1990s socially mixed quarters predominated as a result of controlled rents. Growing feelings of alienation through physical deprivation, social segregation, ethnic discrimination, and also increased stress due to late-modern working conditions are recurring themes in Berlin, where the threat of poverty is 5 per cent higher than the German mean.[15] However, the Berlin administration does not miss a trick when it comes to projecting the city's significance as a fulcrum of international tolerance and multicultural variety. The authorities and the population alike are yearning for global recognition of Berlin's status as a *Weltstadt*. Against oft-repeated talk of its being just a patchwork of parallel communities with little intercultural exchange, Berlin seeks to show the world how cultural diversity can bring about a new creative complexity by synthesising groups in common activities and by proactive public and private events management. Cultural diversity, celebrated most jubilantly at the annual Carnival of Cultures in May, is seen as a positive enrichment for the city. Like the rest of Germany, Berlin is engaged in a long learning process that may yet disprove prominent voices that have declared multiculturalism dead (Horst Seehofer) or failed (Angela Merkel, Thilo Sarrazin, and others).[16]

Since his reorganisation of the state government in 2006, Klaus Wowereit has chosen to absorb the role of senator for culture into his mayoral office. This gives him opportunities to be seen on red-carpet occasions with both representatives of international politics and show-business celebrities. The magnification of the 'creative industries', a mix of IT-based ventures and cultural initiatives, is a central concern in his advocacy of Berlin as a metropolis. In setting out his governmental programme on 12 January 2012, he spoke of Berlin as a 'metropolis open to the world'. His address included statements that do not merely express intent but reflect already ongoing developments:

> Berlin is regarded worldwide as a creative metropolis and a centre of contemporary art. The senate will ensure that the framework is in place for further good work by our operas, theatres, museums and cultural institutions. In collaboration with the Federal government we shall develop the Humboldt Forum as a site of cultural encounters with the non-European cultures of the world. The realisation of the Humboldt Forum will close a large gap in the historical centre of Berlin.
>
> (Berlin gilt weltweit als Kreativmetropole und als Zentrum zeitgenössischer Kunst. Der Senat wird die Rahmenbedingungen für eine weiterhin gute Arbeit unserer Opern, Theater, Museen und Kultureinrichtungen sichern. Gemeinsam mit dem Bund werden wir das Humboldtforum zu einem Ort der kulturellen Begegnung mit den außer-europäischen Kulturen der Welt entwickeln. Die Verwirklichung des Humboldt-Forums schließt eine große Lücke im historischen Kern Berlins.)
>
> (Wowereit 2012)

The tone is one of great confidence, factually supported by the high turnover of the creative industries in Berlin, which matches the city's entire budget (€22.276 billion in 2012 and €22.493 billion in 2013). High-tech clusters plus the networks of art and culture account for a sixth of Berlin's GDP. The international film festival, one of the largest in the world measured by the number of films shown and tickets sold, is part of this impressive staging of creativity. This means that in financial terms the extent of cultural activities cannot be measured solely by the figures in the senate's budget for the cultural affairs section in the mayor's office (€845 million in 2011). This official budget allocation, even when expanded by other budget lines related to culture, like research and development, schools and education, the Olympia Park, town planning, environment and tourism, and social integration, is easily outstripped by the total spend on culture and creative networks in Berlin. Such networks have their own department in the city administration, while the range and status of the cultural institutions that are part-financed by the senate is illustrated by the number of supervisory boards chaired or attended by the secretary for cultural affairs (André Schmitz), which include the board of the celebrated Berlin Philharmonic under Simon Rattle. Mixed-finance structures are the norm for these prestigious institutions. The three opera houses (including the Staatsoper under its director Daniel Barenboim), the Berlin ballet, the Berliner Ensemble, the Deutsches Theater, and the

Friedrichstadt-Palast, with its vast stage for spectacular musicals and shows on ice, are all run as limited companies with their own income streams, topped up by subsidies from the public purse.

The governing authorities are keen to find new sources of revenue, particularly because – according to the annual accounts comparing the finances of the Länder – the city is broke.[17] Under Germany's fiscal transfer mechanisms, which channel resources from the relatively richer regions to those that are deemed 'poorer', Berlin currently receives €3 billion. It is not simply for reasons of prestige that the city looks to culture in all its manifestations as a field that promises to maximise its economic wellbeing: the weight of the cultural industries, which can be defined broadly to encompass anything from the development of high and popular culture to that of innovative software, games, fashion, and advertising, is considered crucial. Two extensive studies on *Kulturwirtschaft in Berlin: Entwicklung und Potentiale* (Cultural Industries in Berlin: Development and Potential) were published in 2005 and 2009 respectively. They are flanked by further studies, expertise and advice offered by the Berlin Chamber of Commerce and Industry. Berlin is neither Germany's financial centre (which is Frankfurt am Main) nor the seat of its highest courts (which is Karlsruhe); culture and the creative industries are therefore major compensatory factors to improve its standing. Strategically, the chosen route to achieve expansion is the composition and promotion of clusters, particularly in the high-tech sector, bringing together individuals with projects, public institutions, and private firms. Innovation in science and technology and innovation in culture are seen as belonging together and are brought under the common heading of *Kreativwirtschaft* (creative industries). This suits city policymakers because, in order to enhance Berlin's status as a place offering critical mass, every effort is being made to attract still more scientific, cultural, and entrepreneurial talent – hence the stress on the already high level of education, the density of research, and the lively intellectual environment in the city.

A cluster strategy is in operation in many fields, not only in Berlin but throughout Germany. The Federal Ministry of Education and Research has subdivided the whole of Germany into metropolitan regions in order to finance and achieve internationally leading high-tech clusters. In Berlin, *Kreativwirtschaft* is itself defined as a cluster and described with the same permanently upbeat optimism typical of cultural policy more generally:

> This cluster represents above average rates of growth. Circa 29,000 mainly small and medium-sized enterprises achieve an annual turnover of €22 billion. This means that the cluster contributes a sixth of the total GDP of Berlin. With over 220,000 employees, it constitutes an important element in the Berlin labour market.

> (Das Cluster steht für überdurchschnittlich hohe Wachstumsraten. Rund 29.000 zumeist kleine und mittelständische Unternehmen erwirtschaften jährlich einen Umsatz von über 22 Mrd. €. Damit trägt das Cluster zu einem Sechstel zum Gesamtbruttosozialprodukt der Berliner Wirtschaft bei. Mit über 220.000 Beschäftigten stellt es einen wichtigen Beschäftigungsfaktor für den Berliner Arbeitsmarkt dar.)[18]

Significantly divorced from the more refined, exuberant, or ironical diction of the actual authors of creativity, the presentation of clusters is framed in the language of 'organisation man' (Whyte 1956), drawing uninhibitedly on Anglo-Americanisms and purpose-built verbal compounds. It is clear that the cultural policy of Berlin is designed to foreground its new identity. The mayor and his secretary of state see culture as having this vital purpose: 'In a metropolis that is marked by its diversity, culture provides both identity and social cohesion' ('Zugleich stiftet die Kultur Identität und Zusammenhalt in einer von Vielfalt geprägten Metropole') (Bürgermeister von Berlin/Senatskanzlei kulturelle Angelegenheiten 2011: 5). Pragmatically, this functionalised concept of culture can be seen as a response to the de facto situation in a city whose inhabitants (like those of some other European and American cities) come from every part of the globe. It is, however, also a positive response to a negative past, from which it marks a determined departure. The memory of intolerance when variety, be it racial, religious, or ideological, was systematically destroyed by different forms of totalitarian regime is used as an implicit exhortation to prevent any kind of repetition of this history. Such memory finds its material expression in an ever growing number of memorial sites selectively inscribing the cityscape with monuments bearing witness to an otherwise unmasterable past. By this remembrance of the past, which has become part of cultural policy, the present authorities, usually in collaboration with private citizens and groups advancing particular commemorative initiatives, hope to strengthen further the commitment to tolerance and democracy in present-day society.

Cultural policy in Berlin is informed by a range of stimuli that by no means conform to a single ideological pattern. Unlike the images of Berlin presented in the contemporary novel or in film, which are based on fictional or documentary depictions of individual experience, the portrait sketched out here critically indicates the designs and intentions for this capital city on the part of its politicians, administrators, and corporate citizens. It is primarily their imagination and their interpretation of various public interests, as well as their need to legitimate their policy procedures and decisions in professional and political discourse, that determines much of the development that is taking place. Such rule by democratic and administrative action is neither beholden strictly to the utility demands of the market nor free of confusion and obfuscation, as is glaringly obvious from the repeated failure to keep to targets and deadlines. The new airport at Schönefeld, the reconstruction of the Berlin state opera house and of the most prestigious cinema (Zoo-Palast), and the new building of the Federal intelligence service are some of the notorious examples cited by critics. Seemingly endemic hitches, which some Germans fear damage their nation's reputation for efficiency (and which were cited by Mayor Klaus Wowereit in his resignation speech of 25 August 2014 as a major factor in his decision to step down the following December) do not contribute to the positive image of a city that prides itself above all on its cultural radiance, a point that Wowereit never ceased to stress during his period of office (2001–14).

The challenge of the metropolitan regions: North Rhine-Westphalia

Unlike Berlin, North Rhine-Westphalia covers a relatively large geographical area, and it has by far the most inhabitants of the Federal Länder. While its population density is lower than that of the German city-states, it is higher (523 inhabitants per square kilometre in 2011) than that of the neighbouring Netherlands (402 inhabitants per square kilometre). North Rhine-Westphalia is divided into 10 subregions that are encouraged to preserve and develop their own cultural distinctiveness, at times challenging Berlin's status as an unquestioned metropolis. Federalism acts as a safeguard against a disproportionate amount of material and cultural wealth being concentrated in the capital city. Outside the capital, certain regions are also able to think of themselves as metropolitan. Within the EU, the label 'metropolitan region' is now applied with somewhat inflationary frequency, but in Germany the sophisticated infrastructure of these regions – sociologically, culturally, or in terms of transport facilities – makes such labelling plausible. It is officially supported by the Federal Office for Building and Regional Planning, which has subdivided Germany into 11 metropolitan regions, of which Rhine-Ruhr is by far the largest and, with its 11.69 million inhabitants, the only one to approach the size of greater London or Paris. 'Metropole Ruhr' has its own website and, as Essen-Ruhrgebiet, was awarded the title European Capital of Culture 2010. Despite the hopes of local intellectuals that its 53 towns would be politically agglomerated into a single *Ruhrstadt*,[19] the region remains an administrative mélange of town councils and locally organised industrial associations parochially holding on to their separateness and their considerable budgetary debts. It is remarkable that the conception of an extensive cultural programme by public and private institutions and individuals was able to weld the region together, at least for the duration of 12 months, to play out the dream of a coordinated metropolis.

Despite its common cultural identity, which is supported by a dense infrastructure of roads, motorways, trams, trains, underground systems, waterways, joint efforts to improve the environment (*Emschergenossenschaft, Lippegenossenschaft, Ruhrverband*), over 100 theatres, a dozen musical stages, three opera houses, and prominent rock and popular music venues, the jealously defended municipal demarcations persist. Although the North Rhine-Westphalian government is committed to encouraging the transformation of the area by increasing its leisure, cultural, educational, and research attractions, it is doubtful whether it can force these municipalities into an administratively synchronised metropolitan unit. However, at least in the field of cultural policy, there remains a determination on the part of organisational and marketing institutions such as *Kultur Ruhr* and public or private trusts to preserve the impetus of *Kulturhauptstadt Ruhr 2010*. This subregion's corporate identity as an area that has enriched the cultural landscapes of Europe and its use of culture as a lever for both creative thinking and material innovation are to be further developed to facilitate the massive restructuring of the economy from heavy to lighter industries. Culture is the stimulant for new thought, new social interconnection, and the transformation and re-use of old industrial structures. This is signally done in the long international festival season entitled *Ruhrtriennale*. Politicians like to stress that culture is no luxury, that it should be accessible to all types of public, and that it must be regarded as 'yeast in the dough', energising the whole of society. At the same time, they have announced cuts in the arts budget for North Rhine-Westphalia, from €198 million to €182.5 million in 2013 – although in the context of the creative industries these figures must be seen as seedcorn money generating its own multipliers by flanking privately financed ventures and public-private foundations that contribute their own funds. Public lotteries also provide support for the arts, which can be funded more easily if networks and clusters of excellence in and between different cultural subregions are established.

The ministry responsible for cultural matters is called the Ministry for the Family, Children, Youth, Culture and Sport, which sometimes works together with the Ministry for Innovation, Science and Research. Although culture appears here as just one area amongst others, it is clear from the actual use of culture as an operative concept guiding governance that it is considered vital as a transforming incentive in all aspects of life. The motto is 'Change through culture and culture through change' (Staatskanzlei des Landes Nordrhein-Westfalen 2009: 7). Since the beginning of the new millennium, the state has been divided into 10 distinct, though not hermetically sealed, cultural landscapes. Apart from representing different types of terrain, both physically and historically, they pursue differently accentuated projects in collaboration with a multiplicity of initiatives designed to meet individuals' demands and improve their quality of life. A special report issued by the ministry in 2011 provided an impressive survey of the state's support for culture, complete with detailed figures (Land Nordrhein-Westfalen 2011). In this report, quite remarkably, the word culture is used to describe the capacity of creative activities to interconnect with all others, and to project the human being as at once a value for enterprise and an enterprising being. Economic and cultural life and the public and private spheres are to be brought into productive communication. Within creative establishments, the same criteria that determine the organisation of labour in industry are to be applied, including the flexibilisation of work times, skills, and tasks. This is illustrated by the way in which government administrators define their role as being to give advice and financial support to cultural institutions like theatres and museums on issues relating to the organisation of work, the management of knowledge, the improvement of health, the coordination of family and professional duties, and the attainment of further qualifications.[20]

In North Rhine-Westphalia there are a number of major cities with claims to metropolitan status, foremost amongst them Cologne, which calls itself the *Kulturmetropole am Rhein*. Its city council approved a detailed cultural development plan in 2009 (Stadt Köln 2009). Despite incessant wrangles between political parties and individuals, largely over public debt, the council is clearly determined to preserve and enhance the cultural attractions of this ancient city. Like Berlin, it tries to combine native traditions with the integration of European and global cultures, while preserving its many historical monuments such as its famous cathedral, its Roman remains, its international museums, and its large arenas and exhibition and media centres. Its many carnival societies, with their rich costumes or countercultural attire, sustain a long season of good-humoured merrymaking, culminating in a huge procession of fools and floats. The history of the carnival provides an example of how a lived culture both complies with and censors the present, an observation that could also be applied to the unique international literary festival (*Literaturfest*) that has taken root in Cologne. Cultural policy here is situated at the interface between administrative institutions and initiatives arising from civic society. This is also true of another metropolis, Düsseldorf. With its Deutsche Oper am Rhein and its ballet, museums, attractions for freelance artists, and extraordinarily active trade fairs, as well as its own carnival season, it, too, has achieved an international presence that is felt well beyond its regional anchorage, and as far away as Moscow and Shanghai (Landeshauptstadt Düsseldorf 2010: 7, 14).

Cultural policy in the new Länder

Unlike in the Federal Republic, cultural policy in the German Democratic Republic was not the prerogative of regional states, which were dissolved in 1952. All policy was determined centrally by the ruling party (SED – Socialist Unity Party of Germany) and implemented at the various levels of the state hierarchy – organised in descending order into *Bezirke* (administrative areas), *Kreise* (districts), and *Kommunen* (municipalities). Supplementing the activities of the state administration, but equally subject to overt control by a centrally directed ideology, were a wealth of cultural facilities affiliated to industrial concerns, agricultural production cooperatives (LPGs), and other, quasi-party organisations such as the Kulturbund der DDR (Cultural Alliance of the GDR)[21], the Demokratische Frauenbund Deutschlands (Democratic Women's Association of Germany), and the Freie Deutsche Gewerkschaftsbund (Union of Free German Trade Unions – with around 250,000 officials involved in organising cultural activities at local level). For all that culture was manifestly conceived of as an instrument of ideological dissemination, the massive state investment in local and regional amenities throughout the 40-year history of the GDR yielded a cultural landscape that, even by West German standards, was both impressive and extensive. To allay fears that this rich cultural infrastructure would simply be swept away by the tide of restructuring attendant on German unification, the Federal government made available substantial funds with which, for a three-year period, culture was to be subsidised in the new Länder. As defined by the German Unification Treaty (Article 35, §2), the purpose of this transitional funding was to ensure that 'no harm should befall the cultural assets [of the new Länder]'. Nevertheless, the process of bringing the cultural sphere in the new Länder into line with the model prevailing in the rest of the Federal Republic – a restructuring that was not concluded until the end of the 1990s – was marked by a number of changes (Strittmatter 2010: 74): concentration (such as the merger of orchestras or the amalgamation of library holdings); administrative relocation (of amenities such as youth centres, which became the responsibility of the local Ministry for Women and Youth, or cinemas, which were now classified as commercial enterprises); closure (above all of the cultural facilities affiliated to factories and trade unions); and expansion (through the founding of new amenities, particularly in the museum sector, and the development of an autonomous cultural scene, the like of which was not allowed to exist in the GDR).

The emphasis given in the Unification Treaty to preserving cultural assets implied a somewhat narrow perspective and created the impression of an exclusive preoccupation with the so-called 'beacons' of culture (*Leuchttürme*), namely those institutions, facilities, and artefacts deemed to be of national and not merely regional or local significance. However, the thinking informing the initiatives taken in some of the new Länder evidenced a more expansive and creative approach to cultural policy. Thus in its lengthy document on *Landeskulturkonzept* (concept of culture for the state), presented to the regional parliament in November 2004, the government of Saxony-Anhalt stressed that its task was not to 'devise conceptually' the cultural development of the Land but rather to 'maintain the preconditions for a varied cultural life':

> For this to happen, it is not enough just to provide funding; it also requires, amongst other things, support for networks, media, and public information work, communication platforms, state-wide initiatives, and targeted support for prioritised, profile-building cultural projects. [. . .] When priorities are set, particular importance attaches to certain kinds of things, especially cultural tourism, cultural values that might help improve the image of the *Land*, and the kinds of facilities that enhance cultural identity.

> (Dies kann keineswegs nur durch die Bereitstellung finanzieller Mittel geschehen, sondern u.a. durch die Unterstützung von Netzwerken, durch Medien- und Öffentlichkeitsarbeit, durch die Errichtung von Kommunikationsplattformen, durch landesweite Initiativen und durch gezielte Förderung von profilbestimmenden Schwerpunkten der Kulturarbeit [. . .] Bei den kulturpolitischen Schwerpunktsetzungen gewinnen allerdings bestimmte Aspekte eine herausgehobene Bedeutung. Das betrifft insbesondere: kulturtouristische Effekte, kulturelle Inhalte, die in der Außenwirkung das Ansehen des Landes verbessern können, Angebote, die besonders geeignet sind, kulturelle Identität zu stiften.)
>
> (Landesregierung von Sachsen–Anhalt 2004: 2–3)

The emphasis here on forging a regional identity is perhaps understandable, for as a relatively recent creation – dating back to 1945, when the Soviet military administration simply bolted on the Prussian parts of Saxony to the state of Anhalt – Saxony-Anhalt lacked the historical roots underpinning other 'new' Länder such as Brandenburg or Saxony. Nevertheless, as their respective cultural policies demonstrated, these states were likewise not content to restrict their agenda to merely preserving their cultural assets. In accordance with Article 34 of its constitution, in which is inscribed the obligation to preserve and promote culture, the state of Brandenburg has gradually evolved a model of cooperative cultural development, which, in different forms, also applies in other Federal states. Like those states, Brandenburg wished to define the collaboration between the Land and municipal cultural authorities. In 2012 the Brandenburg parliament endorsed a prospectus dealing with cultural strategy in which this collaboration is described afresh:

> The state will work in partnership with the municipalities – which also have a constitutional responsibility for cultural affairs – to maintain the region's cultural infrastructure. The aim of the state is to support the municipalities in creating the necessary framework for

universal participation in culture, which the state can shore up additionally on a project-by-project basis.

(Das Land wird die kulturelle Infrastruktur arbeitsteilig mit den Kommunen fördern, die ebenfalls eine verfassungsgemäße Verantwortung für kulturelle Angelegenheiten haben. Ziel des Landes ist es, die Kommunen darin zu unterstützen, die grundlegenden Voraussetzungen für die kulturelle Teilhabe aller bereitzuhalten, auf die die Landesförderung projektbezogen aufsetzen kann.)

(Land Brandenburg Ministerium für Wissenschaft,
Forschung und Kultur 2012: 9)

In the aforementioned report 'Culture in Germany' (Deutscher Bundestag 2007) the Federal commission of inquiry on culture in Germany described Brandenburg's cooperative approach to cultural policy as exemplary. Arguably, however, the most distinctive model is that operated by Saxony. In Article 1 of its constitution, the Free State of Saxony (Freistaat Sachsen) – the title under which the Land proudly announced its reclaimed sovereignty in 1990 – defines itself as 'a democratic and social state founded in law and committed to the protection of the natural foundations of life and to culture'. This self-identification as a 'culture state' reflected not only Saxony's tradition-laden history but also one aspect of its more recent past, for within its boundaries were located more than half of the cultural facilities that had been built up in the GDR (Knoblich 2010: 62). The legislation introduced in 1994, however, marked the clearest possible break with the centralising tendencies of the former socialist state. Moreover, the Culture Areas Law (Kulturraumgesetz) made Saxony unique amongst the Länder in imposing a legal obligation on municipalities to foster culture. This had long been a matter of some debate. The Federal report on culture, for instance, concluded that while a blanket obligation to provide 'all forms of cultural work' did not exist, the remit of the municipalities nevertheless included 'the duty to oversee culture, which was to be discharged through their cultural policy' as they saw fit (Deutscher Bundestag 2007: 90). Beyond its legal ramifications, the 1994 law also enacted crucial administrative and financial measures. Saxony was divided into five rural and three urban 'culture areas' (the latter co-extensive with the towns of Dresden, Chemnitz, and Leipzig).[22] In order that the financial burden of promoting culture should not fall disproportionately on a few municipalities, each rural area was to be party to the overall financial settlement (at a rate that, since 2011, has amounted on average to €8.70 per head of population), while the state government has supplemented the budget with an annual contribution of around €87 million.

For proponents of the Saxon model, its great merit is that it not only serves to strengthen regional identity but also fosters collaboration and solidarity, since the rural culture areas unite economically weaker communities with municipalities possessing greater financial muscle. This compares favourably with the excessively competitive mentality promoted by, for example, the Conurbation Law (Ballungsraumgesetz) enacted in Hesse in 2001, which effectively established the Frankfurt/Rhine-Main region as the state's global player and reduced other municipalities to second-class status.[23] By contrast, as its candidate in the 2010 competition for European Capital of Culture Saxony chose not the historic city of Dresden, or even Leipzig, but the town of Görlitz in the rural culture area of Upper Lusatia-Lower Silesia, whose impressive joint bid with the neighbouring Polish town of Zgorzelec lost out narrowly to Essen-Ruhr in the verdict of the EU jury. Faced with the criticism that the Kulturraumgesetz potentially contradicts the clause in the Basic Law guaranteeing the municipalities the right to administer their own affairs (Article 28, §2), advocates of the Saxon legislation point out that the governing body of each rural culture area is comprised of delegates from the relevant municipalities. Moreover, the interests of the latter are also represented on Saxony's Kultursenat, an advisory committee that is completely independent of the Ministry for Science and Art and liaises between the state government, parliament, and the municipalities. Generally throughout Germany such powerful advisory committees exist at the Federal level (Deutscher Kulturrat), at the Land level (for example, in North Rhine-Westphalia or in Thuringia), and at the municipal level (for example, in Bochum, Cologne, Augsburg, Halberstadt etc.).

Perhaps the most telling indicator of the efficacy of Saxony's cultural policy, however, is a simple statistic: with the exception of the city-state of Berlin (and also that of Hamburg, albeit only by a tiny fraction), Saxony boasts the highest expenditure on culture per head of population in the Federal Republic (Statistische Ämter des Bundes und der Länder 2012: 34). Such lavish funding helps explain how it is able to sustain 14 subsidised public theatres, the same number as the substantially more populous and affluent state of Baden-Württemberg.[24] In the season of 2007–08, the year in which the Kulturraumgesetz was renewed, those theatres put on an astonishing 661 productions, a figure topped only by Germany's largest state, North Rhine-Westphalia (Knoblich 2010: 65). Another branch of culture that has flourished spectacularly – and this is true of the new Länder generally, not just Saxony – is the museum sector, which since unification has experienced a veritable boom in the number and variety of museums as well as in annual attendance figures.[25] As Tobias Knoblich (2010: 67–8) has observed, the remarkable growth in the number of institutions specialising in industry, agriculture, and technology is undoubtedly related to the general process of de-industrialisation that Saxony has undergone since 1990, while the increase in and popularity of *Heimat* museums reflect the renewed interest in local and regional identity that accompanied the municipalities regaining their autonomy. Although institutes devoted to the history of the GDR have predictably fared less well – the Panorama Museum in Bad Frankenhausen (in Thuringia) being a rare survivor[26] – one link with the past has been maintained. The East German regime had always shown great commitment to respecting the rights of the Sorbs, a Slavic minority group in the GDR. In 1999, in a notable example of cross-border collaboration, the states of Saxony and Brandenburg concluded a treaty establishing the Stiftung für das Sorbische Volk (Foundation for the Sorbian People), which was dedicated to the preservation of the language, customs, and traditions of the Sorbs, a goal similarly pursued by two theatres in Upper Lusatia-Lower Silesia, the Deutsch-Sorbische Volkstheater Bautzen and the Sorbische National-Ensemble Bautzen.

The expansion in the museum sector since unification was exceeded by only one other type of cultural activity in the new Länder, the development of socio-culture – for the simple reason that no such activity had existed in the GDR. This phenomenon was associated with the radical democratisation of culture that since the 1970s had been advocated by progressive West German cultural administrators like Hilmar Hoffmann and Hermann Glaser as the guiding principle of cultural policy, above all at the municipal level. In embracing this development, Saxony, like the other new Länder, was able to make use of the cultural clubhouses (*Kulturhäuser*) that had existed in many places in East Germany.[27]

Culture and the quality of life

Glaser became a self-styled 'propagandist of the niche' (Glaser 1976: 189). The notion of socio-culture he advocated was more comprehensive than the narrower idea of high culture. For him it was necessary to acknowledge the way in which life is conducted and creatively developed in particular milieus, typically centred on locality, whether urban, suburban, or rural. Socio-culture was an attempt to provide 'an additional communicative level within pluralist society, which is dissected into diverse individual interests and conflicts and shot through with specific barriers to understanding' (Glaser 1974: 49). Accordingly, culture, freed from its restrictive equation with the privileged sphere of artistic production and aesthetic appreciation, was to be aligned with broader practices in the media, social interaction, and cognitive behaviour. The goal of culture, understood now as a network of communicative practices, was to generate emancipated citizens empowered to think critically about themselves and their position in the contemporary world. A wave of socio-cultural activities that began in the Federal Republic in the 1970s eventually swept through the whole of Germany after unification. Its continuing growth is attested to by the myriad of socio-cultural organisations (currently 470) represented by the Bundesvereinigung Soziokultureller Zentren e.V. (Federal Association of Socio-Cultural Centres). It has its own periodical (*soziokultur*) and other occasional publications, all of them made available online.[28] The association's motto, 'Diversity. A matter of principle' (*Vielfalt. Aus Prinzip*), encapsulates both the immense range of social, cultural, educative, and artistic activities, and the remarkable interactive mix of professionals and laymen/women, officialdom and grassroots, public and private funding involved.

It is clear that, in the whole of contemporary Germany, quality of life is intended to be enhanced by an open-minded cultural policy that is bolstered by the development of cultural industries and socio-cultural initiatives. Municipal, regional, and Federal subsidies are designed to preserve and provide space for the lived identity in distinctiveness, difference, and togetherness, and for the creativity of society as a whole. But while official policy wishes to address cultural needs in every corner of the land, culture resists intrusive administration, for it encompasses creative responses to life and, to retain its vitality, feeds on fundamental spontaneity. Hence under democratic conditions it can neither be fitted neatly into a cultural policy framework, however specifically regional in conception, nor channelled in a single ideological direction.[29] As has been indicated in this chapter, the tensions and contradictions evident in contemporary German society will be expressed even in subsidised cultural practices, artefacts, texts, and events. Culture may be a universe of acquired meanings, articulated in particular patterns of behaviour and in the characteristic structuring of the material environment. But it is also dynamic, generating new ideas by individuals and groups that change tastes, lifestyles, built environments, and modes of interaction. Such change typically originates within urban environments, which, given the way in which funding is distributed under the Federal system, allows metropolitan cultural variety to thrive in many conurbations. To the extent that culture materially and cognitively embeds all aspects of human life, it is larger than any given political or legal structures. It is a primary element of all social constellations, but at the same it is rooted in civic society, which, without political and legal structures, is fatally exposed to disorder. Hence the preference for hybrid associational arrangements in the conduct of cultural life, where official agents of political authority combine with independent organisations of citizens.

The National Council for Culture (Deutscher Kulturrat), frequently consulted by government, reflects this hybridity in the make-up of its executive.[30] Its informative bi-monthly journal, *Politik und Kultur*, regularly publishes lists of cultural institutions in Germany that for one reason or another are threatened with closure. It criticises the loss of jobs in cultural policy administration, but it also makes helpful suggestions about how cultural diversity might be enhanced and legally guaranteed in Germany and Europe. In other words, it echoes the predominant tenor in a nation of culture minded above all to nurture creative impulses in the whole of society. The journal and the institution behind it are another illustration of the way that practices have evolved which both presuppose and engender vibrant participatory discourses resisting the twin threats of economic utilitarianism and ideological rigidity. The chief motivation governing all endeavours in this field is the ideal-type of a *Kulturnation* that actively fosters culture as a non-coercive factor determining the quality of life.

213

Notes

1 A notable exception is Klaus von Beyme (2012).
2 For a critical survey of cultural theories see Nünning and Nünning (2003) and Moebius and Quadflieg (2006).
3 The 'grand coalition' between CDU/CSU and SPD is committed in a major way to culture as a variety of practices and also intends to expand it as a subject of scholarly analysis; see Bundesregierung (2013).
4 See, for example, the comments of Hans Zehetmair (2001: 87), former Minister for Science, Research, and Art in Bavaria. For the same reason, Gau and Weber (2001: 269) prefer the term *Kulturauftrag der Länder*, as proposed by Geis (1992: 524).
5 In addition to the constitutions of Länder cited elsewhere in this chapter, see, for example, Article 40, §2 of the constitution of the Rhineland-Palatinate (1947): 'Die Teilnahme an den Kulturgütern des Lebens ist dem gesamten Volke zu ermöglichen' ('It is the task of the state to facilitate the participation of the entire populace in life's cultural wealth').
6 The Federal Commissioner for Culture and the Media is something of a hybrid between a ministry and a government agency. Although based in Bonn, it is affiliated to the Federal Chancellery.
7 Quoted by Naumann (2001: 104). By 'Wilhelminism' Schirrmacher presumably meant a tendency to cloak the culture of the Federal Republic in the mantle of boastful pomposity and nationalistic pride, as had happened in the era before 1914.
8 Hesse coined the term in his essay 'Der unitarische Bundesstaat', which was first published in 1962 and is reproduced in Hesse (1982).
9 See Zehetmair's unequivocal endorsement of both 'cooperative federalism' and the *Kulturstiftung der Länder* as a paradigmatic example of that principle in practice (Zehetmair 2001: 90).
10 The examples he cites of where such advisory competence is relevant include the tax system, copyright law, foundation law, and the fixed book price agreement.
11 An arrangement based on extra taxation in the whole of Germany, ensuring substantial financial transfers to the economically much weaker new Länder.
12 The citizens of Berlin voted by a slim majority in favour of the merger.
13 See Article 23, § 1 of the Grundgesetz.
14 Pierre Bourdieu (1983), in an article that first appeared in German translation, used this term to point to social inequalities created by individuals having uneven access to culture. By contrast, cultural administrators operate with a very broad, class-neutral definition of culture in an attempt to show that cultural capital can be accessed by all. Critical analysis is needed to establish the validity of such claims.
15 For the relevant statistics see 'Armutsgefährdungsquoten im Bundesmaßstab' (Amt für Statistik Berlin-Brandenburg 2011: 24); for a critical description see Gröschner (2013).
16 For the judgements of Seehofer (Prime Minister of Bavaria) and Merkel (Federal Chancellor) see *Der Spiegel* (2010); see also Sarrazin (2010).
17 See Bundesministerium der Finanzen (2012) for the official statistics.
18 See www.berlin.de/projektzukunft/kreativwirtschaft/clusterstrategien/ (accessed 14 March 2013).
19 See the large and richly illustrated volume *Ruhrstadt: Die andere Metropole*, edited for the Kommunalverband by Gerd Willamowski, Dieter Nellen, and Manfred Bourrée (2000).
20 See www.ostwestfalen-lippe.de/Blogs/OWL-Kulturburo-Blog/unternehmensWert-Mensch-fur-Kreativunternehmen.html (accessed 12 March 2013).
21 This was founded in 1945, renamed as such in 1974, and represented at all levels of government.
22 The rural culture areas are: Vogtland-Zwickau, Erzgebirge-Mittelsachsen, Leipziger Raum, Elbtal-Sächsische Schweiz-Ostergebirge, and Oberlausitz-Niederschlesien.
23 For a comparison of the two laws and their consequences for cultural policy see Kramer (2010: 260–1).
24 Only Bavaria and North Rhine-Westphalia, both of which are considerably larger than Saxony, boast more, with 20 and 26 respectively (Deutscher Bühnenverein 2012: 257).
25 For example, in 1991 Saxony had a total of 265 museums; 20 years later the number had risen to 388 (Staatliche Museen zu Berlin – Preußischer Kulturbesitz 2012: 28).
26 Built on the site of the last battle of the Peasants War of 1525, the museum's prime exhibit is an enormous historical panorama painting by the Leipzig artist Werner Tübke. The museum took 20 years to complete and, ironically, opened barely a month before the fall of the Berlin Wall signalled the end of the socialist state it was designed to celebrate.

27 'Das Konzept Soziokultur resultiert aus den Entwicklungen einer neuen Kulturpolitik der 70er Jahre in den alten Bundesländern und fand in Sachsen eine Erweiterung um Traditionen aus der Klub- und Kulturhausarbeit der ehemaligen DDR. Beiden Entwicklungen ist ein weiter Kulturbegriff gemein.' [The concept of socio-culture was the product of a new approach to culture in the old Federal states during the 1970s, which in Saxony was extended by the culture-club work in the former GDR. Common to both developments is a broad conception of culture] (Landesverband Soziokultur Sachsen e.V. 2013: 32).

28 See www.soziokultur.de/bsz/node/10 (accessed 10 July 2013).

29 The allusion here is to Herbert Marcuse's acerbic analysis (1964). We do not accept his argument but read it as warning of an inherent danger in present-day society. He held that the democratic discourse has in fact been destroyed by technological rationality undermining it.

30 For the composition and the tasks of this organisation see www.kulturrat.de/detail.php?detail=170& rubrik=1 (accessed 24 September 2013).

Bibliography

Adorno, T.W. and Horkheimer, M. (1979) *Dialectic of Enlightenment*, trans. J. Cumming, London: Verso.

Amt für Statistik Berlin-Brandenburg (ed.) (2011) *Regionaler Sozialbericht Berlin und Brandenburg 2011*, Berlin: Kulturbuch Verlag.

Bachmann-Medick, D. (2010) *Cultural Turns. Neuorientierungen in den Kulturwissenschaften*, rowohlts enzyklopädie, 4th edn, Reinbek bei Hamburg: Rowohlt.

BOP Consulting (2012) *World Cities Culture Report 2012*, on behalf of the Mayor of London. Online. Available at http://worldcitiesculturereport.com/cities/Berlin (accessed 15 March 2013).

Bourdieu, P. (1983) 'Ökonomisches Kapital, kulturelles Kapital, soziales Kapital', in R. Kreckel (ed.) *Soziale Ungleichheiten*, Soziale Welt Sonderband 2, Göttingen: Otto Schwartz Verlag, 183–98.

Bundesministerium der Finanzen (2012) 'Die Ausgaben und Einnahmen der Länder für das Haushalts-jahr 2012, 1–4. Quartal'. Online. Available at www.bundesfinanzministerium.de/Content/DE/Standardartikel/Themen/Oeffentliche_Finanzen/Foederale_Finanzbeziehungen/Laenderhaushalte/2012/Einnahmen-Ausgaben-der-Laender-Jahr-2012-endg.Erg.pdf?__blob=publicationFile&v=1 (accessed 8 June 2013).

Bundesregierung (2013) *Deutschlands Zukunft gestalten: Koalitionsvertrag zwischen CDU, CSU und SPD. 18. Legislaturperiode.* Online. Available at www.bundesregierung.de/Content/DE/_Anlagen/2013/2013–12–17-koalitionsvertrag.pdf;jsessionid=717F1CCF800237B9E4A9E9358FC9065F.s1t2?__blob=publicationFile&v=2 (accessed 15 December 2013).

Bundesvereinigung Soziokultureller Zentren e.V. (2013) Online. Available at www.soziokultur.de/bsz/node/10 (accessed 8 June 2013).

Bürgermeister von Berlin (ed.) (2011) *Kulturförderbericht 2011 des Landes Berlin*, Berlin: Senatskanzlei-Kulturelle Angelegenheiten. Online. Available at www.berlin.de/imperia/md/content/sen-kultur/kulturfoerderbericht_2011.pdf (accessed 8 October 2014).

Der Spiegel (2010) 'Integration: Merkel erklärt Multikulti für gescheitert'. Online. Available at www.spiegel.de/politik/deutschland/integration-merkel-erklaert-multikulti-fuer-gescheitert-a-723532.html (accessed 8 June 2013).

Deutscher Bühnenverein (2012) *Theaterstatistik 2010/2011*, Cologne: Deutscher Bühnenverein, Bundes-verband deutscher Theater.

Deutscher Bundestag (2007) *Schlußbericht der Enquete-Kommission 'Kultur in Deutschland'*, Cologne: Bundesanzeiger Verlagsgesellschaft.

Deutscher Kulturrat (2013) 'Was ist der Deutsche Kulturrat e.V.?' Online. Available at www.kulturrat.de/detail.php?detail=170&rubrik=1 (accessed 10 September 2013).

Forschungsgruppe Weltanschauungen in Deutschland (2011) 'Religionszugehörigkeit, Deutschland'. Online. Available at http://fowid.de/fileadmin/datenarchiv/Religionszugehoerigkeit/Religionszugehoerigkeit_Bevoelkerung_1970_2011.pdf (accessed 13 July 2013).

Gau, D. and Weber, J.-I. (2001) 'Die Kulturpolitik der Länder im Spannungsfeld zwischen Bundesebene und Europäischer Gemeinschaft', *Jahrbuch für Kulturpolitik 2001*, 2: 269–77.

Geis, M.-E. (1992) 'Die "Kulturhoheit der Länder". Historische und verfassungsrechtliche Aspekte des Kulturföderalismus am Beispiel der Bundesrepublik Deutschland', *Die öffentliche Verwaltung*, 12: 522–9.

Geis, M.-E. (2001) 'Kulturföderalismus und kulturelle Eigengesetzlichkeit: eine juristische Symbiose', *Jahrbuch der Kulturpolitik 2001*, 2: 139–52.

Glaser, H. (1974) 'Das Unbehagen an der Kulturpolitik', in O. Schwencke, K.H. Revemann, and H. Spielhoff (eds) *Plädoyers für eine neue Kulturpolitik*, Munich: Hanser.

Glaser, H. (1976) 'Document: Joys and Sorrows of a Utopian Cultural Administrator (Copeland Lecture at Amherst College, April 1976)', *International Journal of Cultural Policy* 9(2): 185–94.

Gröschner, A. (2013) 'Berlin – Die entfremdete Stadt', 14 November, Heinrich Böll Stiftung. Online. Available at www.boell.de/de/2013/11/14/berlin-die-entfremdete-stadt (accessed 13 June 2013).

Häberle, P. (2001) 'Kulturhoheit im Bundesstaat – Entwicklungen und Perspektiven', *Jahrbuch der Kulturpolitik 2001*, 2: 115–37.

Hesse, K. (1982) *Konrad Hesse: Ausgewählte Schriften*, ed. P. Häberle and A. Hollerbach, Heidelberg: C.F. Müller.

Knoblich, T.J. (2010) 'Kulturelle Infrastruktur in Sachsen und ihre Entwicklung seit 1990', *Jahrbuch der Kulturpolitik 2010*, 10: 61–72.

Kramer, D. (2010) 'Metropolen und Umland: Kulturanalyse und Kulturpolitik', *Jahrbuch der Kulturpolitik 2006*, 6: 255–64.

Land Brandenburg Ministerium für Wissenschaft, Forschung und Kultur (2012) *Kulturpolitische Strategie 2012*, Potsdam: Brandenburgische Universitätsdruckerei und Verlagsgesellschaft.

Land Nordrhein-Westfalen (2011) *Kulturbericht des Landes Nordrhein-Westfalen. Kulturförderung 2011*, Ministerium für Familie, Kinder, Jugend, Kultur und Sport. Online. Available at www.miz.org/artikel/2013_Kulturbericht_NRW_2011.pdf (accessed 13 June 2013).

Landeshauptstadt Düsseldorf (2010) *Kulturreport 2009/2010. Geschäftsbericht des Kulturdezernates der Landeshauptstadt Düsseldorf*, Düsseldorf: Stadtbetrieb Zentrale Dienste.

Landesregierung von Sachsen-Anhalt (2004) *Leitlinien zur Kulturpolitik des Landes Sachsen-Anhalt (Landeskulturkonzept)*. Online. Available at https://www.sachsen-anhalt.de/fileadmin/Files/Landeskultur konzept_Sachsen-Anhalt.pdf (accessed 27 April 2013).

Landesverband Soziokultur Sachsen e.V. (2013) *Soziokultur in Sachsen 2013*. Online. Available at http://soziokultur-sachsen.de/verband/78-news/news/271-soziokultur-in-sachsen-2013 (accessed 15 November 2013)

Marcuse, H. (1964) *One-Dimensional Man: Studies in the Ideology of Advanced Industrial Society*, Boston: Beacon Press.

Moebius, M. and Quadflieg, D. (eds) (2006) *Kultur: Theorien der Gegenwart*, Wiesbaden: VS Verlag für Sozialwissenschaften.

Mohrshäuser, B. (1998) *Liebeserklärung an eine häßliche Stadt: Berliner Gefühle*, Frankfurt a.m.: Suhrkamp Taschenbuch.

Naumann, M. (2000) 'Zentralismus schadet nicht', *Die Zeit*, 45, 2 November.

Naumann, M. (2001) *Die schönste Form der Freiheit*, Berlin: Siedler.

Nida-Rümelin, J. (2001) 'Perspektiven des Kulturföderalismus in Deutschland', *Jahrbuch der Kulturpolitik 2001*, 2: 63–74.

Nünning, A. and Nünning, V. (eds) (2003) *Konzepte der Kulturwissenschaften: Theoretische Grundlagen – Ansätze – Perspektiven*, Stuttgart and Weimar: Verlag J.B. Metzler.

Sarrazin, T. (2010) *Deutschland schafft sich ab*, Munich: Deutsche Verlagsanstalt.

Staatliche Museen zu Berlin – Preußischer Kulturbesitz. Institut für Museumsforschung (2012) *Statistische Gesamterhebung an den Museen der Bundesrepublik Deutschland für das Jahr 2011*, Berlin: Institut für Museumsforschung.

Staatskanzlei des Landes Nordrhein Westfalen (2009) *Strukturwandel durch Kultur. Städte und Regionen im postindustriellen Wandel*, Düsseldorf.

Stadt Köln (2009) *Kulturmetropole am Rhein. Teil 1: Charta*. Online. Available at www.stadt-koeln.de/media asset/content/pdf41/kulturentwicklungsplan_-_teil_1_-_charta.pdf; *Anhang: Bestandsaufnahme*. Online. Available at www.stadt-koeln.de/mediaasset/content/pdf41/kulturentwicklungsplan_-_anlage.pdf; *Teil 2, Maßnahmenkatalog*. Online. Available at http://offeneskoeln.de/attachments/6/8/pdf142986.pdf; http://offeneskoeln.de/attachments/7/5/pdf178257.pdf (accessed 5 June 2013).

Statistische Ämter des Bundes und der Länder (2012) *Kulturfinanzbericht 2012*, Wiesbaden: Statistisches Bundesamt.

Strittmatter, T. (2010) 'Zur Entwicklung der kulturellen Infrastruktur im Land Brandenburg seit 1990: Aspekte des kulturellen Strukturwandels in den neuen Bundesländern', *Jahrbuch der Kulturpolitik 2010*, 10: 73–92.

Von Beyme, K. (2012) *Kulturpolitik in Deutschland: Von der Staatsförderung zur Kreativwirtschaft*, Wiesbaden: Springer Fachmedien.

Whyte, W.H. (1956) *The Organization Man*, New York: Simon & Schuster.

Willamowski, G., Nellen, D., and Bourrée, M. (eds) (2000) *Ruhrstadt: Die andere Metropole*, Essen: Klartext Verlag.

Wowereit, K. (2012) 'Regierungserklärung des Regierenden Bürgermeisters von Berlin, Klaus Wowereit, am 12. Januar 2012'. Online. Available at www.berlin.de/rbmskzl/regierungserklaerung/ (accessed 12 March 2013).

Zehetmair, H. (2001) 'Föderalismus als unverzichtbares Strukturprinzip moderner Kulturpolitik', *Jahrbuch der Kulturpolitik 2001*, 2: 87–90.

14

Theatre and diversity in the Berlin Republic

Christel Weiler

Translation: Maud Capelle

Theatre in Germany plays an essential role in society and public life, often mirroring contemporary conflicts and debates. In post-Wall Germany, the subject of diversity and theatre needs to be considered with an eye to three different areas: the coexistence of independent and municipal or state theatres; the unification of East and West Germany in 1990; and the question how we conceive of 'German' theatre in an increasingly multi-ethnic society. This chapter explores those three areas, and provides some insight into theatre's place, achievements, and challenges in the Berlin Republic.

You will find a municipal theatre (*Stadttheater*) in almost every German town. Some larger cities number several such institutions, most of them funded by local taxpayers (i.e. by the municipalities). You will also find numerous private theatres, as well as venues funded both by generated income and public subsidies. Berlin's Schaubühne, and Mühlheim's Theater an der Ruhr are examples of the latter. Alongside the more traditional theatres, independent venues – such as Kampnagel in Hamburg, the Mousonturm in Frankfurt, or Hebbel am Ufer (HAU) in Berlin – are a key feature of the German theatre landscape. Well beyond the major cities, even in midsize municipalities such as Jena or Marburg, such venues now make it possible for individuals and groups to realise their visions and their ideas.

While German municipal stages, with their resident companies and specific educational mandate, look back on a long history, independent theatre groups are a relatively recent phenomenon.[1] They emerged against the backdrop of the student protests of the 1960s, the gradual establishment of theatre festivals (which drew theatre-makers from abroad to Germany), and the attendant increased exchange of practices, most notably regarding an experimental approach to the body. In this context, a key role was played by Jerzy Grotowski and Eugenio Barba, and by the idea, inherent in their work, of theatre as a laboratory. Well known in Germany for their books, both artists brought their performances to the country and organised workshops with their lead actors, giving German audiences the opportunity to learn more about Grotowski's and Barba's work.

Every year the *Deutscher Bühnenverein* – the employer association and pressure group for theatres and orchestras – records all existing venues available for the presentation of drama, music, and dance performances. It specifies attendance figures, which plays were staged, how the theatres are funded, which segments of the population are being addressed, how many people are working at the theatres, and so on. The resulting report provides a statistical overview of developments and shifts in (especially municipal) German theatre. According to those figures, in 2012 Germany numbered a total of around 150 municipal theatres with resident companies, funded by the local authorities. Around 250 additional theatres were supported by various sources such as foundations, private sponsors, and other municipal or state funding programmes.[2] Although it is the association's declared aim to preserve, promote, and develop the unique diversity of the German theatre and orchestra landscape and its contribution to cultural life (Deutscher Bühnenverein, n.d.), it fails to account for independent theatres, which contribute significantly to a complex and multifaceted theatre scene. The interests of independent theatres, especially their demand for fair and adequate support, are represented by the *Bundesverband Freier Theater*.

Germany has an extensive support system for the arts and the humanities, which is also available to independent theatre practitioners. The *Deutsches Informationszentrum Kulturförderung* (or DIZK) lists 260 schemes for the performing arts alone. It shows the main financial backers to be the municipalities, the Fund for the Performing Arts (*Fonds Darstellende Künste*), the German Federal Cultural Foundation (*Kulturstiftung des Bundes*) and, specifically for Berlin, the so-called Capital Cultural Fund (*Hauptstadt Kulturfonds*), as well as private foundations. As a rule, these institutions support special ventures and projects – funding is granted on a temporary basis and applicants compete for a share of available funds. Accordingly, the future of independent theatre practitioners is anything but secure. For each new project they must find not only financial backing but also a venue, technical equipment, in short the whole production apparatus required to stage a performance. The most recent attempt to provide a secure economic foundation for theatre work is 'crowd funding', a web-based funding model that has been practised with varying degrees of success.[3]

Even though their economic situation differs significantly from municipal and private theatres, independent theatre practitioners have become powerful and influential cultural players. Independent theatre takes many forms: soloists who organise their work alone; collectives that have been collaborating for several years without being tied to one single establishment (such as the groups SheShePop and Showcase Beat Le Mot); production communities that form around a stage director for a limited period of time, dissolving when the project comes to an end, as in the work of stage direction team Rimini Protokoll; and venues such as Kampnagel in Hamburg, the Mousonturm in Frankfurt, Forum Freies Theater in Düsseldorf, or the Theaterhaus Jena. The independent scene contributes a lot to innovation in German-speaking theatre in general; and it has a significant impact abroad, as it very often serves as cultural ambassador for Germany's Goethe Instituts.

During the 1970s the noble institution of the municipal theatre could still be distinguished clearly from independent theatre, but today the situation is less clear-cut. Boundaries have blurred as theatre's variety and plurality have grown. One sign of this new state of affairs is that the independent scene now has a place in Berlin's annual festival of theatre, the *Theatertreffen*. Looking at the performances staged during the 2012 festival, Barbara Burckhardt (2012) writes: 'in German theatre a structural change is taking place that has aesthetic consequences and whose end is not yet in sight.'

In the following, the term 'theatre' encompasses not only conventional theatre, but also musical theatre, dance, and all experimental forms such as performances that blur the line between theatre and the visual arts. It refers to the traditional city and state theatre system as well as to the independent theatre scene with its new forms of representation, production, and dissemination.

Diversity and the public sphere

Germany has theatres for children, for the elderly, for dance enthusiasts, as well as for the traditional educated middle classes (*Bildungsbürgertum*) interested in the conventional dramatic canon and for urban intellectuals who prefer post-dramatic work. There is theatre that specifically addresses the concerns of women and theatre that deals with migration issues. Theatre aims to entertain, to unsettle, to question or indeed confirm commonly accepted values. There is theatre that meets the desire for audience participation, takes to the streets, peeks into courtyards, and plays in living rooms, churches, or galleries. There is dance and singing, puppets are used and music is played, people discuss and argue. Theatres have long ceased to be places that merely make stages available for plays; they have become forums for discussion, for experimentation, for exchange, and for encounters with the audience. There seems to be no limit to the variety and mix of formats and genres, and to the audience's heterogeneity.

The complex plurality of the performing arts plays an important role in and for Germany's public sphere. In a talk given in May 2010, the sociologist Dirk Baecker (quoted in Schmidt 2013) elaborated on the reflexivity of the institution and enthusiastically called the institution of the theatre 'the ideal form to give shape to the observation of man by man, and thus reintroduce second-order observation in society and there observe society's seduction and contagion, its risks and dangers'[4] ('die Form schlechthin, um der Beobachtung des Menschen durch den Menschen selbst eine Form zu geben und so die Beobachtung zweiter Ordnung in die Gesellschaft wieder einzuführen und dort auf ihre Verführung und Ansteckung, ihre Risiken und Gefahren hin zu beobachten'). For non-German readers this might sound exorbitant, but this second-order observation manifests itself in the specialist journals for German-language theatre such as *Theater heute*, *Theater der Zeit*, *Die Bühne*, *Der Spielplan*, *Double*, *IXYPSILONZETT*, *Opernwelt*, or *Tanz*. These provide outlets for writing and reflecting on the forms and functions of conventional theatre, of children's and youth theatre, of puppet, figure, or object theatre; for highlighting the connections to other arts; for reporting on the filling of leading positions; for feting new discoveries; for spreading gossip and scandals; and last but not least, for regularly raising the question of cui bono. The web portal *Nachtkritik* not only reports daily on premieres taking place in small and large cities, but also takes up politically relevant debates connected to theatre and invites its readers to join the discussion. This is another format in which the 'observation of man by man' is practised and takes effect, using theatrical performances as its starting point.

Berlin – a historical perspective

This chapter has so far given a general picture of the wealth and complex diversity of the current theatre system. The focus now narrows to Berlin's varied theatre scene, which for reasons of space, but also for other reasons I will briefly outline, is central to the remainder of the chapter.

Historically speaking, Berlin has played a particular role in the development of German theatre, and more specifically of its aesthetic diversity. Theatre at the turn of the century and in the Weimar Republic was shaped in Berlin by personalities such as Otto Brahm, Bertolt Brecht, Erwin Piscator, and Max Reinhardt. New dramatic forms were presented and established on Berlin's stages. Brahm called for the portrayal of true-to-life stories and established a completely new acting style; Brecht put an end to illusionism and emphasised the constructedness of events taking place on the stage; Piscator used the advent of film as an opportunity to combine visualisation strategies and commentary; and Reinhardt emphasised the festiveness of theatre performances and the magic that can emanate from the stage, defining in yet another way the relationship with the audience. National Socialism put a brutal end to this diversity. The Nazis exploited theatre for their own interests, forcing many artists to leave the country.

After 1945 and until the fall of the Berlin Wall, energies were focused on rebuilding Germany's theatres and articulating a new aesthetic and political self-conception, also among theatre practitioners. The Berliner Ensemble, under the direction of Bertolt Brecht and after his death Helene Weigel, garnered the greatest international visibility. In the 1960s, the Volksbühne, with Benno Besson at the helm, was another site for experimentation in the city's East. In West Berlin, the Berliner Schaubühne stood out internationally;[5] its director Peter Stein raised the bar for European theatre and gained worldwide recognition. Stein worked with Robert Wilson, at that time a relative unknown, and presented his piece *Death, Destruction & Detroit* to a German audience in 1978. In 1988 Berlin was chosen as European Capital of Culture, and the city was opened up for an aesthetically differentiated and diverse theatre when the Berlin Senate agreed to the enduring use of one specific theatre building for international guest performances: the Hebbel Theater. Nele Hertling, first as general secretary of the Akademie der Künste (Academy of the Arts) and from 1989 as artistic director of the Hebbel Theater, led the way in the internationalisation of Berlin theatre that followed.

The fall of the Berlin Wall in 1989 drastically altered the overall situation. More or less overnight, Germany and its theatre landscape underwent a radical change. Suddenly, Berlin had three opera houses (the Deutsche Oper, the Komische Oper, and the Staatsoper) and five large theatre venues (the Volksbühne, the Deutsches Theater, the Berliner Ensemble am Schiffbauer Damm, the Maxim Gorki Theater, and the Schaubühne), all competing for available funds. The list of 'Federal' theatre cities – Frankfurt, Berlin, Hamburg, Cologne, Düsseldorf, Stuttgart – had to be amended to encompass Leipzig, Jena, Dresden, Weimar, Anklam, and Potsdam. Meanwhile Germany was swept up in a process of transformation that went well beyond its theatre. The cards were reshuffled and a new era began, bringing profound social changes. Not only did the 'rich' west pledge to support financially the 'poor' east, it also became apparent that the country's two halves had evolved very differently over the previous 40 years and that at least two – if not more – 'German (hi)stories' were now rubbing up against each other.

With the fall of the Wall on 9 November 1989, the Bonn Republic was set to become the Berlin Republic. Berlin's official designation as the new capital took place in 1990, and in 1999 the government moved to Berlin. In a publication of the Bundeszentrale für Politische Bildung (German Federal Agency for Civic Education), Manfred Görtemaker (2009: 9) identifies as the essential difference between the two republics 'the novelty of the political, economic, social, and cultural environment in which the German Federal Republic has been operating since 1989–90' ('die Neuartigkeit des politischen, ökonomischen, gesellschaftlichen und kulturellen Umfeldes, in dem die Bundesrepublik seit 1989/90 agiert'). With Berlin as capital, the Federal government, using national (not local) taxpayers' money, established the Capital Cultural Fund (*Hauptstadtkulturfonds* or HKF) to support culture specifically in Berlin. To date, the fund has allocated a total of €126.3 million. Support is given to projects in the fields of conventional theatre, dance, music, the visual arts, media art, and performance. The institution's website (Hauptstadtkulturfonds, n.d.) describes what seems to be a vision for Berlin as Germany's representative city of culture: 'Projects supported by the HKF make up a substantial part of what Berlin currently stands for as an international cultural metropolis' ('Die durch den HKF geförderten Projekte machen einen gewichtigen Teil dessen aus, wofür Berlin als internationale Kulturmetropole heute steht'). Such funds have meant that theatre in Berlin, in contrast to large parts of the country, has been able to develop in remarkably varied ways. Not only the success of the 'alternative' venues such as the Ballhaus Naunynstraße, Sophiensäle, Radialsystem V, or Dock 11, but many well-attended exhibitions, music events, and theatre festivals would have been inconceivable without this support.

Berlin, then, has a very particular status in cultural life and policy. The multi-ethnic capital is where the issues and social conflicts that coexist with aesthetic diversity are most clearly visible. The new frameworks for political and cultural life in Germany are most vividly noticeable there, and while the special funds available mean that conditions in Berlin are not representative of the German theatre scene, the capital remains a point of reference for theatres in other parts of the country. The *Theatertreffen*, for example, established in the 1960s, still takes place annually in Berlin, and presents to a critically demanding Berlin audience the 10 'best' performances from Germany, Austria, and Switzerland. Success at the festival opens many doors.

The new frameworks

With the *Wende*, eastern and western parts of the city became equally accessible to its citizens and presented themselves in all their differences: differences in the architecture, in the clothes, in the names given everyday objects, and especially in the sudden attractiveness of certain neighbourhoods (*Kieze*) such as Prenzlauer Berg or Mitte in the eyes of tourists and art pilgrims from all over the world.

Berlin's inhabitants became reacquainted with their city at the same time as they experienced its rapid transformation. Shops opened and had disappeared one month later, streets were given new names, and memories of the era of repression in the east were erased as Berlin became a party town and a magnet for tourists from all over the world. The Wall was sold piece by piece, and today its remains are displayed in Berlin courtyards as expensive artworks. The eastern part of the city was populated by west Germans, and many former residents of East Berlin moved away because they could no longer afford the rent.

The altered economic situation, especially the generous funding of cultural activities, meant that Berlin drew creative types and artists. Referring to a *bon mot* of Klaus Wowereit (Mayor of Berlin 2001–14), by which Berlin is 'poor but sexy', Ulrich Gutmair (n.d.) has described its transformation after the fall of the Wall:

> As a matter of fact, the contradiction between Berlin's economic reality and its image cannot be described any more succinctly. Compared to most other large German cities, it is a poor city. Nevertheless, since the fall of the Wall, Berlin has evolved into one of the most culturally productive cities in the world. Berlin is famous for its club scene and for the number of musicians, DJs, and visual artists who live here. Hundreds of galleries try to sell art to collectors who are as keen to visit the city as are young tourists from all over the world.

> (In der Tat lässt sich der Widerspruch zwischen der ökonomischen Realität und dem Image, das Berlin prägt, nicht knapper charakterisieren. Berlin ist im Vergleich zu den meisten anderen Großstädten Deutschlands eine arme Stadt. Dennoch hat sich Berlin seit der Maueröffnung zu einer der kulturell produktivsten Städte der Welt entwickelt. Berlin ist berühmt für seine Clubszene und die große Zahl der hier lebenden Musiker, DJs und bildenden Künstler. Hunderte von Galerien versuchen Kunst an Sammler zu verkaufen, die ebenso gern die Stadt besuchen wie junge Touristen aus der ganzen Welt.)

It was clear well before the fall of the Berlin Wall that the East was home to theatre practitioners – directors and playwrights with great artistic potential – whose work did not conform to the politics of the regime under which they were living. Heiner Müller, Einar Schleef, Volker Braun,

B.K. Tragelehn, and Christoph Hein used the stage to create space for a different view of the country. Twenty years after the event, Tobi Müller (2009), writing in *Die Welt* of the subversive potential inherent in theatre, went so far as to suggest that it was the theatres that made the fall of the Wall possible. Certainly, subtle and various forces of resistance came together, which in the end led to Germany's reunification. Theatre was one of them. As early as 1989, a West German festival of new writing called the Heidelberger Stückemarkt revealed that the East was no theatrical desert. The organisers invited theatres from Potsdam, Anklam, Berlin, and Weimar, and thus the West German audience could see with their own eyes how vividly theatre had developed in the East. Its strengths and achievements simply had to be recognised and honoured. Thomas Irmer and Matthias Schmidt were the first German scholars and journalists to document this: their joint work *Die Bühnenrepublik* (The Republic of the Stage) was broadcast nationwide on television in 2003 and is also available in book form.

Under the directorship of Frank Castorf, the Volksbühne Ost (so named to distinguish it from the homonymous venue in the west of the city) has been experiencing a formidable revival since 1992. This success has been due on the one hand to the director's stimulating adaptations of prose texts for the stage, on the other to a style of clever dramaturgy and overall programme design that has become a model and inspiration for other theatres, including the Schaubühne. Castorf's model involves expanding the programme to include discussions, readings, and music performances, collaboration with visual artists and universities, and turning the theatre building into a space able to accommodate a multiplicity of events and encounters. At the Volksbühne, former dramaturges Matthias Lilienthal and Carl Hegemann must take credit for beginning the process of aesthetic diversification, a process continued and enhanced by Christoph Schlingensief's work as a director at the same venue between 1993 and 2006.

With Thomas Langhoff and later Bernd Wilms, the Deutsches Theater, which under the East German dictatorship had also served to house political events, regained its reputation as one of the leading Berlin stages. It garnered special attention with a venue called Baracke, where director Thomas Ostermeier's career was launched with the staging of Mark Ravenhill's *Shopping and Fucking*. Not long after this remarkable directing debut Ostermeier became Andrea Breth's successor as director of the Schaubühne. At the Berliner Ensemble, Heiner Müller, Fritz Marquardt, Matthias Langhoff, Peter Palitzsch, and Peter Zadek briefly shared the position of director, which Heiner Müller then held alone until his death in 1995. Compared with other establishments, the Maxim Gorki Theater initially struggled to develop a profile. Bernd Wilms used it as a springboard to the Deutsches Theater, and Armin Petras attempted to put his stamp on it as both playwright and director, writing and staging mainly Berlin-related stories. Wilms's staging of Döblin's *Berlin Alexanderplatz* in 1999, featuring the actor Ben Becker, caused a major stir because of Becker's popularity as a TV star. Since November 2013, the Maxim Gorki Theater with Shermin Langhoff as director has been breaking new ground.[6]

Since the fall of the Wall, venues in the city's east such as the Volksbühne Ost and the Deutsches Theater have led the development of innovative aesthetic practices. Castorf's stagings of plays adapted from novels have become a model for other directors. René Pollesch, a member of Castorf's company, playwright and director in one, not only involved his actors in the co-creation of dramatic texts, but has developed the idea of post-dramatic theatre: Pollesch's plays depart from classical modes of dialogic representation, and instead offer actors the opportunity to engage in different manners of speaking – at breakneck speed, shouting, in collaboration with the prompter, and so on. Where Castorf and Pollesch seem to cultivate a more abrasive, impure aesthetics on stage, Michael Thalheimer at the Deutsches Theater tests the limits of formalism and purity. Together with his stage designer Olaf Altmann he attempts to expose the fundamental structures of both space and characters. In 2013 Thalheimer moved from the

Deutsches Theater to the Schaubühne (in the former West Berlin), where he now works alongside Ostermeier, who is given credit for introducing the complete works of Sarah Kane to a German audience.

Two venues have been particularly important in the process of internationalisation: the former Hebbel Theater, and the Haus der Kulturen der Welt. Both provided significant markers for diversity. In light of Berlin's present global reputation it seems unimaginable that Berlin audiences were introduced to the work of artists from abroad only in the late 1980s. Nele Hertling (as artistic director of the Hebbel Theater between 1989 and 2003) and her collaborators initiated Berlin's evolution into an internationally visible and recognised city of theatre and (especially) dance. The entire European and American dance avant-garde have been guest performers at the Hebbel Theater: Robert Wilson, the Wooster Group, Jan Fabre, the Belgian Needcompany, and Richard Foreman all won recognition in Germany through the efforts of this venue in the heart of Kreuzberg. The Haus der Kulturen der Welt, established in 1989, has contributed decisively to diversifying the German vision of theatre (and of the arts in general); it is under the supervision of a special agency of the Federal government (Kulturveranstaltungen des Bundes in Berlin GmbH) that works on behalf of cultural concerns and, more particularly, cultural exchange. Since it operates well beyond the field of theatre, however, its contribution to establishing cultural and aesthetic diversity should be considered separately.

All these venues have expanded their programmes to include discussions, talks, and an educational programme that reaches out particularly to schools and to university students. Each has stages that can accommodate varying audience sizes and provide space for the presentation of both the great tragedies and experimental projects. But the Hebbel Theater has a very particular history, which is worth considering in greater detail below.

Aesthetic and social diversity: the Theater Hebbel am Ufer/HAU

Perhaps the most significant impulse towards a different notion of aesthetic and social diversity in theatre emanated from the former Hebbel Theater, now known as the HAU Theater. Matthias Lilienthal took on its artistic direction in 2003, offering in the first instance a continuation of what he had already successfully practised as Frank Castorf's dramaturge at the Volksbühne: the diversification of the programme via the integration of public discussions, the attempt to turn the theatre into a site of encounter, the transgression of boundaries between genres, and thus an expansion of the very notion of theatre.

Lilienthal revolutionised Berlin theatre between 2003 and 2012. He drew in a new audience and created new formats to challenge theatregoers' perceptions of space and time. He has successfully questioned labels such as 'Polish theatre', 'Japanese' theatre, and 'Latin American' theatre by grouping performances from around the world thematically (rather than by national origin); journalist Christine Wahl (2012) observed: 'One had barely formed the feeling of having nailed an alleged truth about the Polish, Latin American, or Japanese status quo, and already it was being at least put into perspective by the next performance.' Lilienthal was interested in binding certain artists to his establishment, and in accompanying and advancing their development in the long term. He supported the directing collective Rimini Protokoll, the director Hans-Werner Kroesinger, the company SheShePop, as well as Tamer Yiğit and Branka Prlić in this way (Wahl 2012). The distinctiveness of this theatre was and is recognised both in Germany and abroad:[7] according to Robert Berkowitz (2013), the HAU under Lilienthal's direction was 'one of the largest, best funded, and [most] risk-taking performance theatre complexes in the world'.

One key element in the HAU's success was that in its production pace, thematic sequence, and the variety of formats it was perfectly aligned with the times. Diversity at the HAU meant reacting to plurality in society with plurality in theatre, accepting a challenge, not viewing entertainment and critical thought as contradictions, and not shying away from the fact that the world is complex and requires you to make your way through the labyrinth while retaining your critical faculties. For ten years, the HAU was Berlin's intellectually most ambitious theatre, and Lilienthal's programme drew attention both to imbalances in the composition of his audience and to the fact that the majority of established theatre artists are white – that even in a multi-ethnic city such as Berlin, theatre is still a quintessentially white institution. Using aesthetic diversity, Lilienthal pointed towards issues linked to social diversity.

Another kind of diversity

In 2006 Lilienthal co-organised the festival 'Beyond Belonging' for the first time, with Shermin Langhoff as its curator. 'Beyond Belonging' opened up the stage for stories linked to Berlin's vibrant migrant culture: families' everyday reality, children's desire for a future, street life, being foreign in Berlin. The festival presented a hip hop spectacle that highlighted some of the recesses of Berlin everyday life, and showcased Berlin-based artists with a migration background who had previously enjoyed little or no visibility.[8] 'Beyond Belonging' took place again in 2007 and was again curated by Shermin Langhoff, but this time it highlighted the life of migrant workers more broadly. Guest performances from Istanbul showcased facets of the Berlin-Istanbul axis. In video installations, in films, and above all in musical performances, a rich artistic culture which so far had been hidden could now be experienced as an integral part of Berlin life. The theatre directors, authors, and playwrights Tamer Yiğit, Neco Çelik, Nurkan Erpulat, and Hakan Savaş Mican made their debut at these two festivals.

In 2008 Shermin Langhoff was named artistic director of the theatre Ballhaus Naunynstrasse, whose reputation now reaches well beyond Germany. The theatre is located in the heart of the Berlin district of Kreuzberg, whose residents mainly belong to Berlin's Turkish- and Arabic-speaking communities. It has set itself the task of producing 'post-migrant' theatre: the artists involved have their roots in migrant families, but they themselves have long been Berlin residents, and they view themselves as part of 'majority' society. Shermin Langhoff (quoted in Donath 2011) has explained her desire to end a situation in which theatre practitioners with a migration background are invisible or are seen as exceptional, but also her interest in

> the stories and perspectives of those who have not themselves migrated, yet carry this migration background as personal knowledge and collective memory. Moreover, in our globalised and above all in our urban lives, 'post-migrant' stands for the entire common space of diversity, beyond the question of origin.

> (Geschichten und Perspektiven derer, die selbst nicht mehr migriert sind, diesen Migrationshintergrund aber als persönliches Wissen und kollektive Erinnerung mitbringen. Darüber hinaus steht 'postmigrantisch' in unserem globalisierten, vor allem urbanen Leben für den gesamten gemeinsamen Raum der Diversität jenseits von Herkunft.)

In 2009 'Beyond Belonging' was organised for what was probably the last time, this time in collaboration with the HAU. The festival once more expanded the possible meanings of 'post-migrant'. While events and performances focused largely on German-Turkish topics, attention was drawn to Berlin as home to a growing community of Asian Berliners, who help shape the urban landscape; for example, a staged 'exploration tour' was conducted through Europe's largest Vietnamese trade centre, the Dong Xuan Centre in Berlin-Lichtenberg. At the same time, a curious audience was able to get to know the Naunynstrasse in more depth. Residents threw open their courtyards, their cellars, and their empty shops for theatre and music. Turkish coffee houses usually open only to men invited mixed audiences in. For one special evening, theatre brought people closer. At the very least, audiences could go home with new insights, also in the literal sense.

Cultural education, along with theatre, is part of what makes the Ballhaus Naunynstrasse remarkable. The venue produces theatre at an ever more professional level – for example, Nurkan Erpulat's extremely successful production *Verrücktes Blut* (Crazy Blood).[9] At the same time it encourages audiences to appropriate means of representation – to learn, that is, to represent themselves – a form of empowerment is thus also at stake. But the Ballhaus Naunynstrasse rejects labels such as 'intercultural education' or 'cross-cultural understanding'. Langhoff (quoted in Donath 2011) says:

> No-one I know belongs to a single, closed cultural space. Our real life has long been transcultural and translocal, regardless of origins. [. . .] We must learn to express ourselves beyond affiliation and origin. If anything, in a country like ours cultural education should now be and be understood as intercultural per se, even without naming it as such'.

> ('Kein Mensch, den ich kenne, gehört einem einzigen, geschlossenen Kulturraum an. Unser wirkliches Leben ist schon längst transkulturell und translokal, und zwar jenseits von Herkunft. [. . .] Wir müssen lernen, uns jenseits von Zugehörigkeiten und Herkunft zu artikulieren. Wenn überhaupt müsste kulturelle Bildung in einem Land wie dem unsrigen heute auch ohne Benennung doch per se interkulturell sein und verstanden werden'.)

It would, then, be wrong to think of the Ballhaus Naunynstrasse as Berlin's theatre for the Turkish community. While it began by calling public attention to phenomena that go hand-in-hand with, for example, Turkish migration and a multi-ethnic population, in its daily work it is a place where social and aesthetic diversity are consistently practised and performed. The team of directors, the artists who work there, the guests who are invited are, like the audiences, multi-ethnic. German, English, and Turkish are spoken in equal measure. In this it differs clearly from most other theatre venues, even though it is by now common for guest directors from all over the world to work temporarily at German municipal theatres.

New impulses

With the establishment of post-migrant theatre, the independent scene has provided an important impetus towards a reorientation of German theatre as a whole, challenging previous assumptions about what theatre is. The Dramaturgische Gesellschaft, 'an open platform for the exchange on artistic work, further developments of aesthetics, methods of production and, last but not least, on the social function of theatre' (dramaturgische gesellschaft, n.d.) devoted its January 2011 general meeting to the question 'Who are WE?' It invited sociologists, psychologists, politicians, and theatre practitioners to address this issue together.

Looking at the composition of casts and companies, at appointments to directorships, or at the staff who administer German municipal theatres, it quickly becomes apparent that we are dealing with an almost exclusively 'white' institution. While on stage theatre may be asking critical questions about social togetherness, those questions are only hesitantly being addressed in practice i.e. in the conditions of production. The institutions themselves – and with them, the production of culture – have, therefore, become a target for criticism. Mark Terkessidis writes: 'One must [. . .] interrogate the core of the institutions, probe them to establish whether their venues, guiding ideas, rules, routines, leadership styles, distribution of resources, and external communication are fair and effective as regards diversity' ('Es gilt [. . .], den Kern der Institutionen zu befragen, sie daraufhin abzuklopfen, ob die Räume, die Leitideen, die Regeln, die Routinen, die Führungsstile, die Ressourcenverteilungen sowie die Kommunikation nach außen im Hinblick auf die Vielheit gerecht und effektiv sind'; Terkessidis 2010: 5).

The debate over 'blackfacing', which has been raging since 2012, is an example of how problematic and precarious the situation can be. It was sparked by what can only be described as an extremely naïve course of action at the Schlosspark Theater Berlin, where director Dieter Hallervorden cast a white actor in the role of a black man in his production of *I'm Not Rappaport* and had him perform in blackface. The explanation that this had been done because no black actor was available and that artistic freedom justified such an approach sparked a wave of criticism, with accusations of racism in Germany's theatre system. The debate was intensified by another instance of blackfacing shortly afterwards, in a production of Dea Loher's *Unschuld* at the Deutsches Theater. Again, white actors were cast to play black people; again, their faces were blacked up. Protest, initiated online mainly by the organisation *Bühnenwatch* (n.d.), was soon joined by *Nachtkritik* (n.d.), which provided a platform for those who criticised this practice as racist. The debate exposed the limited awareness of the theatre practitioners concerned: their apparent failure to recognise that, these days, 'when we consider which kinds of communication to engage in – political or economic, artistic or scientific, athletic or intimate – a "world horizon" [. . .] plays a role, and determines what options may even be entertained' ('bei allen Überlegungen, auf welche Kommunikation man sich politisch oder wirtschaftlich, künstlerisch oder wissenschaftlich, sportlich oder intim einlässt, ein "Welthorizont", wie Niklas Luhmann dies genannt hat, eine Rolle spielt, der bestimmt, welche Möglichkeiten überhaupt in Frage kommen'; Baecker 2011a). Theatre audiences in Germany (and elsewhere) are heterogeneous, also in the sense that they are multi-ethnic; and theatres find themselves called upon to (re)consider notions of artistic freedom in the light of the question: freedom for whom?

Outlook

This chapter has illustrated the different ways in which theatre and diversity may be understood. In German municipal theatre, diversity means first and foremost a varied aesthetic programme whose function in society has long ceased to consist solely in celebrating (or deconstructing) dramatic high culture, but instead meets a wide range of audience requirements. The independent scene further expands that variety, and tends to take a far more critical approach to its own practices or methods of production. The evolution of the independent scene has called greater attention to the multi-ethnic composition of German society. It has sharpened awareness that 'German' theatre is a white institution that, in spite attempts to change, is still far removed from equal participation from those with a different skin colour. The structural changes with which I began this chapter are, therefore, to be seen as the beginning of a process that is far from complete. At the same time, change is happening: not only has the independent scene found its place at the *Theatertreffen*, but more importantly the primacy of the German language on stage has been broken, theatre companies include people of colour, and it is more broadly acknowledged that there is more than one version of (hi)stories for the stage.

Theatre, then, is much more than an effective means for the observation of man by man. It sparks important debates – even when it does so through its own blunders and misconceptions.

Christel Weiler

This makes it on the one hand a forum for public debate in a society undergoing upheaval and change (one way or another, theatre always contributes to society's evolution). More importantly, however, theatre reflects how far a society is willing to be serious in its recognition of diversity. With that in view there is still a lot to be done.

Notes

1 On the history of German theatre, see Fischer-Lichte (1993).
2 For details of German funding policies, see Fonds Darstellende Künste (2007).
3 For details on crowd funding, see www.crowdfunding.de/plattformen/.
4 Unless otherwise stated, all translations are the author's own.
5 For details, see Fischer-Lichte (1998).
6 The theatre tries to acknowledge distinctly the diversity of Berlin inhabitants. Most of the actors come from the Turkish community, and the programme explicitly addresses citizens with experience of migration and tries to reflect on issues of identity.
7 Under the heading 'Five Big Names in the World of German Theatre', Hannah Pilarczyk, arts writer for *Spiegel Online*, wrote in *The Guardian* on 13 March 2011: 'As artistic director of Berlin's three-theatre ensemble HAU, Lilienthal's output is nothing if not diverse: from a musical by raunchy electro pop star Peaches to the latest work by barrier-breakers *Rimini Protokoll*, as well as a conference asking: "What is queer about queer pop?"' (Pilarczyk 2011).
8 Since the 1960s, following the erection of the Wall, Berlin has experienced a high influx of workers from Turkey. Although the Turkish community now numbers around 170,000 members, it was hitherto barely represented in theatre and more generally in the cultural field.
9 *Verrücktes Blut* is remarkable inasmuch as it deals with the attempt to confront the German classics – so-called *Bildungsgut* – with migrant youths. A teacher tries to make her class read and act Friedrich Schiller's drama *Kabale und Liebe*, but this proves to be a not only a dubious endeavour but also a challenge in a number of ways.

Bibliography

Baecker, D. (2011a) 'Das Theater als Trope: Von der Einheit der Institution zur Differenz der Formate', in H. Goebbels, J. Machert, and B. Mundel (eds) *Heart of the City: Recherchen zum Stadttheater der Zukunft*, Berlin: Theater der Zeit, 10–18.
Berkowitz, R. (2013) *The Splintering of Culture*, Hannah Arendt Center. Online. Available at www.hannaharendtcenter.org/?p=11455 (accessed 13 January 2014).
Bühnenwatch (n.d.) *Bühnenwatch*. Online. Available at http://buehnenwatch.com (accessed 13 January 2014).
Burckhardt, B. (2012) *Mirror of Change – The 49th Theater Meeting in Berlin*, Goethe Institut. Online. Available at http://www.goethe.de/kue/the/ibf/en9427652.htm (accessed 13 January 2014).
Deutscher Bühnenverein (n.d.) *Ziele und Aufgaben*. Online. Available at www.buehnenverein.de/de/deutscher-buehnenverein/8.html (accessed 13 January 2014).
Donath, K. (2011) *Die Herkunft spielt keine Rolle – 'Postmigrantisches' Theater im Ballhaus Naunynstraße*, Bundeszentrale für politische Bildung. Online. Available at www.bpb.de/gesellschaft/kultur/kulturelle-bildung/60135/interview-mit-shermin-langhoff?p=all (accessed 13 January 2014).
dramaturgische gesellschaft (n.d.) *about us: the dramaturgs' society – dg*. Online. Available at www.dramaturgische-gesellschaft.de/home/new-contentpage (accessed 13 January 2014).
Fischer-Lichte, E. (1993) *Kurze Geschichte des deutschen Theaters*, Tübingen: A. Francke Verlag.
Fischer-Lichte, E. (1998) 'Berliner Theater im 20. Jahrhundert', in E. Fischer-Lichte, D. Kolesch, and C. Weiler (eds) *Berliner Theater im 20. Jahrhundert*, Berlin: Fannei und Waltz.
Fonds Darstellende Künste (ed.) (2007) *Freies Theater in Deutschland. Förderstrukturen und Perspektiven*, Essen: Klartext Verlag.
Görtemaker, M. (2009) *Die Berliner Republik. Wiedervereinigung und Neuorientierung*, Bonn: Bundeszentrale für Politische Bildung.
Gutmair, U. (n.d.) *Club Berlin – die Stadt als temporäre autonome Zone*, Goethe Institut. Online. Available at www.goethe.de/ins/pl/lp/prj/cit/mpc/pcb/deindex.htm (accessed 13 January 2014).

Haupstadtkulturfonds (n.d.) *Hauptstadtkulturfonds*. Online. Available at www.hauptstadtkulturfonds.berlin.de (accessed 13 January 2014).

Irmer, T. and Schmidt, M. (2003) *Die Bühnenrepublik*, Berlin: Alexanderverlag.

Müller, T. (2009) 'Erst die Theater ermöglichten den Mauerfall', *Die Welt*, 23 October. Online. Available at www.welt.de/kultur/article4910655/Erst-die-Theater-ermoeglichten-den-Mauerfall.html (accessed 13 January 2014).

Nachtkritik.de (n.d.) *Nachtkritik*. Online. Available at www.nachtkritik.de (accessed 13 January 2014).

Pilarczyk, H. (2011) 'Five big names in the world of German theatre', in M. Billington 'Don't mention the phwoar: the future of German theatre', *The Guardian*, 13 March 2011. Online. Available at www.guardian.co.uk/world/2011/mar/13/german-theatre-new-europe-berlin (accessed 13 January 2014).

Schmidt, U. (2013) *Das Theater der nächsten Gesellschaft*. Online. Available at hwww.nachtkritik.de/index.php?view=article&id=8170%3Adirk-baecker-wozu-theater&option=com_content&Itemid=100087 (accessed 13 January 2014).

Terkessidis, M. (2010) *Interkultur*, Berlin: Suhrkamp.

Wahl, C. (2012) 'Theater: Die fünf Revolutionen des Matthias Lilienthal', *Spiegel Online*, 6 January. Available at www.spiegel.de/kultur/gesellschaft/hau-wie-matthias-lilienthal-in-berlin-das-theater-revolutionierte-a-836247.html (accessed 13 January 2014).

15

Religious diversity

Volkhard Krech

Europe is an exceptional continent on the world religious map, and Germany illustrates that exceptionality. The other continents have historically been dynamic and very diverse in religious terms: in Africa, for example, Christianity and Islam exist alongside indigenous religions, while in Asia, Jewish, Christian, and Islamic communities coexist with Hindu religions, Buddhism, and traditional Chinese religion. Europe, by contrast, has long been dominated by Christianity; and yet the religious landscape, including in Germany, has always been more colourful than it seems. A recent growth in religiosity without formal religious affiliation, alongside the increased visibility of smaller religious communities, has made this diversity more visible. It has been further enhanced by immigration, the emergence of new religions, and the establishment of divergent theological currents within the mainline Christian churches.

This chapter offers an historical overview of religious developments in Germany over the last century before looking at the current religious situation and highlighting religious trends. Statistical data is used where available. Due to the legal conditions governing state–church relations in Germany, the two major Christian churches and some other religious communities have the status of public bodies, are organised by formal membership, and are financed by a church tax (*Kirchensteuer*) that is collected as part of general taxation. Formal membership starts with baptism, and people can choose to leave on reaching religious maturity at the age of 14. This explains why statistical data is more available in Germany than in other countries, although not for all religious communities. In the case of the latter, adherence has to be estimated.[1]

Historical developments

The Reformation signalled the start of the 'confessional age' in the Holy Roman Empire of the German Nation (Schilling 1994). At the Peace of Augsburg (1555), the principle of *cuius regio eius religio* was adopted, giving each sovereign the right to determine the official religion (Catholic or Lutheran) of the territory over which he ruled. Following the Thirty Years' War (1618–48), the Peace of Westphalia (1648) modified this principle by extending formal recognition to Reformed Protestantism and prohibiting any change to the religious status quo, even if the ruler himself converted to another faith. Thus the diversity of the religious landscape was strongly connected to the political geography of Germany during the early modern period.

Although the 18th and 19th centuries saw some liberalisation (through the Prussian Religious Edict of 1788, for example), the two major Christian confessions – Lutheran or Reformed Protestantism and Roman Catholicism – were generally privileged. This was the religious back-drop to the process of German nation-building. When the German Empire was established under Otto von Bismarck in 1871, the northern and eastern states were shaped mainly by Protestantism, while the southern states were dominated by Roman Catholicism. During the *Kulturkampf* (1871–8) Bismarck, a Prussian, attempted to restrict the role and power of the Roman Catholic Church, though with limited success. In the remainder of this section, I will look at religious developments in Germany between 1900 and the present, differentiating analytically between the level of the individual and the macro level of society.

Membership of and affiliation to the main Christian churches

Figure 15.1 provides a rough indication of formal church membership during this period.

The chart in Figure 15.1 shows religious affiliation to the Protestant and Roman Catholic churches in the German Empire (*Kaiserreich*), the Weimar Republic, the Third Reich, and (re)unified Germany from 1990 to 2002. Around 1900, the vast majority of the German population still belonged to one of the major Christian churches. There was no significant change in the aggregate membership of the two main German churches until 1910, when it began to fall. This decline continued until 1940, but whereas between 1910 and 1925 the Catholic Church lost members, the Protestant Church gained. The trend was reversed between 1925 and 1939. The biggest change in membership of the two main Christian churches happened between 1945

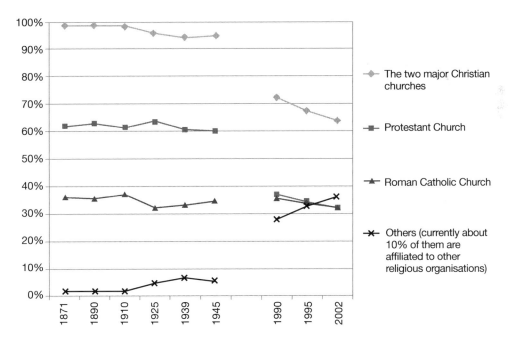

Figure 15.1 Religious affiliation in the German Empire (*Kaiserreich*), the Weimar Republic, the Third Reich, and unified Germany after 1990

Source: Kirchliche Jahrbücher (church statistics); Zentralstelle für Kirchliche Statistik des Katholischen Deutschland; own evaluation

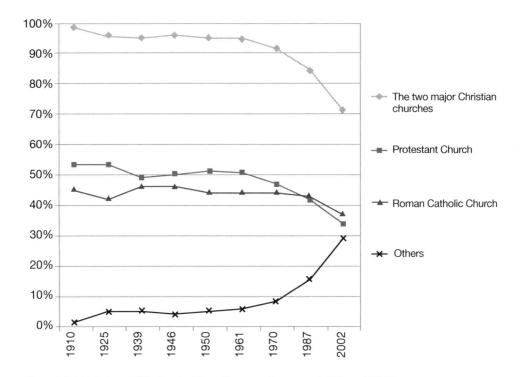

Figure 15.2 Religious affiliation in West Germany between 1900 and 2002

Source: Kirchliche Jahrbücher (church statistics); Zentralstelle für Kirchliche Statistik des Katholischen Deutschland

and 2002, which is hardly surprising: religious politics in the German Democratic Republic (GDR) had a significant influence on church membership, and the Protestant Church lost many, if not most, of its members in the context of socialism and state-decreed atheism. The Roman Catholic Church was less severely affected (but had never been strong in East Germany).

These statistics reflect not so much a process of secularisation as a decline in the importance of religion due to sociopolitical developments. Religious politics in the GDR should be seen not as part of a structural development in modern society (secularisation) but as a cultural factor; in the context of Marxist atheism, religious politics belong to the ideological struggle (*Weltanschauungskampf*). And since atheism can be understood as a system of belief, religious politics in the GDR form part of the modern history of religions. When looking at the process of secularisation, then, it is necessary to isolate religious politics as a factor (see, for example, Dähn and Heise 2003; Pollack 1994). Given the severe dearth of empirical material for the GDR, however, the remainder of this section will focus on the Federal Republic of Germany (FRG).

The statistics for church membership (Figure 15.2) show that, taken together, the two main churches in the FRG experienced no significant change in membership from the end of World War II to the 1960s; when one church lost members, the other one gained. In the early 1970s, as a result of secularisation processes during the 1960s (McLeod 2007), the situation changed. At first only the Protestant Church lost a substantial number of members, but in the early 1990s the Roman Catholic Church experienced the same trend.

Religion in German society: the idea and process of secularisation

A closer look at the societal sphere reveals that secularisation moved from being a focus of discussion to establishing itself as an empirical fact. The idea of secularisation (other than as a legal term) comes from theology – that is, from within the religious sphere. Parallel to church building and the organisation of mass religiosity, Protestantism during the 19th century developed an *idea* of individual religious practice based on authenticity, faith, and integrity, in the light of which *actual* religious practice could only be seen as deficient. Secularisation in this sense means a lifestyle not wholly shaped by religious practice. From within the religious field, the idea of secularisation was used as a societal stimulus for religion among the public; it became an analytical term in the social sciences from the early 1950s onwards. The journey of the idea from the religious sphere, via the public sphere, to the social sciences was reflected in a rapid increase in the production of books on the subject (Figure 15.3).

The sheer volume of books can be considered an indicator of growing interest in the idea of secularisation in the course of the 20th century. After a slow start at the beginning of the century, the curve rises rapidly from the early 1950s until today. Both the proponents and the critics of the idea of secularisation contributed to this development.

There is an interesting correlation between the number of people giving up church membership and the number of books on the subject of secularisation; both also correlate strikingly with the ends of the two world wars (Figure 15.4).

Periods of mass exodus from the church are generally preceded by booms in the production of books on secularisation. In the early 20th century, a period of high demand for such works was followed by the first large wave of departures from the church, beginning in 1918. This was caused mainly by political (especially socialist) movements, but the end of World War I

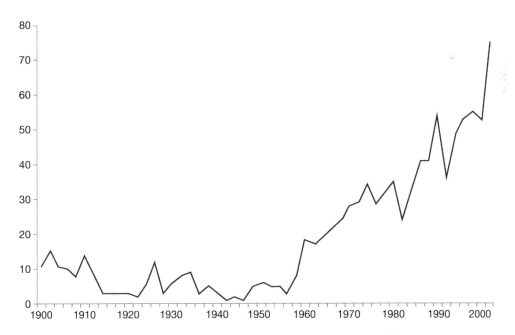

Figure 15.3 German book titles containing the words 'säkular' (secular), 'Säkularisation' (secularisation), or 'Säkularisierung' (secularisation), 1900–2003

Source: Verbundkatalog GBV; own evaluation

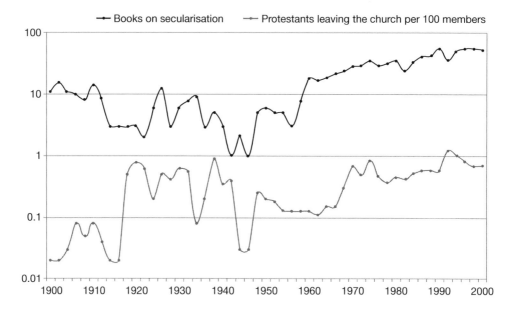

Figure 15.4 Secularisation literature and the decline in church membership (*Austreten*) in Germany, 1900–2000

Logarithmic scale; source: Verbundkatalog GBV and church statistics of the EKD; own evaluation

may also have been a significant factor. After World War II, works on secularisation appeared in ever increasing numbers from the beginning of the 1950s; a corresponding wave of people leaving the church started in the late 1960s. I do not wish to construct a simplistic causal relationship between these two indicators. However, they do tend to support the idea that, in addition to social and religious factors, public discussion of secularisation stimulated church leaving, and vice versa.

One can compare the number of books on religious topics with overall book production (Figure 15.5). The top line shows overall book production in Germany. The middle line shows the production of scholarly literature on religion, and the bottom line, which rises steeply, shows the number of popular and non-scholarly works. While church membership has been in decline since the 1990s, the production of popular religious books has increased. A German consumer polling organisation (the Gesellschaft für Konsumforschung or GfK Group) identified a 20 per cent growth rate for the esoteric book market, and in 1998 the volume of sales in this sector exceeded DM 100 million. If these facts are interpreted as indicating a growing interest in religious topics, it could be argued that organised religion is evolving into 'vagrant religiosity'.

General religiosity

Religiosity has numerous dimensions ranging from religious experience to cultic practice like worship, receiving the sacraments, and so on. This makes it difficult to determine how religious and, in particular, how religiously diverse the population of the Federal Republic of Germany is. An initial indicator is provided by the figures for adherence to particular religious organisations or currents (Table 15.1).

About 59 per cent of the resident population belong to one of the two mainline Christian churches, while the members of other Christian or Christian-affiliated religious communities

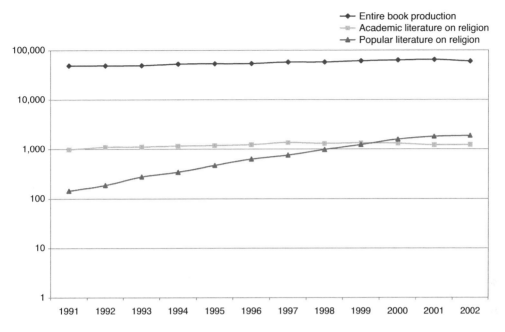

Figure 15.5 Academic and popular literature on religion in relation to total book production in Germany, 1991–2002

Logarithmic scale; source: Verbundkatalog GBV, Amazon, 'Buch und Buchhandel in Zahlen'; own evaluation

Table 15.1 Adherence to a religious organisation or current in Germany 2011

Members of the Protestant Church of Germany		29%
Members of the Roman Catholic Church in Germany		30%
Adherents of other religious communities and currents		10%
These include:		
• Eastern Orthodox, Oriental Orthodox, and Eastern Catholic churches	1.9%	
• Other Christian communities	1.0%	
• Jews	0.2%	
• Muslims	5.5%	
• Buddhists	0.3%	
• Adherents of Hindu religions	0.1%	
• Adherents of new religious movements and the esoteric spectrum	1.0%	
Non-affiliated persons		31%

Source: REMID 2011

comprise about 3 per cent. Islam is the second-largest religion with 5.5 per cent, followed by Buddhism with 0.3 per cent, Judaism with about 0.2 per cent, and Hinduism with 0.1 per cent. New religious communities and currents, as well as the esoteric spectrum, add up to about 1 per cent of the German resident population. Roughly 31 per cent of the German population is not affiliated with any religious community or tendency – a figure far above the global average of 16 per cent. Any increase in this number will have profound implications for the status of religion, but it is impossible to predict future trends based on the data available. The numbers do not say anything specific about the religiosity of people living in Germany: formal membership of or affiliation with a religious organisation can be explained in non-religious terms (social conventions, supporting the sociopolitical participation of religious communities, or a general need for social involvement); and the major religions are always more than just religions – they also mark lines of cultural, political, and sometimes (in Judaism and Hinduism, for example) ethnic identification. Moreover, the category 'without affiliation' does not reveal whether an individual is religious or not; s/he could just as well be cultivating an individualised form of religiosity.

A little more clarity is added by asking how many people consider themselves religious. The German General Social Survey (ALLBUS/GGSS) of 2012 offers the results shown in Table 15.2.

According to this data, about 45 per cent of the German population consider themselves more religious than not religious, and 55 per cent consider themselves more not religious than religious. Ronald Inglehart's studies on value change (namely, from traditional to secular-rational values, and from survival to self-expression values; see Norris and Inglehart 2011) suggest that in Western industrial societies generally the number of those who are rather or very religious has been slightly higher than this – at a constant 55 per cent – for the past 20 years (Inglehart and Minkenberg 2000: 136ff.).

To understand further the influence of religion in Germany we might ask how important religion and church are deemed to be (Figure 15.6 and Table 15.3).

As one might expect, there are significant differences between the eastern and western German population. Whereas about 40 per cent, on average, of the west German population considered religion and the church to be important in the 1980s and 1990s, only about 18 per cent of the

Table 15.2 General religiosity of the German population in 2012

Valid percentage			
Not religious	–1–	22.6	
	–2–	8.6	
	–3–	7.8	
	–4–	4.0	
	–5–	9.5	
More not religious than religious			52.5
	–6–	8.3	
	–7–	11.1	
	–8–	11.7	
	–9–	6.9	
Religious	–10–	9.5	
More religious than not religious			47.5

Source: German General Social Survey 2012 (ALLBUS/GGSS)

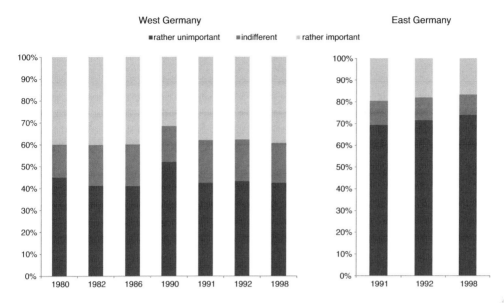

West Germany   East Germany

■rather unimportant   ■indifferent   ▪ rather important

Figure 15.6 Importance of religion and church between 1980 and 1998

Source of data: German General Social Survey (ALLBUS/GGSS)

Table 15.3 Importance of religion and church in Germany 2012

		Valid percentage
Not important	–1–	26.0
	–2–	14.3
	–3–	14.0
	–4–	15.9
	–5–	11.5
	–6–	8.7
Important	–7–	9.6

Source: German General Social Survey (ALLBUS/GGSS)

east German population held the same view. In west Germany, attitudes stayed relatively constant over the 20 years covered by the survey. In 2012 about 54 per cent of the total German population think of religion and church more as not important than as important, and 30 per cent consider religion and church more important than not important.

These figures offer comparatively unambiguous information about religious self-understanding, as well as about the actual importance of religion in people's lives and their attitudes towards religious organisations. However, they also raise the question of what any unspecific indicator of general religiosity actually measures. More specific information is provided by an inquiry into content-specific and concrete statements of faith (Table 15.4).

According to the ALLBUS/GGSS survey of 2012, about 22 per cent of the German population considered themselves theistic and 34 per cent avowed a general belief in a transcendent entity (Table 15.4). Seventeen per cent were agnostic or indecisive, and roughly 27 per cent

Table 15.4 Statements of belief among the German population in 2012

		Valid percentage (rounded)
Theistic faith	(There is a personal God)	23
General faith	(There is some kind of higher being or spiritual power)	31
Agnostic or unsure	(I do not really know what I should believe)	15
Atheism	(I do not believe that there is a personal God, a higher being, or a spiritual power)	31

Source: German General Social Survey (ALLBUS/GGSS)

avowed atheism. There are good reasons to consider atheism another form of faith: after all, atheists do not *not* believe, but rather *believe* that there is no extramundane entity. If we ignore this, however, about 56 per cent of the population are believers as against 44 per cent who are agnostic/unsure and atheists.

Religious communities and currents in Germany

About 70 per cent of the German population, then, belong to a religious community or tendency, but only about half subscribe to any form of religious belief. Today Germany is home to about 230 different religious communities and currents,[2] the largest of which are briefly described below.

The mainline Christian churches

In terms of membership, the two mainline Christian churches account for by far the largest segment of the religiously affiliated population in Germany. However, membership offers only limited insight into a church's sphere of activity. After all, the mainline churches are not only 'service providers' for their members but also collective agents performing relevant tasks in society. It would be difficult to quantify the 'religious factor' in this sphere of activity, so I will limit myself to an outline of membership. I refer to the findings of the fourth church membership survey of the Protestant Church in Germany. Evaluation of the data led to a typology of church membership that differentiates between the five types shown in Figure 15.7 (Höhmann and Krech 2006).

1   The first type is the highly integrated church member. S/he makes up roughly 16 per cent of all church members and corresponds to the classic pattern of what the church expects from its members: s/he espouses traditional Christian beliefs that are mirrored in her or his lived experience. Furthermore, s/he is distinctly attached to the church, regularly attends church services, and participates in church life, at least occasionally.
2   The second type represents about 10 per cent of all church members and is comparatively strongly integrated into the church as an organisation: s/he feels attached to the church, is not inclined to leave the church, frequently attends church services, and occasionally participates in church events. However, s/he does not share the traditional Christian belief in God, so her or his religiosity is less strongly developed than is the case for the first or third (see (3) below) types.

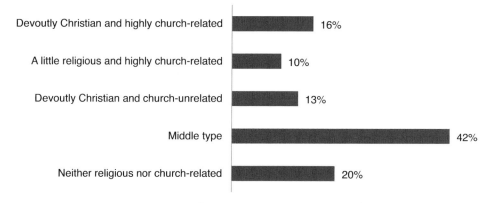

Figure 15.7 Types of membership in the Protestant Church of Germany, 2002

3   The third type, which accounts for around 13 per cent of all church members, follows the Christian faith but is comparatively weakly attached to the church as an organisation. S/he espouses traditional Christian beliefs that are mirrored in her or his daily experience. However, her or his attachment to the church is less strong than that of the first or second type. S/he only occasionally attends church services and, for the most part, does not participate in church activities.
4   The fourth or 'middle' type is the most common, with 42 per cent. This type lacks clearly positive or negative positioning towards Christian beliefs as well as towards an attachment to the church.
5   The fifth type represents about 20 per cent of all church members and is the opposite pole of the first membership type. S/he is neither attached to the church as an organisation nor does s/he particularly follow the Christian faith.

Orthodox Christians

According to statistics published in 2005 by the Evangelische Zentralstelle für Weltanschauungsfragen (a Protestant research institute based in Berlin), the Orthodox Church showed the strongest growth of all Christian churches and communities in Germany between 1993 and 2003, growing from 500,000 to 1.4 million believers. It is now Germany's third-largest Christian church (Thon 2008). This rapid growth is based largely on immigration from eastern European countries: nearly 99 per cent of Orthodox Christians in the Federal Republic have an immigrant background, and two thirds of them have come to Germany in the past 15 years. Only the Greek and a large proportion of the Serbian Orthodox have been living in Germany for decades, having arrived as part of the wave of 'guest workers' (*Gastarbeiter*) that began in the 1960s (see Hansen and Street in this volume).

Immigrants from Greece, Russia, Ukraine, the former Yugoslavia, Romania, Bulgaria, Egypt, Ethiopia, Armenia, Syria, and Eritrea find their religious home in the 17 branches of the Orthodox Church represented in Germany. The different Eastern Orthodox traditions (although not the Oriental Orthodox and Eastern-rite Catholic churches) are united under an umbrella organisation, the Conference of Orthodox Bishops in Germany (Orthodoxe Bischofskonferenz in Deutschland or OBKD), formerly the Commission for Orthodox Churches in Germany (Kommission der Orthodoxen Kirche in Deutschland or KOKiD). Compared with some other religions that have spread in Germany in the wake of immigration, the Orthodox communities are quite well organised. However, in religious terms they are just as active as other faith groups with an immigrant background.

Judaism

The Shoa had a massive impact on the demographics of German Jewry: of the approximately 500,000 Jews living in Germany in 1933, around 300,000 emigrated to escape Nazi persecution, and between 160,000 and 180,000 were murdered in the Holocaust. Nevertheless, Jewish communities began to be re-established in the postwar period, made up partly of Holocaust survivors from Germany itself and partly of Jewish refugees from eastern Europe. The Jewish communities in Germany are largely Conservative or Orthodox theologically; recently, liberal Jews have begun to found their own congregations to reflect their different understanding of the liturgy and issues such as gender relations (Rubinstein 2008). However, the establishment of liberal Jewish congregations is not an entirely new development, since Germany was the birthplace of Reform Judaism in the late 18th and during the 19th century. Up until the early 1990s, the Jewish community in Germany shrank steadily, partly as a result of an ageing population and the emigration of young Jews to Israel, America, or neighbouring European countries, but also because of a high rate of interfaith/mixed marriage. Since the early 1990s, immigration from Russia and other eastern European states has led to a strong growth of Judaism in Germany; more than half of the members of most contemporary congregations belong to this group. This has posed new challenges for the established congregations, as the immigrants often have little knowledge of Jewish tradition. The religious education of migrants has, therefore, become one of the key duties of Jewish congregations. Moreover, the congregations contribute greatly to the integration of immigrants by offering language classes and social services.

Islam

Islam, like Christianity, is a highly diverse faith, with 34 different currents, organisations, and associations represented in the Federal Republic (Chbib 2008). Islam's presence in Germany is essentially the result of immigrant movements, and ethnicity is an important criterion of differentiation. Its adherents' countries of origin range from Turkey (which accounts for a large proportion of German Muslims) to the former Yugoslavia (Bosnia-Herzegovina and Kosovo), Albania, the Arab world (especially Morocco, Lebanon, and Iraq), Iran, various sub-Saharan African countries, Azerbaijan, and Afghanistan. Apart from ethnic plurality, there is a diversity of religious currents. Besides Sunni and Shia orthodoxy, these include Sufism and independent communities that have separated from the mainstreams and developed their own traditions over time (e.g. Alevis and Ahmadis).

Mosques are generally the focal point of Islamic life. Nowadays they offer a number of services apart from Friday prayer, such as pilgrimages, Islamic weddings, corpse washing, and burial rituals. There are often sports activities and youth programmes to choose from: mosques have become a sociopolitical force that goes beyond the purely religious. These social activities are not limited to specifically Islamic interests, as mosques also offer assistance with integration. For example, they provide language and tutoring classes, and often German-speaking contacts are available. This has led to increased co-operation with the municipalities, and there are many mosques and religious associations that now see themselves and are generally recognised as playing a leading role in integration.

Many Islamic congregations are organised into unions. The largest include the Islamische Gemeinschaft Milli Görüş (IGMG), the Türkisch-Islamische Union der Anstalt für Religion (DITIB), and the Verband der Islamischen Kulturzentren (VIKZ). Aside from these, there are a large number of independent congregations. At Federal level, the exact rates of affiliation beyond formal congregational membership are unknown. In March 2007, the Muslim Coordinating Council (Koordinationsrat der Muslime) was founded, which united the unions DITIB and VIKZ with the Central Muslim Council (Zentralrat der Muslime or ZMD) and the Islamic Council (Islamrat). About 98 per cent of all Muslims in Germany live in former West Germany (Haug *et al.* 2009: 106), most of them, due to labour migration, in industrial and urban centres.

Eastern religions

Immigration is also largely responsible for the presence of eastern religions in Germany. Migrants with an eastern religious background have come to Germany from nearly every country in the Far East and south-east Asia, although Hindu Tamils from Sri Lanka and Vietnamese boat people of Buddhist faith are particularly well represented (Kötter 2008). Because of the nature of religious practice in these traditions (for example, the private rites of Shinto devotion) and the infrastructure situation (the few Hindu temples in Germany are widely scattered), the religious life of these communities is centralised only to a small degree, but people do nonetheless gather for important celebrations. For example, the Hindu-Tamil temple in Hamm, which is the largest south Indian temple in Europe, attracts about 20,000 believers to its solemnities. The immigrants find not only a religious home in their place of worship, be it the Hindu temple or the Sikh gurdwara, but also an oasis of familiarity; like many migrants, they find that their religious practice serves a sociopolitical function that goes beyond the purely religious.

There are also German followers of eastern religions, who are for the most part Buddhists. They form a community that is barely connected to the ethnic Hindus and Buddhists and have a very different practice: German converts to Buddhism focus on teachings and ethical conduct (Baumann 1995), whereas ethnic followers of eastern religions are more concerned with worship and community. In times of conflict, the boundaries are very different. Whereas German Buddhists prefer to discuss official interpretations of Buddhist teaching and the right to practise it, migrants' concerns are dominated by the conflicts 'they brought with them', such as the Sri Lanka conflict, the annexation of Tibet, and intra-Indian disputes. And whereas German Buddhists participate in different traditions – they might attend a speech by the Dalai Lama as well as a meditation weekend Zen-style – ethnic Hindus and Buddhists mostly stick to one tradition.

Small religious communities and currents

Among Germany's current population of roughly 82 million inhabitants, about 1.4 per cent represent smaller Christian communities, with between 0.2 per cent and 0.3 per cent – depending on how one estimates – representing new religious communities and the esoteric spectrum. However, we need to take into consideration that for most small religious communities and currents only persons over 14 years of age are accounted for in the data (this is also the age of religious majority in the legal sense). In general, people start consciously to join religious groups, organisations, and movements at that age. This is particularly the case for smaller Christian communities, insofar as they are based on voluntary membership and adult baptism (true of all save for the Methodists and Herrnhuters).

The Christian and Christian-affiliated spectrum

The figures for small Christian and Christian-affiliated communities and tendencies can be broken down as shown in Table 15.5.

For reasons of space, I will not go into statistical details. Instead, I will limit myself to certain key observations on the most numerically significant communities:

1   First, it is notable that the two largest communities, namely the New Apostolic Church with 382,800 members and the Jehovah's Witnesses with 164,000 so-called 'preachers' as active members, connect Christian lore with extrabiblical sources of truth and revelation. Although Jehovah's Witnesses see themselves as scripturalists, they believe that their governing body's interpretations of the Bible are divinely guided. In the case of the New Apostolic Church, living apostles are quasi-official bearers of revelation.

2   Next, the Baptists with roughly 85,000 and the Methodists with 64,000 members represent the largest associations within the classic free church spectrum. They are in third and fourth places in the statistics.[3] The corresponding maps of the *Atlas der Kirchen und der anderen Religionsgemeinschaften in Deutschland* (Henkel 2001: 140ff.) show a concentration of Baptists united in the Union of Evangelical Free Church Congregations in regional strongholds such as East Frisia/Oldenburg, the Bergisches Land, southern Lower Saxony, and south-west Saxony; 56.5 per cent of members live in urban centres, a figure slightly above the German average.

3   The *new* free churches seem to be booming, at least in terms of community formation. Like the traditional free churches, they emphasise their differences from the two major Christian churches (*Volkskirchen*) in the categorical separation of Christian and civic community, the corresponding freedom of the church from the state, voluntary membership, and personal confession of faith.[4] The new free churches are also characterised by a strong commitment to missionary work. Finally – and this is the most important characteristic from a sociological perspective – they are heavily based on the congregationalist principle, that is, they form local and independent congregations and therefore have a comparatively low degree of organisation. Some new free churches, such as the Pentecostal churches and the Union of Free Evangelical Churches, are members of the Association of Evangelical Free Churches (Vereinigung Evangelischer Freikirchen or VEF). Others, such as the Brethren churches, have a critical stance towards both the two major Christian churches and the traditional free churches. The Forum of Free Pentecostal Churches, the largest umbrella organisation of the Pentecostal charismatic congregations, is in fifth place with roughly 50,000 and the Brethren churches in sixth place with 45,000 members. If one adds together the charismatic Pentecostal and the neo-pietist Brethren churches (both of which have a highly developed congregationalist principle) they rank second with nearly 100,000 members and followers.

Not least because of the congregationalist principle, the distribution of these communities varies across the regions. The maps in the *Atlas der Kirchen* (Henkel 2001: 174ff.) show a concentration of congregations belonging to the Forum of Free Pentecostal Churches in Baden-Württemberg. However, the Pentecostal movement in Germany is comparatively evenly spread. The proportion of its members living in urban centres is above average, at roughly 62 per cent.

The highest concentration of Brethren churches can be found in the Bergisches Land and its neighbouring regions, as well as in Saxony. Unlike the Pentecostals, these churches are also

Table 15.5 The Christian and Christian-affiliated spectrum

Smaller Christian religious communities* (partially with elements of neo-revelationism)	Adherents	Source
New Apostolic Church	382,800	REMID
Jehovah's Witnesses	164,000	REMID
Union of Evangelical Free Church Congregations (Baptists; members of the Baptist World Alliance or BWA)	84,975	REMID
United Methodist Church (UMC)	64,100	VEF
Forum Freikirchlicher Pfingstgemeinden (Forum of Free Pentecostal Churches; largest umbrella organisation of Pentecostal charismatic churches):		REMID
– Bund Freikirchlicher Pfingstgemeinden (BFP; Union of Free Pentecostal Churches)	34,600	REMID
– Ecclesia – Gemeinde der Christen e. V.	4,000	REMID/HRGW
– Volksmission entschiedener Christen e. V. (Popular Mission of Convinced Christians)	3,600	REMID
– Mülheim Association of Free Churches and Evangelical Communities	3,000	VEF
– Gemeinde Gottes - Evangelische Freikirche (Church of God – Evangelical Free Church)	3,000	VEF
– Vereinigte Missionsfreunde e. V. (United Friends of the Mission)	1,000	REMID/HRGW
– Apostolische Kirche/Urchristliche Mission (Apostolic Church/Early Christian Mission)	250	REMID/HRGW
– Internationale Jesusgemeinde (International Jesus Church)	36	HRGW
– Jugend-, Missions- und Sozialwerk Altenstieg (Youth, Mission, and Social Relief Altenstieg)		
Brethren churches	45,000	REMID
Selbständige Evangelisch-Lutherische Kirche (SELK; Independent Evangelical-Lutheran Church)	37,460	SELK
Gemeinschaft der Siebenten-Tags-Adventisten (STA; Seventh Day Adventists)	35,948	APD/VEF
Church of Jesus Christ of Latter-day Saints (Mormons)	35,447	REMID
Bund Freier evangelischer Gemeinden (BfeG; Federation of Free Evangelical Churches)	33,107	Idea
Old Catholics (Union of Utrecht)	25,000	REMID
Mennonite Churches (in the Mennonite World Conference)	24,414	REMID
Apostelamt Jesu Christi (Apostle Ministry of Jesus Christ)	20,000	REMID
Christengemeinschaft (Christian Community; anthroposophists)	20,000	HRGW
Arbeitsgemeinschaft Mennonitischer Brüdergemeinden (Association of Mennonite Brethren Churches; outside the Mennonite World Conference)	15,000	REMID
Bund Evangelisch-reformierter Kirchen Deutschlands (Federation of Evangelical Reformed Churches in Germany)	14,000	REMID

continued

Table 15.5 continued

Smaller Christian religious communities* (partially with elements of neo-revelationism)	Adherents	Source
Reformiert-Apostolischer Gemeindebund/Apostolische Gemeinschaft (Reformed Apostolic Church Federation/Apostolic Community	12,000	REMID
Bruno Gröning Freundeskreis (BGF; Bruno Groening Circle of Friends)	12,000	HRGW
Catholic Apostolic Churches (following Edward Irving)	10,000	REMID
Christengemeinden Elim (Elim Christian communities)	10,000	REMID
Pilgermission St. Chrischona/Evangelische Stadtmission (St Chrischona Pilgrim Mission/Evangelical city mission)	9,000	REMID
Free Baptist churches (outside the World Alliance)	8,000	REMID
Evangelisch-Altreformierte Kirche in Niedersachsen (Evangelical Old Reformed Church in Lower Saxony)	7,500	REMID
Evangelische Brüder-Unität (Herrnhuter Brüdergemeine; Moravian Church)	7,200	REMID
Apostelamt Juda/Gemeinschaft des göttlichen Sozialismus (Apostleship of Judah/Community of Divine Socialism)	4,000	HRGW
Universelles Leben (Universal Life)	4,000	REMID
Evangelische Waldenserkirche (Deutsche Waldenserkirche/Freundeskreis der Waldenser; Evangelical Waldensian Church)	3,500	REMID/HRGW
Unitarian:		
– Deutsche Unitarier Religionsgemeinschaft (German Unitarian Religious Community)	2,000	REMID
– Freie Religionsgemeinschaft Alzey (Humanistische Gemeinde Freier Protestanten; Free Religious Community Alzey)	1,000	HRGW
– Bund Deutscher Unitarier – Religionsgemeinschaft europäischen Geistes (German Unitarian Alliance – Religious Community of European Spirit)	300	REMID
– Unitarische Kirche in Berlin e.V. (Berlin Unitarian Church)	100	HRGW
Johannische Kirche (Johannine Church)	3,300	REMID
Churches of Christ/Gemeinden Christi	2,800	REMID/HRGW
Freikirchlicher Bund der Gemeinde Gottes (Free Church Alliance of the Church of God)	2,500	VEF
Church of the Nazarene	2,300	VEF
Evangelisch-Reformiertes Moderamen Berlin-Brandenburg (Evangelical Reformed Moderamen of Berlin-Brandenburg)	2,200	REMID
Salvation Army	2,000	VEF/HRGW
Christian Science/Christliche Wissenschaft	2,000	REMID
Lorber Society	No estimate possible	

continued

Table 15.5 continued

Smaller Christian religious communities* (partially with elements of neo-revelationism)	Adherents	Source
Christliche Gemeinschaft Hirt und Herde (Christian Community of Shepherd and Flock)	1,500	REMID
Reformadventistische Gemeinden (outside the STA; reformed Adventist communities)	800	REMID
Community of Christ (until 2001: Reorganised Church of Jesus Christ of Latter-day Saints)	750	REMID
Fiat Lux	750	REMID
Internationale Gemeinden Christi/Boston Church of Christ	500	HRWG
Religiöse Gesellschaft der Freunde (Quakers)	400	REMID
Worldwide Church of God	400	REMID
Disciples of Christ/Christliche Gemeinde Tübingen	300	REMID
MCC Hamburg – the church (not only) for lesbians and gays	50	REMID
Total	**c.1,164,000**	

* The members of some of these communities are also members of a Protestant regional church.

Sources: REMID (www.remid.de/remid_info_zahlen.htm, accessed 20 October 2010); Reller 2000 (HRGW); Evangelische Zentralstelle für Weltanschauungsfragen, Berlin (EZW); Vereinigung Evangelischer Freikirchen (VEF); Selbständige Evangelisch-Lutherische Kirche (SELK); freikirchlicher Nachrichtendienst der Freikirche der Siebenten-Tags-Adventisten (APD); Evangelische Nachrichtenagentur idea e.V (Idea)

strongly represented in east Germany; nearly half can be found in that area, though these are generally smaller churches. An above-average share of their members (63 per cent) lives in an urban environment (Henkel 2001: 200ff). Overall, the Pentecostal and Brethren churches are fairly evenly distributed across Germany: where one of them is less well represented, the other has a stronger presence.

In conclusion, the statistical findings suggest that those communities within the Christian spectrum that are based on special forms of Christian beliefs (including elements of neo-revelationism and/or stronger local community formation, as well as emphatic practices of communitarisation) are experiencing a boom. The congregationalist principle seems to be particularly attractive because of its 'emotionally supported communality', something people miss in the traditional churches.[5]

Small religions and the esoteric spectrum[6]

I will make just a few key observations on these statistics.

1   If one excludes the Yazidi and the Sikhs as ethnically bound religions, the following communities with numbers of members or followers in at least five figures remain. Ranked first are the Religious Humanists, with 40,000 members. There are neither statistics nor reliable estimates for the German Faith and *Völkisch* groups, unions, and movements. According to the *Handbuch Religiöse Gemeinschaften und Weltanschauungen* (Handbook of religious communities and worldviews) edited by the United Evangelical Lutheran Church, one can reckon with roughly 25,000 followers. Individual circles and associations in this

Table 15.6 Small religions and the esoteric spectrum

Small religions and the esoteric spectrum	Adherents	Source
Religious Humanism	40,000	REMID
German Faith or *Völkisch* groups, unions, and movements	25,000	HRGW
Kurdish Yazidi	20,000	REMID
Freemasons:		
– male lodges	14,500	REMID
– female lodges	350	REMID
– mixed lodges	300	REMID
Scientology	6,000	VS NRW
Bahá'í	5,000	REMID
Sikhs	5,000	REMID
Osho/Neo Sannyas movements	5,000	REMID
Rosicrucians:		
– Lectorium Rosicrucianum	4,200	REMID
– Other Rosicrucian associations	2,000	REMID
Grail Movement	2,300	HRGW
Transcendental Meditation	1,000	REMID
Unification Church (Moon movements)	600	REMID
International Society for Krishna Consciousness (ISKCON)	350	REMID
Divine Light Mission	300	HRGW
Holosophic Society/Kirpal Ruhani Satsang	500	REMID
Brahma Kumaris	300	REMID
Free Zone	200	REMID
Sahaja Yoga	200	REMID
New Church (Swedenborgianism)	200	REMID
Spirituelle Lebensgemeinschaft AUM (Berlin)	200	EZW
Kulturgeister – umbrella organisation for Traditional Paganism	150	EZW
Artgemeinschaft – Germanische Glaubensgemeinschaft wesensgemäßer Lebensgestaltung	140	VS NRW
Ananda Marga	100	REMID
Twelve Tribes	60	REMID
Weltloge Tanatra	28	REMID
The Family (Children of God)	20	REMID
ScienTerra/study group following L. Kin (Scientology secession)	20	REMID
Sathya Sai Baba	No estimate possible	HRGW
Total	**c. 140,000**	

Sources: REMID (http://www.remid.de/remid_info_zahlen.htm; accessed 25 August 2010); Reller 2000 (HRGW); the Evangelische Zentralstelle für Weltanschauungsfragen (EZW); and Verfassungsschutz Nordrhein-Westfalen (VS NRW)

category are kept under observation by the German government agency responsible for safeguarding the constitution (*Verfassungsschutz*) because of their right-wing extremist views. The Freemasons, with about 15,000 members, are ranked third, insofar as they are considered a religious community. Thus the statistics are headlined by religious communities that represent a kind of universal religion and oppose any confessional constriction: the Religious Humanists and the Freemasons. They make up nearly half of the members, in the narrow sense of the term, of neoreligious or syncretic communities.

2   A second large category is represented by associations or movements from the Asian cultural sphere. The Bahá'í religion and the Osho movement, with 5,000 active members each, and Transcendental Meditation, with a narrow circle of 1,000 teachers and 5,000–10,000 'sympathisers', belong in this category.

3   A third category contains esoteric associations like the Rosicrucians, with a total of 6,000 members, and the Grail Movement, with 2,300 members. The Scientology organisation is a special case because it is most heavily influenced by scientism – or rather, by elements of science fiction.

The non-communally constituted esoteric spectrum does not represent the hermetic part of religious history as a whole, but rather that segment of the religious field in which practices such as astrology, rebirthing, reiki, gemstone healing, yoga, pendulums, Ayurveda, channelling, various meditation techniques, tarot, and so on are used. They mostly represent a mixture and an additional interpretation of various (often Asian, but also pagan) traditions. Instead of the binding validity of a religious tradition within which religious beliefs are passed from one generation to the next, a multitude of 'salvation providers' compete with one another for paying clients and customers in an increasingly market-oriented way. Because these forms of interaction are normally only short-term, relatively noncommittal and open to individual needs, this part of the religious spectrum is difficult to quantify. A survey conducted in the department of religious studies at the Ruhr University Bochum on religious diversity in North Rhine-Westphalia showed that the *institutionally bound* following of esoteric practices in the narrow sense accounts for about 0.8–1 per cent of the population of North Rhine-Westphalia (Hero 2008); this figure is probably typical for Germany as a whole.

Summary and outlook

Despite attention from the public and the media, visible and organised religion in Germany is not growing. However, the religious field is becoming more plural, a development that reflects religiosity without affiliation, immigration, the increasing visibility of small religious communities, the emergence of new religions, and the establishment of different milieus and tendencies within the mainline Christian churches.

Whether religiosity is becoming more intense against the backdrop of increasing religious diversity needs to be analysed more closely. Studies on religious diversity in North Rhine-Westphalia have shown that there is a strong connection between religion and immigration (Nagel 2012; Nagel and Jansen 2007; Lehmann 2005): about 43 per cent of immigrants in Germany are involved in religious organisations (Krech 2008). That is more than double the proportion of the overall population who are members of one or other of the mainstream Christian churches (of which 15 to 20 per cent can be considered so-called core members based on the criteria of participation in church activities and a relatively strong faith).

If we look at the majority of members of the two mainstream Christian churches, it seems that the religious situation in Germany is characterised by neither strong identification with a particular religion nor a clear rejection of religion and its organisations but rather by creeping religious indifference or, at most, goodwill towards religion without practical consequences. One can speak of a religious atmosphere of new departures, if at all, only in the Evangelical and Pentecostal charismatic movements. Nonetheless, public interest in and discussion of religion – stimulated by conflicts of (identity) politics on the geo-political global and national levels because of the immigration that Germany has experienced – have increased noticeably. And religion is experiencing a certain boom as a semantic resource to address ethical problems at the borders of instrumental action (on questions of abortion, prenatal diagnostics, manipulation of stem cells, and medically assisted suicide, for example). While a significant increase in religious adherence is unlikely in the near future, one may reckon with a persistence of religion in Germany alongside the various manifestations of the *zeitgeist*.

Notes

1   If not otherwise noted, data are taken from the Religionswissenschaftlicher Medien- und Informationsdienst, Marburg (REMID), as of 2011. See www.remid.de.
2   See, for example, the study on North Rhine-Westphalia (Hero *et al.* 2008); on the whole project, see www.plureligion.net.
3   However, if one adds together all the full and guest member churches of the Association of Evangelical Free Churches, they rank second with 285,000 parishioners and 2,639 congregations (Henkel 2001: 191 with note 9).
4   On the characteristics of traditional free churches see Geldbach (1989). See also Niethammer (1995), who differentiates between the antitypes of the state church, the territorial church, the official church, and the people's church.
5   The term is borrowed from Danièle Hervieu-Léger, cited in Hempelmann (2003: 8).
6   The adherents to some of these communities belong to more than one religious community.

Bibliography

Baumann, M. (1995) *Deutsche Buddhisten: Geschichte und Gemeinschaften*, 2nd edn, Marburg: diagonal Verlag.
Chbib, R. (2008) 'Heimisch werden in Deutschland: Die religiöse Landschaft der Muslime im Wandel', in M. Hero, V. Krech, and H. Zander (eds) *Religiöse Vielfalt in Nordrhein-Westfalen: Empirische Befunde und Perspektiven der Globalisierung vor Ort*, Paderborn: Schöningh, 125–39.
Dähn, H. and Heise, J. (eds) (2003) *Staat und Kirchen in der DDR: Zum Stand der zeithistorischen und sozialwissenschaftlichen Forschung*, Frankfurt a.m.: Peter Lang.
Geldbach, E. (1989) *Freikirchen – Erbe, Gestalt und Wirkung*, Bensheimer Hefte, 70, Göttingen: Vandenhoeck & Ruprecht.
Haug, S., Müssig, S., and Stichs, A. (2009) *Muslimisches Leben in Deutschland: BAMF Forschungsbericht 6*, Nuremberg: Bundesamt für Arbeit und Migration.
Hempelmann, R. (2003) 'Neue Freikirchen als weltanschauliche und ökumenische Herausforderung – eine Bestandsaufnahme', in *Neue Freikirchen als Phänomen innerchristlicher Pluralisierung*, epd-Dokumentation No. 8, 17 February, 5–10.
Henkel, R. (2001) *Atlas der Kirchen und der anderen Religionsgemeinschaften in Deutschland: Eine Religionsgeographie*, Stuttgart: Kohlhammer.
Hero, M. (2008) 'Auf dem Weg zum religiösen Markt? Neue Religiosität und Esoterik', in M. Hero, V. Krech, and H. Zander (eds) *Religiöse Vielfalt in Nordrhein-Westfalen: Empirische Befunde und Perspektiven der Globalisierung vor Ort*, Paderborn: Schöningh, 165–77.
Hero, M., Krech, V., and Zander, H. (eds) (2008) *Religiöse Vielfalt in Nordrhein-Westfalen: Empirische Befunde und Perspektiven der Globalisierung vor Ort*, Paderborn: Schöningh.
Höhmann, P. and Krech, V. (2006) 'Das weite Feld der Kirchenmitgliedschaft. Vermessungsversuche nach Typen, sozialstruktureller Verortung, alltäglicher Lebensführung und religiöser Indifferenz', in W. Huber, J. Friedrich, and P. Steinacker (eds) *Kirche in der Vielfalt der Lebensbezüge: Die vierte EKD-Erhebung über Kirchenmitgliedschaft*, Gütersloh: Gütersloher Verlagshaus, 143–95.
Inglehart, R. and Minkenberg, M. (2000) 'Die Transformation religiöser Werte in entwickelten Industriegesellschaften', in H.-D. Meyer, M. Minkenberg, and I. Ostner (eds) *Jahrbuch für Europa- und*

Nordamerika-Studien 2: Religion und Politik. Zwischen Universalismus und Partikularismus, Opladen: Leske + Budrich, 125–38.

Kötter, R. (2008) 'Identität ohne Abgrenzung: Östliche Religionen', in M. Hero, V. Krech, and H. Zander (eds) *Religiöse Vielfalt in Nordrhein-Westfalen: Empirische Befunde und Perspektiven der Globalisierung vor Ort*, Paderborn: Schöningh, 153–64.

Krech, V. (2008) 'Religion und Zuwanderung: Die politische Dimension religiöser Vielfalt', in M. Hero, V. Krech, and H. Zander (eds) *Religiöse Vielfalt in Nordrhein-Westfalen: Empirische Befunde und Perspektiven der Globalisierung vor Ort*, Paderborn: Schöningh, 190–203.

Lehmann, H. (ed.) (2005) *Migration und Religion im Zeitalter der Globalisierung*, Göttingen: Wallstein-Verlag.

McLeod, H. (2007) *The Religious Crisis of the 1960s*, Oxford: Oxford University Press.

Nagel, A. (ed.) (2012) *Diesseits der Parallelgesellschaft: Neuere Studien zu religiösen Migrantengemeinden in Deutschland* (Bielefeld: transcript).

Nagel, H. and Jansen, M.M. (eds) (2007) *Religion und Migration*, Frankfurt a.m.: Verlag für Akademische Schriften.

Niethammer, H.-M. (1995) *Kirchenmitgliedschaft in der Freikirche: Kirchensoziologische Studie aufgrund einer empirischen Befragung unter Methodisten*, Göttingen: Vandenhoeck und Ruprecht.

Norris, P. and Inglehart, R. (2011) *Sacred and secular: Religion and politics worldwide*, 2nd edn, Cambridge: Cambridge University Press.

Pollack, D. (1994) *Kirche in der Organisationsgesellschaft: Zum Wandel der gesellschaftlichen Lage der evangelischen Kirchen in der DDR*, Stuttgart: Kohlhammer.

Reller, H. (ed.) (2000) *Handbuch Religiöse Gemeinschaften und Weltanschauungen* (HRGW), 5th edn, Gütersloh: Gütersloher Verlagshaus.

Rubinstein, M. (2008) 'Zwischen Normalität und neuem Aufbruch: Das jüdische Gemeindeleben', in M. Hero, V. Krech, and H. Zander (eds) *Religiöse Vielfalt in Nordrhein-Westfalen: Empirische Befunde und Perspektiven der Globalisierung vor Ort*, Paderborn: Schöningh, 140–52.

Schilling, H. (1994) *Aufbruch und Krise. Deutschland 1517–1648*, Berlin: Siedler.

Thon, N. (2008) 'Ethnische Vielfalt und Einheit im Glauben: Die Orthodoxe Kirche', in M. Hero, V. Krech, and H. Zander (eds) *Religiöse Vielfalt in Nordrhein-Westfalen: Empirische Befunde und Perspektiven der Globalisierung vor Ort*, Paderborn: Schöningh, 84–99.

16

Gender and sexuality

Clare Bielby and Frauke Matthes

Gender, sexuality, and Germanness

On 22 November 2005 Angela Merkel became Germany's first female chancellor, dubbed 'Miss Germany' by a national tabloid (*Bild*, 11 October 2005). Ten months previously, Aslı Bayram had become the first woman of non-German descent to win the beauty contest of that title. In the run-up to the Berlin mayoral elections of June 2001, when he would be voted into office, Klaus Wowereit had declared, 'I'm gay and that's just fine'[1] ('Ich bin schwul, und das ist auch gut so'). The Berlin Republic of the 21st century seems a progressive nation as far as gender and sexuality are concerned: women can be voted into the highest political office, women and men with non-German backgrounds can achieve public acclaim, and being openly gay seems to do no harm to your political career.

Delve a little deeper, however, and the situation is less rosy. Wowereit's famous 'coming out' was not as freely volunteered as might be remembered,[2] and reflects an environment in which heterosexuality is still the norm (no politician needs to assert that being heterosexual is 'just fine'). Merkel's success is ascribed by some to feminism – the news magazine *Spiegel* described her chancellorship as a 'triumph of the German women's movement' ('Triumph der deutschen Frauenbewegung'; *Spiegel Online* 2005). Merkel herself, however, avoids being associated with feminism (see her comments in Schwarzer 2009; Ferree 2012: 201–2). And the continued existence of the 'Miss' competition, in Germany as elsewhere, is hardly evidence of progress, even if it can be won by a woman of non-German descent.

In the first decade of the new century, Germany underwent a number of significant political and sociocultural changes. Adjustments in its citizenship law in 2000, for example, mean that citizenship is no longer exclusively dependent on German descent (see Chapter 8). These days only 85 per cent of the German population (even less in major cities) is ethnically German, and ethnic minorities are much more visible than they were in the 1970s (Ferree 2012: 214). Events like 9/11 and the subsequent so-called 'war on terror' had further implications for discourses of German national belonging. It was around the beginning of the century that a shift in the public perception of migrants from Turkey, Germany's largest minority, from 'Turks' to 'Muslims' took place (Yildiz 2009: 474; Chin 2010: 577). Globally, Muslims have turned into 'a source of anxiety' (Yildiz 2009: 475) since 9/11, and this worldwide phenomenon has specific implications in the German context, in which questions around who is inside and outside German culture (which has seen itself as predominately white and Christian) have dominated political discourse. Even the success in the FIFA World Cup of 2010 of the German men's football team, with its players from a variety of ethnic and cultural backgrounds, has helped unsettle the concept of 'Germanness' (see Stehle and Weber 2013), despite Merkel's claim that year that multiculturalism had failed in Germany (*Spiegel Online* 2010).

In this chapter, we explore the categories gender and sexuality as they intersect with class and ethnicity and with questions of national belonging in the Berlin Republic of the early 21st century. Rather than treating gender, sexuality, nationality, race, and class as 'identity categories', discursively constructed or otherwise,[3] this chapter will explore them as something the body 'does' or 'feels', something that affects the body which, in turn, has an effect on the space that body inhabits, the bodies and other objects it comes into contact with, and the world in which that body operates (Ahmed 2004; Deleuze 1992). Poststructuralist theory regards gender, sexuality, and biological sex, but also nationality and ethnicity, as discursively constructed, as fluid and mutually constitutive;[4] that is to say that how masculinity or the 'male' body is 'done' and 'felt' at any given moment is always also about how Germanness, ethnicity (including white Germanness), and class are being 'done' and 'felt'.

Today Germany is part of a transnational world and 'global mediascape' (Stehle 2012a: 3; Appadurai 1996) which shapes national discourses on gender and sexuality. At the fourth UN World Conference on Women in Beijing in 1995, gender was defined as 'the target of equality policy' and gender mainstreaming became a 'central strategic idea' (Ferree 2012: 185). That was endorsed by the European Union two years later in its Treaty of Amsterdam, which named gender mainstreaming a 'primary strategy' (Ferree 2012: 188) and mandated that EU countries pass an anti-discrimination law to outlaw discrimination on the basis of gender, sexuality, nationality and ethnic origin, age, disability, worldview, language, and religion (Germany proved particularly resistant to this law, however, and passed it only in 2006, under Merkel).[5] A paradigm shift attributable to the transnational context of the Berlin Republic has enabled new discursive framings of gender and sexuality: in Beijing in 1995 'gender'[6] rather than 'women' became 'the key word' after feminists had argued successfully for the term on account of the multiplicity and fluidity it enabled (Ferree 2012: 184). The ground had been prepared in Germany by the poststructural approach to gender, sexuality, and the body that American scholars such as Judith Butler had introduced in the early 1990s. Butler's iconic *Gender Trouble* of 1990, in which she set out her ideas of gender as performative, was published in German in 1991 (as *Das Unbehagen der Geschlechter*, Butler 1991), and was hugely influential. Ferree attributes Butler's resonance, particularly amongst younger Germans, to the weakness of the 'macrostructural approaches' of German feminist theory in the context of 'centuries of slow change, deeply institutionalised patterns, and collective identities anchored in material positions'. Ferree also points to the 'increasingly widespread doubt about the unity of interests among women' after feminist interventions by the likes of black and disabled women who did not feel represented by largely white and middle-class feminists (2012: 179). Conceiving of gender as performative, Butler allowed feminists, amongst others, 'to think about choice and change in women's and men's lives' (Ferree 2012: 179). The impact of scholars such as Butler and, more recently, J. Jack Halberstam (1998, 2005) is evident in contemporary Berlin, a hub of the queer activist scene, where, as we will discuss, various — sometimes radical — genders, sexualities, and bodies are lived, felt, and performed, with repercussions for what Berlin and Germany have come to mean internationally.

Femininities in Germany

One of the opening scenes of Kutluğ Ataman's film *Lola and Bilidikid* (1998/1999, *Lola und Bilidikid*) plays with the fluidity of gender, sexuality, ethnicity, and class: three Turkish-German transvestites calling themselves 'die Gastarbeiterinnen' (the (female) guest workers) perform in a queer bar in Berlin's Kreuzberg district. Playing with clichés of the oriental woman, the worker, and the devout Turkish housewife, they reveal femininity, race, ethnicity, and class to be something the body does, regardless of its biology, or something the body 'puts on' – quite literally here in terms of gender: the first sentence spoken by Kalipso, one of the 'Gastarbeiterinnen', in the film is, 'My tits? Where are my tits?' Femininity so overtly performed is clearly marked as drag, and that arguably leads the viewer to see the working-class and ethnic dimensions to the performance also as drag.

But what of more conventional or, to use R.W. Connell's term with regard to gender, 'hegemonic' forms of German femininity, such as motherhood (Connell 2005 [1995])? The authors of *Wir Alphamädchen* (We Alpha Girls; a publication to be seen in the context of new feminisms in Germany, as discussed below), refer critically to the 'Mutter-Kind-Symbiose made in Germany' (mother-child-symbiosis made in Germany) and the complex myth ('komplexer Mythos') of motherhood that exists nowhere as it does in Germany (Haaf *et al.* 2009 [2008]: 223, 164). Telling with regard to the cultural and ideological importance of motherhood is the existence of a word to denote a neglectful mother: '"Rabenmutter"', explains Efstratia Zafeirio, 'is a very German term which incidentally does not exist in any other language' ('"Rabenmutter" ist schon eine sehr deutsche Bezeichnung, die übrigens in keiner anderen Sprache zu finden ist'; cited in Dorn 2006: 273). The central importance of, and emotional investment in, motherhood was clear in public reactions to the liberal family policy proposed by Christian Democrat Ursula von der Leyen, Federal Minister for Family Affairs, Senior Citizens, Women, and Youth from 2005 to 2009 (Ferree 2012: 206–13). In February 2007 she provoked a furore by demanding that the provision of state-financed crèches be extended, thereby breaking with the traditional model of German womanhood as housewife and mother typically propagated by her own party and its Bavarian counterpart, the CSU. Despite protest from within the CDU/CSU as well as from religious commentators, von der Leyen pursued this policy with tenacity. At her initiative, parental benefit (*Elterngeld*) was introduced in January 2007 to replace family allowance (*Erziehungsgeld*), with the stipulation that men take at least two months of the total 14 months as paternity leave for the couple to be eligible, thus further destabilising traditional understandings of gendered roles.

At around the same time, and arguably in response to the policies of von der Leyen, TV presenter Eva Herman (*Das Eva-Prinzip*, 2006; The Eve Principle) and journalist Frank Schirrmacher were arguing that women should return to the home because of a decline in the national birth rate. In his non-fiction bestsellers *Das Methusalem-Komplott* (2004, The Methuselah Plot) and *Minimum* (2006), Schirrmacher railed against the collapse of the German family and the fact that society was getting older, arguing that women should devote themselves to the private sphere. Herman, too, sees the responsibility for Germany's national fate with German women. She called for women to get in touch with their motherly, caring side and to fulfil the 'true purpose' ('wahre Bestimmung') divinely bestowed on them (2006: 27). As the authors of *Wir Alphamädchen* point out, that discussion can be understood as an antifeminist backlash: 'Suddenly a debate about Germans dying out became an argument about women's life roles' ('Plötzlich wurde aus der Debatte ums Aussterben der Deutschen ein Streit um die Lebensmodelle von Frauen'; Haaf *et al.* 2009 [2008]: 156). Even demographers see the framing of this argument in demographic terms as a misrepresentation; societal problems, they claim, are being 'demographised'. Moreover, according to economists, the number of children born has only a minimal impact on economic growth (Haaf *et al.* 2009 [2008]: 157). What might be at stake here is not so much the funding of pensions (tax-paying immigrants could help with that) but, it has been argued, the engagement of German women for the preservation of the German genetic makeup ('Erhaltung des deutschen Genmaterials'; Buttewegge, cited in Haaf *et al.* 2009 [2008]: 157).

Haaf *et al.* are also critical of the discourse on women's 'choice', particularly when it comes to decisions like giving up one's job to devote oneself entirely to motherhood: women are far from on an equal footing with men with regard to making that 'choice', and only certain privileged women can afford the luxury of 'choosing' not to work. An increasing number of women, they argue, are returning to their domestic role as mothers because it is practically impossible both to have enough time to devote to one's children and to have a career, despite the existence of so-called 'new fathers' who are supposedly more involved in childrearing, especially since the introduction of the new parental benefit scheme. The ideology and mythology still surrounding motherhood today, bolstered by more general historically and culturally rooted suspicions about the state's role in childcare provision and the quality of that provision, mean that motherhood becomes, alongside one's career, a 'monster project' (Haaf *et al.* 2009 [2008]: 168–70).

For women to succeed in their career, they need to break through the notorious glass ceiling. Although Germany has a female chancellor and prominent women like Ursula von der Leyen and Andrea Nahles in the cabinet, only 36.5 per cent of politicians in the Bundestag are women (web source 1). In the world of finance, a survey carried out by the Berlin initiative 'Frauen in die Aufsichtsräte' (2011; More women on the boards of directors) found that of 160 market-listed companies, only one had a female CEO and only 6.5 per cent of those on the board of directors were women (*Spiegel Online* 2011). These statistics lend credence to the calls for a Europe-wide female quota in major commercial enterprises, to which – after much heated debate in parliament – the German government is opposed, aiming instead for regulation at the national level (*Spiegel Online* 2013).

In this broad context, a younger generation of largely middle-class, white German women is, once again, withdrawing into the private realm. The 'Biedermeier generation' (Dostert 2010) displays a 'longing for the idyll of the 1950s' ('Sehnsucht nach Fünfziger-Jahre-Idyll'; Haaf *et al.* 2009 [2008]: 21). Films like Ed Herzog's *Schwesterherz* (2006; *Darling Sister*), in which career woman Anna gives up her job and finds fulfilment in married life, as well as the ARD docu-soap *Die Bräuteschule 1958* (2007; Brides' School 1958), in which ten women are 'taken back' to 1958 and drilled in how to become domestic goddesses, propagate what can be called a new social conservatism. The German state has actively encouraged women – or rather certain women – to stay at home and look after their children. Germany's *Ehegattensplitting* – tax breaks for the spouse who is the (main) breadwinner – has financially rewarded a traditionally heterosexual constellation of working husband and housewife. As of 2013, however, the constellation of working wife and housewife/working husband and househusband in same-sex partnerships is also eligible for *Ehegattensplitting*. Since August 2013 a controversial childcare supplement (*Betreuungsgeld*, €100 per month in 2013; €150 per month in 2014) has been paid to parents bringing up children of one to two years at home. This initiative appears to benefit financially privileged families in which one partner can afford not to work; those receiving Hartz IV (combined unemployment and social security benefits introduced in 2005) are not entitled to receive the new childcare supplement.

Clare Bielby and Frauke Matthes

Feminist responses

It is in response to this, but also in the context of global feminist movements and developments in new media, that we can understand a new form of feminism in Germany, with *Wir Alphamädchen* (Haaf *et al.* 2009 [2008]), *Die neue F-Klasse* (Dorn 2006; *The New F-Class*), *Neue Deutsche Mädchen* (Hensel and Raether 2008; *New German Girls*), and the pop-feminist *Missy Magazine* (launched in 2008) leading the way.[7] Haaf *et al.* speak of a 'print hurricane' ('publizistische[n] Orkan'; 2009 [2008]: 9). Contributing to the discussion are German-language feminist blogs such as *Mädchenmannschaft* (*Girls' Team*), founded by the authors of *Wir Alphamädchen* in 2007 (web source 2).[8] Despite their varying quality,[9] the print publications often appear with major publishing houses such as Rowohlt and Piper, suggesting a renewed need or desire (and hence a mainstream market) for feminism in 21st-century Germany, where until very recently post-feminism seemed to have become the new buzzword, and feminism largely meant the persona of Alice Schwarzer and her magazine *Emma*, published since 1977. The majority of new feminist publications seek to differentiate themselves from Schwarzer, and point to her tendency to focus on women as victims (of prostitution, porn, trafficking) and her negativity towards sex, most obvious in the 'PornNo!' campaign (Haaf *et al.* 2009 [2008]; Hensel and Raether 2008). What is more, they demonstrate an increasing desire for men – cis[10] or otherwise – to play an active role in the feminist project, which constitutes quite a break with the Federal Republic's feminist tradition of gender autonomy.[11]

A more recent media hurricane occurred at the start of 2013, when a debate on everyday sexism in Germany raged, leading to an unusual degree of visibility for feminism. Journalist Laura Himmelreich's article for the magazine *Stern* on Rainer Brüderle, parliamentary chairperson of Germany's liberal party (FDP), exposed his sexist behaviour towards her. In response, a feminist blogger in Berlin, Anne Wizorek, started a Twitter stream with the hashtag 'Aufschrei' (outcry), inviting women to tweet their experiences of everyday sexism. The stream attracted over 60,000 tweets in the space of a few days, and Wizorek was invited on to the Günther Jauch political show to discuss that phenomenon.

Other recent examples of German feminisms in a global context include the various 'ladyfests' taking place in German cities since 2003, and annually in the case of Berlin's LaD.I.Yfest. According to their website, 'LaD.I.Yfest is a non-profit, "Do It Yourself" (D.I.Y.) festival of music, art, film, discussions, and workshops. It is organised and orchestrated on a voluntary basis by feminist woman/lesbian/trans★ (wlt★) activists, artists and musicians of various genders'.[12] A more recent, controversial phenomenon embraced by certain German feminists is the so-called 'SlutWalk' (or 'Sl★tWalk'), which started in Toronto in January 2011 after a representative of the Toronto police commented that 'women should avoid dressing like sluts in order not to be victimized' (web source 4). The first German SlutWalk, protesting against the idea that women and their appearance are responsible for rape, took place in July 2011 in Passau and was followed by SlutWalks in other cities, including Berlin, Munich, and Hamburg, on 13 August of that year. The term 'slut' and its potential to be reappropriated has been problematised, particularly by People of Colour activists, who point out that that term has a different and more complex history and present for black women.[13] In the case of the Berlin SlutWalk this led to bitter disputes. Even more contested is the phenomenon 'Femen', a transnational group of feminists founded in Ukraine in 2008 and notorious for their topless protests. The group became active in Germany in the summer of 2012, and was celebrated by Schwarzer's magazine *Emma* for its zero-tolerance approach to sex work and attitude to Islam (*EMMAonline* 2012). As part of their campaign 'Fickt die Sexindustrie!' (Fuck the sex industry!), Femen Germany staged a demonstration on Hamburg's notorious Herbertstraße on 25 January 2013, two days before

International Holocaust Remembrance Day. The choice of date was no coincidence: the full title of the campaign was 'Fickt die Sexindustrie – Der Sexindustriefaschismus des 21sten Jahrhunderts?' (Fuck the sex industry – sex industry fascism of the 21st century?) where a swastika took the place of the 'x' in 'Sexindustrie'. The group hung the words 'Arbeit macht frei', familiar from Auschwitz's notorious arch, at the entry point to the street and carried banners with slogans such as 'Prostitution is genocide'. That instrumentalisation and relativisation of the Holocaust and fascism provoked indignation both inside Germany and further afield (*e*vibes* 2013).

Femen Germany's instrumentalisation of fascism and the Holocaust recalls a similar rhetorical flourish from Schwarzer a few years previously. Schwarzer identified the headscarf as 'the flag of the campaign of the holy warriors' ('die Fahne des Feldzuges der Gotteskrieger') and called 'Islamic crusaders' the 'Fascists of the 21st century' ('[d]iese islamistischen Kreuzzügler [sind] die Faschisten des 21. Jahrhunderts'; Schwarzer 2002). This brings us to a discussion of discourses around Muslim gender relations, and Muslim women in particular. According to Rita Chin, 'Muslim gender relations [. . .] now serve as the most telling symptom of the supposedly intractable clash between European civilisation and Islam' (2010: 558). In that 'gendered framing of difference', the Muslim woman with her headscarf becomes 'a key figure through which objections to Islamic cultural difference have been articulated' (Chin 2010: 557–8). Although there are well educated, high-achieving Muslim women who, as an article in *Die Zeit* announced in 2010, wear the headscarf with 'their head held high' (Schüle 2010), the hip hop singer Sahira Awad being a popular example (*Islamische Zeitung* 2007), many feminists as well as sociologists have assumed that Muslim women have 'virtually no room for individual agency' (Chin 2010: 566). Following in the footsteps of sociological studies on Turkish women in Germany published in the 1970s and 1980s (Chin 2010: 564–70), Necla Kelek's *Die fremde Braut* (2005; The foreign bride) gives what claims to be documentary insight into the living conditions of Muslim women in Germany, who live a life of abuse and oppression under Muslim patriarchy (see Yildiz 2009: 477–81). This kind of 'melodramatic social critique' exists in what is clearly a healthy market alongside autobiographical accounts or 'victim testimonials' (Cheesman 2007: 113–15) by battered Muslim women themselves, representatives of what Karin Yeşilada has termed the 'geschundene Suleika' (maltreated Suleika) (1997; see also Yildiz 2009: 481). These books feed into a discussion of the extent to which non-Western, religiously and culturally 'different' gender relations are compatible with supposedly Western, that is democratic, enlightened values, thus implicitly affirming white, middle-class, Christian German beliefs and practices (Yildiz 2009: 479). Notwithstanding former President Christian Wulff's assertion that Islam belongs to Germany (Wulff 2010: 6), the debates surrounding Muslim gender practices can be read as an expression of national anxieties (Yildiz 2009: 481).

An interesting case study with regard to what might be termed 'other' femininities, that is non-traditionally German femininities, is the Turkish-German journalist, academic, actress, and rap artist Lady Bitch Ray (Reyhan Şahin) who was a media phenomenon for a brief time around 2007–08 (Stehle 2012a: 159). Lady Bitch Ray styled herself a 'hypersexualized "ghetto bitch"' (cited in Stehle 2012a: 158) and deconstructed clichés, found typically in male rap and hip hop, in explicitly sexual and highly ironic ways in her music. For Maria Stehle, Lady Bitch Ray is intentionally a highly perplexing character for Germany, in '[t]he combination of her criticism of German society and her emphasis on being Turkish' (2012a: 160); '[h]er performances worked with and through clichés that are not only gendered, but simultaneously racialized and aimed to challenge the constructions of women, of "Turkish" women, and the co-construction of the Turkish macho-man' (Stehle 2012b: 241). Journalists repeatedly homed in on the question of Lady Bitch Ray's Turkishness and how she was received in the Turkish community.

Interestingly, she repeatedly asserted that it was 'German society' rather than Turks who had a problem with her (Stehle 2012a: 161): 'The German society is all stuck up, they have a tree-trunk up their ass. And I pull that out, piece by piece' (cited in Stehle 2012b: 241). That the phenomenon of Lady Bitch Ray was so short-lived might well suggest that what she represents, particularly in terms of the challenges posed to hegemonic constructions of gender, sexuality, and Germanness, is too radical. Stehle concludes: 'The media frenzy over her performances confirms that Lady Bitch Ray uncovered taboos and for a short amount of time was granted the space to make her intervention; her silencing indicates, however, that ultimately, there is no space for a Turkish-German sexualized and feminist ghetto bitch in Germany' (Stehle 2012a: 161).[14]

Masculinities and Germanness

It is not just with regard to Turkish and Muslim femininities that questions of national and cultural belonging are played out. In May 2012, following a botched procedure by a Muslim doctor, the Cologne district court determined that the circumcision of young boys for religious purposes is bodily harm. That provoked a heated debate about religious freedom in Germany, before, in December 2012, the German parliament passed draft legislation to allow the continued circumcision of Jewish and Muslim boys (web source 5). 'Other' masculinities, like 'other' femininities, have become a canvas on to which questions about Germanness can be projected and on which they can be played out. Following media reports of violence in schools in Berlin's Neukölln district in 2006, as well as media coverage of the Paris riots of 2005, young immigrant men were cast in the German mainstream press as

> sexist and violent – the ultimate perpetrator and the ultimate Other. In discourses about youth violence, the figure of the disenfranchised East-German (sic) Neo-Nazi vanished almost completely; roles for victims and perpetrators were recast. In short, young migrants did not *have* problems any longer, they *were* problems; the protected, contained, and instrumentalized other of the multicultural ideology was transformed into the violent ghetto Turk who cannot and does not want to integrate.
>
> (Stehle 2012a: 14; emphasis in original)

It seems that Germany's 'other men' play a vital new role in the country's perception of itself as a modern, egalitarian, and democratic society.

More mainstream 'German' masculinities are contested in the face of these ethnic, cultural, and religious 'others'. A threat to working-class masculinity, posed by queer masculinity, is explored (for example) in Angelina Maccarone's film *Unveiled* (2005; *Fremde Haut*),[15] in which a lesbian Iranian asylum seeker takes on the identity of a man in order to stay in Germany. The film unsettles a binary understanding of gender (Jeremiah 2011: 591), uncovering its constructed-ness. The main character's unstable, ethnically 'other' (and queer) masculinity challenges German working-class white masculinity and thereby gets to the heart of anxieties in the face of the ethnic and fe/male other. In a similar vein, in conversation with the interview magazine *Galore*, German-Jewish writer Maxim Biller stated: 'I consider Germans to be prudes – German men anyway' ('Ich halte die Deutschen für prüde – die deutschen Männer jedenfalls'; 2008: 25). Biller here destabilises 'the historical German-Jewish opposition where "the Jew" served as a counter-image – a necessity even – in the construction of Germanness' (Matthes 2012: 324). By subverting the power structures underlying the traditional 'German-Other' dyad in some of his fictional writing as well as newspaper columns, Biller, like Lady Bitch Ray, makes the fragility and the precariousness of contemporary German masculinity explicit.

In the context of the challenges posed by so-called 'other' masculinities, as well as the changes that 'hegemonic' German masculinity has undergone in recent years, there appears to be a certain anxiety about, or a will to discuss and pin down, German masculinities today. In January 2013, the English-language magazine *EXBERLINER* published a 14-page special feature on German men. The words 'oh BOY!' – a reference to a film of that name that is set in Berlin and focuses on failed German masculinity (2012) – are printed in large pink font on the front cover, above the face of the most recent Mister Germany (Figure 16.1). The feature includes an article on men as victims of domestic violence perpetrated by women (Riceburg 2013) and an article on how 'new fathers' are discriminated against when it comes to their custody rights (Obermueller 2013). It can, then, be read in the context of an antifeminist backlash. In the quiz 'How much of a German man are you?', the short blurb to describe those who have achieved the most points is as follows:

> You choose function over fashion, reason over spontaneity and principles over romance. Post-war guilt and decades of German feminist upbringing have turned you into a proud, penny-pinching, pontificating *Sitzpinkler* [a man who sits down to urinate]. On the outside, you might come across as a little feminine [. . .] but in bed, your inner beast expresses itself.
> (*EXBERLINER* 2013)

Mister Germany, Jörn Kamphius, explains his preference for foreign women with explicit reference to German women's emancipation: 'It's more to do with the personality of German women. They're constantly trying to show how strong they are. I feel these women are not

Figure 16.1 Mr Germany
Courtesy of *EXBERLINER* www.exberliner.com

themselves and it makes me feel sad. Dealing with them takes too much energy' (O'Donovan and Castellví 2013). Kamphius is styled to present a clear example of 'metrosexual' masculinity: a straight man who pays careful attention to his appearance. His image on the front cover represents a form of masculinity that can be seen in a global context: internationally famous figures like David Beckham, but also the increasing visibility of queer masculinities, have influenced constructions of the masculine far beyond their immediate context.

Old role models no longer seem suitable, but at the same time they are still in place. Women remain at home in over half of German families in which the children are of school age and German wives earn on average only 18 per cent of the family income (Haaf *et al.* 2009 [2008]: 213). Nonetheless, a certain backlash is also emerging from within the Ministry of Family Affairs: in April 2010 Kristina Schröder, then Federal Minister for Family Affairs, pointed to the supposed discrimination that boys at German schools face after years of explicit support for girls (Spiewak 2010). On International Women's Day in 2012, the only public engagement Schröder accepted was an invitation to the ceremony celebrating the 'top fathers of the year' (Wichmann 2012). That should be read in the context of the greater involvement of fathers as part of the 'Elterngeld' policy and as a general encouragement for men to combine their careers with fatherhood more successfully; but it also underlines her political priorities.

A striking example of feminist backlash – a phenomenon that needs to be seen in a global context[16] – is the launch of the German-language website 'wikiMANNia.org' in 2009. Founded on the assumption that women are privileged and men are disadvantaged in politics, law, and society, the aim is to share 'feminism-free knowledge' ('feminismusfreies Wissen') with others, especially 'free men', and to provide 'supporting arguments' ('Argumentationshilfe') for men fighting injustice in, for instance, the workplace, family law, or feminist criticism (web source 6). Probably alluding to the mythopoetic men's movements of the 1980s that developed as a response to feminist efforts of the 1970s and 1980s (Adams and Savran 2002: 5), this website reveals the anxieties that come with the destabilisation of traditional, long-established forms of masculinity.

Queering Germanness

Similar anxieties are evident, and again often couched in national terms, when it comes to what we might refer to as a queering of the traditional German family. In his column for the ultraconservative tabloid *Bild-Zeitung* of 23 August 2012, Franz Josef Wagner effectively tells queer Germans that they should be grateful for what they have: civil partnership, as of August 2001, but with fewer rights than married couples. Wagner invokes the nation: 'what a glorious time it is for you. Nobody locks you up, you love your partner, you are allowed to love them. You are German married partners [. . .]. We've become a better Germany' ('Was für eine glorreiche Zeit für Euch. Niemand steckt Euch ins Gefängnis, Ihr liebt Eure Partner, Ihr dürft sie lieben. Ihr seid deutsche Ehepartner [. . .]. Wir sind ein besseres Deutschland geworden'). But the idea that Germany's queers[17] might overstep the mark, demanding the same rights as heterosexual partners, provokes in Wagner a certain queasiness: 'gay marriage vs. man-&-woman marriage. I don't feel well. Homosexuals, biologically speaking, can't have children' ('Homo-Ehe vs. Mann-&-Frau-Ehe. Ich fühle mich nicht wohl. Homosexuelle kriegen biologisch keine Kinder'; Mentz 2012). Queers, of course, do reproduce, as the existence of a term for queer families – 'rainbow families' ('Regenbogenfamilien') – testifies.[18] In any case, family is not automatically based on biological relations. For some, that is the problem. CDU politician Katherina Reiche contrasts the German (heterosexual) family with same-sex partnerships, which, for her, clearly do not count as families: 'our future lies in the hand of families, not in same-sex partnerships' ('unsere Zukunft liegt in der Hand der Familien, nicht in gleich-geschlechtlichen Lebensgemeinschaften'; cited in Mayer 2012).

While Germany may have had an 'out' gay mayor of Berlin (Wowereit), an 'out' gay former foreign minister (Guido Westerwelle), civil partnerships, and even a lesbian wedding in mainstream soaps like *Verbotene Liebe* (Forbidden Love), Germany's queer citizens do not have equal rights. A civil partnership is not the same as marriage, neither at the level of its cultural meaning nor at that of the rights that those partners have in more tangible terms. Unlike in some other European countries, gay partners are not allowed to adopt a child together; as of 2005, the non-biological parent is allowed to adopt the biological child of their civil partner (*Stiefkindadoption*) and, as determined by the Constitutional Court (*Bundesverfassungsgericht*) in February 2013, a civil partner may adopt an already adopted child (*Sukzessivadoption*) (Schmidt 2013). The Merkel-led CDU looks to be on its way to endorsing gay marriage, or at least to giving those in civil partnerships equal rights (Rietzschel 2013). Some question whether marriage is actually worth striving for, regardless of one's sexual preference (compare Warner 1999), and ask why adoption and childrearing need to be carried out in the context of state-supported two-parent families at all. It is interesting to note that Germany's Green party (Bündnis 90/Die Grünen) favours the introduction of parenthood for more than two parents ('Mehrelternschaft'), which would mean that, in legal terms, a child could have up to four parents.

In fact, the majority of Germany's queer citizens seem content to live socially quite conservative lives. Lisa Duggan has called this stance 'homonormative', defining it as follows: 'A politics that does not contest dominant heteronormative assumptions and institutions, but upholds and sustains them, while promising the possibility of a demobilized gay constituency and a privatized, depoliticized gay culture anchored in domesticity and consumption' (2002: 179). Germany's lesbian magazine *L.MAG*, launched in 2003, regularly includes queer fashion, travel, and wedding features, moving one reader to complain of its similarity to an advertising pamphlet ('wie ein Werbeblatt'; *L.MAG* May/June 2011: 5). *L.MAG* includes political articles and covers a range of political perspectives, but its tendency towards what Heidi Nast has termed 'market virility' (2002: 878) is unmistakeable.

Writing in a US American context, Jasbir K. Puar, combining the terms 'homonormative' and 'nationalism', has coined the term 'homonationalism'. She argues that in the context of the 'war on terror', certain homonormative subjects have been 'folded into' the national imaginary at the expense of other minorities in the USA and more broadly:

> National recognition and inclusion [. . .] is contingent upon the segregation and disqualification of racial and sexual others from the national imaginary. At work in this dynamic is a form of sexual exceptionalism – the emergence of national homosexuality, what I term 'homonationalism' – that corresponds with the coming out of the exceptionalism of American empire.
>
> (2007: 2)

By this logic, certain kinds of homosexuals are accepted as part of the national project at the expense of others. In the German context, a homonationalist stance is evident in Wagner's assertions in the Bild-Zeitung, cited above ('You are German [civilly] married partners [. . .] We've become a better Germany'). Same-sex relationships can also function as paradigmatic examples of German tolerance: Ferree notes that 'same-sex relationships and gender equality are used for "teaching tolerance" to those who are framed as lacking it' in the citizenship classes immigrants are required to take in order to learn about modern European culture (Ferree 2012: 217–19; Brown 2010). Undergirding this strategy is the assumption that those immigrants come from always already homophobic Muslim cultures.

Judith Butler's decision to turn down the prize for civil courage awarded by CSD Berlin (Christopher Street Day, Berlin's gay pride) in June 2010 requires mention, not least because of the public attention it received. Butler turned down the award to take a stance against the racism of groups like Maneo (an emergency telephone line for gay men), which, according to Butler, was fighting homophobia through fighting against other minorities (Hamann 2010), and from which the CSD organising committee had failed to distance itself. In her speech at the event, she drew attention to homonationalism in Germany and elsewhere:

> We've all noticed that homo-, bi-, lesbian-, trans-, queer- people can be used by those who want to wage war: cultural wars against migrants through cultivated Islamophobia and military wars against Iraq and Afghanistan. At such times and through these means we are recruited to nationalism and militarism.

> (Wir haben alle bemerkt, dass Homo-, Bi-, Lesbisch-, Trans-, Queer-Leute benutzt werden können von jenen, die Kriege führen wollen, d. h. kulturelle Kriege gegen Migrant_innen durch forcierte Islamophobie und militärische Kriege gegen Irak und Afghanistan. Während dieser Zeit und durch diese Mittel werden wir rekrutiert für Nationalismus und Militarismus.)
>
> (web source 7)

Butler pointed to groups active in Germany and Berlin to which she would have passed on the award if she had felt in a position to accept it, including GLADT (Gays & Lesbians aus der Türkei), LesMigraS, SUSPECT, and ReachOut, all of which play an active role in Berlin's alternative pride event, *Transgenialer CSD* (Transfabulous CSD).

Situating itself explicitly in the tradition of the 1969 Stonewall Riots in New York's Christopher Street, Berlin's *Transgenialer CSD* emphatically declares itself: 'For the abolishment of the binary gender order! – against heteronormativity [. . .] against every trans*pathologisation! Recognition that homosexuality and transsexuality are reasons to grant asylum!! The right to stay for everyone! [. . .] Fight patriarchy and classism!!' ('Für die Abschaffung der Zwei-geschlechterordnung! – gegen Heteronormativität [. . .] Gegen jede Trans*pathologisierung! Anerkennung von Homosexualität und Transsexualität als Asylgrund!! Bleiberecht für alle! [. . .] Patriarchat und Klassismus bekämpfen!!'; web source 8). That brings us on to the idea of 'trans', with its emphasis on liminality or, better, movement and crossing, with reference to the categories gender, sexuality, the body, but also nationality and ethnicity.

Questions of national, ethnic, religious, and class belonging as they intersect with questions of gender and sexuality are at the centre of a large body of recent cultural production. In the German context, it seems that brown bodies serve as a site on which issues of sex and gender can be played out, certainly in recent films such as *Lola and Bilidikid* and *Unveiled*. Here the idea of 'trans' in relation not only to gender, but also to nationality is of particular interest. 'Trans' allows us, as Christopher Clark has explored in his reading of *Lola and Bilidikid*, to describe 'a moment of in-betweenness, a liminal status that may represent a point in a process of transformation from one category to another' and to understand the 'instability of cultures' (2006: 556). Like 'queer', 'trans', with its emphasis on movement and crossing, enables us to regard sexuality, gender, and bodies, but also culture and nationality, as mutable.

A sense of liminality or movement with regard to gender and the body was apparent at the drag contest organised in 2011 by Berlin's queer magazine *Siegessäule*, where the winner was, according to that magazine,

> a drag person who didn't seem to fit into the queen–king model: Kay P.Rinha, fat, bearded, makeup, showing lots of skin. Was that a plump woman, dressed up as a man who was dressed up as a woman? Or a man, who was a woman portraying a man?
>
> (eine Drag-Person, die so gar nicht in die Queen-King-Schemata zu passen schien: Kay P.Rinha, dick, bärtig, geschminkt, viel Haut zeigend. War das jetzt eine füllige Frau, die sich als Mann verkleidet, der sich als Frau verkleidet? Oder ein Mann, der eine Frau war, die einen Mann darstellt?)
>
> (Göbel 2012: 22)

As the combination of beard and makeup suggest and as the article's rhetorical questions further emphasise, distinctions between masculinity and femininity, but also between 'male' and

Figure 16.2 Ansichtssache (TROUBLE X)
Courtesy of www.trouble-x.info

'female' bodies, recede here. In fact, the body and gender identity – if we want to differentiate between the two at all – of performer Kay P.Rinha can more usefully be seen, following Deleuze and Guattari (1987) and Puar (2007), as a queer 'assemblage'. Berlin's variety of sexual and gendered bodies emerges in an invitation to the queer sex party 'be_cunt' published in *Siegessäule*, embracing 'women, lesbians, trans★, kings, dykes, ladys, genderfucks, femmes, tomboys, and everything in between' ('Frauen, Lesben, Trans★, Kings, Dykes, ladys, Genderfucks, Femmes, Tomboys und alles, was dazwischen liegt'; *Siegessäule*, July 2012: 52). As a patch, to sew onto one's clothing and produced by gender-queer Berlin blogger, activist, and artist, TROUBLE X, asserts, the binary model when it comes to gendered bodies is *Ansichtssache* (a question of opinion) (see Figure 16.2).

While Berlin is probably not 'post-gender' (S.G. 2013: 10), any more than it is post-national, those adjectives might, with some qualification, come close to describing the politics of parts of its queer subculture. However, as Sara Ahmed notes, the very idea of movement and transgression, so central to queer's self-understanding, is itself privileged: 'The idealization of movement, or transformation of movement into a fetish, depends on the exclusion of others who are already positioned as *not free in the same way*' (2004: 152, emphasis in original; see also Puar 2007: 22–3). Berlin is not the only city to have a thriving 'international' queer culture and activist scene where 'international' means largely white and Western. It is important to acknowledge the privileged nature of parts of that scene. 'Queerness' is not desirable or equally accessible to everybody, and it is even possible to talk about what might be termed 'queer-normativity'.[19] Whilst parts of Berlin's queer scene might term themselves 'international' – *Siegessäule* declared it was 'go[ing] international' in November 2012 and now includes an English translation of its calendar of events as well as an English-language column aimed explicitly at 'the international crowd' – that understanding of 'international' is clearly skewed to the Western world. And visitors to Berlin's queer bars and clubs, to its annual queer BDSM festivals, Folsom Europe and the Easter Conference, or to Berlin's Pornfilmfestival, to name but some of Berlin's attractions for queer tourists, are also overwhelmingly white and Western.

Berlin's reputation as a centre of alternative sexualities, genders, and bodies can be traced back to the interwar Weimar period, when a gender-bending Marlene Dietrich donned top hat and suspenders in her iconic role as cabaret performer Lola-Lola in Josef von Sternberg's *The Blue Angel* (1928); when sexologist Magnus Hirschfeld was fighting for gay rights and challenging the notion of binary gender and sexuality through his theory of sexual intermediary types (*sexuelle Zwischenstufen*) at the Institut für Sexualwissenschaft; when Otto Dix and Jeanne Mammen were painting Berlin's queer subcultures in works like *Eldorado* (1927, Dix) and *Sie repräsentiert* (1927, She represents, Mammen). Then, like now, Berlin's thriving queer subculture, as well as its reputation for that, was dependent on movement and crossing. Dietrich would go to Hollywood with Josef von Sternberg, where they would capitalise on and fortify Weimar Berlin's reputation as a centre for queer sexualities and genders (see *Morocco*, 1930, in particular). Christopher Isherwood, resident in Berlin from 1929 to 1933, would retrospectively write *Goodbye to Berlin* (1989 [1939]) and *Mr Norris Changes Trains* (2001 [1935]), which would inspire the Broadway show and then film *Cabaret* (1972). That film has, perhaps more than any other cultural product, secured Weimar Berlin's reputation as an international centre of decadent, alternative sexual practices, genders, and bodies. Berlin still capitalises on that reputation, not least to appeal to tourists, queer or otherwise. Dietrich features prominently and, somewhat fittingly, she seems particularly visible in transitory spaces associated with crossing, movement, and liminality: a large mural of Dietrich in top hat and tails greets the traveller as they walk towards Eberswalder Straße underground station on the U2 line (see Figure 16.3); over-the-shoulder bags with Dietrich's face on them are available to buy from various tourist shops at

Figure 16.3 The Marlene Dietrich mural, Eberswalder Straße
Photograph by Clare Bielby 2013

central crossing points such as Alexanderplatz and Schönefeld airport, where it is one of the last things the traveller sees before they arrive at the departure gate.

Berlin's reputation for alternative genders and sexualities jars with the often still conservative gender politics and the ideological significance of motherhood in contemporary Germany, with which we began. And nonetheless a queer and feminist political scene is thriving in the Berlin Republic, with Berlin itself taking centre stage. It is striking that Berlin's reputation in this regard is dependent on trans(national) bodies, genders, and sexualities. As Ena Lind, DJ and editor of the queer-feminist publication *Bend Over*, asserts in a *Siegessäule* interview, questioned on Berlin's queer scene and whether that scene lives up to its reputation: 'Yes, absolutely. In my view that comes from the constant international exchange, precisely because of Berlin's reputation' ('Eindeutig ja. Meiner Meinung nach kommt das vom ständigen internationalen Austausch, eben wegen ihres Rufes') (*Siegessäule* 2012).

Notes

1 All translations are the authors'.
2 Wowereit was put under considerable pressure by his own party as well as by the press to 'come out' (see Fahrun 2007).
3 Jasbir K. Puar, for example, understands 'queerness' as 'not an identity nor an anti-identity, but an assemblage that is spatially and temporally contingent' in the context of the limitations of 'intersectional identitarian modes' (2007: 204).
4 Our approach draws on poststructuralist gender theory. See in particular Judith Butler (1990, 1993, 2004); and Tamar Mayer (2000).
5 This should not be seen as a feminist gesture, not least because the anti-discrimination law is highly ambivalent in feminist terms, given that gender is demoted to become just one difference amongst others (Ferree 2012: 190, 207).
6 The word 'gender' would normally be translated into German as 'Geschlechtsidentität', but because this is not an entirely satisfactory translation, the English/US term 'gender' tends to be used.
7 See also von Schirach (2007), Koch-Mehrin (2007), Eismann (2007), and Stöcker (2007).
8 As Haaf et al. argue, there is a great deal of potential in new technology for feminist activism, if women can find their way into the traditionally masculine domain of technology (2009 [2008]: 125–36).
9 *Neue Deutsche Mädchen* is a particularly weak example: particularly troubling is how the authors universalise from a white, socially privileged, heterosexual perspective without displaying any interest in women of other sexualities, ethnicities, or social positions. They do not describe their project as feminist.
10 'cis' with regard to gender denotes those who live with the gender they were assigned at birth.
11 As Myra Marx Ferree explores in her study *Varieties of Feminism*, one of the major differences between West German and US forms of second-wave feminism is the former's 'central feminist self-definition as "autonomous"'. Autonomy 'meant naming women as a group whose solidarity had a theoretical justification in their reproductive power and a practical implication in their collective self-determination [. . .] Autonomy also meant a political place that was no longer in thrall to a socialist party and allowed women to determine their own needs apart for [sic] the state's paternalistic care' (Ferree 2012: 22, 80).
12 The first ever ladyfest took place in Olympia, USA in 2000 and has its roots in the US Riot Grrrl movement of the early 90s (web source 3). The asterisk attached to 'trans' 'serves as a placeholder for a wide spectrum of identities, lifestyles, and concepts, including some that may not (wish to) allow themselves to be positioned in terms of gender' (Time and Franzen 2012: 22–3).
13 See, for example, 'An Open Letter from Black Women to the SlutWalk' (2011).
14 In 2012 Lady Bitch Ray brought out the book *Bitchism – Emanzipation: Integration, Masturbation*, which shows she is not completely 'silenced'.
15 The English-language title, *Unveiled*, is interesting. While it clearly has religious connotations, Emily Jeremiah has pointed out that it 'suggests a truth uncovered – the truth of the sexed body – [which] the film itself does not' (2011: 592).
16 See e.g. http://en.wikimannia.org/Main_Page (accessed 13 March 2013).
17 We use the term 'queer' to encompass a wide spectrum of non-heterosexual individuals, from those who consciously reject and/or 'queer' heteronormative ways of being to those whom Puar has termed 'disciplinary queers': 'liberal, homonormative, diasporic' (Puar 2007: xxvii).
18 The term 'Regenbogenfamilien' encompasses queer parents who adopt as well as those who use reproductive technologies such as AI/IVF or surrogacy.
19 On 'Lookism', a disdain for femininity, and normativity in the queer scene and elsewhere, see Göbel (2012).

Bibliography

Adams, R. and Savran, D. (eds) (2002) 'Introduction', in *The Masculinity Studies Reader*, Malden, MA and Oxford: Blackwell Publishers, 1–8.
Ahmed, S. (2004) *The Cultural Politics of Emotion*, Edinburgh: Edinburgh University Press.
'An open letter from black women to the SlutWalk' (2011), 23 September. Online. Available at www.blackwomensblueprint.org/2011/09/23/an-open-letter-from-black-women-to-the-slutwalk/ (accessed 11 March 2013).

Appadurai, A. (1996) *Modernity at Large: Cultural Dimensions of Globalization*, Minneapolis: University of Minnesota Press.

Bild (2012) 'Schlagzeilen, die Geschichte schrieben', 22 June. Online. Available at www.bild.de/news/topics/60-jahre-bild/schlagzeilen-die-geschichte-schrieben-24785042.bild.html (accessed 09 July 2014).

Biller, M. (2008) 'Ich langweile mich zu Tode in diesem Land', interview with Patrick Wildermann, *Galore*, 38: 25–9.

Brown, J.A. (2010) 'Citizenship of the heart and mind: educating Germany's immigrants in the ideological, emotional, and practical components of belongingness', unpublished PhD thesis, University of Wisconsin, Madison.

Butler, J. (1990) *Gender Trouble: Feminism and the Subversion of Identity*, London and New York: Routledge.

Butler, J. (1991) *Das Unbehagen der Geschlechter*, Frankfurt a.M: Suhrkamp.

Butler, J. (1993) *Bodies That Matter: On the Discursive Limits of 'Sex'*, London and New York: Routledge.

Butler, J. (2004) *Undoing Gender*, London and New York: Routledge.

Cabaret (1972) [film], dir. B. Foss, USA/FRG: Allied Artists.

Cheesman, T. (2007) *Novels of Turkish German Settlement: Cosmopolite Fictions*, Rochester, NY: Camden House.

Chin, R. (2010) 'Turkish women, west German feminists, and the gendered discourse on Muslim cultural difference', *Public Culture*, 22(3): 557–81.

Clark, C. (2006) 'Transculturation, *transe* sexuality, and Turkish Germany: Kutluğ Ataman's *Lola und Bilidikid*', *German Life and Letters*, 59(4): 555–72.

Connell, R.W. (2005 [1995]) *Masculinities*, 2nd edn, Cambridge: Polity.

Deleuze, G. (1992) 'Ethology: Spinoza and us', in J. Crary and S. Kwinter (eds), *Incorporations*, New York: Zone Books, 625–33.

Deleuze, G. and Guattari, F. (1987) *A Thousand Plateaus: Capitalism and Schizophrenia*, trans. B. Massumi, Minneapolis: University of Minnesota Press.

Der blaue Engel, (1928) [Film] dir. J. von Sternberg, Germany: UFA-Filmverleih GmbH.

Die Bräuteschule 1958 (2007) [TV series] Germany: Euro Video.

Dorn, T. (2006) *Die neue F-Klasse: Wie die Zukunft von Frauen gemacht wird*, Munich and Zurich: Piper.

Dostert, E. (2010) 'Generation Biedermeier', *Süddeutsche.de*, 11 September, 'Karriere'. Online. Available at http://www.sueddeutsche.de/karriere/studie-zur-jugendkultur-generation-biedermeier-1.998533 (accessed 10 February 2013).

Duggan, L. (2002) 'The new homonormativity: the sexual politics of Neoliberalism', in R. Castronovo and D. Nelson (eds) *Materializing Democracy: Toward a Revitalized Cultural Politics*, Durham, NC: Duke University Press, 175–94.

Eismann, S. (2007) *Hot Topic: Popfeminismus heute*, Mainz: Ventil.

EMMAonline (2012) 'Femen protestieren vor dem Kölner "Pascha"', 25 November. Available at www.emma.de/artikel/femen-protestieren-vor-dem-koelner-pascha-266138 (accessed 12 March 2013).

e*vibes (2013) 'Offener Brief an Femen Germany', 29 January. Online. Available at http://evibes.blogsport.de/2013/01/29/offener-brief-an-femen-germany/ (accessed 12 March 2013).

EXBERLINER (2013) 'How much of a German man are you?', January, 112: 21.

Fahrun, J. (2007) 'Warum sich Klaus Wowereit als schwul outete', *Welt Online*, 19 September. Available at www.welt.de/regionales/berlin/article1481015/Warum-sich-Klaus-Wowereit-als-schwul-outete.html (accessed 18 December 2013).

Ferree, M.M. (2012) *Varieties of Feminisms: German Gender Politics in Global Perspective*, Stanford, CA: Stanford University Press.

Fremde Haut (2005) [film], dir. A. Maccarone, Germany: Ventura Film.

Göbel, M. (2012) 'Anti körper', *Siegessäule*, July, 20–7.

Haaf, M., Klingner, S. and Streidl, B. (2009 [2008]) *Wir Alphamädchen: Warum Feminismus das Leben schöner macht*, Munich: Blanvalet.

Halberstam, J. (1998) *Female Masculinity*, Durham, NC and London: Duke University Press.

Halberstam, J. (2005) *In a Queer Time & Place: Transgender Bodies, Subcultural Lives*, New York and London: New York University Press.

Hamann, K. (2010) 'Interview: "In diesem Kampf gibt es keinen Platz für Rassismus"', *Jungle World*, 29 July. Online. Available at http://jungle-world.com/artikel/2010/30/41420.html (accessed 12 March 2013).

Hensel, J. and Raether, E. (2008) *Neue Deutsche Mädchen*, Reinbek bei Hamburg: Rowohlt.

Herman, E. (2006) *Das Eva-Prinzip: Für eine neue Weiblichkeit*, Munich: Pendo Verlag.

Isherwood, C. (1989 [1939]) *Goodbye to Berlin*, London: Vintage.

Isherwood, C. (2001 [1935]) *Mr Norris Changes Trains*, London: Vintage.

Islamische Zeitung (2007) 'Aufgewachsen im "gut bürgerlichen" Berlin', interview with Sahira Awad, 9 May. Online. Available at www.islamische-zeitung.de/?id=8768 (accessed 15 February 2013).

Jeremiah, E. (2011) 'Touching distance: gender, Germanness, and the gaze in Angelina Maccarone's *Fremde Haut* (2005)', *German Life and Letters*, 64(4): 588–600.

Kelek, N. (2005) *Die fremde Braut: Ein Bericht aus dem Inneren des türkischen Lebens in Deutschland*, Cologne: Kiepenheuer und Witsch.

Koch-Mehrin, S. (2007) *Schwestern: Streitschrift für einen neuen Feminismus*, Berlin: Econ.

Lady Bitch Ray (2012) *Bitchism − Emanzipation. Integration. Masturbation*, Stuttgart: Panini Verlag.

L.MAG (2011) Letter to the editor, May/June: 5.

Lola und Bilidikid (1998/1999) [film], dir. K. Ataman, Germany: Delphi Filmverleih GmbH.

Matthes, F. (2012) '"Echter Südländer − Reb Motke − Deutschmann?" Debating Jewish masculinity in Maxim Biller's *Die Tochter*', *Forum for Modern Language Studies*, 48(3): 323–35.

Mayer, H. (2012) 'Never-ending Story', *Siegessäule*, September, 6.

Mayer, T. (ed.) (2000) *Gender Ironies of Nationalism: Sexing the Nation*, London and New York: Routledge.

Mentz, C. (2012) 'Wagners Unwohlsein', *Siegessäule*, September, 19.

Morocco (1930) [Film] dir. J. von Sternberg, USA: Paramount Pictures.

Nast, H.J. (2002) 'Queer patriarchies, queer racisms, international', special issue, *Antipode: A Radical Journal of Geography*, 34(5): 874–909.

Obermueller, N. (2013) 'The new Berlin dads', *EXBERLINER*, January, 112: 16–17.

O'Donovan, S. and Castellví, T. (2013) 'Herr Deutschland', *EXBERLINER*, January, 112: 13.

Oh Boy! (2012) [Film] dir. J. O. Gerster, Germany: Schiwago Film, Chromosom Filmproduktion, Hessischer Rundfunk (HR), ARTE.

Puar, J.K. (2007) *Terrorist Assemblages: Homonationalism in Queer Times*, Durham, NC and London: Duke University Press.

Riceburg, J. (2013) 'Männer don't cry', *EXBERLINER*, January, 112: 22–3.

Rietzschel, A. (2013) 'Merkel streicht den Konservatismus zusammen', *Süddeutsche.de*, 25 February. Online. Available at www.sueddeutsche.de/politik/diskussion-ueber-die-homo-ehe-merkel-streicht-den-konservatismus-zusammen-1.1608965 (accessed 14 March 2013).

Schirach, A. von (2007) *Der Tanz um die Lust*, Munich: Goldmann Verlag.

Schirrmacher, F. (2004) *Das Methusalem-Komplott*, Munich: Karl Blessing Verlag.

Schirrmacher, F. (2006) *Minimum*, Munich: Karl Blessing Verlag.

Schmidt, F. (2013) 'Adoption: Karlsruhe stärkt Rechte homosexueller Paare', *Faz.net*, 19 February. Online. Available at www.faz.net/aktuell/politik/inland/adoption-karlsruhe-staerkt-rechte-homosexueller-paare-12086176.html (accessed 12 March 2013).

Schüle, C. (2010) 'Kopftuch-Debatte: Mit erhobenem Haupt − Warum sich moderne muslimische Frauen in Deutschland freiwillig für das Kopftuch entscheiden', *Zeit Online* [*Die Zeit*, 19], 6 May, 'Zeitgeschehen'. Available at www.zeit.de/2010/19/DOS-Kopftuch (accessed 09 March 2013).

Schwarzer, A. (2002) 'Islamismus. Die falsche Toleranz'. Online. Available at http://www.aliceschwarzer.de/publikationen/aliceschwarzer-artikel-essays/kernthemen/alice-schwarzer-ueber-islamismus/die-falsche-toleranz/ (accessed 23 August 2013). Taken from the prologue to Schwarzer (2002) *Gotteskrieger und die falsche Toleranz*, Cologne: Kiepenheuer & Witsch.

Schwarzer, A. (2009) 'Das Kanzlerinnen Interview', *Emma*, 5, September/October, 20–6.

Schwesterherz (2006) [film], dir. E. Herzog, Germany: NFP Marketing & Distribution.

S.G. (2013) 'No Girls Allowed', in *EXBERLINER* 112, January, 10–12.

Siegessäule (2012) '. . . meine Stadt', September, 5.

Spiegel Online (2005) 'Neues Deutschlandgefühl: Wir sind Kanzlerin', 23 November. Available at www.spiegel.de/kultur/gesellschaft/neues-deutschlandgefuehl-wir-sind-kanzlerin-a-386466.html (accessed 11 March 2013).

Spiegel Online (2010) 'Integration: Merkel erklärt Multikulti für gescheitert', 16 October. Available at www.spiegel.de/politik/deutschland/integration-merkel-erklaert-multikulti-fuer-gescheitert-a-723532.html (accessed 11 March 2013).

Spiegel Online (2011) 'Frauenanteil in Börsenunternehmen: 160 Firmen, eine Chefin', 17 February. Available at www.spiegel.de/wirtschaft/soziales/frauenanteil-in-boersenunternehmen-160-firmen-eine-chefin-a-746095.html (accessed 12 March 2013).

Spiegel Online (2013) 'Ärger mit Brüssel: Bundesregierung will EU-Frauenquote stoppen', 6 March. Available at www.spiegel.de/politik/ausland/bundesregierung-will-eu-frauenquote-stoppen-a-887122.html (accessed 13 March 2013).

Spiewak, M. (2010) 'Boys Day: Ein Tag für Kerle (Interview mit Familienministerin Kristina Schröder)', *Zeit Online* [*Die Zeit*, 17], 22 April, 'Gesellschaft'. Available at www.zeit.de/2010/17/B-Schroeder-Interview?page=all&print=true (accessed 12 March 2013).

Stehle, M. (2012a) *Ghetto Voices in Contemporary German Culture: Textscapes, Filmscapes, and Soundscapes*, Rochester, NY: Camden House.

Stehle, M. (2012b) 'Pop, porn, and rebellious speech', *Feminist Media Studies*, 12(2): 229–47.

Stehle, M. and Weber, B. (2013) 'German soccer, the 2010 World Cup, and multicultural belonging', *German Studies Review*, 36(1): 103–24.

Stöcker, M. (2007) *Das F-Wort: Feminismus ist Sexy*, Sulzbach: Helmer.

Time, J. and Franzen, J. (eds) (2012) *trans*_homo differenzen, allianzen, widersprüche*, Berlin: NoNo Verlag.

Warner, M. (1999) *The Trouble with Normal*, New York: The Free Press.

Wichmann, M. (2012) 'Frau Schröder, das war . . . Spitze!', *taz.de*, 8 March. Online. Available at www.taz.de/!89178/ (accessed 12 March 2013).

Wulff, C. (2010) '"Vielfalt schätzen – Zusammenhalt fördern": Rede von Bundespräsident Christian Wulff zum 20. Jahrestag der Deutschen Einheit am 3. Oktober 2010 in Bremen'. Online. Available at www.bundespraesident.de/SharedDocs/Reden/DE/Christian-Wulff/Reden/2010/10/20101003_Rede_Anlage.pdf?__blob=publicationFile&v=3 (accessed 23 February 2013).

Yeşilada, K. (1997) '"Die geschundene Suleika": Das Eigenbild der Türkin in der deutschsprachigen Literatur türkischer Autorinnen', in M. Howard (ed.) *Interkulturelle Konfiguration: Zur deutschsprachigen Erzählliteratur von Autoren nichtdeutscher Herkunft*, Munich: Iudicium, 95–114.

Yildiz, Y. (2009) 'Turkish girls, Allah's daughters, and the contemporary German subject: itinerary of a figure', *German Life and Letters*, 62(4): 465–81.

Web sources

Web source 1: www.bundestag.de/bundestag/abgeordnete18/mdb_zahlen/frauen_maenner.html (accessed 18 December 2013).

Web source 2: http://maedchenmannschaft.net (accessed 13 March 2013).

Web source 3: www.ladyfest.net/about/ (accessed 18 February 2013).

Web source 4: www.slutwalktoronto.com/ (accessed 18 February 2013).

Web source 5: www.bundestag.de/dokumente/textarchiv/2012/42042381_kw50_de_beschneidung/index.html (accessed 12 March 2012).

Web source 6: www.wikimannia.org/WikiMANNia (accessed 24 February 2013).

Web source 7: transgenialercsd.wordpress.com/2010/06/19/judith-butler-lehnt-zivilcouragepreis-ab/ (accessed 12 March 2013).

Web source 8: http://transgenialercsd.wordpress.com (accessed 12 March 2013).

17

'Grey' culture

Stuart Taberner

This chapter focuses on the unprecedented demographic ageing of the German population in the present day. It first sets this rapid demographic transformation in the context of the global trend towards older populations, before turning to some of the specific social and political ramifications of the 'ageing society' in the Federal Republic. Subsequently it looks in detail at the ways in which ageing is being debated and represented in film, literature, and other media.

In their landmark report ahead of the 2002 'World Assembly on Ageing', researchers from the Department of Economic and Social Affairs at the United Nations (UN) began by placing the greying of the world's population in its historical perspective:

> Population ageing is unprecedented, without parallel in the history of humanity. Increases in the proportions of older persons (60 years or older) are being accompanied by declines in the proportions of the young (under age 15). By 2050, the number of older persons in the world will exceed the number of young for the first time in history. Moreover, by 1998 this historic reversal in relative proportions of young and old had already taken place in the more developed regions.

In order to illustrate the dramatic shift in the globe's demographic profile that would – quite soon – result, the authors of the report offered a series of eye-catching numbers: 'The proportion of older persons was 8 per cent in 1950 and 10 per cent in 2000, and is projected to reach 21 per cent in 2050'; by the middle of the 21st century just over a fifth of the world's projected 9 billion inhabitants — one in five of all living individuals — would be over 60; and more people than ever before would survive some way beyond this: 'The older population is itself ageing. The fastest growing age group in the world is the oldest-old, those aged 80 years or older. By the middle of the century, one fifth of older persons will be 80 years or older' (United Nations 2002: xxviii–ix).

The trend towards ageing populations is neither entirely uniform nor equally advanced everywhere. It is nevertheless, as Jürgen Kocka suggests, not a national but rather a transnational and, increasingly, global phenomenon (Kocka 2008: 219). For all the West's anxieties about its own evident senectitude, no region of the world is unaffected, including the emerging economic giants in Asia (China) and Latin America (Brazil), around which many of these anxieties ultimately coalesce. The 2012 Report of the United Nations High Commissioner for Human Rights reiterates that a fifth of the world's population will be over 60 by 2050 – an increase from today's 700 million to 2 billion persons – but notes that the fastest increase will take place in Africa. The report adds that in western Asia the population of those aged over 60 will quadruple by 2050; that the proportion of older people in the Asia-Pacific region will rise from 10 per cent today to 24 per cent over the same period; and that a similar profile will become visible in Latin America, which will witness a rise to 25 per cent. It is true that Europe will 'continue to have the oldest population in the world' (OHCHR 2012: 3). But it is by no means *uniquely* predestined for old age and decline, even if that is the fear that seems to motivate much of the public (and popular) debate on the subject of the 'ageing society' across the continent. Sarah Harper, Professor of Gerontology at the Institute of Population Ageing at the University of Oxford, testifies in her report for the International Social Security Association entitled 'Demographic challenges and social security':

> While the predicted increase by 2025 in the per cent of people over 60 for the EU 15 is around 33 per cent, it is a staggering 400 per cent for Indonesia, 350 per cent for Thailand, Kenya and Mexico, 280 per cent for Zimbabwe and up to 250 per cent for India, China and Brazil. It is this rapidity of demographic ageing which will be one of the greatest institutional challenges for less developed and transitional economies.
>
> (Harper 2010: 2)

We are witnessing (in Harper's words) 'a globalisation of population ageing' (Harper 2010: 4) that is generating dramatic challenges not only for Western societies but also for the newly dynamic economies of the East that have only recently reaped the demographic bonus of large numbers of young people combined with low elderly dependency ratios (EDR), that is, relatively few older people to be supported by workers. In the case of China, in particular, *The Economist* claimed in 2012 that 'over the past 30 years, China's total fertility rate – the number of children a woman can expect to have during her lifetime – has fallen from 2.6, well above the rate needed to hold a population steady, to 1.56, well below that rate' and that the country now 'faces a long period of ultra-low fertility, regardless of what happens to its one-child policy' (*The Economist* 2012). One of the primary consequences of this will be that by 2050 China will have a much higher EDR than the United States, where high levels of immigration will continue to depress the country's median age. China will face pressures on its (as yet comparatively undeveloped) social security system similar to those faced in the US, the nation that appears most fearful of its rise.

That population ageing is a global phenomenon does not prevent it from being apprehended first and foremost in relation to national contexts. In the 2012 American presidential elections, for instance, the security of Medicare was once again one of the most controversial issues contested by the Democratic incumbent Barack Obama and his Republican rival Mitt Romney, against the background of President Obama's Affordable Care Act ('Obamacare'), the eligibility of the baby-boomer generation from 2011, and a projected massive rise in costs from 3.7 per cent of gross domestic product (GDP) in 2011 to between 6.7 and 10.4 per cent in 2086 (Medicare Trustees 2012). And it was, of course, no accident that the other key theme of that election was China, typically perceived to be America's chief economic and (potential) military rival and frequently presented as a youthful, more dynamic competitor benefiting from the USA's relative decline. Britain, too, faces the challenges of paying for long-term residential care for the elderly, 'fuel poverty' amongst retirees, and the sustainability of the National Health Service; for example, the number of over-75s admitted to hospital for treatment increased by 66 per cent in the 10 years up to 2010 (NHS 2009).

In Germany, population ageing is debated principally in relation to its supposed significance for the continued strength, and even survival, of the nation.[1] Thus the growing older of the 'native' German population specifically is powerfully associated with a widespread anxiety about the country's low total fertility rate (TFR): 1.39 in 2010, compared with Britain's 1.98, France's 1.98, and America's 1.93 (all below the 'replacement rate' for industrialised countries of 2.1, according to the Population Reference Bureau). And it feeds into a set of concerns relating to the high levels of immigration that Germany has been experiencing in recent years. In the popular imagination (or popular newspapers, at least), ideas about non-white immigration in particular and the supposed danger of *Überfremdung* (the swamping of German society with 'alien' cultures) abound. 'Kinder statt Inder' (children not Indians), the slogan coined by Jürgen Rüttgers during an election campaign in the German state of North Rhine-Westphalia in 2000, continued to resonate more than a decade later,[2] as did the occasional calls from the right (but not only the right) to defend a German *Leitkultur* (a preeminent 'German' culture) against the supposedly Anglo-American ideology of multiculturalism.[3] In his book *Das Methusalem-Komplott* (2004; *The Methuselah Conspiracy*), Frank Schirrmacher, co-editor of a respected broadsheet, the *Frankfurter Allgemeine Zeitung*, argued that Germany was facing a crisis of social cohesion arising from rapid ageing, mass (Muslim) immigration, and a loss of confidence on the part of the 'natives'. And in 2010 onetime Social Democrat (SPD) politician Thilo Sarrazin went even further in *Deutschland schafft sich ab* (*Germany Does Away with Itself*), declaring that the supposed replacement of an ageing and dwindling 'German' population by (non-white) immigrants was leading to a 'dumbing-down' of German society and the collapse of its economy. Sarrazin's book achieved sales of more than 1.5 million within a year.

Certainly, Germany *is* ageing somewhat more quickly than comparable nations, and this will have a dramatic impact on its public finances. Correlating with a high level of 'income adequacy' for pensioners (i.e. high pensions, generally around 66 per cent of pre-retirement earnings, and generous benefits) is the country's poor outlook with regard to its fiscal sustainability. As the Global Aging Initiative of the Center for Strategic and International Studies concludes in its Global Aging Preparedness Index: 'Four of the seven highest-ranking countries on the income adequacy index (the Netherlands, Brazil, Germany, and the UK) are among the seven lowest-ranking countries on the fiscal sustainability index' (CSIS Global Aging Initiative 2010: v). A rapidly ageing population will undoubtedly bring down the size of the labour force, raise the old-age dependency ratio, and reduce economic growth and the country's ability to resource rising living standards (Börsch-Supan 2005). As things stand, by 2050 the number of people of working age in Germany is predicted to decline from 50 to 40 million people – by 20 per cent, that is – and the ratio of over 65s to workers is forecast to rise to around 55 per cent, implying a dependency ratio of just under two workers for every senior (OECD 2005).

In sum, as Helmut Seitz and Martin Werding argue, the German case is 'particularly severe':

> By international standards, the German baby boom was rather late, peaking in the mid-1960s, and also weak. On the other hand, the subsequent decline in fertility was fast and very pronounced. For more than three decades now, the country has had one of the lowest fertility rates in the industrialised world. At the same time, life expectancy has increased, and continues to do so, quite as much as it does elsewhere. As a result, a massive change in the age structure of the German population is already under way that will become fully visible in the period between 2015 and 2035. Unlike many other countries, Germany is actually faced with the prospect of a declining population and, with even higher certainty, a shrinking labour force, processes that will start from now on and probably last until 2050 and even beyond.
> (Seitz and Werding 2008: 2)

Others emphasise the catastrophic collapse in fertility in eastern Germany in the years follow-ing unification as well as the out-migration of younger people from the territory of the former GDR (Höhn *et al.* 2008), or point to 'significant labour supply disincentives for married women' and the poor availability of childcare, which combine to push women 'to decide "either" "or" in respect of paid work and starting a family' (Kreyenfeld and Konietzka 2008: 170). To be sure, fertility and female labour force participation – along with the reforms to retirement age, pensions, and labour force participation rates amongst older people that are already in train – must be addressed if Germany is to adapt to a demographic shift that is as inevitable as it is momentous.

For all of these reasons, and for others relating to the particular social and political context of population ageing in Germany,[4] the discussion in the Federal Republic is characterised by a greater degree of urgency (and contention) than in other countries. At the same time, even if the challenges of population ageing are not (yet) being dealt with as effectively as they might be, they are certainly not being ignored. On the one hand, German government commissions have addressed the issue, most notably the Commission of Inquiry into Demographic Change (*Enquête-Kommission 'Demographischer Wandel'*), which delivered its final report in 2002. The Federal Statistical Service has attempted to assess Germany's ageing in comparison with other EU countries, for example, in its report on older people in Germany and the EU (Statistisches Bundesamt 2009). On the other hand, major research foundations have sponsored studies on Germany's demographic challenges and quality of life issues.[5] University institutes in Munich (the Center for the Economics of Ageing), Jena (the Leibnitz Institute for Age Research), Heidelberg (*Deutsches Zentrum für Alternsforschung*, which closed in 2005), and Cologne (the Max Planck Institute for Biology of Ageing) have been exploring the theme. In 1994, the Federal Government finally added seniors to the portfolio of the Ministry for Families (Bundesministerium für Familie), created in 1953 – young people had been specified in 1957, and women three decades later in 1986. A federal umbrella association of older people's groups (*Bundesarbeitsgemeinschaft der Senioren-Organisationen*) had been supported by the ministry since 1989, with the task of coordinating the lobbying and outreach efforts of more than 100 organisations.

More generally, each of the major political parties has a special section for older people, and Germany's federal organisation for social equality, the *Sozialverband Deutschland*, with over half a million members and 3,000 local branches, campaigns actively on issues affecting older people, such as poverty and social isolation. Groups such as the *Senior Experten Service* seek to re-engage retirees by matching their experience with younger people starting their own businesses or to promote 'active ageing' ('aktives Altern').

Ageing in German culture

Of course, ageing is not only a social or economic issue – it resonates culturally, too. To an even greater extent than in other Western countries, the shelves of German bookshops are filled with volumes on ageing and what it means both for society as a whole and for the individual in particular, ranging from the serious to the decidedly middle-brow. For the most part, the authors of these books are concerned to challenge the prejudice that older people have little to contribute to society, or even that they present a 'burden'.

Most immediately striking is the extent to which businesspeople and politicians have rushed to publish policy solutions to the interaction between Germany's supposedly negative demo-graphic profile and the growing perception that its economy faces a crisis of competitiveness. In *Der Generationen-Pakt: Warum die Alten nicht das Problem, sondern die Lösung sind* (2011, *The Generational Contract: Why Old People are not the Problem but the Solution*), senior manager

Herbert Henzler and CDU (Christian Democrat) politician Lothar Späth outline suggestions for increasing the participation rate of older people in the workforce and for making pensions and welfare more flexible so that retirees might continue to make a valuable contribution to the economy and to the vibrancy of society more generally. From the other end of the political spectrum, the former SPD (Social Democrat) spokesperson, diplomat, and journalist Uwe-Karsten Heye makes a similar case in *Gewonnene Jahre: oder Die revolutionäre Kraft der alternden Gesellschaft* (2008; *Extra Years: Or The Revolutionary Power of the Ageing Society*), albeit with a greater emphasis on the social benefits that might accrue from better integration of older people.

Professor Ernst Pöppel and Dr Beatrice Wagner contribute to a body of 'popular science' books on the subject with *Je älter desto besser* (2012; *The Older, the Better*), whereas Margarete Mitscherlich-Nielsen (famous for her 1967 book *The Inability to Mourn/Die Unfähigkeit zu trauern*, co-written with Alexander Mitscherlich) offers a psychoanalyst's perspective in *Die Radikalität des Alters. Einsichten einer Psychoanalytikerin* (2010; *The Radicalism of Old Age. A Psychoanalyst's Insights*), which was published just before her death, aged 94, in 2012. And Elisabeth Niejahr in *Alt sind nur die anderen* (2004; *Only Other People are Old*) and Claudius Seidl in *Schöne junge Welt* (2005; *Beautiful Young World*) serve up wide-ranging, if rather generalised, sociological analyses. In all three cases, the emphasis once again is on the prejudice suffered by older people in a society obsessed with youth and productivity, and on promoting an alternative vision of old age as a 'transformative' experience, as a life stage in which the individual can draw on decades of experience in order to re-present or even reinvent themselves.

Silvia Bovenschen, a well-known feminist academic, essayist, and author, presents a more philosophical approach in her *Älter werden: Notizen* (2006; *Growing Older: Notes*), thus contributing to a large body of texts dedicated to self-reflection in old age, particularly amongst a generation that, born towards the end of the war or in the first years after 1945, 'grew up' with, and did so much to shape, the two German states that emerged from the ruins of Nazi Germany. Former student activists of the '68 era, intellectuals, and politicians are especially prominent here. More broadly, and as is common in other 'ageing societies', 'ordinary' old people are given the opportunity to speak for themselves in collections of their stories such as Sabine Bode's *Wir Alten: Porträts einer lebenserfahrenen Generation* (2008; *We Old People: Portraits of a Generation with Life Experience*).

Above all, however, the market is dominated by more 'popular' texts. Men might receive guidance from Eckart Hammer's *Männer altern anders: Eine Gebrauchsanweisung* (2007; *Men Age Differently: An Instruction Manual*), whereas women might opt for any number of self-help books, including *Selbstbestimmt und solidarisch. Frauen und das Alter* (2005; *Independent and in Solidarity. Women and Old Age*) by Hanna Habermann, Ute Wannig, and Barbara Heun; Christine Swientek's *Mit 40 depressiv, mit 70 um die Welt: Wie Frauen älter werden* (1991; *Depressed at 40, Around the World at 70: How Women Age*), or Barbara Dribbusch's *Älter werden ist viel schöner, als Sie vorhin in der Umkleidekabine noch dachten* (2012; *Growing Older is much more Beautiful than You just Thought in the Fitting Room*). Both sexes might choose Peter Gross and Karin Fagetti's *Glücksfall Alter: Alte Menschen sind gefährlich, weil sie keine Angst vor der Zukunft haben* (2008; *Lucky in Old Age: Old People are Dangerous because They aren't Afraid of the Future*); Henning Scherf's *Grau ist bunt: Was im Alter möglich ist* (2006; *Grey is Multicoloured: What's Possible in Old Age*); Matthias Irle's *Älterwerden für Anfänger* (2009; *Growing Old for Beginners*), or one of many other comparable books.

On the screen, too, old age is a theme – and here we glimpse the concerns of a cinema-going audience that is itself ageing. Piet Eekmann's 1998 film *Die Männer meiner Oma* (*My Grandma's Men*) addresses the discomfort that younger people often experience with regard to old-age sexuality (and particularly older women's sexuality), as the filmmaker listens to his 78-year-old grandmother's account of her love life, including her most recent fantasies. Similar, but far better known, is Andreas Dresen's *Cloud 9* (*Wolke 9*, 2008), in which Inge (in her mid-60s) cheats on her husband Werner during a highly physical affair with Karl (in his mid-70s). Some members of Dresen's audience were scandalised by the explicit sexual scenes in the first 15 minutes, which show Inge with Karl and then Werner naked and having intercourse, and walked out. (In the United States, HBO's 2007 television series *Tell Me You Love Me* provoked a similar debate.)

Katrin Bühlig's film *Kribbeln im Bauch* (2001; *Butterflies in My Stomach*) examines the reactions of grown-up children to a love affair between a man in his 90s and a woman in her late 80s. In Bühlig's film, the retirement home is a theme, and the implied question of whether there can be a new lease of life in old age. Christoph Englert's *Nebeneinander* (2010; *Next to One Another*) focuses on Alzheimer's disease – a condition that afflicts around 1.2 million of the 16.5 million Germans over 60, according to the German Alzheimer's research institute (Alzheimer Forschung Initiative) – in a moving depiction of Walther's ever less successful efforts to get through to his wife; while Michael Haneke's *Love* (*Liebe/Amour*, 2012), which won the Palme d'Or at Cannes following its première there and an Oscar for Best Foreign Language Film in 2013, explores a husband's inability to cope with his wife's partial paralysis and dementia following a stroke and refuses to offer any prospect that old age might encourage reconciliation, understanding, or even renewed affection. Growing old and ill simply causes his characters to reveal the dissatisfaction with one another they have harboured for many years. And in Sophie Heldman's *Satte Farben vor Schwarz* (2010; *Rich Colours before Black*), the mood is still darker as the film depicts an older couple's struggle to adjust to the husband's debilitating illness and their decision to commit suicide together. Suicide, particularly assisted suicide – *Sterbehilfe* – is, of course, a topic that may be even more controversial in Germany than elsewhere on account of the historical memory of the Nazis' euthanasia programme. Tilmann Jens's book *Demenz* dealing with his father's dementia launched a ferocious debate in 2009 owing to Walter Jens's standing as a leading intellectual of the wartime generation and his previous support for the individual's right to choose the manner of his or her ending.

The French-German co-production *Et si on vivait tous ensemble?/Und wenn wir alle zusammenziehen?* (2011; *All Together*) also thematises dementia, but in a comedy starring Daniel Brühl as the much younger fifth member of a household of oldtimers and occasional object of their (sexual) fantasies. This film, which was a minor international success, illustrates a more recent trend in aesthetic representations of ageing both in Germany and elsewhere, namely the attempt to depict the humorous aspects of growing old, as a means of demonstrating both its everyday normality and older people's humanity.

Ageing is now an increasingly prominent topic on television, in the theatre, and in the visual arts as well. In 2007 Jörg Lühdorff's three-part TV thriller *2030: Aufstand der Alten* (*2030: Uprising of The Old People*) presented a dystopian vision of future solutions to the 'problem' of caring for the elderly: barracks, eerily reminiscent of Hitler's concentration camps, are erected to which old people are sent to die (Germany's social concerns, in this case the treatment of the elderly, are often compressed into the country's ongoing confrontation with its Nazi past). Less elaborate, and more saccharine, is the soap *Rote Rosen* (*Red Roses*), aimed at an older audience, which achieved a market share of 10.1 per cent of viewers in its time slot in 2011, according to the TV station *Das Erste*. In 2011, moreover, the first 'Theaterfestival 60plus' took place in Rudolstadt, featuring 15 productions on old age by nine amateur and professional theatre groups. And visual artists are also engaging with the theme. The photo competition *Neue Bilder vom Alter(n)* (*New Images of Age and Ageing*) sponsored by the academic collaboration 'Altern in

Figure 17.1. Ursula and Siegfried M.
Reprinted with kind permission of Gerhard Weber

Deutschland' attracted more than 400 entries, and an exhibition of 80 images toured Germany through 2012. Gerhard Weber was the winner with his 'Ursula and Siegfried M.', an erotic picture of the elderly couple in their underwear in which their attire contrasts with the old-fashioned setting of their bedroom (Figure 17.1).

Ageing in contemporary German-language literature

Old age is a major theme in contemporary German-language literature. Recent texts build on a tradition that reaches back to classical times — notably Plato, Pindar, Cicero, and Seneca — and was reanimated by writers as diverse as Christoph Martin Wieland (1733–1813), Johann Wolfgang von Goethe (1749–1832), Theodor Storm (1817–88), E.T.A. Hoffmann (1776–1822), Wilhelm Raabe (1831–1910), Adalbert Stifter (1805–68), Theodor Fontane (1819–98), and Thomas Mann (1875–1955).

For the most part, the extensive engagement with growing old that is manifest in recent German-language fiction is issue-driven rather than reflexive. The major concerns are: care and caring for older people, sex and love, gender and old age, family relationships, and physical and mental decline. At the same time, however, there exists a smaller body of writing that is less directly concerned with growing old as a biological and sociological phenomenon and more focused on the broader implications of the fading of the wartime generation and of the generation born towards the end of the war and in its immediate aftermath that did so much to shape German society and politics. This writing *by* older authors (as opposed to more issue-focused writing *about* old age, often in fact by younger authors) is generally more philosophically inclined, featuring a more intensive engagement with the way memory functions, the choices the individual made under Nazism, communist East Germany, or the capitalist West, and the question of what it means to have lived through such historical disruptions for the older person now facing his or her imminent demise.

As far as the larger number of issue-driven texts *about* old age is concerned, we might point first to a very particular genre of 'retirement home' narratives – almost all of them by younger authors – such as Tanja Dückers's short story 'Lux Aeterna' ('Eternal Light', in the collection *Café Brazil*, 2001), Annette Pehnt's *Haus der Schildkröten* (2006; *House of Tortoises*), and Leonie Ossowski's *Die schöne Gegenwart* (2001; *The Beautiful Present*). These texts use the retirement home as a setting to explore a range of social and psychological issues, including dignity in old age, the dissolution of the nuclear family, what happens when parents become dependent and children become carers, and how, in advanced years, lifelong relationships may begin to dissolve as new ties and new ways of living evolve.

A further set of texts deal with love and sex in old age, for example Barbara Bronnen's *Am Ende ein Anfang* (2006; *At the End, a Beginning*), which tells of how former lovers, now aged, glimpse one another at a railway station and begin a correspondence inflected by reminiscence and desire. Frequently the issue at stake in these books is whether children can come to terms with their parents' flowering of sexuality. Or such texts may challenge social expectations, and stereotypes, of older people's sexual desire more generally. Thus we find a striking number of novels featuring older men who are beset by anxiety with regard to their sexual function yet also correspondingly lustful, including many by established older male writers such as Botho Strauß (2003), Günter Grass (2006), Martin Walser (2004, 2006, 2009 [2008]), and Christoph Hein (2011). What is usually also at stake in these intentionally provocative, even outrageous expressions of *Altherrenerotik* (old men's lust), however, is not only an anxiety about growing old, or even about impotence, but rather a more general reluctance to withdraw – the innuendo here is quite deliberate – from the limelight and from the significance, and influence, that these male writers have for decades enjoyed in postwar Germany's rather patriarchal public sphere. For women writers, lust is almost never a central theme – there is no female Philip Roth – though the loss of attractiveness, as society defines it for women, that comes with ageing often bothers female protagonists, such as Christa Wolf's alter ego in *Stadt der Engel* (2010), published in English as *City of Angels* in 2013. An exception here is *Nacktbadestrand* (2010; *Nudists' Beach*) by the elderly Austrian writer Elfriede Vavrik, which was inspired by the adventures that followed her placement of a personal ad.

There is also a set of texts that thematises older people's apparent disengagement from a society that has moved beyond them, as it were. In some of these, the focus is on the psychological interiority of the ageing individual, as in Gerhard Köpf's *Ein alter Herr* (2007; *An Elderly Gentleman*), which portrays the increasing detachment of an elderly male professor, whereas in others disengagement is framed as social critique. For example, Monika Maron's *Endmoränen* (2002; *End Moraines*) and *Ach Glück* (2007; *O Fortune*) ruminate on the sense of redundancy frequently experienced by older east Germans as they confront a post-unification devaluation of their GDR biographies. And finally, a large number of books deal with illness, especially Alzheimer's disease. Georg Diez's *Der Tod meiner Mutter* (2009; *The Death of My Mother*) and Arno Geiger's *Der alte König in seinem Exil* (2011; *The Old King in Exile*), for instance, present autobiographical accounts of a parent's drawn-out death and of the difficulties children have in coming to terms with this process. Harriet Köhler's *Und dann diese Stille* (2010; *And then this Silence*) confronts the same issue in the form of a novel, and dementia is a key theme in Katharina Hacker's *Die Erdbeeren von Antons Mutter* (2010; *The Strawberries of Anton's Mother*), in which a son, a doctor, finds it difficult to deal with the reality that he is unable to help his mother.

As far as texts *by* older writers dealing less with old age as a biological reality than with reflection on the individual's biographical involvement in German history are concerned, we find a recent abundance of texts in which growing old prompts reflection on the importance of generation in a country in which a powerful sense of belonging to a particular historical cohort has been created by dramatic historical caesurae.

First and foremost, we have a series of novels by authors born in the 1940s who would later, in West Germany, become members of the 'generation of '68' – student radicals challenging their parents' complicity in Nazism – and who would have such a powerful influence on reshaping the postwar Federal Republic into a progressive, self-critical democracy. Uwe Timm's *Rot* (2001; *Red*), Peter Schneider's *Skylla* (2005), and F.C. Delius's *Mein Jahr als Mörder* (2004; *My Year as a Murderer*), for example, reassess the revolutionary fervour of the late 1960s, whether their actions were justified in the fight against a West German state that was quick to suppress dissent, and their narrators'/authors' mellowing into old age in the decades that followed 1968. For Monika Maron, a writer of the same generation who grew up in the GDR (she left for West Germany in 1988), the focus is rather on psychological deformation, the feeling of having lived a wasted life, and disorientation in the new (post-unification) present. In Maron's 1996 novel *Animal Triste*, a woman from the former GDR, aged around 50, appears prematurely redundant and withdraws into self-stupefying reminiscences of a love affair with a West German following the fall of the Wall. And in *Endmoränen*, a woman growing into late middle age feels herself to be both sexually and socially redundant as she casts her mind back to her career as a writer of (mildly) subversive biographies during the GDR and wonders what purpose her life might serve after the end of that state. In contrast, the Austrian writer Peter Handke, whose mother was an ethnic Slovenian from Carinthia, sets German and Austrian history, and specifically the Nazi past that was so formative for this generation, within the broader transnational history of violence and ethnic conflict in central and southern Europe that continues into the present day with the wars of the 1990s in the former Yugoslavia. In Handke's quasi-mystical *Die Morawische Nacht* (2008; *The Night on The Morava*) the author's alter ego journeys on the river Morava, conjuring up the voices of those he has known, and looking back on who he has become within the memory landscape of war and genocide into which he was born.

Other writers of the same generation present quite different perspectives on the same historical timespan. The Jewish writer Rafael Seligmann's autobiography, *Deutschland wird dir gefallen* (2010; *You'll Like Germany*) thus reflects on the 'unexpectedness' of a Jew growing old in Germany after Auschwitz. Edgar Hilsenrath, a generation older than Seligmann and an inmate of the ghetto into which the Nazis forced Jews in Czernowitz (Chernivtsi in present-day Ukraine; then in Romania), does the same in *Berlin . . . Endstation* (2006; *End of the Line . . . Berlin*). Ruth Klüger looks back to her childhood in different ghettos and concentration camps, including Auschwitz, in *weiter leben* (1992; Klüger translated the text into English as *Still Alive*,

2001), and in *unterwegs verloren* (2008; *Lost on The Way*) to the discrimination she continued to experience as a Jew *and* a woman following her departure for the United States after 1945.

Hilsenrath and Klüger, in fact, belong to the generation of German-language authors born from the mid-1920s to the mid-1930s – and now in their mid-80s – who are writing memoirs, reflections, and autobiographically inspired texts, acutely conscious that they are now inescapably nearing the end of their lives. Hilsenrath and Klüger, self-evidently and understandably, focus on their experiences *as* Jews and on the persecution they endured during the Nazi period. Some of their non-Jewish peers, on the other hand, tend towards abstraction and a certain timelessness, or perhaps ahistoricity. The work of Austrian poet Friederike Mayröcker, for example, presents a determined, even stubborn rebellion against the passing of time. Thus her 1992 collection *Das besessene Alter* (*Possessed Old Age*) initiated a non-representational, if not abstruse lyrical confrontation with old age, death, and the loss of her partner, the poet Ernst Jandl, that continues to the present. Not quite as involved, but similarly timeless, is Peter Rühmkorf's cycle of poems *Paradiesvogelschiß* (2008; *Fear of the Bird of Paradise*), written while he had terminal cancer.

For the large majority of authors of this generation, however, there is no getting away from 'history'. And here history almost always means National Socialism and the way in which adolescent experiences of the Hitler era shaped the choices made in the postwar period: to opt for communist East Germany (the GDR) over capitalist West Germany (the FRG), with its supposed continuity with the Nazi past; or to prefer West Germany, for all its faults, as a state that had consciously made a democratic break with totalitarianism. Ludwig Harig's *Weh dem, der aus der Reihe tanzt* (1990; *Woe to Him who Dances Out of Line*) and *Wer mit den Wölfen heult, wird Wolf* (1996; *He who Howls with the Wolf Becomes a Wolf*) thus reflect on the author's early indoctrination and involvement in Nazism as a member of the Hitler Youth and army conscript; Günter Grass's *Beim Häuten der Zwiebel* caused an intense debate, even scandal, when it was published in German in 2006 (the English translation, *Peeling The Onion,* appeared in 2007), on account of its very belated revelation that the author – for many decades *the* proponent of the need for Germans to confront their past openly and honestly – had briefly served with the notorious Waffen SS towards the end of the war. In *Zwischenbilanz* (1992; *Taking Stock*) and *Vierzig Jahre* (1996; *Forty Years*), by contrast, Günter de Bruyn describes growing up under National Socialism and how this prompted his resolve to support the GDR, with its insistence that it was the only authentic choice for true anti-fascists. Christa Wolf does something similar in *Stadt der Engel*, though the focus is on the postwar period and even more so on the post-unification period, when she was widely vilified for her decision to remain in East Germany even once it was obvious that the regime had failed to fulfil its promise to break with the past and to create a better, more equal society. Wolf's text, in fact, may be considered to be a very late example of the wave of autobiographical works by members of her generation that appeared immediately after 1990 seeking to justify or defend the choices this generation had made after 1945.

Ageing into the post-postwar?

In these generational texts, we may glimpse, indirectly, something of the *epochal* significance of 'the ageing society' for the way Germany sees itself today. Certainly, the extent to which these two generations – the wartime generation and the generation born from the mid-1940s to the mid-1950s – are looking back over the country's Nazi and postwar past most likely suggests a generalised sense of an approaching historical caesura. Books such as Günter Grass's 'old-age trilogy' *Beim Häuten der Zwiebel* (2006), *Die Box* (2008; *The Box*, 2010), and *Grimms Wörter* of 2010 (*Grimms' Words*), which look back over 80 or so years of German history, or Christa

Wolf's *Stadt der Engel*, which reviews the author's life in the GDR and post-unification, are thus infused with a sense of the past-ness of Germany's tumultuous 20th century. And it is likely that as Germany ages, and leaves behind its difficult past, its self-understanding will change. The extensive and unprecedented diversity of its population as a result of decades of immigration, especially the arrival of refugees, asylum seekers, Jews, and 'ethnic Germans' from eastern Europe over the last 20 years, will be one factor in bringing about this change, as writers of these backgrounds begin to look back in old age on different histories, and especially different displacements and disruptions, rather than on the Nazi past, the GDR, and postwar West Germany. There has been much talk about German 'normalisation' since unification – that is, of the imminent passing of the wartime generation coinciding with a lesser emphasis on the legacy of Nazism and postwar division. But it may be that for Germany, as it enters 'the post-postwar' period, normality will in fact mean that its increasingly elderly population's sense of what it *is*, and of its past, becomes more disparate, even as its concerns become more mundane and future-oriented: namely, how to ensure active and fulfilling lives while remaining open to the world.

Notes

1 Austria and Switzerland face similar demographic pressures; see IMF (2002).
2 In 2013, for example, the *Tagesschau* registered a low level of interest amongst highly qualified Indian students in working in Germany, partly on account of a negative view of Germans' attitudes towards immigrants in general and Indians in particular. See *Tagesschau* (2013).
3 Age and ethnicity are intimately related in the Federal Republic. In 2010, 19.3 per cent of the population had a migration background (*Migrationshintergrund*), that is to say, were immigrants or children of recent immigrants, with a median age of 35 as compared with 45.9 for all other residents (Statistisches Bundesamt 2011). In 2009, conversely, only 4 per cent of people over 65 were not German nationals (Statistisches Bundesamt 2009). (This figure also reflects the fact that very few older immigrants, especially Turks, have been able, or have wanted, to acquire German citizenship).
4 Specifically, public intergenerational transfers that are especially generous to older people, notwithstanding the incremental raising of the retirement age to 67 by 2029.
5 See Roman Herzog Institute (2004); Robert Bosch Foundation (2010); Jacobs Foundation (2006–08).

Bibliography

German research centres on ageing

Deutsches Zentrum für Altersfragen, www.dza.de.
Leibnitz Institute for Age Research, www.fli-leibniz.de.
Max Planck Institute for Biology of Ageing, www.age.mpg.de.
Munich Center for the Economics of Ageing, http://mea.mpisoc.mpg.de.

Organisations for elderly people in Germany

(all websites accessed 25 April 2013)

Bundesarbeitsgemeinschaft der Senioren-Organisationen, www.bagso.de.
Bundesministerium für Familie, Senioren, Frauen und Jugend, www.bmfsfj.de.
Senior Experten Service, www.ses-bonn.de/en/about-us.html.
Sozialverband Deutschland, www.sovd.de/wir_ueber_uns.0.html.

International reports and studies of ageing

(all websites accessed 25 April 2013)

Alzheimer Forschung Initiative (2012) 'Zahlen und Fakten der Alzheimer-Krankheit in Deutschland'. Online. Available at www.alzheimer-forschung.de/alzheimer-krankheit/faktenblatt_zahlen.htm.

CSIS Global Aging Initiative (2010) *The Global Aging Preparedness Index*. Online. Available at http://csis. org/files/publication/101014_GlobalAgingIndex_DL_Jackson_LR.pdf.

Enquête-Kommission (2002) Final Report of the Commission of Enquiry (Enquête-Kommission) 'Demographischer Wandel – Herausforderungen unserer älter werdenden Gesellschaft an den Einzelnen und die Politik'. Online. Available at www.umweltdaten.de/rup/Bericht_Enquete_Kommission 1408800.pdf.

IMF (2002) 'Population Ageing and Long-Term Fiscal Sustainability in Austria'. Online. Available at www.imf.org/external/pubs/ft/wp/2002/wp02216.pdf.

Medicare Trustees (2012) 'The 2012 Annual Report Of The Boards Of Trustees Of The Federal Hospital Insurance And Federal Supplementary Medical Insurance Trust Funds'. Online. Available at www.cms. gov/Research-Statistics-Data-and-Systems/Statistics-Trends-and-Reports/ReportsTrustFunds/ Downloads/TR2012.pdf.

Mitscherlich-Nielsen, A. and Mitscherlich, M. (1967) *Die Unfähigkeit zu trauern*, Munich: R. Piper & Co. Verlag.

NHS (2009) 'Elderly People Account For Bigger Proportion of NHS Hospital Activity Every Year'. Online. Available at www.ic.nhs.uk/news-and-events/news/elderly-people-account-for-bigger-proportion-of-nhs-hospital-activity-every-year-report-shows.

OECD (2005) *Ageing and Employment Policies/Vieillissement et politiques de l'emploi: Germany 2005*, Paris: OECD Publishing.

OHCHR (2012) 'Report of the United Nations High Commissioner for Human Rights'. Online. Available at www.globalaging.org/agingwatch/Articles/Report%20of%20the%20United%20Nations %20High%20Commissioner%20for%20Human.pdf.

Population Reference Bureau (2012) 'Fertility Rates for Low Birth Rate Countries'. Online. Available at www.prb.org/pdf12/TFR_Table2012_update.pdf.

Sarrazin, T. (2010) *Deutschland schafft sich ab: Wie wir unser Land aufs Spiel setzen*, Munich: Deutsche Verlags-Anstalt.

Statistisches Bundesamt (2009) 'Ältere Menschen in Deutschland und der EU'. Online. Available at https://www.destatis.de/DE/Publikationen/Thematisch/Bevoelkerung/Bevoelkerungsstand/Blickpunkt AeltereMenschen1021221119004.pdf;jsessionid=A7B34A80BD7E91128936B05E36F3911E.cae2?__blob =publicationFile.

Statistisches Bundesamt (2011) 'Ein Fünftel der Bevölkerung in Deutschland hatte 2010 einen Migrationshintergrund'. Online. Available at https://www.destatis.de/DE/PresseService/Presse/Presse mitteilungen/2011/09/PD11_355_122.html?nn=50744.

United Nations (2002) Report of the UN Department of Economic and Social Affairs for the 'World Assembly on Ageing'. Online. Available at www.un.org/esa/population/publications/worldageing 19502050/pdf/62executivesummary_english.pdf.

World Bank (2010) 'Some Economic Consequences of Global Ageing'. Online. Available at http:// siteresources.worldbank.org/HEALTHNUTRITIONANDPOPULATION/Resources/281627–10956 98140167/SomeEconomicConsequencesOfGlobalAgeing.pdf.

Publications of German research foundations on ageing

(all websites accessed 25 April 2013)

Jacobs Foundation (2006–08) 'Altern in Deutschland'. Online. Available at www.altern-in-deutsch-land.de/index.html.

Robert Bosch Foundation (2010) 'Leben im Alter'. Online. Available at www.bosch-stiftung.de/content/ language1/html/31385.asp.

Roman Herzog Institute (2004) 'Deutschland altert. Die demographische Herausforderung'. Online. Available at www.romanherzoginstitut.de/publikationen/details/?tx_mspublication_pi1%5BshowUid% 5D=27&cHash=01418ff61a.

Books and articles on demographic ageing and its consequences

(all websites accessed 25 April 2013)

Börsch-Supan, A. (2005) 'The Impact of Global Aging on Labor, Product and Capital Markets'. Online. Available at www.cepr.org/meets/wkcn/1/1624/papers/BoerschSupan.pdf.

Börsch-Supan, A. and Wilke, C.B. (2003) 'The German Public Pension System: How It Was, How It Will Be'. Online. Available at www.mea.mpisoc.mpg.de/uploads/user_mea_discussionpapers/ y8hl3aada9n1acbo_DP_Nr34.pdf.

Cohen, J. *et al.* (2006) 'Trends in acceptance of euthanasia among the general public in 12 European countries (1981–1999)', *European Journal of Public Health*, 16(6): 663–9.

Harper, S. (2010) 'Population Ageing and Social Security', report written for the International Social Security Association. Online. Available at www.issa.int/Resources/Conference-Reports/Demographic-challenges-and-social-security/%28language%29/eng-GB.

Höhn, C., Mai, R., and Micheel, F. (2008) 'Demographic Change in Germany', in I. Hamm, H. Seitz, and M. Werding (eds) *Demographic Change in Germany: The Economic and Fiscal Consequences*, Berlin: Springer-Verlag, 9–33.

Kamann, M. (2009) *Todeskämpfe: Die Politik des Jenseits und der Streit um Sterbehilfe*, Bielefeld: Transcript Verlag. Introduction online. Available at www.transcript-verlag.de/ts1265/ts1265_1.pdf.

Keil, K., Milke, F., Hoffmann, D., Schuegraf, M., and Zoll, M. (2006) *Demografie und Filmwirtschaft: Studie zum demografischen Wandel und seinen Auswirkungen auf Kinopublikum und Filminhalte in Deutschland*, Berlin: Vistas Verlag.

Kiesel, H. (2008) 'Das Alter in der Literatur', in U. Staudinger and H. Häfner (eds) *Was ist Alter(n)? Neue Antworten auf eine scheinbar einfache Frage*, Berlin: Springer-Verlag, 172–88.

Kocka, J. (2008) 'Chancen und Herausforderungen einer alternden Gesellschaft', in U. Staudinger and H. Häfner (eds) *Was ist Alter(n)? Neue Antworten auf eine scheinbar einfache Frage*, Berlin: Springer-Verlag, 217–36. Also online. Available at www.altern-in-deutschland.de/pdf/publikationen/05-HAW18-Kocka-S217-236.pdf.

Kreyenfeld, M. and Konietzka, D. (2008) 'Education and Fertility in Germany', in I. Hamm, H. Seitz, and M. Werding (eds), *Demographic Change in Germany: The Economic and Fiscal Consequences*, Berlin: Springer-Verlag, 165–87.

Peterson, P. (1999) 'The Grey Dawn: A Global Crisis', *Foreign Affairs*, 78:1: 42–55.

Pott, H.G. (2008) *Eigensinn des Alters. Literarische Erkundungen*, Munich: Wilhelm Fink Verlag.

Raffelhuschen, B. and Walliser, J. (1999) 'Unification and Ageing in Germany: Who Pays and When?' Online. Available at www.nber.org/chapters/c6694.pdf.

Seitz, H. and Werding, M. (2008) 'Consequences of Demographic Change in Germany: An Introduction', in I. Hamm, H. Seitz, and M. Werding (eds), *Demographic Change in Germany: The Economic and Fiscal Consequences*, Berlin: Springer-Verlag, 2–7.

Spengler, O. (1922; 1923) *Der Untergang des Abendlandes*, Munich: C.H. Beck Verlag; trans. C.F. Atkinson (1922) *The Decline of the West*, New York: Alfred A. Knopf.

Staudinger, U.M. and Häfner H. (eds) (2008) *Was ist Alter(n)? Neue Antworten auf eine scheinbar einfache Frage*, Springer-Verlag: Berlin.

Tagesschau (2013) 'Die späten Folgen der "Kinder statt Inder"-Kampagne'. Online. Available at www.tagesschau.de/ausland/indien-deutschland102.html.

The Economist (2012) 'China's Achilles heel'. Online. Available at www.economist.com/node/21553056.

Exhibitions

(all websites accessed 25 April 2013)

2012 – Karsten Thormaehlen, in cooperation with the Deutsches Zentrum für Altersfragen, 'Mit hundert hat man noch Träume', www.dza.de/veranstaltungen/fotoausstellung.html.

2012 – Neue Bilder vom Alter(n), www.altern-in-deutschland.de/pdf/neue-bilder-vom-altern_ausstellung.pdf.

Popular political, popular science, and self-help books on 'the ageing society'

Birg, H. (2001) *Die Demographische Zeitenwende,* Berlin: C.H. Beck Verlag.

Birg, H. (2002) 'Schrumpfen oder Waschsen?: Die Lebensbedingungen sind entscheidend,' *Frankfurter Allgemeine Zeitung*. Online. Available at http://pub.uni-bielefeld.de/download/1785223/2314793 (accessed 29 April 2013).

Bode, S. (2008) *Wir Alten: Porträts einer lebenserfahrenen Generation*, Düsseldorf: Patmos Verlag.

Bovenschen, S. (2006) *Älter werden: Notizen*, Frankfurt a.m.: Fischer Verlag.

Dribbusch, B. (2012) *Älter werden ist viel schöner, als Sie vorhin in der Umkleidekabine noch dachten*, Berlin: Mosaik Verlag.

Gross, P. and Fagetti, K. (2008) *Glücksfall Alter: Alte Menschen sind gefährlich, weil sie keine Angst vor der Zukunft haben*, Freiburg, Basel, and Vienna: Herder.

Habermann, H., Wannig, U., and Heun, B. (2005) *Selbstbestimmt und solidarisch: Frauen und das Alter*, Rüsselsheim: Christel Gottert Verlag.

Hammer, E. (2007) *Männer altern anders. Eine Gebrauchsanweisung*, Freiburg, Basel, and Vienna: Herder.

Henzler, H. and Späth, L. (2011) *Der Generationen-Pakt: Warum die Alten nicht das Problem, sondern die Lösung sind*, Munich: Hanser Verlag.

Heye, U.-K. (2008) *Gewonnene Jahre: oder Die revolutionäre Kraft der alternden Gesellschaft*, Munich: Karl Blessing Verlag.

Irle, M. (2009) *Älterwerden für Anfänger*, Reinbek bei Hamburg: Rowohlt Verlag.

Jens, T. (2010) *Demenz*, Munich: Goldmann Verlag.

Jens, W. and Krug, H. (1995) *Menschenwürdig sterben: Ein Plädoyer für Selbstverantwortung*, Munich and Zurich: Piper Verlag.

Miegel, M. (2002) *Die deformierte Gesellschaft*, Munich: Propyläen Verlag.

Mitscherlich-Nielsen, M. (2010) *Die Radikalität des Alters: Einsichten einer Psychoanalytikerin*, Frankfurt a.m.: Fischer Verlag.

Müller, L. (2002) 'Der Fluch des Ibsenweibs', *Süddeutsche Zeitung*, 16 August, 11.

Niejahr, E. (2004) *Alt sind nur die anderen*, Frankfurt a.m.: Fischer Verlag.

Pöppel, E. and Wagner, B. (2012) *Je älter desto besser*, Munich: Goldmann Verlag.

Scherf, H. (2006) *Grau ist bunt: Was im Alter möglich ist*, Freiburg, Basel, and Vienna: Herder.

Schirrmacher, F. (2004) *Das Methusalem-Komplott*, Munich: Karl Blessing Verlag.

Seibt, G. (2002) 'Auf Wiedersehen Schönheit', *Süddeutsche Zeitung*, 10 August, 13.

Seidl, C. (2005) *Schöne junge Welt*, Munich: Goldmann Verlag.

Swientek, C. (1991) *Mit 40 depressiv, mit 70 um die Welt: Wie Frauen älter werden*, Freiburg, Basel, and Vienna: Herder.

Films

2030: Aufstand der Alten (2007) [TV series] J. Lühdorff, Germany: ZDF.

Die Männer meiner Oma (1998) [Film] P. Eekmann, France: ARTE.

Et si on vivait tous ensemble?/Und wenn wir alle zusammenziehen (2011) [Film], S. Robelin, France/Germany: Studio 37.

Kribbeln im Bauch (2001) [Film], K. Bühlig, Germany: Tangram Film.

Liebe/Amour (2012) [Film], M. Haneke, France/Germany/Austria: Les Films du Losange, X-Filme Creative Pool, and Wega Film.

Nebeneinander (2010) [Film] C. Englert, Germany: Film Munich.

Satte Farben vor Schwarz (2010) [Film], S. Heldman, Germany: UNAFILM E.K.

Tell Me You Love Me (2007) [TV series] USA: HBO.

Wolke 9 (2008) [Film] A. Dresen, Germany: Rommel Film.

TV and theatre (all websites accessed 25 April 2013)

Rote Rosen, www.daserste.de/unterhaltung/soaps-telenovelas/rote-rosen/index.html.

'Theaterfestival 60plus', Rudolstadt, www.neues-deutschland.de/artikel/207917.freude-am-altern.html.

Literary texts

Bronnen, B. (2006) *Am Ende ein Anfang*, Zurich: Arche.

De Bruyn, G. (1992) *Zwischenbilanz*, Frankfurt am Main: Fischer Verlag.

De Bruyn, G. (1996) *Vierzig Jahre*, Frankfurt a.m.: Verlag.

Delius, F.C. (2004) *Mein Jahr als Mörder*, Berlin: Rowohlt.

Diez, G. (2009) *Der Tod meiner Mutter*, Cologne: Kiepenheuer & Witsch Verlag.

Dückers, T. (2001) 'Lux Aeterna', in *Café Brazil*, Berlin: Aufbau-Verlag.

Geiger, A. (2011) *Der alte König in seinem Exil*, Munich: Carl Hanser Verlag.

Grass, G. (2006) *Beim Häuten der Zwiebel*, Göttingen: Steidl.

Grass, G. (2008) *Die Box*, Göttingen: Steidl.

Grass, G. (2010) *Grimms Wörter. Eine Liebeserklärung*, Göttingen: Steidl.

Hacker, K, (2010) *Die Erdbeeren von Antons Mutter*, Frankfurt a.m.: Fischer Verlag.

Handke, P. (2008) *Die Morawische Nacht*, Frankfurt a.m.: Suhrkamp.

Harig, L. (1990) *Weh dem, der aus der Reihe tanzt*, Munich: Hanser Verlag.

Harig, L. (1996) *Wer mit den Wölfen heult, wird Wolf*, Munich: Hanser Verlag.

Hein, C. (2011) *Weiskerns Nachlass*, Frankfurt a.m.: Suhrkamp.

Hilsenrath, E. (2006) *Berlin . . . Endstation*, Cologne: Dittrich Verlag.

Klüger, R. (1992) *weiter leben*, Göttingen: Wallstein.

Klüger, R. (2008) *unterwegs verloren*, Göttingen: Wallstein.

Köhler, H. (2010) *Und dann diese Stille*, Cologne: Kiepenheuer & Witsch.

Köpf, G. (2007) *Ein alter Herr*, Tübingen: Klöpfer und Meyer Verlag.

Kospach, J. (2008) *Letzte Dinge. Ilse Aichinger und Friederike Mayröcker: Zwei Gespräche über den Tod*, Vienna: Mandelbaum.

Maron, M. (1996) *Animal Triste*, Berlin: Rowohlt.

Maron, M. (2002) *Endmoränen*, Frankfurt a.m.: Fischer Verlag.

Maron, M. (2007) *Ach Glück*, Frankfurt a.m.: Fischer Verlag.

Mayröcker, F. (1992) *Das besessene* Alter, Frankfurt a.m.: Suhrkamp.

Muschg, A. (1995) *Nur ausziehen wollte sie sich nicht*, Frankfurt a.m.: Suhrkamp.

Ossowski, L. (2001) *Die schöne Gegenwart*, Munich: Piper Verlag.

Pehnt, A. (2006) *Haus der Schildkröten*, Munich: Piper Verlag.

Roche, C. (2008) *Feuchtgebiete*, Cologne: DuMont.

Rühmkorff, P. (2008) *Paradiesvogelschiß*, Frankfurt a.m.: Insel.

Schneider, P. (2005) *Skylla*, Berlin: Rowohlt.

Seligmann, R. (2010) *Deutschland wird dir gefallen*, Berlin: Aufbau Verlag.

Strauß, Botho (2003) *Die Nacht mit Alice, als Julia ums Haus schlich*, Munich: Deutscher Taschenbuch Verlag.

Timm, U. (2001) *Rot*, Cologne: Kiepenheuer & Witsch.

Vavrik, E. (2010) *Nacktbadestrand*, Berlin: Ullstein.

Walser, M. (2004) *Der Augenblick der Liebe*, Reinbek: Rowohlt Verlag.

Walser, M. (2006) *Angstblüte*, Reinbek: Rowohlt Verlag.

Walser, M. (2009 [2008]) *Ein liebender Mann*, Hamburg: Rowohlt Taschenbuch Verlag.

Walser, M. (2011) *Muttersohn*, Reinbek: Rowohlt Verlag.

Wolf, C. (2010) *Stadt der Engel*, Berlin: Suhrkamp.

Part IV

Germany and Europe

18

Germany and Europe

Negotiating identity in a multicultural present

Fatima El-Tayeb

The story of European identity is often told as if it had no exterior. But this tells us more about how cultural identities are constructed – as 'imagined communities', through the marking of difference with others – than it does about the actual relations of unequal exchange and uneven development through which a common European identity was forged.

(Hall 1991)

This chapter explores one instance of the continuous (re)construction of European identity sketched by Stuart Hall in 1991, on the eve of the Maastricht Treaty and the 500-year commemorations of the 'discovery' of the Americas; namely the integration of Germany not only into the centre of contemporary Europe but into a 20th-century European history long framed as a conflict between democratic Europe and the German aggressor. That integration, I argue, has in part worked through reassigning the part of 'undemocratic aggressor' to European Muslims.

European internalist narrative and multicultural reality

While West Germany had been key to the creation of the European Union, through both its political will and its economic power, the German case remained problematic in constructing a post-1945 and then post-1990 transnational European narrative: after all, much of postwar Europe defined itself against Germany, that is, as victim of National Socialist aggression. The western Europe that emerged after World War II stood for everything Nazi Germany had attempted to destroy: freedom, peace, human rights, and democracy. In the Cold War context, it was important for the western European narrative to keep the memory of the war and the 'Nazis vs. Europe' antagonism alive, even while it acknowledged that postwar West Germany was more European than German in that equation. This tension became particularly acute after the fall of the Soviet empire and German reunification, resulting in a newly powerful German nation – and causing fears reflected in François Mauriac's oft-cited quip 'I love Germany so dearly that I hope there will always be two of them' (Isaacson 1989).

Even if it seems increasingly clear that there is no Europe without Germany, the question of what exactly Europe is appears more unresolved than ever. There is an anxiety-ridden debate around threats to a European identity – alternately defined as Christian, secular, and Judeo-Christian and usually, at least implicitly, as white.[1] Accordingly, threats are perceived as coming from those not considered to belong: communities of colour – black, Roma, and currently, in particular, Muslim – as if uncertainty about Europe's economic and political future could be ended by expelling those embodying 'non-Europeanness'. This perception is reflected in European discourses – legal, cultural, social, economical, academic – in which the term 'migrant' describes not only someone who moves across borders, but also racialised Europeans whose branding as second, third, or fourth generation 'migrant' reframes them as permanent new-comers.[2] That status is transmitted across generations and thus increasingly decoupled from the actual event of migration, shifting the meaning of 'migrant' from a term indicating movement to one indicating a static, hereditary state, signifying the failure to have become unambiguously European – a catch-22, since unambiguous Europeanness is impossible to achieve as long as racialised difference is still visible. The most striking example of this is the perception of European Roma and Sinti communities, who after 500 years are still treated as 'foreigners' in virtually every European nation (see European Commission 2004).

Another example is German Chancellor Helmut Kohl's unsuccessful 1982 attempt to halve Germany's 'Turkish' population – a plan based on the assumption that millions of 'guest workers' and their descendants had not become part of German society and that a monetary incentive would thus be sufficient to make them give up the life they had established over decades in order hastily to return 'home' (Hecking 2013). Almost 30 years later, in October 2010, when Chancellor Angela Merkel proclaimed the 'end of multiculturalism', that radical statement was widely reported but caused relatively little controversy. Rather, it seemed to be taken as the belated official recognition of something already part of common knowledge, namely the end of tolerance for those never considered real Europeans in the first place – labour and postcolonial migrants from the Middle East, Asia, and Africa, and their descendants – and a return to a less fractured, more simple and true notion of European culture (Conolly 2010). It is significant that Merkel's remarks were largely perceived as addressing the German variation of a European condition, thus affirming both that Germany had become representative of Europe and that this united Europe faces problems that transcend national borders and require a transnational European response.[3]

This notion of a European Union destabilised by newcomers who after half a century still prove unwilling or unable to become European is in line with Hall's framing of a Europe that constructs a narrative of continental culture as both homogeneous and entirely self-generated, hermetically sealed off from any outside influences. As the story goes,

> Europe is able to produce from within her own borders and resources, both material and spiritual, the conditions for the next phase of social development. This has been the dominant narrative of modernity for some time – an 'internalist' story, with capitalism growing from the womb of feudalism and Europe's self-generating capacity to produce, like a silk-worm, the circumstances of her own evolution from within her own body.
>
> (Hall 1991: 18)

In that story, migrants and their descendants are perceived as living a permanently provisional life, never putting down roots, never shaping or being shaped by their 'host society'. They can therefore make legitimate claims of belonging neither within national space nor within national time – and both aspects are equally important in defining European identity. National belonging revolves around the production and institutionalisation of a common past. Whether minorities find a place in the larger community therefore also depends on their relation to its narrative of national origin. In Europe, migrants and their descendants are routinely denied access to the common history. The internalist story can neither acknowledge the profound interconnectedness of cultures at the heart of the rise of Europe, and of the very idea of Europe itself, nor how colonialism and the transatlantic slave trade shaped not only the new but also the 'old world'. Instead, such a narrative requires a clear separation between what is European and what is not – an impossible task that invariably produces tensions that threaten its coherence. Historically, these tensions have centred on race and religion as markers of non-Europeanness. Therefore, Europeans who are not white and Christian exist not only in a strange place but in a strange temporality: they tend to be eternally read as having just arrived or even as still being elsewhere – if not physically, then at least culturally. The temporal (dis)placement of the Global South into Europe's past allows for the ongoing subsumption of the 'developing' world under a eurocentric time-space notion that confirms a narrative in which constant European progress is measured against a racialised outside that eternally lags behind (and thus always follows, never shapes Europe's path). In this model, religion, secularism, and race are mapped on to one another in a way that produces the white, Christian(ised secular) West as always ahead, always the location of progress.[4]

The desire to create unambiguously European spaces is fundamentally tied to a reconstruction of national memories within the emerging continental European[5] narrative. And while this includes nations that were only (re)created after the fall of the Soviet empire and thus depended on consciously constructing national myths, allowing room for the redefinition of belonging, there is little to no public acknowledgment of the ethnic and religious diversity represented in not only contemporary but also historical Europe. Rather, the supposed ethnic homogeneity of a past Europe is seen as an explanation for the persistent resistance to a multi-ethnic and multi-religious conceptualisation of Europe now. This leads, not only in the continent's East, to exclusionary ethnic essentialism. The repression of the long history of race and racism in Europe produces the continent's contemporary 'multicultural' state (associated with visual markers of non-Europeanness, be they dark skin or a headscarf) as a novelty, which requires adjustment in the best case and resistance in the worst, and which, most importantly, can simply be declared to have 'failed'. Multiculturalism in this sense does not merely describe a reality (which cannot be undone at will), but represents a particular discursive means to manage and control this reality.

Thus there is a causal relation between the declared failure of Europe's multicultural present and the continent's 'racial amnesia', that is, the persistent externalisation of race and racialised populations from Europe's past. That externalisation implements an unquestioned normative Christian(ised) whiteness, thus defining migrants and minority communities as a threat to the very Europe they are part of, their presence only acknowledged as a sign of crisis and forgotten again in the ongoing construction of a new European identity remaining within internalist limits. I propose to zoom in on a particular space and time within this larger formation of domination, namely post-1991 Germany, to show how both global developments – the 'war on terror' and 'humanitarian' NATO interventions – and intra-continental discourses, namely the singling out of European Muslims as a threat to Europe's stability, have contributed to a reframing of (post-) World War II history that sustains Hall's model of an internalist narrative, in which Europe remains eternally superior.

Memory and identity in the Federal Republic after 1945

The complicated and complex production of hegemonic memory is particularly evident in post-World War II West Germany. The German example is unique in that it represents the attempt to produce a historical memory in support of a national identity that does not (only) claim to be based on a common history, shared values, the overcoming of external persecution, and the fight for liberty and unity, but also the memory of Germans as perpetrators of genocide and as destroyers of liberty. That project, admirable as it is, has consistently produced strong tensions and attempts to resolve them.[6] It has also resulted in racialised communities being kept permanently out of national history, treated as eternal outsiders. As Zafer Šenoçak writes with regard to the situation of Turkish Germans: 'One can immigrate into a country, but not to its past. In Germany, history is read as a diary of the "community of fate", the nation's personal experience, to which Others have no access' (Šenoçak 2000: 53). At the same time, however, migrants live with the national past as much as the native population, and rather than remaining outside it, they frequently, yet often unknowingly, partake in a nation's attempts to come to terms with its history. This is particularly evident in post-unification German attempts to deal with the fascist past.

The 2008 global financial crisis led to a renewed focus on Germany as Europe's political powerhouse and economic engine, a perception that confirms a successful normalisation after World War II that began with the founding of the European Economic Community in 1957 and culminated in national unification three decades later, after the fall of the Soviet empire. The unification of East and West Germany in 1990 and the reconstruction of German memory within the European context can be read as a successful attempt to place the unified Germany back in the internalist story of Europe: the history of East Germany is deployed as a narrative representing Germans as victims of an ultimately un-European totalitarianism, that is, Stalinism. On the one hand, this facilitates the integration of the united Germany into emerging European memory by giving it its own 'victimised by an external totalitarian regime' trope. At the same time, the identification of East Germany with Stalinism justifies the wholesale dismissal of 40 years of developments in the GDR, as they can be read as forced on Germans by an outside intervention and thus not truly part of an 'internalist' German history. This perception turned the supposed unification into a de facto annexation. And (again symptomatic of European East/West divisions) while socialist East Germany has ceased to exist, dominant West German discourses identified the failure of East Germans to become instantly westernised as the reason for the east's xenophobia, poverty, political apathy, and general inability to succeed within capitalism; former East Germans are accused of clinging to a misplaced nostalgia for the socialist past that has produced its own term, *Ostalgie* (a compound of the German words for 'east' and 'nostalgia'; see Boyer 2006).

Meanwhile, former East Germans are granted an unambiguous status as German that is still denied to the descendants of labour migrants, who in turn have become a major target for eastern German racist violence. Public discourse admits to this endemic racism in the east largely in order to deemphasise similar violence in the western part of the nation. That is, racism becomes a marker of a temporal displacement of eastern Germans (and eastern Europeans) caused by their location in the former sphere of influence of the (non-European) Soviet empire, which prevented them from advancing towards the tolerant multiculturalism characterising the nation's (and continent's) western part – just as Muslim Germans' proclaimed anti-Semitism is framed as an anachronism, caused by their cultural location in an Orient that failed to move through a secularising Enlightenment. Consequently, both groups are targets of state-funded education programmes meant to move them towards the White Christian western German norm (Özyürek 2005; Partridge 2010).

The temporal and spatial dislocation of racialised Germans is obvious here: while white east German youths are targeted for their 'xenophobic' as well as anti-Semitic attitudes, the focus of state programmes directed at them is on Holocaust education and does not include lessons on the history of racism in Europe or on colonialism. Muslim youths, on the other hand, the primary targets of programmes addressing 'migrant anti-Semitism', are educated about the Holocaust as well as 'the Middle East conflict', thus assuming a correlation, if not equation, of German eliminatory anti-Semitism and contemporary anti-Zionism located in the Middle East. Through this equation, their Middle Eastern background situates Muslim youths in Germany closer to historic German anti-Semitism than white German youths (unless they are eastern German).[7] That assumption is not generally supported by empirical data, which often shows minoritised youths sympathising and identifying with the Jewish victims of fascist persecution on a higher level than majoritarian Germans, who tend to be more ambiguous in their identification (Georgi and Ohliger 2009). However, that does not preclude Muslim youths from – sometimes at the same time – expressing anti-Zionist or even anti-Semitic attitudes in response to Israel's treatment of Palestinians (Partridge 2010). This strongly indicates that the projection of 'historic' Christian/European forms of anti-Semitism on to contemporary Muslim societies – which of course also implies that anti-Semitism in Europe is a thing of the past – is not helpful in addressing either form of anti-Semitism (Bunzl 2005). What this kind of 'anti-anti-Semitism' training does achieve, however, is the placing of majoritarian West Germans in the familiar role of embodying a normative, advanced position that still needs to be achieved by others. To imply instead that contemporary Muslim youths in Germany might be able to teach their white classmates about empathy with persecuted Jews or to supplement lessons on historic Christian anti-Semitism with lessons on historic Muslim empires as spaces of protection for Jews could offer an approach to teaching about the Holocaust (as well as 'national history') more adequate for contemporary 'multicultural' Germany. To get there, however, it would first be necessary to let go of the internalist narrative – on the national as well as the global level.[8]

Western narratives: Hitler's revenants, new fascisms, and the primacy of the European past

The rise of the US empire and of neoliberal multiculturalism in the second half of the 20th century coincided with the reordering of Europe after World War II into West and East, the loss of colonial empires, and, after 1990, another reordering that largely collapsed Europe into the European Union. The latter came to symbolise Europe's successful reformation after the 20th-century crises of totalitarianism, confirming the continent's place as centre and gatekeeper of universal human rights. Simultaneous with the rise of the US as the new global power, western Europe, primarily through the European Union, reconfigured itself as a neutral arbiter: reformed, without interest in world domination, but still uniquely equipped to lead by example as – according to the internalist narrative – it represented an advanced stage of development others were still aspiring to reach. With decolonisation and the beginning of large-scale labour migration, movement became less regulated and more common, requiring a new global system that could incorporate and re-regulate this complex movement. Organisations like the United Nations or the International Monetary Fund are meant to do this work. They are thus situated in a kind of neutral 'international public time/space' (Fabian 1983), in which nations in different developmental stages can come together and work towards creating a more equal playing field. Within this model, this means that the Global South receives help in moving towards a future that is the West's present, while allowing the latter an educational glimpse of its own past. The non-Western world cannot, however, ever offer the West a developmental model for its own future.

Instead, this model justifies Western interventions in the internal affairs of nations of the Global South by framing conflicts as repeating patterns present in the history of the West, therefore giving Western nations a particular authority in deciding on the proper response (the 'X is the new Hitler' argument being the bluntest expression of this). To take away their sovereignty thus becomes the only way to save these nations from repeating the West's mistakes, while helping them to learn from its successes. As Josef Böröcz has observed with regard to the model function western Europe has for the post-socialist East:

> In order to think of any contemporary social form as the desirable 'already' for the desirous reformers of the 'not yet,' it is necessary to assume, as liberal thought does invariably, that the 'backwardness' of those that are 'not-yet' advanced has no causal connection to the previous advancement of the more 'developed' role model. If the achievement of the 'advanced' social forms is acknowledged to be due to benefits derived from somebody else's wretchedness, or if the suffering of the wretched is recognised as having been caused by the 'advancement' of the developed, the teleological blueprint becomes morally unacceptable and even nonsensical.
>
> (Böröcz 2006: 117)

This means that the West's advancement cannot be causally linked to a wilful under-development of the Global South (because then this advancement cannot function as a model for the rest of the world). It also means that 'humanitarian disasters' such as the Holocaust and, receiving much less attention, the transatlantic slave trade cannot be seen as outcomes of Western progress, but must be framed as non-representative aberrations or as descent into 'un-European' barbarism.[9] Accordingly, much of postwar Western domination uses World War II as a main reference point: in the case of the United States, to underscore that its global domination after 'the good war' is due to its antiracist humanitarianism, first expressed in the liberation of the world from fascism; in the case of Europe, to show that important lessons have been learned, that in fact the same uniquely European qualities that caused its downfall can now be mobilised to save the world. In the words of French philosopher Pascal Bruckner:

> Modernity has been self-critical and suspicious of its own ideals for a long time now, denouncing the sacralisation of an insane reason that was blind to its own zeal. In a word, it acquired a certain wisdom and an understanding of its limits. The Enlightenment, in turn, showed itself capable of reviewing its mistakes.
>
> (Bruckner 2007)

Europe needs to be absolved from its past in order to take its place in the new global order and vice versa. Not surprisingly, military interventions led by the US American multicultural, antiracist empire are increasingly framed as 'humanitarian'. Within this framework, (north-west) Europe functions as the global conscience, as is manifest in the location in The Hague of the International Criminal Court, which could have been housed nowhere but in western Europe as the only space *per definitionem* safe from the threat of grave human rights violations both in the present and foreseeable future and, paradoxically, in the past – which means that fascism has to be confirmed as ultimately 'un-European'. To achieve this aim and affirm the continued identification of the West as the space of the 'already', the two aspects of Western domination – US military force and European human rights commitment – have increasingly intersected since the early 1990s. 'Humanitarian' NATO interventions in the First Gulf War and the Kosovo conflict and succeeding international war crimes tribunals suggested that waging war and protecting human rights are not only not mutually exclusive but in fact might need to go together.

These contemporary operations, I suggest, simultaneously did the work of confirming the dominant version of the past sketched above. The wars were explicitly framed as restagings of World War II – Saddam Hussein was quite unsubtly equated with Hitler and the Serbians with the Nazis (Palmbach and Kempf 1994). While it appears that George Bush Sr first introduced the 'Saddam as Hitler' trope in the debate around the Gulf War,[10] it was soon picked up by parts of a German Left suffering from a profound identity crisis after the end of (state) socialism and national reunification, both of which were widely seen as a triumph of capitalism and conservative political forces. The uneasiness with the new status quo produced a return to the key moment of modern German history: National Socialist rule, which both implied a moment of moral superiority of the Left and the moment of its biggest failure. The Gulf War in many ways became the foil for the reorientation of the German (and European) Left and its division into two camps, both of which justified their contemporary position by directly referencing Nazi Germany – and by projecting it into the present and outside of Europe (Schmid 2006). Those protesting against the US intervention did so under the heading 'Nie wieder Krieg!' (never again war!), referencing a German pacifist movement going back to World War I and revived in the Easter March movement of the 1960s. Supporters of the US countered with 'Nie wieder Auschwitz!' (never again Auschwitz!) – picking up the 'Saddam is Hitler' line and identifying the destruction of Israel as the ultimate goal of a process begun with the invasion of Kuwait (Schmid 2006). The latter claim moved beyond Bush's initial use of the comparison, which was meant to present Saddam Hussein as committing atrocities necessitating NATO's intervention on 'humanitarian' grounds, to arguing that Saddam Hussein was intentionally working on fulfilling the original Hitler's plan of eliminating the Jews (Bruhn and Ebermann 1991).

The instrumentalisation of the conflict in the Middle East by both the so-called anti-imperialists and anti-nationalists (later 'anti-Germans') has been analysed elsewhere and is not of key relevance here (see Palmbach and Kempf 1994; Schmid 2006). What is relevant, however, is its contribution to the notion that the end of the Cold War and of state socialism had produced a vacuum that was in acute danger of being filled by 'new Hitlers' if the West was not vigorously alert. This argument was expressed most succinctly by Hans Magnus Enzensberger in a February 1991 piece for the German news magazine *Der Spiegel* entitled 'Hitlers Wiedergänger' (Hitler's Revenants). Enzensberger, one of Germany's most influential literary figures, identified the insistence on the singularity of National Socialist crimes as morally rather than intellectually justified. That is, it had been effective in suppressing comparisons that were meant primarily to minimise the Holocaust. Now, however, a situation had occurred in which the comparison was not only justified but evident. Presenting a small set of criteria, Enzensberger proceeds to make his case, first identifying Saddam Hussein as an enemy of mankind, bent on total destruction – if need be of the whole world, including his own people – then pointing to the obvious parallel with Hitler, mortal enemy of not only Jews, Russians, or Americans, but also Germans. This leads Enzensberger to his second point of comparison: today's Iraqis are presented as the Germans of 1933 to 1945. Moving quickly from Iraq to the Arab world in general, he identifies an overwhelming collective murderous frenzy/death wish and concludes: 'Despite their very different circumstances, his followers are motivated by impulses identical to those of our fathers and grandfathers and they have the same goal. This continuity proves that we are dealing here not with a German or an Arab, but with an anthropological reality.'[11] Following the internalist storyline to the letter, Enzensberger sees Arabs as living through the German past and extrapolates from that a particularly German ability to know what needs to be done – or rather, the responsibility of the minority of Germans aware of the historical lessons to point out that appeasement is never a successful strategy with Hitlers/enemies of mankind.[12]

The move away from the singularity of German crimes against humanity, achieved through postulating a 'legitimate' comparable case (with potentially equally disastrous consequences, averted only by a swift allied reaction to the rise of the new Hitler), can be considered an important step towards a 'normalisation' of post-unification Germany within a continental union that had allied itself politically and militarily with the remaining superpower (the USA). That it was not the last step became evident in 1999 during the mobilisation for the NATO intervention in Kosovo, this time with German military participation. The discursive shift since the Gulf War allowed decision makers like Joschka Fischer, whose position as Foreign Minister confirmed the very success of the peace movement in Germany, to justify the Bundeswehr's first combat mission by explicitly connecting World War II, the Holocaust, and Serbian rule in Kosovo.[13] This was arguably made easier by the location of the conflict. The Balkans frequently function as Europe's internal Other. As such the region historically signifies a barbarism that not only lurks beyond the continental borders but lingers within (Atanasoski 2013). Thus the region gained particular importance as a site that can and must be fully integrated into Europe/the West in order for the latter to control its own demons and successfully project them on to the racialised outside.

While the former Yugoslavia was located outside the Soviet sphere of influence, strictly speaking, its collapse became symptomatic of the threat of 'Balkanisation' facing Europe after the fall of the USSR, a threat whose containment exemplified the new world order. The NATO intervention in Kosovo appeared as the ideal illustration of the methods and values of the modern US empire, using precise and therefore 'humane' high tech military interventions to defend a model of civic multiculturalism represented by its own post-civil rights society against a violent, 'barbaric,' proto-fascist racism, exemplified by Serbian 'ethnic cleansing' (Atanasoski 2013). The unambiguous representation, and reading, of this US-led NATO war, the first on European soil, as 'just' and 'humanitarian' fitted within a larger narrative of not only postwar liberal multi-culturalism but also European internalism; both narrative strands supported the contrast of modern, civilised, 'clean' Western technology with messy, chaotic, dirty, violent Eastern/Oriental ethnic violence and thus built on a view of the continent's East that is deeply ingrained in Western thought (see Böröcz 2006).

The duality thus established in turn facilitated the framing of Kosovo as a reenactment of the paradigmatic 'good war', World War II, the newly united post-Cold War Europe allied with the US against a fascist threat that has finally been successfully moved out of Europe's geographical centre to its eastern periphery, where it seemed naturally to belong. The Kosovo intervention thus functioned as an affirmation of US empire that simultaneously connected it to and separated it from its Western successors, exactly because the Balkans are a site that offers both historic continuity and the ability constantly to rewrite the past based on changing contemporary constellations.[14] Here, the pivotal moment represented by the NATO intervention in Kosovo confirmed a narrative of the new post-socialist world shaped by an alliance between a reunited Europe and an American superpower committed to a humanitarian militarism that would reliably prevent a return to the barbarism represented by fascism and communism (and thus could legitimately act without UN authorisation, the latter body having failed in its mission to protect human rights globally). The less than subtle attempt to rewrite Europe's reaction to the rise of Nazism in the present through a narrative in which the allied (NATO) forces this time immediately intervened in order to protect vulnerable minorities was successful enough to produce the ongoing trope of Europe/the West vs. the 'new fascists', potentially worse than the old ones (most explicit in the 'Islamofascism' trope discussed below). These interventions in the present thus confirmed that Europe had successfully contained its past. There were a number of complications, however, most obviously in Germany's changed position: as part of the allied forces this time, and an increasingly central one (Kosovo was the first military engagement of the Bundeswehr, a monumental shift, symbolising Germany's arrival in the West; see Chapters 25 and 26). The realignment of Germany meant, however, that others had to take its historical place. Muslim communities increasingly became those others. While in Bosnia and Kosovo Muslims were the (European) victims of an aggression framed as the new fascism (and even in the first Gulf War, while Saddam appeared as Hitler, Kuwait was represented as Iraq's Poland), since the attacks on New York's World Trade Center (WTC) of 11 September 2001 Islam has emerged as the new (old) enemy of Western civilisation, its characterisation as '21st-century fascism' ('Islamofascism') popularised by western European intellectuals like Bernard-Henri Lévy, Leon de Winter, and Christopher Hitchens (Hitchens 2007).[15]

Muslims, Europe, and Germany

The current focus on Muslims as antithetical to Europe (both as an ideal and as a reality) is often framed as reactive to events in the US (the attacks on the WTC and the subsequent 'war on terror'). If one focuses on developments within western Europe, however, it becomes obvious that the reframing of Muslims as a threat to European core values comparable only to the devastating aggression of Nazi Germany began much earlier, namely after the fall of the Soviet empire and in the context of the resulting move away from the western European social market economy model. While the end of state socialism in the eastern part of the continent meant a harsh transition to a largely unregulated capitalism for many former Warsaw Pact nations, throughout the 1990s the continent's west slowly moved away from a concept of governance that implied a state responsibility to minimise economic and social inequality (see Chapters 10 and 22). That shift meant a sharp rise in temporary employment, cuts in social programmes, unemployment benefits, and health care plans, and a new emphasis on individual responsibility and on the looming destruction of the welfare state by irresponsible and undeserving groups, which were identified first as migrants in general and then more specifically as the continent's Muslim community. This is strikingly exemplified by the success of Thilo Sarrazin's 2010 book, *Deutschland schafft sich ab* (*Germany Does Away with Itself*). Sarrazin's bestseller follows the model of linear historical progress to an extent that could almost appear satirical. The author, a former Bundesbank board member and leading SPD politician, traces the route of global progress from ancient Egypt through Greece to the Roman Empire, after which development appears to take place only in Europe; Sarrazin omits any Muslim influences when describing Europe's move into modernity and treats Africa as the continent without history. With this the author underscores one of his central points: history shows that some people(s) are more civilised and intelligent than others. Presenting 1950s Germany as an idealised past of national efficiency and self-confidence, Sarrazin moves on to a nightmare scenario, in which plummeting birth rates among authentic German women (and rising rates of single motherhood among those who do reproduce) are contrasted with the excessive fertility of migrants from the Middle East and Africa, migrants who, while being by his account significantly less intelligent and civilised than Germans, are smart enough to know that the welfare state will take care of them, if they can only make it to Germany: 'In particular among the Arabs in Germany, there is a widespread tendency to produce children in order to receive more entitlement transfers, and really, the women, often locked up within the family, barely have anything else to do' ('Insbesondere unter den Arabern in Deutschland ist die Neigung weit verbreitet, Kinder zu zeugen, um mehr Sozialtransfers zu bekommen, und die in der Familie oft eingesperrten Frauen haben im Grunde ja kaum etwas anderes zu tun', Sarrazin 2010: 150; my English translation).

The factual dismantling of a system that defined western Europe's identity – capitalist yet socially responsible; guaranteeing individual freedoms yet defined by a sense of shared responsibility for the community; competitive yet caring; non-interventionist yet committed to global human rights – created a crisis that was solved by a discursive scapegoating of the continent's Muslim population. The projection of a reactionary identity on to Muslims on the one hand allowed the reaffirmation of Western liberal ideals in crisis, on the other justified the move away from exactly those ideals through the claim that excessive liberalism, multiculturalism, and state support for minorities had enabled reactionary, anti-democratic, misogynist, homophobic, non-white, non-Western Muslim groups to threaten the liberal West much more than economic neoliberalism ever could (El-Tayeb 2012). The newly discovered fundamental 'foreignness' not of immigrants but of the already present and established Muslim minority was used to manage this 'sacrificial crisis' of European liberalism.[16] I argue that the discursive shift towards World War II fulfils a function similar to earlier debates around hijab and honour killings in normalising what is conceived of as 'properly' European by defining it against Europe's Muslims, while also confirming the inclusion of the EU in a system of (neo)liberal multiculturalisms and of Germany within this neoliberal Europe. The shift in focus cut short a belated and hesitant exploration of widespread collaboration in German-occupied nations during World War II and its root in a Europe-wide anti-Semitism, an exploration that has been repressed rather than facilitated with the post-1989 transnationalisation of European memory. The trope of Muslim anti-Semitism reconfigures white, Christian Europe as the saviour, not prosecutor of the Jewish minority, stabilising the narrative of a Judeo-Christian European past/inside, challenged constantly by Muslim outsiders. European anti-Semitism thus appears not as structural and ongoing but as a historically contained aberration, and the recent focus on 're-educating' already deviant Muslim male youths confirms that this past has been overcome (Partridge 2010). In its European variation, Santayana's famous 'Those who cannot remember the past are condemned to repeat it' (Santayana 1905: 284) condemns those configured as non-European to repeat the continent's past, unless Europe prevents that through humanitarian interventions or re-education.

The trope, which gained momentum just a few years after nations like France and the Netherlands had finally begun to address their history of collaboration and anti-Semitism during the German occupation, presents Europe as victimised by an external totalitarianism (in which fascism and Stalinism become largely equivalent). It is complemented by the discourse on the internal threat of 'Islamofascism' and anti-Semitism embodied by the continent's Muslim communities. The localisation of anti-Semitism in a discernible group that is already excluded from membership in society allows that society to engage in symbolic condemnations that affirm the innocence of the majority and frame disciplining as the only possible response. Diana Pinto, for example, historian and senior fellow at the Institute for Jewish Policy Research in London, makes a revisionist claim for the existence of a Muslim anti-Semitism that absolves the majority from responsibility while pitting minorities against each other (in part by drawing on racist stereotypes):

> The old anti-Semitism came from above, from the elites, and was used to mobilise the
> lower classes. The people who destroyed synagogues in 1938 did that on orders and had
> wives at home who ironed their brown shirts. The new anti-Semitism comes from below,

from aggressive thugs with a violent potential that is directed towards Jews but not limited to them [. . .]. Over the last ten years, Jew-hatred has been growing among blacks too. It is based on arguments such as: 'Enough of the Holocaust! Our ancestors suffered under slavery; which lasted longer and cost more lives than the Holocaust. That is what we want to talk about!' Black anti-Semitism is lower in numbers than its Muslim counterpart, but is much more violent.

(cited in Schmidt 2008: 14; my translation)[17]

This perception of Muslim anti-Semitism as more aggressive and pervasive than either 'the old anti-Semitism' or that of the contemporary European far right has been gaining traction and seems to have shaped the responses to the brutal beating in August 2012 of a Berlin rabbi, who identified his tormentors as 'Arab-looking youths'. Comments quickly focused on this aspect: in a statement, the director of the antiracist Amadeu Antonio Foundation claimed that it was 'unfortunately mostly young migrants' who were responsible for physical attacks on Jews, and while she hastened to emphasise that growing anti-Semitism was also a problem of 'German society', the tone had been set and the source of the problem was located among 'migrants' (this almost always referenced youths born and raised in Germany), notwithstanding the fact that the vast majority of anti-Semitic attacks, physical, verbal, and symbolic, are committed by the German radical right.[18] The public reaction configured 'Muslim anti-Semitism' as both the same as and worse than historic German anti-Semitism (thereby erasing the latter's survival into the present) and thus as a(nother) lethal threat to the continent posed by culturally and racially foreign minorities. This in turn allows for the disciplining in the name of state antiracism of an already marginalised community, constantly asked either to subject itself to forms of re-education or face the threat of expulsion. Echoing Pinto, the discourse presents 'migrant' anti-Semitism as more dangerous and excessive, indicating that the very presence of these racialised youths is already seen as excess.

The assumption that anti-Semitism among second-generation 'migrant' youths (i.e. youths born and raised in Germany) is caused by their 'foreign' (i.e. Muslim) cultural background and is thus a sign of failed integration ignores the existence of anti-Semitic structures within the dominant society (and the possibility of those being a source of minority anti-Semitism). It also ignores the connections between anti-Semitism and other forms of racism, often directed against these very youths. Positioning Jews and Muslims as antagonists, with majority Germans and the state standing in as mediators educating and controlling Muslims, discursively erases the similarities in the 'racing' of religion directed at both Jews and Muslims as non-Christian minorities – a focus that would place the problem squarely within the dominant Christian(ised) society. Holding Muslims responsible for anti-Semitism also hides the fact that the majority of anti-Semitic acts (and, arguably, anti-Semitic sentiment) can be traced to majoritarian Germans simultaneously holding anti-Semitic, racist, and Islamophobic beliefs – all of which are on the rise in Europe. Instead of addressing the increasing normalisation of racist beliefs and acts across the continent, the crisis of (neo)liberal multiculturalism is thus localised among the population already made most vulnerable by it through economic marginalisation and political disempowerment. Through this culturalist framing of economic exclusions in post-industrial Europe, class is not only racialised but also (de)nationalised, placing an ethnicised underclass literally outside the nation, stigmatised as deviant and dangerous through discourses around hijab, honour killings, and terrorism.

The absence of explicit, state-sanctioned discourses on race in Europe is too often read as a sign that race does not matter there. But (western) Europe shares the spatio-temporality of liberal capitalist modernity and moves within the same system of knowledge production that controls what is a legitimate 'race matter'[19] – and in Europe (almost) nothing is: the continental European discursive and political system is not one that is constructed as managing differently raced populations, but one that, implicitly, marks racialised populations as non-citizens rather than second-class citizens. This makes 'xenophobia' the only officially recognised, albeit inappropriate framework to address violence against them. This means that the racialised individual is recognisable as a rational target only when perceived as a migrant, stranger, non-citizen. The current consensus on the 'failure of multiculturalism', which is blamed on the inability of 'immigrants,' of the third or fourth generation, to live up to European standards – standards to which they remain completely external – is an expression of this assumption. The economic, social, and political marginalisation of, in particular, European Muslim communities is not deemed a worthy subject of antiracism, since these communities failed to subscribe to the European project of liberal multiculturalism and are therefore not only responsible for their marginalised state but have in fact failed 'Europeanness'. Of course, it was never possible for them to pass, as racialised communities are simultaneously forced to affirm their otherness if they want the state to protect them from violence and to deny this otherness in order to become legitimate multicultural subjects who can lay claim to (potentially) belonging to the community of citizens.[20] The seeming consensus on the end of multiculturalism can also be understood, however, as a sign of the end of exactly this imaginary European monoculturalism. In other words, the growing centrality of the migrant as internal threat to Europe might be read as caused by and at the same time hiding an important change: the continent-wide shift to a 'migrant' population that is increasingly minoritarian, consisting of the so-called second and third generations, born and raised in their countries of residence – countries which have, in effect, become multi-ethnic and multi-religious.

Notes

1 While Jews arguably became 'European' post-World War II, the increasingly popular reference to Europe's Judeo-Christian identity, primarily evoked in response to the disruption represented by the contemporary Muslim presence, works discursively to erase the exclusion and persecution of the racialised Jewish minority by the Christian majority that characterised much of Europe's 'Judeo-Christian' history (see Schmidt 2008).

2 In addition, there are specific concepts such as the Dutch 'allochton', referencing those who are Dutch citizens by birth but not entirely of 'autochthonous' Dutch parentage; in practice this is applied to Dutch citizens of colour. The recent German category 'Bürger mit Migrationshintergrund' (citizen with migrant background) similarly turns migration into a pseudo-cultural identity category differentiating between 'real' and second-class Europeans (see El-Tayeb 2011).

3 See also British Prime Minister David Cameron's similar statements a few months later (Cameron 2011).

4 See Fabian (1983). Currently, the Muslim world is represented as 'medieval' (based, of course, on Europe's, not the Middle East's, 'Middle Ages'), while Africa is still frequently placed within the Stone Age.

5 The UK, where there is rather more acknowledgment of historical ethnic and religious diversity, cannot be seen as representative here.

6 The *Historikerstreit* of the mid-1980s likely represents the first sustained attempt to 'normalise' the German past by externalising fascist rule as essentially 'un-European' (more specifically as 'Asiatic' in nature and Stalinist in its political formation). See Nolan (1988).

7 See the German Ministry for Family, Seniors, Women and Youth's 'Vielfalt tut gut' (Diversity is good) initiative for an overview of projects directed at east German and Muslim youths: http://www.dji.de/index.php?id=1459&L=0&print=1 (accessed 8 October 2014).

8 Conversely, as Damani Partridge concludes about official German strategies of commemoration: 'contemporary monumentalisation of, and distancing from Holocaust memory is necessary for contemporary modes of normalised racial exclusion' (Partridge 2010: 821).

9 The recent case for reparations brought by the Caricom nations against France, the Netherlands, and the UK for the slave trade and the genocide of indigenous populations in the Caribbean attempts to change that; see Fox (2013).

10 Bush used the Hitler comparison to claim that the atrocities committed in Kuwait by invading Iraqi soldiers were actually 'worse than what Hitler would have done' (Wette 2003).

11 My translation.

12 Enzensberger's text can be read as an early example of what Jacques Rancière identified as the 'ethical turn of aesthetics and politics', that is 'a reversal of the flow of time: time turned towards the end to be realised – progress, emancipation, or the other – is replaced by time turned towards the catastrophe that is behind us. And it is also a leveling of the very forms of that catastrophe. The extermination of European Jews then appears as the explicit form of a global situation, which also characterises the everyday of our democratic and liberal existence' (Rancière 2006: 9). In a second step, this reversal allows for the postulation of a consensus on human rights that justifies infinite justice/violence against those, and only those, who position themselves as 'enemies of mankind'.

13 Explicitly referencing the earlier rift within the German Left, now threatening to split the Green Party, Fischer stated: 'Auschwitz is unique. But I, I have two principles: Never again war, never again Auschwitz, never again genocide, never again fascism, both belong together for me' ('Auschwitz ist unvergleichbar. Aber in mir – ich stehe auf zwei Grundsätzen: Nie wieder Krieg, nie wieder Auschwitz; nie wieder Völkermord, nie wieder Faschismus: beides gehört bei mir zusammen,' Fischer 1999).

14 Compare Barack Obama's remarks on the occasion of US troop withdrawal from Iraq: 'That's part of what makes us special as Americans. Unlike the old empires, we don't make these sacrifices for territory or for resources. We do it, because it's right' (White House 2011).

15 The genealogy of the term 'Islamofascism' is not entirely clear. Christopher Hitchens traces it back to Anglo-Irish writer Malise Ruthven in 1990 (Hitchens 2007). Probably not surprisingly, the Islamo-fascism argument was picked up especially eagerly by French and Dutch intellectuals. Both nations had seen painful discussions on World War II collaboration during the 1990s; in addition, the Netherlands faced a national crisis after the failure of Dutchbat, the country's UN contingent stationed in Srebrenica, in Bosnia-Herzegovina, to prevent the slaughter of Muslim men and mass rape of Muslim women by Serbian troops in 1995. The proponents of the 'Islamofascism' meme tend, like Enzensberger, to identify a set of criteria 'proving' the fundamental sameness of radical Islam and fascism, though unlike him they see the cause of this affinity in the nature of Islam rather than in human nature. See, for example, Hitchens:

> Both movements are based on a cult of murderous violence that exalts death and destruction and despises the life of the mind. ('Death to the intellect! Long live death!' as General Francisco Franco's sidekick Gonzalo Queipo de Llano so pithily phrased it.) Both are hostile to modernity (except when it comes to the pursuit of weapons), and both are bitterly nostalgic for past empires and lost glories. Both are obsessed with real and imagined 'humiliations' and thirsty for revenge. Both are chronically infected with the toxin of anti-Jewish paranoia (interestingly, also, with its milder cousin, anti-Freemason paranoia). Both are inclined to leader worship and to the exclusive stress on the power of one great book. Both have a strong commitment to sexual repression – especially to the repression of any sexual 'deviance' – and to its counterparts the subordination of the female and contempt for the feminine. Both despise art and literature as symptoms of degeneracy and decadence; both burn books and destroy museums and treasures. (Hitchens 2007)

Moving beyond the propagandistic use of the term Islamofascism, academic interest in collaborations between Nazis and 'the Arab world' has exploded since 9/11 (see Nordbruch 2012). While varying in their conclusions, a majority of these studies focus on Muslim Nazi sympathisers like Amin al-Husayni, the Mufti of Jerusalem, while paying little or no attention to Nazi influence on the Syrian Social Nationalist party or the Lebanese Phalangists, both founded in the 1930s by Christian Arabs and both still active today (see e.g. Herf 2009; Berman 2003).

16 See Bonnie Honig: 'A scapegoat is a figure made to represent some taint borne by the community as a whole, in particular, the loss of distinctions that defines the sacrificial crisis from which the community is trying to recover. The attribution of that taint to a scapegoat allows the community to unanimously disavow it, and the ritual murder of the scapegoat cleanses the community and reestablishes the lines of proper order that had become so dangerously attenuate' (Honig 2001: 34).

17 The reactions to black French comedian Dieudonné, whose performances have been repeatedly banned, seem to illustrate this dynamic, in which anti-Semitic acts by black and Muslim Europeans are perceived as more extreme and threatening not because of their extreme quality but because of the positionality of the perpetrators. There is no doubt that Dieudonné's comedy routines use crude anti-Semitism, but they do not necessarily seem 'much more violent' than others, including those coming from the French far right (to which Dieudonné has grown increasingly close over the course of the last decade); rather what sets them apart is their explicit reliance on the concept referenced by Pinto above, that is, Dieudonné's contrasting of Holocaust commemorations with the lack of attention to the impact of the histories of slavery and colonisation. This is characterised by Michael Rothberg in a much more careful analysis as 'competitive memory', which 'assume[s] that the public sphere in which collective memories are articulated is a scarce resource and that the interaction of different collective memories within that sphere takes the form of a zero-sum struggle for preeminence' (Rothberg 2009: 3). While Rothberg rightly points to the shortfalls of such an approach, it must be conceded that dominant European memory discourses tend to enforce this competitive model (Partridge 2010). The source of one recent scandal around Dieudonné is a tasteless song parodying Holocaust commemoration, 'Shoananas'. What remains unmentioned in mainstream critiques, but no doubt is not lost on many of his fans, is the song's original version, Annie Cordy's 'Chaud cacao', one of many examples of a casual French racism that is not even registered as such (Ball 2014; Cassely 2013).

18 According to the German government, in 2012, there were 865 recorded anti-Semitic incidents, 27 of them violent ('Gewaltdelikte'). Of these, 820, including 23 violent incidents, were committed by perpetrators categorised as extreme right; 26, including four violent ones, by migrants (including Germans 'of migrant background'). Categories used to identify perpetrators are 'extreme right', 'extreme left', 'migrant', and 'others.' The numbers are based on the quarterly inquiry by parliarmentarians from *Die Linke*. More than half of the inquiry is devoted to a discussion of Muslim anti-Semitism and anti-Zionism (see http://www.petrapau.de/17bundestag/ dok/down/2012_zf_antisemitische_straftaten. pdf). Based on these numbers, it seems safe to say that claims to the particular aggressiveness and pervasiveness of migrant or Muslim anti-Semitism are on shaky ground. 2012 was also the year when, after moral panics around oppressed Muslim women and homophobic and violent Muslim youths, the latest iteration of threatening Muslim Otherness emerged in the so-called *Beschneidungsdebatte* on whether circumcision of Muslim (and Jewish) boys violates human rights and should thus be outlawed. The debate overshadowed both the continuing revelations about the Nationalsozialistischer Untergrund, a white supremacist group that committed at least 10 racist murders, eight of which targeted Muslim men, and the 20-year commemorations of the 1992 Mölln arson attack, which cost the lives of three Turkish Germans and injured nine (Çetin, Voß, and Wolter 2012).

19 While white supremacy endorsed and justified racial hierarchies, state antiracism does not deny or excuse the existence of inequality, but instead defines which forms of inequality deserve recognition and correction:

> By controlling what counts as race matter, an antiracist goal, or a truism about racial difference, official antiracisms have structured legitimate knowledges in the domains of law, public policy, economy, and culture. In a society in which normative power is pervasive, control over the means of rationality is as important as, if not more important than, control over other social forces. (Melamed 2011: 16)

20 See, for example, the recent attempt to strike the term 'race' from French laws. Meant to reflect France's supposedly 'colourblind' approach, such a move does nothing to prevent racism; on the contrary, it limits the ability even to discuss it. In Germany, it was only in 2012 that a higher court, overturning earlier decisions, confirmed that the police cannot legally practise racial profiling when looking for 'illegal immigrants' or 'Islamist terrorists' (the state had argued that 'dark skin' was a reasonable marker in identifying both groups); see Rath 2012.

Bibliography

Atanasoski, N. (2013) *Humanitarian Violence. The US Deployment of Diversity*, Minneapolis: University of Minnesota Press.

Ball, S. (2014) 'Dieudonné: from anti-racist to anti-Semitic zealot', *France24*, 6 January. Online. Available at www.france24.com/en/20140104-dieudonne-anti-racist-anti-semitic-zealot/ (accessed January 7, 2014).

Benhabib, S. and Post, R. (2006) *Another Cosmopolitanism: Hospitality, Sovereignty and Democratic Iterations*, Oxford: Oxford University Press.

Berman, P. (2003) *Terror and Liberalism*. New York: W.W. Norton.

Böröcz, J. (2006) 'Goodness is Elsewhere: The Rule of European Difference', *Comparative Studies in Society and History*, 48(1): 110–37.

Boyer, D. (2006) 'Ostalgie and the Politics of the Future in Eastern Germany', *Public Culture*, 18(2): 361–81.

Bruckner, P. (2007) 'Enlightenment fundamentalism or racism of the anti-racists?', Perlentaucher 27 January. Online. Available at www.signandsight.com/features/1146.html (accessed 10 April 2013).

Bruhn, J. and Ebermann, T. (1991) 'Der Golfkrieg, die Linke und der Tod', *Arbeiterkampf*, 331: 34–6.

Bunzl, M. (2005) 'Between Anti-Semitism and Islamophobia: Some Thoughts on the New Europe', *American Ethnologist* 32(4): 499–508.

Cameron, D. (2011) 'PM's Speech at Munich Security Conference', 5 February. Online. Available at http://webarchive.nationalarchives.gov.uk/20130109092234/http://number10.gov.uk/news/pms-speech-at-munich-security-conference/ (accessed 10 January 2014).

Carras, C. (2013) 'Europe poised between union and hegemony', 10 April. Online. Available at www.opendemocracy.net/costa-carras/europe-poised-between-union-and-hegemony (accessed 10 April 2013).

Cassely, J.-L. (2013) 'La dieudonnisation des esprits, une (grosse) quenelle qui vient d'en bas,' *Slate France*, 28 December. Online. Available at www.slate.fr/story/74429/ dieudonne-quenelle (accessed 7 January 2014).

Çetin, Z., Voß, H.-J., and Wolter, S.A. (2012) *Interventionen gegen die deutsche 'Beschneidungsdebatte'*, Berlin: Edition Assemblage.

Conolly, K. (2010) 'Angela Merkel declares death of German multiculturalism', *The Guardian*, 18 October. Online. Available at http://www.theguardian.com/world/2010/oct/17/angela-merkel-germany-multiculturalism-failures (accessed 25 January 2014)

Eder, A. (ed.) (2003) *'Wir sind auch da!' Über das Leben von und mit Migranten in europäischen Großstädten*, Munich: Dölling und Galitz.

El-Tayeb, F. (2001) *Schwarze Deutsche: Der Diskurs um 'Rasse' und nationale Identität, 1890–1933*, Frankfurt a.m.: Campus.

El-Tayeb, F. (2011) *European Others: Queering Ethnicity in Postnational Europe*, Minneapolis: University of Minnesota Press.

El-Tayeb, F. (2012) '"Gays who cannot properly be gay": Queer Muslims in the neoliberal European city', *European Journal of Women's Studies*, February, 19(1): 79–95.

Enzensberger, H.M. (1991) 'Hitlers Wiedergänger', *Der Spiegel*, 4 February, 26–8.

European Commission Directorate-General for Employment and Social Affairs (2004) *The Situation of Roma in an Enlarged European Union*, Luxembourg: Office for Official Publications of the European Communities.

Fabian, J. (1983) *Time and the Other: How Anthropology Makes Its Object*, New York: Columbia University Press.

Fischer, J. (1999) 'Rede auf dem Außerordentlichen Parteitag der Grünen in Bielefeld, 13.5.99'. Online. Available at http://staff-www.uni-marburg.de/~naeser/kos-fisc.htm (accessed 14 December 2013).

Fox, B. (2013) 'Caribbean Countries Seek Slavery Reparations from Three European Countries', *The Grio*, 25 July. Online. Available at http://the grio.com/2013/07/25/caribbean-countries-seek-slavery-reparations-from-three-europen-countries/ (accessed 7 December 2013).

Friedrich, T. and Schürmann, H. (2008) 'Jeder ein Hitler', *Der Tagesspiegel*, 27 September. Online. Available at www.tagesspiegel.de/politik/geschichte/nazivergleich-jeder-ein-hitler/1334614.html (accessed 7 December 2013).

Georgi, V.B. and Ohliger, R. (2009) *Crossover Geschichte: Historisches Bewusstsein Jugendlicher in der Einwanderungsgesellschaft*, Hamburg: Körber-Stiftung.

Hall, S. (1991) 'Europe's Other Self', *Marxism Today* (August), 18–19.

Hecking, C. (2013) 'Secret Thatcher Notes: Kohl Wanted Half of Turks Out of Germany', *Spiegel Online International*, 1 August. Available at www.spiegel.de/international/germany/secret-minutes-chancellor-kohl-wanted-half-of-turks-out-of-germany-a-914376.html (accessed 7 January 2014).

Herf, J. (2009) *Nazi Propaganda for the Arab World*, New Haven: Yale University Press.

Hitchens, C. (2007) 'Defending Islamofascism', *Slate*, 22 October. Online. Available at www.slate.com/articles/news_and_politics/fighting_words/2007/10/defending_islamofascism.html (accessed 7 December 2013).

Honig, B. (2001) *Democracy and the Foreigner*, Princeton: Princeton University Press.

Isaacson, W. (1989) 'Is One Germany Better Than Two?' *Time*, 20 November, 36.

Keaton, T. (2006) *Muslim Girls and the Other France: Race, Identity Politics and Social Exclusion*, Bloomington, IN: Indiana University Press.

Melamed, J. (2011) Represent and Destroy: Rationalizing Violence in the New Racial Capitalism, Minneapolis: University of Minnesota.

Nolan, M. (1988) 'The Historikerstreit and Social History' (special issue), *New German Critique*, 44: 51–80.

Nordbruch, G. (2012) 'The Arab World and National Socialism – Some reflections on an ambiguous relationship', in M. Sing (ed.) *Rethinking Totalitarianism and its Arab Readings*. Online. Available at www.perspectivia.net/content/publikationen/orient-institut-studies/1–2012/nordbruch_arab-world (accessed 9 January 2014).

Özyürek, E. (2005) 'The Politics of Cultural Unification, Secularism, and the Place of Islam in the New Europe', *American Ethnologist*, 32(4): 509–12.

Palmbach, U. and Kempf, W. (1994) 'Die Konstruktion des Feindbildes Saddam', in W. Kempf (ed.) *Manipulierte Wirklichkeiten: Medienpsychologische Untersuchungen der bundesdeutschen Berichterstattung im Golfkrieg*, Münster: LIT-Verlag, 58–81.

Partridge, D. (2010) 'Holocaust Mahnmal (Memorial): Racial Memory Amidst Contemporary Race', *Comparative Studies in Society and History*, 52(4): 820–50.

Povinelli, E. (2011) *Economies of Abandonment: Social Belonging and Endurance in Late Liberalism*, Durham, NC: Duke University Press.

Rancière, J. (2006) 'The Ethical Turn of Aesthetics and Politics', *Critical Horizons*, 7: 1–20.

Rath, C. (2012) 'Urteil zu Kontrollen nach Hautfarbe: Gericht verbietet Polizei-Rassismus', *die tageszeitung*, 30 October. Online. Available at www.taz.de/Urteil-zu-Kontrollen-nach-Hautfarbe/!104549/ (accessed 23 November 2013).

Reddy, C. (2011) *Freedom with Violence: Race, Sexuality, and the US State*, Durham, NC: Duke University Press.

Rothberg, M. (2009) *Multidirectional Memory: Remembering the Holocaust in the Age of Decolonization*, Stanford, CA: Stanford University Press.

Ruz, G. (2006) 'Why 'Islamofascism' May Create New US Enemies', *npr*, 31 October. Online. Available at www.npr.org/templates/story/stry.php?storyId=6412169 (accessed 7 December 2013).

Santayana, G. (1905) *The Life of Reason*, volume 1, New York: Dover.

Sarrazin, T. (2010) *Deutschland schafft sich ab: Wie wir unser Land aufs Spiel setzen*, Munich: Deutsche Verlags-Anstalt.

Schmid, B. (2006) 'Der Nahe Osten als Projektionsfläche', *LabourNet Germany*, 19 August. Online. Available at http://labournet.de/krieg/nahost/projektion.html (accessed 7 January 2014).

Schmidt, J. (2008) 'Der neue Antisemitismus in Frankreich kommt von unten: Die Historikerin Diana Pinto über die Ängste französischer Juden, extremistische Imame und religiöse Bandenkriege in Paris', *Süddeutsche Zeitung*, 18 July, 14.

Šenoçak, Z. (2000) *Atlas of a Tropical Germany: Essays on Politics and Culture, 1990–1998*, trans. and ed. L. Adelson, Lincoln: University of Nebraska Press.

Suleiman, S.R. (2006) *Crises of Memory and the Second World War*, Boston: Harvard University Press.

Wette, W. (2003) 'Wem der Vergleich Saddam Husseins mit Adolf Hitler dient', *Frankfurter Rundschau*, 29 March, 1.

White House, Office of the Press Secretary (2011) 'Remarks by the President and First Lady on the End of the War in Iraq', 14 December. Online. Available at www.whitehouse.gov/the-press-office/2011/12/14/remarks-president-and-first-lady-end-war-iraq (accessed 21 August 2013).

19

The place of Europe in contemporary German film

Paul Cooke

Film plays an important role in Germany. In recent years the nation's films have enjoyed enormous critical and commercial success both at home and abroad. The first half of 2013 saw a rise in the number of people going to the cinema to almost 63 million, the highest ever recorded in the country, generating profits of almost €500 million (again a national record), with around 27 per cent of ticket sales going to German films, an increase of almost 10 per cent on 2012 (FFA 2013). Internationally, the last two decades have seen German productions become regular guests at all the major film festivals, from Sundance to Tokyo, winning awards across the globe. As reviewers are keen to point out, the industry appears once again to be reaching the aesthetic heights that brought it the praise of critics internationally from the late 1960s to the early 1980s. Cinematic success is helping to cement a wider shift in the international perception of Germany, and is an element in its growing 'soft power'.

Commentators agree that the film and cultural industries frequently play a key role in a country's international standing, and thus the influence it can wield (Nye 2004). Film has helped to communicate to the world how Germany continues to reflect critically upon its troubled history, thereby reinforcing the nation's democratic credentials. Historical dramas have tended to be the most successful internationally: if one looks at the German-language films that have either been nominated for, or have won, the 'Best Foreign Language' Oscar since 2000, from Caroline Link's World War II drama *Nowhere in Africa* (*Nirgendwo in Afrika,* 2001) to Florian Henckel von Donnersmarck's GDR conspiracy thriller *The Lives of Others* (*Das Leben der Anderen,* 2006), they have almost without exception been historical dramas, the majority exploring the legacy of the Holocaust and National Socialism. In the films, that period in German history marks a moment of rupture for the nation, which ultimately informs a foundational myth for the present-day Berlin Republic. Indeed, the Holocaust is often presented as a foundational myth for the entire European Union, as we shall see in this chapter, which explores how the film funding landscape in Germany shapes the types of films the country makes, and particularly how those films reflect the nature of the country's relationship with the rest of Europe. That can be seen in a wide range of films, from the big-budget historical epics, which often rely on European funding and sometimes appear to have little to do with that period in history per se, to smaller-scale productions that explore critically the issues facing contemporary German society as the country continues to negotiate its place in the world.

European history and the 'europudding'

It is 16th-century France during the Wars of Religion. Medium shot: Henry of Navarre (played by Julien Boisselier) gallops on horseback across our screen against the bucolic background of a hilltop meadow at dusk. He is followed by three of his closest comrades, the whole group bathed in golden light, accompanied by a non-diegetic soundtrack of swelling strings and an off-screen voice quietly reciting a verse on the transcendent wisdom of God's love. We have just seen Henry escape the violent, claustrophobic, and self-destructive decadence of the French court, where his Huguenot countrymen have been slaughtered for their religious faith during the St Bartholomew's Day massacre, a bloodbath depicted in all its epic proportions. He has returned to his homeland, declaring his intention to rebuild this corner of France according to the values of religious tolerance, community, and social responsibility, values we will see him use to create a unified French nation.

This scene is the centrepiece of Jo Baier's historical epic *Henry of Navarre* (*Henri 4*, 2010), a film that offers a useful starting point for a discussion of the place of Europe in contemporary German film, in terms both of the cultural role played by concepts of Europe and Europeanness on Germany's screens and the pragmatics of film production for the domestic industry. *Henri 4* is a €19 million co-production, supported mainly by a range of German funds, but also by Austria, France, Spain, and the MEDIA programme of the EU. It was almost 10 years in the making, and was the idea of Regina Ziegler, one of Germany's most successful producers, who also invested heavily in the project. Ziegler had long been fascinated by the story of Henry of Navarre, which she discovered as a young woman when she read Heinrich Mann's fictional biography of the French king (*Die Jugend des Königs Henri Quatre/Young Henry of Navarre*, 1935, and *Die Vollendung des Königs Henri Quatre/Henry, King of France*, 1938), written by Mann while in exile in France from Nazi Germany. She bought the rights in 2001 and commissioned Baier, one of Germany's best-known directors of historical dramas for television (*Der Laden/The Shop*, 1998; *Stauffenberg*, 2004), to write the screenplay and direct.

This was intended to be a high-prestige project, with a budget far in excess of those for most domestically produced films, which are generally less than €5 million (Castendyk 2008: 114). It was, Ziegler insists, 'a Babylonian project', a 'pan-European film to defy Hollywood' ('ein babylonisches Projekt', '[ein] gesamteuropäische[r] Film, der Hollywood Paroli bieten kann'), which would herald the return to the big screen for both the director and the producer after decades working in television (Beier 2010). It involved a number of well-regarded actors, including Hannelore Hoger, Joachim Król, Devid Striesow, and Karl Markovics, as well as a very experienced crew. Ziegler also brought in Gernot Roll, a cinematographer who has worked on several high-profile historical dramas, including Caroline Link's *Nowhere in Africa*, and Hans Zimmer, one of Germany's best-known composers, who has worked in Hollywood for years and won awards for his musical scores on films such as *The Lion King* (Roger Allers, Rob Minkoff, 1994), *Gladiator* (Ridley Scott, 2000), and *Inception* (Christopher Nolan, 2010).

But *Henri 4* was a flop, both critically and commercially. It sold a mere 40,000 tickets on its theatrical release in Germany and achieved only a very limited distribution in other parts of the world. It might well have been one of the biggest financial flops in German film history if it had not also been an 'amphibian film', produced – and presold – to appear on television in an extended version. Many critics considered the film crassly exploitative of the historical material, more focused on depicting graphic violence and the sexual exploits of the young king than on offering a serious engagement with history: 'some of this would be better placed in a Bavarian soft-core porn movie from the early 70s than here' ('Da hätte manches besser ins bayerische Lederhosenkino der frühen 70er gepasst, als zu diesem Stoff'), complained Rüdiger Suchsland

(2010). Perhaps the harshest criticism of all came from those who called the film a 'europudding' (Beier 2010), the pejorative term used to describe a trend in European cultural production, particularly visible in the 1990s, towards films and popular songs that seem to trade national specificity for an insipidly artificial form of 'Europeanness'.

Taking as my starting point the way *Henri 4* was funded, this chapter examines the place of German film in Europe, and the relationship between European funding and the complex network of German national and regional film funding bodies. It examines the aims and values of a variety of schemes and looks at how they have helped to support the increased international visibility of German film since 2000. This provides the context for a discussion of some of the types of films this network of funding has helped to produce. On the one hand, we find German production companies supporting the rise of big-budget blockbusting movies such as *Henri 4* that seem intent, for better or worse, on the production of a pan-European identity based on a common understanding of European history; films that risk dismissal as europuddings. On the other, we find often smaller-scale films that self-consciously interrogate the very type of European identity the europudding seems to propagate.

What does Europe mean for German film? Is it even possible to talk of 'German' film within the transnational context of European film funding? Or does the growing importance of transnational funding streams in fact allow us to explore anew that which is specific to the German film tradition?

Europe and the funding of German film

Germany is very well supported in terms of public funding compared with most other European nations. By the end of the 2000s, German institutions were funding the national film industry to the tune of around €290 million (Castendyk 2008: 66), a level that has only ever been topped by France (Gaitanides 2001; Storm 2000; Rahayel 2006). Indeed, if one looks purely at the funding available to cinema production, this is in fact far in excess of France (Castendyk 2008: 129). How then does the present system work? One of the main differences between the contemporary funding landscape and that of the 1960s–1970s (when German film last made a major impact internationally) is, as Randall Halle has described in detail, the transnational turn in the production and distribution of film globally, evidenced most obviously in the German context when national filmmakers use European subsidy schemes (Halle 2008: 30–59). On the European level there are two main funds available to German production companies, both of which have helped consolidate a culture of transnational co-production across the region: the European Union's Measures to Encourage the Development of the European Audiovisual Industry (MEDIA) and the Council of Europe's EURIMAGES.

Henri 4 was supported by the MEDIA scheme. This was set up in 1990 and has gone through various incarnations with slight changes in focus. Its basic remit has remained the same: to 'strength[en] the competitiveness of the European audiovisual sector' as a global player in the face of Hollywood domination, supporting the production and distribution of a film beyond its country of origin. Its current incarnation, MEDIA 2007, enshrines a commitment both to film as commerce and to film as culture within its foundational parameters, wishing to 'contribut[e] to the spread of a business culture for the sector and facilitat[e] private investment', but also 'to preserve and enhance European cultural diversity' (MEDIA 2007). That said, its focus in practice has been on the development of the commercial industry (Miller *et al.* 2005: 187). The main criticism of MEDIA over the years has been the level of funding available; many have suggested that the Commission, for all its warm words, was not really serious about building up a European film industry (Jäckel 2003: 76). In its present incarnation, MEDIA 2007, which replaced MEDIA PLUS (2001–6), the budget has been increased from €454 million to €755 million. However, this has not only to cover a now greatly expanded EU but, along with the development and distribution work of the previous scheme, to accommodate the MEDIA Training programme, which was previously funded separately.

Of more significance to the aesthetic development of European film (although less significant in purely financial terms) has been the Council of Europe's co-production, distribution, and exhibition fund EURIMAGES (Jäckel 2003: 76), a fund that Germany has made great use of. This scheme was set up in 1989 to support the film industries of those countries that decided to join. These include a number of EU states such as Germany and France (but no longer the UK) as well as many others, including Switzerland, Turkey, and Macedonia. Through EURIMAGES, member states provide an annual budget of €25 million for the production, distribution, exhibition, and digitisation of film. In particular, production companies looking for support are actively encouraged to think transnationally since, to apply for funding, a production must involve at least two participating member states. In 2012 EURIMAGES invested €11 million in 33 productions, of which 11 involved a German production company (EURIMAGES 2013). That said, there is a concern among some of the larger participating countries, including Germany, that the level of return does not warrant their financial investment, projects often receiving very low levels of funding. This is one of the reasons why the UK, for example, decided to leave the scheme (De Vinck 2009: 68).

MEDIA and EURIMAGES have, nonetheless, enjoyed a good deal of international critical success over the years through the projects they have supported, particularly in the 2000s, when the emphasis of the schemes changed from full co-production to the 'lighter touch' co-financing of projects. This, as Belén Vidal notes, has 'opened up new possibilities for collaboration with no cultural strings attached' (Vidal 2012: 64). Instead of large committees needing to be involved in decisions about the artistic direction a film would take in return for a film being financed, individual auteurs were able to put together budgets that would allow them to realise ambitious projects without having to give up artistic autonomy. A good example of this shift can been seen in Michael Haneke's film *The White Ribbon* (*Das weisse Band – Eine deutsche Kindergeschichte*, 2009). This was funded by both MEDIA and EURIMAGES. It won prizes at the European Film Awards, Cannes, and the Golden Globes, and was nominated for the 'Best Foreign Language Film' Oscar. There are numerous other successes that could be mentioned. Lars-Olav Beier points to Lars von Trier's *Antichrist* (2010) – a film that had more than 20 production partners from six European countries – as an example of what can be achieved through transnational European funding schemes. These are the types of films that Germany's former Minister for Culture Christina Weiss calls 'natural co-productions': projects that emerge when a group of funders feels convinced by the strength of the story being told, and simply wishes the filmmaker to be able to realise his or her project (Kirschbaum 2005).

Both Haneke and von Trier are, of course, filmmakers whose work has a clear and successful 'signature' with which funders are unlikely to want to interfere. The schemes have, however, also been criticised for continuing to permit precisely this type of interference. For all MEDIA's stated aim to protect cultural diversity, both schemes (MEDIA and EURIMAGES) continue to be accused of furthering the development of the much-maligned europudding. About a third of the films made by German companies are European co-productions, for which the MEDIA and EURIMAGES schemes have been particularly important, helping to put together budgets that have the best chance of allowing European filmmakers to make the type of large-scale 'spectaculars' that have helped Hollywood dominate international markets for decades. *Henri 4* is a good example of such filmmaking. Although its €19 million budget is still small beer by

Hollywood's standards, it is clearly a film with international aspirations, since these are costs that could never be amortised in any one of the domestic spheres that contributed to its production. *Henri 4* was to show the world the large-scale potential of European film. Although production companies, and funders, are clearly learning from past pan-European productions, in *Henri 4* it is evident that the europudding has not completely disappeared, as we shall see when we look at the film in more detail. The film offers an example of what the German actor Daniel Brühl, who has played roles in films across the continent, defines as 'synthetic' cinema, which tries to create an artificial sense of a joint European project (quoted in Beier 2010). Such films often fail to achieve the transnational distribution that might seem to be built into these projects (as co-productions) almost structurally. Germany was the only country where *Henri 4* got anything like a mainstream release. There are any number of reasons for that, from the film's subject matter to the quality of production, but it is a common failing of European films funded by MEDIA and EURIMAGES and points to a key failure in the schemes, which were set up precisely to facilitate transnational circulation (De Vinck 2009).

However, even if we maintain our focus on its funding, the failure of *Henri 4* cannot be laid solely at the door of MEDIA. The film was supported by a complicated network of national and regional financial sponsors. The German industry actively seeks co-production deals with countries around the world (Jäckel 2003: 64) and currently has over 20 formal international co-production treaties with countries including Australia, Brazil, India, Canada, and New Zealand, as well as with numerous EU member states. The most significant of these is France, from which the *Henri 4* project benefited – although, somewhat surprisingly given the subject matter, not much of it was filmed in France, the production team taking advantage of the cheaper production costs of the Czech Republic. But the majority of the funding was German. On the Federal level, it was supported by the main source of national film support, the *Filmförderungsanstalt* (FFA), set up in the 1960s and paid for by a levy on cinema tickets and, latterly, on the video, DVD and Blu-ray market, along with contributions from the public and private television networks. Another important national source of funding from which *Henri 4* benefited, and which has been instrumental in bringing a number of high-prestige co-productions to Germany, is the *Deutscher Filmförderfonds* (German Federal Film Fund, DFFF). This was set up in January 2007 to replace a tax shelter system that had largely benefited Hollywood productions rather than the domestic industry (Cooke 2012: 45–9); €60 million per year is currently made available to allow the recovery of up to 20 per cent of the costs a production incurs in Germany. After initial fears that this would be just another complicated level of state subsidy, inhibiting rather than mobilising the private capital the government has long claimed it wants to attract into the industry (Fischer 2006; *Vermögen & Steuern* 2006), the DFFF is now overwhelmingly praised. Since 2007 the fund has invested over €200 million in film production and has seen a return on that investment of over €1 billion. The films it has supported include *Valkyrie* (Bryan Singer, 2008), starring Tom Cruise, Stephen Daldry's *The Reader* (2008), Tom Tykwer's *The International* (2009), Quentin Tarantino's *Inglourious Basterds* (2009), and Uli Edel's *The Baader Meinhof Complex* (*Der Baader Meinhof Komplex*, 2008), all of which have helped to make Berlin-Brandenburg's Studio Babelsberg one of the most successful European studios, in both financial and critical terms; in 2008, over 20 of the films made with the support of the studio were shown at that year's Berlin Film Festival. Although most of the films supported are English-language international co-productions, the DFFF has also been instrumental in the financing of big-budget German-language films such as *Henri 4*. Moreover, the fund has helped to raise the profile of German actors abroad. These include David Kross, who plays the young Michael in Stephen Daldry's *The Reader* (an adaptation of Bernhard Schlink's international bestselling novel about the legacy of the Holocaust, *Der Vorleser*, 1995), and Christoph Waltz, who was unknown internationally until he played the charming yet menacing Nazi in Tarantino's 'spaghetti' war film *Inglourious Basterds*, for which he won the 'Best Supporting Actor' Oscar.

Of particular importance to the German film industry is a range of regional schemes operated by the Federal states (*Länder*), which provide up to 70 per cent of the public funding available. Some Länder have become more important European film funders than certain national governments, acting as an impetus for transnational co-operation by attracting major international productions to facilities in their part of Germany. Examples in the 2000s include Gurinder Chadha's *Bend it like Beckham* (2002), which was partially supported by *Filmförderung Hamburg* (hence the inclusion of a German football tour in the script), and James McTeigue's British-German co-production *V for Vendetta* (2005). *Henri 4* was financed by regional funders from Baden-Württemberg, Bavaria, Berlin, and North Rhine-Westphalia. Enabled by a mixture of government, private, and public television money, all the major regional film federations tie their funding to a project's 'regional effect', as they see the development of their local economic and artistic infrastructure as a core aim of their support. This generally means that, for every euro they provide, €1.50 has to be spent in the region. Some regions have been extraordinarily successful of late. In 2008 the Bavarian film fund, for example, saw a 300 per cent 'regional effect' return on its €27 million investment in production (*Blickpunkt: Film* 2009: 42). The DFFF has also helped in this regard. About half of the DFFF money allocated to date has, for example, flowed to Berlin-Brandenburg, with the region estimating a 500 per cent 'regional effect' through the many major international productions it has attracted to Babelsberg (*Blickpunkt: Film* 2009).

Around two thirds of the budgets for German feature films come from public subsidies. When one adds up all these various pots of money, the funding available to German production companies is potentially very generous. However, the diffuse nature of the funding structure is regularly attacked by commentators and members of the industry. A production company will invariably need to seek support from a range of sources. This led, particularly in the early 1990s, to what the German Films Service + Marketing (the Federal organisation tasked with promoting German film abroad) criticised as 'a hotchpotch of compromises, a German road movie in the worst sense of the word, the plot making sudden and unexplained relocations just in order to meet a particular fund's requirements'. In a sense, such films replicated on the national level what the europudding created on the transnational. In the last decade, in a similar fashion to the changes in European film funding, there have been attempts to address the criticisms levied at regional funding schemes. The main regional funders have started to work together to allow the trade of 'local effects' between films (Blaney 2002: 8). Nonetheless, it is difficult to overcome this impulse completely (as *Bend it like Beckham* illustrated). What Matthias Kurp calls 'sponsor tourism' continues as film productions travel the country, increasing a film's expenses due to the need to support a mobile film crew, and doing little to build a sustainable film industry with a life beyond the individual project being funded (Kurp 2004).The complexity of the system can still lead to films being made by committee, based on a project's ability to guarantee funding rather than the prospect of either critical or commercial success (and thereby working against the ostensible overall aims of the funding system).

A final source of film funding that was important to *Henri 4* and has also played a role in the international visibility of German film across Europe is public and private television. Television provides a far more stable form of film financing compared with the precarious world of cinematic funding. Currently it is relatively easy for historical epics, in particular, to find both buyers and backers among television networks across the globe, since such productions are considered to have longer shelf lives than feature films aimed at the cinema and can thus more readily amortise their initial costs (Meza 2006). Support can take the form of either a pre-sales agreement or a full co-production, in which case the company will often be heavily involved in the development of a project. In the heyday of the New German Cinema in the 1970s, television played a major role as a film funder and, more importantly, as a medium of exhibition for the work produced. Filmmakers, however, were able to maintain a high degree of artistic autonomy. In the last two decades this has begun to change, with private television companies, in particular, being exercised by the commercial viability of a film project and its attractiveness to a mainstream, primetime audience. The increasing influence of television officials in the decision-making process has had a noticeable effect on the type of films that have been made in Germany, much to the chagrin of many filmmakers. Most fiercely disputed is the role of so-called 'amphibian films' – such as *Henri 4* – which are designed to be released in both cinematic and extended television versions, but are driven primarily by their ability to be transmitted in primetime television slots. This led to a very public feud between Volker Schlöndorff, who was to direct a film based on Donna Woolfolk Cross's novel *Pope Joan* (1996), and producer Günter Rohrbach. Schlöndorff argued that it was impossible to make a film that could work in both formats without a far bigger budget than that available to him, since he was, in effect, being asked to make two movies. The need for the film to work on television was undermining any cinematic aspirations he had for a project to which he had committed eight years of his life.

The 'amphibian film' has, in fact, enjoyed a good degree of commercial success in recent years. Oliver Hirschbiegel's international hit *Downfall* (*Der Untergang*, 2004), for example, was an amphibian. Such productions often enjoy widespread screening across the television networks of Europe. The dominant figure in this area is Nico Hofmann, whose *teamWorx* company regularly re-edits its two-part historical docudramas, invariably marketed within Germany as high-end 'event television', for theatrical release (Cooke 2008). Baier's *teamWorx* production *Stauffenberg*, for example, was sold to 82 countries, and *Dresden*, the company's melodramatic account of the bombing of Dresden (Roland Suso Richter, 2006) to over 100 (Urbe 2006).

The renewed popular success of some television comedy on the big screen has further countered the perception that television has had a wholly negative impact on filmmakers' cinematic aspirations, at least in commercial terms. Tom Gerhardt's *7 Zwerge – Männer allein im Wald* (7 Dwarves, Sven Unterwaldt Jr, 2004), for example, sold over 6 million tickets on its theatrical release. More successful still is the work of Michael 'Bully' Herbig. Herbig is a television comic well known for his ProSieben show *Bullyparade*, the camp characters from which he has used in two films: *Der Schuh des Manitu* (Manitu's Shoe, 2001), a spoof western in the style of the 1960s film versions of Karl May's popular novels, which achieved an audience of 10.5 million, and *(T)Raumschiff Surprise – Periode 1* (Dreamship Surprise – Period 1, 2004), a parody science fiction movie that sold just over 9 million tickets on its theatrical release and references a whole host of US movies and television shows, from *Star Trek* (Gene Roddenberry, 1966–9) and *Star Wars* (George Lucas, 1977) to *Back to the Future* (Robert Zemeckis, 1985) and *Minority Report* (Steven Spielberg, 2002). Highly reminiscent of Jim Abrahams's American parodies *Airplane* (1980) and *Hot Shots!* (1991), *Der Schuh des Manitu* and *(T)Raumschiff Surprise* are the second and third most popular German films with domestic audiences since the 1950s, beaten only by *Otto – Der Film* (Xaver Schwarzenberger and Otto Waalkes), the monster comedy hit of 1985, with its estimated 14 million spectators (FFA 2010). Although both films have been a huge success at home, Herbig has failed to gain the widespread international release he hoped for, offering evidence perhaps of the non-translatability of German comedy. It also suggests the importance of television to the growth of the domestic market for German popular film, with the three most successful German comedies for decades all coming out of successful television shows.

Herbig's success illustrates the shift in the funding ethos away from individual artists towards the popular entertainment and commercial ethos of Hollywood; something which is also reflected in his close working relationship with Bernd Eichinger and Constantin Films. Until his death in 2011, Eichinger was Germany's most important commercial producer, responsible for a large number of the country's international successes, including *Downfall*, *The Baader Meinhof Complex* and Tom Tykwer's *Perfume* (2006). Constantin, the company Eichinger bought in 1978, is the nearest that Germany comes to a major production company in the Hollywood sense, making what in German terms are big-budget, blockbusting 'event movies' for the international market, many of which, like *Perfume* or his adaptation of the Marvel comic strip *Fantastic Four* (Tim Story, 2005) are shot in English and have an international cast.

Constantin is driven by the bottom line, pushing German cinema, for better or worse, towards the international mainstream. Without doubt, this has had knock-on effects for the industry as a whole, helping to increase the visibility of German productions through the commercial success of some of Eichinger's German-language films abroad. This is of potential benefit to all filmmakers, whether they are interested in the production of work with mass appeal or more esoteric fare. Indeed, for all the discussion of a shift away from the art-house sensibility of the New German Cinema since unification, that kind of filmmaking has far from disappeared. On the contrary, in recent years it has been making something of a comeback, albeit often in a far more media-savvy way than the 1970s, with filmmakers and producers attempting to marry the imperatives of the market and the German funding system with their own aesthetic agenda. The most obvious example of this is X-Filme Creative Pool. Although X-Filme clearly has an international outlook, the specifically 'German' nature of its films is also important to its strategy. As Stefan Arndt, one of the company's co-founders, puts it:

> We intended to tackle really authentic German stories that are set in Germany and are about Germany, and we also wanted to find the kind of story ideas which would also function outside of Germany.

> (Halle 2002: 43)

The impulse to approach 'authentic' German stories that will also work abroad is clear, for example, in Haneke's *The White Ribbon* or Wolfgang Becker's international hit *Good Bye, Lenin!* (2003), both of which were produced by X-Filme. *Good Bye, Lenin!* explores the specifically German theme of unification and the legacy of the GDR in present-day German society, *The White Ribbon* life in the German provinces on the eve of World War I. In interviews both filmmakers echo Arndt's comments, playing on what they see as the translatability of their plots, something hinted at in Becker's production from the outset in his use of English in the film's title. For Becker, the GDR is intended largely to provide a backdrop for a universally applicable story: 'It's not so much a story about unification but rather a family story' ('Es ist weniger eine Geschichte zur Wiedervereinigung als eine Familiengeschichte') (quoted in Funck 2003: 35). The film's success abroad might well be attributable at least in part to its translatability. Nonetheless, it is also clear from foreign reviews that the GDR theme gave this universal story a 'unique selling point' on the international market (Bradshaw 2003: 27).

European identity, European history

Spectacular historical dramas such as *Henri 4* can use a specific moment from history to turn a nation's past into a story relevant to present-day international audiences (Vidal 2012: 52). Although clearly that was not realised in the case of Baier's film, more successful examples of this European trend that have had a large degree of German participation might be mentioned, from Jean-Jacques Annaud's depiction of the battle for Stalingrad, *Enemy at the Gates* (2001), to Christian Carion's story of the World War I Christmas truce, *Joyeux Noël/Happy Christmas* (2005). Often in such films, however, a nationally specific 'moral-ethical engagement with the material gives way to entertainment' (Halle 2008: 126) and they can lose their national focus, tending instead to construct a common 'European project' based on a common understanding, and ownership, of modern Europe's historical origins.

At the heart of that European project is frequently what has been described as the 'Europeanisation of the Holocaust' (Probst 2006). With regard to European film production specifically, Thomas Elsaesser notes that 'While thirty years ago, Auschwitz and the persecution of Jews was still very much a catastrophe that the Germans had to show themselves repentant and accountable for in the eyes of the world', historical milestones such as the anniversary of *Kristallnacht* or the liberation of Auschwitz 'have since become European days for joint acts of reflection and solemn commemoration, where Europe can affirm its core values of democracy and commitment to human rights, while condemning totalitarianism in all its forms' (Elsaesser 2005: 73). Even *Joyeux Noël*, which on the face of it would seem to have little to do with that period in history, defines its engagement with the European past with reference to the Holocaust: the shot of the soldiers (including a Jewish officer played by Daniel Brühl) being packed onto a train and transported to the East at the end of the narrative evokes well-known images of Jewish victims being taken to their deaths under National Socialism.

Thus national heterogeneity is subsumed under a form of transnational uniformity in which all European identities, including that of post-unification Germany, can find their democratic self-perception reflected and affirmed. This is an impulse common to numerous German historical dramas of the last decade produced for both the big and the small screen, films that have benefited from the funding constellation outlined and that have tended to have the widest international release. Examples include *Aimée & Jaguar* (Max Färberböck, 1999), the story of a lesbian love affair between a Jewish woman and her non-Jewish lover as the couple negotiate life in war-torn Berlin, or *Rosenstraße* (2003), Margarethe von Trotta's portrayal of the non-Jewish women who protested against the internment of their Jewish husbands. These films present what could be termed *Schindler's List* moments – stories that, like Spielberg's 1993 block-buster, give heroic accounts of non-Jewish solidarity with Jewish victims, thereby suggesting the continuation of a spark of humanity during the period that was not extinguished by the Nazi takeover and has once again taken hold in the present-day German state. One could point to a range of narratives, from Volker Schlöndorff's *Der neunte Tag/The Ninth Day* (2004) to Marc Rothemund's Oscar-nominated *Sophie Scholl – Die letzten Tage/The Final Days* (2005) and Suso Richter's *Dresden*, that present similarly heroic moments but through an overtly Christological prism, offering audiences a narrative of national redemption. While all these stories deal with the German experience of history, it is interesting to note that they all – to a lesser or greater extent – embed their presentation of German history within a wider European context, their stories of noble suffering and sacrifice invariably pointing forward to, and thus providing a moral foundation stone for, a postwar order in which Germany will be central to a future *European* democracy.

Of the films mentioned so far, the construction of the postwar order as an explicitly European project is perhaps at its most explicit in *Dresden*. The film sets the bombing of the city against a somewhat improbable love affair between a German nurse and British airman. The affair itself is doomed to failure – having survived the bombing of the city, the airman dies on a journey back to his lover in the immediate aftermath of the war. However, all is not lost. In the closing moments of the main narrative arc we learn that the nurse is expecting his baby, a child whose existence suggests a future transnational utopia, in which a unified Europe will prevent any future European civil conflicts. In the destruction of the city we find the beginnings of a new German, and ultimately broader European, order of harmony. In the final sequence of the film this is related back to the visual – or more precisely the cinematic – memory of the Holocaust. We are shown footage from the reconsecration of the Frauenkirche on 30 October 2005. This is immediately followed by shots of an elderly crowd standing outside the church, the majority of whom, the film seems to imply, are themselves the real-life survivors of the bombing. Then, as the credits roll, we hear the words of the Federal President Horst Köhler, who makes clear how we are to understand the Frauenkirche today, namely as a symbol of reconciliation with all of Germany's former enemies and of hope for a Berlin Republic embedded in Europe. His multilingual declaration (noticeably including English and Hebrew) of 'peace be with you, shalom aleichem [. . .] Friede sei mit euch' is followed by a claim that Dresden has today become an international symbol of pacifism. The use of Hebrew begins to forge a link between the experience of those who lived through Dresden and those who experienced the Holocaust, a link that is subsequently reinforced in another echo of *Schindler's List*: when watching the faces of the elderly people in the crowd listening to Köhler's words, it is impossible not to be reminded of the final sequence in Spielberg's film, where we see the real Jewish survivors whom Schindler saved paying tribute to the film's eponymous hero. In *Dresden* we are shown a mirror image of the Jewish survivors in Spielberg, both groups united by age and by their understanding of the horror of war. The Frauenkirche acts as the symbolic heart of a nation that is now a beacon of pacifism, not because Germany has accepted its guilt for unleashing the war and committing the crimes of the Holocaust per se, but because it, along with its Jewish citizens, suffered the consequences, consequences that allow the nation to empathise with its former enemies and victims (for further discussion see Cooke 2008).

Henri 4 seems to be a historical drama far removed from this particular version of a European 'project', further even than *Joyeux Noël*. However, in interviews given in the run-up to the film's release, both the director and the producer continually linked the story they wanted to tell back to precisely this moment in European history, positioning Germany's past as a common foundation stone for modern Europe. Baier insists that *Henri 4* is about tolerance in an intolerant time ('Toleranz in einer intoleranten Zeit'), reminding us that it was a story written by Heinrich Mann in France to show an alternative to Nazi barbarism ('ein Gegenentwurf zur Nazibarbarei'; ddp 2008). And, Ziegler insists, at a time when the world is again in the grips of ideological religious wars, Heinrich Mann's story remains a 'timeless fable' (Ziegler 2010). The film's story of the good king, who rules according to humanist, ecumenical values as opposed to ideological, bigoted principles, is offered as a prototype for the values of contemporary Europe, rooted not in 16th-century France but in the formative European tragedy of National Socialism. The unification of France under the enlightened leadership of Henri ultimately provides a model for a European Union built on similar values.

Problematising the European project

At the heart of these films, and particularly many of those funded by MEDIA and EURIMAGES, is the wish to foster a common (if necessarily very loosely defined) European cultural identity. Yet, while the schemes have funded a number of films that engage with the question of Europe, not all are as celebratory of the European project as those already discussed. Particularly in some of the smaller projects that the funds have helped produce, we find a more critical view of the meaning of Europe. Here we might mention several German-led ensemble films, one of the most innovative being the '99 euro films' project. The second of these, *Europe* (2003), brings together nine European directors (including Harry Kümel, Richard Stanley, and Benjamin Quabeck) to present a series of shorts (none of which cost more than €99 to make) that together form a morbid vision of the new Europe consumed by the ghosts of its past. Another notable example to have come out of Germany is Stanisław Mucha's meditation on Europe's spiritual, cultural, and geographical centre as the continent expands eastward, *Die Mitte* (*The Middle*, 2004), a film that ironises the notion of Europe as the home of civilisation, envisioning the search for the centre of the continent as a comic documentary version of Joseph Conrad's *Heart of Darkness*. Finally, Fatih Akin, one of Germany's best-known directors, who has received funding from both MEDIA and EURIMAGES, has repeatedly explored the concept of Europe and European values in relation to non-European culture (*Gegen die Wand/Head-On*, 2004; *Auf der anderen Seite/The Edge of Heaven*, 2007). Specifically he forces the spectator to reflect upon the status of Turkey as either a European or Asian nation, once again challenging any uncritical understanding of Europe as the home of rationality and reason.

With regard to the Holocaust and its place as a foundation stone for present-day Europe, Robert Thalheim's *Am Ende Kommen Touristen/And Along Come Tourists* (2007) provides a particularly interesting counterview to that found in many spectacular historical dramas. Although produced entirely with German money, this low-budget film benefited from coordinated exhibition through Europa Cinemas, a network of theatres set up by the MEDIA scheme in 1992; this shows how transnational structures can help new filmmakers find an audience, and potentially mitigate the homogenising tendencies identified in larger-budget European fare. Of course, as noted by De Vink, such successful coordination is the exception rather than the rule and, in the case of Thalheim's film, circulation remained small-scale by mainstream industry standards (De Vinck 2009). In response to the 'Europeanisation' of the Holocaust, *And Along Come Tourists* asks the question who owns historical memory within present-day Europe, where Germany ultimately stands in a neo-colonial relationship with, particularly, its eastern European neighbours. Set in the Polish town of Oświęcim, better known in the West by its German name Auschwitz, the film tells the story of 19-year-old Sven (Alexander Fehling) as he embarks on a year's civilian service placement (*Zivildienst*; the alternative to military service for young German men) at the concentration camp memorial. Through Sven's eyes, we are given a view of a town that for its German visitors is synonymous with the crimes of the Holocaust, but for its Polish inhabitants is a place where they simply live and work. The camp itself, more often than not, appears as an absent presence in the film, not least because Thalheim, like many filmmakers before him, including most famously Steven Spielberg, was not given permission to film at the memorial. That constraint becomes an important dynamic within the film, helping Thalheim to challenge the spectator's visual expectations of a narrative set in this particular town. In the opening sequence, for example, we are presented with a shot of Oświęcim's railway station, its tracks in the centre of the frame. This immediately calls to mind the archetypal Holocaust image of the Auschwitz railway tracks that brought millions to their death in the camps; but here the tracks bring a bemused Sven to his placement. Oświęcim is presented as a real place, in which real people live, rather than a symbolically charged image of the past, as one might expect it to be in a historical drama. It is a place where the young form bands, go to discos and have fun, just like anywhere else, but where the overwhelming attitude to the population from the outside world is one of condescension and pity. Thus the film asks the spectator to reflect upon well-worn images of the Holocaust anew, exploring how such images circulate in contemporary culture and how they relate to specific individual experience, rather than to a generalised European project.

And Along Come Tourists ultimately leaves open the key question it asks, namely, where does contemporary German society go today with the process of *Vergangenheitsbewältigung* (dealing with the past), if the term is going to mean anything beyond a kind of bland collective reflection on history? What are the specific national constraints on the transnational circulation of Holocaust memory, and how do they relate to a European population faced with diverse social and economic challenges? Thalheim's film provides a useful corrective to europudding, a filmmaking trend that, although no longer as prominent as it was in the 1990s, can still emerge from European funding structures. As we have seen, these are not the only types of films produced. European structures can provide the opportunity for the production of films that otherwise could not be made, or might not otherwise be seen, as well as supporting some that perhaps should not be made. That said, it is important to note that, for all the intention in some of these films to create the sense of a common European project, there is often anything but homogeneity in their reception across Europe. Recent German historical films, for example, have had widely varied critical resonance internationally. Invariably, they are related to local debates. One thinks, for example, of how German history films have sparked discussions about Vichy collaboration in France or Franco in Spain (Paoli 2009). Indeed, even in Germany they have been widely debated, generating competing readings. Consequently, it is clear that, for all the apparently homogenising tendencies within their approach to the presentation of history, even europuddings do not taste the same everywhere. They will be read differently according to where, and by whom, they are consumed. Or they will simply be ignored, their *non-*consumption perhaps ultimately providing the best mechanism for protecting the vibrancy, and diversity, of European film production.

Bibliography

Beier, L.O. (2010) 'Filmgroßprojekt "Henri 4": Riesig, stressing, babylonisch', *Spiegel Online*. Online. Available at www.spiegel.de/kultur/kino/0,1518,681528,00.html (accessed 5 March 2007).

Blaney, M. (2002) 'Regional Film Funding In Germany – the "Big Six"', *German Film Quarterly*, 1: 8–15.

Blickpunkt: Film (2009) 'Filmstandort Nummer eins', 9 February: 38.

Bradshaw, P. (2003) '*Good Bye, Lenin!*', *The Guardian*. Online. Available at www.theguardian.com/culture/2003/jul/25/artsfeatures.dvdreviews (accessed 25 July 2011).

Brug, M. (2007) 'Wenn geschludert wird; Constantin-Film feuert Volker Schlöndorff als "Päpstin"-Regisseur. Der Grund: Kritik an der Multiverwertung von Filmen', *Die Welt*. Online. Available at www.welt.de/welt_print/article1049548/Wenn-geschludert-wird.html (accessed 24 July 2010).

Castendyk, O. (2008) *Die deutsche Filmförderung: eine Evaluation,* Potsdam: Eric Pommer Institute.

Cooke, P. (2008) '*Dresden* (2006), TeamWorx and *Titanic* (1997): German Wartime Suffering as Hollywood Disaster Movie', *German Life and Letters*, 61: 279–94.

Cooke, P. (2012) *Contemporary German Cinema*, Manchester: Manchester University Press.

Cross, D. (1996) *Pope Joan*, New York City: Three Rivers Press.

ddp (2008) 'Es geht um Toleranz in einer intoleranten Zeit', *Basisdienst Nachrichtenfeature*. Online. Available at www.lexisnexis.com/uk/nexis/search/newssubmitForm.do (accessed 3 December 2013).

De Vinck, S. (2009) 'Europudding or Europaradise? A performance evaluation of the EURIMAGES co-production film fund, twenty years after its inception', *Communications*, 34: 257–85.

Elsaesser, T. (2005) *European Cinema Face to Face with Hollywood,* Amsterdam: Amsterdam University Press.

EURIMAGES (2013) 'Co-production funding history'. Online. Available at http://www.coe.int/T/DG4/Eurimages/History/Coproduction/default_en.asp# (accessed 3 December 2013).

FFA (2010) 'DFFF Figures 2007–2009'. Online. Available at www.ffa.de/downloads/dfff/dfffin-zahlen/2010–02–10%20DFF%20Flyer%20Evaluation_engl.pdf (accessed 18 February 2013).

FFA (2013) 'Kino-Halbjahresergebnis'. Online. Available at www.ffa.de/downloads/publikationen/ffa_intern/FFA_info_2_2013.pdf (accessed 27 August 2013).

Fischer, L. (2006) 'Geschäft mit Filmfonds völlig zusammengebrochen', *Die Welt*. Online. Available at www.welt.de/print-welt/article235428/Geschaeft-voellig-zusammengebrochen.html (accessed 12 August 2011).

Funck, G. (2003) 'Im Auge des Sturms: Wird ein Autor entdeckt: Bernd Lichtenbergs Good Bye, Lenin!', *Frankfurter Allgemeine Zeitung*. Online. Available at www.seiten.faz-archiv.de/FAZ/20030215/fd1n 200302151760923.html (accessed 15 February 2013).

Gaitanides, M. (2001) *Ökonomie des Spielfilms*, Munich: Reinhard.

Halle, R. (2002) 'German Film, Aufgehoben: Ensembles of Transnational Cinema', *New German Critique*, 87: 1–48.

Halle, R. (2008) *German Film After Germany: Towards a Transnational Aesthetic*, Urbana, IL: University of Illinois Press.

Jäckel, A. (2003) *European Film Industries*, London: BFI.

Kirschbaum, E. (2005) 'New wave of Euro pix avoids Europudding curse', *Variety*. Online. Available at www.variety.com/article/VR1117931911?refcatid=19 (accessed 30 October 2011).

Kurp, M. (2004) 'Filmförderung erreicht Rekord-Niveau', *Medienmaerkte*. Online. Available at www.medienmaerkte.de/artikel/kino/040502_film_foerderung.html (accessed 2 February 2010).

Mann, H. (1935) [1991] *Die Jugend des Königs Henri Quatre*, Frankfurt a.m.: Fischer.

Mann, H. (1938) [1991] *Die Vollendung des Königs Henri Quatre*, Frankfurt a.m.: Fischer.

MEDIA (2007). Online. Available at http://ec.europa.eu/culture/media/about/index_en.htm (accessed 15 November 2012).

Meza, E. (2006) 'Mojto's mojo working with an eye towards H'w'd', *Daily Variety*, 16 April, 1.

Miller, T., Govil, N., McMurria, J., Maxwell, R., and Wang, T. (2005) *Global Hollywood: No. 2*, London: BFI.

Nye, J. (2004) *Soft Power: The Means to Success in World Politics*, New York: Public Affairs.

Paoli, P. (2009) 'Une histoire qui ne cesse d'évoluer', *Le Figaro*, 21 November, 4.

Probst, L. (2006) '"Normalization" Through Europeanization: The Role of the Holocaust', in S. Taberner and P. Cooke (eds) *German Culture, Politics and Literature into the Twenty-First Century: Beyond Normalization*, Rochester, NY: Camden House, 61–74.

Rahayel, O. (2006) 'Funding Film in Germany', *Goethe Institut*. Online. Available at www.goethe.de/kue/flm/fim/en1394196.htm (accessed 26 August 2013).

Schlink, B. (1995) *Der Vorleser*, Zürich: Diogenes.

Storm, S. (2000) *Stukturen der Filmfinanzierung in Deutschland*, Potsdam: Verlag für Berlin-Brandenburg.

Suchsland, R. (2010) 'Henri 4', *film-dienst*, 5: 35.

Urbe, W. (2006) '*Dresden* und *Stauffenberg* sind weltweit Bestseller', *Berliner Morgenpost*. Online. Available at www.morgenpost.de/printarchiv/kultur/article253547/Dresden-und-Stauffenberg-sind-weltweit-Bestseller.html (accessed 17 October 2009).

Vermögen & Steuern (2006) 'Medienfonds-Resümee: Die erwarteten Traum-renditen hat es für die Anleger nie gegeben', 8: 34–8.

Vidal, B. (2012) *Heritage Film: Nation, Genre and Representation*, London: Wallflower.

Ziegler, R. (2010) 'Statement Regina Ziegler', trailerseite.de. Online. Available at www.trailerseite.de/archiv/trailer-2009/13139-henri-4-film.html (accessed 3 December 2013).

Filmography

7 Zwerge – Männer allein im Wald (2004) [Film] Sven Unterwaldt Jr. Germany: Zipfelmützen GmbH & Co.

Aimée & Jaguar (1999) [Film] Max Färberböck. Germany: Zeitgeist Films.

Airplane (1980) [Film] Jim Abrahams. USA: Paramount Pictures.

Am Ende Kommen Touristen (2007) [Film] Robert Thalheim. Germany: 23/5 Filmproduktion GmbH.

Antichrist (2010) [Film] Lars von Trier. Denmark, Germany, France, Sweden, Italy, Poland: Zentropa Entertainments.

Auf der anderen Seite (2007) [Film] Fatih Akin. Germany, Turkey, Italy: Anka Film.

Back to the Future (1985) [Film] Robert Zemeckis. USA: Universal Pictures.

Bend it like Beckham (2002) [Film] Gurinder Chadha. UK, Germany, USA: Kintop Pictures.

Das Leben der Anderen (2006) [Film] Florian Henckel von Donnersmarck. Germany: Wiedemann & Berg Filmproduktion.

Der Baader Meinhof Komplex (2008) [Film] Uli Edel. Germany, France, Czech Republic: Constantin Film Produktion

Der Laden (1998) [Film] Jo Baier. Germany: Arte.

Der neunte Tag (2004) [Film] Volker Schlöndorff. Germany, Luxembourg, Czech Republic: Provobis Film.

Der Schuh des Manitu (2001) [Film] Michael 'Bully' Herbig. Germany: herbX Medienproduktion GmbH.

313

Paul Cooke

Der Untergang (2004) [Film] Oliver Hirschbiegel. Germany, Austria, Italy: Constantin Film Produktion.

Die Mitte (2004) [Film] Stanisław Mucha. Germany: Arte.

Dresden (2006) [Film] Roland Suso Richter. Germany: teamWorx Produktion für Kino und Fernsehen GmbH.

Enemy at the Gates (2001) [Film] Jacques Annaud. USA, Germany, UK, Ireland: Paramount Pictures.

Europe (2003) [Film] Tony Baillargeat, Nacho Cerdà, Rolf Peter Kahl, Harry Kümel, Benjamin Quabeck, Richard Stanley, Ellen ten Damme, Stephan Wagner, Xawery Żuławski. Austria, Germany: 99euro-films.

Fantastic Four (2005) [Film] Tim Story. USA, Germany: Constantin Film Produktion.

Gegen die Wand (2004) [Film] Fatih Akin. Germany, Turkey: Arte.

Gladiator (2000) [Film] Ridley Scott. UK, USA: Scott Free Productions.

Good Bye, Lenin! (2003) [Film] Wolfgang Becker. Germany: X-Filme Creative Pool.

Henri 4 (2010) [Film] Jo Baier. Germany, France, Austria, Spain: Ziegler Film & Company.

Hot Shots! (1991) [Film] Jim Abrahams. USA: Twentieth Century Fox Film Corporation.

Inception (2010) [Film] Christopher Nolan. UK, USA: Warner Bros.

Inglourious Basterds (2009) [Film] Quentin Tarantino. USA, Germany: The Weinstein Company.

Joyeux Noël (2005) [Film] Christian Carion. France, Germany, UK, Belgium, Romania, Norway: Nord-Ouest Productions.

Minority Report (2002) [Film] Steven Spielberg. USA: Twentieth Century Fox Film Corporation.

Nirgendwo in Afrika (2001) [Film] Caroline Link. Germany: BKM.

Otto – Der Film (1985) [Film] Xaver Schwarzenberger, Otto Waalkes. West Germany: Rialto Film.

Perfume (2006) [Film] Tom Tykwer. Germany, France, Spain: Constantin Film Produktion.

Rosenstraße (2003) [Film] Margarethe von Trotta. Germany, Netherlands: Studio Hamburg Letterbox Filmproduktion.

Schindler's List (1993) [Film] Steven Spielberg. USA: Universal Pictures.

Sophie Scholl – Die letzten Tage (2005) [Film] Marc Rothemund. Germany: Broth Film.

Star Trek (1966–9) [TV] Gene Roddenberry. USA: Desilu Productions.

Star Wars (1977) [Film] George Lucas. USA: Lucasfilm.

Stauffenberg (2004) [Film] Jo Baier. Germany: teamWorx Produktion für Kino und Fernsehen GmbH.

The International (2009) [Film] Tom Tykwer. USA, Germany, UK: Columbia Pictures.

The Lion King (1994) [Film] Roger Allers, Rob Minkoff. USA: Walt Disney Pictures.

The Reader (2008) [Film] Stephen Daldry. USA, Germany: The Weinstein Company

The White Ribbon/Das weisse Band – Eine deutsche Kindergeschichte (2009) [Film] Michael Haneke. Germany, Austria, France, Italy: X-Filme Creative Pool.

(T)Raumschiff Surprise – Periode 1 (2004) [Film]. Michael 'Bully' Herbig, Germany: herbX Medienproduktion GmbH.

V for Vendetta (2005) [Film] James McTeigue. USA, UK, Germany: Warner Bros.

Valkyrie (2008) [Film] Bryan Singer. USA, Germany: MGM.

20

The making of German European policy

William E. Paterson

European policymaking in Britain and France has always reflected a clear aim of identifying the national interest in European integration and then using a highly centralised state machinery to pursue that aim. Germany's European policymaking has been quite different, reflecting quite different aims. Whereas Britain and France have been concerned to preserve sovereignty, after 1949 the infant Federal Republic lacked sovereignty, and European integration was a way of recovering it. The national interest was European cooperation, and the policymaking machinery was not, therefore, designed to identify an(other) explicit national interest but rather to reflect a 'reflexive multilateralism', privileging European integration. It was, accordingly, notably porous and decentralised, although the decentralisation also reflected the *Ressortprinzip* (departmental principle) that is the core principle of governing in Germany. A final unique feature of German policymaking is the large role played by parapublic bodies such as the Bundesbank and the Federal Constitutional Court (*Bundesverfassungsgericht*).

These internal arrangements were flanked by a close alliance with France where Germany was the horse and France (De Gaulle) the coachman. In more recent years this system has come under pressure. The formerly rather technocratic approach at governmental level has been subject to increasing politicisation, as European integration has entered into the nooks and crannies of German life. As Germany has become ever more central in the European Union, there has also been a perception that the present arrangements lack a strategic capacity. The Franco–German relationship has become damagingly asymmetric as the French economy has weakened; it can no longer serve as the anchor of German European policymaking.

European policymaking at governmental level

> Conceptions of sovereignty are linked so closely to domestic structures that it is difficult to untangle the role of ideas from that of political organization and practice.
>
> (Keohane 2003: 322)

> To eat well, to sleep well, and never, never to be alone.
>
> (Michael Stürmer)[1]

German policymaking machinery reflects the circumstances of its origins. In other states the Foreign Ministry played the central role, but Germany's Auswärtiges Amt (Federal Foreign Office) was only created in 1951, and Konrad Adenauer remained foreign minister (as well as chancellor) until 1955. A single-minded concentration on economic recovery and the status of the incumbent minister, Ludwig Erhard, ensured that the key role was played by the Federal Ministry of Economics (Bundesministerium für Wirtschaft). The establishment of the European Economic Community (EEC) and its subsequent expansion gave urgency to the question of coordination and to a definitive agreement on European policy responsibilities. The Ministry of Economics was entrusted with the task of coordinating day-to-day European policy, while the Foreign Office was left with responsibility for long-term-oriented integration policy, including Franco-German relations, with the chancellor retaining the right to set policy guidelines (*Richtlinien-kompetenz*) (Hesse and Goetz 1992). In 1998 a further change took place. The responsibility for coordination of day-to-day policy was transferred from the Ministry of Economics to the Federal Ministry of Finance (Bundesministerium der Finanzen), Division EA 1, with a secondary coordination unit in the Foreign Office (Division E-KR).[2]

Overall the system was characterised by power-sharing between coalition ministries, the principle of ministerial autonomy (enshrined in Article 65 of the Basic Law), and a relatively weak norm of information-sharing between ministries; Bulmer and Paterson (1987) portray it as a system characterised by coalition politics, federalism, departmental sectorisation, and the role of parapublic institutions reflecting the semi-sovereign nature of the Federal Republic. This internal semi-sovereignty and institutional pluralism meshed well with the reflexive multilateralism (pro-integration bias) of Germany's external stance. Peter Katzenstein stressed the congruence between German institutions and those of the European Union at that time:

> Although distinctive, the institutional practices that mark the European polity resemble Germany's on this score. The system of governance in the European polity is based on what one might call 'associated sovereignty', pooled competencies in overlapping domains of power and interest, which is characteristic also of Germany's 'semi–sovereign' state.
>
> (Katzenstein 1997: 33)

Reflexive multilateralism

Reflexive multilateralism was reflected in the weight accorded to the views of European institutions (most obviously when Walter Hallstein was president of the Commission). It was also associated with a 'leadership avoidance reflex' whereby Germany sedulously avoided solo initiatives or a leadership position (Paterson 1993). The exigencies of Germany's institutional pluralism meant that German coordination was post hoc, and a final position emerged very late on in the process, in stark contrast to the British ex ante model, where a tightly unified policy was agreed at the earliest possible opportunity. In an important contribution, Derlien pointed out the advantages of the post hoc strategy, a stance appropriate to the Federal Republic's internal semi-sovereignty and European vocation, over the United Kingdom's defensive stance:

> My contention is that the German pattern of ex post coordination, a policy style resembling management by exception, is ultimately superior to a practice of ex ante coordination of all policy matters regardless of their salience. Such a strategy is counterproductive, for it leaves little room for the recurrent multi issue bargaining process at the European level and the informal norm of reciprocity.
>
> (Derlien 2000: 6)

As the European Union enlarged and expanded its policy scope, however, these advantages were less highly valued and there were increasing calls for reform of the system, which was widely perceived as inefficient and confusing. Those complaints failed to bring about a radical change in the system. There was no trigger, not even German unity, strong enough to disturb the pattern of embedded interests. There were some incremental improvements (Beichelt 2007) but some observers queried how successful they were (Große Hüttmann 2007).

If the formal arrangements remained relatively static, there was, however, one massively significant change. The chancellor had always played a key role in 'historic decisions', but, in line with the *Ressort* principle, substantive policy was largely a matter for the relevant department. This division was associated with a pattern where German success at the level of 'historic decisions' contrasted with a very mixed record in day-to-day politics or *Tagespolitik* (Derlien 2000). From 1998, however, Chancellor Gerhard Schröder chose to intervene at the level of substantive policy: in 1998–9, for example, at the urging of German car producers, he intervened to prevent the implementation of a European directive on the recycling of used cars supported by his environment minister in Brussels. This pattern has continued under Chancellor Merkel, who has played a leading role in attempting to resolve the eurozone crisis alongside her finance minister. Future plans for the governance of the eurozone, involving a significant increase in the number of summits, will ensure a continued central role in these issues for the chancellor. In a speech in Bruges (Merkel 2010), Chancellor Merkel set out her endorsement of the Union method, which involves relying on cooperation between the large member states and signals a decisive break with reflexive multilateralism.

The greater role of the chancellor has been underpinned by a strengthening of the European policy expertise of the *Bundeskanzleramt* (BK; the Federal Chancellor's Office). Division 2 is responsible for foreign and integration policy and Division 4 is responsible for overseeing *Tagespolitik*. Even with the strengthened personnel of these divisions, the BK cannot hope to rival the specialist ministries in policy expertise. It does, however, possess two trump cards: it represents the chancellor, the dominant figure in the German government; and Chancellor Merkel is a figure whose governmental authority bears comparison with that of Adenauer. In making this authority work, the Chancellor's Office has in Peter Altmaier (chief of staff in the BK) and Christoph Heusgen (foreign policy adviser), the two leading European policy thinkers in the Federal government. The BK plays the key role in relations with other member states. This has become ever more central as the role of the Commission has declined. A feature of the eurozone crisis is the high number of bilateral disputes that have been handled by the member states without the mediation of the Commission. The BK is the key agency in the preparation of the ever-increasing number of European councils and emergency summits.

The loosely coordinated, rather porous decision-making machinery that characterised European policymaking in Germany meshed well with a European vocation and a reflexively multilateralist policy style. Over time that European vocation has weakened, however. As Thomas de Maizière, the German interior minister at the time of writing, put it: 'For our European friends, they need to come to terms with the fact that Germany is going to act just as other countries do in Brussels' (Chaffin 2010). This raises the issue whether the current decision-making machinery can survive the emergence of a 'normalised Germany' (Bulmer and Paterson 2010), which – at least in the eurozone – is a potential hegemon. This is an issue to which we will return in the conclusion.

Other actors: the Bundestag

European policymaking in the Federal Republic was a markedly technocratic process centred on the executive. The Bundestag played a key role in treaty ratification but otherwise its role was fairly limited, with scrutiny of European legislation being exercised through the committee system. Such a quietist role could perhaps have been expected, given the very broad pro-European consensus from the 1960s onwards; more than in any other large state, German hopes were focused on the European Parliament. German hopes for reform were placed in that institution, which was expected to provide the necessary democratic legitimacy. Until the 1980s a number of very prominent members of the Federal parliament (*Mitglieder des Bundestages* or MdBs) held dual mandates in the Bundestag and the European Parliament.

That set of priorities has altered in the Federal Republic. As Germany's European vocation has weakened, there is little enthusiasm for the European Parliament. This development is not without irony, as the European Parliament has accrued through the Lisbon Treaty (2007) the powers that generations of the German political class aspired to, and German political parties and individuals like Martin Schulz and Elmar Brok are seen as the most influential actors in the European Parliament. Slowly at first, the tide has turned in favour of a focus on increasing the control and scrutiny powers of the Bundestag. This development owed most to the successive judgments of the Federal Constitutional Court (notably the judgments on the Maastricht and Lisbon Treaties), which centred on the view that as the European Parliament did not possess a demos (people), democratic legitimacy could reside only in the institutions of the Federal Republic, especially the Bundestag.

The reservations of the FCC were reflected in the amendments to Articles 23 and Article 45 of the Basic Law that followed the adoption of the Maastricht Treaty, which was signed in 1992 and came into force in 1993. Basically these amendments and their implementing legislation required the Federal government to inform the Bundestag and the Bundesrat (upper house) at the earliest possible time of any measure likely to have relevance to Germany, to involve the Bundestag at the earliest possible time in the discussion of any proposed measure, and to 'take account' of Bundestag views. Under the new Article 45, the Bundestag set up a Committee on European Affairs in 1994.

These reforms were of very limited effectiveness. EU proposals are very technical and attract little interest. The Committee on European Affairs struggled to manage the division of responsibilities between it and the long-established specialist committees. Crucially, the time given for the Bundestag to respond to proposals never proved enough. An attempt was made to deal with this weakness by setting up a Bundestag liaison office in Brussels in 2007, which is able to make only a limited contribution to bridging the gap.

The Lisbon Treaty judgment of the Federal Constitutional Court has proved something of a landmark moment. The Lisbon Treaty provides for a considerable expansion in the powers of the European Parliament. In its judgment (2009) the FCC reiterated its view that, in the absence of a European demos, legitimacy was anchored in the nation state. In dismissing the claims of the European Parliament, the FCC used notably harsh and vivid language that resonated strongly with elite opinion (mass opinion had been sceptical for a long time). The Court called for the strengthening of the control powers of the Bundestag, especially in the area of the flexibility clause (Article 352 of the Treaty on the Functioning of the European Union or TFEU), bridging clauses, or any future proposals entailing the transfer of sovereignty. The Court also ruled that the state should have sovereignty in the following areas: criminal law, police, military operations, fiscal policy, social policy, education, culture, media, and relations with religious groups. Whilst ruling that the treaty was in conformity with the demands of the Basic Law, it did require an act spelling out the competences of the Bundestag in those areas. An attempt by the Christian Social Union (CSU) to impose a set of provisions that would have significantly further constrained the autonomy of the executive in this area failed. A series of laws and amendments was adopted, culminating in the Act on Cooperation between the Federal government and the

German Bundestag in Matters Concerning the European Union (Gesetz über die Zusammenarbeit von Bundesregierung und Deutschem Bundestag in Angelegenheiten der Europäischen Union or EUZBBG, July 2013).

The Bundestag was used to operating with regard to European matters in a climate of low interest and 'permissive consensus'. This all changed with the advent of the eurozone crisis. A partial politicisation had already occurred as a result of the Federal Constitutional Court's efforts to increase the Bundestag's control power, but the effect of the crisis was to switch attention away from the Committee on European Affairs to the Budgetary Committee (*Haushalts-ausschuss*). The move was partially a response to the demands of German public opinion, but it also reflected the insistence of the Federal Constitutional Court in the Lisbon judgment that responsibility for the budget remain exclusively in the Bundestag. Whilst the Bundestag had exclusive responsibility for the German budget, German insistence on looking at other states' budgets resulted in the Irish budget being publicly available in the Bundestag before it had been presented to the Dáil.

Traditionally the Bundestag has not acted as a major constraint on the executive in European policy, and Chancellor Merkel's mastery of German public opinion has ensured that this has remained the case so far in the eurozone crisis. She has come under little pressure from the Social Democrats, although both the Free Democrats and, to a lesser extent, the CSU have flirted with euroscepticism. The creation of a grand coalition (no doubt one of its attractions) to some extent removes that threat for the foreseeable future, although Bundestag sensibilities will be important on areas like bailouts. A renewed eurozone crisis would have incalculable effects.

The Länder

The central role of the Federal states or Länder in domestic policymaking in the Bonn Republic contrasted with their low-key role in European policymaking. From a Länder perspective, important elements of their legislative power were being ceded to the European level without their being fully involved. They therefore pressed vigorously for their right to be heard by the Federal government, which was equally insistent on preserving the monopoly of international negotiating rights and fiercely resisted any constitutionally binding agreement. The result was a thicket of predominantly informal and bureaucratic procedures that built up incrementally.

The picture changed dramatically with the necessity of securing Länder support for the ratification of the Maastricht Treaty in 1992. The Länder used this opportunity to make reform of Article 23 of the Basic Law a precondition of their agreement. The revised Article 23 (1992) made possible much greater Länder involvement in the making of European policy, allowed for the Länder to represent Germany directly in the Council on matters where they held exclusive domestic competence, and 'ringfenced' federalism from future developments in European integration. The effect of the new Article 23 was to further thicken and complicate decision-making on European policy. This potential for delay was a disadvantage where the Federal government wanted to press ahead, but was a useful prayer in aid when it wanted to slow things up without taking responsibility. Länder representation on the Council was initially bedevilled by the lack of experience of the Länder representatives, and in the domestic debate on reform of German federalism (2006–9) the Federal government tried and failed to restrict the Länder's right of representation.

The Länder have a dual impact on European policy. The necessity for formal ratification gives them huge influence on constitutional issues. They successfully pressed for the establishment of the Committee of the Regions, blocked Chancellor Helmut Kohl's desire to extend majority voting in the Council at the Amsterdam European Council, and were influential in the discussion and decisions leading to the Lisbon Treaty. In terms of *Tagespolitik* they do not possess the nuclear weapon of refusal to ratify, but Article 23 and their key role in the delivery of policies in Germany do confer considerable power.

As European integration penetrated into 'the nooks and crannies' of German economic and political life, the Länder represented a protectionist force. The German economy benefited greatly from the single market programme as it was implemented first in the manufacturing sector, where Germany was strong and had profited from a major influence on standard-setting, but it was now being pursued in the area of services and other areas where Germany was relatively weak. That protectionist force has been especially visible in the attempts by firms and by the Länder in which they are based to evade EU subsidy controls, to protect the regional banks (*Landesbanken*), and to reduce the force of environmental regulations; and, in the attempt by the Länder to redesignate various subsidised regional services as essential public provision (*öffentliche Daseinsvorsorge*), again to evade EU subsidy rules.

In the old Bonn Republic, the Länder (especially Bavaria) benefited greatly from the CAP (Common Agricultural Policy) and the single European market, and they were generally strong supporters of European integration. They were also to some extent observers (their demands were channelled at the European level through the *Länderbeobachter* or Länder observer). Since the revision of Article 23 they are full participants, but in a new and much more competitive EU, where advances in European integration rub up against established privileges and practices. The result is a definite change in Länder preferences, from their pre-Maastricht position of 'let us in' to one of 'leave us alone' (Jeffery 2004).

Franco-German relations: France as the 'outsider insider'

The founding contract of European integration was the European Coal and Steel Community, where the French government proposed that Germany be allowed to recover economic power in a multilateral context. This was an offer that the West German leadership was happy to accept. West Germany needed to escape from a web of discriminatory legislation imposed by the Western occupying powers and to gain access to export markets. On a continuing basis the Franco-German relationship relied on Germany's 'European vocation' and on the assumed objection of other member states to solo German leadership, which required an ally (Paterson 2011). In the absence of the United Kingdom, France became the indispensable partner, with an asymmetrical influence on German preferences.

The Franco-German relationship became part of the European Union's founding myths and resulted in German initiatives normally being presented in Franco-German form. The Franco-German relationship is the most institutionalised bilateral relationship in the world. Yves Boyer calculated that there were 115 meetings between the German chancellor and the French president between 1982 and 1992 (Boyer 1996), and post-Maastricht the number of meetings increased. Links between the German Foreign Ministry and its French counterpart are especially close, but as the role of the European Council increased so did the contacts between the Presidency and the Chancellor's Office. Until relatively recently this intense interaction privileged the French position. The more tightly coordinated French position was normally available at an earlier stage of negotiations than the loosely coordinated, post hoc German machinery could deliver. Moreover, the interaction of the highly centralised French coordination machinery with the institutional pluralism of the German decision-making machinery encouraged increased sectorisation on the part of Germany. The impact of this asymmetry can be seen especially clearly in the agricultural sector. Protection of French agriculture is the thickest 'red line' in French European policy. The BMEL (German Agriculture Ministry) is also protectionist. Early meetings with their French counterparts in advance of an agreed German position have tended to strengthen the protectionist side of the German decision. This was illustrated by the efforts made by the German government to retain a joint position with France despite divergent preferences (Landau 1998).

Gradually the balance of adjustment has shifted away from Germany towards France. The traditional German reflex of relying on the Franco-German relationship lost traction as the European Union enlarged to 28 members. Traditionally, where Franco-German agreement was reached it was normally accepted by other members: a quality that made France seem indispensable to German policymakers. This quality began to fray when the two states used it not as a motor to promote further integration but as an *arrière-garde* to defend their narrow national interests. The most striking example was the defiance by France and Germany of the Stability and Growth Pact rules in 2001–2.

The expansion of the EU to 28 members has been associated with a loss of traction for the Franco-German relationship that became immediately visible in the Iraq crisis, where a cleavage between 'old' and 'new' Europe left France and Germany largely isolated; only Belgium and Luxembourg rallied to their side. The logic of a 'shrinking core and an expanding periphery' (Dyson and Goetz 2003: 376) has weakened the structural power of the Franco-German relationship. This is clearly visible in both the Council of Ministers and the European Parliament (EP). In the EP their share of MEPs has fallen from 29.7 per cent to 23.4 per cent: in the Council their combined weighted votes no longer constitute by themselves a blocking minority (Schild 2010:1374).

The peculiar quality of the Franco-German relationship rested on the assumption that any attempt at solo German leadership would be resisted by other members of the European Union. This assumption came to look outmoded in the salvage operation for the Lisbon Treaty during the German Presidency of 2007, when other member states looked to Chancellor Merkel rather than the Franco-German duo for leadership. The creation of the eurozone, the greatest achievement of the Franco-German relationship, has proved to be its greatest challenge since the onset of recession in 2008. Somewhat unexpectedly, given the degree to which Germany profited from the eurozone, its ideational leadership in the establishment of the eurozone, and the boldness of Chancellor Merkel's leadership in the Lisbon salvage process, the German government has often preferred to adopt a very cautious and defensive role; France responded with a much greater sense of urgency, but its increasing economic weakness greatly constrained its influence. In the past France had benefited from an embedded institutional asymmetry that gave it the leadership role. Economic asymmetry now robbed France of its former privileged position.

A key strength of the Franco-German relationship, its institutionalised character, while helpful in treaty making, has turned out to be ill adapted to the sort of speedy crisis management needed to respond to the financial markets. Even when a Franco-German agreement is reached, it is invariably oversold, and implementation is delayed by the necessarily time-consuming ratification procedures. These difficulties are increased by the fact that neither the French nor the German government possesses the easy familiarity with the financial markets of their Anglo-Saxon counterparts.

The structural drag inherent in such an institutionalised relationship might have been transcended if there had been a 'dynamic duo' at the helm of France and Germany who were focused on economics. Helmut Schmidt criticised the absence of financial markets expertise and argued that, had the crisis occurred when he was chancellor, he would immediately have telephoned Giscard d'Estaing and developed a strategic plan.[3] Such a relationship depends on a very high degree of trust, which has been lacking. Declining mass support for the EU in both countries and the more critical role of the FCC in Germany have also shrunk the degree of executive autonomy the Federal government now enjoys in this area.

The stuttering performance of the Franco-German couple in the eurozone crisis and the increasing asymmetry of the Franco-German relationship have cast doubt on the continued centrality of the relationship. Paterson (2011) argues that Germany has emerged as 'a reluctant hegemon' owing to the eurozone crisis, where its ever-growing economy and principal creditor status have placed it in the driving seat in relation to crisis management. This argument is buttressed by an examination of the increasingly asymmetric Franco-German relationship. The fading of the objections by other states to German leadership noted above is an important precondition for such a role. The implications of the shrinking of the Franco-German role and Germany's emergence as a potential hegemon are huge and will be taken up in the conclusion to this chapter.

Societal forces: political parties

From the mid-1960s there was a solid pro-European consensus in the established political parties in support of European integration. This support was crucial during the extended debates about entry into the eurozone, when support from the political parties remained solid despite an adverse public opinion. In their early years the Greens opposed some aspects of German European policy, but since the advent of Joschka Fischer as foreign minister they have been strong supporters of European integration; they were, for instance, more sympathetic than any other party to Germany taking on a larger share of debt to deal with the eurozone crisis. The PDS (Party of Democratic Socialism), the successor party to the SED (East German communist party) has been a continual critic of the EU, a tradition that has been continued by Die Linke (The Left), the successor to the PDS (see Chapter 7).

Although the consensus appeared unchanged by 2009, it was to some extent 'hollowed out'. In the 2009 election, European integration played a lesser role than in any election since 1949. As the crisis developed, reactions differed within the CDU/CSU–FDP coalition. The FDP came out strongly against Eurobonds. The chancellor and the finance minister were not keen, but did not rule out their introduction at that time. The FDP's attempt to instrumentalise euroscepticism in the Berlin Land election was a dismal failure, and its vote fell from 7.6 per cent in 2006 to 1.8 per cent in September 2011. The CSU, the Bavarian partner of the CDU, has always been more populist than the CDU, and faced with a Land election in September 2013 it struck a critical note at times. When Chancellor Merkel was faced with mobilising support for bailout measures in the Bundestag, she was persuaded by Peter Altmaier, then the chief whip of the CDU/CSU parliamentary party and a noted European, that a more positive approach was needed, and the European element in the party programme was strengthened in 2011. Chancellor Merkel's position was made easier by the attitude of the opposition. In May 2010, the SPD failed to support the coalition in the Bundestag by abstaining on the legislation putting through the €750 million Greek bailout. Since then the opposition has taken a more generous line, although with the approach of the German election it took a notably ungenerous line on the Cyprus bailout.

Until now Germany has lacked a eurosceptic party defined by its opposition to the EU and to European integration, but the unpopularity of the eurozone has led to the creation of a new party, the *Alternative für Deutschland*, committed to the withdrawal of Germany from the eurozone, though it favours continued membership of the EU. The AfD polled 4.7 per cent in the 2013 Federal election, a very creditable performance for a new party, and is likely to do even better in future European elections.

German political parties, while remaining broadly pro-European, are much more sensitive to public opinion than in the past and have moved from unconditional support for the EU to much more conditional support. In the coalition negotiations of autumn 2013, both the CSU and the SPD pressed for the introduction of referendums on any transfer of sovereignty to EU institutions. This request is unlikely to succeed, but it reflects a greatly changed attitude towards the EU. This changed attitude is reported on in a recent euroblog by Sonia Alonso (Alonso 2014), where she notes that there is a long-term downward trend in supportive references to the EU in party manifestos.

Internally, party political influence has become something of a constraint on governmental action, as parties become more sensitive to public opinion. Externally, political parties help to project German preferences and power. The German parties play key roles in the European-level party federations and in the party groups in the European Parliament. Within the European Parliament, German influence is likely to increase following the election of Martin Schulz (SPD) as president of the Parliament. In the meetings of party and governmental leaders that take place on the eve of EU summits, where decisions are often pre-cooked, German leaders are normally especially influential. Finally, the party political foundations are a massive repository of influence for German views on Europe. The foundations have offices in most national capitals, where they act as a filter between the state in question and their German parent. The foundations can be especially important where that state has a conflicted view on the EU, as in the case of the United Kingdom and the Czech Republic; the relaunching of British European policy after the fall of Prime Minister Margaret Thatcher in 1990 was marked by a speech by John Major at the Adenauer Foundation headquarters in Sankt Augustin, for example.

Political parties thus play a partially contradictory role in the making of German European policy. At the European level, German political parties are an important element in the projection of German European policy; their influence is reflected in the ascent of Martin Schulz. The expansionary role of German political parties at a European level contrasts with their role in the domestic arena, where the tendency is to act as a constraint on German European policy.

Parapublic institutions: the Federal Constitutional Court

In his seminal work 'Politics and Policy in West Germany: The Growth of a Semi Sovereign State' (Katzenstein 1987), Peter Katzenstein analysed the taming and decentralisation of political power in the Federal Republic. One key element in this 'taming' was the role of two key parapublic institutions, the Federal Constitutional Court and the Bundesbank.

The lawless and arbitrary character of the Third Reich engendered a very strong commitment to the rule of law in the Federal Republic, which was reflected in the wide powers given to the Federal Constitutional Court. The Basic Law allows wide recourse to the Court, and that is an opportunity which citizens, parties, and groups have been keen to take advantage of. As guardian of the Basic Law, the FCC has profited from the growing attachment to it and is a very self-confident body that enjoys widespread public support. It takes its role as guardian of the Basic Law very seriously, and this has on occasion led it to resist the judicial claims of the European Court of Justice (ECJ). The aim of the Federal Constitutional Court is to ensure that ECJ judgments are compatible with the Basic Law, rather than simply to accept the primacy of European law. A pattern of rivalry with the European Court of Justice developed quite early on, as became clear in the Solange decision of the FCC in 1974, which attempted and over the longer period succeeded in moving the ECJ to adopt its own fundamental rights protection (Davies 2012). The position of the Federal Constitutional Court was strengthened by the revised Article 23 of the Basic Law, adopted after German unification, which prohibited any amendments that would impinge on a number of inviolable constitutional principles that underpin the Basic Law: federalism, democracy, the social state, the rule of law, and human rights.

According to Bulmer *et al.*, 'This no passaran [sic] rule goes far beyond the mere protection of federalism, to imply more broadly that German constitutional organs have a right and duty to monitor and shape the future development of European integration in a far wider sense' (2000: 43). On 12 October 1993 the Federal Constitutional Court, in a widely noted judgment on the conformity of the Maastricht Treaty with the Basic Law, insisted on its right as defender of the Basic Law to rule on the balance of competences between the EU and German institutions.

Whilst the Maastricht judgment influenced the European policy of the Federal government (Harnisch 2001), it did not become a major element of public debate in Germany. The Lisbon judgment of 2009 was to have a greater impact on policymaking and the German discourse on Europe. Its tone, which could now be described as eurosceptic, resonated with a changed public and press opinion. Carl Otto Lenz, a senior German euro lawyer, pointed out that the judgment used the term sovereignty 33 times, despite it not being mentioned in the Basic Law that the FCC exists to defend (Proissl 2010). It also, in line with Article 23, stipulated five reserved areas where it saw no scope for further transfer to the EU. Since the Maastricht judgment, the FCC has insisted on the Bundestag being actively involved in key EU decisions, and the ruling created a number of new control powers for the Bundestag, the effect of which has been to create a new domestic opportunity structure for more politicised debate in the Bundestag. The fear of provoking a recourse to the Federal Constitutional Court has instilled even greater caution on the part of the Federal government. It is not the usual practice of the FCC to rule a policy that the Federal government has assented to as unconstitutional, but rather to set out the conditions that would make policy in the area compatible with the Basic Law. In that sense, the FCC has moved from 'veto player' to co-shaper of German European policy, and the direction it prefers is limitation of further integration.

The Bundesbank

The trauma of the mega-inflation in 1923 has led to an instinctive commitment to 'sound money' and to the strong powers and high public standing of the Bundesbank, the German central bank. As Jacques Delors once quipped, 'not all Germans believe in God but they all believe in the Bundesbank'. So great was its influence that David Marsh referred to 'The Bundesbank: The Bank that Rules Europe' (Marsh 1992). The creation of the European Central Bank threatened to marginalise the Bundesbank and bring the principle of 'sound money' into conflict with the European vocation principle (Van Esch 2012). The reservations of the Bundesbank were to some extent stilled by siting the ECB in Frankfurt and adopting a constitution for it based on that of the Bundesbank. At that point, the epistemic community supporting the European vocation (the chancellor, the Foreign Ministry, and German industry) was much stronger than that supporting the Bundesbank, and some expected the Bundesbank to be relegated to the Frankfurt branch of the ECB (Marsh 2013: 212).

The balance of forces has altered visibly over the intervening period. On the European side, the chancellor is not prepared to defy public opinion in the way that Chancellor Kohl did over the creation of the eurozone. The Foreign Ministry, the key advocate of European integration, has lost influence and under the present incumbent is missing in action and less European than in the past. It has also been replaced in importance by the Finance Ministry. The role of the Bundesbank has been buttressed by ordoliberalism, a liberal German economic philosophy which emphasises the need for the state to ensure the principal role of the free market (see Chapter 24). Ordoliberalism also has a narrow view of the role of central banks. Its adherents argue that they should be independent and should concentrate on pursuing monetary policies with the aim of ensuring monetary stability, while governments should restrict themselves to setting the frameworks for competition and functioning markets. Whereas the support for the European vocation principle is waning, support for sound money ideas remains hugely strong in German public opinion. It is the dominant view among German academic economists and receives strong support from the country's perhaps most respected daily broadsheet, the *Frankfurter Allgemeine Zeitung*. Moreover, while the influence of the Foreign Ministry is shrinking, the Finance Ministry, where support for sound money is most concentrated, is becoming ever more central. This is likely to continue, as Wolfgang Schäuble will remain in the Finance Ministry in the new coalition. What is clear is that the Federal Constitutional Court and the Bundesbank now act as more significant constraints on the taking of decisions in German European policy than at any point in the past.

Conclusion

> The past is a foreign country: they do things differently there.
>
> (L.P. Hartley)

> I fear Germany's power less than her inactivity.
>
> (Sikorski 2011)

Germany's mode of dealing with European policymaking was created in a divided pre-sovereign polity desperate to find markets for its export-oriented industry (Paterson 2005). This weakness dictated a 'European vocation' and a reliance on the Franco-German relationship. In a sense, France was always in the room when German European decisions were taken, as France was invariably central to the German negotiating position. Internally, the decision-making machinery was both more porous, reflecting Germany's reflexive multilateralism, and more loosely coordinated than in France or the United Kingdom. Germany is now united and fully sovereign, and France the supplicant in the Franco-German relationship. Germany is viewed as the 'reluctant hegemon' of the eurozone – it is truly a different country.

All this raises the question whether the decision-making machinery that was appropriate to the infant Federal Republic's weak position is still fit for purpose. Externally Germany is fully sovereign, perhaps too sovereign for some tastes, while internally Germany remains semi-sovereign, arguably with less executive autonomy than in the past. The other actors – the Länder, the Bundesbank, the Federal Constitutional Court, and the political parties – could always have constrained the executive, but the 'European vocation' ensured that 'permissive consensus' ruled in relation to European policy, although the FCC began to challenge this consensus from 1974 onwards. The more recent pushback by German parapublic institutions (the Bundesbank and the Federal Constitutional Court) and the Länder calls into question the pattern of 'associated sovereignty' (Katzenstein 1997) between German and European institutions. It also sets up a tension with the Federal government, which may wish to deepen the integration capacities of the eurozone.

The institutions of the Federal Republic were shaped by an imperative not to repeat the hegemonial drive that had scarred Europe and ruined Germany in the Nazi era, and to emphasise the decentralisation and limitations of power externally and internally. It is not at all clear that the semi-sovereign pluralist institutions or German public opinion are fitted to play the new central role. There has been a perennial discussion as to whether a new European ministry, either as an independent entity or as part of a reinforced Chancellor's Office, should be created to supersede the current parcelling-out of responsibilities for European policy between a number of ministries. This division, reflecting Germany's multilateral policy style, was combined with a close alliance with France. Coordination of European policy classically occurred late in the process, and was usually referred to as post hoc coordination. It had the advantage that Germany could place itself at the centre of emerging constitutive bargains, but the variation in positions sometimes held by different ministries till late on in the process could lead to confusion in other member states. That is not a situation that can be contemplated easily if Germany is playing the leading role. Germany's new central role entails strengthening its strategic capacity and centralising the European policymaking machinery.

A strengthened strategic capacity is required to meet the challenges of the eurozone, and to hold the European Union together in the face of an emerging north-south split and the fragmentation challenge presented by the United Kingdom. This strategy deficit is new. In the original conception of the European Union, strategic orientation was to be provided by the European Commission; but the Commission is now a shadow of its former self and the Union method (Merkel) does not assign it a central strategic role. For much of the history of European integration, strategic leadership was provided by France in the joint Franco-German leadership, but this has now been superseded by Germany's unquestioned leadership position.

The persistence of semi-sovereignty and the role it gives to powerful veto players greatly constrain the strategic element in German European policymaking. Chancellor Merkel is often criticised for lacking a strategic vision in her *Staatskunst* (statecraft) for managing the eurozone crisis, but this ignores the fact that she has always had to anticipate the response of the Federal Constitutional Court. This chapter has described the increased role of Chancellor Merkel and the BK in the making of German European policy, but it has to be borne in mind that the BK is small and does not dispose of the specialist expertise of the other ministries. The result is that the chancellor's attention has to be selective. In the 2007 German Presidency, environmental policy was a *Chefsache* (a matter to be decided at the top level), and now the eurozone crisis and relations with principal member states are *Chefsachen*. There is simply not enough overarching strategic capacity to deal with the scale of the challenges.

Despite Germany's pre-eminent position in the European Union, worrying dilemmas remain. Its domestic policymaking machinery has long been regarded as suboptimal, but the exigencies of coalition government and the role of the key veto players (Länder, Bundesbank, and Federal Constitutional Court) make radical reform unlikely. Part of this gridlock is produced by the constitutionally anchored role of key actors like the Länder and the Federal Constitutional Court. The Basic Law and its interpretation by the Federal Constitutional Court also impart an element of inflexibility to a German leadership role; for example, if Eurobonds are thought to have become necessary, they would run up against the 'eternity clause' (Article 79(3) of the Basic Law), which precludes any transfers of sovereignty from the Bundestag to the EU level that would prevent the Bundestag from exerting its constitutionally guaranteed competences (Article 20 of the Basic Law). In this and a number of other cases prescribed by the 'eternity clause', the transfer of sovereignty requires constitutional change, which raises the question whether the Basic Law itself is ripe for revision. In the Bonn Republic there was a perfect match between what other member states expected of Germany and what its European policymaking machinery, including the Franco-German relationship, was able to produce. None of the dilemmas that confront German European policymaking are likely to be resolved quickly, and the spectre of a powerful Germany, unable to meet the expectations of its partners, will remain.

Notes

1   Michael Stürmer on the aims of German European policy; author's translation of a remark made in the author's presence.
2   For the organisation and responsibilities of divisions in the Ministry of Finance, see www.bundes finanzministerium.de/Content/DE/Downloads/Ministerium/Organigram_engl.pdf?__blob=publication File&v=7; for the organisation of divisions in the Federal Foreign Office, see www.auswaertiges-amt.de/cae/servlet/contentblob/373562/publicationFile/189194/Organigramm-en.pdf (accessed 10 December 2013).
3   *Basler Zeitung*, 29 May 2010.

Bibliography

Alonso, S. (2014) 'German party manifestos are increasingly unlikely to downplay European issues and reflect negative attitudes towards the EU'. Online. Available at http://blogs.lse.ac.uk/europpblog/2014/01/07 (accessed 20 January 2014).

Beichelt, T. (2007) 'Over-Efficiency in German EU Policy Coordination', *German Politics*, 16(4): 421–32.

Boyer, Y. (1996) 'France and Germany', in B. Heurlin (ed.) *Germany in Europe in the Nineties*, Basingstoke: Macmillan, 241–6.

Bulmer, S. and Paterson, W. (1987) *The Federal Republic of Germany and the European Community*, London: Allen and Unwin.

Bulmer, S. and Paterson, W. (2010) 'Germany and the European Union: From Tamed Power to Normalized Power?' *International Affairs*, 86(5): 1051–73.

Bulmer, S., Jeffery, C., and Paterson, W. (2000) *Germany's European Diplomacy: Shaping the Regional Milieu*, Manchester: Manchester University Press.

Chaffin, J. (2010) 'Why a Fearful Germany is Refusing to Rush to the Rescue', *Financial Times*, 25 May, 10.

Davies, W. (2012) *Resisting the European Court of Justice: West Germany's Confrontation with European Law, 1949–79*, Cambridge: Cambridge University Press.

Derlien, H.-U. (2000) 'Failing Successfully?' in H. Kassim, G. Peters, and V. Wright (eds) *The National Coordination of EU Policy: The Domestic Level*, Oxford: Oxford University Press, 54–78.

Dyson, K. and Goetz, K. (eds) (2003) *Germany, Europe and the Politics of Constraint*, Oxford: Oxford University Press.

Große Hüttmann, M.G. (2007) 'Die Koordination der deutschen Europapolitik', *Aus Politik und Zeitgeschichte*, 10: 39–45.

Harnisch, S. (2001) 'Change and Continuity in Post-Unification German Foreign Policy', *German Politics*, 10(1): 135–60.

Hesse, J. and Goetz, K. (1992) 'Early Administrative Adjustment to the European Communities: The Case of the Federal Republic of Germany', *Jahrbuch für Europäische Verwaltungsgeschichte*, 4: 181–206.

Jeffery, C. (2004) 'Regions and the Constitution for Europe: German and British Impacts', *German Politics*, 13(4): 625.

Katzenstein, P. (1987) *Policy and Politics in West Germany: The Growth of a Semi Sovereign State*, Philadelphia: Temple University Press.

Katzenstein, P. (ed.) (1997) *Tamed Power: Germany in Europe*, Ithaca and London: Cornell University Press.

Keohane, R. (2003) 'Ironies of Sovereignty: the EU and the US', in J. Weiler, I. Begg, and J. Peterson (eds) *Integration in an Expanding European Union: Reassessing the Fundamentals*, Oxford: Blackwell.

Landau, A. (1998) 'Bargaining over Power and Policy: The CAP Reform in the Uruguay Round', *International Negotiations*, 3(3): 453–79.

Marsh, D. (1992) *The Bundesbank: The Bank that Rules Europe*, London: Heinemann.

Marsh, D. (2013) *Beim Geld hört der Spass auf*, Berlin: Europa Verlag.

William E. Paterson

Merkel, A. (2010) 'Speech by Federal Chancellor Angela Merkel at the opening ceremony of the 61st academic year of the College of Europe in Bruges on 2 November 2010'. Online. Available at www.bruessel.diplo.de/contentblob/2959854/Daten/ (accessed 10 December 2013).

Paterson, W. (1993) 'Muss Europa Angst vor Deutschland haben?' in R. Hrbek (ed.) *Der Vertrag von Maastricht in der wissenschaftlichen Kontroverse*, Baden-Baden: Nomos, 9–18.

Paterson, W. (2005) 'European Policy Making: Between Associated Sovereignty and Semi Sovereignty', in S. Green and W. Paterson (eds) *Governance in Contemporary Germany: The Semi Sovereign State Revisited*, Cambridge: Cambridge University Press, 261–82.

Paterson, W. (2010) 'Does Germany Still Have a European Vocation?' *German Politics*, 19(1): 41–52.

Paterson, W. (2011) 'The Reluctant Hegemon? Germany Moves Centre Stage in the European Union', *Journal of Common Market Studies*, 49: 57–75.

Proissl, W. (2010) *Why Germany Fell Out of Love with Europe*, Brussels: Bruegel Essay.

Schild, J. (2010) 'Mission Impossible? The Potential for Franco-German Leadership in the Enlarged EU', *Journal of Common Market Studies*, 48(5): 1367–90.

Sikorski, R. (2011) 'I fear Germany's power less than her inactivity', *Financial Times*, 28 November. Available at www.ft.com/cms/s/0/b753cb42–19b3–11e1-ba5d-00144feabdc0.html#axzz2t0dv7MaC (accessed 11 February 2014).

Stürmer, M. and Neal, M. (1996) 'Les conséquences de 1989, les objectifs de la politique étrangère allemande', *Politique Étrangère*, 61(3): 513–19.

Van Esch, F. (2012) 'Why Germany wanted EMU: The Role of Helmut Kohl's Belief System and the Fall of the Berlin Wall', *German Politics*, 10(5): 34–42.

21

German power and 'embedded hegemony' in Europe

Beverly Crawford[1]

With ample evidence of German clout in shaping the outcome of the current euro crisis, there is general agreement that Germany is Europe's economic hegemon: the country with the most resources required for leadership. There has been little effort, however, to define hegemony or the role of a hegemon in the European economy, particularly in a crisis. This chapter describes how Germany's post-Wall European policy has been shaped by its role as the EU's economic hegemon since the 1980s. However, its continued position as a hegemonic leader of the eurozone – and of the single market as a whole – remains to be seen. German patronage and leadership ensured cooperation in creating and maintaining the European single market in good times and, in doing so, shaped the European 'milieu' (Bulmer, Jeffery, and Paterson 2000) in ways that enhanced European cooperation and protected and bolstered German economic interests. In the current European crisis, however, German unwillingness to make the sacrifices necessary to stabilise monetary union in bad times may signal that the era of hegemonic leadership in Europe is coming to an end.

This chapter begins by explaining why the debate over post-Wall German foreign policy is flawed and why an examination of Germany's role as the 'hegemonic leader' in Europe may yield more fruitful analysis and reconcile conflicting positions in the debate. The next section defines what I mean by the term hegemonic leader, why a hegemon is needed to achieve and maintain international cooperation, and what resources it takes to be one. I briefly discuss why hegemonic leaders rarely act alone and the dangers of domestic backlash in hegemonic states. I then turn to an overview of the hallmarks of German regional hegemony in Europe and describe some of the ways in which Germany has played the role of Europe's hegemonic leader. The final section is a case study of Germany's role in the European monetary system, measured by the standards of hegemonic stability theory. I conclude with an overview of the argument and raise the disturbing question whether Germany can and is willing to provide the hegemonic stability that is required for continued monetary union in the EU. I close by suggesting that Germany's unwillingness to provide resources for cooperation in this important issue area has already led to instability in Europe and that, unless Germany takes steps to help regain stability, is likely to result in more instability, defection from cooperation, and the demise of the monetary union.

Continuity or change: the wrong debate over post-Wall German foreign policy

Twice in the 20th century Germany aggressively reached for hegemony in Europe with disastrous results. After 1945, in order to prevent a third attempt, the Allies stripped a defeated, divided, and demilitarised Germany of its sovereignty and bound it to multilateral institutions, setting the direction for German economic and military policy. As the latter half of the century wore on, Germany emerged as Europe's economic powerhouse under the aegis of those institutions. After 1989, when full sovereignty (and the potential military capability to maintain it) was restored, the 'German question' was revived. Would Germany remain bound to treaty institutions that governed its foreign policy and military behaviour? Or would national interests replace its European interest? Many observers believed that Germany's commitment to the European interest was unwavering. Others speculated that Germany, now less dependent on European institutions, would begin asserting its sovereignty and go its own way. But most analysts agreed that, given the besmirched and bungled attempts to dominate its neighbours in the first half of the century, preponderant German power on the continent was to be feared. Analysis of the potential for a powerful Germany to play a *positive* hegemonic role in Europe seemed unthinkable. When evidence of the positive role of German power appeared, most analysts ignored or dismissed it.

This inconceivability of German power as a positive regional force trapped the debate over its foreign policy in a narrow, sterile dichotomy of 'continuity' versus 'change' (for analyses of this debate see Harnisch 2001; Rittberger 2001; Risse 2004; Herborth and Hellmann 2006; Gross 2009; Mauer 2009; Crawford 2010; Mayhew *et al.* 2011; and Chapter 25 in this volume). Observers in the 'continuity' school saw Germany as a 'reflexive multilateralist', still tightly bound to (and dominated by) European institutions. Others saw the potential for change in German foreign policy, equating it with the achievement of 'normality' as a European nation state. They predicted that sovereignty after 1989 would lead Germany to settle into the normal game of power politics, with an eye to serving only its self-interest. Even the most inconsequential German foreign policy decisions were carefully scrutinised, and each act was held up as support for one or the other position. There was little discussion of Germany's foreign policy 'vision' (Karp 2006; Crawford 2010). Although all accepted that the German economy was the 'engine' of the European economy, the function of the engine was rarely defined, and the notion that Germany was providing hegemonic stability within Europe was still inconceivable.

Positive and negative continuity

Within the straitjacket of a continuity versus change debate, each position had a positive and negative variant. Those who saw positive continuity in Germany's ongoing participation in multilateral institutions argued that a powerful Germany had finally relinquished power politics, embedding itself further in those institutions and helping to cement cooperation and consensus in furthering the expansion and integration of the European free market. Pointing to Germany's continued limited military capabilities, some observers argued that, as a corollary, Germany had abandoned militarism and therefore the pursuit of hegemony in Europe.

The more negative variant of the continuity thesis interpreted Germany's reflexive multi-lateralism as an indication that Germany is a free-rider in multilateral institutions, raking in the benefits of cooperation without paying the costs (Vinocur 2006; Leithner 2009; Soros 2012). Pointing to Germany's refusal to join the Iraq invasion or abstention from participation in a no-fly zone over Libya in 2011, critics called Germany a consumer rather than a provider of security. Germany was accused of 'navel gazing', of hiding behind its 'culture of reticence', of refusing to abandon its 'reflexive comfort zone', and of fearing to leave its 'safe house of moral comfort and limited involvement' (Vinocur 2006). In the midst of the euro crisis, Germany was seen as a free-rider on the common currency regime, and accused of being mired in a 'can't do' mode when it came to helping cement European solidarity.

Positive and negative change

The argument that Germany had, in the 21st century, finally shaken off its past to become a 'normal' state had its positive and negative interpretations as well. Those who urged Germany to embrace its 'normality' as a positive development lauded Germany's military participation in the wars of the Yugoslav succession and in Afghanistan. Some suggested that Germany could now take its rightful place among the world's great powers. Many argued that European integration weakens national sovereignty and that the EU is remote, anti-democratic, and elitist, ruled by unelected Brussels bureaucrats; it would therefore be prudent for Germany to loosen its ties to the EU.

Those who interpret normality in a negative light equate every apparent act of self-interest, or behaviour inconsistent with the analyst's views of appropriateness, with either a loosening of the bonds of multilateral cooperation and/or a step in the direction of regional domination. Germany's unilateral recognition of Croatia was cited by this school of thought as an attempt to recreate the World War II alliance with an independent Croatia as part of a divide-and-conquer strategy in the Balkans (see Crawford 1996). The Bundesbank's startling interest rate hike in 1992 that briefly derailed progress towards monetary union was cited as an example of Germany's effort to undermine European integration. Germany's refusal to participate in America's Iraq war in 2002–3 or in NATO's air strikes against Libya was cited as evidence of a dangerous break with multilateralism. Germany's breach of the eurozone's Stability and Growth Pact accompanying the monetary union (EMU) was interpreted as evidence of a weakened European identity and an assertion of naked national self-interest. Germany's approach to the eurozone crisis – not permitting a rise in inflation, precluding the establishment of Eurobonds, hesitating to provide bailouts for crisis countries – is cited as evidence of a declining interest in European cooperation that could be devastating, both in Europe and beyond (Sarotte 2010). George Soros went so far as to blame Germany for keeping 'periphery countries' in a 'permanently subordinated position' (Soros 2012). Kundnani (2011) saw Germany as loosening its ties to multilateral institutions and becoming a geo-economic power.

The four variants of the continuity versus change argument can be summarised in the matrix as shown in Table 21.1.

None of these views, however, captures the essence of Germany's role in Europe in 'good times' or its foreign policy vision. The vision consists of two tightly bound principles: multilateralism and antimilitarism. In the period before 1990, these principles did not conflict; they were vehicles by which West Germany could foster its national interest in the absence of traditional state power and national sovereignty. Indeed, ironically, West Germany maintained the national interest by relinquishing the military and diplomatic forces that maintained it. Particularly in the absence of sovereign control over military force, German leaders and the public at large believed that military solutions to foreign policy problems should be a last resort. With no real foreign policy of its own, Germany's international behaviour was based on civilian practices: trade, foreign aid, peacekeeping, international monitoring, and international law.

The FRG also behaved as a 'normal,' self-interested state *before* unification – and not always in the service of its policy vision. As part of the strategy to increase exports, for example, Germany

Table 21.1 The four variants of the continuity versus change argument

	Germany continues as a 'reflexive multilateralist' (policy continuity)	Germany returns to 'normality' (policy change)
Positive	Germany as a cooperative player in multilateral institutions, maintaining a European identity.	A renewed policy of self-interest and even euroscepticism is healthy. The EU is undemocratic and incompetent. Like other 'normal' states, Germany must look after its own interests and is doing so.
Negative	A powerful and sovereign Germany is a freerider within multilateral institutions, consuming rather than producing the benefits of membership.	Germany's self-interested behaviour will harm Europe and the international community.

– in its role as a 'trading state' – sold arms and dual-use goods and technology abroad – even to unstable countries. In 1989 it was revealed that a West German firm, Imhausen-Chemie, had been providing Libya with the goods and technology to produce poison gas in significant and dangerous quantities. In the thick of the Cold War, the FRG broke with the United States when it chose to assist the Soviet Union in building a pipeline to transport natural gas to Europe. And, as I discuss in more detail below, from the 1970s until the creation of EMU, West Germany riled its European partners by raising interest rates to counter domestic inflation.

Similar examples after 1990 suggest 'continuity' of self-interest in Germany's postwar foreign policy behaviour. But overwhelmingly the evidence suggests that these two principles – multilateralism and antimilitarism – were the dominant guiding principles and held firm in post-Wall German foreign policy (Crawford 2010). When multilateral commitments conflicted with the commitment to antimilitarism, Germany chose the antimilitarist stance but did not renege on its essential multilateral treaty commitments. Although it bent the rules in recognising Croatia and broke them when it breached the eurozone's Stability and Growth Pact, important multilateral treaty commitments within NATO and the EU remained strong. Multilateral cooperation in the invasion of Iraq and the airstrikes in Libya was entirely voluntary: Germany broke no commitments by refusing to engage in military action, nor was alliance security reduced. Germany maintained its military commitment to NATO in Afghanistan, but its rules of engagement were severely restricted to reconnaissance, training, and humanitarian aid. German soldiers were forbidden to fire at anyone who might be a civilian.

The continuity-change dichotomy also misses the chief role that Germany played in the post-Wall period: underwriting the stability of and taking the lead in shaping European institutions. Some analysts have argued that leadership requires a preponderance of regional power – including military power – to call the shots, which Germany does not possess, and others argue that even if Germany has the power to lead, it is unwilling to do so (Paterson 2011; Schönberger 2012). Below I present evidence for the argument that Germany possessed the resources needed to underwrite cooperation in Europe, and used those resources to further European cooperation in the eurozone. It is to this role, which I call 'hegemonic leadership', that the discussion now turns.

Hegemonic leadership

What is a hegemonic leader? Hegemony is a fraught term. When observers of German foreign policy argue about German hegemony or lack thereof, they usually mean it in terms of 'the most powerful state': the one that calls the shots or mobilises advantages to achieve its own interests (Mullins *et al.* 2001; Rachman 2012). Many assume that a hegemon is dominant militarily or has the capability to be so. Others see a hegemon as a dominant ideological power in the Gramscian sense: a state with the ability and willingness to impose its ideology on others (Cox 1983; Engel 2008).

My definition of a hegemonic leader is the standard one used in the field of international relations and first introduced in the literature by Charles Kindleberger (1986), based on Mancur Olsen's theory of collective action (1965), and elaborated by Robert Gilpin *et al.* (2002), Robert Keohane (1984), Barry Eichengreen (1990), and others in Kindleberger's tradition (Krasner 1976; Snidel 1985): *a hegemonic leader is the state powerful enough to pay the costs required for cooperation and shape the rules of multilateral institutions.* Or, more simply, as Jürgen Krönig (2013) writes, hegemony 'requires the ability to define and pursue national interests, [. . .] using the hegemon's greater weight and influence in such a way that it serves the common good'. This definition is based on two assumptions: (1) that states cooperate with one another to achieve goals that individual states cannot achieve (for example, they form multilateral organisations and enter into treaties); and (2) achieving cooperation is difficult because all want the benefits of cooperation while paying the least possible cost for it; or they decide that, although it benefits the group as a whole, cooperation does not promote their *individual* goals as well as unilateral action would. Cooperation is uncertain because each is worried that others will not cooperate, and so is tempted to exit before others do. In a world of sovereign states, members of a cooperative regime can leave at any time, and they do so for those reasons (Olsen and Zeckhauser 1966).[2]

An international monetary union provides an example of cooperation and its difficulties.[3] States that trade with one another want to share a single currency because under national currency systems exchange rate stability is uncertain. Without a single standard defining the value of trading partners' currencies, the costs of doing business – such as transaction and currency exchange costs – are high, especially if exchange rates fluctuate constantly. High transaction costs and exchange rate volatility make the value of traded goods uncertain. One partner in a business transaction will lose money if the currency of his trading partner depreciates. The more a currency's value fluctuates, the more likely this loss is to occur, which eventually makes traders more hesitant to conduct business. For example, prior to the creation of the euro, if a French trader wanted a product from Germany to sell in France, the merchant had to exchange French francs for German deutschmarks (DM) to pay for the product. If a fluctuation in the exchange rate between the franc and the DM caused the DM to be valued higher than the franc, the merchant would lose profit since it would take more francs to purchase the good in question.

Exchange rates can fluctuate because governments manipulate them to meet national economic goals. If unemployment is on the rise, for example, they are tempted to devalue their national currency in order to stimulate exports and create jobs; but currency devaluations are inflationary and contagious and can set off a chain reaction of retaliatory devaluations that will hinder trade. One benefit of monetary unions is that they reduce or eliminate transaction costs, especially those associated with large, unpredictable fluctuations in exchange rates. This was a problem in interstate trade in the United States until monetary union in 1791. Even then, the decision to issue a single currency was a hard-fought political battle. The achievement of monetary union among different sovereign states is even more difficult. Members of such a union – particularly those running trade deficits – will be tempted to leave it to protect their own economies when they deem it necessary to devalue their currencies in order to bring trade into balance.

In fact, collective action among sovereign states is difficult in a number of issue areas (a defence alliance, for example, or a treaty to reduce nuclear weapons, greenhouse gases, or other impediments to free trade). A hegemonic leader can alleviate the uncertainty of collective action by providing the bulk of a collective good: security, in the form of, for example, nuclear weapons reductions or strong environmental laws that limit greenhouse gases – the good that every state wants to cooperate to achieve. What this means is that cooperation requires a particular kind of powerful leader – not one who coerces others to cooperate or simply makes all of the decisions, but rather one who pays the lion's share of the costs of cooperation or offers generous 'side payments' to others as an inducement for them to provide their share of the collective good. As the hegemon continues these practices, it garners legitimacy in the eyes of other regime members, reinforcing their cooperation. A hegemonic leader of a free trade regime, for example, can raise the incentive to cooperate by providing resources (loans, aid, a large import market) for states facing a trade deficit to stimulate their economies and therefore maintain their membership of the regime. In the absence of hegemonic intervention, states in a monetary union who face trade and budget deficits must bear the burden of cooperation. That means that they are forced to take 'austerity measures': deflate their economies, lay off workers, and reduce pensions and incomes in order to halt imports and rein in inflation (which depreciates currency values). This hurts all trading partners, and therefore the temptation to deflate or defect from the regime must be removed. Only a hegemonic leader can provide appropriate incentives to remove that temptation.

But the European Union is not an 'ordinary' regime established to ensure cooperation among states. It is a treaty-based institution that integrates the markets of its members into a single market. Decisions are taken through complex voting procedures established to ensure that no one state will dominate the process; indeed many decisions are taken by consensus. From the beginning, all members were 'embedded' within the institution, beholden to its rules and norms. Many of those rules can be obeyed at low cost to member states. But as we have seen above, a treaty commitment to remain in a regime is simply not enough to ensure cooperation. The EU is essentially a free trade regime, subject to the problems of collective action described above. It is for this reason that the bulk of the EU budget – 41 per cent – is devoted to 'cohesion', measures intended to keep Europe together, by providing aid to weaker regions and sectors. But even with these funds, when the governments of member states perceive that the burden of cooperation is too high, they will be tempted – as Britain has been – to leave the union.

Kindleberger (1986) claimed that in order to remove that temptation, a hegemonic leader must provide five incentives to maintain a free trade regime: a stable exchange rate (to afford certainty in cross-border trade); a market for distress goods (goods that cannot find a buyer), thereby stimulating the potential defector's economy and creating employment; countercyclical long-term lending (to balance deficits and possibly create jobs); macroeconomic policy coordination (to maintain sustainable government debt and build institutional arrangements that allow the correction of emerging imbalances); and real lending of last resort during financial crises. The hegemon might need to run a trade deficit with the crisis country to stimulate that country's exports; it would need extensive capital for countercyclical and last-resort lending. Finally, it would need to provide these incentives in order to gain agreement from other members of the regime to create stable institutions for policy coordination. These and other incentives provide legitimacy for the practice of hegemonic stability.

Why would powerful states take on this role? Because they perceive the benefits of pursuing the common good. A hegemonic leader of an alliance, for example, will pay the costs because a peaceful, cooperative environment is in its best interest, and the costs of providing it are lower than the costs of arms races and wars. In a monetary union, a hegemon will underwrite cooperation in the ways outlined above because the stable currency that cooperation offers will work to its benefit, promoting exports, creating certainty in good times and preventing competitive devaluations in bad. The hegemon of a cooperative regime does not lead alone. Leaders have never had such a preponderance of power that they could provide *all* the resources needed for stability (Eichengreen 1990). Indeed, it would not be a good idea to provide all. *But they must provide a disproportionate share of those resources.* Kindleberger (1981) suggests that shared leadership adds legitimacy and reduces the danger that leadership will be regarded as a cloak for domination. Shared leadership reduces the temptation of hegemons to bully. Shared leadership also reduces the drain on the hegemon's resources. Certainly, cooperation among liberal democratic states requires leadership within institutions in which all members have a say.

It is not altruism but the provision of a *disproportionate* share of resources to underwrite cooperation that characterises hegemonic leadership. Like other members of cooperative arrangements, hegemons gain the intangible benefits of stability, while also garnering reputational benefits and influence as a result of taking on the largest burden. But they also gain tangible benefits. In a free trade regime, for example, although in theory open markets benefit all, they benefit the strongest economy the most: its exports are the most competitive; they provide the most lucrative employment market. But though they gain the most, free trade is not a 'zero-sum game' in which some win and some lose. In fact, it is considered a 'positive–sum game' in which the efficiency and innovation that free markets create benefits all, even if some benefit more than others.

Even with the benefits it receives, paying the lion's share to maintain cooperation will drain the hegemon's resources or lead to a perception of resource drain that can trigger domestic distrust of hegemonic practice and thereby constrain it. In the United States, for example, the US Marshall Plan was initially hotly contested in Congress: on the Senate floor Alexander Wiley of Wisconsin declared 'We are through being "Uncle Sap"'; Senator Homer Capehart of Indiana called the Marshall Plan 'state socialism'; and Frederick Smith of Ohio called it 'outright communism'. Senator Joseph McCarthy of Wisconsin later called it a 'massive and unrewarding boondoggle' that had turned the United States into 'the patsy of the modern world'. The controversy might have gone on and even destroyed the initiative, but in February 1948, at the peak of the debate, communists overthrew the government of Czechoslovakia. Shortly afterwards, Congress moved quickly to fund the plan, but at a lower level than Truman had requested. Even then, a publicity blitz was carried out to convince the American people that the funding would stimulate US exports and help the country escape an impending economic meltdown. Even in this landmark case, then, hegemonic practice narrowly escaped domestic constraints.

A domestic backlash can constrain hegemonic largesse, even when it does not represent a significant resource drain. For example, under pressure from domestic business in the 1970s as trade competition increased, the United States Congress enacted protectionist measures in section 301 of the trade law. Those measures were renewed numerous times under subsequent US governments, even when the US economy grew.

While hegemons provide absolute gains to the system, making their trading partners more competitive, over time they will sustain relative losses by narrowing the wealth gap between themselves and others – even to the point of threatening hegemonic decline. Britain experienced relative decline as the leader of the 19th-century free trade regime as its trading partners grew in economic might. In the last half of the 20th century, many Americans grumbled that US military leadership in NATO and the defence spending required placed an unfair burden on the US, while NATO partners were free to pursue economic growth, thus closing the economic gap between themselves and the US. In the postwar international monetary regime, historical evidence shows that when the US *did* accept the costs of exchange rate stability, those costs ultimately undermined the US economy (Gowa 1983). When losses to hegemonic capability are too great, international cooperation, which depends on hegemonic stability, can become unstable over time as the hegemon balks in the face of his shrinking advantage. This happened to the exchange rate regime under the gold standard when British hegemony declined, eventually leading to the collapse of the regime. It happened to the postwar exchange rate regime under the United States as the US deficit grew and the real value of the dollar weakened. This resource drain – which can destabilise the regime and lead to domestic backlash, with a decline in relative economic power – threatens hegemonic leadership. The hegemon walks a tightrope between providing resources that sustain cooperation and dissipating its own power to provide those resources. Hegemonic leaders cannot retain their hegemonic power in the long run without constructing 'burden-sharing' rules within the cooperative framework to protect them.

Hegemonic leaders often attempt to shape cooperative institutions and rules that institutionalise burden sharing in order to protect themselves from this kind of resource drain. As noted above, paying a disproportionate share to maintain cooperation is not popular in a hegemonic state, and unpopularity threatens its government. Therefore hegemonic leaders try to shape cooperative systems to spread the costs among all members and maintain the economic strength required to provide an anchor for the system and maintain their own interests. But the moment when spreading the costs can lead to defection from cooperation is uncertain. Usually it is signalled by domestic political unrest in weaker countries when the cost of cooperation does not seem worth the benefits. We can only approximate the resources needed to provide the hegemonic leadership needed to prevent defection from the regime, and we have only the 20–20 hindsight of history to tell us when spreading the costs too thickly can lead to the demise of the regime itself.

Germany's hegemonic power

Leadership to strengthen cooperation is called 'hegemonic' because the state willing to provide it has the resources to do so. What are those resources? Keohane lists five kinds of resources that a state must possess in order to deserve the title of hegemon: control over raw materials, control over markets, control over sources of capital, a competitive advantage in the production of highly valued goods, and military superiority. After World War II, the United States was the only state left standing that could boast control in these five areas and showed a willingness to lead; as a result, the US was dubbed the world's hegemon (Gilpin *et al.* 2002). It lowered its trade barriers and ran trade deficits so that the economies of Europe and Japan could grow and cooperate in a free trade regime. It supplied Marshall Plan aid for European reconstruction and military security for its allies. In the creation of the first European Communities, the US acted as the 'external' hegemon, both paying the costs and taking blame for being heavy handed; the US's provision of security and aid prevented any one state within Western Europe from appearing dominant in the cooperative effort.

To assert that Germany has the resources to be a global hegemon would be ludicrous. As the world's fourth largest economy, and second largest exporter, it is considered a global 'great power'; but it lacks the military resources to provide traditional security in a European alliance, or to be a malevolent, land-grabbing imperialist. Military power is not relevant in the context of the European Union. Despite efforts to expand its powers in other issue areas, including a common foreign policy, the EU is organised to achieve the *economic* benefits of a free trade regime for its members first and foremost.[4] What Germany does have is resources to underwrite that effort.

With regard to Keohane's first measure, Germany is, like most EU states, dependent on other nations for raw materials, particularly energy. Indeed, Germany's lack of raw materials has historically been a justification for aggressive expansion. Although Germany may never 'control' sufficient energy resources within its borders, its energy independence is growing faster than in any other industrial nation (Buchan 2012). It is the largest producer of renewable energy in Europe (Eurostat 2012a); its connections with global energy suppliers are geared to assuring a secure energy supply through its export dominance (Germany is the largest exporter to the Middle East) and the expansion of German board memberships in foreign energy corporations. With its interlocking board directorates, 'German capital very much guards the energy back door of the EU, reaping a range of related benefits in [. . .] commercial exchanges' (Van der Pijl *et al.* 2010: 401).

The second of Keohane's measures is control over markets. No two countries benefit equally from a trading relationship. Depending on the size and structure of their economies, one country (usually the one with the lesser economy) may become disproportionately dependent on the other even as it becomes better off than it was before that relationship. When commerce with a larger country accounts for a very large proportion of the total imports and exports of a smaller economy, the latter is increasingly vulnerable to the larger country's influence. Germany and its neighbours find themselves in this position of dominance and vulnerability. Germany exports more goods and services to other EU states than any other member and remains the biggest exporter and import market in Europe. EU countries absorbed 59 per cent of Germany's exports in 2011, and few other European exporters can supply the products that Germany produces at the price that EU and eurozone membership enables. Clearly, Germany's exports also depend on the EU market, but its trade focus is shifting towards Asia and the developing world (see Chapter 25). Germany dominates the EU's global trade, and is the largest exporter to China and Russia. In 2012 Germany had by far the largest trade surplus of any EU member state; France and Britain, the next largest economies in Europe, ran trade deficits (Eurostat 2010; European Commission 2012; Fontes 2013).

The third source of hegemonic power is control over sources of capital. Companies in countries with large capital markets have deep pockets; they can draw on savings and their own export earnings in order to invest both at home and abroad. Governments can leverage large capital markets to advance foreign policy objectives, controlling access to markets in quid pro quo negotiations. Thanks to its booming economy, large trade surplus, and the highest ratio of savings to GDP in Europe (World Bank 2013), Germany is a magnet for foreign capital, rapidly becoming the largest capital market in Europe and providing ample credit for investors both in Europe and in the rest of the world. Germany also became the main supplier of intra-EU foreign direct investment (FDI)[5] *and* Europe's preeminent destination for FDI from both European and non-European firms.[6] Bursting with profits, German firms have achieved an unprecedented global centrality in mergers, acquisitions, and interlocking company directorates (Van der Pijl *et al.* 2010), and because Germany was the only major eurozone nation to escape the credit downgrades that have hit its neighbours, in 2013 foreign investors still overwhelmingly preferred to park their money in German banks.

A hegemon is the largest producer of value-added goods. It imports products that are labour intensive or produced with well-known production techniques. It produces and exports the capital-intensive products and those that will provide the basis for producing even more advanced goods and services in the future. Germany has a competitive advantage in the production of these goods in Europe, and one measure of that advantage is that Germany maintains the largest share of manufactured goods as a percentage of GDP in Europe, a third larger than that of France and Britain (CIA World Fact Book 2012). Additionally, the German industrial worker remains the most productive in Europe, as Germany is the European leader in heavy industry and in the production of high technology manufactured goods. In terms of patent applications per capita, Germany ranks first in Europe; moreover, Germany has the highest percentage of employees in knowledge-intensive services in the EU (Eurostat 2011).

Finally, Keohane notes, a hegemon must possess superior military power. But traditional military power has been rendered increasingly useless in a world where states no longer have a monopoly on violence, where overwhelming modern force cannot defeat tribal combatants living in caves, where computer hackers can potentially shut down a nation, where threats to the 'national interest' can come from the earth's atmosphere, where a crisis of confidence in a single economy (like Greece's) can bring the globe to the brink of economic disaster, and where, as Konrad Jarausch has written, 'havoc created by global capitalism [. . .] is beginning to rival the suffering caused by the nation state' (Jarausch 2006). Asking who won a given war in the last half of the 20th century and in the first decade of the 21st century is like asking who won the San Francisco earthquake. Germany is exceptional in that it has all but abandoned this hallmark of hegemony at a point in history where its usefulness to provide security has increasingly been called into question.

In sum, Germany possesses advantages that permit it to underwrite the free trade regime – or act as a hegemonic leader – in Europe. But has Germany been willing to do so? In what follows, I argue that in the 20 years since the Wall fell, the answer has been yes. Germany takes the lead in shaping the European institutions that bolster free trade, both to stabilise the free trade regime and to serve its own self-interest. It does not, however, shape those institutions alone. And, as I have noted above, hegemonic leadership has an Achilles heel: expenditure of resources to maintain cooperation can drain hegemonic power and cause domestic backlash; and not expending enough resources will cause the hegemon to lose legitimacy in the eyes of its partners, even triggering defection from cooperation. And as we shall see, although Germany has exercised hegemonic leadership in 'good' times, the Achilles heel of hegemony may prompt an unwillingness, or even an inability, to exercise that leadership in bad times.

German hegemony in Europe

Throughout history, states have achieved economic hegemony by the strengths enumerated here, but few have provided the kind of leadership that is necessary for cooperation in a free trade regime like the EU. Germany has supplied that leadership in providing the most support for cooperation as a whole, making side payments for cooperation in specific issue areas, and constructing European institutions that codified cooperation and burden sharing (Paterson 2011; Goetz 2004; Thomson 2010).

Germany is the largest net contributor to the EU budget, consistently paying almost twice as much as it has received. In contrast, France and the UK maintain relative parity between payments and receipts. France, in particular, has reaped the most benefit of any EU member from the Common Agricultural Policy funds to subsidise its farmers so that they would sign on to the cooperative European effort. In the realm of nonproliferation policy and export control, Germany is also the leader in cooperative efforts to stem the tide of weapons proliferation, imposing more stringent restrictions on its own high technology exporters than other members (Crawford 2007). Being by far the largest of the environmentally progressive countries in the EU, it is the most important of the three leaders in EU environmental policymaking. In diplomacy, Germany has been called the most important member of the EU3 negotiating team in the Middle East (Westcott 2008). Germany was the undisputed architect of the European monetary union (EMU). And to assuage fears of its dominance in these and other issue areas, Germany agreed to the relative overweighting of the less populous France, Britain, and Italy in EU voting and is notably underrepresented in qualified majority voting in the Council of

Ministers (Posen 2005). Within the EMU Germany has contributed 27.1 per cent of the ECB's €6.36 billion in capital, but has the same voting rights as Malta, with 1 per cent, and Austria, with 2.1 per cent (Lawton 2012).

Leadership and self-interest in a free trade regime can be quite compatible. Hegemonic leaders benefit from the cooperative arrangements that they support, but that does not mean that others are disadvantaged. Analyses calling Germany a 'political dwarf' in Europe forget that the EU was and continues to be *primarily* a free trade regime. To create and sustain free trade in Europe, the EU was built as an organisation with a rule structure that continues to protect the single (free) market. Production standardisation, standard environmental regulation, standard rules for high technology exports, and cohesion funds to protect the less competitive and stimulate poorer regional economies all work to provide incentives to stabilise the single market. Still, the greatest economy benefits more from free trade than others. Even before unification, Germany as a reflexive multilateralist with the biggest economy benefited from each decision to enlarge and deepen the single market and to make it more efficient. Germany's growing export surplus confirms this.

In guiding policy development for the union, Germany is less than altruistic. For example, in environmental policy, Germany vied to have its standards accepted by the European Community as a whole in order to 'level the playing field' so that German exporters would not suffer from regulatory restraints that its European competitors did not share (Sbragia 1992). The same is true of the export control regime; German controls on high technology exporters were more stringent than those of their European competitors, and exporters wanted European standards to rise to Germany's level. Self-interested? Certainly; but most would agree that stiffer regulations to protect the environment or curb the export of dangerous high technology serve the common good in ways that go beyond creating a level playing field for trade. Finally, although Germany is the top contributor to EU cohesion funds, it is also the top *indirect* beneficiary of cohesion payments. Each euro that Germany pays into EU cohesion funds generates €1.25 in revenues from exports to new member states (EU Business 2012). Germany benefits most, but EU members agree that enlarging the single market benefits all.

Attention to self-interest deflects domestic criticism of hegemonic leadership. Exporters in Germany have benefited tremendously from the single market and from pan-European regulations that rise to German standards in order to create what exporters call a level playing field. These policies support not only domestic interests but deeply entrenched norms: German export philosophy regarded exports as a right of business; all state interventions needed specific and explicit authority. When important social groups benefit and a deeply entrenched worldview is upheld, hegemony is bolstered domestically.

Hegemonic leaders do not lead alone, and Germany is no exception (Pedersen 1998). There are in fact no 'lone' leaders in the EU. It is commonplace to note that Germany and France, as the original founders of the European Coal and Steel Community (ECSC), have long been the two 'pillars' providing dominant support for the European project – with, as Charles de Gaulle noted, Germany the horse and France the coachman of the European 'coach'. This image was fine for public consumption – reflecting France's need to assert great power status and Germany's need to keep a low profile after its defeat in World War II. In reality, however, it was Franco-German *agreement* as equal partners that was required for Europe to move forward.[7]

Germany is a co-leader in a number of issue areas. In diplomacy, Germany is one member of the EU3 with Britain and France, shaping policy together, albeit with Germany in the lead. In EU environmental policy, Germany leads together with Sweden and Denmark, the top three 'green' EU members. Although all 17 members of EMU are represented on the European Central

Bank's governing council, Germany, along with France and Italy, has two votes by virtue of its seat on the executive board.[8]

Only since the gathering storm of the euro crisis have analysts referred to Germany as a 'hegemon'. The reference to Germany as a hegemon is found primarily in journalistic accounts of the crisis and then only in the negative sense discussed above (Pedersen 1998 and Crawford 2007 are the exceptions). In most of these accounts, Germany is described as the dominant but most blatantly self-interested state in Europe, with the power to lead but reluctance to do so. Some reports and opinion pieces – which fit into the analytic category of 'negative change' – read as if Germany has dominated Europe since unification but has acted in a short-sighted, self-interested, self-centred manner, imposing costs on others in order to reap the benefits of disproportionate power. Other pieces read as if self-serving German hegemony arrived full-blown on the scene with the wave of the euro crisis, whereas previously German hegemony was not acknowledged. In contrast to these accounts, I have suggested here that, with ample resources to underwrite cooperation, German foreign policy in Europe has evolved into that of a hegemonic leader as defined in the standard literature on hegemonic stability theory. Germany has been far from reluctant to underwrite cooperation. It assumes the largest financial burden in the EU, provides leadership in key issue areas, and as the largest economy and exporter reaps the benefits of leadership in decisions that enhance the single market. Evidence of self-interest is not evidence of policy 'change' unless self-interest harms the interests of others. Hegemonic stability theory explains why Germany agreed to make the greatest contribution to the EU budget. It explains why Germany does not lead alone, and why it acts to protect its interests in the free trade regime. Germany has been neither a 'reflexive multilateralist', a 'normal' narrowly self-interested power, nor a 'free-rider' on multilateral institutions. German hegemony in Europe has been the long unacknowledged elephant in the room.

The European Monetary Union and financial crisis: continued hegemonic leadership?

Will Germany always be capable and willing to be a hegemonic leader in Europe? On the road towards monetary union, Germany did play a leadership role, calling the shots and underwriting cooperation. But since the onset of the 2009 financial crisis, Germany has stopped short of providing stability to the monetary regime. Like the United States in the post-war international economy, Germany may prove to be a hegemonic leader in Europe only in 'good' times.

From the 'snake' to EMS

The history of monetary union in Europe provides a good case study of German hegemonic leadership – and highlights the consequences of the absence of leadership. As noted above, monetary union supports a free trade regime by lowering transaction costs and eliminating currency volatility. The blueprint for monetary union was a 1969 agreement (the Werner Plan), which was shelved because of disagreements over how the burden of cooperation should be shared – whether surplus (France's position) or deficit (Germany's position) countries should bear the lion's share (Crawford 2007: 124–6). Germany was not strong enough to get its way. In 1972 Germany introduced a substitute, called the 'snake,' which lined up European currencies in bands, allowing for upper and lower limits of currency value. Snake members agreed to joint intervention in exchange rate markets to keep member currencies within the band, buying up currencies that were dropping in value and selling those that were appreciating.

In actuality, 'snake' members did not have the resources to stabilise exchange rates. Liquidity was in short supply, and interventions were few and far between. This meant that the burden of cooperation fell on the deficit countries, which would have to deflate their economies or leave the band altogether. And of course they left rather than deflate. By 1974 the 'snake' had failed, but European countries with export surpluses and therefore intense interest in stable exchange rates pegged the value of their currencies to the DM, creating a zone of exchange rate stability. But the peg to the DM meant that members would have to adhere to German preferences, coordinating macroeconomic policies to tighten belts, if necessary, in order to maintain price stability.

Because this DM zone was German dominated, German Chancellor Helmut Schmidt launched a multilateral initiative in 1978, creating a new common 'band', and a new institution, the European monetary system (EMS), with a new set of rules. Like the rules of the DM zone, the rules of the EMS conformed to German preferences: exchange rate stability would be backed by increased policy harmonisation according to anti-inflationary standards. The EMS was also backed by two safety nets – liquidity and intervention – for those with weakening currencies. Though the EMS was supposed to provide those safety nets, they were actually provided by Germany.

With large surpluses and an economy growing stronger by the day, Germany provided a central source of liquidity for the system. Throughout the 1980s, the Bundesbank bought falling currencies and lowered the discount rate to provide countercyclical lending (Ungerer *et al.* 1986, 1990; Marsh 1992). With Germany taking on the role of the hegemonic leader, the EMS proved to be remarkably successful in stabilising exchange rates. Stable exchange rates, in turn, benefited German exporters, and export surpluses continued to grow. But the single market could not ensure continued economic growth, particularly because the dollar devaluation after 1985 made European exports to the world relatively more expensive. Despite the liquidity that Germany provided, and the currency interventions and discounts that did occur, European exports slowed, unemployment in deficit countries grew, and economic growth was reduced to a snail's pace. As the situation in the deficit countries worsened, Germany proved unwilling to provide them with adequate loans, since German officials believed that increasing liquidity would put inflationary pressure on the system. The increasingly dire situation was exacerbated because the currencies of both deficit and surplus EMS countries were interlocked; economic fluctuations between them were reflected directly in rising unemployment and cuts in the deficit members rather than in a depreciation in value of their currencies. Many analysts attributed the worsening situation to the anti-inflationary (read deflationary) bias of the German-dominated exchange rate system. Although they benefited from the credibility that the DM 'anchor' had given their currencies, deflationary pressures and the pressure on exports rendered adherence to EMS rules increasingly painful for all but Germany, whose exporters continued to accumulate a surplus in intra-regional trade. As Kindleberger's argument would predict, cracks began appearing in the EMS.

From EMS to monetary union

Although Germany took on the hegemonic task of providing stable exchange rates in good times, it was unwilling to undertake the task of stabilising the system in bad times. In Germany's eyes, stability in bad times was the task of deficit, not surplus countries. But the EMS made no provision for deficit countries to tighten their belts in order to bring trade into balance. German leaders began therefore to prefer a tighter monetary union that would *require* deficit countries to deflate their economies. And all deficit countries were demanding more 'voice' in decisions on monetary cooperation in Europe. Indeed, both France and Italy 'complained with increasing vigor that the EMS had invested disproportionate power in Germany' (Grieco 1996: 290). Certainly not wanting to engage in deflationary policies, most EMS members believed (correctly, as it turned out) that monetary union would reduce interest rates – achieved by collectivising risk – which would make it cheaper for them to borrow, both to fund national budgets that fell into deficit and to prime the employment market lost through the failure of uncompetitive businesses. It seemed that the loss of national monetary sovereignty and potentially deflationary practices that Germany required became secondary concerns compared with these benefits. Therefore agreement among both surplus and deficit countries on the net benefits set the stage for monetary union.

In 1988, France and Italy took the initiative that led to EMU and the creation of a European Central Bank (ECB) that would give all members voting rights on the development of EU exchange rate policy. But the core rules of EMU were not subject to a vote, and those rules were constructed according to German policy preferences. Indeed, Germany quickly came on board in order to shape the new system, demanding an independent central bank dedicated to price stability, constraints on members' deficits and inflation (called 'convergence criteria'), and tight sanctions on defectors. Gone were the safety nets of the EMS. Indeed, Germany would not agree to a date for the final stage of monetary union until others agreed that those criteria must be met before a potential entrant could join the eurozone (Crawford 1998).

The 'convergence criteria' for membership of the eurozone represented a German effort to wrest some control over national budgets from member governments in order to achieve 'burden sharing' on the part of deficit countries. The criteria established common rules to ensure that members who made painful economic reforms would not face higher interest rates caused by members who did not make the same reforms. The rules defined 3 per cent of GNP as the upper limit for public deficits and 60 per cent of GNP as the upper limit for public debts. Members also promised to maintain an inflation rate not more than 1.5 per cent above the rate of the three members with the lowest inflation rates. These criteria were strengthened when Germany insisted on a Stability and Growth Pact (SGP) that created sanctions for defection. Any country breaching criteria for three consecutive years was subject to fines that could run to billions of euros. And the ECB as the guardian of price stability was not permitted to provide countercyclical loans or to be a lender of last resort for deficit members breaching the criteria.

In demanding these criteria, Germany relinquished a key function of hegemonic leadership that it had provided under the 'snake' and the EMS; neither Germany nor the ECB would provide loans or intervene in any other way to reduce recessionary pressures on members' economies. The strong German economy did provide one important component of Kindleberger's requirement for hegemonic stability, however: stable exchange rates.

Without loans and currency interventions, countries and regions feeling recessionary pressures had a smaller toolkit for reviving their economies than they had had under EMS. National control of interest rates had come to an end. Hamstrung by wage and labour inflexibility, European governments would normally use fiscal policy to carry much of the load of cushioning recessions, but fiscal policy had become severely circumscribed. Many economists argued that it made no sense to force countries in recession to cut public spending,[9] but eurozone members were not allowed to expand budget deficits beyond 3 per cent of GDP. But something was about to shift. Beginning in 1996, Germany fell into a sustained period of low growth and mounting fiscal burdens as unemployment skyrocketed, the population aged, and healthcare obligations festered. In order to ease the fiscal burden, the German government could have borrowed from within the EU capital market (to which it was the largest contributor), but borrowing would have raised interest rates across the EMU region, further contributing to deflationary pressures. Germany attempted to adhere to the SGP, cutting government spending to meet the requirements, and shoving the economy into deeper crisis. But by 2002 it had violated the pact and refused to pay the fine for doing so, following Portugal's breach and paving the way for France to break the pact as well. Germany flouted the SGP for four years, weakening the very rules for burden sharing that it had created. It would now be difficult to ask other eurozone members with chronic deficits to curb their borrowing and spending.

This did not seem to matter to the German leadership because Germany – as Europe's main exporter – was the chief beneficiary of the lower transaction costs that the euro introduced. And because, according to the director of McKinsey & Company, the value of the euro was 18–25 per cent below what the value of the DM would have been (*The Local* 2011), German exports were cheaper, not only vis-à-vis the exports of other major industrial nations but against all other members of the eurozone (*The Local* 2011; Norris 2011). Rather than providing a market for its trading partners' goods, Germany began to rack up a huge trade surplus with the rest of the EU. German exports increased fourfold from 2002 to 2010. In 2012, Germany's share of the wealth created by the euro was almost half the EU total. McKinsey management consultants attributed two thirds of German growth between 2002 and 2012 to the euro's introduction (Buergin 2012).

During the economic boom of 2003–8, German banks went wild with procyclical lending, extending credit on a massive scale to the eurozone's Mediterranean countries (De Guzman *et al.* 2010). And with that credit, they gobbled up German products, while Germany bought little from them. Between 2000 and 2007, Greece's annual trade deficit with Germany grew from 3 billion euros to 5.5 billion, Italy's doubled, Spain's almost tripled, and Portugal's quadrupled. In Germany, consumption of imports dropped, and the savings rate increased (Eurostat 2012b). But as the financial crisis escalated in 2009, lending abruptly stopped. Germany had failed two tests of a hegemonic leader: providing countercyclical lending and a market for distress goods (Matthijs and Blyth 2011).

The 2009 euro crisis

Recalling Kindleberger's argument, we remember that without hegemonic leadership in the form of a market for distress goods and aid to deficit countries in crisis, a fixed exchange rate system, and by extension a monetary union, will not survive. Germany had no intention of providing a market for distress goods, and, under Germany's direction, EMU had no provisions for such aid. Of course, between 2003 and 2009 it appeared that a hegemonic leader was not needed. As expected, the pooling of risk in the eurozone kept interest rates low, and along with German banks' liberal financing, allowed struggling countries to fund deficits and buy German goods.

But low interest rates were a temporary privilege, given the growing imbalances in the eurozone. In addition to funding the shopping sprees of debtors, low rates also spurred inflation in wages and goods in the economies of Germany's trading partners, which in turn made the exports of the Mediterranean countries more expensive and left imports relatively cheaper. The possibility of currency manipulation had been erased by the euro. In 2009 it became apparent that five members of the eurozone – Greece, Portugal, Ireland, Italy, and Spain – had failed to generate enough economic growth to pay back their debts. Investors were exposed and the threat of bank failures loomed. When the US financial crisis of 2008 hit Europe, a lender of last resort was nowhere to be found.

European leaders held a series of panicky meetings in spring 2010 to find such a lender. German Finance Minister Wolfgang Schäuble (2010) had apparently read his Kindleberger, and declared that the hegemonic stability thesis was more relevant than ever in Europe's current situation: he suggested that Germany and France should revive their old alliance and together become the hegemon of Europe – the hegemon that was missing in the 1930s. But for the next three years, this was not to be. Briefly it appeared that Germany would back the ECB as a lender of last resort. Members pooled their resources to raise €500 billion in conditional loans. And for the first time, the ECB intervened in markets to buy debt. Because Germany provided the largest share of contributions (30 per cent to France's 20 per cent and Italy's 17 per cent), German voters threatened a backlash. Chancellor Merkel insisted on bringing in the International Monetary Fund (IMF), which lent €250 billion in a move meant to ensure that Europeans would not bail out Greece alone.

Soaring interest rates and slowing growth in Spain, Italy, Portugal, Ireland, and France triggered more concerted action within the eurozone to raise bailout funds. In late 2012, eurozone members created the European Stability Mechanism (ESM), a treaty-based organisation capitalised at €700 billion with a lending capacity of €500 billion. Providing the bulk of ESM's capital, Germany retains veto power over its decisions. Borrowers are required to implement austerity measures and belong to the Fiscal Compact, a stricter replacement of the SGP. In addition, the ECB agreed to purchase bonds from countries in distress that promised to undertake austerity measures, in effect, forcing deflation.

One task of a hegemon, according to Kindleberger, is to lead an effort to coordinate macroeconomic policies. Germany insisted on austerity as the coordinating mechanism without any stimulus to spur growth. And austerity in the southern European periphery became the condition for the receipt of bailout funds. By April 2013, the number of unemployed workers in Spain and France had reached all-time highs: the number of unemployed in Spain – with an unemployment rate of 27.16 per cent – topped six million for the first time in history; five million were jobless in France, with an unemployment rate of over 10 per cent. The Greek economy contracted 20 per cent between 2008 and 2013. Meanwhile popular trust in the EU plummeted.[10] Photoshopped images of Chancellor Merkel dressed in a Nazi uniform became a common sight at angry protests across Europe. European support for Germany as the EU's hegemonic leader all but disappeared.

Austerity policies and their consequences signal the deepest failure of German hegemonic leadership in the monetary union: the failure to underwrite cooperation by creating conditions under which countries are better off with cooperation than without it – the failure to serve the common good by alleviating the stresses of free trade for deficit countries. By 2013 the temptation to defect from the monetary union had increased, with little prospect of Germany rising to the occasion to create economic stability. Whether the ESM will prove to be an effective lender of last resort remains to be seen. Germany has provided the bulk of the lending, but has not provided the necessary leadership to stabilise the monetary regime in crisis. But we must not forget that in the past Germany has stepped up to the plate, and the story of monetary union is not yet over.

Conclusion

In sum, the change–continuity debate over current German foreign policy is flawed in that it neglects the three-pillared essence of that policy: antimilitarism, multilateralism, and economic power. German policy clearly departs from 19th- and 20th-century expectations of how great powers should behave and from the policies of its political allies. Indeed, German policy has generally been consistent with its rejection of the hallmarks of power politics. Growing power has both permitted Germany to bear the lion's share of the burden of European cooperation and allowed various German governments to shape the terms of cooperation in the European Union. This does not mean that the rules of cooperation are shaped to serve only Germany's narrow interests – cooperation is a non-zero-sum game. All benefit from the cooperative endeavour and are better off than they were before cooperation, even though some will benefit more than others. We have seen this in issue areas as diverse as environmental policy, EU foreign policy, export control of high technology, and the European single market, to name an important few.

The saga of Germany's role in the European monetary union suggests that Germany has partially carried out its role as hegemonic leader, with its dominant contribution to relief for debtor members and the banks who loaned money to them, and its insistence on making the rules. But Germany may be taking burden sharing too far, in insisting that the burden of cooperation be placed on the backs of deficit countries. Leadership means not only shaping the terms of cooperation, but using resources to stabilise the regime by helping those who are tempted to defect. Will Germany continue in its role as Europe's hegemonic stabiliser?

Notes

1 I would like to thank Benjamin Schaub for his assistance with this essay.
2 Germany violated the Treaty of Versailles; the United States violated all of the treaties it made with Native Americans; it also violated the Convention against Torture in 2006, and the Vienna Convention in 2009; India, Pakistan, and Iran have violated the Nuclear Non-Proliferation Treaty.
3 A monetary union in many ways resembles a fixed exchange rate regime, whereby countries retain national currencies but agree to adjust their relative supply to maintain a desired rate of exchange to which all members adhere. A monetary union is an extreme form of a fixed exchange rate regime, but because the countries switch to a new currency, the cost of abandoning the new system is much higher than for a typical fixed exchange rate regime, providing more confidence that the system will last. See Bergin (2007).
4 In total 94.2 per cent of the EU budget is devoted to shoring up and administering the free trade regime. This includes funding for the Common Agricultural Policy, rural development and fisheries, administration, regional competitiveness, and economic cohesion. The composite effect of these expenditures is to create a regime within which equal standards and economic conditions will allow for efficient free trade (BBC 2012).
5 Foreign direct investment is the net inflows of investment to acquire a lasting management interest (10 per cent or more of voting stock) in an enterprise operating in an economy other than that of the investor.
6 In 2011 Germany was listed as the fifth most attractive destination for foreign investment worldwide (*Research in Germany* 2010).
7 When Germany rejected France's intergovernmental Fouchet Plan, it fell through. The Franco-German Friendship Treaty codified the *equal* status of the two countries. As noted below, as German power grew, Germany got the euro it wanted when France caved in to German conditions. When France attempted to create a European aerospace industry to rival Boeing, Germany rejected it and it fell through. France was not able to convince Germany to join the intervention in Libya. And France was not able to tame Germany's demands for austerity in the eurozone crisis.
8 The executive board of the ECB has six members, and its governing council 23 (the 17 national central bank governors and the six executive board members). The executive board comprises currently one Italian (the president), one Portuguese, one German, one French, one Luxembourg and one Belgian member. *De jure* each country has one vote via its national central bank president; *de facto*, however, Germany has two votes because of its seat on the board.
9 Martin Baily, a former chairman of Bill Clinton's Council of Economic Advisers, called it 'Hoover-era economics' and Francis Mer, the French finance minister, said that the requirement for cutting spending had forced Portugal into an 'irredeemable recession' (quoted in *The Economist* 2003).
10 In a Eurobarometer poll, 42 per cent of Poles, 53 per cent of Italians, 56 per cent of French, 59 per cent of Germans, 69 per cent of Britons, and 72 per cent of Spaniards said they did not trust the EU as an institution.

Bibliography

Baumann, R. (2004) 'The German Way' – Germany's policy in the Iraq Crisis and the Question of Continuity and Change in German Foreign Policy', paper presented at the annual meeting of the International Studies Association, 17 March.

BBC (2012) 'EU Budget for 2013'. Online. Available at www.bbc.co.uk/news/uk-politics-11645975 (accessed 18 December 2012).

Bergin, P. (2007) 'Monetary Union', *The Concise Encyclopedia of Economics*. Online. Available at www.econlib.org/library/Enc/MonetaryUnion.html (accessed 2 December 2012).

Buchan, D. (2012) 'The Energiewende: Germany's Gamble', Oxford: Oxford Institute for Energy Studies. Online. Available at www.oxfordenergy.org/wpcms/wp-content/uploads/2012/06/SP-261.pdf (accessed 11 February 2014).

Buergin, R. (2012) 'Germany Reaped the Most Benefit From Euro Membership, McKinsey Study Shows', Bloomberg, 10 January, 8:33 AM PT. Online. Available at www.bloomberg.com/news/2012–01–10/germany-reaped-most-economic-benefit-from-euro-mckinsey-2010-study-shows.html (accessed 10 December 2012).

Bulmer, S., Jeffery, C., and Paterson, W.E. (2000) *Germany's European Diplomacy: Shaping the Regional Milieu*, Manchester: Manchester University Press.

CIA World Fact Book (2012) 'Germany: Economy Overview'. Online. Available at https://www.cia.gov/library/publications/the-world-factbook/geos/gm.html (accessed 19 January 2013).

Cox, R. (1983) 'Gramsci, Hegemony and International Relations: An Essay in Method', *Millennium – Journal of International Studies 1983* [e-journal] 12(2): 162–75. Available through SAGE Publications.

Crawford, B. (1996) 'Explaining Defection from International Cooperation: Germany's Unilateral Recognition of Croatia', *World Politics*, 48(4): 482–521.

Crawford, B. (1998) Interview with Gerhard Stoltenberg, German Minister of Finance under Chancellor Helmut Kohl, 13 March 1998.

Crawford, B. (2007) *Power and German Foreign Policy: Embedded Hegemony in Europe*, New York: Palgrave Macmillan Publishing.

Crawford, B. (2010) 'Normative power of a Normal State: Power and Revolutionary Vision in Germany's Post-Wall Foreign Policy', *German Politics and Society*, 28(2): 165–84.

De Guzman, J.C., Ross, K., and Waysand, C. (2010) 'IMF European Financial Linkages: A New Look at Imbalances,' *International Monetary Fund*, 1 December. Online. Available at www.imf.org/external/pubs/cat/longres.cfm?sk=24527.0 (accessed 26 December 2012).

Eichengreen, B. (1990) *Is Europe an Optimum Currency Area?* Cambridge, MA: National Bureau of Economic Research, Inc.

Engel, S. (2008) 'The World Bank and Neoliberal Hegemony in Vietnam', in R. Howson and K. Smith (eds) *Hegemony: Studies in Consensus and Coercion*, New York: Routledge.

EU Business (2012) 'Germany Top Indirect Beneficiary of EU Cohesion Funds: Study', 1 March. Online. Available at www.eubusiness.com/news-eu/poland-budget-czech.fhx/ (accessed 30 November 2012).

European Commission (2012) 'EU Bilateral Trade and Trade with the World'. Online. Available at http://trade.ec.europa.eu/doclib/html/147269.htm (accessed 20 December 2012).

Eurostat (2010) 'External and Intra-EU Trade – Statistical Yearbook', 10 December. Online. Available at http://epp.eurostat.ec.europa.eu/portal/page/portal/product_details/publication?p_product_code=KS-GI-10–002 (accessed 20 December 2012).

Eurostat (2011) 'High Tech Statistics', 10 October. Online. Available at http://epp.eurostat.ec.europa.eu/statistics_explained/index.php/High-tech_statistics (accessed 27 November 2012).

Eurostat (2012a) 'Primary Production of Renewable Energy, 2000 and 2010', 10 October. Online. Available at http://epp.eurostat.ec.europa.eu/statistics_explained/index.php?title=File:Primary_production_of_renewable_energy_2000_and_2010.png&filetimestamp=20121012133631 (accessed 15 December 2012).

Eurostat (2012b) 'GDP per capita, consumption per capita and price level indices', December 2012. Online. Available at http://epp.eurostat.ec.europa.eu/statistics_explained/index.php/GDP_per_capita_consumption_per_capita_and_price_level_indices#Relative_volumes_of_consumption_per_capita (accessed 20 December 2012).

Fontes, N. (2013) 'Euro Area Trade Surplus Widens in November', Trading Economics, 15 January. Online. Available at www.tradingeconomics.com/euro-area/balance-of-trade (accessed 16 January 2013).

Gilpin, R., O'Brien, P.K., and Clesse, A. (eds) (2002) 'Chapter 2: The Rise of American Hegemony', in *Two Hegemonies: Britain 1846–1914 and the United States 1941–2001*, Aldershot: Ashgate: 165–82.

Goetz, K.H. (2004) 'The New Member States and the EU', in S. Bulmer and C. Lequesne (eds) *Member States and the European Union*, Oxford: Oxford University Press.

Gowa, J.S. (1983) *Closing the Gold Window: Domestic Politics and the End of Bretton Woods*, Ithaca: Cornell University Press.

Grieco, J. (1996) 'State Interests and Institutional Rule Trajectories: A Neorealist Interpretation of the Maastricht Treaty and European Economic and Monetary Union', *Security Studies*, 5: 261–306.

Gross, E. (2009) *The Europeanization of National Foreign Policy: Continuity and Change in European Crisis Management*, New York: Palgrave Macmillan.

Harnisch, S. (2001) 'Change and continuity in post-unification German foreign policy,' *German Politics*, 10(1): 25–60.

Herborth, B. and Hellmann, G. (2006) 'Taking Process Seriously: Concatenations of Continuity and Change in German Foreign Policy', paper presented at the annual meeting of the International Studies Association, 22 March 2006.

Jarausch, K. (2006), 'Reflections on transnational history', *H-Net Online*, 20 January. Available at http://h-net.msu.edu/cgi-bin/logbrowse.pl?trx=vx&list=H-German&month=0601&week=c&msg=LPkNHirCm1xgSZQKHOGRXQ&user=&pw= (accessed 11 February 2014).

Karp, R. (2006) 'The New German Foreign Policy Consensus', *The Washington Quarterly*, 29(1): 62–82.

Keohane, R. (1984) *After Hegemony: Discord and Cooperation in the World Political Economy*, Princeton: Princeton University Press.

Kindleberger, C. (1981) 'Dominance and Leadership in the International Economy', *International Studies Quarterly*, 25:2: 242–54.

Kindleberger, C. (1986) *The World in Depression*, Berkeley: University of California Press.

Krönig, J. (2013) 'Germany in Europe – the unwilling hegemon', *Policy Network*, 7 May. Online. Available at www.policy-network.net/pno_detail.aspx?ID=4393&title=Germany-in-Europe-%E2%80%93-the-unwilling-hegemon (accessed 11 February 2014).

Krasner, S. (1976) 'State Power and the Structure of International Trade', *World Politics* 28: 317–47.

Kundnani, H. (2011) 'Germany as a geo-economic power', *The Washington Quarterly* (Summer). Online. Available at http://csis.org/files/publication/twq11summerkundnani.pdf (accessed 11 February 2014).

Lawton, C. (2012) 'Nowotny Opens a Can of Worms With Comments on ECB Votes', *The Wall Street Journal*, 6 November. Online. Available at http://blogs.wsj.com/eurocrisis/2012/11/06/nowotny-opens-a-can-of-worms-with-comments-on-ecb-votes/ (accessed 1 December 2012).

Leithner, A. (2009) *Shaping German Foreign Policy: History, Memory, and National Interest*, Boulder, CO: Lynne Rienner Publishers.

Marsh, D. (1992) *The Bundesbank: The Bank that Rules Europe*, London: William Heinemann.

Matthijs, M. and Blyth, M. (2011) 'Why Only Germany Can Fix the Euro', *Foreign Affairs*, 17 November. Online. Available at www.foreignaffairs.com/articles/136685/matthias-matthijs-and-mark-blyth/why-only-germany-can-fix-the-euro (accessed 27 December 2012).

Mauer, V. (2009) 'Continuity and Change: Foreign Policy Since 9/11', Eidgenössische Technische Hochschule Zürich. Digital Library. Online. Available at www.isn.ethz.ch/isn/Digital-Library/Articles/Detail/?ots591=4888caa0-b3db-1461-98b9-e20e7b9c13d4&lng=en&id=123830 (accessed 11 December 2012).

Mayhew, A., Oppermann, K., and Hough, D.T. (2011) 'German foreign policy and leadership of the EU – "You can't always get what you want, but you sometimes get what you need"', Brighton: Sussex European Institute. Online. Available at https://www.sussex.ac.uk/webteam/gateway/file.php?name=sei-working-paper-no-119.pdf&site=266 (accessed 12 December 2012).

Mullins, R.E., Lesser, I.O., and Rosenau, W. (2001) 'Chapter 3: The Role of the Hegemon', in *The Emergence of Peer Competitors: A Framework for Analysis*, Santa Monica, CA: RAND Corporation Press: 45–72.

Norris, F. (2011) 'Euro Benefits Germany More Than Others in Zone,' *The New York Times*, 22 April. Online. Available at www.nytimes.com/2011/04/23/business/global/23charts.html?_r=0 (accessed 10 December 2012).

Olsen, M. (1965) *The Logic of Collective Action: Public Goods and the Theory of Groups*, Cambridge, MA: Harvard University Press.

Olsen, M. and Zeckhauser, R. (1966) 'An Economic Theory of Alliances,' *Review of Economics and Statistics*, 48: 266–79.

Paterson, W.E. (2011) 'The Reluctant Hegemon? Germany Moves Centre Stage in the European Union', *Journal of Common Market Studies*, 49, Issue Supplement 1: 57–75.

Pedersen, T. (1998) *Germany, France and the Integration of Europe*, London: Pinter.

Posen, A. (2005) 'If America Won't, Germany Must', *Internationale Politik* (Summer): 32.

Rachman, G. (2012) 'Welcome to Berlin, Europe's New Capital', *The Financial Times*, 22 October. Online. Available at www.ft.com/cms/s/0/01db45ba-1c32–11e2-a63b-00144feabdc0.html#axzz2JJIiYJL7 (accessed 13 December 2012).

Research in Germany (2010) 'FDI Confidence Index: Investors Rank Germany First in Europe', 23 April. Online. Available at www.research-in-germany.de/news-archive-2010/news-archive-april-2010/45150/2010–04–23–04–22–2010-fdi-confidence-index-investors-rank-germany-first-in-europe-sourcePageId=65148.html (accessed 21 December 2012).

Risse, T. (2004) 'Kontinuität durch Wandel: Eine "neue" deutsche Außenpolitik?' *Aus Politik und Zeitgeschichte*, 11(3): 24–31.

Rittberger, V. (ed.) (2001) *German Foreign Policy since Unification: An Analysis of Foreign Policy Continuity and Change*, Vancouver: University of British Columbia Press.

Sarotte, M.E. (2010) 'Eurozone Crisis as Historical Legacy: The Enduring Impact of German Unification, 20 Years On', *Foreign Affairs*, 29 September. Online. Available at www.foreignaffairs.com/articles/66754/mary-elise-sarotte/eurozone-crisis-as-historical-legacy (accessed 2 December 2012).

Sbragia, A. (ed.) (1992) *Europolitics: Institutions and Policymaking in the 'New' European Political Community*, Washington: Brookings Institute.

Schönberger, C. (2012) 'Hegemon wider Willen: Zur Stellung Deutschlands in der Europäischen Union', *Eurozine*, 1 January. Online. Available at www.eurozine.com/articles/2012–01–10-schonberger-de.html (accessed 2 December 2012).

Snidel, D. (1985) 'The Limits of Hegemonic Stability Theory', *International Organization*, 39: 579–614.

Soros, G. (2012) 'How Europe Can Rescue Europe', Project Syndicate, 24 June. Online. Available at www.project-syndicate.org/commentary/how-europe-can-rescue-europe (accessed 7 August 2012).

The Economist (2003) 'The death of the stability pact', 27 November. Online. Available at www.economist.com/node/2246457 (accessed 11 February 2014).

The Local: Germany's News in English (2011) 'Despite crisis, Germany benefits from euro', 26 December. Online. Available at www.thelocal.de/national/20111226–39735.html#.URFYkOj7jzd (accessed 18 December 2012).

Thomson, R. (2010) 'Opposition through the back door in the transposition of EU directives', *European Union Politics*, 11: 577–96.

Ungerer, H., Evans, E., Mayer, T., and You, P. (1986) *The European Monetary System: Recent Developments*, Washington: International Monetary Fund.

Ungerer, H., Hauvonen, J.J., Lopez-Claros, A., and Mayer, T. (1990) *European Monetary System: Developments & Perspectives*, Washington: International Monetary Fund.

Van der Pijl, K., Holman, O., and Raviv, O. (2010) 'The Resurgence of German Capital in Europe: EU Integration and the Restructuring of Atlantic Networks of Interlocking Directorates After 1991', *Review of International Political Economy*, 18(3): 384–408.

Vinocur, J. (2006) 'Germany Starts Moving Out of the Safe House', *The New York Times*, 19 September. Available at www.nytimes.com/iht/2006/09/19/world/IHT-19politicus.html (accessed 13 February 2014).

Westcott, K. (2008) 'Germany's Success as Mid-East broker', BBC, 16 July. Online. Available at http://news.bbc.co.uk/2/hi/middle_east/7504194.stm (accessed 5 December 2012).

World Bank (2013) Data. Online. Available at http://data.worldbank.org/indicator/NY.GNS.ICTR.ZS (accessed 20 January 2013).

22

The German approach to finance in the European context

Lothar Funk[1]

Hans Magnus Enzensberger has been extremely dissatisfied with the state of Europe recently. On 15 May 2010, he expressed his disappointment and anger in an interview with *The Guardian*: 'Europe is a great achievement but they are messing it up [. . .] it is anti-European because they antagonise people without any reason for doing so. [. . .] it is rolling back liberties which we have acquired.'[2] But who is to blame? For many observers, particularly outside Germany and those northern European countries with a similar financial 'stability culture', the answer appears to be obvious: Germany is at fault.

> Germany has become a major player in this gamble of 'antagonizing Europe', the Europe of ordinary people and political elites alike. The Greek quasi-bailout, the euro turmoil, and the current crisis management among the EU Member States all reveal that 'messing up Europe' is nowadays a – intended? – consequence of German EU policy.
>
> (Morisse-Schilbach 2011: 26)

For such critics, the crisis has been first and foremost a crisis of Germany in the context of both the European Union and the European Monetary Union (EMU) or eurozone. To understand this view, one needs to recall that European integration from the early 1950s was based above all on the idea 'that the only way of taming post-World War II Germany was to link it as closely as possible to its European partners through the intermediary of international institutions' (Morisse-Schilbach 2011: 27).

British experts on German politics suggest that 'it is difficult to understand Germany without reference to the EU' (Miskimmon, Paterson, and Sloam 2010: 496). In an op-ed article in December 2013, the German finance minister Wolfgang Schäuble – paraphrasing the historian Fritz Stern – seemed to agree: 'the Germans have understood that European integration gives us a second chance'. Schäuble emphasised Germany's ongoing 'European vocation' in a well-known mantra that had its origins in West Germany but is still part of the DNA of a huge majority of Germans now: 'We only have a future to the extent that Europe is successful. Germany, too, will do well only if Europe does well' (Schäuble 2013a).[3] The German finance minister, then – as one of the architects of the renewal of financial architecture in the eurozone – continues to believe strongly in the merits of the E(M)U. Experts from abroad nonetheless observe that 'deeper European integration (in particular, with the Single Market and the Single Currency) has led to the Europeanisation of domestic policy and the domestication of European policy' (Miskimmon, Paterson, and Sloam 2010: 497).

Conflict is inevitable when public finances come under stress, as has recently happened in the context of globalisation, Europeanisation, and, in Germany, unification. According to critics of current German economic and financial policies at the European level, there has been a structural break in the way Germany approaches EU economic and financial issues since the financial crisis. One might, however, counter that the basic values that inform German economic policies have, at least in principle and after a passing turn to Keynesianism (Funk 2012: 26–7), hardly changed since the initial phase of the social market economy (SME). This chapter will begin by sketching German economic policy in terms of its 'iron triangle' and social market economy approach. It then analyses the two pillars – political and economic – that support Germany's European vocation, and deals briefly with the Federal Republic's traditional focus on the export market and on price stability. Another brief section considers the limited role of Keynesian demand management ideas in the Federal Republic. From there I move to a discussion of the popular notion of German hegemony, before concluding with an analysis of progress towards a new financial architecture for the EMU.

The pillars of the Federal Republic's economic model

At least in terms of its total economic strength, Germany has been the most populous and most powerful EU member state since unification in 1990.[4] The social market economy was initially the economic programme of the Christian Democratic and Bararian Christian Social parties (CDU/CSU) in the first postwar election. The SME aims at combining individual freedom with a functioning and efficient economic system in a humane social order. In several coalitions (usually with the Free Democrats or FDP) until 1966, the CDU/CSU promoted and defended its emerging main features: an optimal delegation of tasks according to which

1 the central bank should be independent, that is, primarily responsible for keeping inflation down, but not responsible for employment;
2 representatives of employees and employers should have a basic right to freedom in collective bargaining;
3 the state should be limited but strong (Funk 2000: 20–1).

With regard to (3), the state has to be 'limited' to ensure that (a) public expenditure is kept at an efficient, rather low level (the primacy of budgetary discipline, which also supports price stability and prevents the crowding out of private investment); (b) there is no discretionary intervention in response to lobbying by sectoral and other sectional interests; (c) privatisation is implemented wherever reasonable; and (d) market-friendly supply side measures are favoured, in order to promote economic growth and employment in contrast to discretionary demand-side interventions that are regarded as counterproductive most of the time. Ensuring stability also implies a rejection of the idea of ex ante macroeconomic policy coordination (Dyson and Quaglia 2012: 195); but the state has to be 'strong', particularly to create the right conditions for effective competition to decrease inefficiency and unwanted distributional effects of ongoing market power based on artificial entry and exit barriers.

This was based on an 'ordoliberal' paradigm that has had a renaissance within Germany since the financial crisis spread to the Federal Republic in the autumn of 2008 and in 2009. Following the financial and economic shocks in many other countries, that paradigm regained some strength

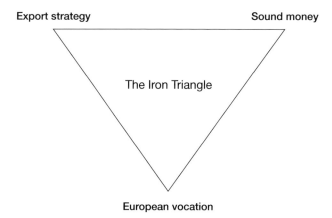

Export strategy

Sound money

The Iron Triangle

European vocation

Figure 22.1 The Iron Triangle of the German Model (based on Paterson 2011: 48)

as an alternative to the 'casino capitalism' (Sinn 2010) of the United States; it has even spread into academic debates, at least in Anglo-Saxon countries (Bonefeld 2013; Siems and Schnyder 2013). Its acceptance remains limited (Blyth 2013: 135–43); but even in the (pre-unification) 'Bonn Republic' the relevant actors usually accepted only the first and second pillars of the ordoliberal SME. The accompanying fundamental regulatory inadequacies had negative effects on Germany's national economic performance that could not be compensated for even by the strengths of the (West) German economy. (The latter included the corporate governance system, vocational training, and other institutional features resulting in 'long-termism' and incremental innovation resulting from 'corporatist' bargains among trade unions, employers' representatives, and the state; Funk 2000: 21.)

In retrospect, the SME has proven more or less compatible with three key principles, namely, an unwavering commitment to price stability; maintaining a large share of exports and imports; and a European vocation in the governing class that prevailed until the current crisis in the eurozone. These features of the (West) German economy have been called a 'self-reinforcing iron triangle' (Figure 22.1), because 'the key principles were derived from the traumatic failures of earlier German polities, notably the Great Inflation of 1923 and murderous and ultimately self-destructive Nazi regime' (Paterson 2011: 48–9).

Indeed, the Federal Republic's economic performance very often benefited from the pick-up of economic growth in the rest of the world, as Siebert observes:

> Traditionally, in the German case an upswing in the business cycle is stimulated by an increase in export demand, which is then followed by a pick-up of investment and eventually leads to less uncertainty, in terms of employment, and to higher income, so that consumer demand increases as well. In the long run, and viewed from the supply side, trade has an impact on growth through different channels.
>
> (Siebert 2005: 7)

Moreover, access to a widening European market has long proved to be a decisive factor for German export successes (Neal 2007: 221–9), and the deepening of European integration has helped increase German exports, especially since the introduction of the euro (Young and Semmler 2011: 10). Losing open markets poses great risks to Germany precisely because of its strong European and international economic involvement. And the country's comparatively strict counter-inflationary policies have resulted in one of the lowest national inflation rates worldwide since the launch of the (West) German currency, the Deutsche Mark or DM. This factor also helped to improve German export strengths.

But to understand the particular role of exports for Germany we must also consider other factors (Gerber 2013: 5f.), not least its geographical position in the centre of Europe with many borders to other nations. Steady innovation and high-quality systems in dominant export industries such as the automobile and metal and electrical industries (Hüther 2011: 13ff.) contribute to good value for money from a foreign customer's point of view; this is true despite high absolute labour costs in industry (corresponding to high labour productivity in German industry) and other factors behind rising prices of German goods for foreign buyers. In a nutshell, one might exaggerate and suggest with Young and Semmler (2011: 12) that 'regardless of whether the Deutsche Mark or the EURO appreciated, German exports are internationally competitive'.

The 'iron triangle' has contributed to Germany's persistently high external competitiveness and ongoing trade surpluses (with the exception of an adjustment period after German unification, which slowed the surge in German exports; Whittock 2008: 8–9). A somewhat broader analysis takes account of further factors, such as the role of demographic factors in societal savings decisions that affect net capital flows and thus net exports to the rest of the world (for a more detailed analysis, see Falke 2009: 202 ff. and Kindleberger 1976 for his structural explanation).

The (limited) impact of Keynesianism

The traditional SME governance model consisted of a set of general guidelines for economic policy rather than precise goals and instructions for policy. This changed, however, during the 1960s, when Keynesian thinking gained some influence in Germany. The goals included in the German Law on Stability and Growth of 1967 still often structure economic policy debates in Germany, even though the law has hardly been applied in practice since the 1970s. It was passed after the first cyclical economic crisis of 1966–7 in West Germany, and was meant to start a shift towards Keynesian demand-side strategy. A law for promoting stability and growth obliged government to smooth out the business cycle (for more detail, see Funk 2012: 12–15).

A high level of employment (often measured in practice by low unemployment) as well as price stability, steady economic growth, and a 'sound' balance in foreign trade (the equilibrium of imports and exports in the medium and longer term) are the four principal economic policy objectives of the government, the so-called 'magic quadrangle' (Figure 22.2). Alongside certain other responsibilities (such as setting and fulfilling ecological goals), the government's task is to ensure an equitable distribution of income and wealth – the 'magic polygon'. The 'magic quadrangle' or rectangle is called magic because of the short-term target conflicts arising in this context (see Figure 22.2). For example, according to the traditional Keynesian trade-off/target conflict view, it was assumed that economic policy could choose between a combination of lower unemployment plus higher inflation, or vice versa. That assumption was proved wrong by the dynamics of the wage bargaining process. As a rule, in the longer term, expansionary monetary and fiscal policies will affect the price level, but not employment. Empirical evidence demonstrated that employees will build inflation forecasts into their expectations and the price level and cost of labour will usually – all other things being equal – rise at a similar rate, at least in the longer term, in labour markets. Thus there is no longer a trade-off between inflation and unemployment – a result that is again in line with orthodox ordoliberal ideas (see Funk 2012: 42).

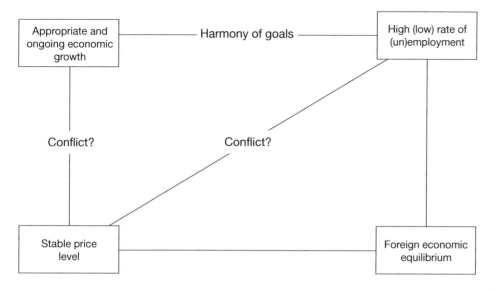

Figure 22.2 Economic stability goals in Germany – a magic rectangle or quadrangle (see Funk 2012: 14)

The two pillars of Germany's European vocation

The EMU, as well as the entire European integration policy within the EU, rests on a political and an economic pillar. James (2012: 1) has argued that

> the quest for European monetary coordination and then for union was a response to genuine (and still existing) problems of currency instability and misalignments at the international level. It was not simply – as it has often been represented – a fundamentally political project. [. . .] That a currency union can be driven by an urgent political concern, overriding economic logic, was demonstrated in a costly way by the case of the 1990 German–German currency union that preceded political unification; but it will be clear in the subsequent account that there was a clear economic as well as political logic behind the creation of a single European currency.

The EMU was expected initially to help overcome the low growth and high unemployment of the 1980s ('eurosclerosis'); in other words, the euro was envisioned with a clear function well before German unification (Hampe 2013a). The contention that unification was the primary factor in Germany's willingness to relinquish the leading European currency, the DM, in favour of a common currency is, therefore, contradicted by the timing, and conspiracy theories that suggest that giving up the DM was the price of unification appear dubious. The situation may nonetheless have suited other member states of the European Community quite well as a way of ending the dominance of both the DM and the German central bank (Bundesbank). Europeanisation had become the Western solution to the 'German problem', by which an untrustworthy former enemy had to be turned into a friend (Birckenbach 2011: 318). German governments concurred, arguing repeatedly that the primary political purpose of the EMU was to make a future European war impossible and uneconomic (James 2012: 1).

In order to demonstrate its political loyalty to the West, the Federal government bid farewell to the so-called coronation theory, by which a joint currency should be established only at the end of a process of integration towards a real political union. The government agreed to a fixed date for the implementation of the single currency based on concrete stability criteria and common institutional rules. By adopting this course of action, it hoped to demonstrate that the unified Germany would be a 'European Germany' and would pursue political integration on the path to political union. At the request of the Federal Constitutional Court (Bundesverfassungsgericht), the German constitution or Basic Law (Grundgesetz) acquired a fresh impulse to European integration in a new Article 23, which states that the EU should become 'committed to democratic, social, and federal principles, to the rule of law, and to the principle of subsidiarity' and that it should guarantee 'a level of protection of basic rights essentially comparable to that afforded by this Basic Law'. All this can be read as an expression of the German will to strengthen the political institutions of the EU, but, as Birckenbach (2011: 328) notes, 'it can also be read as an expression of a German will to export its own political system to the European level. Not every member state has been in favour of such attempts.'

From an economic perspective, the EMU aimed at resolving the trilemma (see Figure 22.3 below) of currency policy within the EU by abolishing nominal exchange rate changes. Since the worldwide depression that started in 1929 and led to the abolition of the gold standard, no convincing solution had been found to the accompanying problems. Neither the Bretton Woods system of adjustable fixed exchange rates nor the flexible exchange rates after 1973 nor the European Monetary System (EMS) after 1979 had convincing results. In principle, an internal market with highly intensive free trade and capital controls can function well even if it is segmented, so long as nominal exchange rates are relatively stable. In order to ensure such stability, the renunciation of nationally autonomous economic policy is needed. This is because such national economic policies usually lead to differing interest and inflation rates that would require changes to nominal exchange rates (Hampe 2013a, 2013b).

The EMS was initiated by Chancellor Helmut Schmidt and French President Valéry Giscard d'Estaing in spring 1978 in order to achieve more stable exchange rates, at least in the European common market, and stronger economic growth. The exchange rate mechanism (ERM) aimed at improved trade relations among the member states, since the constant changes in floating member state currencies were regarded as harmful to international trade within the European economic union, while the participating currencies were to float jointly against the currencies of third countries. According to the European Council of December 1978, the ERM was designed to contribute to more growth while simultaneously maintaining price-level stability; it was also expected to help reduce unemployment and to enhance European integration. One of its pillars was an increased convergence of economic policy. Participants initially included eight member states; southern European countries and the United Kingdom entered later.

However, the system remained fragile as ongoing differences in inflation prevented the desired stability of exchange rates. The gain in convergence was probably much smaller than previously expected by the proponents of the EMS. Between 1979 and 1987, the number of necessary realignments amounted to 14. Overall the DM appreciated against Spain and Italy by 105 per cent, while against the UK and France the appreciation amounted to 65 and 45 per cent respectively. In 1983 France changed course to a 'franc fort' policy in support of increased price stability. That meant that France accepted the DM as the anchor of the system, and thus the policy of the Bundesbank. Politically this subordination was regarded as barely acceptable from the French government's point of view. Fundamental differences in macroeconomic policy after German unification produced currency imbalances that in 1992 led to the exit of Italy and the United Kingdom from the ERM (Owen Smith and Funk 1994: 541–2). As a result, the level of permitted fluctuations in exchange rates had to be increased from ±2.25 per cent to ±15 per cent. Effectively, this meant almost a return to flexible spot rates. In other words, the fundamental solution to the problem the ERM was supposed to address could hardly be achieved with fixed but adjustable exchange rates.

More generally, the analysis of exchange rate regimes shows that it is impossible to achieve all the goals regarded as beneficial for a country at once. This problem is called an 'impossible trinity' (Reinert 2012: 274ff.) and it reveals a fundamental trilemma. The term trilemma 'describes a situation in which someone faces a choice among three options, each of which comes with some inevitable problems' (Mankiw 2011: 712). The trilemma in international finance stems from the fact that it is impossible for a nation to have fixed nominal exchange rates with other countries, free capital flows, and an independent monetary policy at the same time, even if achieving those national economic policy goals simultaneously would be beneficial (Mankiw 2011: 712). This becomes obvious when taking account of the benefits of each of these goals:

- Fixed nominal exchange rates with other countries enable business and households to make better plans for the future, while fluctuating exchange rates caused, for example, by speculation can be a source of broader economic volatility and problems.
- Free capital mobility allows, from a microeconomic perspective, the movement of capital to its most profitable uses and can generally be regarded as welfare-enhancing for societies as a whole.
- Independent national monetary policy is regarded as nationally useful, as decreasing nominal interest rates can help to stabilise an economy in a recession, while raising them can help to deal with a situation of overheating.

The trilemma implies that it is impossible to have it all at once, and that a country must choose one side of the triangle in Figure 22.3 while giving up the opposite corner.

A first important implication is that 'if you pick two of these goals, the inexorable logic of economics forces you to forego the third' (Mankiw 2011: 712); a second is that there is no obvious best way of dealing with this impossible trinity, and 'economists should be cautious

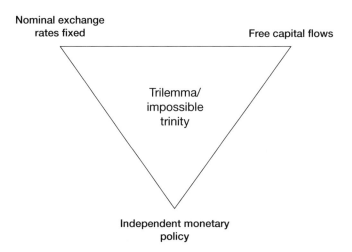

Figure 22.3 The trilemma of international finance or impossible trinity (based on Mankiw 2011: 379; Reinert 2012: 274)

when recommending exchange-rate policy, because it is far from obvious what is best' (Mankiw 2011: 713). One option is to allow free flows of capital and to conduct an independent monetary policy; the United States exemplifies this choice, which implies a floating nominal exchange rate to equilibrate the foreign currency exchange market. A second option chosen, for example, by China, is to restrict the in- and outflow of capital, so that domestic forces decide upon the national interest rate; this allows government both to fix the nominal interest rate and to conduct an independent monetary policy. The third option is the one taken, for example, by the member states of the eurozone: they have eliminated all nominal exchange rate movements within the European monetary union, while capital is free to move at the same time. This has, however, implied all member states relinquishing control over national monetary policy. The US economist N. Gregory Mankiw (2011: 713) notes wisely that 'Americans shouldn't be too harsh when other nations facing the trilemma reach conclusions different from ours. In this area of economic policy, as well as many others, there is room for reasonable nations to disagree'. From a European point of view and with the benefit of hindsight, however, the conclusions reached by the eurozone have proved untenable, as the introduction of (temporary) restrictions on capital movements in the case of the rescue package for Cyprus has demonstrated recently. In other words, more institutional change on this matter can be expected in order to achieve a stable eurozone.

The German hegemony hypothesis re-examined

In spite of experiencing Germany's largest fall in real gross domestic product (GDP) since World War II (−5.1 per cent of real GDP in 2009), the German economy has proved particularly resistant to recent crisis pressures (Funk 2013, 2014). Many German commentators argue that the successful implementation of supply side reforms during the last decade, combined with more traditional elements of its SME, are responsible for Germany's continuing success while much of the euro area's periphery has fallen into deep recession.

The German recession was short-lived and has hardly shown up in the labour market. In contrast to many neighbouring economies, Germany recouped the losses sustained during its recession (limited mainly to 2009) in a subsequent process of strong recovery (an increase in real GDP of 4.2 per cent in 2010 and 3.3 per cent in 2011). Total employment reached record levels in 2010 (and again in the succeeding years), with the highest level of persons employed since unification. The registered unemployment level fell to new lows unequalled since 1991, while simultaneously the number of jobs fully subject to social contributions rose to 28.4 million in 2011, the highest level in the last 15 years. The German Council of Economic Experts (Sachverständigenrat zur Begutachtung der gesamtwirtschaftlichen Entwicklung) particularly emphasises the 'remarkable [. . .] almost continuous rise in employment since the middle of the past decade and [. . .] the fact that the situation is actually better than before the crisis' (German Council of Economic Experts 2011: 19). The pattern of steadily rising structural unemployment was broken for the first time in decades, even though external cooling factors (the crisis in the eurozone and the accompanying tensions in the financial markets, as well as the consolidation efforts in many countries) led to a short-term dip in economic growth to only 0.7 per cent in 2012 and 0.4 per cent in 2013.

The main drivers of the surprisingly stable labour market developments in Germany included – apart from certain direct fiscal policy measures (car scrapping subsidies) in the spirit of Keynesian short-term demand management – a large amount of labour and thus skills hoarding, and the use of short-time work (*Kurzarbeit*). These instruments have been used since the 1970s in western Germany for labour market adjustment purposes, but their widespread use particularly in 2010 was unprecedented in recent decades. The approach worked well because it was based on employers' and government's expectations of a short recession, which proved to be the case. Many of the most affected companies correctly anticipated that the structure of their products was fundamentally appropriate to meet future demand in global markets as well as within Europe and Germany. The increased flexibility of the strategically restructured German labour market (Funk 2003, 2010) contributed considerably to this success, due to the elevated profitability of production prior to the 2008–9 downturn and the accompanying decreased uncertainty for successful entrepreneurship in Germany.

A widely held view within Germany is that the current 'labour market in Germany goes along with a mix of more external flexibility (due to labour market reforms) and more firm-specific internal flexibility (in the course of crisis management)' (Walwei 2011: 563). These factors in particular are held to explain the resilience of the German labour market even despite the steep decline in international trade that depressed German exports in the core areas of machinery and automobile manufacturing. The upswings of 2005 and 2008, combined with wage moderation and increased flexibility as well as the high profits in those sectors before the collapse in demand, were the basis for this rather unique German mode of adjustment. The specific internal experience and mainstream belief within Germany was that controversial structural reforms of the last decade were finally paying off, shortening crisis situations and strengthening the economy. More generally, this may explain why many Germans think that some of the basic lessons of the German experience (such as successfully pursuing supply side orientated measures) should serve as a guideline for national reform efforts in the crisis countries of the euro area (Funk 2012, 2013).

However, the debate outside Germany – particularly among some British commentators as well as leading US Keynesians – was rather different. According to this alternative view, the macroeconomic outlook in Germany brightened after 2004 not only because of the structural reforms that were undertaken but particularly as a result of the simultaneous boom in much of the rest of the eurozone. The latter came about partly because of interest rate convergence after the introduction of the euro, which supported countries with formerly weak currencies (Buti and Sapir 2008: 254) and partly because of the ECB's expansionary monetary policy, which was largely due to macroeconomic imbalances in Germany: 'In short, the ECB's ultralow policy rate had little impact in Germany [. . .] but it was too accommodative for other economies in the eurozone. The result was widely divergent rates of inflation' (Koo 2013: 116). Lack of demand for loans within Germany to finance consumption and private and public investment

> led to capital outflows from Germany, which contributed to the bubbles in the peripheral countries [. . .]. With German producers becoming increasingly competitive relative to those in the booming economies of southern Europe, German exports grew sharply, pulling the nation out of recession. While Germany overtook Japan and China to post the world's largest trade surplus, the growth in the trade surplus was driven mainly by exports to other European countries rather than Asia or North America. This suggests that it was primarily the intra-European inflation differential that gave Germany such a large competitive advantage. In other words, if the ECB had not inflated other Euro zone economies to the extent it did, the German trade surplus would have been much smaller.
>
> (Koo 2013: 116)

Furthermore, a different macroeconomic and structural policy mix in Germany during the post-2000 recession could have limited the monetary effects of Germany's role as the 'sick man of Europe'. Germany was, however, limited also by the rather strict annual budget deficit conditions of the Stability and Growth Pact. If German banks had been able to buy more government bonds at home, they would possibly have bought fewer US subprime papers and fewer bonds in the booming eurozone countries. Koo echoes other critics when he suggests that 'a significant part of today's "competitiveness problem" is attributable to the treaty's 3-percent cap on fiscal deficits, which places unreasonable demands on ECB monetary policy during this type of recession'; the current loss of competitiveness in some countries is to be read in this light, and not (as so often in German official circles) merely as 'the result of poor domestic policy choices (Koo 2013; 117, 111). In other words, according to these critics, Germany contributed at least indirectly to current problems in other European countries and should openly accept this responsibility.

What does all this mean for the contention that Germany is trying to gain hegemony in Europe and shape a 'German Europe'? Even spectators from outside Germany appear to agree that Germany has experienced a turnaround. Since the Federal Republic was established in 1949,

> Germans have embraced a political system and culture in which the values of liberalism, tolerance, openness, and democracy are deeply anchored. Germany has become 'normal' – fundamentally similar to other highly developed western countries like the UK, France, or the United States. [. . .] fundamental structures and values are now shared throughout the West. Thus the old fears that the German 'special path' fostered – the German question – are part of the 'dustbin of history'.
>
> (Conradt and Langenbacher 2013: 363)

In the recent past, Germany has been regarded in a very different, positive sense: 'Many authors even refer to Germany as exemplary – Modell Deutschland' (Conradt and Langenbacher 2013: xi).

Germany's current economic dominance is more likely the unintended consequence of changes and challenges since the adoption of the euro. There are hardly any signs that Germany's current success largely depends on more selfish behaviour than one would find in other member states of the E(M)U. An explanation for the development of the current German position is offered by David P. Conradt and Eric Langenbacher in their recently updated textbook on the German polity. Going back to the German idealist philosopher Georg Wilhelm Friedrich Hegel, they note that his 'cunning reason in history' describes unintended outcomes that may even have an element of irony. Although economists in Germany occasionally saw the euro as a vehicle for greater German export strength (e.g. Eibner 2008: 297), in fact the competitive battle for 'economic superiority' in Europe intensified, and initially Germany lagged behind badly. It is true that German politicians could have done better, but conspiracy theories again seem far-fetched (Norris 2012). Conradt and Langenbacher describe the recent, more elevated German role in the EU as not easily predictable around 10 or 15 years ago, and as an unintended result on (probably) all sides:

> the Euro was supposed to truncate German sovereignty and forever contain German power. [. . .] At first, this is exactly how things played out. Germany had a lacklustre decade after the effects of the immediate postunification economic boom weakened. [. . .] Moreover, the early years of the Euro (after its physical introduction in 2002) produced exactly the wrong monetary policy for the needs of the anemic German economy. [. . .] Under such circumstances, there was little capacity to exert more influence and power.
>
> (Conradt and Langenbacher 2013: xii–xiii)[5]

Since then things have changed, mostly as a result of the delayed positive effects of flexibility-enhancing German reform efforts combined with a good record in terms of emergency measures and longer-term stability-guided policies. The hosting of the football World Cup in 2006 demonstrated a more positive German mood to the rest of the world (see Chapter 27). Despite a growth figure of −5.1 per cent in 2009, Germany was the most positively assessed country in a BBC poll of 27 states (Conradt and Langenbacher 2013: xii). Compared to a decade before that, opinion seemed to have turned around: now there were 'numerous examples of countries emulating German practices, policies, and institutional structures' (Conradt and Langenbacher 2013: xiii). That left Germany well positioned to assume a leadership role in the eurozone crisis. Indeed, Conradt and Langenbacher argue, 'contrary to the intentions of its creators, the Euro has enabled Germany to regain the leading position that it had on the European continent prior to World War II', even if it is now, in William Paterson's phrase, a rather 'reluctant hegemon' (see Chapter 20). Whether that reluctance is 'rapidly falling away', as Conradt and Langenbacher suggest (2013: xiii), will be considered in depth below.

Crucial dilemmas prior to and during the eurozone crisis

Against this background of renewed German strength – at least in the short term, as the problems of an ageing society may soon dominate (Funk 2004) – many academics are warning against German complacency (Eichengreen 2013; Fratzscher 2013). The German economic hegemony hypothesis can hardly be justified when we take into account both the country's record in terms of economic growth (see Table 22.1) and its persistently high and apparently ever rising unemployment until 2005 (details in Funk 2012: 9–10).

Alongside Ireland, some southern member states showed particularly strong economic growth, while – contrary to the oft-repeated claim that Germany benefited particularly from entering the euro – Germany as the largest EMU country exhibited an inferior economic growth performance. Italy performed especially badly, with a worse economic growth performance than Germany and, at the same time, a price level increase almost as high as in Ireland and Portugal, which had the highest average inflation rates in that period, while Germany experienced the lowest.

After reunification and the break-up of the EMS, real currency appreciation had had disastrous effects for the German economy, 'which had to be squeezed for 15 years to restore competitiveness' (Artus 2010: 7). In line with the pillars of the SME and the iron triangle, Germany therefore insisted, initially at least, on rather strict fiscal requirements for entry into

Table 22.1 Total real economic growth and price level increases between 1995 and 2009 in selected countries of the E(M)U

Country	Real economic growth in per cent	Price level increase in per cent
Ireland	105.0	47
Greece	55.6	67
Spain	50.2	57
Portugal	29.5	48
France	27.4	25
Germany	16.2	12
Italy	11.4	44

Source: Hampe 2013a

the EMU and during its operation (in the end, entrants were not actually required to fulfil those strict criteria). It asked in particular for adherence to a Stability and Growth Pact (SGP) adopted by the European Council in 1997, and was adamant that 'no bailout' should be allowed if countries experienced fiscal distress due to disregarding the fiscal straitjacket, which was implemented to ensure medium- and longer-term stability (Buti and Sapir 2008: 254). Many critics nowadays assert that the failure of the SGP was easily foreseeable, but this is not necessarily true. At the start of EMU, the approach was lauded even in Britain; Artis (2002: 155) called the SGP 'one of the most remarkable pieces of policy coordination in world history. Its construction makes it in some respects comparable to the founding of the Bretton Woods system'. Although the mention of Bretton Woods seems a premonition of potential failure, the rationale behind the approach seemed to make sense:

> the 3 per cent of GDP reference value for triggering the excessive deficit procedure should be treated as much as possible as a 'hard ceiling', the breaking of which would put in motion 'a quasi-automatic' mechanism [. . .] for imposing sanctions, with escape clauses defined as narrowly as possible and legally binding deadlines imposed for taking decisions for the countries to implement corrective measures.
>
> (Buti and Sapir 2008: 243–4)

The 3 per cent criterion, which became part of the Maastricht treaty, was hedged later on with discretionary qualifications, and what actually happened differed considerably from what had been planned (for details, see Buti and Sapir 2008: 244–57). Nevertheless, the SGP aimed at enduring stability-orientated fiscal and financial policy, and contained the obligation to achieve a balanced budget at least in the medium term. An early warning system was provided by the duty to submit annual stability and convergence programmes, which would be followed up with recommendations from the Council. Sanctions threatened in the case of excessive budget deficits. In 2005, however, after Germany and France in particular had repeatedly failed to keep to the rules, the pact was reformed. According to critics, the new pact lost its 'bite' and was weakened because additional factors were given consideration and the deficit procedure was prolonged (Hampe 2013b: 335–6).

In January 1999, the currencies of the different member states were linked irrevocably to the euro. After three years of operating as a shadow currency, on 1 January 2002 the new currency finally took the shape of coins and notes, with €1 equal to DM1.95583. Beyond the advantage that there was no longer any nominal exchange rate volatility among member states, the economic advantages of the euro were seen particularly in an ongoing reduction in transaction and information costs, and in expected gains in economic growth. Moreover, there were potential gains due to the euro's use as an international reserve currency with a larger capital market and, all else being equal, lower average interest rates. And the E(M)U and its political representatives, as a unified player, became a more powerful actor in the globalised world.

But the potential disadvantages of the EMU for the respective actors at national level have to be considered as well. Adopting the euro meant renouncing national monetary, interest rate, and exchange rate policies; the adjustment burden in the case of economic imbalances is on public fiscal and structural policies as well as wage and welfare state policies in the different countries. The question was how to achieve the necessary discipline and microeconomic flexibility of production factors at national level (Hampe 2013b: 336–7). Beyond financial and fiscal issues, the adaptability of national production as well as the resources it required had to be addressed through structural policies, in particular wage and social policies. Countries' room for manoeuvre was affected by the Stability and Growth Pact as well as by the no-bailout clause and productivity

Table 22.2 Institutional framework of policy determination in the pre-crisis E(M)U – different levels of actors for microeconomic and macroeconomic policies

	National	E(M)U
Microeconomic	Labour market regulation	Product and capital market regulation
Macroeconomic	Fiscal policy	Monetary policy (EMU only)

Source: based on Sapir 2006: 382; slightly amended

growth developments (which set the leeway for the distribution of real production). The latter depend on the capacity of production factors to adjust to new situations, and on investment in skills and human capital, in particular. All in all, the rules of the game changed considerably with the adoption of the euro.

Beyond budgetary and financial stability at the macroeconomic level, which was addressed by an independent central bank as well as stability-guided fiscal policy, the EU's Lisbon strategy tried to improve microeconomic flexibility by giving incentives for structural reforms at the national level. The ambitious goal set in March 2000 with the Lisbon strategy was to make the EU 'the most competitive and dynamic knowledge-based economy in the world' by 2009–10 (Papadimitriou 2012: 1). A clear division of labour, as set out in Table 22.2, was meant to achieve this goal (for details, see also Owen Smith 2008: 266–9). However, with the weak governance mechanism, based on the open method of coordination (which relied heavily on voluntarism and peer pressure for its implementation), the incentives set largely failed. An interim assessment suggested that

> the Lisbon method was simply too weak to deliver. Five years after its launch in 2000, it has delivered neither a major thrust towards completing the single market nor significant labour market reforms. [. . .] there is little evidence of a link between initial conditions and subsequent reform efforts over the past ten years, with some countries taking only modest measures despite a low starting point and others carrying out ambitious programmes even though their initial conditions were already relatively favourable. [. . .] Moreover, there is no evidence of an acceleration of reforms during the second half of the period, after the launch of the Lisbon strategy, on the contrary.
>
> (Sapir 2006: 386)

Attempts to improve microeconomic flexibility, above all at the national level, have not been successful: 'Since the introduction of the Euro in the late 1990s, the competitiveness gap between the Eurozone's "core" and "periphery" has been growing steadily' (Papadimitriou 2012: 1). Koo's hypothesis that inadequate German fiscal policy has to be regarded as a potential key source for the current crisis in the eurozone needs to be assessed alongside missing microeconomic reform efforts, particularly in the countries that needed reforms most urgently. At the same time, the macroeconomic framework in place before the current crisis proved unable 'to "police" fiscal discipline amongst its Member States' (Papadimitriou 2012: 1). That problem can be traced back to the blurring of incentives in the original Maastricht public finance requirements:

> Meeting the convergence criteria enabled budgetary laggards to join the virtuous countries in the new policy regime, while failure to comply carried the penalty of exclusion from the euro area. Market incentives were also crucial. Countries with high deficit and debt

levels that adopted a credible adjustment programme were able to enjoy a reduction in interest rates which helped lower their public finance imbalances. The structure of incentives changed with entry into the euro area; the convergence of interest rates meant that the market incentives were reduced, the carrot of the prospect of entry was eaten, and the stick of the risk of exclusion was replaced by the much weaker threat of uncertain and delayed sanctions under the SGP. The experience of the early years of EMU showed that the Council was not ready to use the 'nuclear option' of pecuniary sanctions, especially against large countries.

(Buti and Sapir 2008: 254)

Despite an often rather positive interim assessment of the single currency on its tenth birthday, experts knew of the covert structural problems. Table 22.3 summarises important policy fields related to the E(M)U level and the respective governance structures prior to the recent crisis-related reforms.

For many observers, especially in Germany, the crisis in the eurozone is largely the result of failure to observe the explicit and implicit 'rules of the game' of EMU (see also Hampe 2013a, 2013b: 336–41). The trigger was the dramatic interest rate spread against German governmental bonds (bunds) after Greece's admission of a much higher sovereign debt than had been generally assumed until then. The rating agencies 'failed' as guardians of the financial markets, at least in the sense that they did not lead to sufficiently differentiated interest rates, despite differences in countries' risks prior to the crisis. One reason for this was probably that the financial markets never really regarded the no-bailout clause as credible, because the Stability and

Table 22.3 Institutional framework of policy determination in the pre-crisis E(M)U – features of different policy fields and respective levels

Policy field	Features	Level responsible
Monetary policy	• Primary objective of price stability • The eurosystem contributes to financial stability and supervision	Euro area-wide level

Fiscal policy	Fiscal surveillance in order to rule out unsustainable developments
	• No-bailout rule
	• Stability and Growth Pact
	  – Excessive deficit procedure
	  – Stability and convergence programmes
		National level with 'hard' rule-based co-ordination

Structural policy	• Economic policies matter of common concern
	• Integrated guidelines
	  – Broad economic policy
	  – Employment
	• National reform programmes
	• 'Lisbon strategy', followed by 'Europe 2020'
		• National level with 'soft' co-ordination
		• Open method of co-ordination

Prudential policy	Micro-prudential supervision: limit distress of individual institutions	National level

Source: based on Coene 2012: 105; Brunetti 2014

Growth Pact was never in fact enforced (despite 97 cases to 2010 where annual budget deficits were above 3 per cent).

The main causes of the crisis in the euro area and how to cure it

In order to prescribe an appropriate therapy, a parsimonious diagnosis has to be made. The discussion so far has highlighted several issues behind the crisis in the eurozone: first, the very high public debt levels prior to 2009–10 and their dramatic increase especially in Ireland, Italy, Portugal, Greece, and Spain after 2008–9; and second, the increasing divergence (rather than the expected convergence) in the competitiveness of the individual member states. Problems were caused by demanding too much of the available distributional margin based on productivity growth. That implies, third, a failure of national governments to enforce much needed structural reforms to break up the still existing insider–outsider problems, which led to an overburdening of the distributional leeway limit and caused economic distress both for national economic actors and abroad. As one observer has aptly put it: 'the crisis of the southern European euro countries is not simply a sovereign debt crisis; it is also a growth and competitiveness crisis resulting from insider power' (Iversen 2013: 77). This is a neglected factor in the current debate; it mirrors the Federal Republic's experience after the 1980s, until the German insider–outsider problem was overcome in the context of globalisation and Europeanisation, combined with measured reforms of the welfare state and labour markets (Funk 2000, 2010).

The dramatic rise in interest rates for the sovereign debt of the countries in crisis endangered their ability to pay, and the risk of those countries' insolvency threatened the stability of the entire European banking system with its transnational web of loans. With the help of massive rescue measures that critics in Germany, in particular, regard as out of line with the European treaty on monetary union that was agreed at Maastricht in 1991, it has so far been possible to avoid the insolvency of states and systemically important banks. The justification for those measures – buying time to implement the required structural reforms – was accepted by the governments of Germany and of other countries, and to some extent by the German Bundesbank and the German Constitutional Court (Deutsche Bundesbank 2012: 22–3; Sinn 2014). Nevertheless, this approach meant the gradual substitution of private creditors by taxpayers, whereby the latter are bearing more burdens than are probably justified. The crisis is by no means finally resolved. Potential solutions are still being hotly debated. The countries in crisis need to regain their competitiveness – their 'national business models' prior to the crisis have proved unsustainable. The adjustment process must continue, even though the crisis and the adjustment measures taken so far have caused huge losses in the countries particularly affected. A few months of positive economic growth cannot compensate for losses of per capita incomes between 2007 and 2013 of 8 per cent in Spain, 12 per cent in Italy, and almost 24 per cent in Greece, which went hand in hand with very high unemployment (Brunetti 2014). Public and private debt need to reach sustainable levels, and the banking systems have to be both stabilised in the short term and made sustainable in the longer term.

The dilemma is that all the current resolution mechanisms lead away from other important objectives. Thus for many observers there appears to be no 'ideal path' from the perspective of all the countries and actors involved. The following list outlines some of the interrelated problems (Hampe 2013a):

- The euro crisis risks aggravating divisions between the EMU's member states. Promising and ensuring unlimited aid to weakened countries could potentially calm the financial markets, but the strategy might backfire because it is likely to weaken the reform efforts of the countries in crisis and thus to increase the liability risks for stronger countries. The euro crisis may, then, aggravate a splintering of the EMU's member states, and we may well see a further strengthening of anti–euro parties. That will put the parties at the centre under pressure to toughen already tough aid policies, even though the opposite may be needed, at least for some weaker countries. A frightening scenario with sovereign insolvencies due to populist policies is less likely if the necessary austerity measures in the countries in crisis are carried out within a realistic time scale; but putting less pressure on the countries in crisis by offering a more generous timetable may slow down the required structural reforms (Smaghi 2013: 70–4).

- Only a geographically stable EMU offers the lasting advantages of a single currency in the medium and longer term. Stopping financial aid to Greece and its subsequent insolvency would probably lead to a Greek exit from the EU and force creditors to forgo considerable financial demands. Such a situation would increase speculation that other crisis countries could follow suit and might thus contribute to a domino effect that would worsen the situation of other member states.

- A break-up of this kind might do long-term harm to the EU's position in the world. Even if only a few isolated countries whose non-compliance with reform demands was quite obvious were to leave, the EU's reputation might be damaged by its inability to solve a comparatively small problem such as restructuring a country like Greece (with only 2.5 per cent of the gross domestic product of the eurozone as a whole). Proposals for how to deal with such a serious situation remain quite controversial among economists (Sinn 2013). And there is further cause for concern: if large countries within the EMU and countries with populist governments refused to implement the necessary sweeping structural reforms, a break-up might eventually ensue as creditor nations such as Germany with current account surpluses and comparatively sound public budgets lost interest in participating. At least some calculations show that taking the risk of 'Germexit' – Germany leaving the eurozone (possibly followed by other creditor nations) – might pay off for such countries after only a few years (Mayer 2013).

This helps to explain why Chancellor Merkel ignored demands for mutualisation of debt through Eurobonds and decided instead to pursue the step-by-step approach of solidarity for stability. In terms of game theory, this approach can be regarded as a 'chicken game', in which the 'players' seek through their specific interactions to gain at the expense of the other actors involved (Smaghi 2013: 70–4). There is an overall 'super-dilemma' in such situations:

> a choice that seems optimal in the short term becomes counterproductive because it creates perverse incentives in the medium term. This is why the economic policy cannot be subject to too much discretion and should preferably be subject to rules, even if those rules may appear too rigid when the effect is evaluated on a case by case basis.
>
> (Smaghi 2013: 71)

Trying to overcome such problems is at the heart of the German ordoliberal school of thought, which focuses on institutionalising sanctions against (short-term) misbehaviour or free-riding at the expense of others, as this is likely otherwise to cause 'revenge' and thus destroy mutually beneficial gains from economic interactions. If short-term gains hurting others are forgone, in the medium and longer term all actors are usually better off. This approach also explains why German ordoliberals are so reluctant to adopt short-term expansionary fiscal policy to stimulate the economy in a short-term recession, as the result is usually only a passing fancy without lasting positive effects on economic growth or structural (un)employment. As a rule, German mainstream economists as well as governmental authorities limit Keynesian economic policy foremost to very specific situations: "Government investment for the purpose of stimulating the economy is meaningful only – and on a limited scale – in times of extraordinary crisis" (Deutsche Bundesbank 1999: 15).

From the German perspective, the pathway taken in the eurozone crisis was an attempt to minimise (in a situation of huge uncertainty) the costs for Germany, while simultaneously striking a balance between solidarity – since the alternative of strictly applying the EMU's no-bailout rule was regarded as worse for the countries affected – and putting pressure on the countries in crisis to ensure ongoing reforms at the necessary speed.

Towards a more stable financial architecture

For Chancellor Merkel and the finance minister in her two coalitions since 2009, Wolfgang Schäuble, all alternatives to the euro have so far appeared to be worse under realistic conditions. Knowing this may explain Merkel's often repeated and sometimes ridiculed verdict on the issue: 'If the euro breaks, European integration will also break' ('Scheitert der Euro, scheitert Europa'; quoted from Marsh 2013: 20). Economic analysis suggests that the acute dimension of the crisis as a self-fulfilling crisis of confidence with highly destructive potential could indeed have resulted in a break or breaks. The largely German-led crisis management, therefore, based as it was on a 'cautious and muddling-through approach towards a permanent solution', may well have been adequate, and was certainly superior to either the quick exclusion of crisis countries from EMU or the introduction of debt mutualisation (Heinemann 2013: 38; on France, Schild 2013).

The recent crisis has made the new German SME into a kind of role model for other countries, at least to some extent (Rees 2011; and see Anderson in this volume). In fact, Germany's leading role in preparing blueprints for structural reforms was based on lessons learned from Germany's own experience of fighting persistently high unemployment and low economic growth in the past. The 'Brussels consensus view' (Hirschel 2013) that has emerged is to a large extent inspired by the pillars of Germany's SME and by Germany's recent experience of a turnaround, within a period of few years, from having a lagging and sick economy to being the country with the best recovery in Europe during a time of deep crisis in the EU. According to Finance Minister Schäuble, flaws in the euro-architecture have been amended since the start of the crisis. With respect to the euro rescue, he noted in an interview published in November 2012 that 'the puzzle is becoming complete' (Schäuble 2012: 17). Decisive steps that would stabilise the eurozone included, according to Schäuble:

- launching the European Stability Mechanism as a protective shield for the euro;
- tightening up the Stability and Growth Pact;
- implementing the Fiscal Compact, including 'debt brakes' based on the German and Swiss model;
- improved governance mechanisms to ensure comprehensive and ongoing reforms as well as successful consolidation measures throughout the member states (European semester, euro-plus pact);
- an effective European banking supervisor;
- the decision of Germany's Federal Constitutional Court in early September 2012 to declare the German government's strategy to rescue the euro in line with the Basic Law;
- a European Central Bank that 'does its job very well – until now inflation in the eurozone has been lower than inflation with the deutschmark' (Schäuble 2012: 19).

(This last statement indicates that the minister, like the chancellor (Schwarzer 2012), does not support the Bundesbank's harsh criticism of unconventional monetary policy even as a short-term emergency measure.)

According to the finance minister, since Lehman Brothers filed for bankruptcy on 15 September 2008, the financial markets have become a safer place due to much regulatory work.

Lothar Funk

In an article published in November 2013, Schäuble (2013b) notes: 'By improving supervision and adopting more appropriate capital requirements, we are making the financial system more crisis-resistant. Markets and products have become more transparent.' For Schäuble, the euro rescue is in the best interests of Germany, if it is done properly:

> A collapse of the currency union would be substantially more expensive for German citizens than the obligations that have been made so far in the form of credit guarantees. The loans were only granted under very strict conditions, whose implementation should put the recipients back on their feet economically.
>
> (Schäuble 2012: 19)

An important lesson is that the measures summarised in Table 22.4 that (apart from shorter-term stabilisation mechanisms) address structural issues[6] – the special focus of orthodox ordoliberalism – cannot suffice to stop a self-fulfilling crisis of confidence, as such a crisis 'cannot be contained through an improvement of long-run fundamentals alone' (Heinemann 2013: 39).

This is not to suggest that short-term emergency aid suffices or can substitute for structural measures. Additional sweeping reforms will be necessary despite all the efforts that have been made up till now. However, the speed of those reforms may be better adapted than in the initial phase (Brunetti 2014). Brunetti, a Swiss economist, suggests that in addition to national measures to ensure budget consolidation the continuing design faults of the original EMU system have to be removed. We need an answer to the question how a currency union with sovereign member states can ensure sufficient discipline without in practice abolishing fiscal sovereignty at the national level. In the foreseeable future, steps towards a full fiscal union are regarded as politically unenforceable (not only in Germany), and alternative institutional mechanisms will be needed to overcome the depression-like fall in real incomes in the crisis countries as well as their ongoing solvency problems. The announcement of the so-called outright monetary transactions (OMTs) in July 2012 was an emergency measure that, in retrospect, has helped to prevent a break-up

Table 22.4 Important elements of a firewall against financial crises in the European Union

Unified and effective banking supervision and single resolution mechanism
- to be implemented via a banking union that had been agreed at the end of 2013 (supervisory mechanism and complex resolution regime) and further implemented in the medium term

Mandatory introduction of debt brakes and stricter handling of public deficits
- introduced by Fiscal Compact for improved budgetary discipline of 25 EU member states

Implementation of European stabilisation mechanisms, initially temporarily and then permanently
- establishes jointly guaranteed stability mechanisms; loans in return for consolidation measures and structural reforms; aims at achieving short-term financial stabilisation of entire countries and banks in emergencies

Precautionary measures against macroeconomic imbalances
- particularly to fight lasting high current account deficits as well as ongoing very high current account surpluses

Early coordination of budget and economic policies among member states by European Commission
- introduced via the European semester

More effective control of public budgets
- by making the Stability and Growth Pact stricter and simultaneously more effective

Source: based on Europäische Kommission 2012: 5

366

of the eurozone so far. But no more can be achieved by such a rescue measure. Despite the Bundesbank's (and, in February 2014, the German Constitutional Court's) rejection of the OMTs (Sinn 2014; Weidmann 2014), a good number – though most likely not the majority – of German economists regard them as an appropriate emergency measure. The promise of the ECB's president Mario Draghi to do 'whatever it takes' to rescue the euro will not deal with the huge remaining solvency problems, as the ECB can only resolve uncertainties with respect to liquidity; in practice, it will act as a lender of last resort for sovereign debt, something many economists (especially outside Germany) regard as a suitable mode of rescue for financial institutions that can be regarded as solvent but have liquidity problems in panic situations, when investors suddenly remove money from financial institutions. According to Brunetti (2014):

> The liquidity risk was eliminated with OMT considerably; and one has to hope that the Court of European Justice will acknowledge the applicability of this central instrument. The problem remains, however, that this measure can help only in the case of illiquidity of states that are still solvent. If a country is not solvent anymore, however, the ECB's hands are bound by its constitution.

The original 'no bailout' clause has already been replaced, in effect, with a limited joint bailout fund, following the implementation of the European Stability Mechanism and the fiscal pact to improve the enforcement of fiscal goals compared with the original SGP and its successor. Further measures will nevertheless be needed, as prior to the crisis fiscal policy in many member states was structurally deficient. Banking union appears to be indispensable in order to get rid of the link between banking crisis and sovereign debt crisis in the eurozone, which essentially means breaking the 'doom loop' of weak banks and weak governments lending to each other. Apart from the measures already taken in 2013, it will be essential to implement a credibly financed joint single resolution mechanism (SRM) for de facto bankrupt large banks (Brunetti 2014).

Conclusions

The financial crises since 2008 have had only a transitory impact on most important economic indicators in Germany, with the exception of real investment, which has still not entirely recovered. Despite severe fluctuations in real GDP and other values, such as exports, real wages and consumption remained roughly constant even in 2009 (the year of deep crisis) and increased slightly in succeeding years (Funk 2013).

All in all, Germany seems to have benefited from the euro largely in terms of export gains, especially after the abolition of the exchange rate risk that existed prior to the euro. The country was ranked fourth of the relative winners from the adoption of the euro, according to a very rough ranking by Raiffeisen Research in 2012 (see Table 22.5). The ranking assumes an improvement due to the euro if one of the six chosen macroeconomic indicators improved in the period 1999–2011 compared with 1986–98. While this is a broad-brush analysis that neglects other factors (for example, the specific effects of German unification or key reforms potentially independent of the euro), it is of some interest.

How does Germany's performance match up against that of other countries if we compare the periods 1999–2011 and 1986–98? West German exports were at the heart of the Federal Republic's postwar economic success (Funk 2012: 1–2); and this has been true again since the adoption of the euro. Germany is the only country among the initial euro member states plus Greece that was able to increase its real exports between 1999 and 2011, compared with the

Lothar Funk

Table 22.5 Relative success since the adoption of the euro

Rank/country	Real GDP	Employ- ment	Unem- ploy- ment	Inflation	GDP per head in ppp*	Share of exports	Average score
1 Finland	1	1	5	5	2	7	3.6
2 Greece	2	8	12	1	1	11	5.0
3 Austria	5	3	8	8	4	3	5.1
4 Germany	7	7	9	7	3	4	5.8
5 Belgium	3	5	6	10	5	6	5.9
6 Spain	6	9	2	4	8	8	6.3
7 France	4	6	7	6	6	10	6.5
8 Italy	8	2	4	3	11	9	6.8
9 Ireland	10	11	1	9	10	2	7.4
10 Netherlands	8	12	3	11	6	5	7.5
11 Luxembourg	10	4	10	12	8	1	7.6
12 Portugal	12	10	11	2	12	12	9.7

*ppp = purchasing power parity

Source: Raiffeisen Research (Angelé 2012)

13 years prior to the existence of the euro (in 1986–98 Germany lagged behind all other countries in the sample, apart from Austria, in terms of export growth). According to Angelé (2012), this

> clearly hints at the actual advantage which the euro meant for Germany: the risk of exchange rate shocks was excluded. Sudden exchange rate appreciations (with negative consequences for price-competitiveness and thus for German exports) as during the crisis of the EMS in 1992/93 are no threat for the German economy any more.

In other words, the euro can help maintain German export competitiveness within the European monetary union and against the rest of the world because the damaging appreciations that affected Germany prior to the euro (when the country pursued stricter policies to fight inflation) are avoided.

The euro also helps explain why Germany was able rather easily to recoup a considerable temporary fall in real exports by roughly 14 per cent in 2009, compared with 2008, during the financial crisis (Funk 2013: 205): 'Without the euro and with the Deutsch-Mark, the economic effects of the so-called "Great Recession" would have been arguably considerably more serious. The flipside of this is, however, the sovereign debt crisis in the euro zone' (Angelé 2012). That flipside means massive savings packages as well as interventions from the ECB to keep the currency union and the euro alive. It is still too early to know how costly this will be for Germany.

Table 22.5 suggests that simply creating a common currency union cannot guarantee further convergence. If that were so, we would expect to see Portugal, Greece, and Spain in the role of 'catch-up'-countries, while Luxembourg, the Netherlands, and Austria would be at the bottom of the ranking. Both predictions are partly contradicted by the facts. This indicates, as Angelé (2012) has suggested, that 'in many member states the economic and fiscal policy remained suboptimal and had considerable influence on the highly divergent economic development in the single states of the euro zone'. In that light, the focus of the German government – inspired by ordoliberal ideas – as well as of international institutions such as the OECD, the World Bank, and the IMF on the need for meaningful structural reforms seems justified. That does not mean that further German support for the countries in crisis should be resisted (Funk 2013), but simplistic Keynesian recommendations leave unanswered the key question how the troubled countries' structural problems can be resolved; the evidence also suggests that structural reform efforts at home tend to decrease as soon as more foreign aid is made available. It must not be forgotten that the debt crisis has also left the German economy vulnerable (Das 2013; see also Gros 2013).[7] Germany's government could pursue efficiency-enhancing structural economic policies that would serve both Germany and the common good, while also supporting the troubled nations' economies to some extent. This might reduce the kinds of criticisms of Germany that this chapter has highlighted; and such reforms might also address foreseeable future problems for Germany.

Notes

1   I am grateful to the editor for her patience and support during the completion of this chapter.
2   Cited in Morisse-Schilbach (2011): 26. The article is available online at www.theguardian.com/books/ 2010/may/15/hans-magnus-enzensberger-interview (accessed 13 October 2014).
3   'Denn die Deutschen haben begriffen, dass wir – um mit Fritz Stern zu sprechen – unsere zweite Chance durch die Integration in Europa haben. Eine Zukunft haben wir nur in dem Maße, wie Europa gelingt. Auch Deutschland wird es nur dann gut gehen, wenn es Europa gut geht'. Unless otherwise stated, all translations from the German are the author's.
4   On this issue, see Leonhard and Funk (2002).
5   Please note that – in contrast to Koo on the previous page – Conradt and Langenbacher regard the monetary policy at that time as still too contractive from the point of view of the weak, ailing German economy in the early 2000s. Gradually, however, the German export sector helped to get a struggling Germany running again.
6   Particularly inspired by the German ordoliberal discourse is the German finance minister's insistence on 'a high priority on ensuring that shareholders and creditors bear the main responsibility for the costs incurred in winding up troubled banks' (Schäuble 2013b); that is, the importance of manageable and predictable 'bail-ins' for all partners involved.
7   Das (2013) notes: 'Germany's economic power and financial strength is overstated. Germany remains dependent on its neighbours, with 69 per cent of total exports going to European countries, including 57 per cent to the member states of the European Union.' Das adds with respect to the eurozone countries in crisis: 'Continued weakness in these troubled countries will affect German economic prospects. [. . .] Peripheral countries will be forced to rely on the European Stability Mechanism and European Central Bank to provide financing directly or indirectly via cheap funds to banks to purchase government bonds which will be used as collateral for the central bank loans. National central banks will also use the "Target 2" payment system to settle cross border funds flows between eurozone countries financing peripheral countries without access to money markets to fund trade deficits and capital flight. Over time, financing will become concentrated in official agencies, the ECB and national governments or central banks. Risk will shift from the peripheral countries to the core of the eurozone, especially Germany and France.' Given the current weakness of France, the pressure on Germany is likely to grow.

Bibliography

Angelé, J. (2012) 'Wer tatsächlich am meisten vom Euro profitiert', *Börsen-Zeitung*, 5 December, 235: 7.
Artis, M.J. (2002) 'The Stability and Growth Pact: Fiscal Policy in EMU', in F. Breuss, G. Fink, and S. Griller (eds) *Institutional, Legal and Economic Aspects of the EMU*, Vienna and New York: Springer, 101–15.
Artus, P. (2010) 'Germany is different from the rest of the euro zone, but in reality it is not in a position of strength to impose its views', 28 October, *Flash Economic Research*, 580.
Birckenbach, H.-M. (2011) 'Germany and European Integration', in R. Seidelmann (ed.) *The New Germany – History, Economy, Policies*, Baden-Baden: Nomos, 316–34.
Blyth, M. (2013) *Austerity: The History of a Dangerous Idea*, Oxford: Oxford University Press.
Bonefeld, W. (2013) 'On the Strong Liberal State: Beyond Berghahn and Young', *New Political Economy*, 18(5): 679–83.
Brunetti, A. (2014) 'Wirtschaftsaufschwung – wie lange?', *Neue Zürcher Zeitung*, 14 February.
Buti, M. and Sapir, A. (2008) 'Fiscal Policy in Europe', in B. Eichengreen, M. Landesmann, and D. Stiefel (eds) *The European Economy in an American Mirror*, Abingdon: Routledge, 233–58.
Coene, L. (2012) 'Policy Challenges Facing the Euro-Area Economy', *Economic & Financial Review*, 4(19): 103–27.

Conradt, D.P. and Langenbacher, E. (2013) *The Germany Polity*, 10th edn, Lanham, MD: Rowman & Littlefield Publishers, Inc.

Das, S. (2013) 'Debt crisis has left Germany vulnerable', *Financial Times*, November 5, 26.

Deutsche Bundesbank (2009) 'The Development of Government Investment', *Monthly Report*, 61(10): 15–34.

Deutsche Bundesbank (2012) *Safeguarding stability – The Deutsche Bundesbank's responsibilities and activities*, Frankfurt a.m.: Bundesbank.

Dyson, K. and Quaglia, L. (2012) 'Economic and Monetary Union and the Lisbon Strategy', in P. Copeland and D. Papadimitriou (eds) *The EU's Lisbon Strategy – Evaluating Success, Understanding Failure*, Basingstoke: Palgrave/Macmillan, 189–207.

Eibner, W. (2008) *International Economic Integration*, Munich: Oldenbourg.

Eichengreen, B. (2013) 'Germany's Complacency Problem', *Finanz und Wirtschaft*, 15 October. Online. Available at www.fuw.ch/article/germanys-complacency-problem/ (accessed 1 November 2013).

Europäische Kommission (Vertretung in Deutschland) (2012) *EU-Nachrichten*, 20 September, 5.

Falke, A. (2009) 'The Internationalisation of Germany; Adapting to Europeanisation and Globalisation', in A. Miskimmon, W.E. Paterson, and J. Sloam (eds) *Germany's Gathering Crisis*, Basingstoke: Palgrave, 202–19.

Fratzscher, M. (2013) 'Delusional Germany', 13 November, Project Syndicate. Online. Available at www.project-syndicate.org/print/marcel-fratzscher-on-the-three-beliefs-turning-germany-against-the-euro (accessed 15 December 2013).

Funk, L. (2000) 'Economic Reform of *Modell Deutschland*', in R. Harding and W.E. Paterson (eds) *The Future of the German Economy*, Manchester: Manchester University Press, 16–35.

Funk, L. (2001) 'Strategic Policy to Fight Germany's Unemployment Problem', *International Journal of Manpower*, 22(6): 508–25.

Funk, L. (2002) 'Economic Approaches to the Study of Contemporary Germany', in J. Grix (ed.) *Approaches to the Study of Contemporary Germany*, Birmingham: Birmingham University Press, 232–64.

Funk, L. (2003) 'Chancellor Proposes Agenda 2010 to Revive Economy', *EIROnline*, 31 March. Online. Available at www.eurofound.europa.eu/eiro/2003/03/feature/de0303105f.htm (accessed 20 January 2013).

Funk, L. (2004) 'Employment Opportunities for Older Workers. A Comparison of Selected OECD Countries', *Dice-Report – Journal for Institutional Comparisons*, 2(2): 22–33.

Funk, L. (2007) 'Convergence in Employment-related Public Policies? A British-German Comparison', *German Politics* 16(1): 116–36.

Funk, L. (2010) 'Social Market Economy at Sixty: Path Dependence and Path Changes', in C.L. Glossner and D. Gregosz (eds) *Sixty Years of Social Market Economy: Formation, Development and Perspectives of a Peacemaking Formula*, Berlin and Sankt Augustin: Konrad-Adenauer-Stiftung e.V, 85–103.

Funk, L. (2012) *The German Economy During the Financial and Economic Crisis since 2008/2009: An Unexpected Success Story Revisited*, Berlin and Sankt Augustin: Konrad-Adenauer-Stiftung e.V.

Funk, L. (2013) 'Germany: Sweeping Structural Reforms Can Work', in V. Novotný (ed.) *From Reform to Growth – Managing the Economic Crisis in Europe*, Brussels: Centre for European Studies, 201–33.

Funk, L. (2014) 'Why has the German Job Market Done Astonishingly Well Despite the 2008–2009 "Great Recession"? New Economic Miracle, Institutional Transformation or Beggar-thy-Neighbour Policies?', *Perspectives on European Politics and Society*, 15(3): 305–21.

Gerber, J. (2013) *International Economics*, 6th edn, Boston: Pearson Education, Inc.

German Council of Economic Experts (Sachverständigenrat zur Begutachtung der Gesamtwirtschaftlichen Entwicklung) (2011) *Assume Responsibility for Europe – Annual Report*, Chapter 1, Wiesbaden and Paderborn: Statistisches Bundesamt/Bonifatius. Online. Available at www.sachverstaendigenrat-wirtschaft.de (accessed 15 January 2014)

Gros, D. (2013) 'The German Scapegoat', 5 December, Project Syndicate. Online. Available at www.project-syndicate.org/commentary/daniel-gros-argues-that-the-growing-crticism-of-germany-s-external-surplus-is-misplaced (accessed 15 December 2013).

Hampe, P. (2013a) 'Die Krise der Europäischen Währungsunion: Ursachen und Perspektiven', presentation on 19 February, Politische Akademie Tutzing. Online. Available at http://web.apb-tutzing.de/apb/cms/fileadmin/Tagungsmaterialien/2013/1._Quartal/Hampe_Krise_der_Waehrungsunion.pdf (accessed 15 November 2013).

Hampe, P. (2013b) 'Zur Logik der Europäischen Währungsunion und ihrer Krise', *Gesellschaft, Wirtschaft, Politik (GWP)*, 62(3): 331–41.

Heinemann, F. (2013) 'Die Europäische Schuldenkrise: Ursachen und Lösungsstrategien', *Jahrbuch für Wirtschaftswissenschaften*, 63(1): 18–41.

Hirschel, D. (2013) 'Die Risiken des deutschen Zaubertranks', *Frankfurter Allgemeine Zeitung*, 7 January, 20. Online. Available at www.faz.net/aktuell/wirtschaft/eurokrise/standpunkt-dierk-hirschel-die-risiken-des-deutschen-zaubertranks-12016261.html (accessed 15 November 2013).

Hüther, M. (2011) *Die ökonomische Logik lässt sich nicht ausschalten*, Cologne: Institut der deutschen Wirtschaft Köln.

Iversen, T. (2013) 'Combining competitiveness, growth, and solidarity', in Global Progress and Policy Network (eds) *The Politics of Growth, Stability and Reform*, London: Policy Network, 75–8. Online. Available at www.policy-network.net/publications/4361/The-Politics-of-Growth-Stability-and-Reform (accessed 15 January 2014)

James, H. (2012) *Making the European Monetary Union*, Cambridge, MA and London: The Belknap Press of Harvard University Press.

Kindleberger, C.P. (1976) 'Germany's persistent balance-of-payments disequilibrium revisited', *Banca Nazionale del Lavoro Quarterly Review*, 29: 118–50.

Koo, R. (2013) 'Balance Sheet Recessions and the Global Economic Crisis', in H. Flassbeck, P. Davidson, J.K. Galbraith, R. Koo, and J. Ghosh (eds) *Economic Reform Now*, Frankfurt a.m.: Westend Verlag, 85–131.

Leonhard, J. and Funk, L. (eds.) (2002) *Ten Years of German Unification – Transfer – Transformation – Incorporation?* Birmingham: Birmingham University Press.

Mankiw, N.G. (2011) *Principles of Economics*, 6th edn, Mason, OH: South-Western.

Marsh, D. (2013) *Beim Geld hört der Spaß auf: Warum die Eurokrise nicht mehr lösbar ist*, Berlin: Europa Verlag.

Mayer, T. (2013) 'Trapped in the EMU?' *CESifo Forum*, 13(4): 59–63.

Miskimmon, A., Paterson, W.E., and Sloam, J. (2010) 'Germany at a Crossroads: The gathering crisis sharpens', *Comparative European Politics*, 8(4): 491–504.

Morisse-Schilbach, M. (2011) '"Ach Deutschland!": Greece, the Euro crisis, and the costs and benefits of being a benign hegemon', *Internationale Politik und Gesellschaft/International Politics and Society*, 26–41. Online. Available at http://library.fes.de/pdf-files/ipg/ipg-2011-1/2011-1__04_a_morisse-schilbach.pdf (accessed 2 December 2013).

Neal, L. (2007) *The Economics of Europe and the European Union*, Cambridge: Cambridge University Press.

Norris, F. (2012) 'As Europe's Currency Union Frays, Conspiracy Theories Fly', *International Herald Tribune*, 14 June. Online. Available at www.nytimes.com/2012/06/15/business/as-europes-currency-union-frays-conspiracy-theories-fly.html?adxnnl=1&adxnnlx=1392732408-GbMZRM1miDmPC+ByzS/lkA (accessed 16 June 2012).

Owen Smith, E. (2008) 'Germany and the Dynamics of European Economic Integration', in L. Funk (ed.) *Anwendungsorientierte Marktwirtschaftslehre und Neue Politische Ökonomie – Eckhard Knappe zum 65. Geburtstag*, Marburg: Metropolis, 255–323.

Owen Smith, E. and Funk, L. (1994) 'Trade', in E. Owen Smith, *The German Economy*, London: Routledge: 499–522.

Papadimitriou, D. (2012) 'Introduction', in P. Copeland and D. Papadimitriou (eds) *The EU's Lisbon Strategy – Evaluating Success, Understanding Failure*, Basingstoke: Palgrave/Macmillan, 1–7.

Paterson, W.E. (2011) 'Between the Rhineland and the English Channel', in R. Dehousse and E. Fabry (eds) *Where is Germany Heading?* Studies & Research 79, Paris: Notre Europe, 45–52.

Rees, A. (2011) 'German reform success as blueprint for Europe', *Friday Notes*, 4 November, UniCredit, 6–8.

Reinert, K.A. (2012) *An Introduction to International Economics*, New York: Cambridge University Press.

Sapir, A. (2006) 'Globalization and the Reform of European Social Models', *Journal of Common Market Studies*, 44(2): 369–90.

Schäuble, W. (2012) 'We will be successful', *DE-Magazin Deutschland*, Autumn, 3: 16–19.

Schäuble, W. (2013a) 'There is no longer any risk of contagion', German version published in *Süddeutsche Zeitung*, 2 December. Online. Available at www.bundesfinanzministerium.de/Content/EN/Interviews/2013/2013–12-sueddeutsche-zeitung.html (accessed 20 December 2013).

Schäuble, W. (2013b) 'Taking the necessary action", German version published in *Frankfurter Allgemeine Zeitung*, 12 November. Online. Available at www.bundesfinanzministerium.de/Content/EN/Interviews/2013/2013–11–12-faz.html (accessed 20 December 2013).

Schild, J. (2013) 'Leadership in Hard Times', *German Politics and Society*, 31(1): 24–47.

Schwarzer, D. (2012) 'The Euro Area Crises, Shifting Power Relations and Institutional Change in the European Union', *Global Policy*, December, 3(s1): 28–41.

Siebert, H. (2005) *The German Economy: Beyond the Social Market*, Princeton and Oxford: Princeton University Press.

Siems, M. and Schnyder, G. (2013) 'Ordoliberal Lessons for Economic Stability: Different Kinds of Regulation, Not More Regulation', *Governance* 27(3): 377–96. Online. Available at http://onlinelibrary. wiley.com/doi/10.1111/gove.12046/references (accessed 20 November 2013).

Simon, H. (2011) *Die Wirtschaftstrends der Zukunft*, Frankfurt a.m. and New York: Campus.

Sinn, H.-W. (2010) *Casino Capitalism*, Oxford: Oxford University Press.

Sinn, H.-W. (2013) 'Rescuing Europe from the Ground Up', Project Syndicate. Online. Available at www.project-syndicate.org/commentary/hans-werner-sinn-argues-that-reconstructing-the-euro-is-the-only-way-to-save-the-european-integration-project (accessed 25 December 2013).

Sinn, H.-W. (2014) 'Comments by the Ifo Institute and Prof. Hans-Werner Sinn on Today's Statement by Germany's Constitutional Court on the ECB's OMT Programme', Ifo Institute Munich Press Release. Online. Available at www.cesifo-group.de/ifoHome/presse/Pressemitteilungen/Pressemitteil ungen-Archiv/2014/Q1/press_20140207-Stellungnahme-des-ifo-Instituts-und-von-Prof-Hans-Werner-Sinn-zur-heutigen-Erklärung-des-Bundesverfassungsgerichts-zum-OMT-Programm-der-EZB-.html (accessed 12 February 2014).

Smaghi, L.B. (2013) *Austerity – European Democracies against the Wall*, Brussels: Centre for European Policy Studies (CEPS).

Walwei, U. (2011) 'Die veränderte Struktur des Arbeitsmarktes: zukunftsfähig oder doch nicht nachhaltig?' *WSI-Mitteilungen*, 64(11): 563–70.

Weidmann. J. (2014) 'Of dentists and economists – the importance of a consistent economic policy framework', speech at the Juristische Studiengesellschaft, Karlsruhe, on 11 February 2014. Online. Available at www.bundesbank.de/Redaktion/EN/Reden/2014/2014_02_11_weidmann.html?startpage Id=Startseite-EN&startpageAreaId=Teaserbereich&startpageLinkName=2014_02_11_weidmann+167144 (accessed 12 February 2014).

Whittock, J. (2008) 'Germany playing catch-up', *Economic Review*, 26(1), September, 8–11.

Willecke, F.-U. (2011*) Deutschland, Zahlmeister der EU – Abrechnung mit einer ungerechten Lastenverteilung*, Munich: Olzog.

Young, B. and Semmler, W. (2011) 'The European Sovereign Debt Crisis. Is Germany to Blame?' *German Politics and Society*, 29(1): 1–24.

23

Climate protection policy

Ecological modernisation, industrial competitiveness, and Europeanisation

Rainer Hillebrand

National pride is a contested concept in Germany. Nonetheless, many Germans are particularly proud of two of their country's achievements: being recognised internationally as an environmental leader, especially in climate protection, and possessing a successful industrial sector that places the country amongst the leading export nations. Both climate protection and the international competitiveness of industry have played a significant role for at least the last two decades in Germany's self-perception and in political debates.

Successive governments since the late 1980s have committed Germany to increasingly strict reduction targets for greenhouse gas emissions (GHGE) in order to help avoid global warming and its adverse consequences such as melting ice caps, rising sea levels, and extreme weather conditions. At present, Germany plans to curb emissions by 40 per cent by 2020 relative to the base year 1990, thereby rendering the country one of the most determined climate protectors in Europe and beyond (Hey 2010: 211). In 2010 the government unilaterally announced a globally unique reduction goal of 80–95 per cent by 2050, envisaged in the so-called 'Energy Concept' (BMWi and BMU 2010). This programme aims to transform the current conventional energy supply system by replacing fossil fuels as the primary energy source with renewables such as wind and solar power.

At the same time as aspiring to environmental leadership, Germany remains one of the most important hubs for manufacturing worldwide. Industrial production is at the core of Germany's economic growth model, which focuses on the export of manufactured goods such as cars, machinery, and chemicals (Hall 2012; Posen 2008). In 2010 exports amounted to 47 per cent of GDP, with comparable industrial countries such as the UK (30 per cent), France (25 per cent), and the USA (12 per cent) relying far less on foreign demand (World Bank 2013). In addition, Germany's industrial sector contributed 28 per cent both to value creation (per cent of GDP) and to employment (per cent of total employment) – a level that is again significantly higher than that of other industrial countries. Germany's focus on export-led growth has important repercussions for business and politics: in order to remain competitive internationally, companies need continuously to innovate and save costs. In the political sphere, debates on proposed measures tend to concentrate on how they are likely to affect industrial competitiveness.

Against this background, Germany has adopted an environmental policy strategy of so-called 'ecological modernisation' (Jänicke 2010; Schreurs 2010; Wurzel 2010). This aims to overcome the apparent trade-off between costly climate protection and economic competitiveness with the help of environmentally friendly technology, which serves a threefold purpose: first, its use reduces the environmental load of economic activities; second, innovative technology improves the quality of goods and/or lowers their production costs, thus strengthening international competitiveness; third, beyond the effects on the polluting sectors, an environmental industry emerges, supplying green equipment domestically and – ideally – abroad.

In this chapter I acknowledge and outline the progress made to date by Germany's version of ecological modernisation. However, I also point to the limitations and practical shortcomings of this approach, which may endanger the achievement of more ambitious reduction goals such as the envisioned 80–95 per cent emission cuts by 2050. While the goal of far-reaching GHGE reductions is more or less uncontroversial in Germany and not questioned here,[1] the (instrumental) path towards a greener economy is subject to contestation. This is true especially of one of the centrepieces of ecological modernisation: the promotion of renewable energy. The German scheme for renewables subsidisation in the electricity sector, as stipulated in the Renewable Energy Sources Act (*Erneuerbare-Energien-Gesetz* or EEG), is my case in point. I examine it using an environmental economics framework, looking at the EEG's effectiveness and cost efficiency in reaching the predetermined goals. My argument is that so far the build-up of renewables capacities has proven effective in Germany but that it lacks efficiency, involving unnecessarily high costs with negative consequences for industry as well as for the visionary goal of a complete energy transition. This diagnosis leads me to the question of how those shortcomings can be overcome. I suggest the 'Europeanisation' of ecological modernisation as a way forward, in order to achieve both ecological and economic goals more efficiently.

The first section of the chapter addresses the government's approach to ecological modernisation, including the latest energy transition project, with renewable energy promotion at its core. This policy is then critically assessed from an environmental economics perspective, with an outline of Germany's approach to handling the high costs involved for certain sectors of industry in the face of fierce international competition. The last section looks at opportunities for 'Europeanising' ecological modernisation.

Ecological modernisation and renewable energy promotion in Germany

Germany's climate change policy is rooted in the concept of ecological modernisation (Jänicke 2008). In contrast to approaches that emphasise the negative impact of economic activities on the environment and the limits of economic growth – the Club of Rome, the anti-growth movement, and ecological economics, to name a few (Pearce 2002) – ecological modernisation focuses on the idea that ecological and economic goals are synergetic rather than conflicting, and can be achieved simultaneously through 'green growth' (Seippel 2000; Berger *et al.* 2001; York and Rosa 2003). The key is the contribution of technological progress: green technologies help reduce the environmental impact of economic activities and at the same time tap the economic potential of innovative products and processes. The latter produce cost savings due to the reduced need for resources, resulting in improved international competitiveness. What is more, a completely new environmental industry is likely to develop in order to provide the required environmentally friendly equipment and services. At the macroeconomic level, this new industry pays off in the form of innovative (export) goods, jobs, and tax revenue. In times of increasing fossil fuel prices and stricter climate protection worldwide, the existence of an eco-industry offers huge market opportunities for the home country, thereby (as in Germany) reinforcing the export-led growth model (Hey 2010: 216).

While some innovation is carried out by companies voluntarily in order to seek cost advantages and a competitive edge over others, overall eco-investment falls short of the amount required to achieve ambitious environmental goals. This is because companies feel an incentive to innovate only up to the point where they save cost, for instance the cost of purchasing fossil fuels (private costs). However, environmentally harmful activities also cause so-called external costs by burdening bystanders and/or the environment with pollution. Since these negatively affected third parties (rather than the polluters) have to bear the external costs there is no incentive for the polluters to avoid them. In economic terms, external costs constitute a case of market failure, which renders emission-intensive behaviour artificially inexpensive for individual emitters. As a societal project, ecological modernisation therefore necessitates political action in order to 'coerce' polluters to achieve the higher, socially desirable level of innovation (Jänicke 2008: 558). Green technologies have to be subsidised and/or pollution-intensive behaviour has to be punished by environmental instruments such as eco-taxes, pollution permits or allowances, and eco-standards that transfer the external cost onto the emitters.

In fact, Germany has implemented a mix of environmental instruments to steer businesses and consumers towards greener behaviour (for an overview see OECD 2012). With more than 80 per cent of GHGE in Germany originating from fossil fuels such as mineral oil, gas, hard coal, and lignite (BMWi 2013: 25), one set of measures targets the more efficient use, or even avoidance, of such fuels. Thus, the Red-Green government (SPD and Green party, 1998–2005) introduced an ecological tax between 1999 and 2003 excising the use of non-renewable electricity and fuel. In 2005 Germany in collaboration with its European partners established the EU-based Emissions Trading System (EU-ETS), which requires power plant operators and select industries to operate with cost-causing allowances for every tonne of CO_2 emitted. Both measures tend to make emission-intensive energy sources more expensive and thus their consumption less attractive. In addition, various programmes have been launched to promote a more economic use of energy, encompassing subsidies for combined heat and power generation, residential building insulation, and efficient heating and household appliances.

Besides leaning on the demand side of the energy market, in 1991 Germany started to promote the large-scale build-up of an alternative energy supply system, consisting of renewables such as wind, solar, bioenergy, and geothermal power (Stefes 2010). Since green electricity is still more expensive to generate than conventional electricity, which draws on existing infrastructure and cheap primary energy without being allocated the full external costs involved, renewable technologies are subsidised via so-called 'feed-in tariffs'. Utilities are obliged to provide renewable electricity with priority access to their grids and to remunerate green power generators – including cooperatives, farmers with biogas plants or wind turbines, and home-owners with rooftop solar panels – with feed-in rates fixed in the EEG at above market level for conventional electricity. Conventional power plant operators, in turn, are allowed to cover the difference between the feed-in tariffs they have to pay and the market value of the renewable electricity they receive with the help of an add-on to the electricity retail price: the so-called 'EEG surcharge'. Accordingly, the end-use consumers, rather than the taxpayer, pay for subsidisation.

In principle, the subsidy is fixed per renewable installation (such as a wind turbine or rooftop solar panel) for a period of 20 years following the year of commissioning, with just a few exceptions involving decreased tariffs in later years of the subsidisation period for some renewables such as onshore wind. Otherwise, the feed-in tariffs vary primarily by technology type, installation capacity, and year of commissioning. The first two criteria reflect the actual costs of electricity generation incurred by the respective renewables: for instance, more expensive photovoltaic installations commissioned in 2011 yield feed-in tariffs of between 21 and 28.74 cents/kWh, whereas cheaper onshore wind turbines are subsidised by 8.93 cents/kWh for the first five years upon installation and 4.87 cents/kWh for the remaining 15 years (SVR 2011: 247). The year of commissioning is also crucial – a wind turbine installed in 2000 would have been subsidised more heavily than the same installation in 2010. This degressive tariff design is supposed to mirror cost decreases for equipment over time and incentivise innovation (OECD 2012: 124).

With its approach to ecological modernisation, Germany is praised as a showcase of successful climate protection (Jänicke 2010: 137; Hey 2010). In 2010 GHGE were approximately 24 per cent lower than in 1990 (OECD 2012: 17). The country thereby managed to exceed its commitment to a 21 per cent reduction on average for the period 2008–12, as inscribed in the Kyoto and related EU burden-sharing agreements. What is more, the emission cuts have been fully achieved within the country, without recourse to the Clean Development Mechanism and joint implementation. According to the Kyoto Protocol (adopted in 1997 and in force since 2005), these two flexible mechanisms allow countries to reach part of their abatement obligation abroad in order to minimise the impact on the domestic economy. With respect to its subordinate targets, Germany expanded the share of renewable energy sources in total final energy consumption from 1.9 per cent in 1990 to 12.6 per cent in 2012; in terms of gross electricity consumption, renewables contributed 22.9 per cent in 2012 compared with 3.1 per cent in 1990 (BMU 2013a). Progress has also been made with respect to energy efficiency, the second key pillar besides renewables for a more sustainable energy system. Thus, energy productivity, calculated as GDP per unit of primary energy supply, increased by nearly 50 per cent between 1990 and 2012 (BMU 2013b).

These achievements are even more impressive because the 'greening' has taken place while Germany preserves a substantial industrial base, including the steel, chemicals, and car industries. Admittedly, the collapse of the relatively 'dirty' east German conglomerates and energy generation in the early 1990s helped reduce total German GHGE substantially, as did the global economic downturn in 2008–9. The relocation of parts of industry to eastern Europe and elsewhere further reduced production-based emissions within Germany.[2] Irrespective of these 'windfall gains', climate protection policies, including renewable energy promotion, have contributed significantly to the environmental progress made by turning high- into lower-emission industries (OECD 2012: 9). In addition, a new environmental sector has emerged over the last two decades, consisting to a large extent of the renewable energy industry, which acts as a growth driver and, in 2012, provided approximately 378,000 jobs (BMU 2013a). The development of an environmental goods and services sector maintains Germany's export-led growth model. Having reaped a 'first mover' advantage, the environmental industry is world leading in certain segments and highly active in world markets: it exports approximately a third of its production (OECD 2012: 66). Both environmental and economic achievements in Germany seem to support the ecological modernisation hypothesis that a 'greening' of the economy is possible without the loss of international competitiveness. It is this win–win outcome, in particular, that makes the country a recognised climate policy leader worldwide.

In its 2010 Energy Concept, the German government confirmed, and even extended, its commitment to ecological modernisation. According to this programme, the government aims to create 'radically transformed' and decarbonised energy supply structures, while at the same time allowing 'Germany to remain a competitive industrial base' (BMWi and BMU 2010: 3). As noted above, the overriding environmental target is to cut GHGE by 80–95 per cent from 1990 levels by 2050 (BMWi and BMU 2010). That would make Germany the first industrial nation to achieve the central goal of international climate change mitigation: emission cuts that would limit global average temperature increases to 2°C relative to pre-industrial levels (IPCC 2007). The key drivers of ecological modernisation continue to consist in improved energy efficiency and the expansion of renewable capacities. With respect to the latter, government projections foresee a renewable share of 60 per cent of gross final energy consumption and 80 per cent of gross electricity consumption by mid-century (BMWi and BMU 2010: 5). This would involve an increase by factors of five and four respectively from 2011 levels.

While the goals and key elements of energy transition – significant GHGE cuts without giving up on economic viability, as well as the future role of renewables – are widely accepted across the political spectrum, the feasibility and details of the transformation path are more contested, both in politics and in academia (e.g. SVR 2011; SVU 2011; Monopolkommission 2011; Weber and Hey 2012; Deutsche Bank Research 2013).[3] It is to these criticisms that I now turn. In what follows, the key pillar of the Energy Concept – the massive expansion of renewable energy with the help of feed-in tariffs – is analysed from an environmental economics perspective.

Shortcomings of ecological modernisation: the environmental economics perspective on renewable energy promotion

Besides theorising the cause and nature of and the optimal solution for environmental problems from an economic point of view, environmental economics deals with 'the choice of the means of achieving an environmental goal' (Pearce 2002: 72). At this more practical level, the claim to 'optimality' is abandoned and environmental goals are assumed to be determined in the realm of politics or natural sciences rather than from within the discipline of economics. Consequently, the focus is on the effectiveness and efficiency of environmental instruments in achieving predetermined goals. 'Effectiveness' here refers to the capacity of an instrument to have an impact on economic actors and steer them towards the desired goal (European Commission 2008: 24). Economic efficiency demands that the given environmental objective is reached 'at minimum cost to the economy' (Baumol and Oates 1971: 42). In a dynamic perspective, this implies the existence of incentives for polluters to keep searching for new technologies that, in the future, might allow for even cheaper abatement (Pearce 2002: 73).

In the context of Germany's ecological modernisation, effectiveness and efficiency are important criteria. It is the primary aim of German climate protection policies to be effective: that is, actually to achieve GHGE cuts. That requires instruments that have a negative impact on polluters and a positive one on non-polluters. On the efficiency side, 'least-cost' instruments are sought. The least-cost property of an environmental instrument renders the cost burden on the economy as low as possible, thus doing minimal harm to households and firms. This is particularly important for German companies that compete internationally and therefore are concerned about their production costs. The plea for innovation resonates with the key driver for successful ecological modernisation: green technologies. Environmental economics thus provides a useful framework for examining whether the German approach to energy transition, particularly the renewables support scheme, is conducive to the environmental and economic ends of ecological modernisation. In what follows I look at the effectiveness and efficiency of renewable energy promotion in the electricity sector.

The effectiveness of renewable energy promotion

In comparison with quantity-based support schemes such as the UK Renewables Obligation system, Germany's price-based subsidisation of renewables is widely praised as an effective tool for 'greening' the energy sector (European Commission 2008: 8; OECD 2012: 125). This is true at two levels, in that it supports an increase in green electricity (the subordinate target) and supports GHGE reductions (the primary goal, as stipulated in §1 of the EEG). With the help of feed-in tariffs, Germany has achieved a massive expansion of its renewables capacities. The installed capacities for the two most significant sources – onshore wind and photovoltaics – increased from 0.055 GW in 1990 to 31 GW in 2012 for wind and from 0.0006 to 32.6 GWp[4] for photovoltaics (all data in this paragraph from BMU 2013a). Overall, renewables-based capacity for electricity generation multiplied almost 19 times between 1990 and 2012, from approximately 4 to 76 GW. That expansion of capacity is reflected in the rise of green electricity: while renewables contributed 3.1 per cent to gross electricity consumption in 1990, the share rose to 22.9 per cent in 2012. With respect to the primary goal, renewable energy sources led to an abatement of 145.5 million tonnes, equivalent to 15.6 per cent of all GHGE in Germany in 2012. More specifically, the EEG, which promotes green electricity but not green heat and fuel consumption, saved approximately 81 million tonnes of GHGE through the provision of green electricity.[5]

Renewable energy has the advantage of not being subject to the so-called 'rebound effect', which is one of the weak points of other climate protection instruments such as the promotion of energy efficiency. The problem occurs when the instrument triggers incremental innovation so that the emission intensity of an economic activity is reduced rather than driven down to zero as in the case of a radically new technology. For instance, a power plant with improved technology but still based on fossil fuels might have lower GHGE per unit of electricity generated. However, this improvement does not guarantee an absolute GHGE reduction. Indeed, the emission load is even likely to rise if electricity output grows substantially over time, overcompensating for the per unit abatement formerly achieved. In contrast, renewable energy constitutes a radically different technology from conventional electricity generation. Except for the emissions during the production of renewables equipment (Deutscher Bundestag 2007: 14), renewable installations are GHGE-free throughout operation, regardless of the amount of electricity produced over time, thereby rendering their contribution to climate protection permanent.

Despite this in-principle advantage, the ecological effectiveness of renewable energy is in doubt when one looks at the concrete instrumental mix implemented in Europe. Since the introduction of the EU-ETS in 2005, all utilities are required to work with so-called 'allowances' for the units of CO_2 and some other GHGE they emit. When green electricity is fed in, the level of the allowances required by German utilities shrinks, and power plant operators can sell them off to other emitters EU-wide. While emissions might therefore go down in Germany due to the use of renewables, GHGE will rise elsewhere in the EU, thus neutralising any mitigating effect on global warming. This is true not least because the amount of renewable electricity in Germany has risen unexpectedly, most significantly in the area of photovoltaics, where the government systematically underestimated capacity build-up (SVR 2012: 274).[6] Accordingly, it was impossible in advance to factor in fully the contribution of German renewable capacities when the total EU-wide 'cap' was fixed for GHGE traded under the EU-ETS.[7] In other words, the reduction in GHGE units due to an unanticipated use of renewables brings no additional abatement benefit. In this sense, the effectiveness of renewables promotion in Germany can be felt only when their potential contribution to GHGE reductions is reflected in a lower EU-ETS cap.

The economic efficiency of renewable energy promotion

Besides ecological effectiveness, the question arises as to whether the German promotion scheme for renewable energy sources is an economically efficient instrument to the extent that it achieves GHGE reductions (primary goal) and the expansion of renewable capacities (subordinate goal) at the lowest cost possible.

With respect to the goal of mitigating climate change, the economic efficiency of renewables promotion can be assessed by looking at so-called (marginal) abatement costs, defined as the cost of reducing GHGE by an additional unit (Hanley *et al.* 2013: 288). Renewables promotion is the efficient option if there is presently no cheaper way available to cut GHGE from its status quo level, that is, if marginal abatement costs are minimal. However, even though marginal abatement costs are a basic theoretical concept, their calculation is difficult in reality and the results are somewhat ambiguous. This is due to the huge number and complexity of assumptions required regarding, for instance, the technology displaced (e.g. gas or coal), the site of the renewables, and the various cost categories considered (Marcantonini and Ellerman 2013; Torvanger and Meadowcroft 2011). Nevertheless, and sufficient for the argument made here, there is widespread consensus that current renewable technologies imply relatively high abatement costs, well above the level of the benchmark EU-ETS carbon price (e.g. OECD 2012: 126; Helm 2012: 76). For instance, with respect to the German renewables promotion scheme, Marcantonini and Ellerman (2013: 20) estimate the abatement costs of onshore wind technology at €43/tCO$_2$ on average for the years 2006–10, while the equivalent for photovoltaics was €537/tCO$_2$. Frondel *et al.* (2010: 4052–3) calculate abatement costs of €54/tCO$_2$ · for onshore wind and €716/tCO$_2$ for solar power from photovoltaics, whereas the International Energy Agency (IEA) projects costs of €1,000/tCO$_2$ for the latter (IEA 2007: 40).

In contrast, the carbon price in the EU-ETS has not passed the threshold of €30/tCO$_2$ since its inception in 2005 (SVR 2011: 24), although admittedly the low price level is mainly due to an over-generous supply of allowances. Nevertheless, rather than employing subsidised renewable technologies, abatement would currently be achieved more cost-effectively if undertaken via the EU-ETS (Frondel *et al.* 2010: 4053). And further options are available: for instance, according to the IEA even the more cost-intensive building insulation projects in Germany amount to €20–30/tCO$_2$ abated, 'making these policies 30 to 50 times less expensive than the feed-in tariffs for solar PV' (IEA 2007: 74). Given that the geographical location of GHGE does not matter for global warming, it would be even more advantageous to realise cheap abatement abroad, an issue that has been considered far too little in Germany, with its national focus on ecological modernisation. For instance, Helm suggests that the substitution of coal by less emission-intensive gas in power plants is currently the most pressing climate protection measure, in the light of the 'dash-for-coal' (2012: 195) worldwide. In particular, it would positively impact on the costs of climate change mitigation if the scheduled build-up of power stations with a capacity of 1,000 GW in China and India by 2030 was based on natural or shale gas rather than dirty coal as planned (Helm 2012: 195).[8] Abatement might, therefore, take place outside Germany, although this does not mean that the country is freed from its obligation to invest in climate protection, for instance in the form of large-scale research and development (R&D).

Given the variation in costs of currently available GHGE abatement options, the build-up of renewable capacities in Germany – especially photovoltaics – seems an excessively costly way of achieving climate protection, while 'existing low-cost abatement options have not been sufficiently exploited' (OECD 2012: 119). The renewables support scheme might still be justifiable when considering alternative goals such as the expansion of green energy in an economy's energy mix (the subordinate goal). Instead of being an instrument for short-term GHGE reduction, the share of renewables becomes a target in itself. This could be reasonable if one thinks more strategically and in the long term. Renewables might yet be the cheapest abatement option in the future, when all alternatives have been fully exploited but ambitious reduction goals have still not been achieved. Leaving aside climate protection, renewables can be worthy of subsidisation from an industrial policy point of view as they involve innovative technologies with huge potential for exports and job creation. In energy security terms, renewable energy sources such as wind and solar power are available in Germany, and therefore render the country less import dependent on fossil fuels. Assuming that there will be rising global demand for fossil fuels, with an upward impact on the oil price and on the continued technological progress of renewables, green energy might eventually become the cheapest primary energy source, so that the current subsidisation equals an investment with high expected returns in the future (German Advisory Council on Global Change 2011: 4). However, a price hike for fossil fuels cannot be taken for granted. The USA, for instance, has just started exploiting shale gas, which seems abundant and fairly cheap.

In a nutshell, the promotion of renewables capacities would be an investment in an environmentally friendly, secure, and affordable energy system, with additional benefits for climate protection; the direct impact on current GHGE would be of less concern. In fact, all the above reasons have been put forward in Germany as justifications for the renewables promotion scheme, for instance in the debates surrounding the frequent amendments to the EEG or the Energy Concept (e.g. BMU and BMWi 2010; SVR 2012).

The question of economic efficiency thus arises anew with respect to the subordinate target of 'greening' the energy system, whereby the least-cost subsidisation scheme constitutes the most efficient instrument. This is difficult to assess empirically because Germany has retained largely the same system of feed-in tariffs since 1991 and no alternative promotion scheme such as a quantity-based quota[9] has been tried or tested. From an economic point of view, the German system reveals some inefficiency due to the technology-specific nature of feed-in tariffs, which mirror the state-of-the-art of the respective technologies. This means that less competitive solar power from photovoltaics is remunerated more highly than low-cost onshore wind (OECD 2012: 87). Accordingly, subsidies spent on solar power lead to a lesser expansion of the renewables share than the same amount spent on onshore wind. A shift of subsidies would therefore make the German scheme more efficient, resulting in a higher share of green electricity with unaltered, or possibly even lower, feed-in tariffs.[10]

The inefficiency of the feed-in tariff scheme, which has been at the centre of public debates in Germany and beyond (Böhringer 2010), is reflected in the sharp increase in the EEG surcharge imposed on residential electricity consumers. Thus, the apportionment of cost for green electricity rose from 0.2 cents/kWh in 2000 to 5.28 cents/kWh in 2013, resulting in an increase in electricity prices for end-consumers. The key cost driver is photovoltaics: between 2009 and 2011 alone, the installed capacity of solar panels grew by approximately 12 GW. The commissioning during just these three years gives an estimated net cost of €60.7 billion (2011 prices), accumulating until 2031, when the 20-year subsidisation period will have run out (Frondel *et al.* 2013: 31). At the same time, solar electricity from photovoltaics has been of relatively low salience in renewable electricity generation. It contributed only 15.6 per cent of gross electricity consumption from renewables in 2011, with much lower shares in former years; in contrast, more efficient onshore wind supplied 39.1 per cent (BMU 2013a: 12).

The economic inefficiency of the current photovoltaics boom is due to various trends. While the feed-in tariffs, including guaranteed priority access to the grid and fixed prices for 20 years, have a low degression rate with respect to newly commissioned installations in subsequent calendar years, the price of solar panels has decreased sharply since 2007, when China entered the market as a major supplier of photovoltaics equipment. Accordingly, investment in solar panels has become ever more lucrative and peaked in 2012, amounting to €11.2 billion, approximately three times the amount invested in the second most used technology, wind power (BMU 2013a: 37). Eventually, politics had to react to this unanticipated 'investment boom-cum-EEG surcharge explosion' by scaling down the feed-in tariffs for newly commissioned solar panels in a series of amendments to the EEG. While the cost of photovoltaics promotion seems to be under control, despite the ongoing payment obligation for 20 years, biomass and offshore wind energy constitute two additional heavily subsidised but relatively expensive technologies (SVR 2012: 283).

Despite the high growth rate in green electricity generation, especially during the last decade, renewables at present still have a relatively small share in the German energy mix, so the inefficiency problem remains confined. However, this is about to change with the energy transition project. Accordingly, a huge and still unquantifiable rise in cost is to be expected, including additional investment, which is necessary when renewables represent the prime energy source rather than a niche one.

First, the existing electricity network has to be upgraded and attuned to the needs of the generation of green electricity, requiring an expansion of 3,450 km by 2020 (SVR 2011: 228). The conventional electricity system involves a one-directional current flow from the power plant to the consumer, with the electricity generators being located in close proximity to their customers. In contrast, a green energy system consists of a huge number of decentralised small-scale generators, who are, to a large extent, simultaneously consumers, for example, homeowners with rooftop solar panels. Other kinds of renewable energy (onshore and offshore wind) are generated primarily in northern and eastern Germany, where meteorological conditions are more favourable, whereas electricity demand is higher in the south due to the spatial distribution of industry.

Second, because the production of green electricity depends on weather conditions, the amount it is possible to generate at a given time may not be sufficient (or too big) to meet demand. In order to secure electricity supply and grid stability at any time, additional investment is necessary. This can take the form of new flexible coal and gas-fired power stations that can be easily hooked up if there are adverse weather conditions. Storage capacities are needed to even out intermittent demand and supply fluctuations, including pumped-storage power plants, biomass/biogas plants, and batteries for electric vehicles.

Besides being the low-cost option in a given situation, an economically efficient instrument will incentivise polluters to engage continuously in innovation, searching for new and increasingly inexpensive abatement options. While the need for political intervention to trigger innovation is undeniable from an economic standpoint, the German renewables promotion scheme shows deficiencies in that respect (SVR 2012: 280–1). The feed-in tariffs aim to accelerate market penetration for already existing, relatively expensive technologies in early stages of diffusion, thereby realising learning curve effects (OECD 2012: 87). This should eventually render them competitive compared with established conventional technologies, so that in the long term renewables become marketable without subsidisation. In addition, by exploiting economies of scale in the domestic market, renewable technologies potentially acquire a 'first-mover' advantage internationally, with huge business potential in a globally dynamic market.

The stability of the system, including the fixing of tariffs for 20 years, the priority access to the grid, and the independence from public budgets due to the cost apportionment to electricity consumers rather than to taxpayers all provide a protected niche in which investment can thrive. However, this guaranteed return on investment, without price or commercialisation risk, is diverting investment from yet unknown, probably more efficient, renewable technologies. With the help of technology-specific feed-in tariffs, the government 'picks winners' without knowing whether those technologies will prove to be superior and cost efficient in the longer term. In contrast, 'technology-open' R&D programmes are relatively insignificant in Germany in comparison with the amount of funding available under the EEG. Thus, potential future cost reductions for a green energy system might be missed, since the technological status quo is subsidised rather than R&D for new developments such as 'storage and batteries, the electrification of transport, and new electricity-generation technologies' (Helm 2012: 215).

To sum up, Germany's cornerstone policy of energy transition and climate protection – that is, the promotion of renewables – has proven very effective in building green electricity capacities, although less effective in terms of GHGE reductions because of the overlap with the EU-ETS. However, with its technology-specific feed-in tariffs the approach seems overly expensive and thus not economically efficient with respect to either climate protection or the greening of the energy system. This also holds true in a dynamic perspective, concerning the incentives for invention. The high cost places an unnecessary burden on energy consumers, both households and industry. I turn now to the issue of how they have reacted to this cost burden.

Impact on the economy and industrial competitiveness

While households find it relatively hard to evade the cost burden,[11] industry has various options for dealing with it. For one, it can invest in integrated green production technologies that require less electricity input. This is exactly in line with the ideas of ecological modernisation, in that expensive energy triggers innovation that is conducive to both the environment and industrial competitiveness. However, if ecological modernisation is technically impossible or economically unviable, energy-intensive industry has at least two further options, both of which impede ecological modernisation. First, it can relocate energy-intensive parts of its value-added chain abroad, for instance to so-called pollution havens where environmental policy costs are less perceptible. One result of this relocation is the so-called 'carbon leakage' effect: a displacement rather than a reduction of GHGE on a global scale. Moreover, jobs and tax revenue are lost in Germany if companies leave or downsize (Hillebrand 2013: 669). Second, industry can lobby government for exemptions from the instrumental burden – a strategy that is particularly promising for sectors that provide many jobs, and have well-established links with politics and the potential to threaten with relocation. Again, the goals of ecological modernisation are compromised, since the price signal is removed and a greening of industry does not materialise.

In Germany, the 'losers' of ecological modernisation (such as the chemicals, paper, and other energy-intensive industries) have in fact been granted special arrangements. For instance, feed-in tariffs are reduced to less than 10 per cent of the normal EEG surcharge for companies with an electricity consumption of more than 1 GW per year and electricity costs surmounting 14 per cent of their gross value added. For 2014, 2,367 companies applied for the surcharge rebate, significantly more than in former years (Balser 2013). If the rebate is granted, companies are relieved of approximately €5 billion of their electricity costs, which then have to be apportioned to households and other non-exempted businesses. Similar exemptions apply for other climate protection instruments. The eco-tax provides tax relief for energy-intensive industries such as chemicals and steel amounting to approximately €2.3 billion per year (Grossarth 2012). German governments have also intervened time and again in the EU decision-making process on behalf of the car industry, in order to achieve more lenient CO_2 standards for fuel-consuming German luxury brands (Hey 2010). And the German government has used its influence in Brussels to get generous allocations of emission allowances in successive trading periods of the EU-ETS (Schreurs 2010). While this handling of costs might help industry in terms of securing (international) competitiveness, it erodes ecological modernisation as it 'limits the scope and effects of environmental policy' (Jänicke 2008: 564). The scale of the already existing exemptions is noteworthy relative to the magnitude that is to be expected in the case of a complete transformation of the energy system (at present the ecological modernisation project in Germany is still in its infancy). In fact, recent debates about the energy transition project have focused on cost issues rather than on its ecological and economic potential (Gawel and Hansjürgens 2013: 284), and both government and opposition have discussed ways of making policies more efficient. One solution might lie in the 'Europeanisation' of ecological modernisation.

The need for Europeanisation

Germany is one of the most ambitious countries in the world when it comes to climate protection. With its unilateral energy transformation project, the government underlined its claim to international environmental leadership, with positive effects expected for the environment as well as for industry. However, the overlap of instruments in Europe and the scope of investment required for a renewables-based energy system mean that nationally confined ecological modernisation has been stretched to its limits in terms of effectiveness and economic efficiency. For energy transition to be a viable option, an international dimension is now necessary (BMWi and BMU 2010; Häder 2010; SVR 2011). This is true for several reasons.

As far as the ecological goal is concerned, the German share of 2.4 per cent of worldwide GHGE in 2009 is relatively insignificant, with China (25.6 per cent) and the USA (17.6 per cent) at the top (my calculations, based on data from World Bank 2013). Accordingly, Germany's emission cuts may provide evidence that climate protection is feasible in an industrialised country and may exert moral pressure on others to join in, but this is a far cry from sufficing to mitigate global warming. Without international commitment, the public good of climate change mitigation cannot be achieved.

With respect to the cost of ecological modernisation, renewable energy could be generated more cheaply if installations were located in sites with ideal topography and climate conditions, irrespective of territorial boundaries. Photovoltaics, for example, can be maintained more effi-ciently in sun-rich areas of southern Europe or the Maghreb than in Germany. Wind turbines generate cheaper energy in high-wind regions. Intermittency problems as a result of naturally fluctuating wind and solar supplies could be more easily evened out if more diverse sites were included. Topography in countries such as Norway or Switzerland would allow for inexpensive load balancing, thanks to cheap pumped-storage capacities and hydroelectricity.

In addition, industry would suffer less from high energy costs if competitors were subject to a comparable policy regime. Assuming a level playing field, exemptions from eco-standards, taxes, and surcharges would be unjustifiable. In fact, energy-intensive industries in Germany and beyond would have to bear the cost increases similarly and – if investment in green processes proved technologically impossible – suffer from a price-induced downturn in demand, leading to a downsizing of dirty industries worldwide, rather than displacement in the form of carbon leakage. At the same time, Germany's environmental goods and services sector would benefit from a rise in demand for green technologies if legislators abroad kept a tighter rein on emissions (Hillebrand 2004). With 'de-growth' taking place in resource-intensive industries and cleaner production on the rise, globally effective green growth would occur (Jänicke 2012: 98).

While it seems clear that ecological modernisation in general and energy transition in particular require international backing, the question arises how this can be achieved. So far Germany has been a strong supporter of the global Kyoto/post-Kyoto processes as the first-best solution, with the EU taking the lead in negotiations. Those processes involve internationally agreed GHGE reduction goals that are broken down into national or regional obligations and enforced with the help of nationally implemented instruments. Germany pressed ahead in 1997 by accepting a 21 per cent reduction target for 2008–12 under the EU burden-sharing agreement that enforced the Kyoto Protocol. With respect to the (still ongoing) post-Kyoto negotiations, Germany pushed the EU during its 2007 presidency to offer a 30 per cent GHGE cut, provided that other emitters reduce their emissions by 20 per cent. However, given past experiences and other emitters' apparent lack of interest in committing to change, it is questionable whether a meaningful global agreement can be reached any time soon (Feld *et al.* 2011; Helm 2012).

Even though, in principle, climate protection remains a global challenge requiring a global effort, nations may have to look for alternative solutions, and regional cooperation in Europe might provide 'a practical first step' (Prat 2010: 34). Both the effectiveness and the efficiency of energy transition would benefit if the project were more deeply embedded in the European context – in contrast to the predominantly national design of energy policies in EU member states that we see today. Attuning instruments with goals on a European scale would avoid the distorting effects of an overlap of instruments (such as the overlap between the German EEG and the EU-ETS). The latter – or, alternatively, a carbon tax – could target the primary goal of GHGE cuts, while renewables and their future development could be promoted as a strategic, long-term option. Ambitious goals for the use of green energy – such as the EU's goal of a 20 per cent share of renewables in gross final energy consumption by 2020 – could be achieved more easily if advantage were taken of local conditions EU-wide for wind and solar power (Weber and Hey 2012: 50). The physical and regulatory integration of the EU energy market beyond its still fractured state would help exploit regional advantages and balance out intermittency problems. From an economic perspective, the Europeanisation of ecological modernisation would lead to greater efficiency in achieving environmental goals, involving lower costs overall.

Conclusion

With respect to climate policies, Germany is currently characterised by a high degree of conformity. Most Germans perceive global warming as a major threat to humanity and climate protection as a key policy goal. For more than two decades, all major political parties have agreed on the need to cut down on GHGE and to engage internationally for a global climate agreement. With energy consumption providing the most important source of GHGE in Germany, consensus also extends to the instrumental level – at least after the dispute concerning the role of nuclear energy was settled in 2011 following the nuclear fallout in Japan. Government and opposition parties agree on the need for ecological modernisation, with the transformation of the energy system towards renewables at its core. The energy transition project coincides with the economic tier of ecological modernisation in that it triggers energy savings and leads to the emergence of a modern environmental industry. In the German context this is particularly desirable, since the country's economy relies heavily on the export of manufactured goods, with green products adding new business potential.

Despite some caveats, ecological modernisation has been a success in Germany to date, in that it has helped increase the share of green energy while at the same time safeguarding industrial competitiveness and the development of a new environmental industry. However, the devil is in the detail. From an environmental economics perspective, the key instrument – renewable energy promotion with feed-in tariffs – has severe shortcomings that make the energy transformation project more expensive than is necessary. This is a particular problem for Germany, a still heavily industrialised country preoccupied with competitiveness concerns.

Because a matching commitment from other polluting nations and thus an international level playing field is lacking, the cost burden environmental instruments bring has generated political opposition from German industry as the 'loser' in ecological modernisation. Thus, some energy-intensive industries have managed to achieve exemptions from the eco-tax as well as from the feed-in tariffs cost apportionment, at the expense of households and other unprivileged sectors. This hollows out the ecological modernisation project and bodes ill for the more substantial transformation of the whole energy system by 2050.

A way forward in Germany's pursuit of 'ecological modernisation in international competition' can be found in further internationalisation and Europeanisation. If the country expands its agenda to the EU level and beyond, ecological modernisation will become more effective in climate protection terms. In addition, the costs of renewables could be reduced substantially and a level playing field for industry would become more likely. The key to Germany's success in ecological modernisation, therefore, lies in the export of this very model.

Notes

1 For another opinion see, for example, Feld *et al.* (2011), who question the viability of climate change mitigation with the help of ambitious GHGE cuts, especially if undertaken unilaterally. Rather, they suggest that adaptation measures to global warming be considered.

2 The relocation of industry reduces Germany's production-based GHGE, but the fact that goods produced abroad are (re-)imported and consumed domestically makes Germany's (consumption-based) emission load rise. However, for Germany the difference between consumption- and production-based counts is relatively low due to the country's excellent export performance (OECD 2012: 115).

3 Another long-standing issue in German energy policy regarding nuclear energy was resolved in 2011 (Jahn and Korolczuk 2012). While in the initial version of the Energy Concept the conservative-liberal government (2009–13) assigned an important role to nuclear power as a so-called 'bridge technology' to the age of renewables – a proposal heavily contested by the opposition parties – the nuclear disaster of Fukushima in March 2011 'forced' government to make a sharp U-turn. Thus, Chancellor Merkel announced the end of nuclear power in Germany by 2022, a near-restoration of the initial phase-out plan agreed in 2000 by the then Red-Green government and major utilities. With the legal enactment of the phase-out plan by an overwhelming majority in the German Bundestag in June 2011, the end of nuclear power in Germany is all but sealed.

4 The symbol GWp stands for gigawatt-peak, which is regularly used to signify the nominal power of photovoltaics installations. The nominal power is the power generated by photovoltaic panels under certain standard conditions such as when the temperature of the cells is 25°C and the light intensity amounts to $1000W/m^2$.

5 Besides green electricity, government promotes the use of biofuels and heat from renewables with a separate set of instruments, including tax exemptions for biofuels and the Act on the Promotion of Renewable Energies in the Heat Sector (EEWärmeG). However, the promotion of green electricity via the EEG has so far been the most important and effective policy tool.

6 While government expected an additional accumulation of 0.6 GW in photovoltaic installations in 2008, the actual increase amounted to more than 2.9 GW. In the following years, this trend exploded, showing an annual growth in installed capacity of 3.8 (2009), 7.3 (2010), and 7.5 GW (2011) (SVR 2012: 274).

7 Some scholars argue that the contribution of renewables towards GHGE reduction has been factored into the amount of ETS allowances issued and that the EEG is required as an instrument to reduce CO_2 emissions despite the existence of the EU-ETS (e.g. Weber and Hey 2012).

8 In this context, the large-scale exploitation of shale gas in the USA, and prospectively in China, might be a positive development for climate protection, though possibly not for other environmental concerns such as the use of water and chemicals. However, as Helm (2012: 195–212) outlines, gas is still a carbon fuel and therefore might act only as a transitional option until carbon-free technologies are cheaply available.

9 In a quota system, a market for certificates for green electricity is established. On the demand side, utilities are obligated to source a certain amount of electricity from renewables. In order to fulfil this

obligation they have to obtain green certificates and hand them in to the government at the end of a trading period (e.g. a year). On the supply side, renewable electricity producers offer these green certificates which they receive from government or another institution for the amount of green electricity generated. Renewable electricity producers thus do not receive a fixed feed-in tariff but a varying price from utilities, depending on supply and demand for green certificates (SVR 2011: 256–9).

10 Alternative views exist. For instance, the European Commission in its 2008 report on renewables subsidisation in the EU comes to the conclusion that 'well-adapted feed in tariff regimes are generally the most efficient and effective support schemes for promoting renewable electricity' (European Commission 2008: 3). The report states that the German approach is one of the most successful with respect to onshore wind and photovoltaic energy, amongst other things.

11 Households can invest in more energy-efficient household appliances and better insulation as well as in their own rooftop photovoltaics, benefiting from the renewables boom. However, this strategy is confined to homeowners, which means that the renewables promotion scheme acts regressively and redistributes costs from homeowners and big industry to non-homeowning electricity consumers and SMEs (Helm 2012: 89). In addition, households tend to have less influence in the political process.

Bibliography

Balser, M. (2013) 'Immer mehr Konzerne fordern Strompreis-Rabatte', *Süddeutsche Zeitung*, 12 July. Online. Available at www.sueddeutsche.de/wirtschaft/oekostrom-umlage-immer-mehr-konzerne-fordern-strompreis-rabatte-1.1719644 (accessed 21 July 2013).

Baumol, W.J. and Oates, W.E. (1971) 'The use of standards and prices for protection of the environment', *The Swedish Journal of Economics*, 73(1): 42–54.

Berger, G., Flynn, A., Hines, F., and Johns, R. (2001) 'Ecological modernization as a basis for environmental policy: Current environmental discourse and policy and the implications on environmental supply chain management', *Innovation*, 14(1): 55–72.

BMU (Federal Ministry for the Environment, Nature Conservation and Nuclear Safety) (2013a) *Development of Renewable Energy Sources in Germany 2012*, February 2013 version. Online. Available at www.erneuerbare-energien.de/fileadmin/Daten_EE/Dokumente__PDFs_/20130328_hgp_e_ppt_2012_fin_bf.pdf (accessed 9 July 2013).

BMU (2013b) 'Energieproduktivität und Wirtschaftswachstum'. Online. Available at www.bmu.de/fileadmin/bmu-import/files/bilder/allgemein/image/jpeg/grafik_energieeffizienz.jpg (accessed 8 July 2013).

BMWi (Federal Ministry of Economics and Technology) (2013) 'Energiedaten: ausgewählte Grafiken'. Online. Available at www.bmwi.de/BMWi/Redaktion/PDF/E/energiedaten-ausgewaehlte-grafiken,property=pdf,bereich=bmwi2012,sprache=de,rwb=true.pdf (accessed 10 July 2013).

BMWi and BMU (2010) *Energy Concept for an Environmentally Sound, Reliable and Affordable Energy Supply*. Online. Available at www.bmu.de/files/english/pdf/application/pdf/energiekonzept_bundesregierung_en.pdf (accessed 29 September 2011).

Böhringer, C. (2010) '1990 bis 2010: Eine Bestandsaufnahme von zwei Jahrzehnten europäischer Klimapolitik', *Perspektiven der Wirtschaftspolitik*, 11(s1): 56–74.

Deutsche Bank Research (2013) 'Energy turnaround: Uncommon similarities, but significant differences in the detail', *German Policy Watch*, 24 June. Online. Available at www.dbresearch.de/PROD/DBR_INTERNET_EN-PROD/PROD0000000000315772.pdf;jsessionid=62C127B1B07CD23B2C3D65B3E69B9B41.srv-net-dbr-de (accessed 5 July 2013).

Deutscher Bundestag (2007) *CO2-Bilanzen verschiedener Energieträger im Vergleich: Zur Klimafreundlichkeit von fossilen Energien, Kernenergie und erneuerbaren Energien*, Info-Brief WD 8–056/2007, Wissenschaftliche Dienste, Berlin: Deutscher Bundestag.

European Commission (2008) *The support of electricity from renewable energy sources*, Commission Staff Working Document, SEC(2008) 57, Brussels: Commission of the European Communities.

Feld, L.P., Konrad, K.A., and Thum, M. (2011) 'Umdenken in der Klimapolitik nach dem Gipfel von Cancun!' *ifo schnelldienst*, 64(5): 8–11.

Frondel, M., Ritter, N., Schmidt, C.M., and Vance, C. (2010) 'Economic impacts form the promotion of renewable energy technologies: the German experience', *Energy Policy*, 38: 4048–56.

Frondel, M., Schmidt, C.M., and Aus dem Moore, N. (2013) 'Marktwirtschaftliche Energiewende: Ein Wettbewerbsrahmen für die Stromversorgung mit alternativen Technologien', *Zeitschrift für Energiewirtschaft*, 37: 27–41.

Gawel, E. and Hansjürgens, B. (2013) 'Projekt "Energiewende": Schneckentempo und Zickzackkurs statt klarer Konzepte für die Systemtransformation?', *Wirtschaftsdienst*, 93(5): 283–8.

German Advisory Council on Global Change (2011) *Transforming Energy Systems*. Online. Available at www.wbgu.de/fileadmin/templates/dateien/veroeffentlichungen/factsheets/fs2011-fs2/WBGU_FS2_2011_Energie_en.pdf (accessed 25 October 2011).

Grossarth, J. (2012) 'Bundesregierung verlängert Ausnahmen bei der Ökosteuer', *Frankfurter Allgemeine Zeitung*, 1 August. Online. Available at www.faz.net/aktuell/wirtschaft/wirtschaftspolitik/oekosteuer-ausnahmen-fuer-energieintensive-unternehmen-verlaengert-11840604.html (accessed 11 July 2013).

Häder, M. (2010) 'Das Energiekonzept der Bundesregierung – Darstellung und ökonomische Bewertung', *Orientierungen zur Wirtschafts- und Gesellschaftspolitik*, 126: 36–42.

Hall, P. (2012) 'The economics and politics of the euro crisis', *German Politics*, 21(4): 355–71.

Hanley, N., Shogren, J., and White, B. (2013) *Introduction to Environmental Economics*, 2nd edn, Oxford: Oxford University Press.

Helm, D. (2012) *The Carbon Crunch: How We're Getting Climate Change Wrong – And How to Fix It*, New Haven: Yale University Press.

Hey, C. (2010) 'The green paradox: climate leader and green car laggard', in S. Oberthür and M. Paellemaerts (eds) *The New Climate Policies of the European Union: Internal Legislation and Climate Diplomacy*, Brussels: Brussels University Press, 211–30.

Hillebrand, R. (2004) *Rationale Umweltpolitik und Globalisierung der Wirtschaftsbeziehungen: eine Analyse ausgewählter Umweltpolitikansätze*, Frankfurt a.m.: Peter Lang.

Hillebrand, R. (2013) 'Climate protection, energy security and Germany's policy of ecological modernisation', *Environmental Politics*, 22(4): 664–82.

IEA (International Energy Agency) (2007) *Energy Policies of IEA Countries: Germany*. Online. Available at www.iea.org/publications/freepublications/publication/germany2007.pdf (accessed 24 July 2012).

IPCC (2007) *Climate Change 2007: Mitigation*, contribution of Working Group III to the Fourth Assessment Report of the Intergovernmental Panel on Climate Change (IPCC), Cambridge: Cambridge University Press.

Jahn, D. and Korolczuk, S. (2012) 'German exceptionalism: the end of nuclear energy in Germany!', *Environmental Politics*, 21(1): 159–64.

Jänicke, M. (2008) 'Ecological modernisation: new perspectives', *Journal of Cleaner Production*, 16: 557–65.

Jänicke, M. (2010) 'German climate change policy: political and economic leadership', in R. Wurzel and J. Connolly (eds) *The EU as a Leader in International Climate Change Policy*, London: Routledge, 129–46.

Jänicke, M. (2012) *Megatrend Umweltinnovation: Zur ökologischen Modernisierung von Wirtschaft und Staat*, 2nd edn, Munich: oekom.

Marcantonini, C. and Ellerman, A.D. (2013) *The Cost of Abating CO2 Emissions by Renewable Energy Incentives in Germany*, EUI Working Paper RSCAS 2013/05, European University Institute. Online. Available at http://cadmus.eui.eu/bitstream/handle/1814/25842/RSCAS_2013_05rev.pdf?sequence=1 (accessed 21 July 2013).

Monopolkommission (2011) *Energie 2011: Wettbewerbsentwicklung mit Licht und Schatten*, Special Report No. 59, Baden-Baden: Nomos.

OECD (2012) *OECD Environmental Performance Reviews: Germany 2012*. Online. Available at http://dx.doi.org/10.1787/9789264169302-en (accessed 12 March 2013).

Pearce, D. (2002) 'An intellectual history of environmental economics', *Annual Review of Energy and the Environment*, 27: 57–81.

Posen, A. (2008) 'Exportweltmeister – so what? Better goals for German foreign economic policy', in R. Schettkat and J. Langkau (eds) *Economic policy proposals for Germany and Europe*, London: Routledge, 119–43.

Prat, A.G. (2010) 'Effective regional energy governance – not global environmental governance – is what we need right now for climate change', *Global Environmental Change*, 20: 33–5.

Schreurs, M.A. (2010) 'German perspectives on ecological modernization, technology transfer, and intellectual property rights in the case of climate change', in American Institute for Contemporary German Studies (ed.) *AICGS Policy Report No 45*, Washington: The Johns Hopkins University, 61–77.

Seippel, Ø. (2000) 'Ecological modernization as a theoretical device: strengths and weaknesses', *Journal of Environmental Policy & Planning*, 2: 287–302.

Stefes, C.H. (2010) 'Bypassing Germany's Reformstau: The remarkable rise of renewable energy', *German Politics*, 19(2): 148–63.

SVR (Sachverständigenrat zur Begutachtung der gesamtwirtschaftlichen Entwicklung) (2011) *Verantwortung für Europa wahrnehmen*. Online. Available at www.sachverstaendigenrat-wirtschaft.de/fileadmin/ dateiablage/Sonstiges/chapter_six_2011.pdf (accessed 15 March 2013).

SVR (2012) *Stabile Architektur in Europa – Handlungsbedarf im Inland*. Online. Available at www.sach verstaendigenrat-wirtschaft.de/fileadmin/dateiablage/gutachten/ga201213/ga12_ges.pdf (accessed 25 November 2012).

SVU (Sachverständigenrat für Umweltfragen) (2011) *Wege zur 100% erneuerbaren Stromversorgung*, Special Report. Online. Available at www.umweltrat.de/SharedDocs/Downloads/DE/02_Sondergutachten/ 2011_07_SG_Wege_zur_100_Prozent_erneuerbaren_Stromversorgung.pdf;jsessionid=F0333D6E19D 7500FD90B75FC07915AFB.1_cid325?__blob=publicationFile (accessed 10 June 2012).

Torvanger, A. and Meadowcroft, J. (2011) 'The political economy of technology support: making decisions about carbon capture and storage and low carbon energy technologies', *Global Environmental Change*, 21: 303–12.

Weber, M. and Hey, C. (2012) 'Effektive und effiziente Klimapolitik: Instrumentenmix, EEG und Subsidiarität', *Wirtschaftsdienst*, 92(13): 43–51.

World Bank (2013) 'World Development Indicators'. Online. Available at http://databank.worldbank. org/data/views/reports/tableview.aspx (accessed 22 July 2013).

Wurzel, R.K.W. (2010) 'Environmental, climate and energy policies: path-dependent incrementalism or quantum leap?' *German Politics*, 19(3): 460–78.

York, R. and Rosa, E.A. (2003) 'Key challenges to ecological modernization theory', *Organization & Environment*, 16(3): 273–88.

Part V

Germany and
the world

24

Europeanisation and globalisation as drivers of the German growth model

Kurt Hübner[1]

The times they are a-changing. During the 'golden age' of capitalism, from the mid-1950s to the early 1970s, the western part of Germany turned into an economic powerhouse that swiftly adjusted to the recessionary effects of the first Great Crisis in 1971–3 and then became a widely admired 'model Germany'. By the early 1980s, however, much of this fascination had vanished, and Germany had become a synonym for the 'eurosclerosis' that threatened social and economic achievements in most parts of Europe. German unification and the costs of merging two economies that differed in their institutional settings and level of development caused the state of the economy to deteriorate further. Political reforms were initiated by an incoming 'Red-Green' (Social Democratic and Green party) coalition, but without immediately apparent economic outcomes. Some observers concluded that the German growth model had come to an end. It needed another Great Crisis, the Second Great Contraction that started in 2008 and expanded quickly to become the crisis of the eurozone in 2010, for Germany to recover its previous status as an economic powerhouse. Rather than falling into a growth trap like other eurozone economies, Germany benefited, the argument goes, from the 'Red-Green' labour market and welfare state reforms that lifted its economy out of recession (Blanchard, Jaumotte, and Loungani 2013).

Unlike in the period immediately after World War II, economic strength was now tightly coupled with political power at the European level. This chapter argues that the most recent developments are not so much the outcome of radical changes in the political economy of Germany as the result of smooth adjustment processes in the social, economic, and political features of 'model Germany' (see Chapter 5) that have driven this growth regime from the very beginning. Those changes in the institutional setting were driven by opportunities and challenges created by processes of Europeanisation and globalisation. Rather than the end of model Germany, as anticipated by writers like Streeck (1997), we saw the resurrection of the German growth regime. Unlike other modes of capitalism, model Germany was successfully adapted to the new situation. The particular strength of model Germany is accompanied by economic as well as political weaknesses, however, that may give rise to fundamental economic and political problems.

The institutional setting of the German growth model

The concepts provided by the French regulation approach (Hübner 1990), which were modified and refined by the 'varieties of capitalism' (VoC) approach taken by Hall and Soskice (2001), make the case that economy-specific institutional settings can explain the relative success of national economies in the global division of labour. Within the dual framework of VoC, Germany exemplifies a so-called coordinated market economy that comes with a particular set of political-economic institutions: (i) wages are set at the industry level in the context of corporatism-like employer–employee relations; (ii) bank–industry relations are close and tight; (iii) vocational training is organised and provided within the legal framework of state–industry/profession relations; (iv) there is a well-established signalling relationship between central bank and wage-setting agencies; and (v) there are inclusive industrial relations based on codetermination. The overall effect of those institutions is a high level of economic and social trust, which translates into steady private investment and relatively good industrial relations. The emergence of such a set of institutions after World War II was driven by the self-interest of employers' and workers' organisations, which helped to produce a broad range of compromises, encapsulated in a specific social contract.[2] The emergence of this set of political-economic institutions was embedded in the German discourse of ordoliberalism – a particular German economic-philosophical strand favouring a capitalist market economy, which provided the intellectual basis for what has become the brand 'social market economy' (Biebricher 2012). Ordoliberalism sees markets as threatened by tendencies towards monopolies and oligopolies. It is the task of the state to ensure the proper functioning of markets, hence the emphasis on competition policy. Due to their theoretically based scepticism towards active fiscal and monetary policy, ordoliberals were instrumental in giving the German central bank (Bundesbank) a narrow mandate in terms of price stability and in making the central bank independent of government. Representatives of ordoliberalism were in favour of a strong state, and in some respects close to the versions of political corporatism that eventually fostered the design and practice of collective bargaining (Bonefeld 2012).

The particular German set of political-economic institutions provided the basis not only for the 'economic miracle' after World War II but also for the success of particular lead sectors characterised as 'high trust' segments of the German economy. Overall, the economic data for the period 1950 to 1973 point to a German success story. Real gross domestic product (GDP) grew by 5 per cent per annum; hourly labour productivity rose by an astounding 6 per cent per annum; the average unemployment rate was as low as 1.75 per cent, and even lower in the years after the reintegration of refugees had been completed; the average inflation rate was 2.7 per cent; and the economy-wide capital stock grew by 6.1 per cent on an annual basis. The combination of real wage increases that were close to but still below the annual growth rates of hourly productivity and economies of scale and scope effects due to export-driven market extensions resulted in rising profit shares in conjunction with increasing profit rates, which in turn fed the steady growth of the capital stock.

However, it was not only Germany that experienced an economic miracle in this period (Toniolo 1998). As a matter of fact, all mature capitalist market economies had their own 'miracles' during these years. What has become known as the 'golden age' of capitalism (Glyn *et al.* 1988) was more than a coincidence of national success stories; rather, it was the outcome of an international constellation often described as the 'Bretton Woods regime of embedded liberalism' (Ruggie 1982). At the core of this regime was a fixed exchange rate system closely tied to the US dollar as well as forms of capital controls that were meant not only to prevent destabilising capital flows but also to hedge national financial industries in the face of outside pressures. This exchange rate mechanism evolved hand in hand with social programmes that not only enhanced the German version of the welfare state but also added to the increasing level of social trust. Germany, in particular, benefited from this regime, as the chosen US dollar–deutschmark exchange rate turned out to undervalue the potential of the German economy and consequently provided a strong push for its export sectors. The international demand for capital goods in the period of reconstruction and catching up of the mid-1950s to the late 1960s was well suited to German industry's specialisation profile. The average annual growth rate of German exports in the period of the 'golden age' was 12.4 per cent. As early as 1954, close to 30 per cent of the gross production of the chemical and electrical industries was exported; in the iron and steel sector, exports accounted for 37.2 per cent of gross production, while in the machine and car industries the figure was 31.4 per cent (Abelshauser 2004: 265). Early on, exports were the German growth model's daily bread and moved its trade balance into a structural surplus.

Germany in many respects is an open economy, and the level of openness has increased drastically since 1970 (see Figure 24.1).[3] From a political-economic perspective, Germany is typical of a coordinated market economy that combines economic openness with a relatively strong welfare state with the financial capacity to compensate losers (Pierson 2001). Traditionally, political parties across the spectrum have supported trade policies that result in more openness, in terms of exports as well as imports. Only political parties to the far right and far left of centre have raised concerns about open trade policies, but without being able to get them on to the mainstream political agenda. Europeanisation as well as globalisation can be seen as part of Germany's political-economic DNA and are well embedded in the social contract. This is not surprising, given that more than half of all jobs in the industrial sector depend directly or indirectly on exports; about a quarter of all jobs in the German economy are export dependent (Federal Ministry of Economics and Technology 2012).

The German *Wirtschaftswunder* benefited not only from its particular institutional setting and the advantageous structure of the newly emerging liberal world economy, but also from the modernisation effects of the Nazi Government's war machinery. In 1948 industrial capacity in West Germany was 13 per cent higher than before World War II, partly due to a steady growth

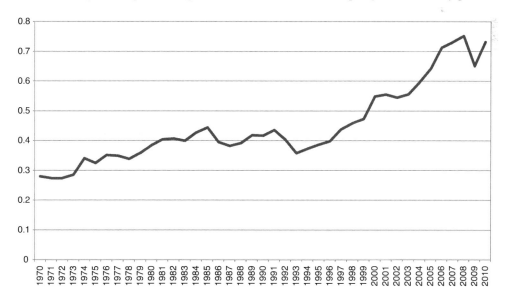

Figure 24.1 Openness ratio (Exports + Imports)/GDP

Source: Eurostat

in the capital stock in order to feed the war machinery, but also because Germany's industry was far less badly damaged than its cities by the war (Eichengreen and Ritschl 2008). The relatively new capital stock became the basis for the strong productivity catch-up in the post-World War II era, which resulted in a steady improvement in international competitiveness.

Europeanisation and globalisation: the economic dimension

It is a well-established axiom in economic trade theory that the creation of trading blocs will cause an increase in trade volume (Viner 1950). In this regard, the launch of a European customs union as early as 1957 and the subsequent creation of a European single market are widely seen as an example where trade creation as well as trade diversion led to overall positive economic effects for the member states of the EU. The pure effects of European integration over the period 1960 to 2010 were strong, not least due to the number of enlargements that occurred in this period. According to Egger and Pfaffermayr (2013), EU integration added significantly to the economic growth of its member states; they also cite empirical evidence that 'northern' member states experienced stronger positive trade effects than 'southern' member states. Member states were deeply affected by the integration projects of both deepening and widening and experienced over time an increase in economic openness, not only with regard to cross-border trade in goods and services but also with regard to capital and labour. Germany. in particular, benefited from those projects, as its private business sector made extensive use of the opportunities afforded by the 'milestones of European integration', especially the Maastricht treaty, which launched the single market in the EU (Hiller and Kruse 2010). The increase in market size triggered efficiency gains (economies of scale) and strengthened economies of scope, making the EU the most highly integrated economic space in the global economy (Eichengreen 2007).

Trade with member economies of the EU is critical for German export sectors. Its importance is reflected in the share of intra-EU trade within the German private business sector. Data from the late 1990s onwards show that the share of intra-EU trade is very high, even though the share of extra-EU trade has also increased slightly over the last few years (see Figure 24.2). In terms of trade, Germany is a highly Europeanised economy.

Germany's large trade surpluses over a long period have their origin within the single market, where the surplus is consistently higher than the overall surplus with extra-EU economies. Even though the share of intra-EU exports (and even more the share of intra-EU imports) has decreased over the last 10 years, seven out of Germany's 10 most important export destinations in 2012 are still member economies of the EU,[4] with France ranked first and the UK and the Netherlands ranked third and fourth, followed by Austria, Italy, Belgium, and Poland (Statistisches Bundesamt 2013a). Of this group only the Netherlands and China register a surplus with Germany; in the case of the Netherlands, this may only reflect the 'Rotterdam effect', by which certain German imports are listed as coming from the Netherlands because the shipping destination for goods from outside the EU is often the port of Rotterdam. With the exception of the Netherlands and China, Germany achieved trade surpluses with all its major trading partners, including the US. The deficit with China has decreased since the early 1990s and was down to €14 billion in 2012.

Germany's dominant export position in Europe, and thus its structural surplus in the trade balance, has not been without challenges. During the 1980s and then again in the mid-1990s to the early 2000s, the German political economy was labelled the 'sick man of Europe'. A long line of academics provided a list of indicators that were supposed to demonstrate the decline of German competitiveness.[5]

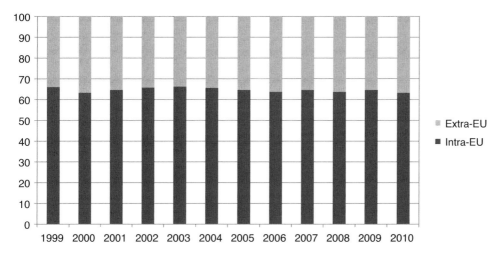

Figure 24.2 Intra-EU and extra-EU trade

Source: Eurostat

Germany's external position, most prominently expressed in its current account, showed quite accentuated swings, moving from a significant surplus, expressed as a share of GDP, to a deficit in 1991. However, this swing did not result from a dramatic negative change in the economic 'fundamentals' that had driven Germany's export performance for a long time. Rather, the path into deficit reflected a domestic 'political victory' that simultaneously changed geopolitics: German unification. What should be seen as a political success came with huge economic costs that transformed the economic landscape not only in former East Germany but in all of Germany, as well as transforming the global political economy. The combination of rapid de-industrialisation in the eastern part of Germany due to a lack of overall competitiveness, the mode of currency unification, which favoured consumption over investment, and the political promises of a catch-up in welfare state entitlements and wages resulted in a huge and long-lasting gap between the GDP of the new Federal states (*neue Länder*) and their actual absorption of economic resources. This gap was closed by capital transfers from west to east that redirected Germany's resource allocation and led to a sharp and sudden increase in public debt (Hübner 1992).

German unification turned out to be an economic burden with far-reaching political and economic implications. The catch-up consumption mode of the eastern part of Germany, supported by wage agreements in the east that were driven not by economic rationale but by political motives, had an adverse effect on price competitiveness. When in the early 1990s this domestic process was confronted with a weakening of global growth and thus a reduction in the demand for German exports, the trade balance, as well as the current account, lost stamina.

The implosion of the former Soviet bloc transformed the global economic and political landscape in dramatic ways. It can be argued that Germany, despite its own domestic transformation problems, made good use of the new opportunities not only through exports of goods and services but also by building up a production network that embraced Europe and prominent areas of the global economy. The sharp increase in outgoing foreign direct investment (FDI) should be interpreted as a strength of the German model, rather than as a sign of a weak domestic production regime. It allowed export-oriented companies to optimise their cost structure and to get immediate access to new growth markets. Since the second half of the 1990s, there has been a rather dramatic rise in outward FDI stock as a share of GDP (see Figure 24.3), which has resulted in a strong net investment position for Germany.

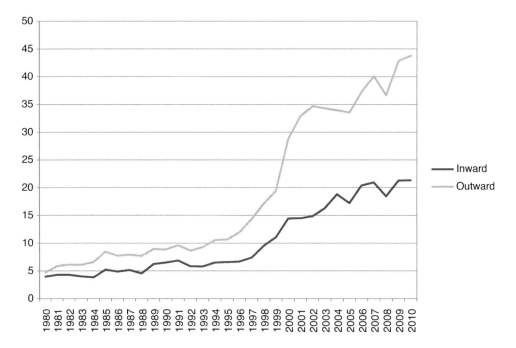

Figure 24.3 FDI stock as a share of GDP, 1980–2010

Source: Eurostat

Data provided by Eurostat indicate that the vast majority of outward FDI stays within the boundaries of the EU. Prominent target markets for German affiliations abroad are Great Britain and Austria, each of which hosts about 15 per cent of the total, closely followed by the US. Outward FDI shows a similar pattern to German exports, and hence a similar mixture of Europeanisation and globalisation (Godart and Görg 2011).

The introduction of the euro in 1999 was another milestone of European integration, insofar as it combined the single market with a common currency zone for a group of member states. This deepening process did not result in a jump in trade volumes for Germany with other member states of the eurozone, even though data indicate that the overall intra-eurozone trade volume increased quite strongly (Baldwin *et al.* 2008).[6] However, the launch of the euro changed the *qualitative* position of Germany within the EU and the economies of the eurozone. With the euro came a turnaround in Germany's current account with the other members of this 'club'. In the period from the launch of the euro (1999) to the outbreak of the global financial crisis (2008), the current account for Greece changed by minus 7.7 percentage points; for Ireland the change was minus 5 percentage points; for Italy minus 3 percentage points; for Spain minus 6.2 percentage points; and for France minus 3.9 percentage points. In the same period Germany registered an improvement in its current account of 8.1 percentage points (Chen *et al.* 2013). Germany accumulated significant surpluses from year to year. Only the global financial crisis of 2008 and then the outbreak of the eurozone crisis slowed down this process, without resulting in a total turnaround.

The various milestones of European integration, as well as the acceleration of economic globalisation since the drastic geo-economic and geopolitical changes at the end of the 1980s, generated fundamental challenges but also offered tremendous opportunities for the established varieties of capitalism. As it turned out, the German production and regulation model did much better than many other models of capitalism. Dealing with structural challenges and seizing opportunities made Germany into an economic powerhouse, at least in Europe. How can this transformation from 'the sick man of Europe' into the continent's dominant economic and political power be explained?

Economic factors in the rise of Germany as a regional power

For most of the period after World War II, Germany was seen as an 'economic giant and political dwarf', and the political class was more than willing to accept the implications of this picture. The situation started to change early in the 21st century, when the Red–Green coalition began to 'normalise' its foreign policy as well as to restructure some features of the institutional setting of model Germany. It needed the eurozone crisis, however, to move Germany to the centre of the EU and to establish its central position, albeit in a more modest way, on the global level. Being the largest and strongest economy in the EU did not come without political implications. Even before the Greek crisis started the eurozone disaster, Germany belonged to the (small) group of core economies that determined the political–economic path the EU and, more particularly, the eurozone should take. Since 2010 Germany has become the critical political actor in the management of the eurozone. Its constraining power sets the policy direction for the eurozone (Hübner 2012), not least due to the weakening economic position of France.

The most popular explanation for the revival in Germany's economic strength is a drastic improvement in cost competitiveness. One argument in support of this view points to the development of relative unit wage costs since the launch of the euro. Another refers to the labour market and welfare state reforms that were put in place under the Red–Green coalition: 'Germany's restrained wages amid healthy productivity gains – which reflect its government–

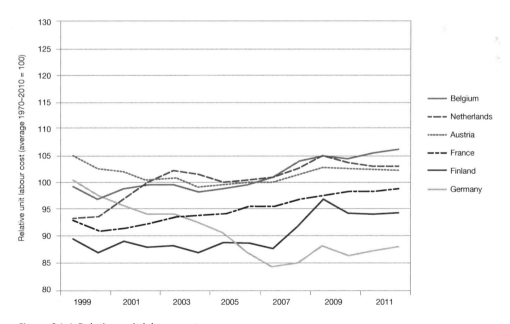

Figure 24.4 Relative unit labour costs

Source: European Commission, Ameco, from De Grauwe (2012)

labour union relations, labour laws and regulations compared to other EU nations – are what have distinguished the country' (Levy 2012). Empirical findings confirm that Germany took a distinct path on unit labour costs, not only in comparison with the crisis-prone southern economies of the eurozone but also in comparison with the remainder of the northern core (see Figure 24.4).

An impressive strand of literature explains this singular development with reference to the cooperative features of model Germany, which allowed the Red-Green coalition during its tenure (1998–2005) to introduce far-reaching reforms of the labour market as well as the German *Sozialstaat* that were designed to help Germany regain international competitiveness (Jackson and Sorge 2012). Compared with the last period of the Kohl Government, the Red-Green coalition introduced a large number of reforms in quick time, as well as encouraging voluntary agreements between unions and employer associations that resembled patterns of concession bargaining established in liberal market economies such as the US (Deeg 2005). However, those reforms still met with strong resistance from the trade unions and social movements, as well as from the traditional left wing of the Social Democratic Party. The main economic effect of the reform package was the large increase in the number of low-income employees as a proportion of the total. According to Eurostat, this employment category's share of overall employment was 22.2 per cent in 2010. Only Estonia, Cyprus, Lithuania, Latvia, Poland, Romania, and Slovakia had similar values (Eurostat 2011). The emergence of a low-wage sector and its steady rise added to the competition pressure on labour markets that kept the rise in nominal wage down. More importantly, the wave of low-wage employment had a restraining effect on private consumption that added to the overall weak effective domestic demand since the early 2000s.

In purely economic terms, the argument can be made that the relative decrease in unit wage costs since the launch of the euro has at least as much to do with the effects of ECB monetary policy as with the wage restraints operated by trade unions in highly competitive labour markets. Unit wage costs are usually expressed as the nominal wage bill in relation to real GDP. However, it is well established that such an indicator is not very helpful in measuring price competitiveness, not least because it does not take into account the real effective exchange rate that exists even between member states of a common currency union. This is relevant also because most member economies of the eurozone are not direct competitors, as they trade in different categories of goods (Felipe and Kumar 2011). Moreover, a breakdown of relative unit labour costs shows that Germany has experienced by far the lowest increase in its price deflator since the launch of the euro. The relatively low increase in inflation greatly improved the nominal price competitiveness of the German business sector, even more strongly than the real price competitiveness (Wyplosz 2013). Unlike Wyplosz, who explains this favourable price development with reference to the policy of wage restraint in Germany, one can argue that the inflation rate in Germany was strongly influenced by the ECB's interest rate policy. The latter is driven not by nominal wage developments in a particular member economy of the currency zone but by a range of (nationally) weighted price factors for all member states. As a result, the interest rate set by the ECB was too high for Germany from the outset of the common currency; for some other countries, the interest rate was set too low (Moons and Van Poeck 2008). Those divergences manifested themselves in starkly varying national inflation rates, which then set the pace for wage negotiations. In the German case, low inflation rates prompted further low nominal wage increases that, in combination with steady productivity increases, drove unit wage costs downwards. In the case of southern members of the eurozone (as well as Ireland), the private credit boom jumpstarted inflation rates and drove up nominal wages ahead of productivity rates, hence the relatively strong increases in unit wage costs. The credit booms also slowed political reform processes in credit-hungry economies (Fernandez-Villaverde *et al.* 2013). But the downside to easy access to cheap credit was that the credit–driven accumulation process eventually resulted in national private debt crises that then turned into public debt crises (Hübner 2013).

This qualification does not undermine the argument that internal devaluation contributed to the improvement in competitiveness; it adds a further component that takes the effects of outsourcing into consideration. Back in the early 1990s, the German business sector started to make extensive use of the skill and cost advantages of transition economies in eastern Europe and put in place a European value chain, particularly by outsourcing standardised parts of the production process to low-wage/high-subsidy/low-tax economies in the east (Marin 2005). The entry of eastern countries into the EU in 2004 and ongoing economic progress in those economies encouraged German companies to outsource more and more operations, including skill-intensive operations. That generated income losses for skilled workers in Germany estimated at 41 per cent of the relative wages of skilled workers (Marin 2010). This strong effect reflects to some degree the restricted mobility of labour from eastern EU economies to Germany, which led to strong foreign direct investment flows into those economies in order to make use of the cost advantages. The Europeanisation of the German value chain was interpreted as a transformation of Germany into a 'bazaar economy', where German companies supposedly make extensive use of production outside Germany (Sinn 2005). Rather than interpreting the out-sourcing as a weakening of model Germany, it can be understood as a strength that allowed the German industrial sector to optimise its cost structure. The increase in outsourcing-oriented FDI was accepted by trade unions, not least because this increase was not accompanied by proportional decreases in domestic investments. Both bargaining parties agreed to a number of so-called company pacts (*betriebliche Bündnisse*), that undertook to keep the level of investment of key exporting companies constant in exchange for wage concessions on the side of the unions.

The economic rise of Germany, particularly since the global financial crisis of 2008, cannot be explained solely by advantageous cost factors. It also reflects strong global demand, particularly from rapidly developing economies, for products offered by German firms. The demand from those types of economies differs from other export demand by its relatively lower price elasticity. With regard to capital goods, quality and service considerations are more important than simple price calculations. With regard to specific consumption goods, it is the symbolic value of those goods that is critical for buyers. In other words, German export sectors were able to make use of fast-growing economies (see Figure 24.5). Due to their specialisation profile, with capital goods and automotives playing a prominent role, German companies were able to meet the strong demand from the private business sectors of those economies for investment goods, as well as the demand for prestigious consumer goods fed by strong and growing economic inequalities. In 2011 vehicles and vehicle parts made up 17.4 per cent of all exported goods; machines had a share of 15.2 per cent, followed by chemical products with 9.5 per cent (Federal Ministry of Economics and Technology 2012). The specialisation profile of Germany is almost perfectly suited to the needs of rapidly growing economies, which need both sophisticated and basic capital goods and infrastructure provision. Given that this group of catch-up economies also shows the steepest increases in Gini coefficients, it comes as no surprise that the German automotive industry won an impressive proportion of the global market for luxury goods (Erber and Schrooten 2012).

The German success story with BRICS is best illustrated by the case of China (Figure 24.6). Like all other EU economies, Germany suffered deficits in its trade balance with China, but they were smaller than the deficits of other European economies. Moreover, since the financial crisis of 2008 the deficit has shrunk rapidly; by early 2013, it had even turned into a surplus. Given that close to 50 per cent of all EU exports to China are provided by German firms, it

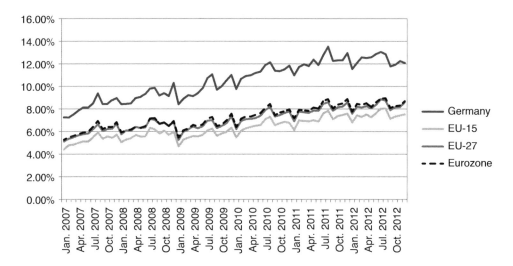

Figure 24.5 German exports to BRICS

Source: Eurostat

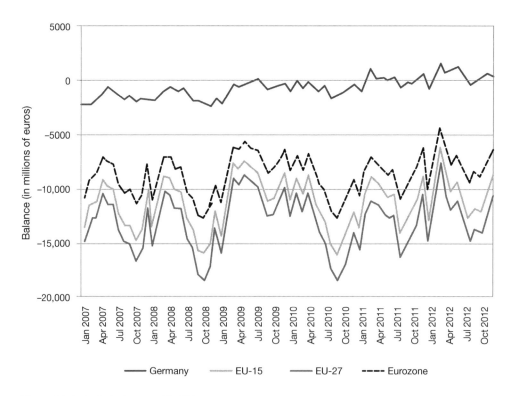

Figure 24.6 Trade balance with China

Source: Eurostat

is impressive that the balance has shifted into potentially positive territory. Germany is the only EU member economy that could generate such a shift.

The combination of (i) changes and adjustments to the institutional setting of model Germany, (ii) making use of value chain opportunities in low-wage medium-skill areas of eastern Europe, and (iii) the complementarity of its product portfolio with demand from fast-growing economies made Germany into an economic powerhouse during the 2000s. Unlike in the decades immediately after World War II, when Germany was seen as an economic giant and a political dwarf, the country was now willing to use its economic power for political purposes.

Regional imperial power or regional hegemon?

The vast literature on hegemony in the global political economy stresses the notion that an ensemble of capitalist market economies needs a political-institutional framework and setting that is controlled and secured by a hegemon, in the form of a leading nation-state, in order to secure a stable growth trajectory (Kindleberger 1981; see also Chapter 21). The hegemonic nation-state provides leadership that is not solely focused on its own national interests but offers political-economic space for interests of other actors. Moreover, unlike in an imperial order, the leader is willing and able to carry a disproportionate share of stabilisation costs. In other words, hegemonic leaders allow other members a certain degree of free-riding as a mode of securing cooperation.

One can argue that the project of European integration differs from imperialist as well as from hegemonic regimes insofar as from the outset the project was about shared power and the transfer of national sovereignty from the nation-state to newly created supranational or intergovernmental bodies (Zielonka 2013). From a *realpolitik* perspective, European integration was all about dealing with the 'German question' (i.e. how to deal with a large and potentially strong nation-state in the middle of Europe). For quite a long time the German question seemed to be settled, not least because German political parties across all camps agreed on a politically low profile for Germany in Europe. The fall of the Wall in 1989 and the rapid process of German unification in 1990 started to change the German position in Europe fundamentally. Simultaneously, the project of European integration changed, most notably with the launch of the common currency (Gamble 2012). The euro can be seen as a means of minimising the power of the Bundesbank and thus domesticating a potentially more powerful Germany inside European institutions. France, in particular, pushed for a political set-up within the newly created European Central Bank where each member would have only one vote.[7] At the same time, Germany accepted that it would have the same number of votes as France in the European Council, even though it was larger in terms of GDP and population (Guerot and Leonard 2011).

It needed only two crises to show that neither the institutional setting of the EU nor the institutional setting of the eurozone was able to deal adequately with the economic and political fallout of crises. The financial crisis of 2008 was an event best handled by nation-states, but because the implications of policy responses were not restricted to nation-states it still needed responses on the part of the EU. When the crisis eventually hit relatively vulnerable EU member states, it was quickly obvious that the structures in place could not deal successfully with the challenges. Moreover, it became clear that the EU was badly in need of economic and political leadership in order to find a constructive and consensual way out of the crisis. Rather than fearing the economic and political power of Germany, many European nation-states were actively hoping that the most powerful economy in the EU would assume a leadership role. 'I demand of Germany', said the Polish Foreign Minister Radosław Sikorski, 'that, for your own sake and for ours, you help it [the eurozone] survive and prosper. You know full well that nobody else can do it. I will probably be the first Polish foreign minister in history to say so, but here it is: I fear German power less than I am beginning to fear German inactivity. You have become Europe's indispensable nation' (Peel *et al.* 2011).

Given the institutional shortcomings of the eurozone and the wide gap between leadership demand and supply, it seemed reasonable to push the economically most powerful nation-state into a more active and responsible position. This strong demand for German leadership, however, was not met by an equally strong willingness on the part of Germany to take the lead in crisis management. At the start of the eurozone crisis, when the incoming Socialist Greek government declared that it had serious problems with the debt criteria of the Maastricht treaty, the Merkel Government demonstrated clear reluctance to engage in any Europe-wide crisis management and was even more resistant to Germany playing an active role in solving the Greek problem. Rather than providing EU leadership, the German government demonstratively gave priority to national interests and simple election calculations (Hübner 2012). The deepening and widening of the eurozone crisis made such a strategy untenable, however. On the contrary, the more the crisis deepened and widened, the more central Germany became to crisis management of the eurozone. For quite a while, the pretence was upheld that the economic philosophy and the political tone of the exercise would be decided by the Franco-German axis. The replacement of President Sarkozy by François Hollande and, more importantly, the decreasing strength of the French economy due to structural problems with its growth model (Bibow 2013) placed both countries on opposing, or at least divergent, political crisis management trajectories.

The management of the eurozone crisis since 2010 should not be described as a German takeover, nor should it be interpreted as Germany's rise to the position of a European hegemon. Still, the Merkel Government set the agenda and provided as well as monitored the underlying economic policy philosophy of broad austerity. Rather than accepting the differences between the various crisis economies, the German approach was from the beginning universal, and detected the root of all problems in fiscal irresponsibility. The politics of social engineering by the Merkel Government are governed by (i) national interests; (ii) a particular reading and interpretation of underlying principles of economic policy (the 'Swabian housewife' [*schwäbische Hausfrau*] approach); and (iii) the political views stemming from an export-oriented growth regime. Those factors and the endogenous structure of moral hazard in a situation where debtors and potential reformers may cease to deliver reforms in exchange for financial support made Germany into the foremost proponent of austerity, within Europe and on a global scale. Unfortunately, the German insistence on unfettered austerity came with a host of unintended consequences that not only undermined the economic case for austerity but also generated deep and fundamental rifts in the eurozone and across the EU.

Given the high public debt to GDP ratios across the eurozone, as well as the high budget deficits since the outbreak of the financial crisis in 2008, the case for austerity seems straightforward. Only a return to fiscal responsibility would calm the financial markets and bring down risk premiums to a growth-enhancing level. This view was supported by standard economic theory, particularly the 90 per cent rule formulated by Reinhart and Rogoff (2010), which was widely accepted by European politicians in general and German politicians in particular. The high level of compliance is not surprising in the light of the German economic revival since 2008. It is astounding, however, in the light of German budget history since the launch of the euro. Germany registered a public budget deficit in 11 of the 14 years between 1999 and 2012; in seven out of those 11 years of public deficits, the German deficit value breached the maximum of 3 per cent under the Maastricht treaty.[8] So the 'Swabian housewife' approach has no basis in German budget history, at least since the launch of the euro. As a matter of fact,

Germany's public budget behaviour since 1999 ranks it below the middle group of eurozone member economies. Until the financial crisis of 2008 hit, economies such as Ireland and Spain were significantly better at complying with the Maastricht criteria.

There is always the chance that politicians will reinterpret history in order to use it as a political tool in debates. In the case of the German bias in favour of austerity, one can argue that the project of the common currency drastically reduced the toolkit of national governments, with the result that austerity seemed the only strategy available in times of crisis. By definition, a common currency area no longer has external devaluation available as a tool to deal with internal imbalances. The substitute for external devaluation is internal devaluation, where fiscal policy responses are key. The two policies differ fundamentally. Whereas external devaluation works through the exchange rate and eventually shifts adjustment burdens to outsiders by processes of currency depreciation, internal devaluation works through wages and prices, and moves adjustment costs to insiders. This is critical to understanding the German stance on crisis management. 'Putting one's own house in order' is the overarching imperative for all member states. This crisis directive comes with the advantage that economic and social adjustment costs are borne primarily by various sectors in the crisis economies. Rather than accepting that the common currency created a truly unified economic space with shared responsibilities, Germany's crisis management approach was nation-state oriented. This is best illustrated by Germany's resistance to all proposals that include an element of mutualisation of debt and risks, such as suggestions for various forms of Eurobonds or for a joint deposit security fund in the framework of a banking union. Proposals by its own German Council of Economic Experts for a redemption fund (Franz *et al.* 2011) as well as initiatives for so-called 'stability bonds' from the Commission (European Commission 2011) met with iron political resistance from Berlin. This political stance can be seen as overly committed to national interests that do not overlap with the stability requirements of the eurozone (Hübner 2013). At the same time, it is clear that all those proposals include a stark political problem that is best described as a moral hazard: how can Germany be assured that national governments will continue with their austerity policies in exchange for the mutualisation of debt? Some of the reform measures to the institutional setting of the eurozone and the EU pushed by the German government targeted exactly this moral hazard problem by transferring large elements of fiscal responsibility from the national level to the European level.

Other German political inputs into eurozone crisis management have their roots in the German export model and its emphasis on competitiveness. As has been shown, the German growth path strongly depends on a flourishing export industry whose activities result in a trade surplus. Competitiveness across a wide range of indicators is key to such a strategy. However, it is a simple principle of mathematics that not all economies can have surpluses in their trade balances at the same time. Improved competitiveness in a highly dynamic global economy is an ongoing requirement, but it is not a recipe for overcoming the crises in eurozone economies. Between the introduction of the common currency and 2008, the share of Germany's trade surplus accounted for by eurozone economies increased from around 18 per cent in 1997 to about 45 per cent, and only the crises in a number of eurozone economies reduced the importance of the eurozone as a destination for German exports (Guerrieri and Esposito 2012). Any successful attempt to rebalance the eurozone thus requires (i) not only a further reduction in the German trade surplus but (ii) the eventual acceptance of trade deficits. The latter can only be achieved if Germany's growth model switches to a more inward-looking regime – a transformation far beyond any political fantasy.

The German insistence on austerity created a fundamental shift in political agency in the EU. The combination of political unwillingness on the part of Germany to act as lender of last resort and misguided economic policy recipes resulted in a wave of sovereign debt insolvency crises that threatened the sustainability and sheer existence of the eurozone. The more official crisis management turned towards strict austerity, the greater the loss in GDP and, consequently, the greater the increase in the public debt ratio. As De Grauwe and Ji (2013) have convincingly demonstrated, the fallacies of the German-inspired austerity strategy resulted in ever higher debt ratios that induced waves of panic attacks in financial markets, which in turn prompted even fiercer rounds of austerity. Ironically, those unintended outcomes propelled the European Central Bank (ECB) to the core of crisis management. To the distress of the Bundesbank, the ECB quickly embarked on a thoroughgoing reinterpretation of its mandate. Rather than simply focusing on price stability, the ECB, following established practices of other central banks, engaged in asset purchases and various forms of quantitative easing, and acted as the ultimate guarantor of the euro. In its advisory opinion (Deutsche Bundesbank 2012) to the German Constitutional Court about the legal range of the ECB's so-called 'outright monetary transaction' programme, the Bundesbank made clear that some of the operations were not covered by the Maastricht treaty and implied huge financial risks for Germany that threatened the sustainability of the German economy. The Merkel Government, on the other hand, was willing to tolerate the new course of the ECB, as its policies and guarantees were the only tools available to rebuild trust in the financial markets. The more impotent national fiscal policies proved to be, the more important the ECB became. Given Germany's insistence on austerity, such a shift in power was unavoidable. In committees of the eurozone and the European Council, Germany's economic power is closely related to its political power, but in the ECB each member has only one vote, regardless of the size of its economy. This institutional set-up implies that Germany very much dominated fiscal policy discourse at the level of the EU and the eurozone, but was unable to set the agenda for monetary policy.

If we stay with our definition of a hegemonic regime as one in which the hegemon is willing and able to bear a disproportionate share of adjustment costs and to offer a political project that takes account of the national interests of all regime members, it is obvious that Germany has not turned into a European hegemon. Rather than being inclusive, the German focus on austerity was driven by narrowly defined national interests. Nor does such a characterisation of the chosen policy path imply that Germany has become a regional imperial power. Despite Germany's agenda-setting power, the Merkel Government had to compromise and, critically, had to accept the implementation by the ECB of a radical policy turnaround that sharply contradicts the German reading and interpretation of the Maastricht treaty. The more the crises drag on and the higher the implied social costs, the stronger the pressure on Germany to allow some flexibility. Since early 2013, there have been growing signs of a German willingness to compromise without giving up the underlying concept of austerity. Rather than demanding a relentless continuation of internal devaluation, both the Merkel Government and the EU Commission have offered flexibility on deadlines for fulfilling the Maastricht criteria. Agenda-setting power and flexibility with regard to the implementation of fiscal consolidation seem to have become the most recent traits of Germany's crisis management. This is still a far cry from being a hegemon in Europe. Rather than proposing an inclusive policy approach, Germany is willing only to allow some more breathing space so that the crisis-ridden economies can stay on the austerity track.

Conclusions

Ironically, the overall German response to the eurozone crisis has the potential to undermine one of the pillars of model Germany's success, namely its exports. The German-inspired austerity strategy ordered by the EU and seconded by the ECB not only resulted in shrinking

GDPs across the eurozone but also destroyed and devalued human skills and capital, with the result that most of the economies switched to a medium-term growth path that is far lower than could have been expected before the crisis hit (Pichelmann 2013). All things being equal, lower growth in the eurozone implies lower export growth for Germany. In order to keep model Germany running, market value losses in the eurozone and in the EU as a whole need be compensated for. More and more, it will be up to extra-EU economic spaces to compensate for smaller export markets in Europe. So far German export industries have demonstrated that they can handle the challenges. However, this would substitute one form of dependence for another. Given the fragile political and economic situation in the US, as well as the economic and, still more, the political challenges faced by the fast-growing economies of Asia and Latin America, it will become increasingly difficult for Germany to extend its export market reach. Rather than focus all its attention on the EU, Germany may intensify its efforts to improve its institutional and treaty relations with other parts of the world.

Notes

1   I am grateful for the excellent research assistance of Jeffrey Mitchell. Please record all errors and omissions on my balance sheet.
2   Proper institutions and 'good governance' are not automatically drivers of growth in a causal sense, even though some authors provide statistical evidence for this (d'Agostino and Scarlato 2012). I argue that particular sets of institutions provide the social environment for capitalist accumulation and economic growth. Those institutional sets differ from economy to economy, and, more importantly, they are not fixed forever.
3   National statistics suggest that the degree of openness is even higher. For example, the Federal Ministry of Economics and Technology provides data from the Federal Statistical Office that show an export ratio of 50.1 per cent in 2011 and an import ratio of 45 per cent, hence a degree of openness of 95.1 per cent (Federal Ministry of Economics and Technology 2012).
4   Switzerland holds rank 8 in 2012. This neighbouring economy is not part of the EU but, due to its membership of the EFTA, it enjoys many of the advantages of membership.
5   Prominent among them was Hans-Werner Sinn, one of the most outspoken neoclassical economists in Germany (for an overview, see Sinn 2005), whose rather bleak publications set the terms for an intense political debate in Germany about a fundamental change in the institutional setting of model Germany.
6   Quantifying trade effects for the eurozone has proven to be rather difficult. Since the publication of Rose's piece on trade effects of currency unions (Rose 2000), which came up with significantly high increases, the debate about euro effects has become quite heated. The consensus seems to be that actual trade effects are positive but much smaller than suggested by the Rose paper (see Frankel 2008). Between 1999 and 2012, intra-eurozone trade increased from a value of 15 per cent of aggregate GDP to about 20 per cent of aggregate GDP; in the same period, however, trade with extra-eurozone economies increased at an even faster rate. This unequal growth results in a decrease in the share of overall EU trade accounted for by intra-eurozone trade (ECB 2013).
7   In the words of Martin Feldstein (2013: 8): 'Substituting the euro for national currencies would also require Germany to give up the Deutsche Mark and to allow a European Central Bank to substitute for the dominant role of the Bundesbank. President Mitterand forced Germany to accept the euro by making that a condition for French support of German unification.'
8   Data for general government net lending as a share of GDP provided by Eurostat.

Bibliography

Abelshauser, W. (2004) *Deutsche Wirtschaftsgeschichte: seit 1945*, Munich: C.H. Beck.
Baldwin, R., DiNino, V., Fontagné, L., De Santis, R.A., and Taglion, D. (2008) *Study on the Impact of the Euro on Trade and Foreign Direct Investment*, Economic Papers 321, Brussels: European Commission.
Berger, H. and Schindler, M. (2010) 'Return to Form', *Finance & Development*. Online. Available at www.imf.org/external/pubs/ft/fandd/2010/09/berger.htm (accessed 2 May 2013).

Bibow, J. (2013) 'On the Franco-German Euro Contradictions and Ultimate Euro Battleground', working paper, Levy Economics Institute of Bard College. Online. Available at www.levyinstitute.org/publications/?docid=1740 (accessed 2 May 2013).

Biebricher, T. (2012) Neoliberalismus zur Einführung, Hamburg: Junius Verlag.

Blanchard, O.J., Jaumotte, F., and Loungani, P. (2013) 'Labor Market Policies and IMF Advice in Advanced Economies during the Great Recession', IMF Staff Discussion Notes 13/02, International Monetary Fund.

Bonefeld, W. (2012) 'Freedom and the Strong State: On German Ordoliberalism', New Political Economy, 17(5): 633–56.

Brown, B.E. (2013) 'Ordeal of the European Union', American Foreign Policy Interests, 35: 21–30.

Buti, M. and Pichelmann, K. (2013) 'European prosperity reloaded: an optimistic glance at EMU@20', ECFIN Economic Brief, 19.

Chen, R., Milesi Ferretti, G.M., and Tressel, T. (2013) 'External Imbalances in the Eurozone', Economic Policy 28(73): 101–42.

d'Agostino, G. and Scarlato, M. (2012) 'Inclusive Institutions, Innovation and Economic Growth: Estimates for European Countries' MPRA Archive. Online. Available at http://mpra.ub.uni-muenchen.de/43098/1/MPRA_paper_43098.pdf (accessed 3 October 2013).

Deeg, R. (2005) 'The comeback of Modell Deutschland? The New German Political Economy in the EU', German Politics, 14(3): 332–53.

De Grauwe, P. (2012) In search of symmetry in the eurozone, CEPS Policy Briefs Online. Available at www.ceps.eu/book/search-symmetry-eurozone (accessed 2 May 2013).

De Grauwe, P. and Ji, Y. (2013) 'Panic-driven austerity in the Eurozone and its implications', VOX. Online. Available at www.voxeu.org/article/panic-driven-austerity-eurozone-and-its-implications (accessed 7 May 2013).

Deutsche Bundesbank (2012) Stellungnahme gegenüber dem Bundesverfassungsgericht. Online. Available at www.handelsblatt.com/downloads/8124832/1/stellungnahme-bundesbank_handelsblatt-online.pdf (accessed 7 May 2013).

DIW Berlin (2013) Germany's Economy in Pole Position, DIW Economic Bulletin. Online. Available at www.diw.de/documents/publikationen/73/diw_01.c.415234.de/diw_econ_bull_2013–02.pdf (accessed 2 May 2013).

ECB (2013) Intra-Euro Area Trade Linkages and External Adjustments. Online. Available at www.ecb.int/pub/pdf/other/art2_mb201301en_pp59–74en.pdf (accessed 2 May 2013).

Egger, P.H. and Pfaffermayr, M. (2013) 'The Pure Effects of European Integration on Intra-EU Core and Periphery Trade', The World Economy, 36.

Eichengreen, B. (2007) The European Economy since 1945: Coordinated Capitalism and Beyond, Princeton: Princeton University Press.

Eichengreen, B. and Ritschl, A. (2008) 'Understanding West German economic growth in the 1950s', SFB 649 discussion paper. Online. Available at www.econstor.eu/dspace/bitstream/10419/25311/1/590225650.PDF (accessed 3 October 2013).

Erber, G. and Schrooten, M. (2012) 'Germany Profits from Growth in Brazil, Russia, India, China and South Africa – But for How Much Longer?' DIW Economic Bulletin, 2(10): 16–22.

European Commission (2011) European Commission Green Paper on the feasibility of introducing Stability Bonds. Online. Available at http://ec.europa.eu/europe2020/pdf/green_paper_en.pdf (accessed 7 May 2013).

Eurostat Statistical Books (2011) External and intra-EU trade: A statistical yearbook, Data 1985–2010. Online. Available at http://epp.eurostat.ec.europa.eu/cache/ITY_OFFPUB/KS-GI-11–001/EN/KS-GI-11–001-EN.PDF (accessed 2 May 2013).

Federal Ministry of Economics and Technology (2012) Facts about German foreign trade in 2011. Online. Available at www.bmwi.de/English/Redaktion/Pdf/facts-about-german-foreign-trade-in-2011,property=pdf,bereich=bmwi,sprache=en,rwb=true.pdf (accessed 2 May 2013).

Feldstein, M. (2013) 'Coordination in the European Union', working paper, National Bureau of Economic Research. Online. Available at www.nber.org/papers/w18672 (accessed 2 May 2013).

Felipe, J. and Kumar, U. (2011) 'Unit Labor Costs in the Eurozone: The Competitiveness Debate Again', Levi Economics Institute of Bard College. Online. Available at www.levyinstitute.org/pubs/wp_651.pdf (accessed 2 May 2013).

Fernandez-Villaverde, J., Garicano, L., and Santos, T. (2013) 'Did the euro kill governance in the periphery?', VOX. Online. Available at www.voxeu.org/article/did-euro-kill-governance-periphery (accessed 2 May 2013).

Frankel, J. (2008) 'The Euro at ten: Why do effects on trade between members appear smaller than historical estimates among smaller countries?', *VOX*. Online. Available at http://voxeu.org/article/euro-ten-why-such-small-trade-effects (accessed 2 May 2013).

Franz, W., Bofinger, P., Feld, L.P., Schmidt, C.M., and Weder, B. (2011) 'A European Redemption Pact', *VOX*. Online. Available at www.voxeu.org/article/european-redemption-pact (accessed 7 May 2013).

Gamble, A. (2012) 'The Changing World Order: From the Opening of the Berlin Wall to the Financial Crash', in M. Telo (ed.) *State, Globalization and Multilateralism: The Challenges of Institutionalizing Regionalism*, United Nations University Series on Regionalism 5, Dordrecht: Springer. pp. 45–60.

Glyn, A., Hughes, A., Lipietz, A., and Singh, A. (1988) 'The Rise and Fall of the Golden Age', in S. Marglin and J.B Schor (eds) (1991) *The Golden Age of Capitalism: Reinterpreting the Postwar Experience*, Oxford: Oxford University Press, pp. 39–125.

Godart, O. and Görg, H. (2011) 'The role of global value chains for German manufacturing' Online. Available at http://papers.ssrn.com/sol3/papers.cfm?abstract_id=2179948 (accessed 3 October 2013).

Guerot, U. and Leonard, M. (2011) *The New German Question: How Europe can get the Germany it needs*, European Council on Foreign Relations. Online. Available at http://ecfr.eu/content/entry/the_new_german_question_how_europe_can_get_the_germany_it_needs (accessed 2 May 2013).

Guerrieri, P. and Esposito, P. (2012) 'Intra-European imbalances, adjustment, and growth in the eurozone', *Oxford Review of Economic Policy*, 28(3): 532–50.

Gullberg, A.T. (2013) 'The political feasibility of Norway as the "green battery" of Europe', *Energy Policy*, 53: 615–23.

Hall, P. and Soskice, D. (2001) *Varieties of Capitalism. The Institutional Foundation of Comparative Advantage*, Oxford: Oxford University Press.

Hassel, A. (2012) 'The Paradox of Liberalization – Understanding Dualism and the Recovery of the German Political Economy', *British Journal of Industrial Relations*, 55.

Hiller, S. and Kruse, R. (2010) 'Milestones of European Integration: Which matters most for trade openness?' Online. Available at www.qass.org.uk/2010-May_Brunel-conference/kruse.pdf (accessed 2 May 2013).

Hübner, K. (1990). *Theorie der Regulation: eine kritische Rekonstruktion eines neuen Ansatzes der politischen Ökonomie*, Berlin: Sigma Verlag.

Hübner, K. (1992). 'Die neuen Länder und der alte Osten. Politisch-ökonomische Transformations-blockaden im Vergleich', in W. Schulz and L. Vollmer (eds) *Entwickeln statt abwickeln: Wirtschaftspolitische und ökologische Umbau-Konzepte für die fünf neuen Länder*, Berlin: Ch. Links, pp. 44–55.

Hübner, K. (2012) 'German Crisis Management and Leadership – from Ignorance to Procrastination to Action', *Asia Europe Journal*, 9(2–4): 159–77.

Hübner, K. (2013) 'Eurozone: Creeping Decay, Sudden Death or Magical Solution?' in Laursen, F. (ed.) *The EU and the Eurozone Crisis*, Farnham: Ashgate, pp. 25–44.

Ito, T. and Okubo, T. (2012) 'New Aspects of Intra-industry Trade in EU Countries', *The World Economy*, 35(9): 1126–38.

Jackson, G. and Deeg, R. (2012) 'The Long-Term Trajectories of Institutional Change in European Capitalism', *Journal of European Public Policy*, 19(8): 1109–25.

Jackson, G. and Sorge, A. (2012) 'The Trajectory of Institutional Change in Germany, 1979–2009', *Journal of European Integration*, 19(8): 1146–67.

Kindleberger, C. (1981) 'Dominance and Leadership in the International Economy: Exploitation, Public Goods, and Free Rides', *International Studies Quarterly*, 25(2): 242–54.

Lehndorff, S. (2012) 'Europe speaks German now!', *'Beyond the Crisis: Developing Sustainable Alternatives'* unpublished conference paper.

Levy, M. (2012) 'Diverging Competitiveness among EU Nations: Constraining Wages is the Key', *VOX*. Online. Available at www.voxeu.org/article/how-restore-competitiveness-eu (accessed 2 May 2013).

Lewney, R. (2011) *Study on the Cost Competitiveness of European Industry in the Globalization Era – Empirical Evidence on the Basis of Relative Unit Labour Costs (ULC) at Sectoral Level: Final Report*. Online. Available at http://ec.europa.eu/enterprise/newsroom/cf/_getdocument.cfm?doc_id=7060 (accessed 2 May 2013).

Marin, D. (2005) *A New International Division of Labor in Europe: Offshoring and Outsourcing to Eastern Europe*, Department of Economics, University of Munich. Online. Available at http://epub.ub.uni-muenchen.de/714 (accessed 2 May 2013).

Marin, D. (2010) *The Opening Up of Eastern Europe at 20 – Jobs, Skills, and 'Reverse Maquiladoras' in Austria and Germany*, Department of Economics, University of Munich. Online. Available at http://epub.ub.uni-muenchen.de/11435/ (accessed 2 May 2013).

Moons, C. and Van Poeck, A. (2008) 'Does one size fit all? A Taylor-rule based Analysis of Monetary Policy for Current and Future EMU Members', *Applied Economics*, 40: 193–9.

New York Times (2012) 'Off the Charts: Germany's Trade within the Euro Zone Falls, 11 May. Online. Available at www.nytimes.com/interactive/2012/05/11/business/Germanys-Trade-Within-the-Euro-Zone-Falls.html?_r=0 (accessed 2 May 2013).

Peel, Q., Cienski, J. and Cohen, N. (2011) 'Germany told to act to save Europe', *Financial Times*, 28 November. Online. Available at www.ft.com/intl/cms/s/0/d29da7fc-19ee-11e1-b9d7-00144feabdc0.html#axzz2SBLkhfTK (accessed 2 May 2013).

Pichelmann, K. (2013) 'Economic Growth Perspectives for Europe', *ECFIN Economic Brief*, 21.

Pierson, P. (2001) *The New Politics of the Welfare State*, Oxford: Oxford University Press.

Reinhart, C.M. and Rogoff, K.S. (2010) 'Growth in a Time of Debt', working paper, National Bureau of Economic Research. Online. Available at www.nber.org/papers/w15639.pdf?new_window=1 (accessed 2 May 2013).

Rose, A.K. (2000) 'One Money, One Market: Estimating the Effect of Common Currencies on Trade', *Economic Policy*. Online. Available at www.nber.org/papers/w7432.pdf. (accessed 13 May 2013).

Ruggie, J.G. (1982) 'International Regimes, Transactions, and Changes: Embedded Liberalism in the Postwar Economic Order', *International Organization*, 36(2): 379–415.

Saull, R. (2012) 'Rethinking Hegemony: Uneven Development, Historical Blocs, and the World Economic Crisis', *International Studies Quarterly*, 56: 323–38.

Schirm, S.A. (2012) 'Leaders in Need of Followers: Emerging Powers in Global Governance', in E. Fels, J.F. Kremer, and K. Kronenberg (eds) *Power in the 21st Century: International Security and International Political Economy in a Changing World*, Berlin: Springer, pp. 211–36.

Singh, A. (2008) 'Historical Examination of the Golden Age of Full Employment in Western Europe', in P. Arestis and J. McCombie (eds) (2009) *Missing Links in the Unemployment Relationship*, Basingstoke: Palgrave Macmillan, pp. 51–71.

Sinn, H.-W. (2005) *Basar-Ökonomie Deutschland: Exportweltmeister oder Schlusslicht*, Berlin: Econ.

Statistisches Bundesamt (2013a) *Germany's Most Important Trading Partners 2012*. Online. Available at https://www.destatis.de/EN/FactsFigures/NationalEconomyEnvironment/ForeignTrade/TradingPartners/Current.html (accessed 2 May 2013).

Statistisches Bundesamt (2013b) *Share of intra-EU trade*. Online. Available at https://www.destatis.de/EN/FactsFigures/NationalEconomyEnvironment/ForeignTrade/ForeignTradeIndicators/EUTrade.html (accessed 2 May 2013).

Steffens, T. (2008) *Chart in Focus: EU driving Germany's trade surpluses*, Deutsche Bank Research. Online. Available at www.dbresearch.com/PROD/DBR_INTERNET_EN-PROD/PROD000000000022 1516.pdf (accessed 2 May 2013).

Streeck, W. (1997) 'German Capitalism: Does It Exist? Can It Survive?' *New Political Economy*, 2(2): 237–56.

Thelen, K. (2012) 'Varieties of Capitalism: Trajectories of Liberalization and the New Politics of Social Solidarity', *Annual Review of Political Science*, 15: 137–59.

Toniolo, G. (1998) 'Europe's Golden Age, 1950–1973: Speculations from a Long-run Perspective', *The Economic History Review*, 51(2): 252–67.

Trade Policy Research (2011) *Global Value Chains: Impacts and Implications*, Foreign Affairs and International Trade Canada. Online. Available at www.international.gc.ca/economist-economiste/analysis-analyse/policy-politique/TPR_2011_GVC_ToC.aspx (accessed 2 May 2013).

Viner, J. (1950) *The Customs Union Issue*, New York: Carnegie.

Wyplosz, C. (2013) 'Eurozone Crisis: It's About Demand, not Competitiveness', working paper. Online. Available at www.tcd.ie/Economics/assets/pdf/Not_competitiveness.pdf (accessed 2 May 2013).

Zielonka, J. (2013) 'The International system in Europe: Westphalian Anarchy or Medieval Chaos?' *Journal of European Integration*, 35(1): 1–18.

25

Foreign policy

From 'civilian power' to 'trading state'?

Hanns W. Maull

Since its inception in 1949, the foreign policy of the Federal Republic of Germany has been driven by its rejection of Germany's militarist and expansionist past and its integration into Western liberal democratic institutions. The catastrophic consequences of National Socialism, war, and defeat led to a fundamental revision of Germany's political identity and therefore produced an entirely new foreign policy. This policy built on the constraints imposed on Germany by occupation and the Cold War, but used them shrewdly to promote (West) Germany's own objectives of rehabilitation, prosperity, security, peace, and, eventually, reunification. The resulting 'grand strategy' or foreign policy role concept has often been described as that of a 'civilian power', built around three central guidelines: 'never again', 'never alone', and 'politics before force'. This chapter explores (West) German foreign policies towards Israel, towards pan-European security cooperation, and in the context of the United Nations. It also looks at Germany's role in world trade. (Relations with the United States and NATO are covered by Chapter 26, while Chapters 20–22 focus on Germany's policies in and towards the European Union.)

(West) Germany's foreign policy role concept as a 'civilian power'

When the Federal Republic of Germany (FRG) and the German Democratic Republic (GDR) were founded in 1949, the two German states were products of the Cold War, created by the competing foreign and security policies of the two new superpowers, the United States and the Soviet Union (Hanrieder 1989: 37–42; Haftendorn 2006: 9–17). The 'two Germanies' had no policy options outside the confines of the East–West conflict, as defined by their respective founding powers, whose political and economic systems they were obliged to replicate. Their political sovereignty, one of the essential assets of independent statehood, was heavily compromised, and the other two most fundamental foreign policy objectives of any state, prosperity and security, were to be achieved through integration into the respective military and economic alliance systems built up by the two superpowers: NATO, the European Community, and the international economic order of Bretton Woods for West Germany (Hanrieder 1989; Von Bredow 2006: 82–90), the Warsaw Pact and Comecon for East Germany (Scholtyseck 2003: 80–5). The fourth principal foreign policy concern of any state, territorial integrity, above all implied unification of the two German states, but also raised other issues (such as the Sarre (Saarland) region held by France, or the eastern parts of Germany in 1937, now absorbed into the Soviet Union and Poland).

It quickly became clear that the constraints faced by West Germany were significantly less onerous than those imposed by the Soviet Union on the GDR, for the simple reason that the Western democratic capitalist model was more effective both economically and politically. The FRG was able to rebuild and become prosperous much more quickly, which in turn helped further to legitimise the democratic political order of West Germany. By the mid-1950s at the latest, the West German political system enjoyed widespread support, while the East German system needed to be backed up by Soviet tanks (in June 1953) and stabilised by border fortifications (in August 1961). The success and legitimacy of West Germany's political order were also enhanced by the Cold War, which made it easier for the West German elite and its people to accept the new foreign policy guidelines of limited sovereignty, Western integration, and a preference for individual freedom over national unity. Led by Konrad Adenauer, West Germany's first chancellor (from 1949) and foreign minister (from 1951, alongside his chancellorship), the Germans eventually came to support those constraints out of conviction, rather than as impositions (Schweigler 1985).

Ultimately, the innate advantages of the Western liberal order in terms of individual freedom and material prosperity allowed West Germany to develop an extraordinarily successful foreign policy. To do so, it had first to accept the constraints imposed on it by the Cold War and Germany's historical and geopolitical position, and then to find ways to turn those constraints into assets. It did both in the grand foreign policy strategy developed, in its essential features, by Adenauer. West Germany's grand strategy – which has been described as the foreign policy role concept of a 'civilian power' (Maull 1990/91) – was built around three axiomatic guidelines: 'never again' was (West) Germany to fall back into the clutches of totalitarianism (which included not only Nazi fascism, but also communism) and military expansionism; in its foreign policy, (West) Germany should act 'never alone', but only in closest coordination above all with its Western allies; and there should be 'politics before force' – Germany should keep its distance, as far as possible, from military force, which had brought so much destruction not only to Germany itself, but to the whole of Europe during two world wars (Maull 2006).

'Never again', the first guideline, was about regaining respectability, recognition and, eventually, status as a major power in international affairs. This precept had particularly important implications for the FRG's relations, before and after unification, with the state of Israel, born out of the Holocaust and inhabited by many of its survivors. (This special relationship will be taken up in greater detail below.) 'Never again' also explains why the Basic Law (Grundgesetz) integrates international law prominently into the German legal system (its norms have precedence over all German laws other than the constitution itself), and underpins Germany's vocal support for human rights and the rule of law in international affairs through its foreign policy.

'Never alone' provided the foundations of West Germany's multilateralist foreign, security, and defence policies, built around membership of NATO and West Germany's integration into the European Communities. But multilateralism also constituted a key aspect of the liberal international economic order designed by the United States and Great Britain in 1944, and implemented through the Marshall Plan from 1948 onwards. Integration into this open world economy was, given the geopolitical realities of the Cold War, impossible to reject for West Germany. But it was also very much to its advantage, as it allowed the country quickly to rebuild its traditional industries and gear them to export markets. West Germany thus became a 'trading state' (Rosecrance 1986) fortunate enough to operate in a multilateral economic order; we will take this up in greater detail below.

Initially West Germany would probably have preferred to remain unarmed, but this turned out to be impossible in the context of the Cold War: rearmament was the price the country had to pay for the security guarantees provided by the United States, eventually through extended nuclear deterrence. But Konrad Adenauer also recognised the political utility of West German rearmament, and cleverly used it to advance his own agenda of rehabilitation and integration. Rearmament caused the first and most bitter foreign policy debate in West Germany, when anti-militarist and pacifist opponents of rearmament mobilised against the plans to create the Bundeswehr as part of the Western military alliance (Winkler 2000: 144–6). They narrowly lost, but scepticism concerning any use of force, and the deployment of German soldiers in combat, in particular, remains deeply ingrained within the German body politic to this day (Colschen 2010: 352–80).

'Never again': (West) Germany's special relationship with the state of Israel

'Every Federal government and every Federal chancellor before me was committed (*verpflichtet*) to the security of Israel due to Germany's special historical responsibility. This historical responsibility of Germany is *raison d'état* (*Staatsraison*) for my country. This means for me as German Federal chancellor that the security of Israel is never negotiable' (*Die Welt* 2008; my translation). Thus Chancellor Angela Merkel on 18 March 2008 during her address to the Knesset (the Israeli parliament). Never before had the Knesset allowed a foreign head of government to speak to it; its rules of procedure had to be changed to accommodate that event. Her visit in 2008 took three days and resulted in an extraordinary institutionalisation of the 'special relationship' between Germany and the state of Israel. Frameworks for closer cooperation were established in a whole range of policy areas, including science and technology, defence and foreign policy, and education. Governments were to consult annually, and each side appointed a coordinator to deepen the bilateral relationship. Among the issues discussed were arms supplies, notably German submarines capable of deploying nuclear-tipped cruise missiles for second strikes (Colschen 2010: 272).

The special relationship had come a long way (Deutschkron 1983; Hansen 2002; Jelinek 2004; Weingardt 2002). The crucial first steps were taken as early as 1949, when Chancellor Adenauer committed Germany to compensate the state of Israel and the Jewish people for the atrocities of the Nazi state (*Wiedergutmachung*). Negotiations between the two governments, which at the time were highly controversial in Israel, began in the spring of 1952 and concluded with the Luxembourg agreement of 10 September 1952, which committed West Germany to payments of 3.45 billion Deutsche Mark (DM) over a period of 10 years (Wolfssohn and Brechenmacher 2007: 506ff). In 1957 Israel approached the Bonn government for arms deliveries for the first time. This caused a massive crisis within Israel, but arms deliveries were nevertheless eventually arranged in secret in 1962, still without formal diplomatic relations between the two countries. The issue was controversial in Israel and difficult in West Germany, which enjoyed good relations with the Arab world and was constrained by its commitment to break off diplomatic relations with any country that recognised the GDR (the Hallstein Doctrine of non-recognition) – a commitment used by Arab states to put pressure on Bonn not to open formal relations with Israel. Diplomatic relations were finally established in 1965 (causing a major crisis in West German relations with the Arab world); they rapidly solidified and normalised, helped by a wave of public sympathy and admiration for Israel's victory over the combined forces of Egypt, Syria, and Jordan in the Six-Day War in June 1967.

The 1967 Israeli–Arab war resulted in the occupation of the Egyptian Gaza strip (settled mostly by several hundred thousand Palestinians in refugee camps) and Sinai Peninsula, the Jordanian West Bank, and the Syrian Golan Heights. This fundamentally transformed the Israeli–Arab conflict, and West Germany henceforth had to consider its special relationship with Israel against the background of its desire to see the conflict resolved. The Yom Kippur War (October 1973) reminded Germany (as well as the other members of the European Communities) of Europe's critical dependence on Arab oil supplies and thus pushed the conflict further up the German foreign policy agenda. Bonn's response to this dilemma was to 'Europeanise' its policy towards the Israeli–Arab and Israeli–Palestinian conflict, acting through the European political cooperation (EPC) machinery, which produced coordinated European Community positions. This allowed the West German government to balance its traditionally close relations with the Arab world and its pursuit of a political settlement for the Israeli–Arab conflict against its special relationship with Israel (Maull 2003). Unfortunately, however, the Europeans were unable to exercise much influence over the conflict, while efforts by the United States (which resulted in separate peace treaties between Israel and Egypt and Israel and Jordan) did not solve but merely transformed it, reducing it to its festering core: the struggle between Israel and the Palestinians over the former mandate Palestine. When the European Community, including West Germany, came out in favour of a two-state solution and the recognition of the Palestinian people in the late 1970s, relations between Israel and West Germany turned sour. Tensions escalated further when in 1981 German Chancellor Helmut Schmidt (who never visited Israel as chancellor, and never met with then Israeli Prime Minister Menachem Begin) considered selling German Leopard II tanks to Saudi Arabia (Colschen 2010: 260–4).

The early 1980s probably marked the lowest point overall in this special relationship. It started to improve soon after the change in government in Bonn from Helmut Schmidt to Helmut Kohl, and survived both the first Palestinian uprising in the occupied territories (*intifadah*) in 1987 and the unification of Germany in 1989–90 reasonably well. Although the *intifadah* drew attention to the festering conflict and added urgency to efforts to resolve it, the West German government during its last years acted more cautiously than in the 1970s, again using the European Community as its conduit for diplomacy, but restraining new European initiatives (Colschen 2010: 264–8).

Since then, the special relationship has been further consolidated, despite its inherent conflict with other important elements of German foreign policy. Germany's willingness to supply Israel with weapons contradicted its declared policy to refrain from arms sales to areas of political tension; its commitment to a special relationship with Israel clashed with its support for a common European approach to the Israeli–Arab conflict; and its strategic and economic interests in having a stable and peaceful Middle East were at times difficult to square with a policy of unconditional support for Israeli security. Indeed, Germany's principled commitment to Israel's security could even imply disagreements and tensions with the Israeli government of the day when its policies (as in the case of the expansion of Israeli settlements in the West Bank) were taken by the German government as undermining the foundations for a durable peace through a two-state arrangement.

The first serious crisis for Germany concerning Israeli security came with the Iraqi invasion of Kuwait and Iraq's defeat at the hands of a massive military coalition led by the United States in 1991. During this war, Iraq fired Scud missiles at Israel. It emerged that not only had the range of those Soviet-made missiles been enhanced with the aid of West German technology and companies: Iraq had also been helped by West Germans in its development of chemical weapons. Thus there was a distinct possibility of Jewish loss of life due to German-supported chemical weapons delivered by missiles enabled with German technology. Fortunately, that did not materialise: Saddam Hussein was apparently deterred from using chemical weapons against Israel by American warnings. But it was enough to send German Foreign Minister Hans-Dietrich Genscher scrambling to Israel in January 1991, promising immediate financial and military support, including German air-defence missiles and two submarines (Colschen 2010: 267). Today the security of the state of Israel seems endangered by the continuing Israeli-Palestinian deadlock over the future of Palestine and the threat from the Iranian nuclear program, which could ignite a further proliferation of nuclear weapons in the Middle East and undermine Israel's present posture of undeclared nuclear capacity.[1] Germany's historical responsibility towards Israel demands that the Jewish state enjoy durable peace, not just security through military superiority. Yet Israel seems unwilling or unable to search for peace through accommodation, preferring security through strength.

'Never alone': (West) Germany in the wider Europe and in the world

Germany and pan-European stability

Germany's almost reflexive multilateralism, like so many other aspects of its policies, seems rooted in West Germany's rejection of its totalitarian, anti-Western past. It found its strongest expressions in West Germany's integration in Europe and in the transatlantic security community of NATO, but it also appears in many other areas of German foreign policy. Indeed, one often finds efforts to complement or even embed policies that by definition are bilateral – such as Germany's special relationship with Israel – within a multilateral context. This was also the case with West Germany's most important bilateral foreign policy project: *Ostpolitik* (policy regarding eastern Europe and the USSR). *Ostpolitik* began when Konrad Adenauer negotiated the return of German prisoners of war from the Soviet Union in exchange for the establishment of diplomatic relations with Moscow, but it gained momentum only under the SPD/FDP (social democratic/ liberal democrat) coalition government headed by Chancellor Willy Brandt from 1969 onwards (Bender 1986). *Ostpolitik* consisted in a number of bilateral negotiations and treaties with the Soviet Union, Poland, Czechoslovakia, and the GDR. It was inspired by two fundamental concerns: to defuse the risk of major war in a Europe divided by the Cold War, and to create political circumstances that would allow a peaceful reunification of Germany (*Wandel durch Annäherung*). Those concerns were shared sufficiently widely across the divide to allow the establishment of a framework for multilateral negotiations 'from the Atlantic to the Urals' on pan-European stability, peace, and cooperation: the Commission on Security and Cooperation in Europe (CSCE). Those negotiations were opened in 1973, and Germany played an important role. The first major result was the Helsinki Final Act of 1975, which defined the principles of cooperation in Europe ('Basket One'), laid out parameters for economic cooperation ('Basket Two'), and set forth criteria for the treatment of citizens within their own boundaries ('Basket Three'). A second, parallel but somewhat narrower multilateral effort, which was confined to member states of the two military alliances in Europe (the CSCE also included the neutral European countries) focused – initially rather less successfully – on conventional arms control (Von Bredow 1996).

The CSCE process continued after 1975. It went through several follow-up conferences and survived the vicissitudes of the 'Second Cold War' during the first half of the 1980s. Its impact on East–West relations was significant and lasting, and it undoubtedly contributed to the end of the Cold War. Initially West Germany's role in this context of pan-European stability and cooperation was highly ambiguous: the policy objective of reunification, which was constitutionally enshrined, fundamentally challenged the post-World War II boundaries and thus the status quo. This had unsettling territorial implications for Poland and the Soviet Union, and for the very existence of East Germany. But West German economic interests in trade and investment with eastern Europe and concern about the risk of war between the two blocs, which (regardless of which side eventually 'won') would have devastated the whole of Germany, provided strong incentives for German foreign policy to seek a relaxation of tensions (*détente*) and mutual accommodation for the sake of pan-European stability. *Ostpolitik* squared that circle: by recognising the territorial status quo, it made possible *détente* and the expansion of East–West trade, while by upholding the possibility of peaceful change and self-determination it undermined the legitimacy of the communist order and opened the gates for the eventual transformation of the East–West conflict through change from below and at the top. During that critical phase (1987–91), the CSCE provided institutional foundations for cooperation and thus helped to channel change in Europe peacefully (Roloff 1996). The Balkan wars of disintegration of the former Yugoslavia from 1991 to 1999 later demonstrated that peaceful change under such circumstances was far from inevitable.

In retrospect, this phase turned out to be the high point of the CSCE process. German foreign policy, in particular, looked to the CSCE to provide a framework for pan-European stability, security, and cooperation to balance the strengthening of Western institutions such as the European Community (which in 1993 became the European Union) and NATO. The Paris Charter of 1990, inspired by the liberal ideas of peace, democracy, human rights, and international cooperation, provided the legal and political foundations for such a framework, but in practice the CSCE process, which in 1995 was upgraded and further institutionalized to create the Organisation for Security and Cooperation in Europe (OSCE), soon lost its momentum. The transformation of Russia and many other member states of the former Soviet Union into liberal democracies and market economies soon stalled, and residual distrust derailed efforts to transcend the old divides comprehensively. Still, pan-European stability and its core issue, the full integration of Russia into a stable framework, continues to be a key concern for German foreign policy, which it tries to pursue both through its bilateral links with Russia and multilaterally through the development of institutionalised cooperation between Russia, the EU, and NATO.

Germany in the United Nations

In many ways, West Germany's 'civilian power' foreign policy role concept made it a perfect member of the United Nations. It had already joined all the major Western institutions, including the World Bank and the IMF, during the first half of the 1950s, and had established its claim to UN membership through a permanent diplomatic mission in New York as early as 1952. It had full membership in (and made significant financial contributions to) most UN specialised agencies. But it took until 1973 for the FRG to overcome Soviet objections and be admitted, together with the GDR, as a full member to the UN. Since then, the UN has been a major focal point of (West) German foreign policy, and Germany has repeatedly served two-year turns as a temporary member of the UN Security Council (UNSC), most recently from 2010 to 2012 (while the FRG had already served in this capacity twice before unification, the GDR joined the UNSC only once, from 1980 to 1981). (West) Germany's first participation in a UN peacekeeping mission came before the end of the Cold War and unification in 1989, when it contributed police forces to a mission to supervise the decolonisation of Namibia (Colschen 2010: 297–303).

From 3 October 1990 onwards, united Germany promised to shoulder greater international responsibilities, not least in the context of the UN (Andreae 2002; Colschen 2010: 304–15). Initially, this primarily meant important financial contributions; from 1992 onward, it also involved the participation of the Bundeswehr in UN peacekeeping operations, such as the UN Transitional Authority in Cambodia (UNTAC). After 1992, the German government (or, more precisely, the Free Democratic successor to Hans-Dietrich Genscher, Foreign Minister Klaus Kinkel) expressed interest in joining a reorganised UNSC as a permanent member. Given demanding procedural requirements and a host of directly competing claimants (Brazil/Argentina and Mexico; Germany/Italy; Nigeria/South Africa/Egypt), this project had little chance of success and therefore never received the full support of Chancellor Kohl. Somewhat surprisingly, the claim was taken up by his successor at the head of a Red-Green (i.e. SPD and Green party) coalition government from 1998 to 2006, Chancellor Gerhard Schröder. His government's last formal effort to secure this objective was a joint proposal to the UN General Assembly by the so-called G-4 (the most insistent aspirants to permanent membership: Brazil, Germany, India, and Japan) for the reform of the UNSC. Again the proposal failed to secure the necessary majority in the General Assembly, thus sparing the present permanent members the need to vote (China would almost certainly have cast a veto against the membership of Japan) (Hellmann and Roos 2007). Schröder's successor Angela Merkel and her coalition governments (first, the grand coalition of CDU/CSU/SPD of 2006–09, then the CDU/CSU/FDP government of 2009–13) have continued to express their willingness to assume more international responsibility in the UN, including the Security Council, but have given up pushing the objective of permanent member status.

The 'trading state': (West) Germany in the liberal international economic order

In its pursuit of prosperity, West Germany relied primarily on exports of industrial goods, and thus exhibited the characteristics of a trading state (Rosecrance 1986; Staack 2000). A trading state's primary concern is with wealth, rather than with power; it accepts the facts of interdependence and therefore seeks to promote its objectives cooperatively within the context of an international division of labour. The task of its foreign policy is to assist business in its efforts to create wealth through trade, but also to get out of the way when politics threaten to muddy the waters of trade. In the case of West Germany, it seems more appropriate to talk about a trading state role *segment* in the context of its broader role *concept* as a civilian power. Particularly in its first two decades, the foreign policy aims of the FRG – such as integration into the Western alliance system, containment of Soviet power in Europe, and the rehabilitation of Germany and its acceptance as a coequal partner – were pursued largely by economic means. Yet this is different from what the role segment of the 'trading state' prescribes, namely the pursuit of wealth and prosperity as an end in itself.

Growth through trade for the FRG came to serve a whole range of domestic and foreign policy objectives; but it was also an aim in itself. The massive destruction caused by World War II and the need to integrate a large refugee population of about 14 million Germans from the east demanded rapid economic growth. In this, West Germany succeeded spectacularly. Two key catalysts for the German 'economic miracle' were the currency reform (introduction of the DM) in 1948 and the outbreak of the Korean War in June 1950. Building on the traditional strengths of German heavy industries (such as iron and steel, cars and trucks, chemicals, and machinery) but with a new, liberal economic policy framework (ordoliberalism; see Chapters 22 and 24), important reforms to traditional German industrial relations, and an expansion of the welfare state, West Germany's economy was rapidly rebuilt and expanded into old and new export markets. It benefited enormously from an international economic environment characterised by open markets, particularly in western Europe and America, and the Bretton Woods regime of stable exchange rates that enhanced Germany's export strengths.

In its economic policymaking, Germany has been strongly influenced by a specific 'economic culture': a set of principles and norms that shape policy behaviour. The core of this economic culture consists of the quest for monetary stability, something that has produced a persistent anti-inflationary bias in economic policy. This includes the norm of a strong currency, as currency devaluation is seen as leading to higher inflation. A second core norm holds that export surpluses are virtuous, external deficits a sign of weakness. The third norm is 'competitiveness': shorthand for the traditional German virtues of hard work and thriftiness. The role segment of the trading state together with those specific characteristics of German economic culture turned the FRG, as Wilhelm Hankel has observed, from a liberal into a highly successful but subtly mercantilist state (Hanrieder 1995: 276 and 535, fn33).

Table 25.1 shows the remarkable expansion of German external trade and the persistently growing trade surpluses from the early 1950s, but also the shift of trade from Europe towards world markets since 1990. This expansion took place against the background of several significant political constraints, such as the Hallstein Doctrine, multilateral restrictions on trade with the Eastern bloc through CoCom,[2] and restrictive arms export policies. It served purposes of wealth creation, but also the promotion of all the key political objectives of Germany as a civilian power: its integration into the Western alliance, its acceptance, its rehabilitation as a coequal partner, its resilience as a bulwark against Soviet expansionism, but also its pursuit of interdependence as a means of fostering political stability, rapprochement, and cooperation across the East–West divide in Germany and Europe, and even its pursuit of unification through rapprochement.

Yet this very success also created new policy dilemmas for the FRG, and later for united Germany: should it seek economic integration primarily within Europe, or within the global economy? If the former, to what extent and how should European integration include elements of a political union? If the latter, how much and in what way should Germany contribute to maintaining and developing the international economic order? In fact, Germany has always tried to have it both ways, as it did in the context of its primary foreign policy orientations between Europe/France and the Atlantic Alliance/America: (West) Germany's economic integration took place in the European and the global context more or less simultaneously. Tensions between regional and global efforts to shape economic interdependence, and between demands on Germany and its willingness to contribute to the international economic order, have surfaced repeatedly over the last few decades, and they continue to challenge German foreign economic policy, in the European debt crisis and beyond.

The contribution Germany has made towards what might be called 'system maintenance' of the international economic order has been surprisingly modest so far: overall, Bonn and then Berlin have been happy to let the United States take the lead and carry much of the weight of providing the required public goods. (West) Germany did revalue the DM reluctantly once during the 1960s, responding to repeated and strong speculative pressures and underlying macro-economic imbalances; and (unlike France) it refrained from rocking the monetary boat of stable but adjustable exchange rate relations (for example, by accumulating dollar reserves without insisting on their redemption from US gold reserves). This may have helped to defer but did not prevent the eventual collapse of the international monetary order of Bretton Woods in 1972–3. The FRG did support efforts to reconstruct a stable monetary order at the European Communities level from the early 1970s onward (first through the Werner Plan and then through

Table 25.1 Evolution of German trade, exports, trade surpluses/deficits, and export destinations

Year:	External trade, total (mill.)	Exports, total (mill.)	Balance of trade (± = surplus/deficit) (mill.)	Share of exports (% of total):				
				EU (15)	Other Europe	USA	Asia of which:	China
1950	19,736	8,362	– 3,012	53.8	15.2	5.1	n.a.	0.57
1960	90,669	47,946	+ 5,223	53.1	15.2	7.8	9.8	0.84
1970	234,882	125,276	+ 15,670	59.5	13.7	9.1	7.0	0.49
1980	691,708	350,328	+ 8,948	60.5	13.4	6.3	6.9	0.59
1990	1,254,336	680,857	+ 107,378	60.9	11.7	7.5	9.5	1.09
2000	1,135,824	597,481	+ 59,138	57.1	14.6	10.3	10.4	1.58
2010	1,765,661	680,857	+ 153,333	49.2	17.5	6.8	15.4	5.60

Note: Data to 1990 are in DM, for 2000 and 2010 in euros. 'Other Europe' excludes the Soviet Union/Russia, other non-European post-Soviet states, and Turkey, but includes Ukraine, Moldova, and Belarus for 2000 and 2010.

Source: Own calculations, based on: Statistisches Bundesamt, Statistische Jahrbücher, various years (available at https://www.destatis.de/DE/Publikationen/Statistischesjahrbuch Statistischesjahrbuch_AeltereAusgaben.html)

the creation of the EMS), but to this day it has been both insistent on imposing strict monetary disciplines and economic policy integration on its partners and unwilling to abolish monetary sovereignty. Germany's *inability* to impose its own monetary economic culture and behaviour on its partners, combined with its *unwillingness* to truly Europeanise monetary affairs, was at the core of the European debt crisis when it exploded in early 2010 (Dyson 1994, 2002: 173–211).

A similar picture emerges for the international trade order (Falke 2006; Lütticken 2006). Germany has been one of the principal beneficiaries of the GATT/WTO liberal economic order, but nevertheless has not played a strong leadership role. Formally, of course, international trade policy has been conducted at the European level since 1972, but European positions have been shaped by the member countries. The FRG has been consistently unwilling to confront France over its protectionist agricultural policies, as this was part of the fundamental economic bargain at the core of European integration: France would insist on protection and market access for its agricultural sector, while the FRG would get French market access and support for its industrial exports. But Germany could also hide behind French agricultural protectionism as a convenient cover to protect its own (politically influential) farm interests. France and Germany also worked together closely on promoting the European civilian aircraft industry through industrial policies. Of course, Germany has been supportive of international initiatives to liberalise industrial markets and has helped to tilt EU external trade policies in a broadly liberal direction, but this has probably reflected more the interests of German industry than any normative conviction about the advantages of market liberalisation. Overall, as Andreas Falke has argued, Germany's foreign trade policies have been pragmatic–eclectic and low-profile, rather than principled and forceful (Falke 2006: 187ff).

Since 2010, the bifurcation in German foreign economic policies has become particularly pronounced. On the one hand, Germany has been deeply enmeshed in the euro debt crisis, and has assumed a clear leadership role in crisis management efforts to save the euro at limited cost and risk to the German taxpayer (Müller-Brandeck-Boquet 2012). On the other hand, Berlin has pursued a strategy of developing 'strategic partnerships' with rising powers such as China, which the government likes to call *Gestaltungsmächte*, implying that Germany itself is such an 'influential power'. The government document spelling out that strategy (Government of the Federal Republic of Germany 2012) puts it in the traditional context of a pro-European and multilateralist foreign policy. It not only presents the strategic partnerships as compatible with similar efforts by the European Union (without, however, explaining why national partnerships are necessary at all if they are to be pursued at the European level) but justifies them as geared towards promoting closer international cooperation in the interests of a sustainable global order. Yet in terms of substance, there can be no doubt that economics, broadly defined, are at the core of those partnerships.

'Politics before force': Germany's military power 'out of area'

During the first half of 1955, a battle between the government and strong neutralist and pacifist forces in the opposition parties and in German society raged over plans by Konrad Adenauer to rearm West Germany. The government won, but the opposition need not have worried. The new Bundeswehr was very different from any of Germany's previous armed forces, and certainly not an instrument of force in the pursuit of national sovereign interests. Objections to German rearmament were not confined to domestic opposition and the Warsaw Pact; many of the FRG's Western neighbours were deeply concerned about any revival of German national military power. To accommodate those concerns (which Adenauer himself, who distrusted the German people, shared), the Bundeswehr was fully integrated into a newly created NATO military command structure to defend Germany and western Europe against Soviet conventional military superiority. Even if the German government had intended to deploy the Bundeswehr autonomously, it would have been unable to do so (Hanrieder 1989: 29–62). But postwar German foreign policy has been characterised by a profoundly sceptical attitude towards the utility of military force in general and towards German use of force in particular (Berger 1998). During the 1970s and 1980s, the FRG fielded western Europe's strongest army, with close to half a million men under arms at its peak level; that was politically acceptable because those forces were there to *deter* war, rather than fight it. Strictly speaking, the Bundeswehr and NATO as a whole would have failed in their mission if a major war had broken out between the two blocs in Europe. But deterrence needed to be psychologically credible, forcing NATO into elaborate preparations for prevailing in such a conflict. This could not be done below the nuclear threshold, and NATO therefore linked its defence of Europe to the threat to use nuclear weapons. To make this threat credible, it was felt that tactical nuclear weapons were needed, and that those also had to be deployed in West Germany.

The modernisation of tactical weapons, decided by NATO in 1979, caused the second major debate in West Germany's security policy in the early 1980s. This time, the opposition mostly came from civil society and extraparliamentary forces, but it also gained traction within the Social Democratic Party. As a result, the Social Democrat Chancellor Helmut Schmidt lost his majority in the Bundestag and the Christian Democrats returned under Chancellor Helmut Kohl. They won the battle for modernisation and deployment of tactical nuclear weapons. Again, however, the opposition need not have worried: those weapons were soon to be scrapped in the context of major advances in disarmament agreed between East and West during the last years of the 1980s (Haftendorn 2006).

With the unification of Germany in 1990, German security policy and the Bundeswehr simultaneously faced three major challenges (Meiers 2006). First, the Bundeswehr, with its theoretical strength of about 470,000 men under arms (which, however, was never fully achieved) had to take over and merge with the East German National People's Army (*Nationale Volksarmee*, NVA), which theoretically numbered 170,000. Second, those new armed forces had to be reduced to the maximum of 370,000 permitted under the 2+4 Treaty. And third, those forces had to be restructured and retooled in line with the new defence and security requirements facing NATO and the Western alliance system, within which Germany – and the Bundeswehr – remained firmly integrated. Two major crises, which broke out almost simultaneously with the unification of Germany and Europe in 1990, quickly showed that the new security environment after the end of the Cold War included the actual use of military force. In August 1990, Iraq invaded and tried to annex Kuwait, and in the summer of 1991, the former Socialist Federal Republic of Yugoslavia began to disintegrate into violence as a result of the ambitious machinations of Serbian leader Slobodan Milošević, who wanted to create an ethnically pure 'Greater Serbia'. Kuwait was liberated in a major multilateral military campaign orchestrated and led by the US government and military. Many other NATO states participated in the campaign, but the Bundeswehr did not: Germany instead contributed a massive $17 billion to the collective war effort. In the wars of disintegration of the former Yugoslavia, the West as a whole hesitated until NATO finally decided to halt the fighting and atrocities in Bosnia through military intervention in 1995 (Operation Deliberate Force). In this intervention, German Tornado aircraft participated in combat missions: for the first time since 1945, German armed forces had become involved in war.

Germany's willingness to participate in multilateral peacekeeping and peace enforcement missions was the result of the third major debate within Germany (now united) over military security policies. Contrary to a widely held view, Germany's reluctance to participate in what used to be called, during the Cold War, out-of-area operations,[3] dates only from the 1970s. Before that period, the West German government on two occasions approved participation of Bundeswehr units in collective Western out-of-area operations, namely in the contexts of the Cyprus crisis in 1964 and of the Egyptian blockade of the Gulf of Aqaba that preceded the Israeli-Arab war in June 1967 (Rühl 1998: 95). Neither mission materialised, but the decisions of the Bonn government at the time were not considered constitutionally or politically problematic. The more restrictive interpretation of Articles 24 and 87a of the Basic Law (Grundgesetz), which the Constitutional Court struck down in 1994, originated during the rule of the Social Democrat/liberal coalitions led by Chancellors Willy Brandt and Helmut Schmidt (1969–82), primarily as a means to avoid German entanglement in the Vietnam war.

From 1990 to 1995, Germany's political elites and public opinion gradually came to accept that under certain circumstances the use of force was the best available option to keep or even to enforce the peace (Philippi 1996). Increasingly persuaded that the ghastly carnage of the unfolding wars in former Yugoslavia needed to be halted, the foreign policy establishment in all major parliamentary parties with the exception of the East German PDS (the successor of the former East German communist party) came to accept that under certain circumstances the Bundeswehr had to be deployed in multilateral missions. Led by then Minister of Defence Volker Rühe (1992–8), this learning process took place through what Rühe himself called his 'salami tactics' of gradually enlarging the quantity and quality of Bundeswehr participation in multilateral missions: first, the missions were traditional UN peacekeeping missions, such as in Cambodia (1992) or Somalia (1993), but then enforcement elements – and thus the possibility of military combat operations – began to creep into NATO missions with Bundeswehr participation, such as enforcement of UN-mandated sanctions through NATO at sea and in the air over former Yugoslavia. Domestic political controversies over those missions were settled by the Constitutional Court with its decision to permit Bundeswehr participation in collective security efforts to secure the peace, but to require for all such missions approval by the Bundestag (12 July 1994). Since then, the Court has been repeatedly called upon to restrain Bundeswehr participation in multilateral missions, but has refused to impose additional constraints on governments and the Bundestag.

In 1999 Germany's willingness to accept the deployment of the Bundeswehr in combat missions surmounted another threshold, when German combat aircraft participated in NATO Operation Allied Force: a full-scale air war to impose a political settlement of the fighting and ethnic cleansing in Kosovo on Serbia. For the first time, NATO intervened militarily without a clear mandate from the UN Security Council. Yet the majority of the German political establishment and a large part of the public were willing to support the mission. After Serbia's defeat and capitulation, the Bundeswehr also contributed significantly, and presently sends by far the largest national contingent to KFOR, the NATO peacekeeping operation in Kosovo (Maull 2000).

Another major turning point in Germany's attitude towards the deployment of the Bundeswehr abroad came with the terrorist attacks on New York and Washington on 11 September 2001 (Rudolf 2005). Initially, the attacks seemed to provide further support for those who were willing to send the Bundeswehr abroad: in response to 9/11, the US and its allies – including a small contingent of German special forces – attacked Afghanistan, helped topple the Taliban government and went after al-Qaeda cells and leaders (Operation Enduring Freedom). The Bundeswehr also participated in other aspects of the US-led 'global war on terror', particularly in naval operations off the Horn of Africa. Yet in retrospect it becomes clear that the military interventions in Kosovo and Afghanistan had strained the 'culture of restraint' (*Kultur der Zurückhaltung*) that continues to characterise Germany's foreign policy culture and role concept. To secure a majority in his governing Social Democrat-Green coalition government in the Bundestag vote on the mandate for Bundeswehr participation in Operation Enduring Freedom, Chancellor Gerhard Schröder had to link the issue to a vote of confidence in his government, indicating significant unease within the coalition about this extensive mandate involving a maximum of 4,900 men and women in uniform. (The overall majority in the Bundestag for the mandate was not at issue, since the opposition supported Bundeswehr participation; see Szabo 2004.)

The Bundeswehr also joined the International Security Assistance Force (ISAF), the international peacekeeping mission in Kabul from 2002, whose mandate was eventually expanded to encompass all of Afghanistan (Von Krause 2011). ISAF, which was later merged with US military efforts to search out and destroy the remnants of al-Qaeda and the Taliban regime in Afghanistan, increasingly turned into a counterinsurgency war not only in the south and east, but also in the north of the country, where the Bundeswehr was deployed. As a result, the Bundeswehr for the first time experienced significant casualties. The NATO air attack on two hijacked tankers near Kunduz ordered by the Bundeswehr officer in command on 4 September 2009, which apparently caused close to 100 Afghan civilian casualties, dramatised the realities of the war for the German public and ignited the first serious debate about the mission at home (Noetzel 2011). Support for the mission declined as public opinion reverted to its traditional scepticism, and government also became more reluctant to deploy the Bundeswehr abroad in potentially risky and dangerous missions, as Germany's abstention from the Western military intervention in Libya in the spring of 2011 showed. It would be misleading to take Berlin's defection from the common Western position in the UN Security Council vote on UNSC Resolution 1973 on Libya as representative of a new German policy line: the government has since agreed to send a small mission to Turkey in 2013 to strengthen Turkey's air defences against Syria, and at the time of writing is considering participation in an EU mission to support the government of Mali against an Islamist insurgency in the north of the country. Yet scepticism towards the use of military force in the pursuit of non-vital foreign policy objectives has again grown significantly over the last decade, both within the government and among the public (Maull 2011).

As of December 2012, the Bundeswehr had a total of 6,108 soldiers participating in about a dozen smaller (mostly in Africa) and four major missions: ISAF in Afghanistan (4,322), KFOR in Kosovo (1,210), Atalanta, the EU operation against piracy off Somalia's coast (324), and the UN operations in and off the coast of Lebanon (324). The largest number of soldiers on missions abroad (more than 10,000) was reached in 2002, and at any time during the last decade several thousand Bundeswehr soldiers were serving abroad. Up to December 2012, 99 soldiers had been killed in action, more than half of them in Afghanistan.

Conclusion: German foreign policy – continuity and change

How has German foreign policy changed over the last six decades? The question whether continuity or change has characterised German foreign policy after unification has been at the centre of a long and lively debate among scholars, which continues to this day (see Chapter 21). It is unlikely to be settled for good, for there have obviously been significant continuities (in the basic orientations of German foreign policy) as well as important changes (notably with regard to the use of force). From the theoretical perspective followed here, continuities have dominated. National foreign policy role concepts are usually 'sticky': that is, they change only slowly. Dramatic discontinuities do happen occasionally, as with German foreign policy in 1933 and again in 1949, but they are exceptional and usually related to similarly profound domestic discontinuities.

There are two important reasons why national foreign policy role concepts usually change very incrementally: first, they are anchored in national identities, which gives them considerable weight and stability; but secondly, they are also malleable and open to – indeed, usually in need of – authoritative interpretation by decision-makers. Role concepts are complex: they combine several key norms and guidelines. Those are often in tension with one another, and there is a need to interpret and order them hierarchically in any given situation (e.g. which of our principles is at stake here, and which is the most important in this context?). The malleability of role concepts helps explain the paradox of continuity in (West) German foreign policy: why should Germany continue to pursue, broadly speaking, the 'civilian power' role concept of the old FRG after unification, in a situation in which Germany's external environment had changed so fundamentally? In fact, the basic norms and policy guidelines that we have used to structure this analysis of German foreign policy could be reinterpreted by different decision-makers and governments, the emphasis could be subtly shifted, and tensions between norms could be creatively exploited.

Yet over the last decade or so, something more fundamental may be gathering momentum in German foreign policy, which seems to be drifting away from its traditional moorings. This is not about a significant reinterpretation, let alone a fundamental reversal of the 'civilian power' role concept. Rather, it is a hollowing-out of the tradition, a loss of prescriptive strength of the normative framework guiding German foreign policymaking under the imperative of domestic political concerns and pressures. This 'domestication' of foreign policy decisions, which is not confined to Germany alone, appears to weaken, and at times to overwhelm, the ability of German foreign policy to define and then to keep to its course.

Notes

1 Israel officially denies possession of nuclear weapons, but it is well known that the country has a nuclear arsenal of 100 to 200 warheads and delivery systems capable of deploying those nuclear weapons across distances of several hundred kilometres, and that the Israeli government would probably use them if confronted with something it saw as an existential threat to the state of Israel. See Cohen (2009).
2 CoCom (Coordinating Committee for Multilateral Export Controls) was established during the Cold War to prevent the export of arms, munitions, and militarily sensitive technologies to the Warsaw Pact states.
3 The term relates to military operations involving troops from NATO member states in missions outside NATO's collective defence responsibilities as defined by the NATO treaty. To exclude member states' colonial possessions from those shared responsibilities, the treaty defined the area in which NATO mutual obligations for collective security applied in geographic terms as the 'area north of the topic of Cancer' (North Atlantic Treaty, Art. VI).

Bibliography

Andreae, L. (2002) *Reform in der Warteschleife: Ein deutscher Sitz im UN-Sicherheitsrat?* (Schriften des Forschungsinstituts der DGAP, Reihe Internationale Politik und Wirtschaft Band 69), Munich: Oldenbourg.
Bender, P. (1986) *Neue Postpolitik: Vom Mauerbau bis zum Moskauer Vertrag*, Munich: dtv.
Berger, T. (1998) *The Cultures of Antimilitarism: National Security in Germany and Japan*, Baltimore: Johns Hopkins UP.
Cohen, A. (2009) 'Israel, A sui generis Proliferator', in M. Alagappa (ed.) *The Long Shadow: Nuclear Weapons and Security in 21st Century Asia*, Stanford, CA: Stanford University Press: 241–68.
Colschen, L. (2010) *Deutsche Außenpolitik*, Paderborn: Wilhelm Fink.

Deutschkron, I. (1983) *Israel und die Deutschen: Das schwierige Verhältnis*, Hamburg: Verlag Wissenschaft und Politik.

Die Welt (2008) 'Das sagte Kanzlerin Angela Merkel vor der Knesset', 18 March (speech of Chancellor Angela Merkel in the Israeli parliament). Online. Available at www.welt.de/politik/article1814071/Das-sagte-Kanzlerin-Angela-Merkel-vor-der-Knesset.html (accessed 19 April 2013).

Dyson, K. (1994) *Elusive Union: The Process of European Economic and Monetary Integration*, New York, Longman.

Dyson, K. (ed.) (2002) *European States and the Euro: Europeanization, Variation, and Convergence*, Oxford: Oxford University Press.

Falke, A. (2006), 'German Trade Policy: The Decline of Liberal Leadership', in H.W. Maull (ed) *Germany's Uncertain Power: Foreign Policy of the Berlin Republic*, Houndmills: Palgrave Macmillan: 185–98.

Government of the Federal Republic of Germany (2012) *Shaping Globalization – Expanding Partnerships – Sharing Responsibility, A strategy paper by the German Government*, Berlin: Federal Foreign Office. Online. Available at https://www.auswaertiges-amt.de/cae/servlet/contentblob/616558/publicationFile/169957/Gestaltungsmaechtekonzept%20engl.pdf (accessed 25 September 2013)

Haftendorn, H. (2006) *Coming of Age, German Foreign Policy Since 1945*, Lanham, MD: Rowman & Littlefield.

Hanrieder, W.F. (1989) *Germany, America, Europe: Forty Years of German Foreign Policy*, New Haven: Yale University Press.

Hanrieder, W.F. (1995*) Deutschland, Amerika, Europa: Die Außenpolitik der Bundesrepublik Deutschland, 1949 bis 1994*, Paderborn: Schöningh.

Hansen, N. (2002) *Aus dem Schatten der Katastrophe: Die deutsch-israelischen Beziehungen in der Ära Konrad Adenauer und David Ben Gurion*, Düsseldorf: Droste.

Hellmann, G. and Roos, U. (2007) *Das deutsche Streben nach einem ständigen Sitz im Sicherheitsrat: Analyse eines Irrwegs und Skizzen eines Auswegs* (INEF-Report 92/2007), Universität Duisburg-Essen: Institut für Entwicklung und Frieden.

Jelinek, Y.A. (2004) *Deutschland und Israel 1945–1965: Ein neurotisches Verhältnis*, Munich: Oldenbourg.

Lütticken, F. (2006) *Die europäische Handelspolitik in GATT/WTO*, Baden-Baden: Nomos.

Maull, H.W. (1990/91) 'Germany and Japan: The New Civilian Powers', *Foreign Affairs*, 69(5): 91–106.

Maull, H.W. (2000) 'Germany and the Use of Force: Still a "Civilian Power"?' *Survival*, 42(2): 56–80.

Maull, H.W. (2003) 'Die deutsche Nahostpolitik: Gescheiterte Ambitionen', in H.W. Maull, S. Harnisch, and C. Grund (eds) *Deutschland im Abseits? Rot-grüne Außenpolitik 1998–2003*, Baden-Baden: Nomos, 121–32.

Maull, H.W. (2006) 'Die prekäre Kontinuität: Deutsche Außenpolitik zwischen Pfadabhängigkeit und Anpassungsdruck', in M.G. Schmidt and R. Zohlnhöfer (eds) *Regieren in der Bundesrepublik Deutschland: Innen- und Außenpolitik seit 1949*, Wiesbaden: VS Verlag, 413–37.

Maull, H.W. (2011) 'Deutsche Außenpolitik: Orientierungslos', *Zeitschrift für Politikwissenschaft*, 1: 93–114.

Meiers, F.-J. (2006) *Zu neuen Ufern? Die deutsche Sicherheits- und Verteidigungspolitik in einer Welt des Wandels, 1990–2000*, Paderborn: Schöningh.

Müller-Brandeck-Boquet, G. (2012) 'Deutschland – Europas einzige Führungsmacht?', *Aus Politik und Zeitgeschichte*, 62(10): 16–22.

Noetzel, T. (2011) 'The German Politics of War: Kunduz and the War in Afghanistan', *International Affairs*, 87(2): 397–418.

Philippi, N. (1996) *Bundeswehr-Auslandseinsätze als außen- und sicherheitspolitisches Problem des geeinten Deutschland* (Europäische Hochschulschriften, Reihe 31, Band 318), Frankfurt a.m.: Peter Lang.

Roloff, R. (1996) *Auf dem Weg zur Neuordnung Europas: Die Regierungen Kohl/Genscher und die KSZE-Politik der Bundesrepublik Deutschland von 1988 bis 1992*, Cologne: SH-Verlag.

Rosecrance, R. (1986) *The Rise of the Trading State: Commerce and Conquest in the Modern World*, New York: Basic Books.

Rudolf, P. (2005) 'The Myth of the "German Way": German Foreign Policy and Transatlantic Relations', *Survival* 47(1): 133–52.

Rühl, L. (1998) 'Sicherheitspolitik: Nationale Strukturen und multilaterale Verflechtung', in W.-D. Eberwein and K. Kaiser (eds) *Deutschlands neue Außenpolitik, Band 4: Institutionen und Ressourcen*, Munich: Oldenbourg, 87–99.

Scholtyseck, J. (2003) *Die Außenpolitik der DDR*, Munich: Oldenbourg.

Schweigler, G. (1985) *Grundlagen der außenpolitischen Orientierung der Bundesrepublik Deutschland: Rahmenbedingungen, Motive, Einstellungen*, Baden-Baden: Nomos.

Hanns W. Maull

Staack, M. (2000) *Handelsstaat Deutschland: Deutsche Außenpolitik in einem neuen internationalen System*, Paderborn: Schöningh.
Szabo, S.F. (2004) *Parting Ways: The Crisis in German-American Relations*, Washington: Brookings.
Von Bredow, W. (1996) *Der KSZE-Prozeß: Von der Zähmung zur Auflösung des Ost-West-Konfliktes*, Darmstadt: Wissenschaftliche Buchgesellschaft.
Von Bredow, W. (2006) *Die Außenpolitik der Bundesrepublik Deutschland: Eine Einführung*, Wiesbaden: VS Verlag.
Von Krause, U. (2011) *Die Afghanistaneinsätze der Bundeswehr: Politischer Entscheidungsprozess mit Eskalationsdynamik*, Wiesbaden: VS Verlag.
Von Staden, B. (1990) *Der Helsinki-Prozeß*, Munich: Oldenbourg.
Weingardt, M.A. (2002) *Deutsche Israel- und Nahostpolitik: die Geschichte einer Gratwanderung seit 1949*, Frankfurt a.m.: Campus.
Winkler, H.A. (2000) *Der lange Weg nach Westen II: Deutsche Geschichte vom 'Dritten Reich' zur Wiedervereinigung*, Munich: C.H. Beck.
Wolfssohn, M. and Brechenmacher, T. (2007) 'Israel', in S. Schmidt, G. Hellmann, and R. Wolf (eds) *Handbuch zur deutschen Außenpolitik*, Wiesbaden: VS Verlag: 506–20.

26

Germany and America, 1949–2012

James Sperling

This chapter considers Germany's position within the Atlantic order, particularly its relationship to the United States. The analysis is framed by the dynamic interaction of the geostrategic and geo-economic interests of the United States and Germany. The trajectory of the postwar order inexorably elevated Germany's geostrategic importance to the United States, particularly with respect to its policy of containment. Germany's geo-economic importance was the product of the 'economic miracle' of the 1950s in conjunction with the strategic over-extension of the United States, particularly in south-east Asia. The economic consequences of the US strategy of containment eventually manifested as the abandonment of the Bretton Woods fixed exchange rate system in 1973 and engendered conflicts between the United States and Germany on the management of the transatlantic economy and the distribution of the costs attending the defence of the West. The Cold War centrality that Germany enjoyed in US foreign policy calculations was challenged by the changed post-Cold War strategic context, the rising strategic and economic importance of China for the United States, and Germany's continuing inability and unwillingness to assume a proportionately robust and responsible role in meeting the challenges posed by growing global disorder. This change in Germany's salience to the United States can be traced to two bilateral factors: first, disagreements on macro-economic management after the collapse of the international financial system in 2008, conjoined to the parochialism of German economic statecraft when dealing with the eurozone debt crisis; and the highly caveated German participation in NATO out-of-area operations, which has shifted US attentions to France and Britain as America's most important and dependable allies. The cumulative impact of these developments has been Germany's relative decline as a key partner on many issues at the top of the American foreign policy agenda.

The postwar importance of the Federal Republic of Germany (FRG) in US foreign policy calculations was derived in part from the American grand strategy of containing the expansion of Soviet power (a key component of which was the forward defence of the United States (US) from German territory), in part from the sustained uncertainty over the strategic and diplomatic consequences of German domestic political developments, and in part from the postwar emergence of Germany as an economic power and possessor of the second most important reserve currency after the dollar.[1] Americans viewed the Federal Republic as a partner (in managing the transatlantic economy), a subaltern (in acquiescing to shifts in the American deterrence strategy), and an ATM (in financing European integration and America's informal empire). Post-Cold War, however, the German role has undergone a significant change, although the change has been more pronounced in the realm of security than in economy (where German policy rarely deviated from a narrow national interest). Germany has shed the roles of subaltern and ATM, and has redefined the content and limits of its partnership with the US on military-strategic issues. These changes may be attributed to a shift in structure (the end of bipolarity, the transformation of NATO into a voluntary alliance, and the fluidity of the contemporary international system), in status (unification and the eradication of the vestigial elements of the occupation regime), and in expectations (German responsibility for supplying regional and global order).

The transatlantic economy

The entrenched metanarrative of Germany's postwar foreign economic policy revolves around the rising trajectory of its economic capacity and gradual emergence as a joint manager of the transatlantic economy. That narrative, with significant caveats, was carried over into the post-unification period, but also anticipated the emergence of a dominant if not hegemonic Germany in Europe and its unqualified status as America's most important European partner. The primary source of postwar German leverage with the US was economic. American macro-economic policy and the management of the dollar episodically vexed the transatlantic relationship between 1957, when American Treasury Secretary Robert B. Anderson first pressed for a revaluation of the Deutsche Mark (DM) to ease the American balance of payments deficit, and 2002, when the euro replaced the DM. The twin goals of German macro-economic policy – a stable DM–dollar exchange rate and domestic price stability – brought Bonn into persistent conflict with Washington over American macro-economic policies geared to sustaining full employment and economic growth at the expense of price stability, the financing of overseas military operations – notably the wars in Korea, Vietnam, Iraq, and Afghanistan – with borrowing on global markets, and escalating American demands for burden sharing to offset the costs of containment until 1989 and global governance thereafter.

1949–1989

The deterioration of Soviet-American relations in the late 1940s and the outbreak of the Korean War in 1950 enabled Chancellor Konrad Adenauer to exploit the military and economic potential of West Germany to gain American support for the interrelated objectives of rearmament, reunification, and full sovereignty (Hanrieder 1989). America and Germany enjoyed convergent economic interests for most of the 1950s: both promoted the multilateralisation of the European trade and payments system as the first step towards the goal of European economic integration and the eventual convertibility of Europe's currencies. German and American trade and monetary preferences, paradoxically perhaps, began to diverge with the success of those policies by 1958. During this decade, Germany successfully linked security and economic policies in German-American relations, but that linkage slowly became a source of American leverage as the American payments position continued to deteriorate and Germany's remained in chronic surplus. Successive German governments acceded to administration demands that Germany support the dollar in exchange for security; in the 1967 Blessing Letter, the Bundesbank (German central bank) promised to refrain from converting excessive dollar balances into gold. That promise eased the international strain on the dollar and enabled the Johnson Administration to continue financing the war in Vietnam and Great Society programmes without regard to the requirements of external equilibrium.

The centrality of the dollar in the Bretton Woods fixed-rate monetary regime lent the US an ability to finance its payments deficits with its own liabilities. Although successive German governments fretted over the danger of 'imported inflation' in the 1950s, American macro-economic policy went seriously awry in the 1960s. At the same time, the Bundesbank, with the support of the Chancellors Ludwig Erhard and Kurt Georg Kiesinger, pursued a single-minded anti-inflationary policy (consistent with societal expectations and the provisions of the Bundesbankgesetz) that placed increasing pressure on the $–DM rate and the Bretton Woods fixed exchange rate system generally. Moreover, the German unwillingness to accommodate inflation and revalue a seriously undervalued DM left the Bundesbank in a policy bind that could be solved only in Washington. As the American payments position deteriorated, inflationary pressures continued unabated, and American macro-economic policies remained unmindful of its external consequences, frictions arose between the US and Germany that were played out in tedious negotiations over defence burden sharing reinforced by congressional threats, in the form of the perennial Mansfield Amendment, to reduce unilaterally the number of American troops stationed in Europe.

President Richard Nixon initiated a retrenchment of American commitments consistent with the progressive erosion of America's hegemonic position. The Nixon-Kissinger strategy encoded a subtle change in the American attitude towards Europe and accepted that an economically powerful Europe marked the 'end of American tutelage and the end of an era of automatic unity' (Nixon 1972: 40). The downgrading of US commitments and the shedding of responsibilities, embodied in the Nixon Doctrine, paired American retrenchment with the expectation that Europe would assume greater responsibilities for supporting the trade and monetary regimes created and supported by US power since 1945. The Nixon Administration endeavoured to force Europeans to assume greater responsibility for their own military and economic security and to pay a higher price for a hedged American security guarantee.

When the Nixon Administration declared 1973 to be the 'Year of Europe', it made explicit the American desire to rebalance American-European relations. Just as military-strategic parity with the Soviet Union necessitated the acceptance of the military and political status quo in Europe, economic parity within the Atlantic economy required a revision of the rules governing the postwar monetary and trade systems and the redistribution of the burdens attending an open world economy. The administration warned that if outstanding trade and monetary disputes were left unresolved they would inevitably spill over into other areas, including the American security guarantee. Chancellor Willy Brandt (1973: 689) acknowledged the need for such a recalibration to avoid a permanent rift in the Atlantic community, but also wanted to restrict that re-ordering to the 'Atlantic zone of partnership' that defined the boundaries of Germany's legal obligations under the North Atlantic Treaty.

The continuing US reluctance to relinquish its hegemonic prerogatives despite its relative decline vis-à-vis Europe generated open and acrimonious debates on the reform of the international monetary system, the American elevation of fair trade as the organising concept of the Atlantic trading system, the (un)desirability of increased trade with the Soviet Union, the response of the NATO member states to the oil crisis in 1973, and the discord surrounding the appropriate macro-economic response (accommodation or adjustment) to the quadrupling of oil prices in 1973–4. The key expression of German dissatisfaction with the management of the American economy was the effort to achieve some form of monetary autonomy from the US. The 1969 Werner Plan, the first major step towards European monetary union, fell victim to the monetary turbulence of the 1970s. The travails of the dollar forced Germany to float the DM unilaterally in May 1971. The Nixon shock in August 1971, which negated the pledge to exchange gold for dollars held by central banks, was followed by the generalised float of the dollar in 1973, a rapid rise in the value of the DM, and an unwanted reserve role for the DM. The task of aligning Germany's trading and currency interests was first addressed with the joint float of most European currencies in 1973, and the eventual emergence of a DM-dominated currency bloc performed the triple trick of buffering the DM and German economy from the gyrations of the dollar, preserving the price competitiveness of German goods in its major European market, and enabling the Germans to export their deflationary bias in macro-economic policy to Europe.

German vulnerability to energy supply disruptions provided another source of discord in German-American relations in the 1970s, particularly after the US announced that it would no longer guarantee European oil supplies in the event of a Middle East oil embargo or supply disruption, an eventuality that became a reality with the October 1973 Arab-Israeli war. The subsequent oil embargo and quadrupling of oil prices brought to the surface the contradictions and tensions not only of Germany's energy security policy, but of its economic and strategic interdependence with the US. A secure supply of oil required, at a minimum, that Germany remain classified as a neutral in the conflict by the Arab states and avoid alienating its primary source of natural gas, the embargoed Netherlands. After the Dutch threatened to suspend natural gas deliveries to the rest of the European Community, West Germany implemented a policy of energy diversification that clashed with US foreign policy preferences, particularly when the Reagan Administration sought (and failed) to impose an embargo on the sale of large-diameter pipe to the Soviet Union in 1982. Germany resisted American pressure owing to a number of factors: diversification was essential for national security, the sale of Soviet natural gas and oil on the European market would provide hard currency for the purchase of German exports, closer commercial relations with the Soviet Union would help insulate German-Soviet relations from the Reagan Administration's bellicosity, and Germany lacked a compelling reason to follow the American lead owing to the degraded security guarantee and what was perceived as a fickle and dangerous foreign policy.

This decade-long conflict over energy policy paralleled continuing macro-economic conflicts. The Carter Administration's hapless stewardship of the American economy reinforced the German view that only a European solution would insulate Germany from the twin dangers of imported inflation (exacerbated by the oil crisis) and export non-competitiveness posed by a rising DM. The decision to create the European Monetary System (EMS) at the 1978 Bremen summit represented a German-led declaration of monetary independence from the US and the dollar. President Carter's belated rescue package for the dollar in November 1978 and initial EMS success in creating a European 'zone of monetary stability' introduced a brief period of economic comity in the Atlantic economy that was promptly undone by the Reagan Administration.

The Reagan Administration's monetary and fiscal policies confronted Germany with a macro-economic nightmare: an anti-inflationary macro-economic policy and budget deficits occasioned by deep tax cuts that required high American interest rates which, in turn, distorted German macro-economic policy and the dollar–DM exchange rate. By 1983 the Bundesbank regularly described the DM as the 'antipolar' currency of the dollar: that is, the value of the DM was invariably inversely related to the value of the dollar and no longer reflected German macro-economic conditions. It was also believed that an ever-appreciating dollar and high US interest rates forced the Bundesbank to follow more restrictive policies than domestic conditions required; the antipolar role of the DM subordinated the Bundesbank's monetary policy to the requirements of external balance rather than to the domestic goals of economic growth and reducing structural unemployment.

The Reagan Administration dismayed the Germans with continued denials that there was a connection between high real interest rates, an overvalued dollar, and massive American trade deficits. Moreover, different political and economic priorities at either end of Pennsylvania Avenue ruled out any significant reduction of the budget deficit, the dollar's overvaluation, or the trade deficit. Once the administration acknowledged that a 'strong' dollar did not translate into a 'strong' America as fears of deindustrialisation and a rising Japan accelerated, the US retreated from its earlier insistence that the market determine the dollar's value. When Washington turned to Bonn and Tokyo to reverse the dollar's climb in September 1985, it found a reluctant and suspicious partner in the Federal Republic. The difficulties of striking a sustainable bargain with the Plaza Agreement in 1985 and Louvre Agreement in 1987, particularly the inability of the US to make good the promise to implement macro-economic policies consistent with internal and external balance and the October 1987 stock market crash, led Germany to question the American leadership role in the transatlantic economy. In 1988 the German economics minister, for example, noted that the absence of a *legitimate* hegemon in the international system required cooperation among the major industrialised economies and heralded the emergence of a multipolar world. Although America's pre-eminence was not challenged, the legitimacy of an American leadership role was made contingent upon the ability of the US to reduce its budget deficit, 'the *conditio sine qua non* for more order and balance in the world economy' (Bangemann 1988: 849). This assessment was not shared in the US; American Treasury Secretary Nicholas Brady noted that concerns over the American deficits were 'exaggerated or unwarranted' (Sperling 1990: 91).

The task facing the Federal government and Bundesbank in the 1980s was to strike a balance between the economic imperatives of price stability, exchange rate stability, and policy convergence within the EMS on the one hand, and the political imperative of monetary coordination with the US on the other. German experience demonstrated that the drive to sustain Germany's commercial dominance of Europe and to maintain stable cross exchange rates could not be conducted independently of American macro-economic policies. This asymmetrical interdependence of West German and American macro-economic policies helps explain not only a recurring source of German-American economic conflicts and frictions between 1958 and 1989, but the German willingness to exchange the DM for the euro with the Maastricht Treaty, signed in 1992 and implemented in 1993.

1990–2012

The postwar *Wirtschaftswunder* gave way to the *Wirtschaft ohne Wunder* for most of the 1990s. The global recession in the early 1990s created yet another period of German-American discord on macro-economic policy: while the Federal Reserve implemented countercyclical interest rate policies to fulfil its growth mandate, the Bundesbank – with the blessing of the Kohl Government – raised interest rates to combat the inflation attending unification. For the Americans, German policy presented a barrier to a Europe-wide recovery; for the Germans, the Bundesbank was simply discharging its sole responsibility to protect the internal value of the DM. Ironically, the US and a unified Germany traded places in the early 1990s: the Americans criticised the Germans for following a Reaganesque macro-economic policy of high interest rates and unsustainable budget deficits. By the end of 1992, the Germans, Americans, and Japanese had abandoned the coordination of macro-economic rate policies and adopted the Sinatra Doctrine: each state would pursue macro-economic policies dictated by domestic rather than systemic conditions. Despite the global economic recovery in the second half of the 1990s, German governments faced slow economic growth and unemployment attributed to structural rigidities in the economy compounded by the mistakes of unification, particularly the unwarranted rise in eastern German wages by government fiat and the undeserved purchasing power lent eastern Germans with the favourable rate of exchange between the West and East German marks. Moreover, the Kohl Government assumed that the *Fonds Deutsche Einheit*, capitalised at DM100 billion, would cover the costs of unification. Instead, those costs amounted to almost $1.9 trillion between 1990 and 2009 (Reuters 2009). The attending indebtedness ended Germany's cheque-book diplomacy – its postwar source of diplomatic leverage – and contributed to the relative 'failure' of the German strategy for European Monetary Union (Sperling 1994 and 2010). Rather than creating a hard currency area comprising France, Germany, and the Netherlands, which the convergence criteria all but guaranteed in 1992, Germany was saddled with a monetary union that allowed almost any state to join irrespective of its fiscal circumstances (see Chapter 22). Moreover, the EMU removed the one source of leverage that Germany could directly and autonomously exercise vis-à-vis the US: namely, the ability to discipline American macro-economic and exchange rate policies owing to the growing reserve and transaction roles of the DM inside and outside Europe. A hard currency area comprising a few like-minded countries would have produced a European central bank immune to American pressures to adopt macro-economic policies inconsistent with the needs of the European economy, and capable of enforcing Europe-wide conformity with German macro-economic preferences without the fiscal liabilities that became all too apparent with the eurocrisis.

The onset of the deepest recession since the 20th century's Great Depression in 2007 – the collapse of Lehman Brothers and subsequent meltdown of the global financial system in 2008 – and the largely uncoordinated policy responses of the world's major economies represented the first major post-unification macro-economic crisis in German-American relations. In this iteration, however, American policymakers were relatively indifferent to German economic interests or policy preferences. This relative decline of Germany in American macro-economic calculations reflects one important institutional change and a number of structural developments: the European Central Bank (ECB) manages Europe's money, London rather than Frankfurt remains Europe's most important financial centre, the German role in the real and financial sectors of the American economy has declined since 1989, and most critically, American macro-economic policy is increasingly oriented towards reassuring its Pacific creditors.

The German government insisted that the causes of the financial crisis were 'made in America': the Federal Reserve pursued a too-expansive monetary policy; the regulatory frameworks governing banks and non-banks in the financial system were ineffective; and the domestic sub-prime crisis led to a $1.4 trillion loss that spread to the eurozone economies (BMWi 2008). Chancellor Angela Merkel also blamed 'reckless speculation' on the American property market, a lack of transparency in American financial markets, and excessive deficit spending in the wake of 11 September 2001 as contributory factors (*Financial Times* 2009). These specific criticisms of American macro-economic policy eventually took the shape of a full-blown German critique of the Anglo-Saxon economic model and the joint Franco-German suggestion that America (and Britain) 'bow to the European model' (*Financial Times* 2009; Sanger and Landler 2009). Yet German criticisms of American policy ignored Germany's own culpability in the crisis: a global 'savings glut' (attributed to unsustainable Chinese, German, and Japanese current account surpluses) provided the source of easy credit that fuelled the financial bubble that burst in 2008 (Furceri and Mourougane 2009: paras 15–25).

The growing German distemper with the American response to these crises, particularly in the person of Finance Minister Peer Steinbrück, revealed a persistent rhetorical division between the US and Germany with respect to the most appropriate macro-economic and regulatory policy responses to the financial crisis and recession. By the time of the April 2009 G-20 summit, Chancellor Merkel, along with French President Nicolas Sarkozy, insisted that a return to economic growth depended upon the creation of an effective regulatory framework that restored confidence to global financial markets; they rejected both the efficacy and necessity of additional fiscal stimulus. American President Barack Obama, with qualified support from British Prime Minister Gordon Brown, preferred a two-track strategy that shared the Franco-German goal of restoring stability to the financial markets via regulatory reform, but also pushed for a coordinated fiscal stimulus among the G-20 countries to prevent the recession from descending into depression. Chancellor Merkel resisted additional German fiscal stimulus: an economic recovery in Germany, given the openness of the national economy, depended upon the recovery of foreign demand for German exports rather than an up-tick in domestic consumption. Consequently, she encouraged other countries to adopt more expansive fiscal policies to increase global demand, suggesting in March 2009 that China 'do more' because the Chinese government could avoid increasing its level of debt *and* China had a greater growth potential than Germany (Wolf 2009). German resistance to increased deficit spending was not entirely unreasonable: first, the German fiscal packages for the period 2009–10 amounted to 3.5 per cent of national GDP; and second, the output gap in the German economy, which had shrunk to 3.3 per cent (lower than any country other than France), did not justify additional fiscal stimulus (Benoit 2009; BMWi 2008).

The deterioration of the American fiscal position was the joint product of the tax cuts introduced during the George W. Bush Administration, the total costs of stabilising the national banking system, the loss of revenue and higher financial outlays attending the recession and slow economic growth, and the concurrent wars in Iraq and Afghanistan. The American budget deficit as a share of GDP amounted to almost 14 per cent in 2009, and US Federal gross debt as a share of GDP rose from 69.7 per cent in 2008 ($9.98 trillion) to 107.4 per cent in 2013 ($17.6 trillion).[2] The looming fiscal crisis in the US has been aggravated by the inability of President Barack Obama and the US Congress to enact a budget that would restore fiscal balance without pushing the economy back into recession. At the same time, the unsustainable fiscal positions of the southern eurozone countries, particularly Greece, underscored the difficulty of protecting the single currency until the ECB could credibly claim to be the lender of last resort during the process of fiscal rebalancing.[3] These European macro-economic imbalances, the purgatory of uncertainty plaguing the euro, and the inability of the US to put its fiscal house in order differed from past macro-economic crises in the Atlantic economy: neither the US nor Germany could exert any meaningful influence on the policy choices of the other, since those policy choices remain hostage to internal political and institutional dysfunctions.

Transatlantic security

Germany straddled the major fault line of the Soviet-American contestation for European hegemony. The American policy of containment sought to halt the expansion of Soviet power and deny the Soviet Union access to the resource-rich and industrialised regions of the world, foremost among them western Europe. Postwar American diplomacy encouraged western European political and military integration as the means of strengthening the European pillar of the Western alliance, allaying French concerns over a renascent Germany, restoring German sovereignty on terms mutually acceptable to Germany and its neighbours, and embedding Germany in binding multilateral frameworks. Over the course of the 1950s and 1960s, German and American diplomacy was largely complementary, although that concordance was increasingly strained as Washington accommodated the strategic consequences of nuclear parity with the Soviet Union in the 1970s and 1980s. The end of the Cold War and the growing strategic salience of extra-European developments have revealed deep and abiding conflicts over security policy and the purposes of the Atlantic alliance.

1949–1989

The most immediate postwar Allied objectives were German disarmament and the demilitarisation of the German economy. The exigencies of the Cold War required a policy reversal, but German rearmament took place within a NATO in which Germany was not quite equal: of the NATO member states, only German armed forces were directly responsible to a NATO commander, rather than a national general staff, and the Allies retained the right to scrutinise the categories of armaments Germany could possess or manufacture. This state of affairs only ended in 1990 with the Treaty on the Final Settlement with Respect to Germany.

The American goal of an Atlantic community resting on the twin pillars of NATO and European economic integration suited German interests. Germany's centrality for the US pivoted on containment's negative purpose of denying the Soviet Union access to European human and industrial capital with the positive goal of enhancing the security and welfare of the entire transatlantic area. Washington's desire to rearm Germany, particularly after the outbreak of the Korean War, reflected the recognition that America was unable to defend Asia and Europe simultaneously. But rearmament confronted the US with the dilemma of simultaneously providing security *for* and *from* Germany (Hanrieder 1989: 39). After the failure of the European Defence Community (a French-designed multilateral framework controlling a rearmed Germany), German sovereignty was returned, with significant caveats, with the 1954 Paris Treaty. Germany was only then permitted to join NATO and rearm.

The Soviet launch of Sputnik in 1957 called into question the American strategy of 'massive retaliation' and the credibility of the extended nuclear deterrent. To remedy the strategic fallout from Sputnik, the Kennedy Administration replaced massive retaliation with the dual strategies of 'mutually assured destruction' with respect to strategic nuclear weapons and 'flexible response' with respect to the forward defence of Europe. While these two strategies were complementary and enhanced the credibility of the US security guarantee, they also created two separable geostrategic spaces. To allay the fear of abandonment, the Kennedy Administration offered Europe President Dwight D. Eisenhower's plan for a NATO-based multilateral nuclear force. The offer caused disquiet in Moscow; it interested neither Paris nor London, but found favour in Bonn. When the Johnson Administration unceremoniously dropped the proposal in 1963 without prior consultation with Chancellor Erhard, an enthusiastic supporter, it did nothing to assuage Bonn's doubts about the constancy of the American guarantee.

Despite the general congruity of German and American strategic objectives in Europe, conflicts did arise when Bonn was forced on occasion to choose between Paris (without which no progress on European integration was possible) and Washington (the only credible guarantor of German security). But the underlying diplomatic tension in German-American relations revolved around the appropriate level of engagement with the Soviet Union and Warsaw Pact member states. When the Hallstein Doctrine was unveiled in 1955 after the establishment of the German Democratic Republic (GDR), that policy of withholding or withdrawing diplomatic recognition from any state recognising the GDR was not inconsistent with American diplomacy. Yet as both the US and the Soviet Union became more interested in stabilising the European diplomatic and military-strategic status quo, the Hallstein Doctrine and West Germany's preoccupation with unification threatened the unspoken Soviet-American solution to the 'German problem' – a permanently divided Germany. The *Ostpolitik* initiated by the grand coalition in 1966 and accelerated after the election of Willy Brandt as Chancellor in 1969 raised fears in Washington that Germany might be tempted to exchange its loyalty to the West (*Westbindung*) for unification.

As the Soviet Union and the US fast approached nuclear parity, the US began its 'retreat from empire' in 1968 with the election of President Richard Nixon (Osgood 1973). The Nixon Doctrine, which reduced America's global military commitments, inevitably caused alarm in German foreign policy circles, raising fears of a Nixon Doctrine for Europe (Kaltefleiter 1973). Despite the fundamental convergence of German–American strategic interests in Europe and the unfulfilled fear of an American strategic retrenchment from Europe, the 1970s revealed divergent interests *outside* Europe that foreshadowed conflicts after 1989 over 'out-of-area' operations (see below).

The oil crisis, and the 1973 Middle East war precipitating it, sparked a serious diplomatic crisis when the US transhipped military materiel to Israel from German territory. This episode, sparked by Germany's desire to retain its 'neutral' status in the Middle East conflict and protect its oil supply, revealed a willingness to resist American policy outside Europe when German national interests were at stake. The deterioration in German–American relations – the joint product of nuclear parity, a palpable American weariness with foreign entanglements, and the conflicts that emerged over the 1973 war and its aftermath – accelerated with the election of President Jimmy Carter in 1976.

Chancellor Helmut Schmidt had difficulty concealing his contempt for Carter, particularly after the latter's decisions to deploy and then not deploy the neutron bomb. That inconstancy cost Schmidt political capital at home, threatened, in Schmidt's estimation, the eurostrategic nuclear balance, and set the stage for intense conflicts over the deployment of intermediate nuclear forces (INF) in the early 1980s. Schmidt's collateral suspicions regarding American intentions were sustained with the leak of Presidential Review Memorandum 10, which proposed sacrificing a third of Germany's territory before the first use of tactical nuclear weapons, and an emergent eurostrategic imbalance favouring the Soviet Union. Schmidt's 'two-track' proposal to modernise theatre nuclear weapons and restore the strategic balance in Europe had two components: NATO would forgo INF modernisation in exchange for the withdrawal of Soviet INF already deployed in the European theatre; in the absence of such a bargain, NATO would deploy Pershing II and cruise missiles in Europe.

NATO adopted Schmidt's proposal, but it required the US to enter into good faith negotiations with the Soviet Union, which were not forthcoming. The Reagan Administration's intemperate and vilifying rhetoric ushered in a 'new' Cold War, made all the more precarious by the unveiling of the strategic defence initiative, which itself threatened to upend the strategic balance of terror that had maintained the postwar status quo. Moreover, the Reagan Administration was convinced of the strategic utility of deploying modernised INF in Europe. Chancellor Schmidt reasonably concluded that the US had not acted in good faith, had failed to meet the conditional aspect of his proposal, and had provided the grounds for non-deployment on German soil. The departure of Chancellor Schmidt in October 1982 and the 1983 election of Helmut Kohl as chancellor eventually reintroduced diplomatic calm to German–American relations. Bonn agreed to the deployment of Pershing missiles after a fierce domestic debate, but the subsequent Soviet-American double-zero agreement in 1988 compelled the Germans not only to accept the withdrawal of the Pershing IIs stationed in Germany, but to surrender the Pershing IAs under German control. This American *volte-face* on nuclear weapons deepened existing suspicions that the American security guarantee was hedged and stoked fears of singularisation: a nuclear war in Europe would be restricted to German territory. President Ronald Reagan's more circumspect and constructive diplomacy vis-à-vis the Soviet Union in his second term hastened the end of the Cold War, the dissolution of the Soviet Union, and the unification of Germany – an outcome embraced in Washington and Bonn if nowhere else.

1990–2012

NATO cohesion and West German obeisance to American strategic preferences depended upon the persistence of three postwar conditions: Europe remained the prize in the superpower competition, the division of Germany was a perpetual feature of the European state system, and German neutrality was not an option. The end of the Cold War and unification negated each condition. Just as the strategy of containment had elevated Germany's strategic importance to the US, its post-1992 redundancy diminished it. Germany went from being at the epicentre of the Cold War to merely occupying the centre of Europe.

The 1990 treaty liberated Germany from many of the postwar legal, institutional, and psychological inhibitions imposed upon it by NATO membership and from a non-negotiable dependence upon the American security guarantee. All postwar restrictions on German sovereignty remaining from the end of World War II evaporated. In exchange, Germany reaffirmed its adherence to the Non-Proliferation Treaty (NPT) and accepted the restriction of the German armed forces to 370,000 individuals under arms in the Conventional Forces in Europe Treaty (CFE). The NPT did not preclude German possession of nuclear weapons within a politically unified EU, and the limitations placed on Germany by the CFE Treaty were neither onerous and punitive nor one-sided. The Berlin Republic remains embedded in NATO as a full, equal, voluntary partner, but also enjoys the hypothetical option of exit.

The Cold War devalued the German contribution to a NATO bereft of an existential threat and preoccupied with the projection of force for peacekeeping and crisis management operations 'out of area'. The US Defense Department identified Germany as America's most capable conventional military ally during the Cold War, but those assessments neither considered German force projection capabilities nor expected Germany to acquire them. Post-unification, the US Defense Department focused on Germany's marginal contributions to allied force projection capabilities, the development of which constituted the primary goal of the NATO defence capabilities initiative. Even though Germany still contributes the largest European share of NATO ground combat forces, four factors limit the utility of that contribution: first, German forces were trained and equipped to fight the wrong kind of war in the wrong place at the end of the Cold War; secondly, the post-Cold War transformation of the German armed forces has fallen foul of budgetary constraints; thirdly, the Bundeswehr can deploy only approximately 10 per cent of its armed forces (far below NATO's 50 per cent deployability goal); and finally, German forces are subject to some of the most restrictive caveats in combat operations (Sperling 2010; Sperling and Webber 2009).

One irony of post-unification German foreign policy is that a Red-Green coalition first embraced the use of German military power out of area.[4] How did Germany make the journey from refusing to provide anything other than logistical or financial support for out-of-area operations, notably in the first Gulf War and non-combatant roles in the former Republic of Yugoslavia between 1992 and 1995, to becoming a regular participant in NATO-sponsored peacekeeping and peacemaking missions? As Lothar Rühl (2001: 110) has noted, the Erhard and Kiesinger Governments committed the German military to peacekeeping operations in Cyprus (1964) and to a NATO naval formation in response to a blockade of Israel (1967). But restrictions on the use of German military force out of area became a quasi-constitutional principle over the course of the SPD/FDP tenure between 1969 and 1982. That principle was inviolate until the 1994 Federal Constitutional Court decision. It found no barrier to the participation of German troops out of area, subject to a UN mandate authorising the use of force and Bundestag approval. Germany thereafter committed combat troops to NATO operations in Afghanistan (2001–14), Bosnia-Herzegovina (1995–2004), the former Yugoslav Republic of Macedonia

(2001–3) and Kosovo (1999-present), and has participated in allied naval operations in the eastern Mediterranean (2001-present) and the Horn of Africa (2001-present).

The amicable relationship between Chancellor Helmut Kohl and Presidents George H.W. Bush and Bill Clinton did not survive the elections of Chancellor Gerhard Schröder and President George W. Bush. Schröder's decision to challenge the Bush Administration's Iraq policy during the 2002 German parliamentary elections poisoned bilateral relations; the German chancellor promised German non-participation in an American-led operation even *with* a UN mandate, and US Defense Secretary Rumsfeld dismissed Germany (and France) as 'old Europe'. Germany aligned itself with France and the Russian Federation against the US at the United Nations and then blocked (along with Belgium and France) the American request in the North Atlantic Council to provide military assistance to Turkey prior to the war. It is probably impossible to know whether a mismatch of personalities aggravated already manifest divergences of German and American interests outside Europe (see Merkl 2005; Szabo 2007). In any event, this episode blighted German-American relations until Chancellor Angela Merkel charted an Atlanticist course correction. Merkel nonetheless avoided becoming a direct party to the American occupation of Iraq. The most important lesson, however, is not the immediate cause or aftermath of the German-American fissure, but the relative unimportance of Germany to the US when it decided to push ahead with the Iraq invasion, and the negligible costs incurred by German defiance of American demands.

NATO operations in Afghanistan (2002–14) and Libya (2011), as well as the stationing of Patriot missiles in Turkey in 2013, reveal the continuing evolution of Germany's assessment of its security role and definition of its obligations to the US outside Europe. Turkey and Afghanistan demonstrate Germany's commitment to NATO's collective defence obligation arising from Article 4 and 5 contingencies respectively. Libya demonstrated that Germany will abstain from participation in a NATO military operation if it falls outside collective defence, if it violates the German national interest, or if buck passing is a viable option.

The Carter Administration's adverse reaction to the Soviet invasion of Afghanistan reportedly led Chancellor Helmut Schmidt to declare 'Kabul ist nicht Bonn'. Chancellor Gerhard Schröder did not have the option of declaring similarly that 'Kabul ist nicht Berlin' after 11 September 2001. The invocation of Article 5 and the safe haven afforded al-Qaeda by the ruling Taliban made German participation in Operation Enduring Freedom (OEF) and the follow-on UN-mandated International Security Assistance Force (ISAF) a critical test of its fidelity to the alliance and the US. The Bush Administration, despite the invocation of Article 5, chose to conduct a national operation to evict the Taliban from Afghanistan, but welcomed national contributions tightly aligned with American military objectives. A limited number of NATO allies, including Germany, made significant contributions to ground combat operations and devoted an impressive share of national naval and air assets to OEF. American gratitude for that German contribution to the eviction of the Taliban was relatively short-lived once high intensity combat operations had ceased. NATO assumed command of ISAF in 2003, and the task of stabilising and reconstructing Afghanistan commenced.

The German contribution to ISAF (as well as that of other allies) initiated a new round of recriminations over burden sharing within the alliance and contributed to renewed American doubts about NATO's future. Although Germany contributed the second largest number of NATO-Europe troops to ISAF after the United Kingdom, closely followed by France, Germany did not contribute a proportionate share of troops based on the common measure of burden sharing.[5] Afghanistan also renewed the debate begun in the Balkan conflicts over intra–alliance risk-sharing. Germany was a primary target for US discontent: then US Defense Secretary Robert Gates claimed that the level of risk avoidance in Afghanistan foreshadowed a two-tier alliance,

435

where some allies do the fighting while others stand aside. German armed forces operated almost exclusively in the 'safe' northern and western regional commands, and have been subject to a large number of caveats on their deployment and to some of the most restrictive rules of engagement of the major NATO states. Afghanistan also revealed a gap between the German theory and practice of networked security: the German level of bilateral and multilateral aid for the purposes of reconstruction and stabilisation neither set it apart from the other major NATO states nor matched the German position that the underlying problem in Afghanistan (and elsewhere) requires a broad approach favouring the civilian instruments of statecraft.

Libya underscored the lack of allied consensus on member-state obligations in those cases where a military operation serves milieu-shaping policies rather than collective defence. NATO's Operation Unified Protector (OUP), the first UN-authorised military intervention against a ruling government on the basis of the 'responsibility to protect', initiated a crisis of participation within the alliance that went far beyond earlier burden sharing debates. Only 13 NATO allies made any direct military contribution (Belgium, Bulgaria, Canada, Denmark, France, Greece, Italy, the Netherlands, Romania, Spain, Turkey, the UK, and the US), and five of those 10 European states – Bulgaria, Spain, Greece, Romania, and Turkey – abjured a direct combat role, while Italy assumed one only reluctantly in late April 2011. Even more troubling were the allies with significant military capabilities, notably Germany and Poland, who declined to participate.

Germany's non-participation underscored an apparent scepticism towards utility of force as an instrument of statecraft, illustrated the political and constitutional limitations on the use of force, revealed the gap between German rhetoric and action with respect to international law, and raised the suspicion that Germany sought to further its commercial interests by siding with China, Russia, India, and Brazil on the UN Security Council. With the commencement of OUP, Berlin withdrew from NATO command all German naval and air force personnel in the Mediterranean as a matter of constitutional necessity, but in exchange offered to redeploy German AWACS crews to Afghanistan as a sign of 'alliance solidarity'. The Merkel Government concluded that it did not have a positive obligation to enforce UNSCR 1973 and the 'responsibility to protect' was not viewed as a compelling principle of action. These doubts were widely shared in the Bundestag and most agreed with the coalition government's assessment that enhanced economic sanctions alone could achieve the goals of UNSCR 1973 (Merkel 2011; Deutscher Bundestag 2011a: 10815–16, 10819–20, 10825–6; 2011b: 11140–2, 11145, 11149–52).

The German Ministry of Defence, in revised defence policy guidelines published after the onset of the NATO mission in Libya, established that the future use of force must answer in the affirmative 'the question of whether German interests require and justify an operation and [determine] what the consequences of non-action would be' (German Ministry of Defence 2011: 4). The government and opposition (in varying degrees) justified German inaction via a fourfold reinterpretation of multilateralism. First, Germany delegated responsibility for enforcing UN Security Council Resolution (UNSCR) 1973 to a coalition of regional actors (notably Persian Gulf states) and questioned whether it was a Western responsibility to intervene. Second, Germany was required only to observe UNSCR 1973, not to enforce it. Third, Germany was acting multilaterally insofar as it joined approximately one half of the NATO member states in abstaining from OUP, supported the formation of an EU military humanitarian force for Libya (EUFOR Libya), and cast an abstention on UNSCR 1973 with four other rising powers – Russia, China, Brazil, and India. And finally, Germany's NATO membership no longer meant that wherever NATO led, Germany would automatically follow (Deutscher Bundestag 2011b: 11145).

The foreign policy elite was more critical of the German abstention at the UN and withdrawal of German forces from NATO command than the Obama Administration. Former

Foreign Minister Joschka Fischer (2011) called the decision the 'greatest debacle since the founding of the Federal Republic', while others claimed that Germany was an 'undependable alliance partner' (Schmidt 2011; Varwick 2011) and 'the funeral director of alliance politics' (Stefan Kornelis, cited in Erlanger and Dempsey 2011). Eighteen months later, the Merkel Government – perhaps chastened – quickly agreed (along with the US and the Netherlands) to provide Turkey with Patriot missiles and up to 400 German support personnel to deter a Syrian attack on Turkish territory (Deutscher Bundestag 2012b: 3–4). The government carefully identified the international legal obligation (the Turkish request for an Article 4 consultation) and constitutional propriety (Article 24(2) of the German constitution) of the action (Deutscher Bundestag 2012b: 1). In the parliamentary debate authorising the deployment, members of the government claimed that this action demonstrated Germany's reliability as an alliance partner and that the alliance could depend upon the Bundestag to act responsibly and with dispatch (Deutscher Bundestag 2012c: 26553; 26560).

Conclusion: German multilateralism and German–American relations

Scholarly literature on the transatlantic relationship has tried to capture the limits of Germany's role in Europe and possibilities for partnership with the US, both before and after 1990. Some scholars focus on Germany's structural position in the Atlantic economy, describing it as a hegemonic or dominant power (Hütter 1978; Markovits and Reich 1997; Kreile 1978), while others focus on German behaviour, describing Germany as a 'reluctant power' or 'reluctant hegemon' (Meiers 1995; Bulmer and Paterson 2013), a 'civilian power' (Harnisch and Maull 2001), a Europeanised power (Bulmer *et al.* 2000), a 'normalized power' (Bulmer and Paterson 2011; Opperman 2012) or a 'responsible power' (Ischinger 2012). Despite these various assessments, there is a general consensus in the scholarly community – with notable exceptions – that German foreign policy has exhibited a reflexive multilateralism, a self-imposed 'culture of restraint', a profound scepticism towards the use of force, and the eschewal of a narrow *raison d'état* in favour of *raison de communauté*.

These components of German foreign policy have undergone subtle and not-so-subtle evolutions since unification: the reflexive multilateralism of the postwar period has been replaced with a flexible multilateralism that is not solely defined by the *Westbindung* (Sandschneider 2012), the exercise of German power in the national interest has modified the 'culture of restraint' to include the option of not acting with its allies or the broader international community, and fidelity to international law has been narrowly defined as conformity with law rather than a responsibility to enforce it. German policy responses to the postwar monetary crises and macro-economic policy conflicts were narrowly national in purpose and instrumentally multilateral. This narrow conception of economic interest was in full view during the 2008 financial crisis and has framed the German response to the eurocrisis. The Merkel Government, like those before it, insists that the lessons of Germany's historically disastrous *Sonderweg* frame the multilateral debate on the management of the global economy and euro, and excuse Germany from taking robust and effective military action in Afghanistan (and indirectly in Libya). This privileging of German history is matched by an unwillingness to accept as equally valid other national metanarratives or the policy preferences embedded in them; German governments, for example, appear indifferent to the toll austerity programmes are taking on fragile democracies in southern Europe.

So long as German governments could credibly claim, as they could over the course of the postwar period, to be America's most important NATO ally and macro-economic counterpart, their 'lessons' of history had to be taken seriously in Washington and elsewhere. Neither claim is as credible today. The changed structure of power, the resiliency of German democracy, and the successful unification of Germany have removed the security pathologies that originally lent the transatlantic bargain its force. The crises testing the German–American relationship in the early 21st century reflect the changed contexts of that bilateral relationship. Just as Germany is no longer dependent upon the American security guarantee, America has become increasingly dependent upon its Asian creditors to finance domestic consumption and wary of rising powers along the Eurasian periphery. Nonetheless, America and Germany remain allied militarily for good reason and are linked economically out of necessity. But the essential nature of that relationship is undergoing a transformation that will either contribute to a stronger transatlantic community built upon a foundation of greater equality or engender an estrangement arising out of mutual indifference and strategic drift.

Notes

1   With the end of the World War II, Germany was truncated and divided into the American, British, French, and Soviet zones of military occupation. The Americans, British, and French combined their zones of occupation and formed the Federal Republic of Germany in 1949, while the Soviet zone of occupation eventually became the German Democratic Republic (GDR). To avoid any confusion, this chapter uses Germany and the Federal Republic interchangeably; any reference to the GDR will be explicit.
2   The level of publicly held debt amounted to 40.5 per cent and 74 per cent of GDP in 2008 and 2012, respectively, while the amount of publicly held debt rose from $5.8 trillion to $12.6 trillion between 2008 and 2012 (OMB 2012).
3   That claim gained credibility after ECB President Mario Draghi promised that the bank would do 'whatever it takes' to protect the euro (*Wall Street Journal* 2012).
4   The 1998 parliamentary election produced a coalition government between the Social Democratic Party and Alliance 90/The Greens; it is commonly referred to as the Red-Green coalition, reflecting the colour associated with each party respectively.
5   The burden sharing index for Germany (derived from the German share of troops/share of NATO GDP) was less than unity (.64) and reveals a significant level of free-riding (Sperling 2010: 56–8).

Bibliography

Bangemann, M. (1988) 'Weltwirtschaft im Wandel', *Bulletin*, 91 (1 July): 849–52.
Benoit, B. (2009) 'Berlin warns US on inflation spiral', *Financial Times*, 18 March.
Brandt, W. (1973) 'Exchange of toasts between Chancellor Brandt and President Nixon at the White House', *Department of State Bulletin*, 68 (28 May): 688–9.
Bulmer, S. and Paterson, W.E. (2011) 'Germany and the European Union: from "tamed power" to normalized power?' *International Affairs*, 86(5): 1051–73.
Bulmer, S. and Paterson, W.E. (2013) 'Germany as the EU's reluctant hegemon? Of economic strength and political constraints', *Journal of European Public Policy*, 20(10): 1387–1405.
Bulmer, S., Jeffery, C., and Paterson, W.E. (2000) *Germany's European Diplomacy: Shaping the Regional Milieu*, Manchester: Manchester University Press.
Bundesministerium für Wirtschaft und Technologie (BMWi) (2008) *Schlaglichter der Wirtschaftspolitik: Sonderheft Finanzkrise*, 13 November, Berlin: BMWi.
Deutscher Bundestag (2011a) *Stenografischer Bericht, Plenarprotokoll 17/95*, 95. Sitzung, 17. Wahlperiode, 16 March, Berlin: Deutscher Bundestag.
Deutscher Bundestag (2011b) *Stenografischer Bericht. Plenarprotokoll 17/97*, 97. Sitzung, 17. Wahlperiode, 18 March, Berlin: Deutscher Bundestag.
Deutscher Bundestag (2012a) 'Antrag der Bundesregierung. Entsendung bewaffneter deutscher Streitkräfte ... vom 4. December 2012', *Drucksache 17/11783*, 17. Wahlperiode, 6 December, Berlin: Deutscher Bundestag.
Deutscher Bundestag (2012b) 'Beschlussempfehlung und Bericht des Auswärtigen Ausschusses (3. Ausschuss)', *Drucksache 17/11892*, 17. Wahlperiode, 6 December, Berlin: Deutscher Bundestag.

Deutscher Bundestag (2012c) *Stenografischer Bericht, Plenarprotokoll 17/215*, 215 Sitzung, 17. Wahlperiode, 14 December, Berlin: Deutscher Bundestag.

Erlanger, S. and Dempsey, J. (2011) 'Germany Steps Away from European Unity', *New York Times*, 23 March. Online. Available at www.nytimes.com/2011/03/24/world/europe/24germany.html?page wanted=all (accessed 23 September 2013).

Financial Times (2009) 'We all want to put the global economy back on its feet' (interview with Angela Merkel), 28–9 March.

Fischer, J. (2011) 'Deutsche Aussenpolitik – eine Farce'. Online. Available at www.sueddeutsche.de/politik/streitfall-libyen-einsatz-deutsche-aussenpolitik-eine-farce-1.1075362 (accessed 23 September 2013).

Furceri, D. and Mourougane, A. (2009) 'Financial Crises: Past Lessons and Policy Implications', *Economics Department Working Papers No. 668*, ECO/WKP(2009)9.

German Ministry of Defence (2006) *White Paper 2006 on German Security Policy and the Future of the Bundeswehr*, Berlin: Ministry of Defence.

German Ministry of Defence (2011) *Defense Policy Guidelines*, Berlin: Ministry of Defence.

Hanrieder, W. (1989) *Germany, Europe, America: Forty Years of West German Foreign Policy*, New Haven: Yale University Press.

Harnisch, S. and Maull, H.W. (eds) (2001) *Germany as a Civilian Power? The foreign policy of the Berlin Republic*, Manchester: Manchester University Press.

Hellman, G. (1996) 'Goodbye Bismarck? The Foreign Policy of Contemporary Germany', *Mershon International Studies Review*, 40 (supplement 1): 1–39.

Hütter, J. (1978) 'Die Stellung der Bundesrepublik Deutschland in Westeuropa: Hegemonie durch wirtschaftliche Dominanz?', *Aus Politik und Zeitgeschichte*, 2 (13 January): 103–13.

Ischinger, W. (2012) 'Germany after Libya: Still a responsible power?', in T. Valasek (ed.) *All alone? What US retrenchment means for Europe and NATO*, London: Centre for European Reform, pp. 45–60.

Kaltefleiter, W. (1973) 'Europe and the Nixon Doctrine: A German Point of View', *Orbis*, 18: 75–94.

Kreile, M. (1978) 'Die Bundesrepublik Deutschland – eine "économie dominante" in Westeuropa?', *Politische Vierteljahreschrift*, Sonderheft 9: 236–56.

Markovits, A.S. and Reich, S. (1997) *The German Predicament: Memory and Power in the New Europe*, Ithaca: Cornell University Press.

Maull, H.W. (2001) 'Germany's foreign policy, post-Kosovo: still a "Civilian Power"?' in S. Harnisch and H.W. Maull (eds) *Germany as a Civilian Power? The Foreign Policy of the Berlin Republic*, Manchester: Manchester University Press, pp. 106–27.

Meiers, F.-J. (1995) 'Germany: The Reluctant Power', *Survival*, 37: 82–103.

Merkel, A. (2011) 'Regierungserklärung von Bundeskanzlerin Angela Merkel zum Europäischen Rat am 24./25. März 2011 in Brüssel', 24 March. Online. Available at www.bundesregierung.de/Content/DE/Regierungserklaerung/2011/2011–03–24-merkel-europaeischer-rat.html (accessed 23 September 2013).

Merkl, P. (2005) *The Rift Between America and Old Europe: The Distracted Eagle*, Abingdon: Routledge.

Nixon, R. (1972) *US Foreign Policy for the 1970s: The Emerging Structure of Peace. A Report to the Congress by Richard Nixon, President of the United States*, Washington: White House.

Office of Management and Budget (OMB) (2012) *Historical Tables. Budget of the US Government Fiscal Year 2013*, Washington: OMB. Online. Available at www.whitehouse.gov/omb/budget/Historicals (accessed 23 September 2013).

Opperman, K. (2012) 'National Role Conceptions, Domestic Constraints and the New "Normalcy" in German Foreign Policy: the Eurozone Crisis, Libya and Beyond', *German Politics*, 21(4): 502–19.

Osgood, R.E. (1973) *Retreat from Empire? The First Nixon Administration*, Baltimore: Johns Hopkins University Press.

Reuters (2009) 'Study Shows High Cost of German Reunification', 7 November. Online. Available at www.reuters.com/article/2009/11/07/us-germany-wall-idUSTRE5A613B20091107 (accessed 23 September 2013).

Rühl, L. (2001) 'Security Policy: National Structures and Multilateral Integration', in W.-D. Eberwein and K. Kaiser (eds) *Germany's New Foreign Policy: Decision-Making in an Interdependent World*, Basingstoke: Palgrave Press, pp. 102–16.

Sandschneider, E. (2012) 'Deutschland: Gestaltungsmacht in der Kontinuitätsfalle', *Aus Politik und Zeitgeschichte*, 62(10): 3–9.

Sanger, D.E. and Landler, M. (2009) 'In Europe, Obama Faces Calls for Rules on Finance', *New York Times*, 2 April.

Schmidt, H. (2011) 'The opposite of calculability: An interview with former German chancellor Helmut Schmidt', *Internationale Politik*, 4: 47–53.

Sperling, J. (1990) 'West German Foreign Economic Policy during the Reagan Administration', *German Studies Review*, 13: 85–110.

Sperling, J. (1994) 'German Foreign Economic Policy after Unification: The End of "Cheque Book" Diplomacy?' *West European Politics*, 17(1): 73–97.

Sperling, J. (2010) 'Germany and America in the Twenty-first Century: Repeating the Post-war Patterns of Conflict and Cooperation', *German Politics*, 19(1): 53–71.

Sperling, J. and Webber, M. (2009) 'NATO – From Kosovo to Kabul', *International Affairs*, 85(3): 491–511.

Szabo, S.F. (2007) 'The German American Relationship after Iraq' in H.W. Maull (ed.), *Germany's Uncertain Power: Foreign Policy of the Berlin Republic*, Basingstoke: Palgrave, pp. 122–36.

Varwick, J. (2011) 'Unzuverlässiger Bündnispartner: Ist Deutschland aussenpolitich isoliert?' *IP-Journal*, 22 August. Online. Available at https://zeitschrift-ip.dgap.org/de/article/19225/print (accessed 29 September 2013)

Wall Street Journal (2012) 'Stock Futures Jump on Draghi's "Whatever It Takes" comment', 26 July. Online. Available at http://blogs.wsj.com/marketbeat/2012/07/26/stocks-jump-on-draghis-whatever-it-takes-comment/ (accessed 29 September 2013)

Wolf, M. (2009) 'Why G20 leaders will fail to deal with the big challenge', *Financial Times*, 1 April.

27

Sport politics

Jonathan Grix

This chapter looks at the unusually important role that Germany has played in manipulating sport for non-sporting ends. It argues that Germany has played a major role in influencing the manner in which other states have used sport for political aims. The core focus will be on two case studies: an in-depth discussion of the role of the German Democratic Republic (GDR) in fostering the political use of sport; and the more recent example of Germany's hosting of the 2006 FIFA World Cup. If the 1936 Berlin Olympics are looked upon as the first mega-event in sports history, the GDR can be understood as the first state systematically to exploit (elite) sport for political purposes. In fact, it is fair to suggest that, without the unprecedented global success of GDR athletes, East Germany might never have been recognised as a *de jure* state in the first place. The second case study deals with the successful leveraging of a major sports event (the 2006 World Cup) to change Germany's poor national image abroad as a result of the atrocities wrought by the Nazi regime. It is argued that the success of 2006 has influenced a number of other states to bid for and host sports mega-events in order to alter and improve their international image.

Germany has played a central role in the use of sport for political ends. Four key examples illustrate Germany's impact on the development of sport and on sport's manipulation for political purposes: first, the so-called 'Hitler Olympics' of 1936, arguably the first sports mega-event, which has influenced subsequent sports mega-events (these generally refer to the Olympics and the FIFA World Cup, but they include so-called 'second order' events (Black 2008) such as the Commonwealth or Pan American Games); second, the Munich Olympics, held in democratic West Germany in 1972, which saw the first political use of a major sporting event by terrorists and greatly influenced the manner in which subsequent such events have been 'securitised' (Cornelissen 2011; Houlihan and Giulianotti 2012); third, the manipulation of elite sport in East Germany for political gains, which resulted in arguably the most successful sports system ever known (the key characteristics of this system – minus the systematic doping – are to be found today in most advanced capitalist states); and finally, Germany's hosting of the 2006 FIFA World Cup. The success of this and the impact it had on Germany's international image, it could be argued, have influenced recent and future mega-event hosts from 'emerging' states. In what follows, the unprecedented politicisation of sport by East Germany is the backdrop for a discussion of unified Germany's successful attempt to use a sports mega-event to change its (negative) image abroad.

By way of introduction, it is worth reflecting briefly on the two German Olympics. Although the Nazi dictatorship (1933–45) lasted only 12 years, it produced one of the very first politicised sports mega-events in modern history: the 1936 Olympic Games in Berlin. The so-called 'Hitler Olympics' (or 'Nazi Olympics') is widely recognised as the first and most blatant use of sport for political purposes. Young (2010: 96) labels the event 'the pinnacle of Olympic spectacle', comparable to the 'Hollywood show' of Los Angeles in 1984 (also known as the most commercial Games up until that time) and Beijing's bombastic affair in 2008. The Berlin Olympics were immortalised by Leni Riefenstahl's beautiful, and extremely controversial, documentary of the whole event, *Olympia* (Riefenstahl 1938/2006). Both Riefenstahl and Joseph Goebbels, Hitler's infamous propaganda minister, worked hard to create the impression of a link between the philosophical and aesthetic Greek origins of the Olympic Games and the emerging Third Reich. Riefenstahl, the author of infamous propaganda films such as *Triumph of the Will* (*Triumph des Willens*, 1935), begins her epic documentary-style film of the Games by making a transition from ancient Greece to modern Germany, the prologue capturing physically perfect athletes against a backdrop that includes shots of ancient Olympia. Riefenstahl's link with antiquity ties in with the symbolism of Olympism and the lofty ideals of world peace espoused by the movement. Goebbels oversaw the introduction of the torch relay, the idea for which is generally credited to the sports administrator Carl Diem. The practice continues to this day (Hilton 2008), and sees a torch lit in Athens and carried by a succession of runners to the country in which the Games are taking place. Miah and Garcia (2012) point out the difference between the original motives for instigating the relay, which were to propagate the Nazi regime, and its use now, as an integral part of community engagement by the Olympic movement, in an attempt to whip up enthusiasm for the event rather than the hosts.

Adolf Hitler's sporting dictum, recorded in his prison-penned biography, *Mein Kampf* (My Struggle), was as follows: 'Not a day should go by in which a young person does not receive at least one hour of physical training in the morning and one hour in the afternoon, covering every type of sport and gymnastics' ('Es dürfte kein Tag vergehen, an dem der junge Mensch nicht mindestens vormittags und abends je eine Stunde lang körperlich geschult wird, und zwar in jeder Art von Sport und Turnen'; Hitler 1926: 410); this sentiment was echoed in Walter Ulbricht's (East German head of state, 1960–73) rather more catchy slogan (in the original German, that is): 'everyone, everywhere, should take part in sport once a week' ('Jeder Mann, an jedem Ort, einmal in der Woche Sport'; DDR-Wissen 2013). Hitler, like Ulbricht, was fully aware of the political potential of sport. Although Hitler was not known as a sporty type, he recognised the enthusiasm that accompanied national success in sports such as football. And sport fitted well with an ideology based on a cult of youth, strength, and genetic and racial endowments. Sport lends itself to the simplistic narratives of dictatorships. The binary opposites available in the arena of sport assist in drawing comparisons: contestants meet 'one-to-one', they go 'head-to-head'; usually sport is 'black and white', with clear rules and a clear winner or loser; participants' performances are judged as good or bad; and so on. Modern sport, with its emphasis on 'measuring' or 'quantifying' performance, exact times, national, European, and world records, distances, and, above all, medal tables, appears to fit well with the crass racial distinctions made by the Nazis and the simplistic *Klassenkampf* (class war) mentality of the Socialist Unity Party (Dennis and Grix 2012). Interestingly, in his study of the 1936 Games, Young concludes that the extravagant show put on by the Nazis – including 10,000 dancers performing a play and a 3,000-strong choir (Senn 1999) – did little to change perceptions of the country abroad, despite intense propaganda efforts (Young 2010). Yet in the 21st century, showcasing the host nation and attempting to improve a state's international image are what drives hosts of sports mega-events more than any other reason for hosting (Grix 2012).

The events that took place in Munich in 1972 are a reminder of the Janus-faced nature of sports mega-events, especially the Olympic Games. Schiller and Young (2010), in their excellent in-depth study, carefully trace and uncover the meticulous planning and considerable effort Germany put into preparations for the 1972 Games. A few days prior to the deaths of 11 Israeli Olympic team members and one West German policeman during a kidnap attempt by the Palestinian group Black September (five group members were also killed), a 16-year-old German had won the Olympic high jump. Had the event finished there, the 'joyous leap to victory might well have stood as a metaphor for West Germany's successful rehabilitation on the world stage through the Olympics' (Schiller and Young 2010: 2). Unfortunately, politics viciously interrupted sport, completely overshadowing the planned 'coming out' party for the Germans, who were hoping to use the event to signal their successful transformation from defeated aggressor to democratic economic powerhouse.

The brief description possible here does little to unravel the complexities of what the 1972 Games meant: the bitter German-German rivalry and the GDR's delight at being able to use its own insignia for the first time in an Olympics, or deeper debates about 'overcoming' or 'mastering' Germany's recent history and how this affected the institutional and psychological development of Germany and the Germans. But it reminds us of the risks involved in staging a major sports event and the legacies of Munich. Munich can be read as the starting point for the 'securitisation' of mega-events, which reached its apogee at the recent London 2012 Games. In London, measures taken to prevent a Munich-type security disaster included surrounding the Olympic park with an 11-mile, £80 million, 5,000-volt electric fence, and providing more troops than those deployed at the time for the war in Afghanistan (approximately 13,500). The UK even stationed anti-aircraft missiles on residential roofs close to the Olympic park (Graham 2012).

East Germany and the politicisation of sport

The East German dictatorship, founded in 1949, the same year as the Federal Republic, lasted almost four times as long as the Third Reich (1933–45). The 'German Democratic Republic' was initially a pariah state in terms of international political legitimacy. Its founders were well aware of the power and potential of sport as a political tool, and as early as 1948 Erich Honecker, then Head of the Free German Youth movement (*Freie Deutsche Jugend* or FDJ) in the Soviet zone and a future leader of the Socialist Unity Party (SED) and the East German state, declared that 'sport is not an end in itself, but the means to an end' (Holzweissig 2005: 1), effectively anticipating the politically focused use of sport by the GDR just prior to its inception.

East Germany's political instrumentalisation of sport for international recognition and legitimacy remains unparalleled. I shall argue that East Germany's success in elite sport has had far-reaching and unintended consequences, and that the sports model developed and refined in the GDR continues to shape modern-day elite sports in advanced capitalist states. There is a certain irony in the fact that East Germany collapsed, yet its sporting legacy continues to influence its erstwhile opponents. Mike Carlson, who wrote the obituary for *The Guardian* on the death in 2002 of Manfred Ewald, the architect of much of the GDR sport model, aptly observed that 'despite being disgraced, in the end he [Ewald] had won, because the entire sporting world followed down the path he had blazed' (Carlson 2008; Younge 2002). Not only do the central tenets of this system live on in the 21st century, but it would appear that the most successful elite sports systems globally are beginning to converge around a GDR-influenced model.

Success in elite sport was intended to promote the tiny state of about 17 million citizens and gain it desperately needed recognition, as it was constantly in the shadow of its richer and bigger neighbour, West Germany. Examples of sport as a central part of nation-building abound – take Australia and its rather more recent attempts to construct a sense of community around sporting success (Stewart *et al.* 2004) – but none compare with the efforts of East Germany, with its serious legitimacy deficit and lack of a cohesive 'national' history or culture, to gain *de jure* international recognition. Andrew Strenk perhaps overstated the 'soft power' role of sport when he suggested, as early as 1978, that the usual measures of 'trade, commerce, diplomacy and negotiation were not available to the GDR for use in influencing the world beyond the borders of Eastern Europe', so it instead 'turned to sports as a medium of cultural diplomacy to obtain [its] foreign policy goals' (Strenk 1978: 348–9). Nonetheless, in 1969 official East German documents demanded not only that elite sport should contribute more to an 'increase in the international authority and image of the GDR', but also that sporting success ought to indicate the 'growing strength of the GDR' (Dennis and Grix 2012: 19) – clear indications that elite sport success was intended to influence world opinion on East Germany.

This was achieved by making a swift and impressive impact on the world of elite sport, improving from seven summer Olympic medals in 1956 (as part of a 'unified' German team) to a staggering 102 at the state's last Olympics in Seoul in 1988 (Dennis and Grix 2012; see also Beamish and Ritchie 2006). The 1970s can be understood as the period in which the GDR finally began to gain the recognition from the international community that it craved. After formal recognition of the East German Olympic Committee by the International Olympic Committee in 1965, East Germany had to wait until the Munich Olympics, organised by its *Klassenfeind* (class enemy), West Germany, in 1972, before it was able to compete as a wholly independent national team, complete with national flag, national anthem, and national kit (Riordan 1999).[1] While the Munich Olympics in 1972 can be understood as the beginning of the securitisation of the Games, it also signals a high point in the pursuit of politics through elite sport by the GDR. The GDR not only beat its West German neighbours at their home Games, but the GDR flag and national anthem became commonplace and were televised around the world to a global audience watching and listening to the event. It is quite clear that the GDR leadership perceived a positive correlation between the achievement of their sportsmen and -women and the international standing of the state, with East German sport representatives dubbed 'diplomats in tracksuits' (Holzweissig 1981) because of their contribution to breaking the diplomatic deadlock and isolation of their country (Dennis 1988). Yet in an official document from 1970, in the run-up to Munich, East German sport officials rather hypocritically accused their cousins next door of 'using sport and sports performances for the purpose of underpinning the political aims of West German imperialism' (Dennis and Grix 2012: 20).

Another East German legacy that has relevance for sport politics today is the intense and successful propaganda undertaken by the regime via the elaborate provision of mass sport in a unique combination with elite sport, where the former provided a 'throughput' of raw material for the latter. This has had a clear impact on how politicians and governments in advanced capitalist states view sport policy. A majority of states, including the UK, now build their sports policies on the premise that elite sport success inspires the masses to take up sport and thereby produces a 'pool' of potential talent whence future Olympians will come. This 'virtuous cycle' of sport (Grix and Carmichael 2012) has its roots, in part, in a misreading of GDR sport history. It impacts directly on, for example, the UK's Olympic legacy claims (see below). Stewart *et al.* (2004: 53) provide a clear example of how Australia, too, was taken in by the GDR's propaganda when it came to assessing the link between community or mass sport and elite sporting success: in the 1970s the Confederation of Australian Sport, making the case for more sport funding, even 'cited East Germany as an exemplar of good sport policy since it funded both elite and community sport'. While East Germany was at pains to explain its success in terms of an harmonious and mutually beneficial relationship between elite and mass sport – in part to cover up a systematic doping programme – in fact part of the success of the system was keeping elite sport separate from mass sport, channelling the majority of scarce resources into elite sport, and focusing on specific sports with the best chance of medal success.

The East German model and its impact on contemporary sport politics[2]

If the belief in a 'virtuous cycle' of sport discussed above is a GDR legacy, then another and perhaps more profound one is the influence the GDR sports model has had and continues to exert on the majority of states that excel at elite sport (apart from the US, which depends on its collegiate system). Most states successful in elite sport exhibit systems based on the core characteristics of the East German model. Table 27.1 below indicates the similarities between modern-day sports systems and the GDR and places them in context by comparing them with a range of different regime types. Of the 10 areas of influence listed in the table, the following can be understood as generic characteristics that have stood the test of time:

• a government-led sport policy;
• government funding for sports and full-time athletes;
• a system of talent identification;
• the professionalisation of coaching;
• the integration of sports science/medicine in attempting to improve athletes' performance.

These core tenets of an elite sport development model can be found in, or have been employed in, advanced capitalist states such as the UK, Canada, New Zealand, Australia, Norway, the Netherlands, and unified Germany, as well as in China, which despite its consumer approach to communism is still a dictatorship. It is around such tenets that successful elite sports models appear to be 'converging' (for an earlier comparative discussion of elite sport models and the influence of East Germany on them see also the work of Green and Oakley 2001; Green and Houlihan 2005; Collins and Green 2007).

The clearest example of the GDR's impact on modern elite sports systems is Australia, which studied the East German set-up carefully and took steps to introduce an up-to-date, technologically advanced version of the sports 'miracle' (Dennis and Grix 2012). Interestingly, the UK – and for Olympic purposes, Great Britain – has adopted many of the characteristics of the Australian (and by default, the East German) model of sport. However, the UK rarely (and never positively) mentions the GDR in UK sport policy documents, while Australia is held in very high regard, even revered. The UK Government Department for Culture, Media and Sport (DCMS) produced a strategy document in 2002 in which the authors asserted:

> we can learn lessons from Australia. Their purposeful pursuit of sporting excellence, sustained by Government in partnership with sporting bodies, has resulted in Australia becoming, on a per capita basis, by far the most successful sporting nation in the world.
>
> (DCMS 2002: 7)

An indicator of East Germany's influence on Australia came in the run-up to the Sydney Olympics in 2000 when Ekkart Arbeit, the former East German coach, was controversially signed up as their director of coaching (*Independent* 1997).

Table 27.1 Key characteristics of select countries' sports models (GDR, Australia, UK, China and the US)

	East Germany	Australia	UK/GB	China	US
Regime type	Socialist dictatorship	Democracy	Democracy	Communist dictatorship	Democracy
1 Rationale for investment in elite sport	International prestige; domestic 'feelgood' factor/identity	International prestige; domestic 'feelgood' factor/identity participation/health	International prestige; domestic 'feelgood' factor/identity participation/health	International prestige; domestic 'feelgood' factor/identity	International prestige; domestic 'feelgood' factor/identity
2 Policy type	Olympic-driven, Government-led sport policy	Olympic-driven, Government-led sport policy	Olympic-driven, Government-led sport policy	Olympic-driven, Government-led sport policy	Distinct lack of Government involvement in elite sport; US Olympic Committee drives sport policy
3 Management/ governance type	Technical-rational/ instrumental approach ('Old' PM)	New Public Management	New Public Management	Technical-rational/ instrumental approach	Not applicable
4 Underlying philosophy	Ideologically-driven (socialist) professionalism/ win at all costs attitude	Ideologically-driven (capitalist) professionalism/ win at all costs attitude; 'virtuous cycle' of sport	Ideologically-driven (capitalist) professionalism/ win at all costs attitude; 'virtuous cycle' of sport	Ideologically-driven (consumer communist) professionalism/win at all costs attitude	Ideologically-driven (capitalist) professionalism/ win at all costs attitude; focus almost exclusively on elite sport in colleges/ universities
5 Talent ID	Systematic talent ID and youth development (initially drawing on USSR)	Well developed, systematic talent ID programme built on GDR model	Outline of a talent ID system that draws on Australia and Canada	Systematic talent ID and youth development (similar original roots as GDR)	Well developed talent ID systems through professional sport/high school/universities

6 (Central) State funding for sport and athletes	Athletes effectively full time or given jobs to suit	Athletes offered scholarships and career and education support	Very small group on tiered funding scheme according to their chances to 'medal'	All 'professional' athletes full time and receive wages directly from the state	Funding administered by USOC to NGBs. Tiered funding scheme according to NGB medal success.
7 Coaching and Training	Comprehensive system of coaching and coaches; training treated as a science	Funded athletes given access to top-level coaching and training facilities	Funded athletes given access to top-level coaching and training facilities	Comprehensive system of state coaching and training	College/university athletes given access to top-level coaching and training facilities
8 Sport science/medicine	Advanced and integrated sport science and medicine	Comprehensive system attempting to mesh sports science and medicine	Fledgling system of science and sport medicine	Advanced and integrated sport science and medicine	There is a lack of integrated sport science and medicine programmes
9 Sport facilities and competition	Top-class sport facilities; wide network of sport schools; frequent competition from young age	Network of state of the art facilities	Loose network of English Institutes of Sport based on Australian example	Top-class sport facilities; wide network of sport schools; frequent competition from young age	Top-class and wide-ranging sport facilities; wide network of college and inter-collegiate/university sport; frequent competition
10 Focus on specific sports	1969 decree to split sports into funded and non-funded crucial to later success	AIS decision to focus on specific Olympic sports	Game Plan discusses the need to focus on 'medal intensive' sports	China remains world leading in specific sports: table tennis, gymnastics; traditionally focused on specific events	Sports leading to professional career favoured

Source: Dennis and Grix, 2012; Stotlar et al., 2006 and Sparvero, Chalip and Green, 2008

An excellent example of policy transfer from the GDR to contemporary sports systems is the area of coaching. The GDR set the standard for the professionalisation of coaching in terms of both quality and quantity, with literally thousands of coaches propping up the sport system, many of them volunteers. Australia's coaching system, which influenced the UK, was in turn influenced by Canada's system. Canada, whose high level of state involvement in sport earned it the nickname the 'GDR of the Commonwealth' (Macintosh *et al.* 1987), is yet another advanced capitalist state to draw upon the East German dictatorship's sport system for inspiration. The GDR is thus the starting point for a chain of policy transfer: Canada adopts and develops its own specific coaching system based on the East German model; this is then imported and adapted in Australia; and that in turn influences thinking about how to shape the UK coaching system. A glance at Table 27.1 above reveals, however, that the US, still the most dominant Olympic superpower, has not been affected by the global developments and trends towards a convergence of elite sport development systems. In fact, Sparvero *et al.* suggest the US has developed elite sport 'amid the chaos' (2008: 260), a reference to the seemingly haphazard and uncoordinated make-up of the sport landscape in the US. Interestingly, perhaps, in the place one would presume East Germany's system to have had the most impact, unified Germany, there does not appear to have been much transfer from the sports 'miracle'. According to Busse (2010), Germany failed to pick out the best aspects of the East German model and implement them in the new, unified Germany. A dynamic German Olympic squad could have been produced consisting of the best of both Germanies. Busse picks up on many of the cornerstones of East Germany's success discussed above, such as the development of children and youths, and suggests that Germany should have learned lessons. It does appear, however, that a much watered-down version of the successful elite sports schools has been kept in Germany, with the *New York Times* claiming in 2002 that 'East Germany may be gone, but its sports system is being resurrected' (Pohl 2002). Forty-one 'sports schools' exist in unified Germany today, 18 of them taken over from the GDR (Deutscher Olympischer Sportbund 2013).

The 'sporting arms race' of the Cold War (Collins and Green 2007), led by the successes of East Germany, has clearly influenced the UK and a majority of advanced capitalist states in their sport policies. In the UK, for example, elite sport policy has been and remains the clear focus of attention for successive governments. Community sport and school sport, on the other hand, are of secondary importance. Evidence of this can be found in key UK sports policy documents: the Labour Government's *Game Plan* (2002) and *Playing to Win* (2008), both issued by the Department for Culture, Media and Sport. Both documents leave little doubt about whether international success through sport should be a key policy aim; rather, they discuss the process by which that can best be achieved.

The UK's new approach to funding athletes, which underpins the shift towards striving for elite sport success, is based on a so-called 'no-compromise' management system clearly linked to an Olympic-driven sport policy. It finds parallels in Australian, New Zealand, and Canadian sport policies. UK Sport is very clear that it intends to ensure that no national governing bodies of sport underperform, and that they are held accountable for the monies they receive, by publishing a

> series of 'Funding Release Triggers' that will ensure that the planning and governance of all the governing bodies is carefully monitored. *Those not able to meet the criteria over a range of key issues will have performance funding withheld as they modernise their practices and performance systems.* The triggers – which also require performance targets to be achieved – look to set in place a range of sound governance processes.
>
> (UK Sport 2008; my emphasis)

Two key points are to be taken from this. First, the manner in which sport is 'managed' and the associated discourse are very similar to practices in the GDR (see the discussion of the GDR's 'Old Public Management' in Dennis and Grix 2012). Target setting, checks and balances, feedback loops, reviews, reassessments, and so on are employed to ensure a continuous progression and improvement of the system (see also Bergsgard *et al.* 2007). Secondly, the elite-driven discourse in sport policy that underlies and affects most policy decisions remains unquestioned. Few dispute the underlying logic of the virtuous cycle of sport (see above); few outside academia appear interested in the fact that elite sport success and the holding of mega-sporting events do not appear to be linked to an upsurge in sustained mass participation. Evidence for the long-term effects of elite sport success on participation is hard to come by, but a report commissioned by Sport Canada came to the conclusion that 'there is little empirical evidence to support the anecdotal claims that high performance sport leads to social benefits such as building national pride [. . .] and encouraging healthy behaviours' (Bloom *et al.* 2006: ii). The lack of evidence for the 'elite sport–mass sport' causality has not, however, dampened governments' appetite for investment in elite sport, as the heavy investment in Olympic sports and the fierce competition to host sports mega-events by a range of states around the world testify.

The 2006 FIFA World Cup: improving Germany's image abroad

The final example of how Germany has been and continues to be influential in sport is the country's hosting of the FIFA World Cup in 2006. Once again Germany turned to sport for political purposes: it attempted – successfully – to use a sports mega-event to improve its negative and stereotypical image abroad. In particular, and importantly, the event was designed to effect a change in a negative international image based mostly on atrocities carried out during the Nazi era over 50 years before. The Germans adopted an innovative leveraging strategy (discussed in depth in Grix 2013a) – that is, a strategy that involved long-term, well planned campaigns to 'leverage' as much as possible out of the sports mega-event. This should be understood as an attempt actively to gain from hosting the event, rather than hoping for post-event 'legacies'. Germany prepared for hosting the 2006 World Cup by putting in place measures designed to improve the country's image and ensure an efficient, smooth-running event: a fan-centred approach, whereby fans were not seen as a 'problem' but were central to the success of the image improvement campaigns; and the generation of a 'feel good' factor among fans, visitors, and Germans alike.

Germany had started planning *before* it was even awarded the right to host the 2006 World Cup. Unlike many states, it took a proactive approach to hosting a mega-event. One key example of this will suffice. Horst R. Schmidt, Vice Chair of the 2006 FWC organising committee, described the strategy developed with the aim of improving Germany's image in the world and ensuring the success of the event thus:

> We developed a cluster of specific measures to achieve this. We launched a 'welcome tour' to *all* 31 countries qualified for the tournament. Franz Beckenbauer, the Chair of the organising committee, visited every country and received a high-level reception; he went to the countries to welcome them to Germany [. . .] this greatly influenced the media coverage of the event positively.
>
> (author interview with Schmidt, 2012; Grix 2013a: 297)

The 'cluster' of measures Schmidt refers to included several high-level campaigns that brought together politics, business, NGOs, civil society, and cultural organisations (Brauer and Brauer

2008). Well-orchestrated and resourced national and international campaigns were put together, funded, in the main, by the Federal government, but also with partners from business, FIFA, and the German Football Federation.

Interestingly, what the Germans were attempting – to alter a national image based in great part on outdated stereotypes – is conventionally deemed either impossible or extremely difficult to do (see Manzenreiter 2010 for the case of China; also Fan 2006). The Barcelona Olympics in 1992 is usually cited as the only exception to this rule (Horne and Manzenreiter 2006). However, given that Germany had suffered from an extremely negative image abroad for many years prior to 2006, it had little to lose and much to gain. Grix and Lacroix, writing before the event, note that to suggest

> that Germany has an image problem abroad would not be new. It remains the case that the legacy of the Third Reich, the barbarity of the Nazis and the bellicose behaviour in the early part of the 20th century has etched itself deep into the psyche of Germans themselves and that of their international partners. Germany's rich cultural history and her spectacular rise from ruins during the post-war period rarely figure in foreigners' perception of modern-day Germany, especially it seems in Britain.
>
> (Grix and Lacroix 2006: 373)

Given Germany's traumatic past, it had much to gain from attempting to reforge a national image that had 'remained fixed in the stereotypes established in two world wars' (Watt 1965: 114). Germany's postwar identity was built around the export-driven 'German model', based on a successful (social) democratic economic model also known as 'corporatism' (Hutton 1996). By 2006, however, the Germans wanted to move on from an image derived from history and the ability to make things. In 2004 the incoming Federal president, Horst Köhler, had suggested Germany should become 'more than the land of poets and thinkers' ('mehr als das Land der Dichter und Denker') and more than just 'Made in Germany' (Köhler 2004).

Postwar Germany was characterised by its lack of 'hard' power, by a strong commitment to multilateral institutional arrangements and the expanding European Union, and by its consistent efforts to convince foreign elites and publics alike that it had changed. 'Soft power' resources, in the shape of academic and cultural exchanges, were and remain the object of heavy investment with the purpose of changing Germany's negative image abroad (see Chapter 28). Organisations such as the German Academic Exchange Service and the Goethe Institut (receiving around €200 million per year; author interview with the German Foreign Office 2011) have set up cultural centres and undertaken campaigns throughout the world, and act as ambassadors for German culture and language (DAAD 2013; Goethe Institut 2013).

Indices of success?

Clearly one of the ways to dispel myths about foreign nationals, their nations, culture, and habits is to visit the country concerned. This section discusses how the World Cup provided the catalyst for Germany to showcase itself externally and, at the same time, offer an event that encouraged non-German nationals to travel to and around Germany, acquainting themselves with the nation and its people. Central to Germany's leveraging strategy was to improve its poor external image and break down entrenched stereotypical depictions of the Germans. Reports on Germany and the Germans in the British press, for example, have for decades touched on World War II and Nazism, or employed the stereotypical monikers of a 'dominant', 'arrogant', and 'dull' people. It is noticeable that since 2006 the British press, the worst offenders in the world for 'German bashing' – according to Gary Younge, the 'last "acceptable" prejudice' (Younge 2002) – appear to have become much better disposed towards Germany (Grix 2013a).

Incoming tourists and overnight stays by international travellers increased greatly in the context of this sports mega-event. Overnight stays by visitors from the UK rose in June and July 2006 by 35.9 per cent, the highest among Germany's 10 most important source markets (Federal Ministry of the Interior 2006)). There appears to have been a steady increase in the number of incoming tourists and overnight stays by international travellers in Germany since the event, with the former increasing slowly but tourists clearly staying longer (and spending more). The two million foreign tourists who travelled to Germany during the month-long tournament are estimated to have spent €600 million (Deutsche Welle 2006). While it is notoriously difficult to find accurate data on the exact economic impact of the World Cup on a nation's economy, half of the companies that reported a positive 'World Cup' effect on their business thought reputational gain for Germany and its products was 'the underlying reason for the economic success of this mega event' (Federal Ministry of the Interior 2006: 24). The head of sport at the national news magazine *Der Spiegel* believes that the World Cup acted as a catalyst in breaking down stereotypes of Germans and building up a positive sense of home-grown patriotism: 'I think we are happy about the change to our image in the world – everybody knows already that we can organise the World Cup, but the image of a modern, friendly, party-loving nation is new' (author interview with Gerhard Pfeil, 2011).

The evidence appears to confirm that the World Cup acted as a turning-point in the relationship of foreigners with Germany and of the Germans with their own self-image. All available indices suggest that the 2006 FIFA World Cup was successful. For example, the Anholt–GfK Roper Nation Brands Index (2004–11), which measures foreigners' views of Germany in respect of six dimensions (governance; people; exports; culture and heritage; tourism; and investment and immigration) shows how Germany fared before and during the World Cup, and how it has fared since.

The graph indicates that being chosen to host the 2006 FIFA World Cup, including the run-up to the event in 2006, led to an upward trajectory in Germany's image abroad. A survey

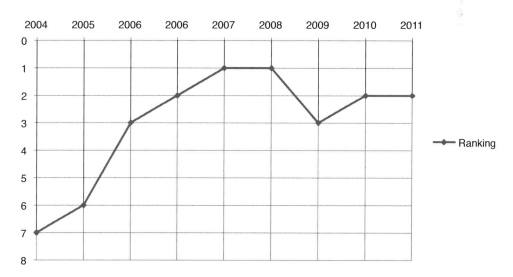

Figure 27.1 Germany's image abroad

Source: Anholt-GfK Roper Nation Brands Index (2004–11)

taken just before the event in 2006 placed Germany third in the world, while a survey round after the event saw an immediate improvement to second place and then a two-year reign at the top of the index. Subsequent years, although with some fluctuation, show a much improved international image of Germany, which maintains a level way above that of pre-tournament times. There is little evidence of any other event or reason that helps explain this turnaround in international image other than the well-planned, well-executed 'leveraging' of the sports mega-event of 2006. Some five years after the event, with Germany due to host the FIFA women's World Cup in 2011, Petra Hedorfer, Chair of the German National Tourist Board, suggested that the men's World Cup in 2006 'proved to great effect how an event of this kind can improve the international perception of Germany' (FVW 2013). The German National Tourist Board was equally pleased to note that the external perception of Germany and the Germans had improved markedly due to the World Cup, unexpectedly so among the bordering nations of the French and Dutch; the only exceptions, where a negative image of Germans remained, were (perhaps understandably given the history of its relations with Germany) neighbouring Poland, and Italy (Federal Ministry of the Interior 2006).

The atmosphere around the mega-event, helped by the Fan Zones and public viewing areas – and the fact that the home side got off to a very successful start – impacted not only on the non-German perception of Germany, but also on the German self-image. All nine interviewees in an in-depth study of the 2006 World Cup spoke of the new, confident flag-waving (sporting) patriotism that accompanied this mega-event (Grix 2013a). Patriotism is normal for the vast majority of countries, but in Germany it has been suppressed because of the country's Nazi past. When they were brought together in 1990 after a separation by high walls and barbed wire of some 40 years, East and West Germans exhibited very different social and political attitudes accrued via socialisation processes in diametrically opposed political systems (see, for example, Grix 2000). The World Cup was 16 years on from formal unification, but differences between former 'Ossis' and 'Wessis' remained. Robert Ide, sports correspondent with the leading Berlin daily *Der Tagesspiegel*, was in a good position to reflect on the effect of the World Cup on the 'inner unity' (*innere Einheit*) of the Germans. Born in East Germany, Ide wrote a bestselling novel depicting his difficulties in coming to terms with the collapse of his former state and in dealing with being an outsider in the new, unified Germany (Ide 2007). In a subsequent interview with the author, he recalled how a spontaneous meeting of Croatian, Australian, and German fans at the railway station after a match in Stuttgart turned into a party. Hundreds of fans followed a local brass band around the huge railway station. The Australian fans, whose team had just lost to Croatia, mixed happily with Croatian and German fans. Ide comments:

> a lot of people were so delighted that something like this could happen in Germany [. . .] as the brass band weaved its way around the railway station with all those different fans in tow, I caught sight of an old man, who must have been 70 or 80. He had tears of joy in his eyes and he said to me, 'I've never experienced anything like this in Germany, ever. Astonishing, this is my country, I can't believe it.' I felt the same way, and as I sat in a beer garden later and heard our national anthem, I thought, yeah, I'm going to sing along, this is somehow my country as well [. . .]. That was the first time for me that I sang the national anthem, because it wasn't our [i.e. those from East Germany's] national anthem, it was West Germany's, along with all their laws and so on.
>
> (author interview with Robert Ide, 2011)

It would appear that this sports mega-event *has* altered Germany's image abroad, contrary to what many commentators believe (Fan 2006; Manzenreiter 2010). The German Embassy in

London suggested that not since the Berlin Wall fell had there been such an 'intensive and positive impact on Germany's image', which had 'turned into almost enthusiastic perception' (cited in Federal Ministry of the Interior 2006: 25). Patrick Spaven, called before the UK Foreign Affairs Committee as an expert witness, identifies what this section has attempted to show, a deliberate and calculated leveraging of a sports mega-event to change Germany's image abroad:

> Germany's status [. . .] seems to be significantly better off in image terms now than it was in late 2005. The only factor that I can find to explain that is the 2006 FIFA World Cup, around which it managed public diplomacy, in a very broad sense – international influence – as well as I've seen any country, and in a purposeful way. What happened in Barcelona was almost incidental; it wasn't a grand strategy. Germany had a grand strategy, which I think they designed and pulled off very well.
>
> (Foreign Affairs Committee 2010: Q33)

While many hope the impact of hosting a sports mega-event will be positive, the German use of the 2006 FIFA World Cup to shape Germany's image abroad left little to chance. Its effects are now being felt in other spheres, seven years on: a recent *Guardian* article describes a 'shift' in the perception of German cultural output and an 'invasion' of the UK by German cultural influence in the form of music, dance, and art. Cultural commentators 'believe[s] the 2006 World Cup helped popularise German culture beyond artistic and intellectual circles' (Needham 2012).

Germany's influence on world sport politics continues: the 'emerging' states now bidding for and winning the right to host sports mega-events show a shift away from the belief that their primary functions are to leverage economic gains, bring forward urban regeneration projects, and inspire the masses to take up physical activity. The so-called 'new lands' (FIFA President Sepp Blatter, cited in Longman 2010) of Qatar, China, Brazil, Russia, and so on are moved by a desire not only to put themselves on the map, but also to improve their image among foreign publics abroad (Grix 2013b, Grix and Lee 2013).

Conclusion

This chapter has argued that Germany's global influence on sport politics has been substantial. Other scholars have analysed at length the impact both German Olympics have had on subsequent sports mega-events (Young 2010). The Hitler Olympics can be read as the first in a long line of bombastic uses of sporting spectacle to showcase a nation and its values; the most recent example is the £60 million opening ceremony by China in 2008. The Munich Olympics signals the start of what has been termed the 'securitisation' of mega-events; the culmination of this development was witnessed in London 2012, where the army had to be called in to secure the Games after the private security company G4S failed to provide the necessary personnel. The chapter has also discussed in detail two further German examples of sport politics. The first, and perhaps the least advertised, is the unprecedented influence the East German model of sport has had on modern-day sports models. No official, commentator, or athlete would admit to the similarities between the 21st century's elite sport development systems and East Germany's, but there is little doubt that the GDR was some 40 years ahead of its time in terms of producing world-class athletes. The final example of Germany's influence on sport politics is the recent (2006) staging of the FWC, which showed other states what a successful sports mega-event can achieve. The next group of mega-event hosts, including Qatar, Russia, and Brazil, are looking to such events to put their states on the world map and to burnish their respective images for the benefit of foreign publics. Germany, a democratic state since 1949, has been able to project and alter its image abroad; whether others will fare as well when exposed to the scrutiny of the global media remains to be seen.

Notes

1   The GDR did compete as an independent team in Mexico in 1968, but without GDR insignia. In previous Olympics a joint German team had competed, using a German flag adorned with Olympic rings and Beethoven's 'Ode to Joy' as an anthem, to be played at medal ceremonies in lieu of the German national anthem; see Balbier 2007.
2   This section rests heavily on Dennis and Grix 2012: 176–85, but also updates and expands on it.

Bibliography

Anholt-GfK Roper Nation Brands Index (2004–11). Online. Available at www.gfkamerica.com/practice_areas/roper_pam/nbi_index/index.en.html (accessed 1 March 2012).
Balbier, A. (2007) *Kalter Krieg auf der Aschenbahn: Der Deutsch-Deutsche Sport 1950–1972*, Paderborn: Schöningh.
Beamish, R. and Ritchie, I. (2006) *Fastest, Highest, Strongest. A Critique of High-performance Sport*, New York and Abingdon: Routledge.
Bergsgard, N.A., Houlihan, B., Mangset, P., Nodland, S.I., and Rommetvedt, H. (2007) *Sport Policy. A Comparative Analysis of Stability and Change*, Oxford: Butterworth and Heinemann.
Black, D. (2008) 'Dreaming big: the pursuit of "second order" games as a strategic response to globalisation', *Sport in Society*, 11(4): 467–80.
Bloom, M., Gagnon, N., and Hughes, D. (2006) *Achieving Excellence: Valuing Canada's Participation in High Performance Sport*, Ottawa: The Conference Board of Canada.
Bloyce, D. and Smith, A. (2010) *Sport Policy and Development: An Introduction*, London: Routledge.
Brauer, S. and Brauer, G. (2008) 'Sport and national reputation: The 2006 FIFA World Cup and Germany's image worldwide'. Online. Available at www.fifa.com/mm/document/afmarketing/marketing/83/31/80/sportverlagenglisch-trackchanges.doc (accessed 13 February 2012).
Busse, P. (2010) 'Wie steht es um das Erbe des erfolgreichen DDR-Sports?' *Deutschland Archiv*, 43(5), pp. 884–8.
Carlson, M. (2002) 'Obituary: Manfred Ewald. East Germany's drug-based sports mastermind', *The Guardian*, 29 October. Online. Available at www.guardian.co.uk/news/2002/oct/29/guardianobituaries.sport (accessed 21 January 2011).
Carlson, M. (2008) 'From GDR to GBR. A New Perspective on Britain's Olympic Success'. Online. Available at http://mcarlson-andoverhere.blogspot.com/2008/08/from-gdr-to-gbr-new-perspective-on.html (accessed 21 January 2011).
Collins, S. and Green, M. (2007) 'The Australian Institute of Sport', *Journal of the Academy of Social Sciences in Australia*, 26(2): 4–14.
Cornelissen, S. (2011) 'Mega Event Securitisation in a Third World Setting: Glocal Processes and Ramifications during the 2010 FIFA World Cup', *Urban Studies*, 48(15): 3221–40.
DAAD (2013). Online. Available at http://www.daad.de/en/ (accessed 8 February 2013).
DCMS (Department for Culture, Media and Sport) (2002) *Game Plan, a strategy for delivering Government's sport and physical activity objectives*, produced by the DCMS and the Strategy Unit, London: Cabinet Office.
DCMS (Department for Culture, Media and Sport) (2008) *Playing to Win: A New Era for Sport*, London: DCMS.
DDR-Wissen (2013) 'DDR-Lexikon. Sport'. Online. Available at www.ddr-wissen.de/wiki/ddr.pl?Sport (accessed 11 November 2013).
Dennis, M. (1988) *The German Democratic Republic*, London: Pinter Publishers.
Dennis, M. and Grix, J. (2012) *Sport Under Communism: Behind the East German 'Miracle'*, Basingstoke: Palgrave.
Deutsche Welle (2006) FWC Reports. Online. Available at www.dw-world.de (accessed 2 March 2012).
Deutscher Olympischer Sportbund (2013) '"Eliteschule des Sports": Daten, Zahlen, Fakten'. Online. Available at www.dosb.de/de/eliteschule-des-sports/hintergrund/daten-zahlen-fakten/ (accessed 21 November 2013).

Fan, Y. (2006) 'Branding the nation: what is being branded?' *Journal of Vacation Marketing,* 12(1): 5–14.

Federal Ministry of the Interior (Germany) (2006) 'Die Welt war zu Gast bei Freunden – Bilanz der Bundesregierung zur Fußball-Weltmeisterschaft 2006', Berlin: Federal Ministry of the Interior.

Foreign Affairs Committee (2010) 'FCO Public Diplomacy: The Olympics', London: TSO. Online. Available at www.publications.parliament.uk/pa/cm201011/cmselect/cmfaff/581/10111002.htm (accessed 8 February 2013)

FVW (2013) 'Germany sets new goals'. Online. Available at www.fvw.com/tourism-boss-hails-country-as-european-superstar-germany-sets-new-goals/393/86299/11245 (accessed 5 December 2013).

Goethe Institut (2013). Online. Available at www.goethe.de/enindex.htm (accessed 8 February 2013).

Graham, S. (2012) 'Olympics 2012 Security: Welcome to Lockdown London', *The Guardian,* 12 March. Online. Available at www.guardian.co.uk/sport/2012/mar/12/london-olympics-security-lockdown-london (accessed 6 February 2013).

Green, M. and Houlihan, B. (2005) *Elite sport development. Policy learning and political priorities,* London and New York: Routledge.

Green, M. and Oakley, B. (2001) 'Elite sport development systems and playing to win: uniformity and diversity in international approaches', *Leisure Studies,* 20: 247–68.

Grix, J. (2000) 'East German Political Attitudes. Socialist Legacies vs. Situational Factors: A False Antithesis', *German Politics,* 9(2): 109–24.

Grix, J. (2012) 'The Politics of Sports Mega-events', *Political Insight,* 3(1): 4–7.

Grix, J. (2013a) '"Image" Leveraging and Sports Mega-Events: Germany and the 2006 World Cup', *Journal of Sport and Tourism,* 17: 298–312.

Grix, J. (2013b) 'Sports Politics and the Olympics', *Political Studies Review,* 11: 15–25.

Grix, J. and Carmichael, F. (2012) 'Why Do Governments Invest in Elite Sport? A Polemic', *International Journal of Sport Policy and Politics,* 4(1): 73–90.

Grix, J. and Lacroix, C. (2006) 'Constructing Germany's Image in the British Press: An Empirical Analysis of Stereotypical Reporting on Germany', *Journal of Contemporary European Studies,* 14(3): 373–92.

Grix, J. and Lee, D. (2013) 'Soft Power, Sports Mega-Events and Emerging States: The Lure of the Politics of Attraction', *Global Society,* 27(4): 521–36. Online. Available at http://dx.doi.org/10.1080/13600826.2013.827632.

Hilton, C. (2008) *Hitler's Olympics. The 1936 Berlin Olympic Games,* Gloucester: Sutton Publishing.

Hitler, A. (1926) *Mein Kampf,* trans. R. Manheim (2001), New York: Houghton Mifflin.

Holzweissig, G. (1981) *Diplomatie im Trainingsanzug. Sport als politisches Instrument der DDR in den innerdeutschen und internationalen Beziehungen,* Munich: Oldenbourg Press.

Holzweissig, G. (2005) 'Sport – Gesellschaftliche Rolle und politische Funktion', *Horch und Guck,* 51: 1–9.

Horne, J. and Manzenreiter, W. (eds) (2006) *Sports Mega-Events: Social Scientific Analyses of a Global Phenomenon,* Oxford: Blackwell.

Houlihan, B. and Giulianotti, R. (2012) 'Politics and the London 2012 Olympics: the (in)security Games', *International Affairs,* 88(4): 701–17.

Hutton, W. (1996) *The State We're In,* London: Vintage Publishers.

Ide, R. (2007) *Geteilte Träume,* Munich: Luchterhand Publishers.

Köhler, H. (2004) 'Deutschland soll ein Land der Ideen werden'. Online. Available at www.sueddeutsche.de/politik/die-rede-von-koehler-deutschland-soll-ein-land-der-ideen-werden-1.299287 (accessed 28 September 2012).

Longman, J. (2010) 'Russia and Qatar win World Cup bids', *New York Times.* Online. Available at www.nytimes.com/2010/12/03/sports/soccer/03worldcup.html?pagewanted=all&_r=0 (accessed 8 February 2013).

Macintosh, D., Bedecki, T., and Franks, C.E.S. (1987) *Sport and politics in Canada,* Montreal: Queen's-McGill Universities Press.

Manzenreiter, W. (2010) 'The Beijing Games in the Western Imagination of China: The Weak Power of Soft Power', *Journal of Sport and Social Issues,* 34(1): 29–48.

Miah, A. and Garcia, B. (2012) *The Olympics. The basics,* London and New York: Routledge.

National Audit Office (2005) *UK Sport: supporting elite athletes,* London: TSO.

Needham, A. (2012) 'Cultural invasion of Britain celebrates Germany's big shift', *The Guardian,* 4 March. Online. Available at www.guardian.co.uk/world/2012/mar/04/german-cultural-invasion-london (accessed 8 February 2013).

Pohl, O. (2002) 'Olympics: Germans Resurrect the East's Methods', *New York Times,* 10 September. Online. Available at www.nytimes.com/2002/09/10/sports/olympics-germans-resurrect-the-e-s-methods.html?pagewanted=all&src=pm (accessed 21 November 2013).

Riefenstahl, L. (1938/2006) *Olympia*, Arthaus DVD.

Riordan, J. (1999) *The International Politics of Sport in the Twentieth Century*, London: Spon Press.

Schiller, K. and Young, C. (2010) *The 1972 Olympics and the Making of Germany*, Berkeley: University of California Press.

Senn, A.E. (1999) *Power, Politics and the Olympic Games*, Leeds: Human Kinetics.

Sparvero, E., Chalip, L., and Green, B.C. (2008) 'United States', in B. Houlihan and M. Green (eds) *Comparative Elite Sport Development*, London: Butterworth-Heinemann.

Stewart, B., Nicholson, M., Smith, A., and Westerbeek, H. (2004) *Australian Sport: Better by Design? The Evolution of Australian Sport Policy*, London: Routledge.

Stotlar, D. K., Wonders, A. and Babkes, M. (2006) 'Developing elite athletes: A content analysis of US national governing body systems', *International Journal of Applied Sport Sciences* 18: 121–44.

Strenk, A. (1978) 'Diplomats in Track Suits', in B. Lowe, D. Kanin, and A. Strenk (eds) *Sport and International Relations*, Champaign, IL: Stipes Publishing.

The Independent (1997) 'Athletics: Australia Sign Coach Linked to Drug Abuse', 3 October. Online. Available at www.independent.co.uk/sport/athletics-australia-sign-coach-linked-to-drug-abuse-1233683.html (accessed 7 November 2013).

Triumph des Willens (1935) [Film] Leni Riefenstahl, Germany: UFA.

UK Sport (2008) 'World Class Governance'. Online. Available at www.uksport.gov.uk/pages/world_class_governance/ (accessed 3 June 2011).

Watt, D.C. (1965) *Britain Looks to Germany: British Opinion and Policy towards Germany since 1945*, London: Oswald Wolff.

Young, C. (2010) *Berlin 1936*, in A. Bairner and G. Molnar (eds) *The Politics of the Olympics: A Survey*, London and New York: Routledge.

Younge, G. (2002) 'Bet you won't be shouting for this lot on Sunday', *The Guardian*, 28 June. Online. Available at www.guardian.co.uk/uk/2002/jun/28/race.germany (accessed 8 February 2013).

Interviewees

1 Desk Officer at the German Foreign Office (Culture and Education Policy, Communication, and Germany's Image Abroad), Berlin, August 2011.

2 Robert Ide (Chief Sports Editor, *Tagesspiegel*), Berlin, August 2011.

3 Gerhard Pfeil (Chief Sports Editor, *Der Spiegel*), Hamburg, August 2011.

4 Horst R. Schmidt, Secretary of the German Football Federation and Vice President of the FIFA 2006 organising committee (currently treasurer of the German Football Federation) (telephone interview, September 2012).

28

Cultural outreach

Overcoming the past?

Gregory Paschalidis

According to the BBC World Service Poll, which has been tracking opinions about country influence in the world since 2005, Germany was seen as the country with the most positive influence in the world during the whole of the period 2008–13, with the exception of 2012, when it fell to second place, behind Japan.[1] Excepting Greece, every country polled had a favourable view of Germany. The picture becomes even more impressive if we look across continents. The BBC's findings approximate those of the Transatlantic Trends survey of 2012, according to which Germany was tied with the United States as the most favourably viewed country, rated favourably by 74 per cent of Europeans, 67 per cent of Americans, and 71 per cent of Russians. What cost Germany the top place was the significantly lower score it got in Spain (38 per cent), Portugal (40 per cent), and Italy (43 per cent). Those responses, like the response of Greece in the 2013 BBC poll, reflected popular discontent with Chancellor Angela Merkel's handling of the public debt crisis in the countries of southern Europe.

In the span of just two generations, since the end of World War II, Germany has succeeded in transforming its international image from that of a rogue state, stigmatised as the perpetrator of obscene crimes and ferocious destruction, to that of an (almost) universally appreciated moral authority. It is a success story unequalled in modern history. Although it is not unrelated to the towering role of the German economy in global trade, it also represents a prime example of the rewards of soft power.

The Adenauer era: Weimar's second life

Recounting his years amidst the ruins and deprivations of early postwar Germany, Oskar Matzerath, the dwarfish hero of *The Tin Drum*, the first and best-known novel of Nobel Prize-winning author Günter Grass, recalls that he educated himself 'in the company of thousands determined to learn, to make up for the education they'd missed, took courses in night school, was a regular visitor at the British Centre, called *Die Brücke*, or The Bridge' (Grass 2009: 398). By October 1946, a network of 35 information and education centres, suggestively named *Die Brücke*, had been set up by the British Embassy's Cultural Relations Department in cities across the British occupation zone. Most of them contained no more than a few books and British newspapers, but those in Berlin and other major cities offered substantial libraries, English classes, films, lectures, theatre, and exhibitions. A similar assortment of cultural fare was provided by a host of US-run reading rooms and information centres called *Amerika Häuser*, and by a growing number of French cultural institutes. In 1950 Germany had 64 *Brücken*, 48 *Amerika Häuser* and 110 reading rooms, as well as 18 French cultural institutes.

At a time when most of Germany's cultural infrastructure lay in ruins, these Allied-built cultural networks proved highly popular among the Germans who, like Oskar Matzerath, felt a *Nachholbedürfnis* (need to catch up) after the prohibitions of the Nazi period, and a hunger for culture 'more acute than the need for coal, food, and water' (Beal 2000: 108). The rationale for this massive Allied cultural presence derived from the denazification objectives set by the Potsdam Agreement (August 1945). In tandem with the purge of ex-Nazi cadres from civil service and public institutions, these cultural networks were part of a wide-ranging re-education policy aimed at the cultural and spiritual detoxification of the German psyche and its inculcation with the values of democracy and liberalism. For the British and the French, in particular, 're-education' also involved a hefty measure of traditional *rayonnement culturelle*, aimed at securing their cultural influence over the vanquished.

Before long, though, Allied missionary zeal to redeem the soul of postwar Germany mutated into intra-Allied competition for coaxing it into another war. Starting in 1946, with the fierce clashes between Western and Soviet-controlled press, radio, and theatre venues, and culminating in the autumn of 1947, with the ban on the communist front organisation *Kulturbund* from operating in the British and American zones (Caute 2003: 105–10), the battle for the 'hearts and minds' of Germans became the prelude to the Cold War. The cultural outposts established by the Allies as part of their common denazification mission became the basis for open cultural-ideological rivalry, in a process that would lead to the Berlin blockade (June 1948-May 1949), and, in 1949, to the creation of two separate German states.

The cultural outreach of the Federal Republic of Germany (FRG) commenced soon after the first postwar elections were held on 14 August 1949. To deal with the task, Konrad Adenauer's government rebuilt an infrastructure of organisations that had previously been responsible for cultural diplomacy in the Weimar Republic. Because they had been taken over by the Nazi propaganda apparatus, all of these organisations had been dissolved by the Allies in 1945, and they had to be refounded, sometimes redefined, and even renamed, to erase the vexed memories of their recent past.

The German Foreign Institute (*Deutsches Ausland-Institut* or DAI) was established in Stuttgart in 1917 as an academic think-tank for documenting and maintaining cultural ties with German communities abroad (*Auslandsdeutschtum*). Greatly favoured and upsized by the Nazi regime, the DAI was turned into a strategic instrument for the advancement of its expansionist and racial policies in eastern Europe (Gesche 2006). In 1949 the DAI was refounded as the Institute for Foreign Cultural Relations (*Institut für Auslandsbeziehungen* or ifa) and charged with organising exhibitions and seminars, and providing books and teachers for German schools abroad.

The Academic Exchange Service (*Akademischer Austauschdienst* or AAD) was originally founded in 1925 to support the exchange of political science students between German and American universities. In 1930 the AAD merged with the Alexander von Humboldt Foundation and the German Universities Overseas Office (*Deutsche Akademische Auslandsstelle des Verbandes der deutschen Hochschulen* or DAASt), and was renamed the German Academic Exchange Service (*Deutscher Akademischer Austauschdienst* or DAAD). It expanded to cover academic exchanges for all fields of study with other countries as well. During the Nazi period, despite the dramatic decline in the number of foreign students coming to study in Germany (Bodo 2003), the DAAD continued to open new branches abroad, which served as active disseminators of Nazi propaganda. In November 1943, the DAAD's headquarters in Berlin was bombed and its records destroyed, causing the suspension of its activities. With the energetic endorsement of the academic community of the UK and the USA, who viewed it as a vital part of Allied re-education policy, the DAAD was refounded on 5 August 1950, once again with a focus on German-American student exchanges.

The Goethe Institut (*Goethe Institut zur Fortbildung Ausländischer Deutschlehrer*) was originally founded on the 100th anniversary of Goethe's death, in 1932, as the German language teacher training division of the German Academy (*Deutsche Akademie* or DA), a non-governmental organisation established by nationalist scientists in Munich, in May 1925, to foster 'Germanness' abroad, especially among German minorities in eastern, central, and southeastern Europe. The establishment of the Goethe Institut reflected the DA's growing emphasis on propagating the German language abroad, a task which earned it the financial support of the German Foreign Office (*Auswärtiges Amt*). Under the Nazis, the DA expanded to become 'the biggest cultural propaganda institution of the Third Reich with more than 250 language schools in Europe' (Michels 2004: 207). As in the case of the DAI, the DA was dissolved in 1945 for being so closely enmeshed in Nazi war policy. In 1951 the Goethe Institut was refounded and resumed its original mission of teacher training, as well as the DA's lectureships abroad programme.

The Alexander von Humboldt Foundation for Nature Research and Travel (*Alexander von Humboldt-Stiftung für Naturforschung und Reisen*), initially founded in 1860 by Humboldt's friends and colleagues, with the aim of supporting young scientists, lost its original endowment in the German hyper-inflation of 1923. Re-established under the Weimar Republic in 1925, it focused on supporting foreign academics to pursue their research in Germany, but when the Nazis took it over it was turned into a vehicle for the recruitment of a racially pure foreign student elite who would become the ideological disseminators of a Nazi-ruled 'New Europe' (Impekoven 2012). At the behest of former Humboldt guest academics it was resurrected again in 1953, and continued to provide grants to leading foreign academics to conduct research in Germany.

In the same period, two important agencies for public diplomacy were also established. InterNationes was founded in 1952 as an independent, non-profit institution whose remit was to publish and distribute information about the Federal Republic to foreign politicians, academics, and journalists, as well as to cultural and educational establishments. In 1953 the shortwave station Deutsche Welle first went on air, addressing itself originally to listeners with German roots, but soon after to a wide range of international audiences in its foreign-language programmes.

The most pressing need felt by the Federal Republic in the context of its newly regained sovereignty was its reintegration into the international community and the restoration of its grievously tarnished foreign image. Most of the aforementioned organisations of cultural diplomacy that were put to the task had in fact originally been set up to help Germany deal with a similar exigency, in the wake of its defeat in World War I. Their redeployment by the young Bonn Republic signalled, in effect, a return to the Weimar Republic's policy of using culture as an autonomous national asset capable of redeeming Germany's international image (Düwell 1976).

During the early 1950s, as these organisations gradually resumed their historical responsibilities, the Allied cultural presence began to dwindle. In 1955, when the *Besatzungszeit* (occupation period) ended and West Germany was declared a fully sovereign state, there were only 16 *Amerika Häuser* left in the FRG, while by 1959, when *The Tin Drum* was published, the *Brücken* were already a thing of the past, the British Council having taken over the few surviving ones. The blatantly unidirectional and paternalist model of cultural communication practised by the Allies during the re-education phase was giving way to a more symmetrical model of cultural exchange. In March 1957, as a result of Chancellor Adenauer's steadfast policy of strengthening ties with western Europe, Federal Germany became one of the founding members of the EEC, and a realignment of its foreign cultural policy priorities became noticeable. Its focus shifted from the Atlantic to Europe, a shift that was reflected in the DAAD's new emphasis on exchanges with European neighbours (Aguilar 1996: 139).

A milestone in this eurocentric turn was the signing of the Franco-German Friendship Treaty by Chancellor Konrad Adenauer and General Charles de Gaulle on 22 January 1963. The so-called Elysée Treaty heralded the beginning of a new era in the turbulent history of Franco-German relations, putting an end to entrenched animosity and inaugurating a 'special relationship' that has since become the bedrock of European integration and stability. It stipulated close cooperation in the areas of defence and foreign policy, as well as in culture and youth policy, placing special emphasis on educational exchanges and cultural contact between the two countries. Hundreds of schools and towns were twinned, scores of Franco-German high schools were established, and a Franco-German Youth Office was set up to facilitate visits to the partner country by thousands of young people of all ages and educational levels.

The cultural and educational provisions of the Elysée Treaty constitute the most pathbreaking and far-reaching event of cultural diplomacy during the Adenauer era, which was otherwise characterised by caution and traditionalism. In his study of Germany's participation in the first postwar World Exhibition in Brussels in 1958, Johannes Paulmann describes the pains taken to avoid any echoes of Germany's notoriously self-aggrandising participation in the Paris World Exhibition of 1937. The style of national self-presentation chosen would advance Germany's reintegration into the international community 'by attempting not to emulate others or to demonstrate exceptional achievement, but by fitting in and exercising restraint'. A spare, transparent architectural plan was selected to connote the openness of the Federal Republic, while the emphasis was not on 'technological feats' but on quality, everyday products that 'signified the country's return to normality' (Paulmann 2007: 182, 191). Perhaps the most telling example of what Paulmann calls an 'attitude of restraint' (*Haltung der Zurückhaltung*), was Bonn's reluctance to capitalise on the German national football team's win in the 1954 World Cup, after defeating the overwhelming favourites Hungary. Despite the popular enthusiasm stirred by the so-called 'Miracle of Berne', which many regard as the decisive moment in the remaking of national identity in postwar West Germany, the official handling of the event was markedly subdued, emphasising its purely sporting dimension (Balbier 2006).

The heightened self-consciousness shown in these cases of national self-display was also noticeable in Bonn's reaction to anything that might compromise the country's international rehabilitation process. It was a reaction that, more often than not, backfired. In May 1956, Alain Resnais's *Night and Fog* documentary on the extermination camps was withdrawn from the Cannes Film Festival at the request of the West German Foreign Ministry. Suggesting that it would 'disturb the international harmony of the festival by its emphatic reminder of a painful past' (Fehrenbach 1995: 222), the Ministry demanded the film's withdrawal under Article 5 of the Festival regulations, which allowed for such an action if a film was deemed offensive to the sensibilities of a participating country (Leahy 2003). In view of the public scandal that ensued, and the selection committee's threat to resign, the film was finally allowed to be shown at Cannes, but in an 'out of competition' slot.

The effort to keep the lid on the entire war guilt issue was behind another of the Bonn Foreign Ministry's memorable blunders, this time concerning the international fallout of the 'Fischer controversy', the German historians' dispute triggered by Fritz Fischer's iconoclastic thesis about Germany's responsibility for World War I. In February 1964, the Foreign Minister Gerhard Schröder withdrew the Goethe Institut travel grant awarded to Fischer for a lecture tour in the United States, heeding the alarmed remonstrances of Fischer's 'patriotically concerned' rivals that this tour would bring 'national disaster' (Herwig 1996: 114). The cancellation provoked concerted protest from American historians, who secured financial support for Fischer's tour, and led to a much publicised debate about restrictions on academic freedom in the Federal Republic (Stelzel 2003).

The Weimar Republic's foreign policy, masterminded by the foreign minister and 1926 Nobel Peace laureate Gustav Stresemann (1924–9), placed excessive emphasis on the preservation of the cultural identity of the *Auslandsdeutschen,* the German-speaking minorities living abroad. By, in effect, vivifying the prospect of their eventual annexation to the fatherland, Stresemann's policy ended up undermining his otherwise pacifist intentions. The Bonn Republic's analogous shadow were the Germans living in the German Democratic Republic (GDR), a bitter ideological adversary which cast the FRG as the sole heir of the Nazi past and questioned the sincerity of its democratic transformation, all the while claiming to be the only true representative of German culture. At the same time, the GDR was seen as an integral, unrelinquishable part of Germany. This ambivalence was the source of constant tension and made the FRG's cultural self-representation a delicate balancing act between contention and inclusiveness, challenge and negotiation.

The two German states were crossing swords on the airwaves by the mid-1950s. The launch of Deutsche Welle's foreign-language programming in October 1954 provoked the creation of the Foreign Languages Service of the GDR's Radio, in April 1956. When the latter was replaced by Radio Berlin International in May 1959 the contest spiralled, with both German stations broadcasting in an increasing variety of languages, including Arabic, Swahili, and Hindi. The choice of these languages indicated another arena of fierce inter-German rivalry. After the building of the Berlin Wall in 1961, the GDR's foreign policy targeted the developing countries of Asia and Africa not so much because of the wider relocation of the Cold War towards the periphery but primarily in an effort to secure international diplomatic recognition as an independent state. In 1961 the Foreign Students' Institute (*Institut für Ausländerstudium*) was renamed the Herder Institute and charged with training German language teachers and promoting the German language abroad. Consequently, the Herder Institute established a secure footing in eastern Europe and spearheaded the GDR's inroads into the Third World, becoming the main instrument of the GDR's foreign cultural, educational, and language policy and a counterweight to the Goethe Institut (Altmayer 2009). By 1970, however, the FRG had established 18 cultural institutes in Africa compared with the GDR's four, while the FRG's superiority extended also to the substantially larger amount of funds, experts, and scholarships offered to the developing countries (Winrow 1990: 50–1). The concomitant transformation of the Goethe Institut from a parochial German language training school into a powerful frontline international network was the single-handed achievement of one person.

Dieter Sattler (1906–68) was the most influential cultural politician in the early Federal Republic. A trained architect who had served as State Secretary for Fine Arts in the Bavarian Ministry of Education and Culture (1947–50), President of the German Theatre Association (1950–2), and Chairman of the Bavarian Radio Broadcasting Council (1951–2), as well as cultural attaché to the German Embassy in Rome (1952–9), Sattler assumed his post as Head of the Cultural Department of the Foreign Office (1959–66) as an outsider (*Quereinsteiger*) among the ministry's career bureaucrats and diplomats (Stoll 2005). Unburdened by their entrenched routines or Nazi past associations, he combined an expertise and vision that made him the architect of the FRG's foreign cultural policy. In a landmark lecture in 1960, poignantly titled 'The Hour of Cultural Policy', Sattler described international cultural relations as the 'third stage' (*dritte Bühne*) of world politics, 'upon which the dramas being acted out were just as important as

461

those on the stages of diplomacy and economics' (Arnold 1979: 134). He thus underlined his belief in the critical contribution foreign cultural policy could make to the Cold War effort.

Sattler's policy instrument of choice was the Goethe Institut, which he promptly made the main agency for showcasing German culture abroad, assigning to it all 35 cultural institutes that the Foreign Ministry ran abroad and generously supporting its international expansion. With this, Sattler not only successfully countered the GDR's cultural offensive but propelled the Goethe Institut to the status of a global cultural agency, in the same league as the British Council and the Institut Français. At the same time, he pressed the government to raise the budget of his department to 1 per cent of the defence budget. Despite his frequent quarrels with foreign minister Gerhard Schröder (1961–6), he managed an astonishing increase from 58.8 million marks in 1958 to 230.3 million marks in 1966 (Aguilar 1996: 277).

The Brandt era: foreign cultural policy as a two-way street

In 1949, returning to Frankfurt after 15 years of exile, the Frankfurt School philosopher Theodor Adorno was relieved to see that interest in high culture had not been eroded by entertainment mass culture in Germany.[2] He was troubled, however, that the widespread postwar *Hunger nach Kultur* (hunger for culture) went in tandem with political apathy and apparent indifference to the vibrant legacy of Weimar modernism. The widely acclaimed resurrection of culture, he feared, was but the pursuit of the 'dangerous and ambivalent solace of taking refuge in provincialism' ('gefährlichen und zweideutigen Trost der Geborgenheit im Provinziellen') (Adorno 1950: 471, my translation). A retreat into politically uncontroversial high culture certainly permeated Germany's cultural self-projection abroad. The first and most favoured cultural ambassador of Federal Germany abroad in this period, sponsored personally by Konrad Adenauer, was the Berlin Philharmonic Orchestra. Starting as early as 1948, with its English tour, the Philharmonic's highly popular performance of German classical music was ideally a non-controversial and universally appreciated means of rebuilding Germany's international reputation (Frede 2007). For cultural conservatives like Sattler and his predecessors, reaffirming the national symbolic capital associated with the German classical heritage and adhering to the time-cherished promotion of the German language were essential to restoring the image of the *Land der Dichter und Denker* (land of poets and thinkers) as a *Kulturnation* (Schulte 2000: 45). The same was true for the GDR, which felt a perhaps even more urgent need for national self-assertion. The heritage turn was further reinforced by the propaganda imperatives of the cultural Cold War, whose arsenal, in a curious juxtaposition to the menacing stockpiles of nuclear weapons, consisted mainly of the noble heirlooms of European high culture: great art and literature, classical music and dance. All this was to change in the 1970s, however, when a new concept of culture became the hallmark of West Germany's new cultural policy both at home and abroad.

Soon after he began his tenure as Foreign Minister (1966–9) in Kurt Kiesinger's coalition government, Willy Brandt described foreign cultural policy as the 'third pillar' of foreign policy (*die dritte Saüle der Außenpolitik*), next to diplomacy and economic relations. Brandt's valorisation of foreign cultural policy appears to sum up the implicit wisdom of the previous half century and offer a fitting epigraph to the way foreign cultural policy had been promoted during the cultural Cold War. However, if Sattler's notion of 'the third stage' of world politics had been geared to the exigencies of the Cold War, Brandt's notion of 'the third pillar' was meant as a way out of the Cold War mindset. Far from endorsing the customary deployment of culture in either propaganda drives or the kind of dazzling gestures of *détente* that characterised relations between the USA and the USSR in the 1950s, Brandt's intention was to underscore the role of cultural relations in his *Wandel durch Annäherung* (change through rapprochement) policy, which he hoped would overcome the division of Germany and of Europe at large.

Brandt's 'active peace policy' in the context of East–West relations – conventionally remembered as *Ostpolitik* – was inspired by the success of the Elysée Treaty between West Germany and France. Assessing the first five years of its operation, Brandt notes that, by contrast to the limited benefits it had at the political level, its achievements at the societal level – such as the surge of youth, cultural, and educational exchanges, as well as the manifold economic, scientific, and technological partnerships – were indisputable, and reflected in the feelings of trust and conciliation that had taken root in the two countries (Brandt 1969: 39–40). Casting aside, moreover, the historical association of foreign cultural policy with ideological and cultural propaganda, Brandt stressed the need to redefine it on the basis of mutuality and collaboration (Brandt 1969: 198).

During Brandt's chancellorship (1969–74) the reform of the FRG's foreign cultural policy progressed more methodically. In December 1970, the parliamentary secretary (*Staatsminister*) of the Foreign Ministry and eminent sociologist Ralf Dahrendorf submitted his reform proposals in the *Guidelines for Foreign Cultural Policy* (*Leitsätze für die auswärtige Kulturpolitik*). Dismissing the traditional German notion of *Kultur* for its elitist focus on artistic and intellectual achievement, Dahrendorf proposed an 'expanded concept of culture' (*erweiterter Kulturbegriff*) encompassing contemporary sociocultural processes and issues. In harmony, also, with Brandt's ideas, Dahrendorf redefined the role of foreign cultural policy, shifting its traditional focus on unidirectional information and cultural export towards a bilateral model of exchange, dialogue, and cooperation. He upset the Goethe Institut by prioritising the cultural programmes organised abroad rather than the promotion of the German language. The latter, he suggested, was the means and not the end of foreign cultural policy.

Dahrendorf's *Guidelines* formed the basis for a comprehensive review of the FRG's foreign cultural policy undertaken by a parliamentary commission of inquiry. Its report, submitted in October 1975, while reaffirming the importance that German diplomacy should give to cultural relations, reinstated the role of the German language in foreign cultural policy. Most of its 130 recommendations, however, concerned the simplification and better coordination of the extremely complex and decentralised system of the country's cultural representation abroad, and the Foreign Ministry's role in setting overall objectives and supervising their implementation. Little was done with regard to the contentious issue of the autonomy of the numerous and often overlapping intermediary agencies. The creation of a centralised agency was, in any case, impossible, given the constitutional stipulation that culture and education were solely the responsibility of the Länder (see Chapter 13). A new cooperation agreement was concluded between the Federal government and the Goethe Institut in 1976. Although it safeguarded the institute's independence, it included a veto clause allowing an ambassador to veto a specific event 'if he has a good political, not artistic or aesthetic reason, to believe that damage can be done by this event to the image of Germany abroad' (Witte 1999: 54). The institute's mission was modified to reflect the newly expanded notion of foreign cultural policy. Its original description, set down on the occasion of its refounding in 1951, was 'the cultivation of German language abroad' ('zur Pflege der deutschen Sprache im Ausland'). In 1961, after Sattler extended the institute's remit to include cultural representation, it was reformulated as 'the cultivation of German language and culture abroad'. While retaining the language part, the reference to culture was now replaced by 'support for international cultural cooperation' ('Förderung der internationalen kulturellen Zusammenarbeit') (Michels 2013).

The changes in the Goethe Institut's cultural programming that ensued have since become the hallmark of its international identity. Scores of hitherto excluded avant-garde artists like Anselm Kiefer and Joseph Beuys, critical writers like Hans Magnus Enzensberger, Heinrich Böll, Peter Handke, and Günter Grass, and iconoclastic filmmakers like Rainer Werner Fassbinder, Werner Herzog, and Wim Wenders went on tour around the world communicating not only a realistic picture of Federal Germany's highly diversified cultural landscape but also the image of a distinctly reflexive and self-critical country that was boldly interrogating its past and present. The inclusion of programmes relating to environmental problems and issues of immigration and development, of technological change and scientific ethics, projected the image of a country with a high degree of sensitivity and responsibility regarding matters of global relevance and concern. The close ties with civil society abroad that the Goethe Institut begun to forge during the 1970s are attested to by the fact that its branches in Athens under the Colonels, in Lisbon under Salazar, and in Tehran under the Shah provided a forum and a refuge for dissident groups and ideas.

The Brandt era was a watershed in Federal Germany's foreign cultural policy and shaped the country's cultural outreach for years to come. In the mid-1970s France, Britain, and the United States also took steps to re-evaluate and reform their cultural representation abroad. None, however, succeeded in bringing it in tune with the sentiments and challenges of international society as effectively as the Federal Republic. Another instance of the vision of Brandt's new cultural diplomacy was the creation of the Washington-based German Marshall Fund (GMF), a permanent memorial to the United States' initiative to help the recovery of war-torn Germany and Europe through the generous economic and material aid supplied by the Marshall Plan (1947–51). With the unanimous backing of the Bundestag, Brandt pledged 150 million marks for the first 15 years of the fund's operation, whose objective was 'to promote American-European study and research projects' and 'strengthen relations between not only Germany and the United States, but among the transatlantic community as a whole' (Siegel 2012: 6). Besides being a widely lauded gesture of gratitude, the creation of the GMF was intended to reaffirm the importance of the German-American alliance, which had been severely strained by Brandt's single-handed pursuit of *Ostpolitik*. More than that, it signalled a radical change in the status of Federal Germany: just two decades after it was founded and the Marshall Plan ended, it had transformed itself from the beneficiary of aid into a generous donor, from the recipient of a unidirectional 're-education' into an equal partner in cultural and educational exchange. In his speech at Harvard on 5 June 1972 marking the establishment of the GMF, Brandt drove home the point: 'America needs a self-confident Europe capable of forming a common political will [. . .] it waits for Europe to grow into an equal partner with whom it can share the burden of responsibility for world affairs' (Brandt 1972). Three months later, Germany's new self-confidence and the optimism exuded by Brandt's speech were to be severely tested.

Germany and Japan were excluded from the first postwar Olympic Games, held in London in 1948, because of their role as aggressors in World War II. Just as the 1964 Tokyo Olympics signalled Japan's readmission to world society and re-emergence as an international power, the 1972 Munich Olympics was seen as an event of truly global prestige and significance that would affirm West Germany's new identity and international standing. It was, in fact, in the context of the preparations for the Games, in the late 1960s, that the FRG came to accept sport as a form and an arena of national self-representation to the outside world (Balbier 2006: 5–6; see also Chapter 27). Compared to the international representation secured through the FRG's membership of NATO and the EEC, or the usual forms of cultural diplomacy, 'the symbolic capital on offer via the Olympic Games was immeasurable', giving the opportunity 'to overlay residual images of the recent past with new narratives about the country's political, economic, social and cultural acumen' (Schiller and Young 2010: 2–4). The organising committee's publicity campaign aimed 'to win friends for the Federal Republic', to use this unique occasion 'to refine or, where necessary, correct the image' of the nation abroad, and increase tourism (Schiller and Young 2010: 48). Their overriding concern, though, was to avoid any comparison with the 1936 Berlin Olympics. In contrast to the propaganda-laden grandiloquence of 1936, the Munich Olympics should have the festive feel of *heitere Spiele* (jolly Games).

It was the first postwar Olympic Games where West and East Germany would take part with separate teams and their own national flags and anthems. All the usual flag-waving and national rituals, however, were deliberately avoided, and the opening ceremony was carefully designed as a postnational event (Balbier 2005). Jesse Owens, the iconic African–American athlete who had crushed Hitler's myth of Aryan superiority at the 1936 Olympics, figured prominently among the guests. Otl Aicher, responsible for the overall aesthetic concept of the Games – embracing architecture, uniforms, emblems, posters, slogans, advertisements, and so on – combined the visual modernism of Bauhaus with the social vision of a broad, all-inclusive democracy, with the intention of turning the Munich Olympics 'into a huge playground, in which spectators and athletes could interact freely and regardless of nationality, race, or creed' (Schiller and Young 2010: 103–4). Even his choice of colours – the rainbow colour scheme and the light blue – was meant to project a playful feeling and avoid the aggressive and authoritarian associations of red, white, and black (Balbier 2006: 6). Halfway through the Games, however, all these expectations and hopes turned into a nightmare. On 5 September, the attack by the Palestinian terrorist organisation Black September left 11 Israeli athletes and one German police officer dead. The tragedy is still remembered as one of the darkest days in the history of the Federal Republic. If the Berlin Olympics had proved the most controversial Games ever, the Munich Olympics, designed to cancel and redress the former's legacy, became the most traumatic Games in the history of the modern Olympic movement.

While the Munich Olympics failed to be a 'jolly' occasion, they did impress upon the millions of visitors and spectators abroad the image of a peace-loving, open, and pluralist West Germany, an image most powerfully established by the principal bridge-builder of the times, the 1971 Nobel Peace laureate Willy Brandt. From Brandt's *Kniefall* (his spontaneous act of kneeling at the memorial to the Warsaw Ghetto uprising) in 1970, to Chancellor Helmut Schmidt's speech at Auschwitz in 1977, the pursuit of a new peace politics was integrally linked with the pursuit of a new memory politics. By contrast to the silence about the Nazi past that marked the Adenauer years, a silence that bred the frustration and angry protests of the *Achtundsechziger* (the 1968 generation), the Social Democrat-liberal years were characterised by an unprecedented openness about and engagement with it. In the period of conservative rule inaugurated by the election of Helmut Kohl as chancellor in 1982, this attitude was significantly modified. Thinking of reconciliation as the delivery of the present from the weight of history, Kohl underlined Germany's wish to 'fill in the graves of the past' (Feldman 2012: 40). The *Historikerstreit* (historians' controversy) of the late 1980s, triggered by the denial of the singularity of Nazi crimes by certain right-wing intellectuals, is revealing of 'the growing desire of the conservatives for a '"usable past", [for] a new, proud "normal" national identity' (Rabinbach 1988: 4). Accordingly, objections to the Goethe Institut's perceived 'leftiness' grew more regular, and motions that it should be pressed to adhere more closely to Bonn's policies more vocal (Mitchell 1986: 75–6). At the same time, there was a renewed emphasis on German language promotion, and a return to high culture as a means of projecting the national image (Schulte 2000: 59).

From Brandt to branding: refashioning Germany

When the two German states of the Cold War period reunited in October 1990, a heated debate ensued, both domestically and internationally, regarding the future directions of German foreign policy. After 40 years of consistently pursuing a *Verantwortungspolitik* (foreign policy of responsibility) committed to restraint and multilateralism, Germany's unification was widely seen as opening the way to its return to the disquieting assertiveness that had characterised its pre-war status as the powerhouse of Europe, hence the repeated and emphatic government assurances throughout the 1990s of its commitment to foreign policy continuity (Lantis 2002: 2–3).

It was with a similar commitment to continuity that Hilmar Hoffmann, in his inaugural speech as president of the Goethe Institut on 1 July 1993, identified cultural policy as the 'third pillar' of German foreign policy. Evidently, the champion of the 1970s slogan *Kultur für alle* thought it imperative to affirm his loyalty to the foundational principle of Germany's most prolific period of cultural diplomacy. But in 2001, just before the end of his nine-year term of office, the Goethe Institut merged with InterNationes, as a money-saving measure, while the total number of its branches around the world was reduced from 150 to 130. What stamped Hoffman's tenure in office was discontinuity rather than continuity with the Brandt era.

Following unification, the DAAD took over the East German scholarship programmes, Deutsche Welle inherited the transmission facilities of Berlin International, while the Goethe Institut moved into the countries of central and eastern Europe and the Commonwealth of Independent States (CIS) hitherto covered by the Herder Institute. In the period 1991–2002, a total of 13 Goethe Instituts opened in this region – in Warsaw, Prague, Cracow, Budapest, Moscow, Almaty, Sarajevo, Minsk, Ryazan, Vilnius, Tashkent, Tallinn, and Ljubljana – and two in east Asia (Seoul, Ho Chi Minh City). The expansion east, however, occurred at the cost of closing down branches in the US, Australia, and Africa. In western Europe between 1990 and 2002, the number of Goethe Instituts was reduced from 43 to 34.

Financing the economic and social integration of the two Germanies proved extremely costly. As a result, government support for cultural programmes was drastically reduced, but it was significantly increased for language teaching abroad, especially in central and eastern Europe. For example, 42 per cent of all recipients of Goethe Institut scholarships for teachers of German in 1997 were from central and eastern Europe and the CIS. A similar combination of downsizing and relocation was followed by the cultural agencies. After undergoing restructuring, ifa targeted its activities on central and eastern Europe. After taking the ambitious steps of starting television programming in both English and German (1992) and going online (1994), Deutsche Welle had to reduce its radio broadcasting in western European languages. Subsequently, though, it expanded its Russian programme and also started broadcasting in Ukraine (2000) and Belarus (2005).

The dramatic decline of Russian after the collapse of the USSR from its status as the lingua franca of central and eastern Europe opened up a vast new space of linguistic competition between Britain, France, and Germany. Far more than a contest for new territory between the leading international languages, the 'scramble for the East' was about gaining a communication advantage in the race to tap into the huge potential of the CEE market. During the period 1990–2008, the central and eastern European region proved the primary growth market for the German economy. While fast becoming the favourite destination of German investment, second only to the US, by 2009 the region had come to be as important for German exports as Germany's two largest trading partners, France and the USA, combined. Simultaneously, Germany has become central and eastern Europe's principal trading partner, far outstripping France or the UK (German Foreign Trade Office 2010). A considerable share of this success is down to the activities of the Goethe Institut and the DAAD. Geographical proximity, close economic ties, and deep-seated historical bonds have helped German to be in high demand in most central and eastern European countries, coming second only to English. To further support the promotion of German in central and eastern Europe, synergies were developed with the book industry, book fairs organised and translations subsidised, while special funds were made available for the creation of academic libraries and for reading rooms in 40 central and eastern European cities (Wood 2007: 113).

These powerful links between foreign economic and cultural policy were forcefully articulated and pursued by Foreign Minister Klaus Kinkel (1992–98). Identifying CEE and the CIS as the two top regional priorities for Germany's foreign cultural policy, he declared culture a critical factor in the shaping and advertising of *Standort* Germany – in the branding of Germany as a means to attract foreign capital and promote its exports (Kinkel 1997). Rainer Hülsse views Kinkel's instrumentalisation of foreign cultural policy for economic purposes as a decisive rupture in Germany's postwar external self-representation. Whereas during the Cold War period, under pressure for international rehabilitation and security, Germany's foreign image policy was based on the classical instruments of foreign cultural policy, from the mid-1990s onwards it has been based on the instruments of public relations, marketing, and advertising. If previously the goal was to build the image of a 'normal' country, the goal now is 'to turn Germany into a brand'. The official rationale for this drastic change was to reinforce the country's competitiveness in view of 'the challenges and necessities of an increasingly globalized economy' (Hülsse 2009: 304).

During the 1990s, nation-branding was developed as an innovative approach to public diplomacy, whereby culture is used as part of an elaborate strategy to enhance a country's trade advantage. Most famously used in Great Britain's 1997 'Cool Britannia' campaign, it was subsequently established as the most widespread form of national self-presentation. In this respect, Kinkel's initiative to develop links between cultural policy and the economy was not simply an expression of the German liberal party's traditional support for the business community, but a reflection of how national identities had come to be refashioned in the post-ideological world of economic globalisation. Quite unsurprisingly, then, the new approach to national image-making has since been pursued with increasing vigour by all subsequent German governments, its high point being the 'Germany – Land of Ideas' campaign.

In 2005, the advertising agency Scholz and Friends, one of the biggest in Europe, developed a nation-branding campaign to coincide with Germany's hosting of the 2006 football World Cup. The campaign, under the patronage of the then German President Horst Köhler, was a collaboration between the German government and the National Federation of German Industries (BDI), supported by the Foreign Ministry, the Ministry of Education and Research, corporations like BASF and ThyssenKrupp, Deutsche Welle, and the Goethe Institut. The campaign's aim was to make Germany 'visible and identifiable domestically and internationally as a powerful innovator and creative force'.[3] Its main actions included the 'Walk of Ideas' sculpture park in Berlin, the '365 Landmarks in the Land of Ideas' event series, joint actions with the government's 'Invest in Germany' marketing agency, and finally, a 10-minute film called 'Welcome to Germany', in which celebrities like the former national football player Oliver Bierhoff and the top model Heidi Klum presented the sights, culture, science, economy, sport, and lifestyle of Germany.[4] The arts and culture programme, entitled 'Time to make friends', that was prepared to promote and accompany the 2006 football World Cup involved around

50 different projects, the most important being 'the 'FC Deutschland 06' campaign. The Goethe Institut contributed by organising an international festival of football-related films and the touring photo exhibition 'World Language Football' (Eggers 2006).

The exhaustive deployment of the image-making mechanism, combined with a high degree of international media exposure, ensured that the hosting of the 2006 World Cup boosted Germany's image enormously. There was a striking distance between the official restraint in the face of the 1954 'miracle of Berne', or even at the 1974 World Cup final in Munich, and the public expression of national pride marking the 2006 event. Focused on the bounded character of 'soccer nationalism', the German media rehabilitated the flag and the national hymn, encouraging a therapeutic experience of rebirth into a shared national identity (Zambon 2012; see also Chapter 27). The outbreak of this highly emotional 'new German patriotism' prompted a nationwide debate about the relaxed, unabashed relationship of contemporary Germans with their national symbols and their national identity.

The 'Germany – Land of Ideas' campaign continued with a series of follow-up projects, such as the '365 Landmarks in the Land of Ideas' competition and the 'Innovationskraftwerk' open innovation platform for new business ideas from around the world. This indicates that the campaign's significance is best appreciated in the context of the FRG's wider nation-branding strategy of enhancing its status as a hub of scientific learning, research, and innovation. The first step in this direction was taken in 1998, when, in response to the accelerating internationalisation of tertiary education and the need to recruit high-quality researchers and professionals, Professor Max Huber was appointed as federal commissioner for international university marketing. The subsequent launch of GATE-Germany (2001), a joint initiative of the DAAD and the German Rectors' Conference, contributed to making Germany the third most favoured destination for international students in the world, after the USA and the UK (OECD Indicators 2010). One in eight of the quarter of a million foreign students studying in Germany in 2009 was funded by scholarship from the DAAD, which has now become the world's largest academic exchange organisation, represented on all continents in the world through 14 offices and 50 information centres.

Another crucial step was taken in 2009, with the opening of German Houses of Science and Innovation (DWIH) at specific high-profile international locations – to date, New York, São Paulo, New Delhi, Tokyo, and Moscow – under the 'Land of Ideas' motto. Sponsored by the Foreign Ministry and in cooperation with German science and business organisations, as well as the DAAD and the Alexander von Humboldt Foundation, the objective of DWIH is to showcase 'the achievements of German science, research and research-based companies' and promote 'collaboration with innovative German organizations'.[5]

The post-Cold War period is characterised not only by the methodical economic instrumentalisation of culture and the consequent rise of nation-branding to the status of a fourth pillar of foreign policy, but by the equally methodical political instrumentalisation of culture as a vital element in the exercise of 'soft power'. If Kinkel's insistence on the link between culture and the economy was a telling instance of the former, Joschka Fischer's insistence on cultural relations as part and parcel of international relations offers a supreme example of the intense politicisation of cultural diplomacy implied by the latter. In his 'Konzeption 2000' (Concept 2000), the foreign minister in the Social Democratic-Green coalition (1998–2005) underlined the central role of Germany's cultural diplomacy as 'an integral element of a foreign policy that aims at the prevention of conflict and the securing of peace'. Foreign cultural policy is not about 'the good, the beautiful and the true', but about scientific exchange and the promotion of civil society. The guiding principles of cultural and educational foreign policy should be the promotion of democracy, the establishment of human rights, poverty alleviation, participation in scientific-technological progress, and the protection of natural resources (Fischer 2000).

In certain crucial respects *Konzeption 2000* represents a resurgence of the Brandt/Dahrendorf agenda for foreign cultural policy. Specifically, it suggests a revived vision for cultural relations in the era of the new acute global challenges to peace, security, democracy, and development. Germany's response to the post-9/11 era of 'the clash of civilisations' has been to initiate a broad variety of projects and programmes concerning intercultural dialogue, most recently the 'Ernst Reuter Initiative for Intercultural Dialogue and Understanding', organised jointly by the German and the Turkish governments. Especially important, also, has been both ifa's and the Goethe Institut's recent focus on building civil society. The vast variety of projects developed by the Goethe Institut since 2008 under the 'Culture and Development' umbrella are specifically targeted at conflict-ridden and poverty-stricken regions – at countries in which civil societies are only just beginning to emerge. In the late 2000s, after a long period of almost continuous downsizing and restructuring, the Goethe Institut's international presence began to regain its strength; at the time of writing it has 158 branches in 93 countries. Most significantly, it has resumed its place in the frontline of international cultural relations with initiatives that recall its pioneering work from the 1970s and 1980s.

Epilogue

Federal Germany's postwar foreign cultural policy has been one outcome of the two most cataclysmic events in modern European history: World War II and the Cold War. Its paramount objectives were the international rehabilitation of the country from the stigma of the aggressor and its recognition as an agent of peace and cooperation. Even though it lacked France's or Britain's transcontinental network of ex-colonies and linguistic communities, Germany succeeded in developing an impressively resourceful and multidimensional foreign cultural policy, characterised by its engaged multilateralism and its expansion, beyond the confines of conventional cultural diplomacy, into social, economic, scientific, and political issues of global significance but also local relevance. A critical factor in this success has been the unwavering reliance on a multitude of non-governmental, Länder-based organisations. Despite the resultant 'unclear, even illogical' distribution of responsibilities (Aguilar 1996: 81), duplication, and frequent antagonism, this pluralism of civil society actors ensured the diversity, independence, and innovation that make for effective and trustworthy cultural relations.

In January 2013, France and Germany celebrated the 50th anniversary of the Elysée Treaty, perhaps the paramount modern example of civil society-driven cultural diplomacy. Since 1963, the French-German Youth Office has enabled more than 8 million young people from France and Germany to take part in 300,000 exchange programmes. After German unification, cultural contact and exchange between the two countries was further intensified by the creation of the Franco-German television channel Arte (1991) and of the Franco-German University (1999), a network of 160 German and French universities offering integrated courses in both countries. Brandt's intuition was right: reconciliation, understanding, and cooperation are best served not by politics but by becoming an integral part of people's everyday life. To commemorate the anniversary France and Germany issued a joint postage stamp, bearing the picture of a man and a woman, side by side, peering through binoculars coloured respectively blue, white, and red, and black, red, and gold. That was a fitting depiction not only of the two countries' rapport but also of what cultural diplomacy is all about: farsightedness, and seeing things from the other's point of view.

Gregory Paschalidis

Notes

1 Germany scored 56 per cent in 2008 (the first year it was rated), 61 per cent in 2009, 59 per cent in 2010, 62 per cent in 2011, 56 per cent in 2012, and 58 per cent in 2013.
2 Frankfurt's Institut für Sozialforschung (Institute of Social Research), commonly known as the Frankfurt School, was closed down by the Nazis soon after they assumed power in March 1933. To avoid persecution, its members left Germany and most of them, such as Adorno, Herbert Marcuse, Max Horkheimer, Leo Löwenthal, and Friedrich Pollock, moved to the USA, where they continued their work during the war at the New School for Social Research in New York.
3 See www.land-der-ideen.de/en/about-us (accessed 13 October 2014).
4 See www.broadview.tv/en/production/welcome-to-germany-land-of-ideas/ (accessed 13 October 2014).
5 See www.germaninnovation.org/about-us/german-houses-of-science-and-innovation (accessed 13 October 2014).

Bibliography

Adorno, T. (1950) 'Auferstehung der Kultur in Deutschland?', *Frankfurter Hefte*, 5(5): 469–76.
Aguilar, M. (1996) *Cultural Diplomacy and Foreign Policy. German-American Relations, 1955–1968*, New York: Peter Lang.
Altmayer, C. (2009) 'World's First Chair of German as a Foreign Language: The History of the Herder-Institut'. Online. Available at www.goethe.de/ges/spa/dos/daf/ges/en4618725.html (accessed 15 December 2013).
Arnold, H. (1979) *Foreign cultural policy. A survey from a German point of view*, trans. K. Hamnett, London: Oswald Wolff.
Balbier, U.A. (2005) 'Der Welt das moderne Deutschland vorstellen: Die Eröffnungsfeier der Spiele der XX. Olympiade in München 1972', in J. Paulmann (ed.) *Auswärtige Repräsentationen. Deutsche Kulturdiplomatie nach 1945*, Cologne: Böhlau.
Balbier, U.A. (2006) '"Zu Gast bei Freunden". How the Federal Republic of Germany learned to take sport seriously', *Eurozine*, June. Online. Available at www.eurozine.com/articles/2006–06–09-balbier-en.html (accessed 15 December 2013).
Beal, A. (2000) 'Negotiating Cultural Allies: American Music in Darmstadt, 1946–1956', *Journal of the American Musicological Society*, 53(1): 105–39.
Bodo, B. (2003) 'Foreign Students in Nazi Germany', *East European Quarterly*, 37(1): 19–42.
Brandt, W. (1969) *A Peace Policy for Europe,* trans. J. Carmichael, New York: Holt, Rinehart & Winston.
Brandt, W. (1972) '1945 Different than 1918', Speech at Harvard University, Cambridge, MA. Online. Available at www.loc.gov/exhibits/marshall/m15.html (accessed 15 December 2013).
Caute, D. (2003) *The Dancer Defects. The Struggle for Cultural Supremacy during the Cold War*, Oxford and New York: Oxford University Press.
Düwell, K. (1976) *Deutschlands auswärtige Kulturpolitik, 1918–1932: Grundlinien und Dokumente*, Cologne: Böhlau.
Eggers, E. (2006) 'All around the Globus: a foretaste of the German football imagination, c.2006', in A. Tomlinson and C. Young (eds) *German Football. History, Culture, Society*, London and New York: Routledge.
Fehrenbach, H. (1995) *Cinema in Democratizing Germany. Reconstructing National Identity after Hitler*, Chapel Hill and London: University of North Carolina Press.
Feldman, L.G. (2012) *Germany's Foreign Policy of Reconciliation: From Enmity to Amity*, Plymouth: Rowman & Littlefield.
Fischer, J. (2000) 'Rede des Bundesministers des Auswärtigen', in *Forum: Zukunft der Auswärtigen Kulturpolik*. Online. Available at www.ifa.de/fileadmin/pdf/aa/ akbp_zukunft2000.pdf (accessed 15 December 2013).
Frede, L. (2007) 'Botschafter der Music': The Berlin Philharmonic Orchestra and the Role of Classical Music in Post-War German Identity, *MHRA Working Papers in the Humanities*, 2, 19–29.
German Foreign Trade Office (2010) *Report on the Economy CEE*. Online. Available at www.ahk-balt.org/fileadmin/ahk_baltikum/Publikationen/Konjunkturumfrage/Konjunkturbericht_MOE_2010_ENG_02.pdf (accessed 15 December 2013).
Gesche, K. (2006) *Kultur als Instrument der Außenpolitik totalitärer Staaten. Das Deutsche Auslands-Institut 1933–1945*, Cologne: Böhlau.

Grass, G. (2009) *The Tin Drum,* trans. B. Mitchell, Boston and New York: Houghton Mifflin Harcourt.

Herwig, H. (1996) 'Self-Censorship in Germany after the Great War', in K. Wilson (ed.) *Forging Collective Memory. Government and International Historians through Two World Wars,* Oxford: Berghahn Books.

Hülsse, R. (2009) 'The Catwalk Power: Germany's new foreign image policy', *Journal of International Relations and Development,* 12: 293–316.

Impekoven, H. (2012) *Die Alexander von Humboldt Stiftung und das Ausländerstudium in Deutschland 1925–1945,* Gottingen: V & R Unipress.

Kinkel, K. (1997) 'Zehn Thesen zur Auswärtigen Kulturpolitik', *Bulletin,* 20 March.

Lantis, J. (2002) *Strategic dilemmas and the evolution of German foreign policy since unification,* Westport, CT: Praeger Publishers.

Leahy, J. (2003) 'Nuit et Bruillard', *Senses of Cinema,* 26. Online. Available at http://sensesofcinema. com/2003/cteq/nuit_et_brouillard/ (accessed 15 December 2013).

Michels, E. (2004) 'Deutsch als Weltsprache? Franz Thierfelder, the Deutsche Akademie in Munich and the Promotion of the German Language Abroad, 1923–1945', *German History,* 22(2): 206–28.

Michels, E. (2013) 'Goethe-Institut', in *Historisches Lexikon Bayerns.* Online. Available at www.historisches-lexikon-bayerns.de/artikel/artikel_44721 (accessed 15 December 2013).

Mitchell, J.M. (1986) *International Cultural Relations,* London: Allen & Unwin.

OECD Indicators (2010) *Education at a glance.* Online. Available at www.oecd.org/education/skills-beyond-school/45926093.pdf. (accessed 1 December 2013).

Paulmann, J. (2007) 'Representation without Emulation. German Cultural Diplomacy in Search of Integration and Self-Assurance during the Adenauer Era', *German Politics and Society,* 25:2: 168–200.

Rabinbach, A. (1988) 'Editor's Introduction', *New German Critique,* 44: 3–4 (special issue on the *Historikerstreit).*

Schiller, K. and Young, C. (2010) *The 1972 Munich Olympics and the Making of Modern Germany,* Berkeley: University of California Press.

Schulte, K.-S. (2000) *Auswärtige Kulturpolitik im politischen System der Bundesrepublik Deutschland,* Berlin: VWF.

Siegel, N. (2012) *The German Marshall Fund of the United States. A Brief History.* Online. Available at www.gmfus.org/wp-content/blogs.dir/1/files_mf/1336582663GMF_history_publication_web.pdf (accessed 15 December 2013).

Sölter, A. (2008) 'The Renaissance of Soft Power. Rediscovering Cultural Diplomacy in Transatlantic Perspective', CMG Workshop, Goethe-Institut, Toronto. Online. Available at www.culturaldiplomacy. org/canadameetsgermany/content/articles/program-archive/2008/Renaissance_of_Soft_Power.pdf (accessed 25 November 2013).

Stelzel, P. (2003) 'Fritz Fischer and the American historical profession: tracing the transatlantic dimension of the Fischer-Kontroverse', *Storia della Storiografia,* 44: 67–84.

Stoll, U. (2005) *Kulturpolitik als Beruf. Dieter Sattler (1906–1968) in München, Bonn und Rom,* Paderborn: Ferdinand Schöningh.

Winrow, G.M. (1990) *The Foreign Policy of the GDR in Africa,* Cambridge: Cambridge University Press.

Witte, B. (1999) 'How to represent Germany as a *Kulturstaat* abroad', in F. Trommler (ed.) *The Cultural Legitimacy of the Federal Republic: Assessing the German Kulturstaat,* Washington: American Institute for Contemporary German Studies/The Johns Hopkins University.

Wood, S. (2004) *Germany and East-Central Europe: Political, Economic and Socio-Cultural Relations in the Era of EU Enlargement,* Aldershot: Ashgate.

Wood, S. (2007) 'The "Bundeskulturminister" and other stories: Observations on the politics of culture in Germany', *German Politics,* 8(3): 43–58.

Zambon, K. 'Constructing Patriotism Above Reproach: The Rehabilitation of German National Pride in the 2006 World Cup', paper presented at ICA Conference, Phoenix, AZ, May 2012.

Index